538 WAYS TO

LIVE WORK AND PLAY

LIKE A LIBERAL

BY JUSTIN KREBS

CO-FOUNDER OF LivingLIBERALLY

Skyhorse Publishing

All Rights Reserved. No part of this book may be reproduced in any manner without the express written consent of the publisher, except in the case of brief excerpts in critical reviews or articles. All inquiries should be addressed to Skyhorse Publishing, 555 Eighth Avenue, Suite 903, New York, NY 10018.

Skyhorse publishing books may be purchased in bulk at special discounts for sales promotion, corporate gifts, fund-raising, or educational purposes. Special editions can also be created to specifications. For details, contact the Special Sales Department, Skyhorse Publishing, 555 Eighth Avenue, Suite 903, New York, NY 10018 or info@skyhorsepublishing.com

www.skyhorsepublishing.com

10   9   8   7   6   5   4   3   2   1

Library of Congress Cataloging-in-Publication Data

Krebs, Justin.

538 ways to live, work & play like a liberal / by Justin Krebs.

p. cm.

ISBN 978-1-60239-982-2 (PBK. : ALK. PAPER)

1. Liberalism--United States. I. Title. II. Title: Five hundred thirty-eight ways to live, work & play like a liberal.

JC574.2.U6.K75   2010

320.51'30973 — DC22

2010005918

Printed in Canada

INTRO DUCTION

My name is Justin Krebs . . . and I'm a proud American liberal.

If you think you just read the opening words of a support group—well, maybe you have. When you're politically vocal in this country, you sometimes need all the support you can get. Especially when you are willing to use the original "L Word."

Liberal. It's a dirty word that's finding its way back into fashion. Sure, it was once hurled as an insult, but that is so 1988. We're in a new millennium, a new presidency, and there are new cultural and political norms on the rise. It's not so bad to be liberal anymore.

While many once shunned it, more and more of us embrace the liberal label—"Proud Liberal" . . . "Unapologetic Liberal" . . . "Card-carrying Liberal."

What does it actually mean?

Does it mean to be engaged in the humanities in a well-rounded way like the "liberal arts"? Or is it a brand of thoughtless, reckless social programming as Reagan and his conservative cadre would have snarled? In the 1800s, it indicated hands-off economic policies; in the 1950s, it was the national consensus at the center of which President Eisenhower found himself. In Canada, it's the conservative-centrist party. In 2008, it was a label Senators (and leading presidential candidates) Obama and Clinton saw as too leftist for their campaigns.

For all that folks toss the word around, few try to define it. We generally agree that it's to the left on our political spectrum, but do we know what it is beyond that? More than "not being conservative" or—as was popular for eight years—"being different than President George W. Bush," what do liberals believe?

Most people would rather not have to define labels too carefully, whether they are flinging them at others or applying to themselves. But if I'm going to make the claim that this book will relate how you can "live liberally" in your everyday life, I better give a try at a definition.

So here goes.

> **Liberals believe that we are better off when we live for each other than when we live only for ourselves.**

There. That was simple.

Wait! That definition was short and straightforward! It didn't tackle every possible policy consideration, didn't articulate a four-point plan, and isn't rooted in the most tangled political arguments of today!

If that's what you were thinking, you're in for a surprise. "Liberal," as a political approach, isn't strictly tied to current debates. Liberals don't define our political principles by the stances we take on particular issues. Issues come and go . . . one election you're arguing over civil unions, and the next year there's consensus on that and you're arguing over marriage equality. Instead, our stances flow from this principle: We all are in this together.

Being liberal is not only a political philosophy—liberal is how you live your life and interact with neighbors, coworkers, and strangers on the street. It's not just how you vote on Election Day, but how you vote with your wallet every day. It's not only what you chant at a rally, but what you laugh at or rock out to on your iPod.

It all comes down to an approach to life that acknowledges that we're sharing this planet, sharing our cities and roads, sharing our fortunes and even our misfortunes, sharing our resources and our surpluses, our creative impulses and pleasures, even sharing our weather, with those around us. We all truly are in it—in all of it—together.

We are better off when we live for each other than when we live only for ourselves. Liberals believe that government is a tool to advance common prosperity. We believe that diversity—in backgrounds and of ideas—is a strength. We believe that creativity and science are necessary assets for creating more wealth and opportunity for all people. We believe that where one comes from shouldn't lock him or her out of the chance to succeed. We believe that we are all in the same boat, and we want everyone else to prosper as well because our fates are interlocked. This means cherishing the environment, cultivating peace, and working with other nations, other communities, and our neighbors to develop solutions that work well for all of us.

And that's just the political side. As a lifestyle, "living liberally" is

★ living collectively—investing in and drawing from common resources

- ★ living creatively and expressively, because communication and connection build community

- ★ living sustainably, because we need to green our society so it will work for all of us and for future generations—not just 50 years from now, but 500, even 5,000

- ★ living diversely, because what unites us is strengthened by the range of experiences and cultures we represent

- ★ living freely and joyously, because life's too short to be unhappy.

This is not a historical definition of liberal. It's not an etymological definition. I hope it's not a temporal definition. It's my belief—and it's the set of values that drives so many good people and shapes so many strong communities.

It's how I try to live liberally . . . and I hope over the next 538 ideas, tips, and steps, it may become how you, more consciously, live liberally too.

What You're Going to Find in This Book

I fully believe that every day, in some of the most routine activities, you can be living out your progressive values. And I believe that there are some ways you're already doing so and might not know it.

The purpose of this book is to spark your imagination with a combination of anecdotes and examples of how others are living liberally, some simple steps you could consider, and some ways I'm trying to make my politics personal and my personal politics public.

There is no one way to be "liberal," of course—that's in the very nature of being liberal. And life can be full of contradictions. Is it more important to buy a book by a progressive author to support those ideas, or to not buy it because you want to reduce consumption and could just borrow it from the library? Should we celebrate cars that run on renewable energy, or push to decrease car culture entirely? Is it better to vote for an independent party candidate for the diversity of ideas, or to become the liberal wing of a more powerful party?

I welcome those debates and look forward to well-meaning liberals disagreeing with a healthy portion of this book. These aren't "the ways" to live like a liberal—they are "some ways."

Some are startlingly simple, and that's as it should be. Nobody should expect you to dramatically and suddenly change your life; I'm not sure I have ever suddenly changed my lifestyle. But by doing a few of the easier acts regularly, it may create new habits that will come to feel routine.

Some of the ideas are hard, or even uncomfortable. You don't have to do them all. Just think about them. If you try some of them, ask yourself, "why not try more?" Alternatively, suggest a way you can do something similar that's more comfortable and accessible for you.

The numbered ideas running throughout this book include things to read, watch, and buy; questions to ask; and new ways to relate to friends, coworkers, and neighbors. The magic number "538" is a weighted political number: the total electoral votes we tally each presidential election. However, our politics shapes our lives on more than just Election Day, so these 538 ideas are concepts to play with, organizations to learn about, and choices to consider in your everyday life. There will be anecdotes. There will be how-to sections. There will be lists, sidebars, and the occasional guest contributor. There will not be everything.

There are thousands of businesses and grassroots groups doing incredible work, and I only mention a few; there are thousands of considerations as to what you buy, what you teach your children, where you can go for vacation, and I only have so much room. Amazing innovations take place around the country, but a disproportionate number included here are New York City–centric . . . because it's what I know best. I do look forward to hearing from you about what you know best—because I know there are incredible examples of the liberal life in all fifty states.

So where you see those gaps, do the most liberal thing you can: share your knowledge. Share it with me, share it with other friends, share it with whomever you give the book to next. This would be a dull conversation if I were the only person who had anything to say.

So Let's Get Started

. . . But before we do, I want to share one other pretty good definition of liberal floating around (but if I'd written it first, you would have ignored mine). It was spoken by a man who had been insulted as a "liberal" and decided not to roll over, but to defend himself:

> *"What do our opponents mean when they apply to us the label 'Liberal?' If by 'Liberal' they mean, as they want people to believe, someone who is soft in his policies abroad, who is against local government, and who is unconcerned with the taxpayer's*

> *dollar, then . . . we are not that kind of 'Liberal.' But*
> *if by a 'Liberal' they mean someone who looks ahead*
> *and not behind, someone who welcomes new ideas*
> *without rigid reactions, someone who cares about*
> *the welfare of the people—their health, their housing,*
> *their schools, their jobs, their civil rights, and their*
> *civil liberties—someone who believes we can break*
> *through the stalemate and suspicions that grip us in*
> *our policies abroad, if that is what they mean by a*
> *'Liberal,' then I'm proud to say I'm a 'Liberal.'"*

That was then-senator John F. Kennedy in September 1960. He believed in living liberally.

CHAPTER 1
LIVING LIBERALLY

> *Somebody came along and said "liberal" means "soft on crime, soft on drugs, soft on Communism, soft on defense, and we're gonna tax you back to the Stone Age because people shouldn't have to go to work if they don't want to." And instead of saying, "Well, excuse me, you right-wing, reactionary, xenophobic, homophobic, anti-education, anti-choice, pro-gun,* Leave it to Beaver *trip back to the '50s," we cowered in the corner and said, "Please don't hurt me."*
>
> —BRUNO GIANELLI, THE WEST WING

This impulse to make politics fun was on our minds when my friend Matt O'Neill and I decided to start a weekly political drinking club in 2003. Fun wasn't the end goal; it was the essential means.

We were frustrated New York liberals. We had just seen our country march to the drumbeat of war and invade a country we didn't need to attack. We felt that the authoritarianism and arrogance of the Bush administration needed a response, and yet the public and press seemed speechless. Where were the effective leaders of the left?

We wanted to vent, and we wanted to find a way to make a difference. We believed that there was more that liberals in New York—with a surplus of time and creativity—could do. But we also realized we couldn't change national politics until we started locally.

Many of our own friends weren't even talking politics. We knew they shared our values and our frustration, yet we weren't engaging with them around the issues that pushed all of us. We wondered why. In truth, even in a liberal city, you're not "supposed" to talk politics in social settings. This was driven home one night when a friend and I brought voter registration forms to a bar. We approached a circle of twenty-somethings, one of whom we knew, and asked if they were registered to vote. All of them said yes, except one. When we asked if he'd like to take a minute, he said he didn't believe in voting. When— clearly shocked—we asked why, the woman we knew in the circle spoke up.

"Hey, let's not talk about politics. We're out at a bar . . . we all came here to have fun."

Furthermore, people are busy. Our friends had jobs, and in addition to their workdays, they had relationships and time at the gym and volunteer projects. Asking them to get more involved in political conversation sounded like asking them to make more time in their week . . . which they just didn't have.

Finally, the opportunities to step up into politics were slim. If you have limited time, do you want to start dedicating it to those over-earnest screechers that think politics is all work and no play? We attended a few meetings of groups aimed at younger progressives and found out they typically seemed like a high school Model United Nations club, deeply concerned with following *Robert's Rules of Order* and filled with people eager to become part of the party machinery. I remember one meeting that spent a good amount of time determining whether the agenda was in the proper order.

Politics wasn't fun; people were busy; young political groups were lame . . . so how could Matt and I get our friends a little more politically involved?

We figured we needed to bring politics to the natural habitat of our generation: a bar. We needed to make it part of our friends' social life, not something they suspended their life to join. We needed to make it easy and fun. So we decided to start a weekly gathering in our local dive bar where people knew politics would be on the table.

From the start, there was no hard-driving agenda. We figured that folks who decided to come would probably bring their own agendas . . . and they did. Other people, who had spent their days spitting mad at their computer screens, came and vented and shared and found out they weren't alone.

It also made it an easy place for less political people to come. If you were interested in politics, but felt like you didn't know much, we gave you an easy way in. You're not asked to make a presentation or debate an issue; you very naturally learn more about the topics of the day from other attendees.

And if you didn't want to talk politics, you didn't have to. You might just start showing up because you know it's a group of friends and friends-of-friends who are welcoming, social, chatty. We didn't see those less-political folks as a distraction. We understood from the start that we needed a scene open to all . . . and we just had to believe that even if you didn't come for the politics, just by being there some of the politics would rub off on you.

We decided to meet every week. We wanted the regularity so people would always know when and where it was. They wouldn't have to come to any given Thursday, because they would know it was *every* Thursday. It made it easier to drop in and drop out, and it meant people didn't have to join an e-mail list. They always knew where we'd be.

The frequency created a sense of continuity. It was like an ongoing conversation. People could pick up where they'd left off the week before. Folks would start recognizing each other. We were really building a community.

We chose the perfect bar for it. Rudy's, a classic dive bar in Hell's Kitchen, on the west side of Manhattan, was known for cheap beer by the pitcher and free hot dogs. It had a great backyard that made gatherings of unpredictable size easy to fit in, and management that liked us because we were already regulars. It was a storied place: it was a speakeasy during Prohibition and became one of the first legitimate bars in the city after Prohibition was repealed. It was also known for a colorful, mixed crowd—Hell's Kitchen old-timers sharing the bar with aspiring actors working in the nearby theater district, joined by some folks in transit uniforms getting off long shifts on the subways, and others in suits who represented the neighborhood's newly gentrifying population. These people were used to sharing the crowded bar, sometimes sharing the few booths, and even sharing a pitcher. What better place to stir up inclusive, diverse, political conversation?

Rudy's had had the informal slogan: "Is the person next to you an artist, a poet, or just a drunk? You never know at Rudy's." Now they could add "liberal" to the list.

In May 2003, we began our weekly democratic drinking club. Our friends came, and soon after they brought their friends.

Then we started getting people who'd heard about us—in a newspaper listing, a forwarded e-mail, or on the nascent blogs. As strangers started arriving to become our companions, our meetings really took off.

It was one of those regulars—a guy named Owen Roth who had learned about us from the blogger Atrios—who said: "You guys need a better name for this," rather than "Democrats and Drinks" or "Buttons and Beer," as we sometimes called it.

"OK, come up with one," we said.

"How about 'Drinking Liberally'?" Thank goodness we had no egos and could grab a good idea when we heard it, and thank goodness Owen was willing to share his good idea for the greater good.

And Drinking Liberally was born.

1

Over the next year, the weekly meetings at Rudy's became a destination for liberals looking for new friends, activists with big ideas they wanted to bounce off people who would listen, candidates and their staff seeking to tap into a new pool of political energy, and reporters who wanted to get the liberal reaction to something in the news—at that time, chiefly, the Democratic presidential primary.

Authors wanted to stop by and speak. Filmmakers asked how they could attract our community to their run at a local independent movie theater. Office-seekers asked if they could say a few words. Entrepreneurs came by to peddle politically themed gifts. The growing network of other new progressive groups—born in that same era of frustration, empowered by the internet and energized by the upcoming election—collaborated with us on debate-watch parties, fundraisers, and media events.

A full year later, we were still doing what was at our core: meeting every Thursday night. By then, we were also a planning hub for progressive activities during the Republican National Convention, which was coming to New York. We had become known to blogs around the country, including the growing phenomenon of Daily Kos. By the summer of 2004, what had started as our small group of friends marked its anniversary by overcrowding the backyard of Rudy's. One of the attendees was a *Newsweek* reporter—and a few weeks later, a photograph of a button boasting "I Only Drink With Liberals" appeared in the magazine.

The new and traditional media gave the club a boost, but something more personal changed our organization's course. A friend named Andrew Hoppin moved from New York to San Francisco and asked to start a Drinking Liberally chapter there because he'd miss coming to Rudy's. We said yes, of course, then quickly figured out what "rules" he'd need to follow to be a chapter.

We were also fortunate that a new friend and ally named David Alpert had recently teamed up with us. David created a quick and easy website that showcased a map of the country with dots for the Drinking Liberally chapters: one in New York City and one in San Francisco.

"David," I asked, "should we really make the map so prominent? It does confirm the idea that liberals are only on the coasts."

"It will fill in," David replied confidently.

Our national network was born.

Since then, the map has filled in. We expanded to Oakland, then to our first "red state" chapter in Houston. Then our fifth group launched in September 2004, in Boise, Idaho. That's when we knew we were really onto something. Soon enough we were in all the predictable places for a progressive social club: Philadelphia, Boston, Ithaca. But we were also finding strong clusters in Iowa, defiant liberals in rural Texas, and a dynamic group in Salt Lake City, at the heart of a state not known for liberals or drinking. Another friend we had bonded with through our weekly gatherings, Katrina Baker, joined us as a partner and gave us a link to our liberal siblings across the United States.

Drinking Liberally has expanded to all fifty states and has several international chapters (the deputy prime minister of New Zealand has attended his local gathering). There are more than three hundred happy hours that meet in big cities and small towns. Some meet weekly, some monthly; all keep that feature of regularity. Each is organized by local volunteer hosts who contacted us to start a chapter; those hosts set the vibe, which varies widely from city to city.

When we started we said we were a group for young people looking to socialize around progressive politics. When the Pittsburgh chapter sent us a group photo and we saw six beefy, gray-bearded men at a table, we knew we shouldn't think of ourselves as a young persons' club anymore.

We've become intergenerational. In many of the smaller towns and redder states, the hosts are middle-aged or older, people who have fought liberal battles for decades but often felt alone. Drinking Liberally helps them find their community.

In some cities like Kansas City, chapters even choose family-friendly restaurants so children can hear people talking politics . . . and join the conversation.

Some chapters, like those in Minneapolis and Philadelphia, have guest speakers and regularly invite candidates for Senate and Congress. Others, including New York City, keep it purely social. The flexibility has allowed Drinking Liberally to grow.

As people have brought their own ideas to it, it has expanded with their imprint.

This sense of expansion led us to create other "Liberally" events. Drinking Liberally has never been about the drinking . . . it's about progressive politics in a social setting. Why not other social settings, like comedy clubs? Thus, "Laughing Liberally" was born. Featuring a mix of established and up-and-coming comedians, these shows serve the performers as much as the audience. Comics are often told to stay away from political material in mainstream clubs; we give them the chance to go as far left as they want. Attendees have the opportunity to know they're not going to suffer an evening of homophobic and sexist material and that they can comfortably meet the other liberals sitting around them.

Chapters around the country started hosting book clubs— "Reading Liberally." These gatherings promote progressive voices and often support independent publishers. They have become natural destinations for book tours as well. Authors who have made Reading Liberally a core partner to their tours range from Andy Stern, the head of the labor union SEIU, to top blogger Markos Moulitsas Zuniga of Daily Kos, to Jeffrey Feldman, a smart, insightful blogger/author whose small publisher may not otherwise have had resources to create events around the country.

Other chapters decided that in addition to drinking they wanted to watch films, and "Screening Liberally" came to life. Whether gathering around wide releases or independent documentaries, these clubs offer one more avenue for the non-drinker to find a local liberal community. Moreover, these groups have become a resource for distributors of progressive films by connecting such work with an audience hungry for it. From the widely publicized *Food, Inc.,* to the Oscar-nominated *Trouble the Water,* to the high-profile *Milk,* to the lesser-known but critically acclaimed

Crawford, films find a willing partner in Screening Liberally events across the country.

In New York, a couple that loved the idea of Drinking Liberally but didn't like to drink on an empty stomach started "Eating Liberally," which hosts meals, guest speakers, and films around food, policy, and sustainability issues. They also happen to be amazing cooks, and every event features food that reflects our political and gustatory tastes.

As this network grew, our vision of it grew as well, and Matt, Katrina, David, and I formed "Living Liberally," a network of social communities and events, a hub for the happy hours, book tours, cycling clubs, and everything else our chapters were inventing. It was definitely no longer focused on drinking. We are out there to make sure wherever you live and whatever your interests, you can find or start a chapter that works for you. We want to make sure that whatever you're doing, however you're living, you're able to live liberally.

These past seven years taught me about our country, and about being liberal. It was clear to me what a liberal should be doing in New York City: we had to register voters, support candidates, attend forums. The experiences of our other chapters around the country have taught me to expand the vision of what a liberal is. A woman in Idaho had to write a letter to the editor of her local paper to argue that one could be a liberal and a god-fearing Christian, after her politics were denigrated in an editorial. Another woman in Natchez, Mississippi, had difficulty finding a bar where white and black Democrats would feel comfortable sharing a drink. For these communities, being liberal was more of a battle than it was to those of us in New York or San Francisco.

I also learned from our red-state friends that even the most conservative communities have ways that locals can live liberally. Des Moines, Iowa, has more than one lesbian bar active in supporting local social and political causes. Lincoln, Nebraska, has a thriving green market that would rival Union Square in New York. Laramie, Wyoming, is a hotbed of peace activists. In Savannah, Georgia, folks are fighting for more locally grown, sustainable school lunches.

Additionally, as Drinking Liberally evolved into Living Liberally, I realized how much more one could do to embody liberal values beyond voting and campaigning. I can consume food and entertainment that reflect my values. I can choose media, retail, and community resources free from corporate control.

I can also bring that spirit that first motivated Drinking Liberally into other walks of life. The spirit of creating and embracing a diverse community, of learning from each other, of forming social bonds that lead to collective action and progressive change, and of doing all this with a sense of fun along the way—these impulses can flow through how we work and play, learn and spend.

Across the United States, people are already Living Liberally—some intentionally, others without realizing it. If we start to recognize where these liberal impulses are in our everyday lives, and where we can take measures to live more liberally, then, step by step, we will create liberal communities, a liberal country, and a more liberal world.

That's not to say we're no longer Drinking Liberally. We still meet every Thursday, 7:30 PM onward, at the same dive bar on 9th Avenue between 44th and 45th streets. Pitchers have gone up a dollar in the past seven years. Hot dogs are still free. Come on by.

CHAPTER 2
LIVING LIBERALLY
IN YOUR EVERY-DAY LIFE

Of all the varieties of virtues, liberalism is the most beloved.
—ARISTOTLE

You wake up to your alarm clock playing National Public Radio, and you start your day. After twenty minutes of yoga, twenty more of Zen meditation, and a calm look through the *New York Times*, you have your Fair Trade latte and leave your home—powered half with solar energy, half with wind—to head off in your hybrid—no, make that your bicycle—to your nonprofit social service job.

You have woken up in Liberal America.

Seriously . . . who really has time for leisurely yoga and the *New York Times*? I don't have that many hours in my day, much less my morning. A solar-wind hybrid home? Is that even possible?

That morning routine may sound like a dream to you—or it may be your nightmare. Either way, it's not the typical liberal morning. I'm not sure if there is one typically liberal way to start your day . . . but there are easy steps to start your day off on the left foot.

Yes, I do like NPR; no, I don't do yoga; I don't drink lattes; my crowded NYC apartment is neither solar-nor wind-powered; and I take public transportation to work. Does that make me more or less liberal than the stereotype above? Not sure . . . but it is more real.

Here are some real ideas for **Waking Liberally:**

Choose Your Morning News

Whether you wake up to a blaring alarm or to music, if you're like most people you pretty quickly switch on a radio or television. The voice helps ease you into the day . . . and may give you some insights into what's going on in the world.

Consciously deciding whose voice and views start your day is a good place to start your Liberal Morning. What you listen to, watch, or read helps set your mood. You could listen to DJs gossip about the previous night's reality TV, or you could listen to radio that will inform your conversations later in the day. Listening to NPR—yes, a stereotype, but a good one—offers you insights and information that may help you engage and influence the members of your car pool, coworkers at your water cooler, and family members at the dinner table. Good radio becomes a source of contagious conversation.

I emphasize "listening" over "watching" because there is something dangerous in that seductive, addictive drug called television. You might consider covering your television to lessen your impulse to just flick it on. Once you do, the hours drain away. Another good tactic is to leave magazines out and open around your house. Just as TV can suck you in, I hope that *The Nation* or *Mother Jones* can, too.

That said, if you do prefer television to radio, there are still choices you can make. You could choose local stations to become informed about your community or public television for coverage that tends to be less sensational than cable news. If you want a dose of fear and anger, start with Fox News, or switch off Fox and watch just about anything else to improve your morning.

If you do have time to read the paper or the news online, why not? Sadly, many of us are in too much of a rush ... but reading is the best way to get a sense of the world, as you can skim and scan through various stories and synthesize them for yourself.

Make Your Lunch

Breakfast starts your day, but think ahead to lunch. If you prepare lunch at home, it's a cost-saving move, and also spares your wastebasket, given how much trash each take-out meal produces. Use a reusable lunch bag for extra green points. Plus, make sure to compost to reduce and reuse your food waste.

Not everything is compostable, of course, so also know your recycling rules. Many municipalities remain mediocre when it comes to recycling. The best way you can help is by sorting properly so they don't have any excuse.

Turn Off Your House

As you leave each morning for work, let your home take some time to rest. Shutting down your house for the day saves energy costs and sets a pattern of conscious, sustainable choices that will follow you through your day.

15 Why control the climate of an empty house? Turn off the AC or
16 turn down the thermostat. Turn off lights. We all should have
learned that one already.

17 Remember to unplug things that don't need to be left on. Unplug
everything? Really? Well, no need to get obsessive. But the fact
is that most appliances, televisions, even cell phone and laptop
chargers continue to waste electricity when they're not being
used. If you don't want to be the manic person who unplugs
18 her television every time she's not watching, consider surge
protectors and power strips, which stop burning electricity in
the off position.

19 You can make this easier if you use an Energy Hub. While we
may be a few years away from these being common commercial
products, the basic idea is appealing: you run all your appliances through this little device that helps turn them on and off
in environmentally conscious and lifestyle-affirming ways. It
can change your AC settings during the night, or get it cooling
just before you come home. It will power down TVs and DVD
players. It may even start your coffeemaker for you while you
sleep . . .

20 Bigger picture: monitor your energy use to save waste and money.
There are great groups like Earth Aid that monitor your use for
you, offer you information on how much your neighbors are
using, give you tips to reduce, and reward you (financially!) if you
21 reduce your use and beat out your neighbors. Make the switch
22 to compact fluorescents and low-flow showerheads to start, and
23 ask your power company about alternative energy. Most power
companies will allow you to request your electricity come from
wind power or other alternative sources. This creates a market
for that energy, which will bring down the cost over time.

One more fun idea, as you're unplugging your phones and iPods
24 and carrying them off for the day: There are backpacks with

solar panels on them that build up enough current to charge your mobile devices while you're on the go. Buy one of those and you never run down, you save money and electricity, and you definitely start some conversations.

Commute Liberally

Maybe you work from home, telecommuting in your PJs all day—what a way to save yourself some peace of mind, and save the planet your carbon emissions. No? Then maybe you get to bicycle to work, exercising while you head to the office. But in most places, that's just not practical.

Use public transportation when you can—what's more communal than mass transit? You literally share space with neighbors and strangers alike. But the reality is that many people have to drive. Furthermore, not everyone can afford a hybrid vehicle.

All is not lost: that's why the car pool was created. It creates a little community of fellow travelers who save fuel and money, look out for each other, and share news, stories, and the road.

You also save time: dedicated high-occupancy vehicle (HOV) or carpool lanes whisk you and your teammates along the fast track. Makes you want to advocate for more of those in your area . . .

Sure, people who go it alone have their own car, their own climate control, their own radio, their own schedule . . . and they'll sit in traffic a whole lot longer.

Caffeinate Liberally

You may have noticed I skipped one critical step in the morning ritual: coffee. Worry not: if you're like me, you didn't get as far as a car pool without first stopping by the coffeepot. I saved this for the last of the morning rituals because our relationship to coffee is so sacred, it deserves its own section.

To the detriment of my health, my wallet, and at times my morals, I am a compulsive coffee drinker. So I want to make sure liberal values are percolating along with the grounds.

A few tips to make the most of your morning joe.

Brew your own. Save money and packaging by making your own coffee, rather than stopping at the coffee shop along the way. You can even enjoy a cup while reading the *Times* and fill up another for the road. Which brings up a good point . . .

Use a travel mug. A travel mug keeps the coffee going strong as you go long. And if you didn't have time to brew, or if you run low, you can go into a store and ask them to refill your mug, saving on yet another paper cup. Often, the cashier won't know what to charge you at first . . . but she'll figure it out. And if many more of us start carrying our own vessels, we'll form a large enough group to start lobbying for discounts. After all, we're saving them money too.

Know your brew. Make your own decisions about which coffee tastes best; but be aware of which labor and environmental practices would leave a bad taste in your mouth. Keep an eye out for phrases like Fair Trade—it makes a big difference. Fair Trade coffee is sold by collectives of local farmers—the purchase rate is higher than they might otherwise receive, and the money is reinvested into their local communities. Another term to look for: shade grown, which means farmers did not clear fields to cultivate coffee. Excessive clearing leads to erosion and decimates the health benefits of trees for our air and ecosystems. Coffee can eat up your insides physically . . . no need for it to do so morally.

Make more than you need. Wait, wait, wait . . . isn't producing too much wasteful, therefore un-green, ergo un-liberal? Well, it would be if we were throwing it out. But when you make more, you share more. Why not bring a travel mug to your carpool-mate (and maybe tomorrow, she'll bring one for you)? Or take a thermos to the office? We're a caffeine culture. . . . I'm not out to starve that addiction; I just want to make it a little more communal.

With a little more research, you'll find ways to liberalize your morning rituals. The government's Energy Star program is full of ideas for reducing consumption at your home. And I still remember reading *50 Simple Things You Can Do to Save the Earth* when I was in the single digits, and as a result diligently turning off the sink faucet as I brushed my teeth. I still do feel a little pang of guilt when I let water run in a trickle as I shave . . . a sign of how effective that book was getting into my subconscious more than twenty years ago.

Maybe twenty years from now, someone will need to explain to their kids why they brew so much coffee. . . .

Who Are the People in Your Neighborhood?

Inside your house, most of what you do is about making progressive politics personal. The next thing you do each morning is enter the outside world—where progressive politics becomes public—where "you" and "I" become "we."

Even before you head to work—before you climb into your carpool vehicle, power up your hybrid, or hop on your bicycle—look around your home and ask the question sung by those great liberal Muppets on *Sesame Street*: "Who are the people in your neighborhood?"

Do you know your neighbors? Do you smile at them? Say hi? Know their names? Invite them over? I'm not just being nosy here. . . . I'm asking questions that are directly connected to your happiness.

There are studies that have demonstrated that happiness is contagious. When your neighbors are happy, it rubs off on you, and you become happy. That's good incentive to know who is on your block. It's not enough just to be near them, though . . . you need to know their names and what's going on in their lives. So, say hello for a healthier life.

Look around: who are the people in your neighborhood, the people who you meet as you're walking down the street? Do you even walk down the street? Or do you depart from an attached garage in a car with windows closed, AC on, and Neighbor Radar turned off? Do you see your neighbors and wave, or has the high fence between your homes successfully hidden you from all contact?

My mother recalls growing up in an old neighborhood in East New York, an area of Brooklyn that, at the time, had a large Jewish population. Kids played in the streets, but they were safe. Both my grandparents worked, but my mom wasn't unsupervised. All the neighbors kept an eye on each other. The grandmothers on the block sat on their stoops and shouted to the kids when they were being too rambunctious. And the kids—rather than ignoring some old lady yelling at them—listened. Why? Because that old lady knew their parents.

This community supervision is celebrated by Jane Jacobs in her book *The Death and Life of Great American Cities*. Incidental [45] policing provides a sense of safety. It's also self-perpetuating: if those old ladies needed anything, the kids would be there to help.

There's something else wonderfully liberal that happens in the best of neighborhoods: people are exposed to the diversity of other families. Sure, my mom's block felt Jewish, but in the spray fountains of the playground one block over, Jewish, black, and Italian kids ran around together.

You don't need a scene out of a Neil Simon play to have a good neighborhood. Just look around for the features that create shared space . . . literally the "common ground" that can help turn strangers into neighbors and neighbors into friends. These democratic spaces allow—even encourage— people to meet and mingle, share concerns and hopes, discuss community affairs, plan events, and extend invitations. And no, these magical spaces I discuss are nothing more remarkable than that spray fountain in Brooklyn in the 1950s.

Visit your neighborhood parks. Parks are true community [46] assets. They help us breathe easier; trees and green pathways contribute to public health. They give children a place to play, seniors a way to get outside, and families and neighbors a destination to visit together. All over the country, neighborhood parks are the easiest way to create common ground.

Backyards are terrific . . . but inherently private. You have your swing set for your kids. Your children aren't asked to share, they don't learn to socialize with new friends. Not that you should never hang out in your backyard, but give your public park a chance.

Play in your area playgrounds. Playgrounds, in addition to parks, fulfill this liberal ideal. The first public playgrounds were built in New York City at the start of the nineteenth century. They were specifically situated in the city's poorest, most crowded areas, usually populated by immigrants, to ensure that children got out for exercise, fresh air, and a good dose of civic engagement.

Now, the importance of play is a real public policy concern and not only for the poorest communities. The impact of play and playgrounds is so widely understood that advocacy groups are increasingly succeeding in making access to playgrounds a public commitment. The organization KaBOOM!, which builds playgrounds—often in needy areas like post-Katrina New Orleans—has been getting mayors to sign on to their "Play Cities" agenda, part of which assures playgrounds and play opportunities in close proximity to every child.

Of course, creating that prevalence of playgrounds and parks requires space. In cities, open space can be a tight commodity, and in small towns and suburbs, it still takes a lot of resources to create, preserve, maintain, and program shared spaces. Consequently, local representatives need to be reminded again and again how important these areas are, and, sometimes, we can't just leave it to our public officials.

Visit a community garden. All across the country, citizens are finding creative solutions to open-space shortages. Community gardens are often born in vacant lots. Sometimes, they begin with the permission of an owner or city agency that has no use for the lot. Sometimes, communities just take over abandoned areas, clean them up, and claim them for public use. The New York–based "Green Guerillas" used the latter method to create dozens of such gardens.

Without public funding, these gardens are truly supported by the "public"—that is, the public citizens who create self-governing methods to maintain these spaces. In many cases, they really do become gardens, growing vegetables and flowers. They provide opportunities for people to grow their own organic produce and learn more about what "organic" means. At the very least, they also provide the opportunity for people to enjoy open space that they collectively created.

Create a play street. Play streets are another communal vision for how to open shared spaces in your neighborhood. In New York City, this phenomenon has closed down city blocks over the summer for decades, giving congested neighborhoods the outdoor space they need . . . right outside their front doors. Like the streets my mom remembers, or the streets I grew up on in small-town New Jersey, these avenues become places to play team sports and board games, learn from each other, or just hang out.

51

In the summer of 2009, the *New York Times* profiled one such play street in the Bronx, a street that had run for thirty-three summers, largely thanks to the perseverance of one local woman who insisted on it and organized her neighbors to support it. But she couldn't do it alone. To close the street, she needed 51 percent of the residents of the block to sign a petition. How's that for the benefits of knowing your neighbors?

You don't have to live in a city or push yourself into public parks to develop bonds with your neighbors. Gated communities make it difficult to feel the democratic flow of different people, income levels, and backgrounds. Life in a McMansion may mean you never even pass your neighbors on the street. Wherever you live, you can at least take some steps to answer the question, "Who are the people in your neighborhood?" and then ask a second question, oft-intoned by that great liberal, Mr. Rogers: "Won't you be my neighbor?"

Left Detour

Mr. Rogers. Fred Rogers, the beloved children's television host who asked us to make believe and to open our imaginations and our welcoming spirits and in an unassuming cardigan taught us how to be a good neighbor, passed away in February 2003. A few weeks later, on what would have been his seventy-fifth birthday, March 20, I sent around an e-mail to everyone in my address list letting people know it was "Won't You Be My Neighbor Day," a tribute to Mr. Rogers that you celebrated by doing neighborly acts while wearing sneakers and a cardigan.

I had made the holiday up; I thought someone should. I wore a zip-up sweatshirt that day (I didn't own a cardigan), but, as far as I knew, the day never caught on. That said, a cursory Google search reveals that Family Communications (fci.org) continues to promote an annual event of the same name and even offers a "Caring Neighbor Checklist" with such recommendations as "Share a Hug," "Volunteer at a Senior Center," and "Visit Your Local Library."

I'd love to believe my e-mail and lone celebration was forwarded to them. More likely, I should recognize that if you have a good idea, chances are someone else had it, too. I'm just glad they saw it through.

Want to invite your neighbors into your life? Or inject yourself into theirs a little bit more? Here are a few ideas that don't take much time or ask you to change your life too much. Each action helps cultivate a liberal landscape, one in which we embrace the idea: We better get to know one another since we're all in this together. And that would make Mr. Rogers proud.

Sit on your porch. Yes, inside is climate controlled and the remote is only an arm's length away. But you already know what you'll see if you stay inside . . . who knows what you may find when you turn outward? It makes it more likely you'll see your neighbors and they'll see you. It will increase your appreciation of the rhythm of your street. People around you feel safer and more welcome (assuming you don't grimace at them), thereby lowering those barriers so that happiness can be as contagious as possible.

53

If you're in a city, fear not. The stoop counts. I've met friends on my stoop—one of them is now on our block association and organizes movie screenings in our local playground. All because I was sitting out front rather than out back or up on my fire escape. Oh, and because she said hello. Which brings us to point two:

Say hi to your neighbors. Sounds obvious. But do you do it? If you're like me, there are days when you just want to keep your head down. You're a little scared: if you say hi, next thing you know you'll have to say, "How are you?" Then you're making small talk . . . and that can sometimes be annoying.

54

However, think about what you can get for those few seconds of annoyance. You might make a new friend. Or recruit someone to a neighborhood association (or be recruited yourself). You create a connection with someone who will hold a set of your keys, or help you carry your groceries, or take in your mail while you're gone. Yes, saying hello is never just saying hello . . . it's a slippery slope into full-fledged community. But you know what? I bet it will cause you more smiles than aggravation in the end.

Although, if a few moments of conversation is too much for you, you're going to hate the next idea:

Invite your neighbors over. Whoa, whoa, whoa. My home is my castle. The point of a castle is to keep people out. And if I want to interact with neighbors, isn't that what parks are for? You spent pages telling us to go to our local playgrounds . . . now you want us to stay inside?

Realistically, you're not going to spend your whole life outside. Winter comes. And there's a lot of quality time that is better served inside: meals, games, TV. Yes . . . TV. I'm a liberal, but I'm not a Puritan!

Personally, I don't cook, so I'd be a hypocrite if I encouraged everyone to invite neighbors over for a meal (though I would gladly accept such invitations). But there is plenty I do in my own home that could be shared with my neighbors . . . and would even be improved by my neighbors' presence.

I like chess. I can't play alone. Would my neighbor enjoy a game? I should ask.

I love charades, celebrity, salad bowl, and all those other games when groups of people shout out answers at each other's absurd clues and gestures. If I shouted guesses at myself, that may be too easy . . . and a little crazy. However, if I'm inviting other friends over anyway, why not knock next door? The worst that happens is that Duane (my next-door neighbor) will say no. The best? He may be able to mime "*To Kill a Mockingbird*" or "Ronald Reagan" really well.

Here's an even wackier idea: invite neighbors over to watch TV. People do this with sporting events all the time . . . how about with the news? Or a good comedy? Or even better: comedy news? *The Daily Show* is a dish best served shared—when you can laugh together . . . and discuss it afterward.

It may be weird to invite neighbors over to watch the Jim Lehrer *NewsHour*, but *The Daily Show* is entertainment. And—it's short. You'll only be entertaining guests for half an hour.

You invite them over for *The Daily Show*, and maybe they'll invite you over to see some of those programs on premium cable that you can't afford.

Now, what does swapping TV times have to do with living liberally?

★ It makes television a shared resource. You've just socialized HBO.

★ It transforms a very inward, private activity into a public, shared one . . . you can discuss and debate.

★ It creates community. What starts with watching TV together can become attending a community meeting or organizing a letter-writing campaign. You start organizing a community and before you know it, you're—gasp!—a community organizer.

Bonus: buy a projector, and turn TV shows into big-screen experiences. It's just more fun that way.

Make enough food to share. As a non-cook, this is a little outside of my skill set. But several times I've been the beneficiary of neighbors who have knocked on my door, announced that they made too much food, and asked if I would like to share it with them.

Did they really overcook, or were they looking for an excuse to reach out? Either way, the result was the same: I was fed. I also developed a sense of warmth for these people I passed in the halls each day. It made me want to help them—carry bags up the stairs, or check in on their family's health. It made me a better neighbor.

The quickest way to my heart was indeed through my stomach.

60 **Share an internet connection and wi-fi router** with your neighbor. You know you want high-speed connectivity at home ... but why shoulder the cost alone? This becomes one more resource that **61** you and neighbors can share. If you feel really liberal, leave it unlocked and make someone else very happy.

62 **Think public.** As you make choices about schooling, recreation, and resources outside your home, consider the public option. When you participate in shared programs and venues, you meet people in your community, come to see issues from their perspectives, and begin to share needs and goals.

This is one of the appeals of public parks—it also extends to public recreation centers. In many cities, where there are not municipal recreation options, the local YMCAs (or their equivalent) serve this role. Many of them offer sliding-scale memberships, so nobody gets turned away. They are more affordable than private fitness centers and create an environment where you and your family will meet people you might not encounter on your street or at your workplace.

This is also true, of course, of one of our country's greatest assets: our public schools. They are our best hope for teaching democracy. They give everyone a level playing field, encourage kids of different backgrounds to meet, and remind a community that all its members are invested in a single resource.

There are plenty of reasons why private schools can be attractive. You might be in an area where the public schools are underfunded or where drug activity gets in the way of learning. You may want your children to have a religious education, or they may have special needs that a private school can meet. I went to a private high school, and had an incredible experience; I also know that it allowed me privileges that not everyone shared. It's a complicated question, because parents want what's best for their children, as they should. Staying invested in the public school is often the way to improve it.

Every family will have to make its own choice, but at least think about public schools. Try them out. You'll discover devoted teachers and the potential for strong community bonds, and your kids deserve to be part of this great experience of democracy.

As you're thinking about public facilities, you can also think about public health. The costs of health care are overwhelming and heavily tax us all. Fortunately, we can protect ourselves, prevent disease among our neighbors, and reduce our communal health care costs at the same time. Get vaccinations to prevent [63] the spread of disease; you might not be at risk yourself, but you do not want to carry diseases to more vulnerable members of society. Don't smoke—not only does it hurt you, but it hurts those [64] around you and incurs incredible health costs down the road. Pick up trash in your community. Don't go to work when you're [65] [66] sick. Preventing contagion improves everyone's health and saves everyone money. (One more reason to advocate for paid sick [67] days for all employees.) Thinking about the public good is an important way of living for others, not just for yourself.

How Large Is Your 'Hoodprint?

Over the past couple years, you've probably heard about your "carbon footprint." That's shorthand for how much greenhouse

gas you are personally responsible for, directly or indirectly. So
you take steps to reduce your carbon footprint on our planet.

More recently, food activists, concerned about access to healthy,
local foods and about the impact of our food system on the environment, have asked us to mind our "foodprint"—the ecological
impact of production and delivery of the food we eat.

Has anyone ever defined a "'hoodprint"—the boundaries of
the neighborhood (physical or virtual) in which you live? I'm a
global, cosmopolitan, big-city guy, so I'm not saying you should
stick close to home all the time, but there is something nice about
the grocer you recognize, or the mail carrier who calls you by
name. There's strength in a community where you can walk to
school, a park, and a movie theater. There are smart environmental and financial consequences to a walk/bike lifestyle as
well as societal advantages that are harder to quantify.

Are there ways you can shrink your 'hoodprint? Can you shop at
a local mom-and-pop rather than drive out to the big-box store?
Can you get some pleasure attending a local minor-league game,
or seeing a show at the local community center? No need to cut
out Major League and Broadway altogether, but are there ways
you can take from—and in doing so, invest in—your community?
The subsequent chapters are filled with reasons to go local . . .
and in doing so, shrink your 'hoodprint.

Though he didn't use the term 'hoodprint, one social scientist
first made me think about the concept. Actually, he's a friend:
David Alpert, one of the partners who took Living Liberally
national, and the publisher of Greater Greater Washington, a
website devoted to discussions of smart city planning.

He once wrote about his friend who lived in a small town—
population about 8,000. His friend had lived there for a number
of years, and his parents had worked there when he was growing

up. He saw people he knew while he walked down the street. He inquired after them, and they checked in on how his family was doing. His supermarket, movie theater, favorite diner and bar, clinic and playground were all within walking distance, and he knew by name many of the people who served him coffee and eggs . . . and they knew how he wanted them.

This sounded familiar, because it sounded a little like the town where I grew up, Highland Park, New Jersey. It was a small walkable town, over the river from New Brunswick, the larger "city" where Rutgers University is based. In Highland Park, I could walk to my friends' homes at an early age, walk to school, and walk to the store. I knew my friends' parents, and in many cases their grandparents, and they knew mine, because some of the kids I knew in preschool, I knew through all of childhood. It was a town where you could play in the street (as well as the backyard).

So I knew what David was talking about. Turned out, though, I knew better than I had realized. David's essay had a twist: the friend was me, and the small town was Hell's Kitchen, on the bustling, crowded west side of Manhattan, just blocks from Times Square and the Broadway theater district. He'd looked up the census data for my few square blocks—and realized I'd created a small-town feel, with neighbors, familiar strangers, regular haunts.

I'd gotten my 'hoodprint to eight blocks.

I live in the center of a big city, and yet some days don't venture more than a few streets from my home. There are the environmental savings of not driving and the convenience of the tight radius. Then there is the real benefit: in a world where more and more people say they feel alienated from neighbors, where people build walls between themselves and others, I feel like I have a home. And that's Living Liberally.

Living Liberally in the Larger World

Being neighborly is at the core of being liberal—but it is not the exclusive domain of liberals. A conservative all-white neighborhood might have good community spirit, but is a far cry from the diverse, inclusive world a liberal envisions.

We have to extend our thinking. If we see value in creating a connection with our neighbors, we should see the similar worth in our neighborhood and the next neighborhood working together, to share resources, help each other out, and tackle problems bigger than either neighborhood could handle on its own. This is why towns need to work together, why states seek solutions to larger problems through the federal government, and why different countries ultimately recognize we need to collaborate across borders.

Additionally, the truth of the world in which we live is that we cannot choose a life shaped only by other people and forces we select. A racist may wish to live in an all-white enclave, but that is not the reality of the arc of history (nor should it be). I may enjoy my eight-block 'hoodprint, but everything from the cost of my food to the quality of my air, from the entertainment I enjoy to the traffic on my street, is influenced by far more than that parcel I call home.

We are all subject to the decisions of people we may never meet and to conditions created by choices made outside our neighborhood. Similarly, we affect the lives of others every day. That is why when we recognize "we are all in this together," we do not only mean "our block" or "our race" or "our religion." In a complex, interconnected world, an approach that embraces diversity and encourages everyone to think about a greater good is not just pleasant, but necessary.

So when you <u>attend your Block Association</u> or <u>help a neighbor with a chore</u>, you are taking steps to create a society where we look out for each other; the key is then taking those same impulses beyond the neighborhood you see and the people you know, and applying those same values to the larger world.

On the surface, this may not seem radical—or even overtly political. However, if you look around our culture, you see many trends that show we are not looking out for each other and are, instead, living for ourselves alone:

★ The popularity of larger cars, such as SUVs, which have countered efforts at fuel-efficiency so these tank-like vehicles can fulfill a fantasy of "owning the road."

★ The decrease, over the past half-century, in participation in civic associations and community social events, coupled with the increase in insular television consumption.

★ The prevalence of gated communities with isolated mansions and private security forces that prevent the natural flow of commerce, people, and ideas.

These patterns of wanting one's own control, privilege, and separation come at the expense of community and the environment, make it easier to segregate oneself from people who are different, and allow one to escape from engaging in larger social issues.

If you look around, you will see choices we make that suggest we are *not* living for one another. That mind-set then seeps into our public discourse, and many of our toughest political questions divide those who believe we should care for one another and those who believe we must only care for ourselves.

Climate Change. When you're all in the same boat, nobody ignores the leak. It's only when you have your personal yacht that you can ignore the ship sinking next to you. If we were all invested in the fortunes of those around us, would anyone spend their time and money denying the impact of global warming? We would be working hard to tackle climate change in order to prevent disastrous water shortages and social unrest that might be the result of inaction. The only folks who have reason to fight action are companies looking after their short-term bottom line ahead of the common good.

Health care. Shouldn't one of the signs of a great country be its ability to support the health of our fellow citizens? Yet, opponents of universal coverage call it "big-government, socialized medicine." There are economic costs to all of us when people are unable to afford health insurance. They often miss out on preventative care, and end up in worsening situations by the time they turn to public hospitals. These become real costs to all of us: in the care they receive later in their illness, in the loss of healthy workers to our economy. Beyond the bottom line, though, there is the moral question: why should anyone die because they cannot get care? We would not accept that in our household or in our neighborhood—why accept it anywhere?

Immigration. Would you imagine people arguing against providing education for children of immigrants if we really believed we were in this together? You don't ask your new neighbor for a passport before helping them carry in bags of groceries or letting them into a local park. Why would that change for their children's ability to get an education and become contributing members of our larger society? When we agree that we are better off in a world where we all succeed, we not only feel a moral and humane obligation to those around us regardless of their citizenship, but realize that undereducated children would be a larger social problem than opening our schools to new students.

Estate Tax. This tax only affected the wealthiest few percent of our country, returning a portion of their estate to the public good at the time of their death, acknowledging that personal wealth is accumulated with the support of public infrastructure. Conservatives rebranded it the "death tax." They convinced middle-class people that it would affect them, which was largely not the case; that it would leave their kids with nothing, which was never true; and that it was "their money, they earned it" — with no regard to how society's investment in infrastructure, regulations, and stability had helped them earn "their" money. They decimated the estate tax and effectively exacerbated wealth disparity in America. If we were interested in what's best for the greater good, we would support the estate tax as a fair, necessary measure. [77]

Progressive Taxation. We say "taxes" like they are a bad thing. Yet, they help pay for the safety of our food, water, and air, the usability of our roads and transit, the protection of our country, the functionality of our courts, and the depth of our scientific inquiry. Supreme Court Justice Oliver Wendell Holmes once opined, "Taxes are what we pay for a civilized society." Less famously, my childhood friend's father once said, "Stop whining and pay your taxes." Why should we approach tax day with dread, when that is what invests in our country, shared fortune, and future? We should cheer on progressive taxation. [78] We are all in this together — and that means we all need to invest together.

A common conservative argument is to accuse good ideas of being "socialist." The very word sets off alarm bells. Americans have a gut reflex against the word. Is that because of decades of facing off against the "Evil Empire"? (Reagan's words, not mine . . . I've always found Russians to be quite hospitable.) Is it because of our Horatio Alger "pull yourself up by your boot-straps" American ideal? Or is it because political leaders are so scared of certain words that once the right wing calls something "socialist," it becomes too hard to defend the idea?

They call expanding health care a "socialist plan to create government-run health care." They accuse environmental regulations, school funding, and progressive tax structures of being "socialist" because they would require our government to supervise more regulations and invest more in national infra-structure.

What they object to as "socialist" are services that are "shared," "supported by all," "serving all," and often "structured by govern-ment." The irony is that there are already many great aspects of the American way of life that fit that description.

While there are pervasive conservative trends in America, we are not ultimately a go-it-alone, every-man-for-himself society. There are strong liberal instincts in America as well. These liberal tendencies live in many of our country's great institutions. We don't call them "liberal" per se, but they embody those values. They pool our resources to deliver strong, public services. They serve all of us, not discriminating by our income, race, neigh-borhood, or nationality. They are services often strengthened by our participation, frequently benefiting from the democratic engagement of those they serve. These institutions invest in the common good and are proof that we are better off when we live, work, and contribute together.

What are some examples of these shared services for the common good?

79 Let's start with our National Park Service. There are vast tracts of land throughout our country preserved for the public's

enjoyment: for our recreation, for beautiful vistas that leave us breathless, for opportunities to learn about a wild America that pre-dated us all.

Admission costs are kept low. Paths are maintained. Rangers are present, friendly, and helpful. Families enjoy unique experiences that go beyond what they'd find in their hometown and surpass what many of them could afford if they had to fly to a remote destination or rent an expensive hotel.

Our "Big Government" has succeeded in giving us "socialized" national parks.

You don't have to head off to the national parks in Wyoming, the land of Dick Cheney, or Alaska, the land of Sarah Palin, to find such "socialized" programs at work. Shared programs are at the core of our communities everywhere. Just look around your hometown. . .

Firefighters. In a great bit, Laughing Liberally comedian Lee Camp jokes about what it would be like if fire departments worked like health care: Before they put out your fire, they have to check your insurance; you may not get full coverage; maybe your fire was a preexisting condition. [80]

We salute and celebrate our firefighters for a reason, and it's not because they only help those who pay or lecture people about "putting your fire out by your bootstraps." They are a community good. In many areas, you can volunteer for your fire department. Volunteer firefighters embody the spirit that we all have to look out for each other. [81]

Police. Do you have to use the "government-run" police force? No—you can opt out of that "public option" and hire your own private security, which many wealthier communities do. Most Americans see a value in a police force that works for everyone. [82]

A private security firm would be happy enough to push a problem along to another neighborhood. Public safety, inherently, cannot be private or segregated; it must protect us all.

83 **Libraries.** Would you accuse your local librarian of being a communist? We have private bookstores, of course, but still value our libraries and do not consider them unfair competition. Pooling knowledge and making information available to the public is good for society.

84 In addition to using your local library, lending a hand and donating to your book drive are liberal acts: actions that support a communal resource that prizes community over commerce.

85 **Schools.** Unless we're all going to send our kids to private schools, we need this "government program." As with most of the institutions listed, it's not enough to pay taxes and let it ride. Schools need parental and community involvement. School systems that shut out parents are rightly criticized. When schools serve as a resource for parents who want to engage in their **86** **87** child's education, they're at their best. Join a PTA. Offer to be **88** a guest speaker. Open your business for a class trip.

89 **Food pantries.** Why would you donate canned goods to people you may not even know? Because you—and your church— believe that it is important to look out for the less fortunate. This is an example that isn't necessarily government-run; often places of worship embody liberal characteristics.

90 **Soup kitchens.** You would never ask why those in need of a meal don't go to a restaurant instead. The volunteers who staff kitchens and shelters are doing tremendous work. Don't just take that from a political lefty; every religious institution in the country would call it the "Lord's work" to feed and house the hungry and homeless.

We learn our political beliefs through the interactions we have and the conversations that lead us in new directions. I would find it hard to believe that someone who worked extensively in a soup kitchen didn't come away believing the people he or she served deserved a chance to make the most of their lives. When you don't talk to homeless people, it's easy to detach from them—they are the "other," unlike us, uninterested in working or pulling themselves together. When you talk to them over a meal, you can't help but realize they are human, like you or me.

91

Does that mean you'll believe in our current welfare system as it works? Not necessarily. Policies and programs are flawed. However, you will come away believing that there should be services that give these folks a chance and the support they need to find new opportunities. And whether or not you believe those services should be government supported, you're already on the right track of knowing that we do have to look out for our fellow citizens.

Public access TV. As goofy as it can be (and justifiably lampooned in *Wayne's World*), public access is one more institution that engages community creativity and delivers back some community good. It teaches skills, builds self-esteem and confidence, promotes community dialogue, and usually does so without commercialization.

92

Seed banks. Of this list, seed banks are the least likely sentinel of socialism to reach your neighborhood, not yet as common as libraries and food pantries. The idea is to create a library of seeds—so if you want to grow vegetables or flowers, you use the seeds collectively shared and catalogued. At the end of the season, you return seeds for others to use. It's beautifully self-perpetuating, encourages curiosity, and is a surprising opportunity to pool natural resources.

93

What makes it truly radical, though, is how these banks cut out agribusiness. There is an "Agricultural Industrial Complex," and they want to own seeds. It sounds absurd . . . but these companies genetically modify seeds to resist weather or disease and patent those creations. So, most seeds you buy are "designer seeds"—and believe it or not, they remain the intellectual property of the companies. If you want to share your seeds, they could legally stop you. This isn't just theoretical . . . agribusiness has done it.

Regardless of the legal arguments, something just seems wrong about that. And seed banks are an institution out to set it right.

All of these examples demonstrate two points:

1) Collectivist institutions are all around us despite the stamping and shouting that we can't have "socialized government programs."

2) It's not enough that they exist. We need to engage with them. We need to improve them and contribute to them. Using our shared resources is a hallmark of a liberal lifestyle; supporting these resources is truly living like a liberal.

94   95   You drive on big-government roads to get to a collectivist post office and people in your family enjoy government-run programs like Social Security, Medicare, and Head Start. It was the "greater good" spirit that led to government involvement in supervising safety in food, water, air, and airlines, and in cleaning up Superfund toxic sites. When you stop to think about how much you benefit from a government motivated by an "all in this together" attitude, you don't need to declare yourself a socialist. Just declare yourself a liberal.

CHAPTER 3
WORKING LIBERALLY

Here's a wild-eyed vision: a workplace where employees could dedicate some of their time at the office to independent projects. They are not told what to do with every moment; rather, their supervisors trust that if given the latitude to experiment, these employees will come up with something good for the company.

Imagine if this were not the only flexibility in their workday. They can come in when they want, as long as they stay late as well. They may wear what they want. Plus, they are well compensated.

What if the company provided, in addition to generous wages, free meals—lunch every day, and dinner for employees who stay late? Periodically, the office would close and take everyone to the movies.

What could make this dreamier? Jars full of jelly beans and coolers of refreshing fruit drinks around the workplace . . . all for free . . .

If these ideas seem crazy . . . then Google is the craziest company I've ever heard of. Google—not the verb that it's become, but the business behemoth that has changed our lives—has a workplace culture that would seem anathema to the button-up world of traditional offices. "Button-up" most definitely wouldn't apply, given that there's no dress code. There is a casual, comfortable feel that earns their California compound the description "campus."

It's almost like they want to make their employees happy.

Their dining halls are well stocked and meals are well known for being tasty and healthy. So their programmers—who are, after all, human and love free food—stay late. At their Mountainview campus, they even have a mobile dentist and mobile barber come periodically.

Now, it's not all altruistic. These services keep employees from having to make appointments and save them trips "off-campus," thus maximizing the time they spend contributing to the company. And they make the staff feel some gratitude, even loyalty. They have social outings and barbecues together, and, if you haven't heard, the company is making money.

It's not that Google is an inherently liberal company. Google sometimes behaves very liberally—it challenged the Bush administration over privacy issues—and sometimes less so, as when it worked with the Chinese government to censor web searches. Al Gore may be a longtime advisor, but Google is also a growing enterprise that has had its own examples of stamping out competition.

As a workplace, though, it offers ideas on how to build a sense of community, allow flexibility, encourage creativity, and respect its employees.

It doesn't require a world-renowned brand name to create this type of work environment. There are some steps that any employee could advocate for and any employer could implement to create an environment that is working liberally.

Get your office recycling. Everyone buys into it at this point, but not every commercial establishment knows how to do it. Learning the rules and making it easy saves money, reduces waste, and sets a good example.

96

Make energy-saving improvements. Most people know about lightbulb savings: buy efficient bulbs, install motion-activated lights in restrooms and closets, turn off lights at night. How about bathroom improvements: invest in low-flush toilets and urinals, hand driers instead of paper towels, and timed faucets, all of which save electricity and water and can improve public health? Or institute policies for turning off computers at night?

97
98 99
100
101
102 103
104

Improve the kitchen. Many offices assume you'll just eat out (or some assume you won't eat at all). Having a functional kitchen cuts down on your lunch costs and may also increase your productivity since you don't have to run to the gourmet deli down the block. This means more than having a refrigerator (which, by the way, should be an energy-efficient fridge). The kitchen needs to invite the staff to use it. Stock dishware to reduce waste and develop a system for cleaning the dishes. Have real utensils and provide common condiments and other frequently used items like milk for cereal.

105
106
107
108

And by all means, invest in a coffeemaker. I would reduce my own personal trash, expenses, and waste of time if there were always a pot of coffee brewing and I didn't need to run down the street.

109

Get rid of the water cooler. OK, water cooler conversation is important . . . it's often the best place to engage colleagues. But we don't actually need a water cooler to do it.

Bottled water is bad business. They take regular water. They truck it over many miles. Then they sell it to you, even though your water is fine to begin with. This creates waste, pollution, and, in some areas, water shortages. A water cooler is better than individually bottled water, but it's time to fight the aqua-industrial complex.

Unsure how you feel about tap water? Convince your office to invest in a filtering container or a filter that attaches to the faucet. Do your research, and you will find the cost savings come quickly.

Relax the dress code. If you work in a formal office, chances are that on your way to work on a hot day, you can't wait to get inside. You're overdressed for the heat, and you're in need of another shower after you crowd into public transportation or hop off your bicycle. The reason you're excited to get inside is because your office is blasting AC: drawing electricity, spewing pollutants, and generally wasting resources.

What if people could dress comfortably? Allowing staff to dress down has enabled businesses to relax the climate control. It saves money for the business and allows people to feel more at home . . . at work.

Create avenues for staff feedback. Every office will benefit from its staff feeling a sense of ownership—and that comes from including staff in discussions and decisions. If you work some-place, you should feel invested in it, and you have a perspective that should be valued. Whether a committee structure or a feedback box, there should be some mechanism by which management hears from its team.

Provide flex time. Why do you arrive at nine and leave at five? Is it so you have something in common with the Dolly Parton song? Or is it because everyone assumes you should?

Working the same hours as everyone else can have its advantages: it makes meetings easier to coordinate, and the office saves resources by only being open certain hours.

There are drawbacks. You all commute during the busiest hours of the day, adding time to your travel and maybe increasing the expense of your peak-hour tolls and train tickets. It also means someone who might moonlight at a night job is working the same hours as someone anxious to get home to be with their kids after school. Why shouldn't the mom or dad come in earlier and leave earlier, while the part-time DJ rolls in, fresher, later in the morning?

Technology makes this more possible. People can telecommute more easily or join meetings outside of their regular hours. And this "flex" approach to scheduling is making workers happier and more productive.

Dedicate a staff lounge. Wait—this place is called "work," so shouldn't we be working here? Most of your workspace is aimed at your job . . . but you don't sit at a desk all day. You go out for meals, hover in the kitchen, linger over the water cooler (or its enviro-friendly replacement).

A comfortable space for the staff facilitates the opportunity to turn your coworkers from fellow drones to potential friends. And since you tossed your water cooler, you need someplace to talk about the TV shows from the night before.

Allow independent time. What if 10–20 percent of your work hours were unstructured? You wouldn't have an assignment, but you'd be at work . . . and whatever you worked on would be contributed to the company.

Would you innovate something new for your department, or come up with a new project your business should be involved in? Would you dream up a new marketing scheme, build a company Facebook page, or imagine some cost-saving measures? Would you conjure ideas for greening your workplace and research low-flow toilets?

Businesses need innovation from the people who know the businesses best and are invested in their success. If companies want innovation, they have to create room for it.

Organize staff outings. Sure, you have an office holiday party. But do you leave early on summer days for your office soft-ball team? Or go as a group on the first day a new movie is released? Building community with your coworkers is like building community anywhere: it leads to greater investment in each other's lives, respect for each other, and ultimately makes you better organized as you push to liberalize your workplace further. Seemingly silly measures like getting off early to go picnic together make your business stronger.

You may not do all of these ideas right off the bat, but starting with any of them is a good beginning. By the way, if people laugh at these ideas as silly, hippie pipe dreams, just ask if that means they do not want to become the next Google.

Organizing Liberally

Jonah had worked at a major telecommunications company for years. He wasn't proud of it. He wasn't ashamed of it. It was his job; it wasn't his life. He had a social life and loved to read and talk about theater and arts and ideas with whomever he could find at his local coffee shop.

Then the 2004 election came around. Like many Americans, for the first time Jonah felt motivated to get involved. He began to volunteer for a campaign for the first time since he'd been in college in the late seventies. He spent evenings making phone calls and took weekend trips to Pennsylvania.

But there were still those eight hours a day, five days a week that he had to spend at work. So he decided to make the most use of his time, and he started engaging his coworkers in political discussions.

He looked around and saw smart, able people who were not giving a second thought to the larger political world, or their potential to have an impact on it. So he started asking them about their politics. It startled them, because nobody at the office much talked with each other unless they had to. When it wasn't business, it was small talk. But Jonah asked them what they thought of current events. More frequently, he told them what he thought. Unapologetically and unasked, he shared his opinions.

More than once he found himself in an animated diatribe in the office kitchen, confronting people who hadn't even disagreed with him . . . they probably hadn't said much of anything. They all knew better than to talk politics with Jonah.

Jonah does not regret how extreme he was getting. "My goal," he said, "wasn't to convince them. They weren't willing to have a conversation, how could I convince them of anything? My goal was to at least make them stop and think. I wanted them to say, 'Hey, what's Jonah so worked up about?' and reflect on the issues. I wanted to make them a little uncomfortable."

I like Jonah a lot. However, this section is not about becoming Jonah. In fact, in some ways, this is about *not* being Jonah. You can bring progressive political views into your work life in ways that make you comfortable and fulfilled and make your coworkers comfortable as well.

There are plenty of places to start that can make your work experience—whatever it is—more communal, more conscientious, and more reflective of your beliefs. Usually, your efforts in this direction will be more successful if you can bring some people along with you.

120
When I was graduating from college, there was a movement to sign on to the "green pledge." It didn't ask you to dedicate your life to a nonprofit field; it understood that people would move into all industries. Whatever discipline you joined, there was room for you to carry your values and consider the environmental and human rights impact of your work. We signed a pledge: "I pledge to explore and take into account the social and environmental consequences of any job I consider and will try to improve these aspects of any organizations for which I work."

Beyond the pledge, though, how do you make this real? Even if you are not working in a "green industry," is there room for you to liberalize your work experience?

You want your business to be a better political, social, and environmental actor in the larger world. First, though, start locally . . . by liberalizing your own office. The ideas above are a place to start. Some are simple pitches on environmental grounds; others pose greater challenges to how an office operates. Begin with the simple ones, get a feel for how to make change within your workplace, and it will be a natural next step to push your business to become more responsible on all fronts.

Excited by these ideas? Or dreaming up new innovations of your own? Whatever you're looking to accomplish—small, or large, in how your workplace operates, how your employers treat employees, or how your business relates to the world—you'll need to follow three simple steps: Advocate, Engage, Organize.

Advocate. You may not be the person who decides what bulbs to use, but if you know how to use the internet, you can make a really strong case for making the switch. You have the ability to research greener business practices and bring them to the powers-that-be. You don't want to make a demand every day, but if you smartly advocate your case, you'll have a greener workplace in no time.

> **Research.** Whether it's asking for recycling or getting the company to ditch the water cooler in favor of a water filter, start by knowing the facts. Find out the environmental benefits and the financial costs. Look up other businesses that have done the same, so that you have case studies showing that these aren't far-fetched ideas. It's not hard to find this information—even the government is in the game. Visit Business.gov for tips on greening a workplace. If the government is putting it out there, it's not too radical for your office.

> **Anticipate.** What will your employers ask? We know they'll ask how much it will cost to make a switch. We know they'll ask how you know it will be an improvement. They'll ask whether other employees will object. Gather all the facts to see it from their perspective and be prepared for their questions.

> **Invest.** Step up and offer to take responsibility for the pilot program—whether that's making a

run for supplies, creating signs, or educating your coworkers. Not only does this make it easy for the boss to say yes, but by investing in it, you're more likely to see follow-through. You lead by example and others will get invested, too. That is the kind of gumption that's worth showing at work—you impress your office while you improve it.

Of course, advocating to your bosses is only one method of liberalizing your work—but a liberal workplace isn't caused by convincing the execs of top-down changes. Like your neighborhood, your workplace is liberal because of how you engage with those who work with you.

126 **Engage.** You see these people at some of your most frustrated moments, in the doldrums of a routine day. You just want to keep your head down and keep to yourself.

If you do that, you'll never bring your progressive values into your workplace.

Don't go all Jonah on them right away. Building a connection is the first step in starting a conversation, which is a step toward creating a community, which is a step toward making change.

Carpool. If you are already planning to share the road, why not include your colleagues? Spend some time with coworkers outside cubicles and corporate culture. Learn to trust and rely on each other. Save on gas and get to use the carpool lanes.

127 **Make coffee for your coworkers.** Whether you make it at home and bring the thermos in to share, or you're the first to get the pot brewing in the office kitchen, create that shared resource. Get everyone invested in keeping the pot full. Save money and waste. Before you know it, people will be saying please and thank you and spending some time sipping and chatting together. If you start brewing coffee for others, they'll start brewing, too, and the pot will never go empty.

Start a lunch co-op. Could you coordinate your colleagues into an office potluck, giving you an opportunity to share and connect? If you don't make lunch, take turns buying or see who wants to eat with you when you get up from your desk. Part of living liberally is integrating your views and values into all the moments of your life—don't let work be an alienating, isolating exception. Take advantage of the social opportunity that lunch provides.

128

Host work socials. Whether your company organizes these or not, you can. If weekend plans seem a little too ambitious, start with an after-work happy hour. Coordinate birthday celebrations around the office. Let your coworkers see you in a different light. Don't just work together, play together.

129

Spike the water cooler conversation. People might not want to carpool or go out together, but in the course of the workday, they can't help but make small talk with you. Can you talk about more than who won *American Idol*? Could you talk about current events?

130

After you've engaged your coworkers a little, it's easier to talk politics. Don't lecture them as Jonah did, but draw them out. Find some common ground. If you diverge on a policy, learn the principles behind the policies you do agree on. If you conflict on a candidate, find out what topics matter most to your coworkers and speak to those issues.

131

The nice thing is that you know you'll see them again. When you knock on doors for a campaign, you have thirty seconds. When you start engaging coworkers, take your time—you'll see them tomorrow and tomorrow and tomorrow . . . and as long as you don't yell at them, they'll probably keep talking to you.

132 · One last note on engagement: **make sure your coworkers are registered to vote.** Put forms on the front desk of the office, and offer to send them in. Don't be shy about asking every colleague if she or he is registered. Much like we accept recycling as a virtue, most people accept that voting is important. If you find someone unregistered or who moved and needs to re-register, you're doing him a favor.

Even if everyone is registered already, nobody will be annoyed that you're reaching out. Plus it's one more great way to start a conversation about politics.

133 · **Organize.** You're becoming an advocate on your own and starting the road to engagement. Now, pull them together . . .

- ★ Your advocacy will be more effective if there are more of you . . .

- ★ Once you engage people, take them to a next step . . .

Now you're ready to . . . uh-oh, that scary word . . . organize!

We all know that President Barack Obama was a community organizer, a fact first celebrated by his supporters, then reviled by the right wing. All that really means is that he spoke to people who shared goals and met common obstacles. He helped them develop a strategy and work together. He helped empower them to move themselves forward.

Organizing in a workplace is much the same, whether your common goal is getting a new coffeepot or raising your wages.

You can circulate letters or petitions to get coworkers to sign on. You can enlist others to help you research solutions and propose alternatives to management. You can collaboratively imagine what would make your workplace a more comfortable environment and take the responsibility to make it happen.

That's all organizing is.

When you talk about organizing in a workplace, you may also be talking about labor unions, the collaborative force most responsible for improving working conditions, raising wages, distributing wealth, and creating a solid middle class over the past century.

Much of the organizing you do might have no connection to unions, and unions are by no means the only way to "work liberally." But they have been a great force in promoting progressive values in and beyond the workplace, and you can't talk about working liberally without talking about them.

The union movement in America grew out of the industrial era, as people crammed into cities to work in factories and realized they were being taken advantage of. By becoming a team, they were able to collectively negotiate for higher wages and better working conditions.

You might not be part of a union, but there's probably still reason you might want to thank them. A few of the accomplishments of organized labor:

★ weekends

★ paid holidays

★ minimum wage

★ child labor laws

Today, one out of eight Americans in our workforce is a member of a union—and new unions are forming all the time. However, not everyone will join a union—and creating a union at your workplace is not necessarily the best use of your time. That does not mean your organizing stops there, and it does not mean the labor movement means nothing to you, nor you to it. Unions know that their cause cannot be only about their members, and they fight beyond one contract at a time. Unions have been at the forefront of comprehensive immigration reform, expansion of health care, and the increase in the minimum wage . . . even though their members are documented American citizens, who often have employer-covered care and work for salaries above the minimum wage.

They are taking on battles that assume "we all are living for each other." Why do they engage these fights? To a certain extent, these are strategic. They don't want to have their own members and the good jobs they fought hard to create to get caught in a "race to the bottom" against plentiful low-paid work. On a larger level they recognize that they need to exist in a system where work is respected and working families can pay their way. They see that by fighting against underpaid work and undervalued workers in general, they help the larger cause.

That's why they've created ways for nonunion members to add their voices to the causes labor champions. Working America, a program of the AFL-CIO, is one example: a research and advocacy initiative that pushes for progress on issues that face all working families. It's a place where union and nonunion workers can fuse their interests and show that we're all in this together. You could join and bring coworkers with you—not because it impacts your own workplace, but because it's a way you can improve the workplaces of others.

You don't need a union card in order to start organizing in your own work life. You don't need to use tactics as confrontational as strikes and negotiations. Organizing is simply getting more people involved in the same agenda—and that involvement can lead to personal investment, which helps create a community of colleagues along the way.

Whether your fight is to get rid of the water cooler or get day care on-site, here are five ways you can start organizing today:

Talk with your coworkers. This is the simplest, but it's also the most essential step, which is why we keep returning to it. Share your concerns, and ask them what's on their mind. As you find where your interests overlap, you're naturally starting the process. All good organizing begins when people identify their own needs and goals for change. 136

Delegate. Remember all those steps to become an advocate? Researching solutions, anticipating concerns, stepping up to take responsibility . . . all of these are easier when you're not doing them alone. As soon as you identify areas where you and colleagues want to make change together, make sure everyone has a task. When everyone has a role, everyone has skin in the game. It's harder to back out, and more likely that everyone will lead and innovate in his or her own way. 137

Circulate a petition. Nothing like getting a good old-fashioned John Hancock down on paper to show you're serious about something. You can collect signatures from all coworkers, or have a letter-writing campaign in which everyone writes a letter on the same topic. Provide talking points or templates so the letters are on the same page. This is a basic, easy, and effective step toward organizing. It makes your ideas "real" to have people attach their names. As a practical matter, you could spend a lot of time explaining to each coworker, or explaining to management, what you're asking for. Have it written down, and it saves time. It feels more official. People take it more seriously. 138

139

And the petition doesn't need to be strident. You're not Thomas Jefferson listing the grievances against King George. It can be funny. Charming. Persuasive. Find the tone that fits you and your workplace. There's no reason your boss should feel defensive upon receiving these letters. The letters demonstrate there is an issue people are taking seriously enough that they took the time to put it in writing.

Identify targets and allies. In any setting—a workplace, a neighborhood, Congress—there is a constellation of different players who might be involved in your cause. Maybe they're naturally sympathetic, or they are the skeptics you have to convince. Maybe they're the ones who can give a green light, or just the ones who lob criticism but have no real authority. Take the time to map out who your potential allies are that you should recruit; who your real targets are that you need to convince; and who you might be able to ignore completely.

Don't waste time engaging the CEO if the office manager can make the change you want. Go to her directly. Or, if the topic does need the CEO's approval and relates to the work of the office manager, get her on your side first. Present the case and make her an ally—since the CEO will probably ask her opinion, and you don't want her to feel blindsided.

Just do it. Is there a change you could foster with your allies without requiring a green light? If so, make it happen. I think of the Green Guerillas, who took over abandoned lots and built community gardens. They never would have received permission, but once these flourishing green spaces existed, it was harder to take it away from them. Where is that opportunity in your workplace?

No, you can't change wages or vacation policy or flex time on your own. But you can improve the kitchen and environmental practices. You can start a feedback box or maybe even spruce up an area to make it a lounge. If you and your partners in crime can take initiative, it puts other people in the position of having to say no after the fact, which can be just as unlikely as them saying yes beforehand.

Owning Liberally

Owning a business can make working liberally easier—you could just <u>say yes</u> to any of the ideas in the previous section; or can make it harder—you're now staring at the bottom line and caught in the 1,001 details of keeping a business afloat that get in the way of loftier goals.

142

Some would even argue that as a business owner, you shouldn't worry about being liberal; that your responsibility is straight-forward: to make money—and that's the only metric by which you should be measured. If you have investors or shareholders your responsibility is to them and to making them money . . . not to workers, unions, the environment, or any one of a number of external constituencies.

I first heard this argument when I was about twelve. At Passover one year, my one conservative uncle (a great guy who very will-ingly debated with the younger liberals in the family . . . also, by the 1990s, he was a Clinton voter, so "conservative" is a relative concept) and my father were debating business ethics.

My uncle asserted that you should treat employees well and be honest with them, as well as with investors and partners. Beyond that, business did not need to factor in "ethics." The mission of business was simply to make money.

My father had a different perspective. He had spent much of his life producing Off-Broadway theater, professional productions on a smaller, less expensive scale than Broadway.

He asked my uncle what he should do if he had a million dollars: produce one Broadway production or ten Off-Broadway productions? (The numbers would be much higher today ... remember, this was 1990!) My uncle asked which had the greater chance of success; what makes a show successful; would the greater investment in one place guarantee a profit? I suspected, as a twelve-year-old, that investing big would make a show better known and give a greater chance of profits.

My father didn't argue which would or wouldn't make money. Instead he suggested asking fundamentally different questions.

If you invest in ten shows instead of one, how many more people do you employ? Ten times as many designers, directors, performers, stage managers—and because you're filling ten times as many theaters, you're also employing ten times as many box office managers, house managers, and janitors. You're putting more money into the hands of more working people who are now spending that money, and probably setting lower ticket prices that make it accessible for more audience members, who also eat at local restaurants and support that local economy. And you're making ten times the cultural offering to the world, able to bring a diversity of playwrights' voices, ideas, and issues into public discourse.

He could have made an economic argument about not putting all your eggs in one basket and diversifying investment to hedge bets. That didn't interest him. His work had dimensions other than profit. It was about the community—both the creative community and the community of professional workers—in which he was situated.

[143] Working liberally, for an owner, is about understanding your business in a landscape that includes its workers, customers, and community.

Despite the stories we hear of corporate greed and indifference almost every day, there are still businesses that are trying to do right: to share the prosperity and opportunities that come with success. The businesses don't have to be behemoths like Google. Often it's the local stores that do best, because these shops know their community and care individually about their workers.

In Seattle, a greasy fast-food counter on Capital Hill shows that a business doesn't just have to go with the flow. Hourly servers often have the worst-paid and worst-respected kinds of jobs. At McDonald's, the servers are turned, as much as possible, into robots (read *Fast Food Nation* for more on that) and compensated poorly. Counter jobs are often the reason we need to fight so hard to raise the minimum wage.

Dick's, a fast-food joint in an orange hut that looks like a archetypal 1950s drive-through, does it differently. It has a sign in its window boasting of the benefits it offers employees. Dick's pays significantly higher than the minimum wage, offers health benefits and child care support to hourly employees, and compensates employees for time spent on their education.

They are not merely giving workers time off for education. They are not paying for professional development days that keep their workers in the corporate structure. They are paying for time workers spend improving themselves outside the work environment.

That's a sign of believing in investing in workers and cultivating loyalty that keeps them working there. Dick's prides itself on being a family business. Its employees become part of that family. Its website boasts sections on "community impact" and "giving." Its turnover rate is much lower than elsewhere across the fast-food industry.

Dick's burgers are greasy. They are not locally grown, grass-fed beef. This place isn't doing everything right. But when it comes to respecting labor, there's no question that Dick's has found a liberal way to be an employer.

Across the country, another business that takes working liberally in a different direction is Blue State Coffee. This company peddles Fair Trade coffee, opens its venue to community meetings, and supports positive environmental practices. Blue State does more to engage its customers and share their values: it donates a portion of its profits to local nonprofits.

Charitable giving by companies is nothing new. Blue State Coffee has added a fun twist. When you buy something, you're given a token—and you "vote" with that coin, dropping it into a container for one of several nonprofit recipients. Blue State makes its gifts based on what the customers vote for. Secondly, it's decided at each store to emphasize local causes. It is using this very routine act—buying coffee—to draw its customers, its neighborhood, its product, and profits into one ecosystem.

From the local burger joint to an internet giant, you can work liberally as a business owner. If you do it right, it's not a distraction from running your operation—the liberal approach should become an asset. It involves more people, engenders more goodwill, and returns rewards to the business. Here are five ideas where you can start:

Respect work. Compensate your employees well.

Listen to your workers. Ask for their ideas. Challenge them to improve the business.

Share the wealth. Limit your own compensation as you create ownership stakes for those who work for you.

Know your community. If you build relationships with your neighborhood, industry, and workers, it will pay back. Customers will pay more or will rally around you if you're in trouble. Your business is benefiting in many ways from community security, so you should be a partner in that. [154]

Have a longer—and larger—view. Nothing creates greed as quickly as a short view. The best and most profitable businesses take a longer view. They share their success with their communities. These businesses affirm that we are all working for one another. [155]

There are a growing number of networks to help business leaders share ideas for using their business to change the world. If you join Net Impact, for example, you find yourself part of a global organization that believes business can inspire positive [156] change. Or consider the Social Venture Network if you want [157] to learn from other social and business entrepreneurs who believe that the common good and the bottom line don't need to be adversaries.

Freelancing Liberally

There is another route besides being an employee or an employer that in some ways is the most liberal lifestyle of all: being a freelancer. Work from home, so there's no commute. Stroll to the coffee shop, where all the other freelancers (or, as they're sometimes called, "unemployed") have their Macs open, writing, designing, surfing the web. Make your own hours, wear whatever you want, take long vacations, and drink lots of organic coffee. Now that's the life.

Unfortunately, that's not really the life of most freelancers. Without a doubt, this scene is repeated again and again among underemployed twenty- and thirty-somethings in metropolitan areas, but most freelancers aren't quite so carefree.

I should note what I mean by freelancers. There's an insidious movement for major corporations to categorize more and more employees as "independent contractors"—this gets them around all sorts of rights and protections accorded to salaried payroll workers. So you have hotel chains that call the cleaning crews independent contractors and make them buy their own supplies . . . as though those crews have any control over their own hours or working conditions.

That's a sad, very un-liberal, and quite different story. I'm focused on people who may choose to work for themselves. They don't want to be in an office environment, they're trying to start up their own business, or their skill set is just more suited to a project-by-project basis. Not every freelancer wants to be independent, but there are many who are. Regardless of whether you're there by choice or by circumstance, there's plenty you can do to work liberally . . . and it doesn't require owning a Mac or camping out at a coffee shop.

First, there are the obvious environmental and cost savings:

- ★ Shorten, or eliminate, your commute. 158

- ★ Eliminate office rent and utilities costs. 159

- ★ Waste less paper, or at least have more opportunity to keep track of everything electronically. 160

- ★ Limit investment in conference phones and additional lines (if you don't know about FreeConference.com, go there now!). 161

- ★ Make your flexible time fit your family schedule. 162

Those are all personal advantages (that come with the disadvantages of irregular paychecks, higher taxes, and more pressure to keep receipts). Can there be communal advantages as well? As a freelancer, where's your community? It's probably other freelancers.

You already see that in the coffee shops mentioned above: people feel camaraderie in those settings. Many freelancers find communal solutions for the services an office would normally provide: they often share printers, newspaper subscriptions, passes to research centers or websites, and bookkeeping services. Freelancers quickly realized that liberal truth: that freelancing together is better than freelancing alone. In several cases, they organized. 163

164   **Coworking.** You may not want the overhead of an office, but it sure is nice to leave the confines of your apartment. Sometimes, the coffee shop doesn't cut it.

The coworking phenomenon is the arrangement of a shared space. It probably has a printer/fax /copier everyone can use. It has desks, but also flexible seating areas. It definitely has wi-fi. If it's worth its salt, it has coffee.

You don't simply come, take coffee, and leave. You pay by the month, week, or day for the ability to share these resources.

Costs are low; there's a collective spirit; everyone knows the rules and helps clean up, supervises, and provides security for one another. Many coworking spaces have added on cultural, social, and artistic elements: presentations at the end of the day; happy hours; transforming the office into galleries, hosting performances or parties at night.

This makes sense. The folks who share coffee and couches share culture; they are a community; and by having events there, they make it a home.

165   **The Freelancers Union.** Yes, you can laugh: it's sort of funny at first. Unions are for employees at huge companies. Freelancers are the opposite. But the Freelancers Union creates that delightful oxymoron with real reason: to tell those independent workers that they deserve the security and support of their peers in traditional labor and to create the collective mechanism to get it for them.

Artisan guilds for years helped set prices and guidelines for independent skilled workers, so it's not so absurd that such workers would join together. In modern America, it makes even more sense. Many workers have their health care, pension, and advocacy for workplace rights tied to their jobs. In this scenario, who speaks for the freelancer?

Founded in 2001, the Freelancers Union now represents more than 12,000 members, providing medical, dental, and other insurance at low costs. It's hard for an individual to get health care, and there's a reason that insurance companies pool risk. In the Freelancers Union, you pool your risk with your new community—you go into it together.

The Freelancers Union also advocates for the interests of their members in public policy discussions. In 2009, they scored a big victory when New York City eliminated the Unincorporated Business Tax for many freelancers. This had amounted to a double tax for many workers; now, many individuals will save up to $3,400 thanks to this collective effort. As labor unions fight for their constituents for better contracts and safeguards, this new union does the same for its members. You might work alone, but you're not alone.

Volunteering Liberally

There's one other important way to work liberally—wherever you are in the labor chain. Living liberally means not living for yourself alone; working liberally means working for others as well. You have professional skills: now **volunteer** them.

Sure, there are volunteering opportunities to clean parks and paint schools. Are you a landscaper or a painter? No—you're an accountant, so volunteer to keep the books for a small nonprofit. You're a graphic designer, so make the posters for the community arts center. You're a nuclear physicist, so tutor kids in science.

Your work life should feed into this spirit of giving. It will make you feel better about your work in the end as well.

Yes, at the end of the day, you're tired of work—that's why they call it "work." But if you can work for the greater good—which you aren't always able to do in the course of your typical day—you'll be working liberally.

CHAPTER 4
PLAYING LIBERALLY

> So keep fightin' for freedom and justice, beloveds, but don't you forget to have fun doin' it. Lord, let your laughter ring forth. Be outrageous, ridicule the fraidy-cats, rejoice in all the oddities that freedom can produce. And when you get through kickin' ass and celebratin' the sheer joy of a good fight, be sure to tell those who come after how much fun it was.
>
> —MOLLY IVINS

> If I can't dance, I don't want to be part of your revolution.
>
> —EMMA GOLDMAN

Liberals are somber, dour people who see the end of the world in every unseasonably hot day. They are judgmental fanatics who tsk-tsk your use of disposable plastic plates and reprimand you for not following the news. They are screechy activists who make your water-cooler talk uncomfortable.

Those stereotypes have haunted liberals and probably chase anyone active in politics, left or right. In fairness, there are a good number of humorless, overly earnest lefties and quite a few folks who think being a do-gooder means being a goody-two-shoes.

Those people may have liberal political beliefs, and their intentions may be in the right place . . . but they are not living liberally.

Being liberal isn't just about activism twenty-four hours a day. Nor is it only about working hard and making a difference through your labor. Living liberally requires that you connect to your community and celebrate the diversity, creativity, and joy you find there. It's working hard to ensure everyone has opportunities; but also making sure those opportunities include the chance to enjoy. In short, being liberal should also be about having fun.

The signers of our Declaration of Independence spoke of our inalienable rights: life, liberty—and here's the one we can sometimes forget—the pursuit of happiness.

Greed, self-interest, hoarding money, and wasting resources may be the conservative pursuit of happiness, but it's not the only way. We can pursue happiness in ways that respect the earth and our community and spread happiness to others.

Socializing Liberally

167 Here's one idea to pursue happiness like a liberal: buy a pitcher of beer.

When you arrive at Rudy's and find Drinking Liberally, I promise you someone will offer you a beer before you even make it to the bartender. What inspires this generosity? It's in the spirit of the event to share, to welcome newcomers. And the bar also makes it easy—by serving pitchers.

Pitchers of beer—especially cheap pitchers (Rudy's, with $7 pitchers of Rudy's Blonde and $9 pitchers of our favorite, Rudy's Red, is incomprehensibly inexpensive for Manhattan)—embody the ideals of "drinking liberally." First of all, it just makes economic sense to buy by the pitcher. It's cheaper than buying four pints . . . and despite conservative rhetoric, liberals are good with making the most of our money.

Once you have a pitcher in hand, it's imperative that you share it. Before you know it, you've made three new friends. They're all delighted you just poured them a pint, and are eager to return the favor. You've created a welcoming environment that has pulled people immediately into your community. This generosity self-perpetuates: those three are very likely to order pitchers when they sense it's their "turn."

When your pitcher finally runs dry, some member of your community will refill it. You are all drawing from a shared resource, just like a well of drinking water in the center of town. If that well runs dry, everyone suffers, and similarly everyone is affected when your pitcher goes empty. So now you're not the only one looking after it—everyone is. More people invested in replenishing your resources, everyone with the shared purpose of making sure everyone is drinking.

Do you get the best beer when you order by the pitcher? Not necessarily. Do you get exactly what you want? Probably not. So if you want to forgo the communal experience, you can buy a beer of your choosing; you can purchase a bottle of a pricier, more refined, more exclusive brew. You'll have the gated community of beers—in a bottle, open to your lips and nobody else's. While everyone else is on the public transit of beer, you're whisking by in your Mercedes. Alone.

Which is fine if that's what you want to do. But nobody will care when your bottle is empty. And nobody will instinctively offer to pour you a refill. And when that cute girl walks into Drinking Liberally for the first time, you have nothing to offer her that says, "Welcome to our liberal community."

Drinking Liberally wasn't the first organization to realize that alcohol, in addition to being a social lubricant, is social glue. There's a long history of associations in America that use social bonds to foment a sense of identity and community.

There are the traditional "fraternal orders" like the Elks or Masons, membership-based societies with lodges and traditions. There is the Rotary Club, founded to bring together civic leaders to support efforts to promote peace, prosperity, and humanitarian causes. In a very different atmosphere, the union halls were a social/political space for many workingmen and workingwomen for many decades in the twentieth century. Traditional political clubs were social centers for their members.

168

So why did our idea seem so fresh and new if it's just a rehash of an idea that's been around for centuries? It seems that our generation never learned about these clubs . . . or maybe society had forgotten about them entirely. In *Bowling Alone,* a book that inspired many of us, Robert Putnam explored this topic. As he documented, from the 1960s through the turn of the century, participation in "associations" declined precipitously— civic associations, parent-teacher associations, even bowling leagues . . . hence the title *Bowling Alone.*

People weren't becoming Rotarians or Elks anymore. Union membership had declined. "Membership" had come to mean something very different over those decades. If you were liberal, you might be a member of the Sierra Club or National Organization of Women or People For the American Way, which meant you sent them a check every year and let their professional staff handle the advocacy. Nothing against professional advocates—we need them. However, it reduced the concept of "joining" to donating. You were rarely asked to do anything in person, so it was less likely you felt a connection to your fellow members.

Even if you were a "card-carrying member of the ACLU," you didn't go to movies about civil liberties together. The card, in some ways a badge of honor, was also a joke—it didn't create any shared experience with other cardholders beyond simply sharing a card.

Matt O'Neill and I, when we started our weekly club, had read *Bowling Alone* and viewed what we were doing as a response to the problems Putnam raised. We were reawakening a yearning felt by older liberals to reclaim that sense of fraternity. At the same time, we were offering it like a fresh course to younger liberals. However, by no means were we the only ones inspired to try to recreate social capital in America.

Scott Heiferman was a programmer and developer who had read Putnam as well. His solution: Meetup.com—a website that allowed people to self-organize around their particular interests. It wasn't a chat room or group blog where you could virtually meet others who wanted to practice French or share their love of Vonnegut or trade tips on raising pugs. It was a site that empowered people to arrange face-to-face gatherings. . . . to "meet up."

169

Meetups gained more national attention, especially in the political world, when supporters of Howard Dean in the summer of 2003 started using the platform to attract and engage allies. Dean Meetups were so successful that some people thought Meetup was created by Dean or was specific to politics (political clubs have never been their biggest gatherings). It is a coincidence, but no accident, that Dean Meetups and Drinking Liberally began at the same time. Concomitantly, people were organizing around concerts with "Music for America" and soon after there were jogging groups called "Run Against Bush." There was no vast left-wing conspiracy to create self-organized, localized, progressive events for each social preference. There was a shared desire . . . and suddenly tools that allowed us to realize our desires weren't so unique or absurd after all.

This spirit was not limited to anti-Bush energy in the summer of '03. Green Drinks was already thinking—and drinking—along the same lines, with monthly happy hours for people interested in the environment and sustainability.

Since the launch and success of Drinking Liberally, there have been copycat groups. Drinking Freely is a libertarian drinking club that openly cops to being a rip-off of our model. Not sure that they're taking off, but it's good to know that they are trying. Someone should tell them that libertarians are welcome to come to Drinking Liberally. Over a pint, we may find how much we have in common. Drinking Skeptically gives skeptics a chance to get together. We often get asked if there's an equivalent right-wing group. There isn't: Drinking Conservatively just doesn't sound like that much fun.

While drinking is a great social lubricant, it's of course not the only one. Food works as well. Eating Liberally is only one of a rich collection of groups that organize supper clubs, potlucks, picnics, and outings around healthy, local, and sustainable food practices.

One other such group is Slow Food USA. If you've never heard of Slow Food, think "fast food"—then think the opposite. As advocates, Slow Food is part of a movement to make us think about where our food comes from and our place in a larger food ecosystem. But I imagine foodies sometimes suffer the same stereotypes that liberals weather: that they're no fun. They want to take our sweets away and push us into an ascetic lifestyle.

Foodies would be shocked by that characterization as many quite deliberately make the case that their food tastes better than mass-produced, factory-farmed products of agribusiness. Slow Food's social network of local chapters combines their advocacy mission with the pleasure food can bring in a social setting to form bonds and build the overall movement.

Slow Food chapters talk about issues — and eat and drink along the way, whether through potlucks or outings to local establishments. They realized food politics wouldn't be as much fun if it were only politics . . . it needs the food as well.

We often say that Drinking Liberally is not the end point of political activism; we don't want people just to drink. We believe it's more likely that they'll make calls or knock on doors when friends invite them. In the bar, we build that community. We put newcomers and experienced activists into a position where they share a beer. We watch people walk down the slippery slope from a political conversation to a political conversion.

We're the gateway into liberal political activism. It's easy to have a drink. Then you meet someone who gets you to come to a meeting, and there someone convinces you to canvass. Before you know it, you're handing out fliers on a dark street corner in the icy rain on the first Tuesday in November.

We're not yet the Rotarians, helping fund worthy causes, or the Masons, with secret signs and lodges. We can dream. Someday, I hope people will wear their liberal identification as proudly as many have worn their union affiliations. I hope that in addition to taking action together, we'll also open our doors to each other. I know that if anyone identified themselves to me as a member of the Fraternal Order of Liberals, I'd give them a couch to crash on. I'd also buy them a beer.

The Personal(s) is Political

Finding a mate for your bleeding heart

by guest contributor Katie Halper, Laughing Liberally

What's a liberal girl gotta do to get a date around here? I mean, it's Valentine's Day and I don't have anyone with whom I can share my bleeding heart, exchange Fair Trade chocolates, recite the poems of Pablo Neruda, celebrate Valentine's Day, and, of course, more importantly, V-Day and Freedom to Marry day.

Sadly, you really can't judge a book—or zine or manifesto—by its cover. Someone who makes all the right moves politically can make all the wrong moves romantically, as I've learned from many a bad date. Having no luck in my search for Mr. Right, or Mr. Left, I decided to search online for liberal-friendly dating sites, in the hopes that by taking action, I could get some action. Well, here's what I found:

1. **Act For Love** stole my aforementioned pun and uses "Take Action. Get Action," as their motto. The site is basically a hipster wolf in an activist sheep's clothing. All it is, is a filtered version of the people who are already members of the online dating consortium shared by www.nerve.com, *The Onion*, *Time Out New York*, and the *Village Voice*. So if it's snarky love you're looking for, you may be in luck (and get lucky).

2. **Care2.com Singles** bills itself as a place to "find others who Care2 make a difference for good causes!" The

site is part of www.Care2.com, the environmentally oriented search engine, forum, and directory, with a shopping service that donates a portion of its sales to environmental and progressive causes. This site is not for the rabid horn-dog, because it bombards you with petitions before letting you get to their personals page. But I guess that's a good way to filter out the committed activists from the commitment-phobic wham-bam-thank-you-ma'am-ers. I don't know about the romance potential, but the site is great, so I joined anyway. Their motto should be Care2.com Singles: Come for the free online dating, stay for the free e-mail account, blog, photo sharing, and action alerts.

3. There are tons of vegan and veggie dating sites for people looking to give or get a hot tofurky injection. **Veg Connect** describes itself as "Free Vegan and Vegetarian Personals—Make Rad Friends and Meet Awesome Singles." The site features PETA's "Don't Be a Milk Sucker" campaign—a cautionary tale that demonstrates how milk harms people, through Garbage Pail Kids–esque milk victims like Chubby Charlie, Lactose Intolerant Latoya, Ear Infection Enrique, Windy Wanda, and Pimply Patty. I also caught the surprisingly funny pro-animal, anti-veal, mafia spoof movie *Veal: Fughedaboutit*. So if you're a meat eater, or a milk sucker, you may want to "fughedabout" this site.

I would have liked to have ended this column with an encouraging "So what are you waiting for? Liberal love is only a username, password, and 'why you should get to know me' description away." But I guess my mother was right: a good liberal online dating site is hard to find.

> For now, Let's just hope I'm not forced to "pull a Lieberman" (switch teams) and sign up on Republican Passions (even if it is an oxymoron), DatingRepublicans.com, or Hannidate (brought to you by the lovable Sean Hannity).

Entertaining Liberally

Popular culture is called that for a reason: it's popular. Liberal culture doesn't need to stand in opposition to that. It may appear that politics and culture mostly meet in staid ways: slow, heavy-handed documentaries or exhibits on weighty themes. If that's the case, then it's a combination of culture and politics that brings out the worst in both.

When you connect the two you should experience all the joy of good entertainment, with the shared experience, creativity, diversity, and social consciousness of good politics. We know from *The Daily Show* and *The Colbert Report* that political humor doesn't have to be pedantic. If you know how to look, it isn't hard to find progressive cultural experiences that don't skimp on the entertainment factor.

Comedy

Since I've mentioned Jon Stewart and Stephen Colbert, let's continue on this laugh track. They epitomize the power of using entertainment—and humor in particular—as a vehicle for real ideas. It's another one of those "gateway" moments: people who might never tune in to a show about politics will tune in to a show that makes them laugh. If the comedy can carry in it nuggets of truth—which is what good comedy has always done—then jokes play the role of the Trojan horse. The audience lets in the laughter, and discovers political messaging in its belly.

This is a terrific way to reach younger Americans. Studies have shown that for young Americans, *The Daily Show* is one of the major sources of news. Other studies have also concluded that people who consider *The Daily Show* their primary news source are significantly better informed than people who consider *The O'Reilly Factor* their primary news source. And young voters have been increasingly liberal in the last three election cycles.

Humor and liberal values go hand in hand. Talk radio, the domain of the right wing, often involves an authoritarian host who allows no room for shades of gray. He offers tirades that play off of fear, hate, and division, all of which are well suited for talk radio.

Liberal views tend to consider a larger context and are less black-and-white. They are more complicated, so tirades don't always suit them as well. They are less hateful, so require a more upbeat, joyful medium. These are characteristics of the best comedians, who subvert social settings, expose hypocrisy, overturn authority, and try to please, not frighten, their audience.

Have you seen conservative comedians? They're just not as funny. There are strong conservative strains through much of the comedy-club scene: misogyny, racial stereotypes, antigay rhetoric. It's ugly. It doesn't connect people. It's like a little boy who is so frightened that people won't like him that he becomes a bully and picks on the weaker kid in the schoolyard.

Sadly, that kind of comedy gets easy laughs. Furthermore, many comedy club owners want to play to a lowest common denominator. They worry that political humor will lose people, but everyone can join in a good fart joke or a rant about a woman being a "bitch."

The idea that comedy could be used to effectively promote progressive values inspired the creation of Laughing Liberally. Additionally, we wanted to give comedians the incentive to do more thoughtful comedy. Much as Drinking Liberally told people it wasn't taboo to talk politics in a bar, Laughing Liberally told comedians it wasn't taboo to talk politics in their set. Laughing Liberally sometimes plays to liberal audiences, where it serves the role of rallying and rousing the faithful. Other times, the comedians work to politically agnostic crowds, where the goal is to get the audience in for the comedy and make them leave with the politics.

Once again, this "new" idea wasn't so new. Nor are Stewart and Colbert the innovators behind this. One guy who has been doing it longer than any of us just got elected to the U.S. Senate from Minnesota. He was building off a longer history that has always seen the best comedians use their acts to speak truth to power . . . humorously. So check out some of these classics. They may turn your conservative uncle red in the face, or may just make him laugh himself to the left.

A Few of America's National Comedy Treasures

Mort Sahl. At the Hungry I in San Francisco in the 1950s, "while other comedians joked about their wives, Mort joked about the president." He kept it up through his career, blazing a trail for others on this list. He was pointed without being too controversial, a Will Rogers manner with a smirk, red v-neck sweater, a *New York Times* rolled up under his arm, and a sharp jab. Lampooning the House committee that fueled the communist hunts, he quipped: "Every time the Russians throw an

American in jail, the Committee throws an American in jail to get even."

Lenny Bruce brought religion, race, and political ranting to the stage in an era that was shocked by it—the late 1950s. His use of the word "cocksucker" got him arrested for obscenity in the 1960s. A later charge resulted in an obscenity conviction that was only overturned in the late 1990s, thirty years after his death. [178]

Dick Gregory in the 1960s was one of the first black comedians whom white audiences got to know—and he used that popularity to talk about civil rights through his material. [179]

George Carlin. Famous for his routine that used the seven words you couldn't say on TV, his set made it all the way to the Supreme Court. He used his comedy to rebel, to critique, and to challenge convention. [180]

The Smothers Brothers have made a half-century career of comedy—no small feat given that their antiwar leanings got their TV show canceled forty years ago. [181]

Richard Pryor made a comedy career by discussing racism—yet despite profanity and provocation remained relevant enough that he won the Mark Twain Award for American Humor late in his career. [182]

Ellen DeGeneres used her platform to challenge America when she and the character she portrayed came out on a mainstream national sitcom. [183]

Tina Fey may have delivered the fatal blow to the McCain-Palin campaign as she delivered lines that will resonate longer than Palin's actual speeches and are destined to follow Palin into her doomed 2012 presidential bid. [184]

Movies

We all love the movies. They are delightfully escapist fantasies and can bring diverse views and ideas to the general public. *Guess Who's Coming to Dinner* featured a white family facing the fact that their daughter was bringing home her black fiancé. *Philadelphia*, with Tom Hanks, put the crisis of AIDS more firmly in the mind of mainstream America. Films can also have explicitly conservative themes, celebrating militarism as the later *Rambo* films did, demonizing "the other," and frequently portraying gays as sources of derision. These themes can be unintentional: take an example like the "comedy" *I Now Pronounce You Chuck and Larry,* which traded on gay stereotypes ostensibly to make a point about inclusion and tolerance.

Despite Hollywood's reputation as a liberal mecca and the left-leaning views of many actors and directors, most films work hard to be apolitical—avoiding tough issues, sticking with the mainstream, and pleasing the lowest common denominator. Even apolitical films, though, can be viewed through a progressive lens.

We highlight these ideas with Screening Liberally. In our film reviews, we don't just cover the latest Michael Moore creation or human rights film festivals. We also talk about whatever the mainstream is viewing with a liberal perspective. For example, we praised *Superbad* not just for its comedic qualities, but also for portraying male heroes who did not fall into chauvinist conventions.

Sure, when you go to a film you might want to support directors who reflect your values (Ron Howard shot an ad in which he dressed up as his old characters from *Andy Griffith* and *Happy Days* to discuss why they would support Barack Obama). Or you might skip films by those who don't (Mel Gibson's anti-Semitic, antigay tirades may sour you on his on-screen work). Or you might want to support certain companies; Participant Films, involved in *An Inconvenient Truth* and the feature *Good Night, and Good Luck,* has socially conscious cinema in its mission.

Separate from the political views of the actors, directors, and companies, here are things you can look for in the film to decide whether it's worth screening liberally:

Portrayal of women. Do female characters exhibit leadership, or are they always victims? Are they real characters with desires, or are they just objects in a game played by the men?

Portrayal of people of color. If the most prominent black character in a film is a large, sassy black woman, it might be time to ask what's with our society's obsession with that stereotyped body type. If the only two characters of color in a film pair up with each other, we might ask why it's so inconceivable for a white and black character to get together.

Portrayal of gay and lesbian characters. You realize you know a gay person in your life, right? If you don't think you do, then that's just more proof that not every gay person is a limp-wristed sex fiend—though so many of them in movies are.

Deference to authority. Many films—even fun, enjoyable ones— ultimately contain themes like "Know your place" or "Stick to your own kind" or "You should have listened to the authority figure all along." Not every film needs to have *One Flew Over the Cuckoo's Nest* levels of rebellion, but it is worth noting when the status quo is a little too celebrated or when the point of a film is that the character who rocked the boat really learned her lesson in the end. Even in a charming film like *Forrest Gump* with a known liberal star, Tom Hanks, these themes prevail. Jenny, after being involved in activism, is the lost soul. Forrest, who avoids challenging society, is the hero.

Does it trade on love or on violence? Sure, there is too much sappy sentimentality in many films . . . but ultimately, they often are supporting a world in which love is a driving force. It may be bad filmmaking, but it's not a bad theme. Films with wanton violence, though, send a different message. Michael Bay action flicks ask us to care more about explosions than emotions.

Before you go to the movies, check out reviews for these themes. Look at the posters or the coming attractions for signs of objectifying women or the next crass joke. When you see a film, share

what you saw with others—let your friends see through your liberal lens.

In addition to the mainstream movies, there are other ways of downing a dose of feature films that truly reflect your politics. One way to screen liberally is to screen socially.

Movie clubs. Just as we have drinking clubs and comedy outings, there are plenty of groups organizing to see movies together. Some of them see socially conscious flicks, and others attend the latest new release in socially conscious company. These create the opportunities to share the experience, form bonds and friendships, and continue the conversation after the lights come up.

Putnam bemoaned bowling alone. Isn't viewing together better than viewing alone?

This interest spawned Screening Liberally, a network of film clubs. Chapters host independent documentaries to support emerging filmmakers around liberal themes, attend advance screenings of films that seek to reach a political audience, organize outings to wide-release films, and arrange group screenings at homes or other intimate settings of classics, or political features released to DVD or via download.

Plenty of local groups host these types of events, and you could find them at Meetup.com without too much trouble. One particularly impressive group is Brave New Films. BNF is a group that uses film as a medium to influence political discussions. It was founded by Robert Greenwald, a filmmaker who became well known for *OutFOXed*, which exposed explicit right-wing bias in Fox News. Since then Greenwald and BNF have produced features around labor practices and the Iraq war, then began to experiment with short videos that used the potential of the internet to go viral. They teamed up with different advocacy campaigns and helped create material more engaging than your typical e-blast or position paper—whether targeting the war in Afghanistan, the greed of finance tycoons, or the hypocrisy of television anchors.

They aren't just content producers, though; they are conveners as well. When they released *Iraq for Sale*, a film about the dangers of our reliance on military contractors, they bypassed the effort to be released in movie theaters and went directly to grassroots organizers. Brave New Films encouraged people to host house parties to show the film, gave them ideas for how to shape conversations and take follow-up actions, and made it very easy to use their website to organize and promote a screening. Thousands of events brought the film, and its ideas, across the country.

While house parties are a great do-it-yourself approach, there is something about the big screen. If your progressive movie club wants a night out, consider choosing a cinema that will match your values: independent movie theaters.

Most cities have these. Sometimes they are called the art-house cinema, the indie movie theater, or even the second-run theater. If a film's message isn't mainstream enough to get the big money and wide distribution, this might be the place to find them. Just as frequently, though, these theaters do show wide releases—they may skip the latest torture-porn horror flick, but show the same quirky comedy or Oscar-bait drama as the larger houses.

Why support independent theaters? They are often the mom-and-pops. They have reason to be invested in a local community. They are more likely to host community events and support local nonprofits. They're more likely to think about how their business affects their neighbors. They're also more likely to show the independent films that might not get featured elsewhere. When you see even the wide releases at the small houses, you show the mom-and-pops that you appreciate their work and you keep them going!

Because of their personality, many of these theaters have already cast a liberal lens onto the films they're showing . . . so they will include *Superbad* . . . and probably pass on *I Now Pronounce You Chuck and Larry*.

You don't only have to rely on what the movie theaters are showing. If you want to see something at your local theater—something that might have more appeal than your living room can hold—you should go ahead and ask. Like any cause you want to promote, all you have to do is organize.

Big Screen on Demand

203
a) **Research the film you want shown.** Find out if there is a distributor or if the filmmaker can give you the rights herself. Sometimes through the film's website you can learn if there are fees or restrictions associated with showing it publicly.

204
b) **Don't go it alone.** Ask friends if they'd commit to seeing the film if it came to town. Reach out to groups that might work

on the issues the film tackles and see if they would help host or promote a screening.

c) **Approach the local theater.** You're doing far more than submitting a suggestion to a box at this point; you're coming with information and with allies. Figure out who makes these decisions at the theater—owner, manager, curator. They're probably very interested in hearing what the community wants to see and would be delighted to know somebody wants to help.

205

There is a rich history of classic liberal films in America. Whether they think of themselves as liberal (*The Grapes of Wrath* about the Depression) or just happen to embody a liberal theme (*Footloose*—how can you not see political value in the rebellious city kid fighting for the right to dance in a puritanical town?), they deserve a second look.

206

207

Of course, there are so many, where to begin? Well, why not with the calendar? Below are a few selections that pair well with annual holidays. Watch them with your families and neighbors, or ask the local theater to host a screening series.

Excerpted from "Progressive Films Throughout the Calendar Year" by Josh Bolotsky, Living Liberally

> **Martin Luther King Jr. Day**—Spike Lee's *4 Little Girls* provides a historical context to the 16th Street Church bombing in 1964, reminding us of the events

208

leading up to it and its legacy for the country. Rather than tsk-tsking those who either actively aided oppression or stood on the sidelines, Lee lets them dig their own graves, including a remarkable interview with former Governor George Wallace that one must see to believe.

Valentine's Day—For a film that breaks out of the heterosexist paradigm of most screen romances, check out ***But I'm a Cheerleader***, the (beyond-camp) story of a budding lesbian romance. Two teenagers—one from the punk subculture, the other from a household of perfect grooming and cheerleader drills—are both sent to a "heterosexual reeducation" camp, where they find themselves rebelling with the other gay teenagers against the be-someone-else dogma, all while falling in crazy, exuberant teenage love.

Presidents' Day—***Dave,*** a delightful what-if comedy about an impersonator of a George H. W. Bush–like president who gets to take the real president's place—and slowly but surely tweaks the administration to one that cares about people over profits. Kevin Kline is great as both the president and his look-alike, the film's protagonist. This hilarious film is one of the best early works of Gary Ross, who would later make the excellent, progressive parable *Pleasantville.*

Earth Day—***The Age of Stupid*** is a chilling call to action, reminding us just how little time we have, and just how dire and potentially catastrophic the consequences are if we don't radically change course in response to climate change. Pete Postlethwaite plays a one of the few surviving humans in 2050, in a giant Noah's Ark–like archive of what's left of human civilization, tracing just how and why we didn't take the threat of climate change seriously enough, and waxing philosophical about just how it was that humanity consciously committed suicide. Beyond chilling—required viewing, watch it now.

Memorial Day—The best tribute we can pay our brave men and women in uniform is ensuring that we only ask them to make the ultimate sacrifice when there is no resort left. ***The Great Dictator***, one of Charlie Chaplin's best comedies (and certainly his best talkie), is a film made about one of those times. When supporting Hitler was not particularly controversial in public life, before Pearl Harbor and before the widespread knowledge of the horrors of Nazi Germany, Chaplin had the courage to make a film that not only directly parodies Hitler and fascism but also speaks eloquently of human brother- and sisterhood, and against bigotry in all forms, which includes a Jewish protagonist at a time where this was decidedly not the norm.

Independence Day—There are all sorts of great films made about physical courage in the service of patriotism, and all of them would be fine choices for the day: *Born On The Fourth of July, 1776, Saving Private Ryan.* Less recognized, however, are films made about civic courage, about those whose patriotism meant challenging the status quo to make America a better place, often at great personal risk. In that vein, I strongly recommend ***Good Night, and Good Luck***, a reminder of just how much risk to self it meant to publicly denounce McCarthyism. In the era of Glenn Beck and Sarah Palin conservatism, where Van Jones has to step down as Bush goes unprosecuted, it serves as a reminder that it requires courage to take on those who fight against democracy and in favor of public fear.

Labor Day—***Norma Rae*** is one of those films that is now largely remembered solely as a source of Oscar montage clips—we see the picture of Sally Field with the scrawled UNION sign, and half-remember that this was from some important movie or another. Which is quite a shame, because *Norma Rae* is so much more than that. It's influenced just about every I'm-Taking-a-Courageous Stand, I-Am-Woman-Hear-Me-Roar film made since. As such, watching *Norma Rae* can be like watching a lot of seminal genre films—we can't help but think it's cheesy because we've seen this stuff so many times, until we realize that this film was there first.

Halloween—It's not a particularly original thought that horror tends to be the most innately political of genres—when it's all about finding the root of what scares us most, is there any quicker expressway to our politics? For a film that takes this observation and goes about as far with it as one can imagine, check out *The Last Supper,* a twisted mélange of black comedy, horror, and political satire that is truly sui generis in its originality, and not something you are likely to see replicated anytime soon. This is one of those films whose premise is so delicious that to even mention the main plot would be a little bit like blurting out the punchline before the setup is even finished. Let's leave it at this: The film is about a fear that every serious political thinker has at least once in his or her life: is political dialogue with those we disagree sometimes pointless? What about those fanatics with whom you can't reason? What if the simple fact is, that democracy can't deal with the fact that the world is simply better off without certain viewpoints being represented?

Thanksgiving—It's important for progressives to mention/remember that Thanksgiving can have a very different meaning for Native Americans. Chris Eyre's *Smoke Signals*, with a screenplay by Sherman Alexie, is one of the very few films ever made by Native Americans about Native American characters—and it happens to be a very funny family comedy that reminds us of how often these communities have been left out of the discussion entirely.

Holiday Season (Christmas, Hanukkah, Kwanzaa, Winter Solstice, etc.)—Can one even try to do better than *It's a Wonderful Life*? Where to even start? The protagonist fights to save his community in a time of widespread poverty, finds that wealthy entrenched power (as embodied by Mr. Potter) tries to undercut

> him at every turn, and realizes that wealth isn't as important as how much you help others in this life. A classic. (The fact that the FBI considered the film communist propaganda is worth noting.)

Television

The big screen immediately offers more screening liberally potential than the small screen, but we shouldn't cut out a popular medium just because we don't like it as much. Sure, Robert Putnam points to television as a major factor in the decline of social capital, but there are plenty of ways of Tele-visioning Liberally.

There are occasions that will be broadcast over television that hold public interest, like people gathering in 1969 to follow the moon landing. This regularly happens with nonpolitical occasions: the Super Bowl and other sporting events or episodes of *The Sopranos* when people with HBO suddenly realized they were everyone's best friends.

Starting a few years ago, another community event started springing up once a year: the State of the Union. People were fed up with and scared of President Bush—but they felt like they had to watch. They had to know his next horrifying lie (yellow-cake uranium) or newest out-of-the-blue distraction (manned travel to Mars). We felt a morbid duty to watch this speech.

We couldn't watch alone. Instinctively people started hosting watch parties—in their homes, in public spaces, even in bars. By Bush's second term, it was common for bars—which would have

once said politics was bad for business—to tune into the address
as patrons played a State of the Union Drinking Game. 218

It all comes back to booze.

Sip if he pronounces the word "nu-kyu-ler." Sip when he talks
about "evil-doers." Chug if he invokes Jesus. Finish your drink
if he adds a new country to the Axis of Evil.

This type of game proliferated from 2003 and 2008, and gave
people an outlet other than screaming at the television. It gave
them reason to share the night and led to people joining discussions and getting more involved in politics.

All thanks to the power of the television.

Election years provide countless opportunities for these gatherings. Every primary night and debate night became a cause
to convene around televisions, like you were watching a sports
tournament up to the championship game: election night parties,
complete with winners and losers, game-time commentary, and
chanting all across the country. 220 219

221

Not every year will have that same level of political television—but there are other opportunities to create these communal
events. It might not parallel Barack Obama's acceptance speech,
but it might still make good TV.

We all have televisions. . . . let's put them to work. Here are a
few other ideas to make that omnipresent tube work for the
greater good:

Presidential press conferences. When the president addresses
the nation, he always does so in prime time. It's called "prime"
for a reason. Watch it with your neighbors. You can answer each
other's questions and share your reactions. 222

Premium politics. If you have HBO, you have a resource that you owe it to your friends to share. HBO produces and programs terrific documentaries that you might not otherwise see: *Baghdad ER*, about our military's emergency room doctors, or *Trouble the Water*, about Hurricane Katrina. In an era of watered-down news coverage, these films are some of the best journalism on television.

Screening Liberally Oscar Night. In addition to one-off events, there is some programming you can predict. Every year there will be an Oscar Night, and about 30 percent of your heart wants to watch. You want to see celebrities, you want to be in on the cultural moment, but you may not want to focus all of your attention on it. Watch it with others and make a game of it, just as people do with the State of the Union. Share some political movie trivia throughout the night. Compare notes on which nominated films had the most liberal themes. Guess at whose speeches will be the most radical. It's a night where you can invite the people who enjoy watching press conferences to come to something political . . . but also a little more popular.

Share your favorite liberal shows. Just as you're allowed to enjoy movies that aren't explicitly political, the same applies to TV. *The West Wing* was a liberal fantasy, especially since so much of it aired during the Bush years. Other shows—ones that promote diversity, include themes of subverting authority, or provoke debate in general—can be just as political without being as explicit. *Battlestar Galactica* got people debating torture and occupation. *The Wire* makes you ask questions about the drug war. Sitcoms can even be the source of good liberal values . . . how can we forget *Family Ties*? Pick your favorite weekly features and share them around.

Additionally, getting a group together is a great way to watch some of the best documentaries TV has to offer. PBS consistently runs compelling programming, including their series *P.O.V.*, and if you have HBO, you have access to some of the best documentary work being produced. These are programs that will get you talking and sharing, and they are good opportunities to cultivate your local political community.

State of the Union. We might not groan, grimace, and giggle as much without W. to kick around, but the president's annual address to the joint session of Congress is still a must-watch. Even with someone articulate behind the podium, it doesn't hurt to have a drink in hand.

Big Picture for the Small Screen: You know that *The Daily Show* and *The Colbert Report* will do a better job delivering you the day's events than most news stations, and Keith Olbermann and Rachel Maddow have brought the right's feisty fight to the left, with charm, smarts, and good ratings. But when you decide to queue up Netflix and delve back into TV land, here are a few suggestions from our Liberal TV Guide:

__All in the Family.__ Archie Bunker was a typical American guy in a world run wild: a white, middle-class father, he had to confront civil rights, student unrest, and a constantly changing society. The creation of Norman Lear (who later founded People For the American Way to battle the impact of the religious right), this show gave us the lovable curmudgeon who kept learning new lessons about our new America and brought us all along with him.

__Murphy Brown.__ Any sitcom that picked a fight with a sitting vice president must have done something well. Dan

Quayle's criticisms of Murphy's single-mom status seem almost quaint now. At the time, it reminded us that TV characters could have articulate (and entertaining) arguments on-screen. It also provided the fantasy of reporters who really pursued the story, with little regard to the network's bottom line.

235 ***The West Wing.*** You would watch how Jed Bartlett's moments of indecision inevitably end with him returning, more forcefully than ever, to a passionate, committed, bold agenda. And you would wish that this show's writers were advising the Clinton White House, and not vice versa (or were now advising Team Obama). Infectious dialogue and engaging characters get to play on a stage of global importance . . . and in the end, more often than not, create an America that would make us proud.

236 ***Maude.*** Another Norman Lear creation, this show featured Bea Arthur (later of *Golden Girls* glory) as a liberated woman—outspoken, opinionated, and not afraid to bring up issues to those around her . . . and those watching at home. Famously, a number of episodes dealt with Maude having an abortion, bringing a level of honesty to the discussion that is rarely seen in the more cautious accidental-baby tales of today like *Knocked Up* and *Juno*.

237 ***Family Ties.*** Someday, I hope some young Republican explains to me why they love Alex P. Keaton, Michael J. Fox's breakout character, a young conservative who kept learning liberal lessons by each episode's end. Not that liberals were wholly loved—his ex-hippie parents were teased for being too flighty and far-out—but overall it was a show that talked about equal rights, elitism, wealth disparity, and electoral politics.

The Simpsons. One episode brings us to "Springfield Republican Headquarters," an underground lair populated by a rogue's gallery of villains: corporate (Monty Burns), oil (the Texan), and just creepy (Dracula). No party or politician is spared lampooning, but generally we get to follow Homer as his accidentally right-wing antics, like heading up a local militia, lead him into trouble. Thankfully, the sensibilities of more communal-minded characters with progressive perspectives, like Homer's daughter Lisa, save the day.

238

Saturday Night Live. Before there was _The Daily Show_ and _The Colbert Report,_ Dan Ackroyd was Richard Nixon and Chevy Chase took falls as Gerald Ford. The dead-on satire of the Clarence Thomas hearings, the 1992 Democratic debate where candidates competed to not lose to George Bush, and the Bush-Gore debates of 2000, which gave us "strategery," will live on as vividly as the real events they mocked.

239

Sesame Street. Teaching kids to read and count is one thing; teaching them to do it in Spanish is a little radical. Everything about _Sesame Street_'s early years was a little radical: it gave us an interracial and inter-human–Muppet vision of city life, taught us to embrace differences, to be kind to each other, to accept all sorts of lifestyles, and to love one another: whether you're green, blue, yellow, feathered, or furry.

240

Arts Collectives/Theater

TV and movies have mass appeal because they use mass media. We'd be foolish not to support liberal lessons in such a widespread form. There is also, though, something special and remarkable about the experience of live performance. You feel that thrill of seeing the actors right in front of you, and you know they feel the energy off the audience, hear the laughter, applause, and gasps. Audience and performer are more genuinely connected in live theater, allowing at times for greater sincerity and emotional pull. It also creates a bond: you are not only sharing the experience with other theatergoers, you're sharing it with those onstage. There is a reason why rock concerts can transport people, why live comedy can bring you to uncontrollable fits of laughter, and theater can move and shock and engage you. That genuineness stays with you longer, in many cases, because it feels more immediate.

Theater also has a long history of carrying social messages: whether through satire or allegory, from the Greeks through the labor playwrights of the Depression, upending the social order in Shakespeare or offering a look into a world upended as theater discussed gender, race, and AIDS with greater honesty at the end of the twentieth century.

Unfortunately, many people view theater as a rarefied experience—and that's often a justifiable impression. Theater is usually more expensive than a movie; that's just the economy of live performance.

Fortunately there are alternatives that make theater, and other live performances, accessible. Art collectives around the country rely on volunteer energy, artists who are ready to take risks, and maybe some nonprofit funding to showcase performances you might not see elsewhere. Moreover, these venues sometimes compete financially with a night at the movies.

In New York, Living Liberally has had a sibling in the nonprofit venue The Tank, an organization I helped start in 2003. The Tank is a home for performances and public affairs across disciplines: theater, film, comedy, music, dance, mixed media, puppetry, reading, speakers, forums, debates, meetings, and parties. Ticket prices are capped, so that taking a risk at The Tank feels as affordable as taking a risk at the AMC. Performers aren't paid, but they aren't charged, either. The door is shared between the venue to cover costs and the performers to recoup their expenses. It's a setup where nobody gets rich, but nobody— including the audience—goes broke. [241]

The goal of this financial structure is to serve as a place that prizes creativity, collaboration, and experimentation over commercialism. More than four hundred shows a year take place at The Tank, serving more than a thousand artists and tens of thousands of audience members. It's more than just a home for the arts; it strives to be a center of free expression and community involvement. It strives to be a democratic space.

This type of cultural offering should not be seen as the unique possession of a big city. Though they take different forms, this same spirit—and sometimes the same model—exists around the country.

Look to Iowa, the state in which Kevin Costner once said, "If you build it, they will come." Zach Manheimmer, a transplant from the off-off-Broadway theater world, must have seen *Field of Dreams* too often, because he took that advice. With the help of local partners, activists, funders, and loads of volunteers, he took over a sprawling office space—which had been home to both Obama and Dean's presidential campaigns in the Hawkeye State—and started the Des Moines Social Club. [242]

What is it? You could call it a theater. It has plays. It also has circus classes, poetry slams, and music. So maybe it's a performance venue. Then how do you explain the lounge where cheap local brews are poured, informal organizing meetings are held, and a small stage in the corner tantalizingly suggests an open floor—a Speaker's Box with amplification? There's also the gallery. So it's an art house . . . or a creative playground. It also has meeting rooms for conference and community gatherings, and soon will have classroom space. You could call it a community center . . . but it feels too cool.

There's a reason they called it a "social club"—they had visions of some public space that shared all these attributes. They felt the need to create a space that housed all manner of arts, but not only arts. They wanted a venue that encouraged a liberal sensibility, but wasn't explicitly political. They wanted to make everyone who walked in the door not only feel that they wanted to come back but also believe they were one of the owners, in some way responsible for coming back to contribute to the community.

In the heart of Iowa.

There are different models of how volunteers take ownership over creating a cultural experience for a larger community. It may not be Broadway, but it's more affordable and open, more involved and interactive, and in all of these ways, it's liberal.

A First Act on Liberal Theater

Nothing wrong with an old-fashioned play, if you can afford to go. Whether you catch it at your community theater or make it to a professional house, there are great works of drama that fill out your liberal arts education. Bertolt Brecht, the German playwright, once said he didn't want to create a play that angered or inspired audiences just long enough for them to make it to their car outside the theater, then forget about it on their drive home. Here are a few plays you don't forget about—and inspire us to Live Liberally.

Lysistrata. Originally performed in 411 B.C.E., Aristophanes' comedy tells of efforts of the women of Greece to end war by withholding sex from the men until the war is over. 243

Inherit the Wind. Based on the Scopes Monkey Trial, it recounts a small town putting evolution on trial—and with it, free-thinking, intellectual curiosity, and science. 244

Mother Courage and Her Children. Bertolt Brecht creates a story of a woman who seeks to profit from a devastating war but only meets further devastation. 245

The Cradle Will Rock. A 1937 musical by Mark Blitzstein, it was set to be directed by Orson Welles and produced by John Houseman. The political nature of it—and possibly pro-communist themes—got it closed down. The production company famously rented another theater and did a reading of it. As famous for its context as for its content, it is a reminder that some people find theater so powerful they seek to stop it. 246

Waiting for Lefty. Clifford Odets is one of the playwrights most associated with the WPA era, and this is one of his most famous works, which actually led to audiences shouting "strike" in solidarity with the characters in the play. 247

Twelve Angry Men. Inside the jury room, as jurors' personal prejudices shape their willingness to convict, one skeptical juror stands to make his case.

Master Harold and the Boys. Athol Fugard brought the reality of apartheid South Africa to the American stage with this beautiful play about how racism and segregation infect everyone in society.

Hair. Let the sun shine in! *Hair* caused a stir as it depicted the hippie counterculture of the late 1960s, introduced a slew of new American slang and profanity to the American stage, and ended act 1 with a fully nude cast. The antiwar message resonates over the years, as does the embrace of freedom and peace and questions about how characters should live and love in today's world.

Les Misérables. The setting is one where the poor are wrongly imprisoned, persecuted, and oppressed. The protagonists, however naively, try to make the system right.

Rent. Written at a time when contracting AIDS was a death warrant, this musical features characters who sing about life—about making every moment count. And in "La Vie Bohème," lyrics praise Maya Angelou, Václav Havel, and antipretension iconoclasm. Try to make all that rhyme.

Music

Theater has had to fight to feel little-d democratic at times. Music, though, has always been a populist force. Maybe it's because you don't need sets and lights, you can just pick up an instrument, and so more ragtag bands find a way to be heard. Maybe it's because there is something raw and emotional that accompanies music, or because for so many teens music is a countercultural escape.

You can find the independent venues near you or find the playlist that speaks to you online. Here are a few suggestions for to add to your **Soundtrack for a Liberal America.** This mix was assembled by activist, technologist, and music-lover Franz Hartl with additional contributions from other allies who want you to Rock Liberally.

Public Enemy — *Fear of a Black Planet.* Chuck D is the godfather of revolutionary music, and this album is as sonically dense and aggressive as any album released since.

Black Star — *Black Star.* Before he went to Hollywood, Mos Def highlighted a new political consciousness in hip-hop. Talib Kweli is *THE* dominant political rapper today. Together, they made an album that set the stage for a lot of what Brooklyn is about today.

Le Tigre — *From The Desk of Mr. Lady EP.* While some will say that Kathleen Hanna's best work was with riot grrrl pioneers Bikini Kill, there's no beating her later band Le Tigre for danceable left-wing politics. "Get off the internet! Destroy the right wing!" Yes.

OutKast — *Stankonia.* "Bombs over Baghdad" is an eerily accurate political description of 2010, even though it came out in 2000.

Radiohead — *Kid A.* Arguably the most significant band of the past twenty years. The album showed you how dark and cold things were going to become without being bleak. But letting you know, at the same time, we are going to win (eventually).

258   **The Clash—** *London Calling*. When punk kids said they got their news from The Clash, this is what they were talking about.

259   **Discount—** *Love, Billy*. Allison Mosshart's pop-punk anthems are so sweetly melodic that you can easily lose sight of her politically astute lyrics. Get this for the cover of "Waiting For the Great Leap Forward" alone—then get all their other stuff for good measure.

260   **Marvin Gaye—** *What's Going On*. Can we be sexy and political? Yes, we can.

261   **Fela Kuti—** *Expensive Shit*. People need to KNOW the Fela Kuti story. Required learning, no exceptions.

262   **TV on the Radio—** *Return to Cookie Mountain*. So we had the Iraq war and Katrina, we were fighting back, and the dialect created by fighting back was making us into something new. This is the sonic interpretation of what the post-9/11 decade felt like.

263   **Dar Williams—** *Mortal City*. To be listened to right before debating a right-wing uncle on Thanksgiving, especially the wonderful track "The Christians & the Pagans." Her songs are punchy stories, brimming with insight, wit, and empathy.

264   **Rage Against the Machine—** *Evil Empire*. Politically uncompromising and aggressive.

265   **Bruce Springsteen—** *The Ghost of Tom Joad*. A reminder of what we are fighting to preserve.

266   **Ani DiFranco—** *Up Up Up Up Up Up*. The first track, "'Tis of Thee," is for when the battle seems unwinnable and you need to keep on going regardless.

Traveling Liberally

When you're ready to break away from the everyday and find new playing fields, it is time for your liberal getaway.

You could venture into the wilds of our "big government" national parks. You could take a road trip to great historical sites from the civil rights or suffrage movements. You could vacation to a place where you volunteer building homes part of the time with an organization like Habitat for Humanity. You could find tips for environmentally friendly hiking (carry out what you carry in; respect paths so you will not harm wildlife); or socially conscious hunting (walk to the hunting grounds rather than driving in). You could join Karma Krew, a group that combines yoga with community service. You could tour minor league ballparks to get your fill of sports while supporting smaller markets, local businesses, and less-corporate teams. Or you can just go to the beach . . . and not feel guilty. It's your vacation! You don't have to work or learn every moment. But wherever you go, there are a few things you can do:

Find the local diner. There can be an instinct to go with what you know: Look, a McDonald's! A Starbucks! An Applebee's! You'll have a much richer experience, though, when you go local. You support the local economy in a more meaningful way, spending at places with roots in the community. You're also more likely to get an authentic view of the area. You can ask for stories about where you're visiting, hear the political views of the waitstaff or other patrons, and learn about local happenings you might not have known about. And, in the end, the food will be better than at Applebee's.

274 **Read the local paper.** You're on vacation to avoid reading, I know, but pick up the local paper—whether it's a one-paper town, or a mid-sized city with free alternative weekly. This is where you'll learn what's going on. I'm not saying you need to become an activist in your four days someplace, but it's nice to know what the local folks are talking about. Once you have some grounding, ask them about it. Strike up a conversation. They'll be pleasantly surprised you know anything about their area at all, and usually they're more than eager to share.

275 **Reuse and recycle.** Vacations offer easy opportunities to drop all your good habits . . . and maybe that's part of why you go on vacation. That said, don't take a break from recycling. Hotels don't always make it easy to do—so ask them. Ask whether trash gets sorted or if there's a way for you to sort. Look around for recycling on the street if your hotel doesn't offer it. It may take a little work, but it'll make you feel better. And by asking, maybe it will put pressure on the hotel to make it easier for their guests. Hotels can change their behavior. Somewhere along the way hotels realized they shouldn't launder towels every day. It was probably a cost-saving measure disguised as environmental awareness, but why shouldn't we tie those two goals together?

276 **CouchSurf.** Want to save money, meet some like-minded, inclusive folks, and participate in a great collectivist social experiment?

People have always crashed on the couches of friends and friends-of-friends. Now you can do it by becoming part of a community of CouchSurfers who offer their beds to others and ask for that same courtesy in return. Rather than word of mouth, there are websites like CouchSurfing.org that make it easy to do. You're not swapping per se—rather you're entering a large market of people who are willing to trust and open their homes to one another.

Would you rather just stay in a hotel, not have to talk to strangers, have a guaranteed experience? Sometimes, yes. Other times, you end up in a new town, and it would sure be helpful to have someone who knows the area, the sites, the transit, the nightlife . . . and someone who, because they're a CouchSurfer too, probably gets where you're coming from.

Tip well. Every country and culture has a different approach to tipping. But don't be fooled: if Europeans don't tip waitstaff, it's because their servers are paid well. Ours are not. Nor are our cleaning crews, doormen, porters, drivers . . . and their employers justify their low pay by arguing that they should factor in tips. So support the local economy and show your love of labor by respecting their work. Plus there are enough insults hurled about tourists; do your part to buck that trend. 277

Wear sunscreen. Skin cancer's no good. And public health threats ultimately cost us all. Be smarter than that. 278

Imagination Gone Wild

A section on Playing Liberally isn't complete with a few examples of simply absurd playfulness. In 2003, the flash mob was popularized. A store clerk would look up to see that 150 people had just crowded into her store, and one minute later they were all gone. In a park, fifty people would simultaneously pull out 279 their phones and shout "Sell, sell, sell." These absurd acts of coordination were a mix of street theater, public prank, and well-organized group dynamic. People would receive an e-mail or text message with odd directions, and they would do what they were told. Why? Because it was fun.

Is it liberal? People who never met before were working in concert. They were creating a public experience that they and innocent onlookers shared. They made people think about public space in a different light. They were leaving a residue of trust and joy . . . people came away smiling at strangers, feeling like there was value in engaging the outside world. So, yes, it's liberal.

280 One particular group that has used this method well is Improv Everywhere, which has executed a series of stunts, most notably the No Pants Subway Ride. People receive instructions to board a certain car of a certain train . . . wearing no pants. Eventually the other riders start to notice that not just one or two people are pantless, but dozens. At first it's odd, or alarming. Then it's amusing. As more people get on at each stop, it's downright entertaining, even astounding, and people find themselves laughing together on a subway car. Finally, a man enters the subway with a stack of clothes: "Pants for sale," he shouts, and everyone bursts into hysterics.

Why not? Why not draw people into a surprising comedy and make them feel a connection they didn't know was there?

281 What would happen if this energy was turned to politics? One street activist group that did just that was the Billionaires for Bush, a satiric guerrilla group that would counterprotest liberal demonstrations with signs promoting greed and oligarchy. In 2004, they built a community around protesting and having fun. On tax day, they staged rallies at the post office, "thanking"

regular people for paying taxes so "billionaires" wouldn't have to. During the Republican Convention, when protestors were denied a permit to rally in Central Park, the Billionaires set up a game of croquet and thanked the city for keeping the rabble out of "their" park. Billionaire teams popped up around the country—with guidance and inspiration from the originators, but with the charge to make their own mischief locally. People had the chance to play dress up and get media coverage that contributed to political discourse. (In the health care debate, they turned into Billionaires for Wealthcare, showing up at the "Tea Party" rallies with slogans like "Let them eat Advil" and "Cigna / Palin 2012.")

Shortly after the 2008 election, New Yorkers found themselves being handed free issues of the *New York Times* as they entered subway stations. What they hadn't realized was that the paper was for a date in the future. They soon saw, though, that the paper was from an alternate reality: one where the Iraq war had ended, the Bush team was being prosecuted for their crimes, luxury taxes were imposed on the wealthy, and subsidies were going to green jobs and farmers' markets.

It was a taste of what the world could look like, a prank of possibility. And it was pulled off by some established pranksters, working with advocacy groups, and getting hundreds of volunteers to distribute the papers throughout the city.

You saw people on the subway smile and laugh; some looked concerned, while others looked hopeful. It earned media coverage, which only helped the stories travel more widely and sent people to the online version—an exact replica of www.NYTimes.com with a host of phony, and quite inspirational, stories.

The creators were pranksters and politicos. . . . and they were playing liberally.

CHAPTER 5
LEARNING LIBERALLY

> *As Mankind becomes more liberal,*
> *they will be more apt to allow that*
> *all those who conduct themselves as*
> *worthy members of the community*
> *are equally entitled to the protections*
> *of civil government. I hope ever to see*
> *America among the foremost*
> *nations of justice and liberality.*
> —GEORGE WASHINGTON

These pages provide some playful ideas for liberalizing your life, and there are plenty of other guides to going green, making a difference, saving and sustaining, making friends, and influencing people. Let me be honest: any how-to book can only urge you along a bit. It can open your eyes, suggest a few steps, but rarely will it transform you.

Your worldview and your daily lifestyle are shaped by more than a quick read. They are the results of a host of influences, some which have been lifelong, and some which bombard you every day. How you were raised, whom you speak with and listen to on a daily basis, where you turn for news or inspiration or to discover how to solve a problem—these are the influences that more deeply shape your engagement with the world.

You can't do much about how you were raised, but you can think seriously about how you'll raise others. You can make choices about where you go for information and insights, and think about when and how to challenge the status quo. In this way, day in and day out, you will be living liberally as a result of learning liberally.

Before we get into what you can try out on your own each day, let's tackle some big issues: without question, we're raised with certain conservative biases. I don't mean that you need to get out from under the shadow of a religious-zealot mom or Reagan-loving dad. I mean that our society—our schooling, our cultural inheritance, the habits we pick up before we know any better—contains significant right-wing lessons.

Conservative Falsehoods We Need to Unlearn

- ★ **America is a nation of rugged individuals.** In fact, our greatest successes have always been collective in spirit or action.

- ★ **In America, you pull yourself up by your boot-straps.** Actually, we see how education and opportunity are often either passed down as legacies of the wealthy or are provided to all by the efforts of the state.

- ★ **"In God we trust,"** as emblazoned on our currency. America's origins and proudest moments have often been when we have allowed people to keep their religious beliefs as private choices, out of the public sphere.

There are also some terrific liberal messages we're raised with as gospel, whether they are true or not. Conservative messages are often proven a lie by the realities of how America works; but our liberal ideals have often fallen short through our history of segregation, disenfranchisement, wealth disparity, and militarism.

Liberal Ideals We Want to Believe

★ **"All men are created equal,"** and America is on a march to greater and greater enfranchisement and rights.

★ **We have a country of laws, not of men,** and even our highest law can be amended because laws need to reflect a changing country.

★ **"Life, liberty and the pursuit of happiness,"** "e pluribus unum," and "truth, justice and the American way," are our shared language suggesting a nation of common fortunes, mutual respect, and tremendous tolerance.

America is often not as good as our principles. We are, however, far better than our more conservative myths. So there is really a double mission in learning liberally:

1) discredit and dismiss the conservative tropes and

2) honestly assess where we fall short of the liberal values.

Criticizing our country isn't "anti-American"—from the beginning, our founders were often outspoken about their concerns for the direction of the nation, and every great change—abolition, women's suffrage—grew out of people offering thoughtful critiques of our country.

Even if your goal is to emphasize the liberal legacy of our great nation, it doesn't hurt that cause to point out where we're lacking. Hold up those liberal themes as the ideal. Then the story of how America improves is part of the liberal lesson about our country.

It would be a separate project to catalog and disassemble the conservative lies that have snuck into our national consciousness. It would be an additional separate project to tell the story of America through the liberal lens, and where we still have further to go to reach the rhetoric of our nation. We're not going to do it all right here, but let's start by looking at what we've "learned" and maybe by unlearning a bit.

Growing up, I—like so many public elementary school kids— said the Pledge of Allegiance. The Pledge could be viewed as a great liberalizing force that creates a shared experience for all schoolchildren and asserts they are all part of a greater society; or it could be an authoritarian tool to brainwash us into submission. The fact is, it often becomes an act of repetition. Kids race to say it as quickly as they can. Most mumble through without thinking about the meaning, and many might not be speaking the correct words at all.

One of the few times as a child I was forced to stop and think about the Pledge was when a substitute teacher taught our third grade class. Mrs. Ginsburg was a regular substitute, and many of us had known her since first grade. When she led the Pledge that day, though, we noticed that she skipped a few words.

"And to the republic for which it stands, one nation," she intoned, then paused. Then continued, "indivisible, with liberty . . ."

She'd forgotten to say "under God," and we noticed. But we figured: she's old—chuckle and let it pass.

However, after the Pledge, she pushed us. "Did anyone notice what I did differently?" Nobody wanted to speak up and embarrass her with the fact she'd forgotten the words. "Did anyone notice what I didn't say?"

Finally, one student piped up. We all felt a little sorry for her that she'd flubbed it, and were confused why she was making such a big deal. She, though, wasn't embarrassed at all. "We have a separation of church and state in this country. You can practice whatever religion you want, or no religion, and the country protects your right to do so. But that also means you shouldn't have to say 'under God' when you pledge allegiance to your country."

That day wasn't a game-changer for any of us. We laughed it off, and wondered why we were spending so much time on it. It has, however, stayed with me. Over the years, as I learned more about our country, and the church-state separation, as I came into a political consciousness that was more concerned with those issues, I remembered what Mrs. Ginsburg hadn't said . . . and was thankful to her.

Mrs. Ginsburg wasn't being a radical. In some ways, she was the more traditional one. The words "under God" were added to the Pledge under the Eisenhower administration, as we strove to distinguish ourselves from the "godless communists." It's not that long a tradition, and you could argue—as some have tried, all the way to the Supreme Court—that it has no place in the public expression of belief in our country.

I tend to take a live-and-let-live approach. If you believe that God is watching over us and joining our journey, then say "under God." If you don't, or don't think it's appropriate, skip it. Hopefully, someone will hear that pause in your oath and ask you why, and maybe you'll plant a seed that will undo their formal education down the road. If it makes your Pledge more intentional, and you truly consider what you're saying and why, that itself is a liberal step forward.

Restoring an agnostic Pledge isn't the most important battle in pulling our education to the left. It's more an example of how one person can help you scrutinize the world in a new way, how she can encourage you to think outside the box and ask non-obvious questions. That's a key ingredient to learning liberally.

With that spirit in mind, and with the honest acknowledgment that we're not going to tackle our entire upbringing in this chapter, here are a few places to start in your reimagining of America.

Our liberal history: Ten great moments and why they make us proud liberal Americans.

The Declaration of Independence. There was more than one reason the American colonies sought separation from the British, and they ranged from what we might consider the left (more representation) to what we might call the right (antitax). When the project of drafting this Declaration was handed to a young Thomas Jefferson, America was set on a liberal course. Asserting that "all men are created equal," suggesting a society based on commitment to one another and not loyalty to a crown, and assuming that participatory, representative democracy was a greater form of governance, T. J. laid out a fundamental set of liberal values that our country has been working to live up to ever since.

The Revolution of 1800. In America's earliest days, there were some who imagined a president would be as enshrined as royalty. George Washington's decision to only stand for two terms confounded that expectation, and quickly political parties emerged as a new test for the cohesion of our young democracy.

John Adams won the election in 1796; then in 1800, when Jefferson beat him, we faced a new unknown: how a transfer of power across parties would work in our country. Despite the high rhetoric and deep passions of some of Adams's supporters, and the fears some harbored about Jefferson, there was no violence. There was no need for military intervention and no judicial stalemate (as there would be in 2000). Our country proved itself more integrated than its factions and more stable as a result.

Abolition. The matter of slavery stained the first century of our national history, and its legacy has been a burden we've never lifted. The debate stretches back to before our Declaration and Constitution, and shaped many of the debates about our expansion, our commerce, and our interstate relations through the 1800s. Ultimately, it took a bloody, costly Civil War to end slavery. The end of slavery showed that we could strive for the "more perfect union" suggested in the Preamble of our Constitution. It overturned existing social orders and provided a fundamental challenge to our country—one that we survived. The result was one step forward in respecting all people, promoting dignity and equality, and recognizing a shared fortune for black and white in these United States.

Breaking up the trusts. "Trusts"—what an innocuous, almost positive name for the anticompetitive, anticonsumer monopolies created by big businesses to aggregate wealth. The extreme wealth stratification of the Gilded Age created a cadre of robber barons who controlled entire markets: steel, oil, railways. Not only were these trusts bad for business, they were bad for America. Teddy Roosevelt (and others, but he's most famously associated with this effort) became a "trust-buster," suing to break up these monopolies. He wanted a free market and saw these powerful figures as impeding this goal—so the government had a responsibility to be a tool that created a structure of fairness. When the government proactively intercedes for the greater good, as opposed to acting to protect the wealthy elites, we see America at its best.

Women's suffrage. It took us almost a century and a half before out country was able to see past "all men are created equal" to include all people. Half the population had been excluded from our political decisions: women, who ran households and businesses, formed communities and followed local issues, strengthened families and were every bit as entitled as any man to fair treatment. In 1920, the amendment guaranteeing women the right to vote was again proof that though it may be slow, the arc of history moves toward greater equality, inclusion, and respect.

The New Deal. It's hard to imagine what our country would be like without the reforms that elevated people out of poverty, regulated the greed of the banking industries (well, we've recently seen what life's like when banks go wild), and asserted that the federal government must play a role in shaping education and opportunity for all its citizens. Franklin Delano Roosevelt's advancements in the 1930s—joined later by Johnson's Great Society programs in the 1960s—created a network of safety nets, labor reforms, minimum wage, Social Security, and other pillars that have stabilized our society. Both sets of reforms asserted that we needed to tackle these problems together . . . and when the next great set of reforms expand health care to all and comprehensively transform our energy policy, they will be in the same lineage as these momentous agendas.

Our entrance into World War II. There have long been competing approaches to international relations in our country, a tension between those who support neutrality and isolation against those who support intervention and the exportation of democracy. It's not that one side is liberal or the other conservative. The approach—whether we go it alone or work with allies in the international community—is what makes it a liberal act. As do our intentions: we are always acting for our own security, but are we also acting to amass wealth or to promote human rights, are we fighting to protect the powerful or defend the helpless?

In World War II, our struggle was not ours alone . . . in fact we were a little late to it. After Pearl Harbor, we saw that there was a struggle for peace and for rights, against aggression and against genocide, and we joined the European theater as well as the Pacific. We also understood that peace and security couldn't be left to one country alone—we had to work with allies to succeed in such a monumental effort. Investing in international, multi-lateral forces is a liberal approach to foreign policy, because it depends on seeing beyond our own self-interest. And, after the war, the creation of the United Nations was an effort to invest in a permanent structure of international collaboration.

The aftermath of World War II: The Marshall Plan and the GI Bill. World War II is a rich chapter in our history that makes all Americans proud. The aftermath of the war should compound that pride. Domestically, we passed a sweeping GI Bill that gave returning soldiers the opportunity for higher education. This expansive and expensive program ushered in an economic boom, created the workers needed for a new economy, and built a strong middle class—all because of redistribution of wealth through a government program. Internationally, the Marshall Plan to invest in the European countries that had just come through such a great conflict demonstrated our belief that spending large sums of money would pay back in peace and prosperity. Rather than exacting revenge for the war, or pulling back to our own isolating borders, we showed the world that we understood that we needed to look out for each other's interests and invest in each other's prosperity. We created a more stable, successful Europe as a result.

Civil rights. There are few Americans now who would openly argue against the right of a black person to vote, to shop at a restaurant, or to hold a job (though now those same prejudices sometimes exist toward immigrants). What a different America we were in the 1950s and 1960s, when students were barred from schools, and protestors were met with hoses and police dogs. Dramatic change in America never comes easily. We are fortunate that brave members of the civil rights movement, with effective leaders, focused strategies, and a passion for justice, dragged our country forward. If the struggle between conservative and liberal forces is characterized by status quo vs. change, authority vs. protest, self interest vs. communal good, the sanctity of individual preference vs. the embrace of a common goal, the civil rights movement showed that this can be a liberal country. Though there is always more work to do.

294**The moon landing.** You might say that the dramatic events of 1969 which captured the world's imagination were the triumph of science, not liberalism. True—though we do need to remember that Bush administration right-wingers waged a war against science at every turn. The real reason to include this event is embodied in Neil Armstrong's famous words: "One small step for man, one giant leap for mankind." Armstrong was, perhaps inadvertently, creating what should become an enduring liberal slogan: embodying the fact that a greater good is often more remarkable than individual accomplishments. Truly, the moon landing was remarkable—and took place not because of independent entrepreneurship or innovation, but because of great communal effort, government resources, and common national purpose, set forth by President Kennedy's declaration at the start of the 1960s that by the end of the decade we'd put a man on the moon. It symbolizes what we are capable of when we invest in each other and in our country and when our country invests in us. All thanks to our socialized, big-government space program.

While the events above are generally agreed to be "Great Moments in American History," they also should be seen as examples of the collectivist, inclusive, diverse, and freethinking characteristics that shape a liberal vision of our country.

Furthermore, there are plenty of figures and incidents that embody an America we can be proud of that are not yet among our canon of "Great Moments." Here are a few I hope more high school history books will spend time praising in the future.

Thoreau's antiwar activism. Henry David Thoreau is best known for *Walden*, his journal on living in the woods, embodying that American trope of self-reliance. What Thoreau is less noted for was his principled opposition to the Mexican War in the 1840s, an unnecessary war, sold on false premises by a conservative government looking to increase wealth for its most elite constituents. Sound familiar? Thoreau refused to pay taxes because he didn't wish to fund the war, and went to jail for it. That political dissent should be as discussed as his year in the woods.

295

The achievements of Frances Perkins. Franklin Roosevelt's labor secretary, Perkins was the first woman to serve in the U.S. cabinet. She used that role as a powerful advocate for working families and was a critical partner in New Deal initiatives. She was the champion who helped pass progressive changes such as the minimum wage and overtime laws, which we still enjoy today.

296

The repeal of Prohibition. It all comes back to the booze. In 1919, a puritanical streak in our country sparked an amendment to our Constitution prohibiting the manufacture and sale of alcohol. Thankfully, in 1933, Americans undid that decision. In addition to allowing for the creation of projects like Drinking Liberally, the repeal also sent an important message: Let's not create a culture of prohibition. Making behavior illegal often creates unregulated, dangerous underground networks and criminalizes our population. Within the law, risky behavior can be properly supervised and regulated, taxed for the common

297

good, and made safe for all. Ideally, that will someday extend to the more common and less harmful drugs that are prevalent in all walks of life in our country. Some celebrate December 5, the day the 21st Amendment repealed the 18th, as Repeal Day . . . a holiday we can all toast.

298 **Loving v. Virginia.** In 1967, Mildred Delores Jeter and Richard Perry Loving came before the Supreme Court to petition for their right to marry. The aptly named "Loving" case ultimately overturned laws barring interracial marriage, a holdover from an earlier era. This decision brought us closer to being a country where all races are treated equally and where the mixing of people of different backgrounds is a strength. In Idaho Falls, local progressives from the Drinking Liberally chapter celebrate "Loving Day" as a chance to honor these liberal heroes. We hope this case will be fully honored in the history books of future generations.

299 **The resignation of Richard Nixon.** This was a momentous event, but is often looked at as a sad moment for America. It seems to me to showcase America at its best.

If a liberal country believes that we share prosperity and purpose, then we also must share laws. Just as nobody—not even the largest trusts—may abuse our shared economy, nobody—not even the president—is above our common justice. Richard Nixon didn't believe that, as he demonstrated again and again in his actions. As he famously said in an interview several years after his presidency: "If the president does it, it isn't illegal."

Fortunately, our country proves again and again that when we make mistakes, we have ways to right them. In Nixon's case, we made the mistake of electing him twice, but we also made the more critical mistake of giving him enough latitude to abuse his power: to spy on political enemies, undercut democratic practices, and obstruct the processes of investigation and justice.

So we corrected it: proactive journalism followed by public organizing created pressure on Congress and a political climate in which Richard Nixon became the first president to step down in disgrace before the end of his term. As we had seen in 1800, we saw again in 1974 that the system can work, power can be transferred, no elite is enshrined, and the country is stronger than any one individual.

Very recently, Americans had the opportunity to add another mark to our liberal history: **the election of Barack Obama**. You don't have to like his policies, be a member of his party, or even have voted for him to recognize Obama's election as a remarkable moment in America. He is the face of the new American dream: interracial, with parents of diverse backgrounds, he grew from humble origins to take advantage of educational opportunities, give back to his community, come to serve as a representative, and then ascend to the presidency, reflecting the hopes of millions. Those that fear him most—like the "birthers" who challenge his citizenship—are really fearful that their country is changing: that new colors and names are emerging from a melting pot of languages and cultures. Liberals aren't scared, though: there is strength in our diversity. You see it in the new tone President Obama can strike when speaking to the Middle East and Africa. You see it in the disenfranchised communities that now believe they have a stake in the American project. We are a better country for our mixing of races, religions, ethnicities, and histories—by mixing, we share; by sharing, we strengthen. Our president now reflects that truth about America.

We will have to wait to learn whether history judges him a great president, and a liberal one . . . but his election itself was a remarkable feat in the pursuit of a better country.

In addition to the moments we celebrate, there are the myths we hear as well. It's not enough to embrace our liberal heritage;

we have to actively delete the conservative lies that threaten to distort our honest understanding of our country.

Let's throw these conservative myths out of the history books.

300 **It's not true that our founders were all slave owners.** Some people make the argument that nobody can be blamed for slavery since everyone was doing it. Thomas Jefferson embodies how complicated the case is: on one hand, trying to oppose slavery in the Declaration of Independence; on the other, being a slave owner himself. The fact is, though, that there were those who opposed slavery from the beginning, including Aaron Burr. We need to own up to our country's mistakes, and not allow ourselves to fall into the easy trap of assuming that because "everyone" was committing the same crime, that somehow made it OK. Only by acknowledging that even our greatest founders were guilty can we honestly assess and address the tensions built into our country.

301 **Actually, the yeoman farmer was not the ideal early American.** As much as liberals love Thomas Jefferson, he was guilty of a little rhetorical fraud. He was supposedly the champion of the yeoman farmer, the prototypical "rugged individual" that built our country. How did these farmers, pioneers, and trailblazers have land to explore? They were aided by the Louisiana Purchase, an unprecedented land deal that expanded the borders of our country. It was a huge government program presided over by President Thomas Jefferson and paid for by the national coffers, strengthened by commerce from the cities. As often happens throughout American history, the dreams of the individual are subsidized by the efforts of the government, paid for by our common wealth.

302 **False: Baseball was born in the countryside.** I love baseball. I grew up with all the myths about it: how it was created in the

innocent countryside, how it's always been a national booster in times of trouble, how teams have built up cities, and how the sport has supported America. However, we know that from the beginning, baseball was a business and the patriotic flag-waving has often been a marketing stunt. The greatest bit of public relations work had to do with the origins of the game. Before it was played by Abner Doubleday in the rolling hills of upstate New York farmland, it was played by immigrants and laborers in the streets of New York City. However, even then, the crowded, diverse cities somehow didn't sell as well as the images of rural, white America (or what Sarah Palin might call "real America"), so baseball businessmen made up a different story. We need to keep debunking such myths. We should restore city life as central to, not destructive of, American life. In the urban environments, resources are shared, classes mingle, and immigrants find a home. In cities, the American experiment is often at its most diverse, innovative, and successful.

The 1950s were a time of great peace and prosperity . . . not quite. There was a liberal consensus, a popular president, a booming economy—unless, of course, you were black. The 1950s may live on in our cultural imagination as *Leave it to Beaver*, but the serene surface masked deeper traumas: Jim Crow laws persevered. Violence against blacks was common and ignored. A conservative reading of history suggests that the civil rights movement created new problems that ruptured the beauty of the 1950s. In fact, the 1960s exposed tensions that were already there.

No, Ronald Reagan did not end the Cold War. Conservatives love Ronald Reagan, but his policies to consolidate wealth, bust unions, race-bait, and demonize social programs make him less loved among liberals. Boosters believe they have a trump card: the decline of the Soviet Union. But really the person who could take far more credit than Ronald Reagan is Mikhail Gorbachev, the Soviet premier. Pervasive structural problems had weakened the Soviet economy before Reagan stepped into office, and that economic pressure opened the way for social pressures to liberalize the Soviet Union. Through his two policies of perestroika (reform) and glasnost (openness), Gorbachev courageously ushered in an era that would usher him out; he was a leader who took steps that would limit his own powers. Reagan just happened to be on the other side of the ocean.

A "Liberal" Arts Education

Ideally, your high school education isn't only from textbooks, which tend to take the "story" out of "history." All students should graduate having read books that ask them to question what they learn, challenge authority, and make their own discoveries.

Below is a small selection of works that inspire and challenge, offer a view of another America that exists or could exist, and are just good reads. Many were, at one time, banned from schools, and some of them still are. Thankfully, a number of these books now appear in many high school curricula, reminding us that progress is possible.

1984. George Orwell's compelling antiauthoritarian parable leaves you with chills as you contemplate how the examples of "Big Brother" in today's world try to force us into silence and conformity.

Catch-22. War may be absurd, not just glorious. The retelling of it can make you laugh and cry at once. Joseph

Heller's acclaimed novel asks us to take a new look at old battles and gives us a shared language to despise senseless bureaucracy.

The Grapes of Wrath. An argument by the great John Steinbeck that when people struggle, not only do they need the kindness of others, they also need large-scale reform that we can only provide together.

307

Slaughterhouse-Five. Kurt Vonnegut's most lasting novel describes his experience witnessing America firebomb a city during World War II . . . and the time- and space-traveling fantasy that allows him to deal with the horror. Plus it's really funny.

308

No Name in the Street. James Baldwin's essays, written after he decided to return from his successful expatriate days in Europe to the civil rights–era South, address his struggle to define American identity and ask the reader to struggle as well.

309

To Kill a Mockingbird. Harper Lee creates the enduring protagonist of a young girl who learns not to judge people based on race or fears or that which divides us. The novel offers a picture of a different era of racial bigotry in America, and some sad lessons on what happens when justice isn't served.

310

Fahrenheit 451. Ray Bradbury's tale of a society in which a "fireman" is a book-burner. After you read it, check out BannedBooksWeek.org and find something to read that's still being banned in America today.

311

312 **Beloved.** This work won Toni Morrison the Pulitzer Prize and is President Obama's favorite novel. Yet this story about the brutality of slavery and the challenge of building a life after escaping from it continues to be removed from school library shelves for its language and violence. Read a banned book . . . it will also give you something to discuss with the president.

313 **The Shock Doctrine.** Naomi Klein's assessment of the interlocking power grabs, vast profits, and wars that have shaped global dynamics for the past forty years will make you rethink what you've learned in history class.

314 **A People's History of The United States** by Howard Zinn. Because there's more truth than in our current history books.

Reading Liberally

We may challenge our educational upbringing, but we cannot change or erase it entirely. Therefore, we need to focus on what we can do in our daily lives to continue to learn liberally. Where do we go for information? How do we filter, and whom should we trust? If conservative bias is deep in our cultural psyche, will we be able to recognize it?

315 The short answer: there is no right answer. As the great liberal American poet Walt Whitman suggested, "listen to all sides and filter them from yourself." You should take healthy skepti-
316 cism and scrutiny into all lessons. Talk out your thoughts or

confusions with others. A benefit of a liberal community is that you have more people to bounce ideas off.

A good starting place, though, is to read. There's a reason you get more out of what you read than what you watch or hear: TV and radio set their own pace; in reading, you set the pace. You can return to a question, underline a thought, stop and pick up again later. TV and radio exist in time; texts exist outside of time and allow you to engage with them when and how you want.

So, what should you read?

Magazines

In addition to a newspaper, why not try a few magazines?

★ It's hard to be a daily paper. It's a constant race to keep up with deadlines, which means depth is sometimes sacrificed for immediacy. The pressure to boost sales often pushes sensationalism to the forefront. Magazines have the time to dig more deeply, and more thoughtfully, to offer longer articles with more nuanced themes.

- ★ Magazines support investigative journalism. In some ways, with news, we get what we pay for. In an era of free media, there might not be funding for as much deep, probing journalism as our democracy deserves. Magazines are not always a solution—but in the run-up to the Iraq war, the revelations of torture, the concerns about a neoconservative push to militarily engage Iran, magazines were at the forefront of these stories. We need investigative journalists, so we need to help support institutions that pay them.

- ★ Magazines are sharable. Sure, you might pass on a newspaper in the course of an afternoon, but it's old news by the next day. The longer shelf life of a magazine makes it more likely you'll pass it along and be able to engage in substantive conversations with neighbors or colleagues about what you read.

319 Which magazines? Go explore a newspaper stand and find some you like . . . but here are a few suggestions:

320 **Mother Jones,** a Bay Area–based publication, is a clear alternative to mainstream media. While many newspapers choose to cover the same stories as each other, in a race to conformity, in *Mother Jones* you're more like to find a piece that will challenge the norms.

321 **The Nation** for well over a century has been a constant progressive voice, and in its pages creates space for vibrant political discourse, including divergent views within the left.

322 **The New Yorker.** I used to think *The New Yorker* was a fashionable accessory for people who wanted to demonstrate they lived among an intellectual upper crust. Turns out that I was being a jerk. *The New Yorker* breaks stories, and gives more pages to serious topics than newspapers can afford. Each week, its lengthy articles give you a chance to explore issues you may not have considered and give you the terms and tools to make sense of those topics.

Do you need to have subscriptions to all these? No, of course not. There's also the guilt felt by most subscribers that they don't get to read each issue, and the piles of untouched magazines grow in the corner of your home, a reminder of your personal failings.

Fortunately, that's what public libraries are for. Go on in and leaf through a magazine. Pick up some conservative rags as well—it's worth knowing their arguments in order to make ours stronger.

One tip for when you're done reading a liberal magazine, and this comes from John Javna's *50 Simple Things You Can Do to Fight the Right*: leave the magazine out and open on a library table. For one, when librarians clear up after you, it shows them that people were reading *Mother Jones*, and makes them more likely to renew the subscription or mention to other librarians that it's a popular title.

Second, when you leave a magazine out and open, you never know who might come by to pick it up. You may have just lured someone new into Reading Liberally.

Books

You can bring more than magazine advocacy to your local library. Organize in order to use your library's purchasing power to push all manner of published progressivism. Research what titles are being released and drop a note for your librarian. Ask ten friends to request it. Libraries work on a very local level, and many librarians have a good amount of discretion in what they purchase. They want to buy what will be read—if it is of value to their customers, it is of value to their institution. Create a market for the next titles by progressive radio personalities like Tom Hartmann, or new releases from an independent, progressive publisher like Ig Publishing. The library is going to spend its money somewhere; it might as well support publishers that support good work.

You can also become your own library. Anytime you own a book, think about its fate. Should it be exiled to a pile or a high shelf dusty with years of accumulation? Instead, is there a way the book can live on? Lending libraries and book swaps are organized grassroots avenues to give that book new purpose. Pass a book along to friends, or set up a swap with your neighbors or carpoolers. One nice touch is to put a name and date on the inside back cover; if you feel really forward, include contact info as well. As the book lives again and again in new hands, there's something amusing about seeing where it's been. You never know when you may want to talk to somebody about it, and there's a list of people you could e-mail.

Reading groups. The desire to talk about books and share the experience of reading is behind the proliferation of book clubs nationwide. We are part of this trend with Reading Liberally book groups. There are many of us who fondly remember discussions sections from college and miss the ability to trade ideas in our grown-up life. There are others who read something and don't know what to do next. They desire a community to help them make sense of the book and think about its consequences. You have other folks as well who only read if they're given a deadline. Whatever reason, a book club is a simple way to make the individual act of reading into a shared act of community building.

When we started Reading Liberally chapters, we provided recommendations of books that we thought groups would enjoy. We quickly remembered liberals don't like to march in lockstep.

While we thought it would be cool if dozens of chapters read the same book to be part of a national discussion, each group quickly made clear they had their own interests and considerations. Fair enough—they are stronger as a result of being self-organized.

The amusing part is that the hosts who rebelled against our push for conformity soon found the tables turned. When local Reading Liberally organizers suggested books for their own members to read, they got push-back from members demanding to know why they should all read the same book within the club. Why not choose a theme, suggest a few readings, and let anyone then read whatever they wanted, bringing more information and a wider array of insights into the conversation? Herding liberals is never easy.

Whether you choose one book together, or have people bring in different source materials, there are some simple steps to liberalize your local literary crew.

Choose something the library stocks. Not everyone wants to buy a book each month, and you don't want to lose members over that. Make your selection something available at the local library. This will keep more members engaged, and will send the librarians a message about what people are reading. 330

Support liberal publishers. Liberal books are published by major companies when they are written by big names like Al Franken or a Kennedy. There are many other strong, interesting liberal voices that aren't yet known quantities and major publishers might not take the risk. Smaller publishing houses like Chelsea Green, a Vermont-based publisher best known for food and environmental works, and Ig Publishing, a Brooklyn business that's been turning bloggers into print authors, present terrific work that just doesn't get around as much. Help spread the word and keep these publishers in business. 331

332 **Don't be too dry.** There is an endless number of good policy works out there, but reading only policy is a quick way to lose steam. While a work on climate change followed by a tome on health policy followed by a discourse on education would be valuable, it may also be dull. Mix in fiction, memoirs, poetry. Keep your selections varied and fresh, and that will keep the conversation lively and the group going strong.

333 **Make everyone the decider.** Some book clubs attempt to find consensus each month. Unfortunately, that can lead to less inspired choices and fewer risks. What if each month you pass the decision-making power to a different member? You'll receive a wider range of choices and a few surprises. These selections may be less well known but quite worth the risk. Plus, everyone becomes an owner of the club—in addition to choosing a book, everyone leads discussions, prepares questions or thoughts, does supplementary research. Groups are stronger when everyone contributes.

334 **Mix in some living authors.** One could read for years from the
335 336 great works of the past: from Frederick Douglass to John
337 338 Steinbeck, Elizabeth Cady Stanton to Upton Sinclair. By all means, steep yourself in that history. Also, though, consider the added benefits of living authors. By buying their books, you're supporting and encouraging them, and by reading their works, you have more opportunity to join in a current dialogue. You might be able to reach out to them directly, or see them speak. Fundamentally, you become part of a movement that keeps them producing and keeps fostering new liberal views and voices.

339 One last note for a liberal book club: food . . . and drink. Do it potluck—from each according to his ability, to each according to his appetite.

Host an author. In addition to a regular club that meets at cafés or homes, Reading Liberally also hosts authors on tours. Many progressive authors would love to connect to a live audience, and outside a few major cities, many don't have networks that can host them. Getting into a new city has value for them—it might give them an excuse to get on area radio or in the local paper, it may create buzz among local bloggers, and it might sell some books. They also, honestly, just enjoy knowing that people care about their work.

You don't need to be a major organization to host authors. Why not reach out to them, and give it a try? What do you have to lose? It's easy to do:

★ Write to them through their websites or publishers.

★ Be clear with them about expectations. What type of event are you inviting them to? How many people might be there?

★ Offer more help, if you can. Can you send press releases to the local paper, or make introductions to the local radio station? Can you get an event scheduled at a bookstore? These are good incentives, but offer only if you can really follow through.

★ Start local. Many authors have no travel budget, so start with folks who might be a short commute away. See which local faculty members at area colleges have recently published books.

And yes . . . all of these tricks would work on me. If you throw in a free dinner and beer, I'm definitely there.

The Internet

There's more information in the world than is printed on dead trees. While books give you longer views and deeper insights, the web is more likely your immediate source for news. The internet has unparalleled power to connect you with stories and voices around the world and to give you up-to-the moment coverage, commentary, audio, and video. The internet breaks any monopoly a few agencies can have on the news by empowering anyone and everyone to publish their own news and opinions. By opening the gates wide to people with a range of experiences and expertise, theoretically we could find more accurate information than we could from a few channels and a handful of papers.

Then there is the fear that we could get more inaccuracies; that a world without formal editors and publishers is a world without standards. There is such a glut of information, how do you find what's most important?

Those are legitimate concerns, but surmountable ones. The fact is that our professional papers with publishers and editors get things wrong, as do well-known encyclopedias. Print media has its corporate ties to deal with, and every profession is at risk of groupthink.

The online encyclopedia, Wikipedia, has addressed these challenges and become a trusted source for information. That's not saying you should trust everything on those pages, but there is a community built around the site that monitors it for quality.

Wikipedia is like any common resource: if anyone poisons it, nobody can use it; but if everyone participates, contributes to, and protects it, we all benefit. As with any research you do, don't assume everything on Wikipedia is accurate.

Take similar caution when reading blogs, and you will be able to put similar faith in them. There are inaccuracies, there are agendas, there are opinions disguised as coverage and pay-for-play alliances unannounced. All of that exists on the NBC nightly news as well, so as with any information, you just have to figure out whom to trust.

For example, if you read the *New York Times*, you decide there are some columnists you tend to believe more than others. You draw that conclusion after reading them over time, considering their arguments, weighing them against information you learn, and deciding who seems trustworthy.

The same standard applies to blogs. Take recommendations from friends you trust. Read a handful and question what they tell you. Make blogs earn your loyalty. When you do find someone who gets it right consistently, see whom he or she trusts by seeing who they link to.

Online media may feel fresh and seem to break the mold, but the ground rules are basically the same. If someone regularly publishes false reports, stop reading them and tell other people to stop reading them too.

Once you feel confident enough to stray from the major media websites, you will discover great sources for liberal perspectives on the day's events.

Daily Kos. This high-traffic progressive blog is loved and loathed by political allies and enemies respectively. Kos has more readers than many daily papers, and among the audience are influential readers: policy makers, advocates, elected officials.

Kos, short for the site's founder "Markos," is a community blog. Anyone can sign up for an account and publish diaries on any subject they please. Only a handful of authors have "front page" privileges to create the content that regularly appears on the first page of the website. All other diaries, though, still have a home: they are listed in a side column on the front page. Readers can "recommend" diaries, helping keep the posts on the front page longer.

This system enables independent authors to develop followings. Some writers focus on particular topics and become trusted on specific issues. Others become known for their tone. Hundreds of regular readers comment on all the posts, joining and enlarging the conversation.

While most posts offer analysis or opinion, Daily Kos will at times provide original coverage; it regularly offers videos; and it also conducts independent professional polling.

Think Progress. A project of the Center for American Progress, a Washington, D.C.–based think tank, this site is more news than opinion. It chooses news stories that focus on a liberal agenda: exposing the hypocrisy of the right, discussing movement on progressive initiatives and conservative obstacles. The stories are presented factually and are well resourced, and these posts frequently cover topics that may be overlooked in the general press.

Talking Points Memo proved that a website could also conduct real investigative journalism. Founded by a former traditional media journalist, TPM was a leader in making a real story out of the U.S. Attorney firings. TPM proved that you didn't need heavy printing machinery to be a vital source of news.

FireDogLake, or FDL as it is colloquially called, empowers its readers to become activist journalists. Readers call and confront members of Congress to create public records of where those representatives stand on different issues. The site is an activist hub and a news source, ensuring its readers have the best information to act as the best advocates.

Jack & Jill Politics brings a black political voice to the topics of the day. Mixing humor and style into their writing, J&J has become an important vehicle for black perspectives, which are often missing from media coverage—even when discussing issues involving the black community.

345

Empty Wheel. Marcy Wheeler, the author of this blog, was the authority on the Plame affair and Libby trial, and since then has been recognized with prestigious journalism awards. She's proof that blogs are more than self-interested unemployed recent college grads in their bathrobes.

346

Feministing offers a young, hip, feminist view on the world of politics and on the portrayal and continued stereotypes of women in society. A good source for stories of overt sexism, and a great source of enjoyable reading.

347

Open Left is a progressive strategy blog, discussing how to move forward a left-leaning agenda. This site is far from serving as a Democratic mouthpiece. Open Left writers spend more time confronting conservative and compromising Dems for selling their party and supporters short than they do criticizing Republicans, whose right-wing leanings aren't worth arguing against.

348

FiveThirtyEight became a phenomenon in the lead-up to the '08 election as a smart, focused, exciting site about polling. It took its name from the total number of electoral votes. FiveThirty Eight gave number-lovers something to feast on each day and continues to analyze polls, votes, and current races.

349

Crooks and Liars is your go-to place for video. You can find the best clips from the TV talk shows (without having to suffer through the entire programs) and the best videos being

350

produced by progressive groups. It's the television channel of the movement.

Eschaton is whip-fast rapid response of biting snark hitting all the events of the news cycle. And Atrios, the founder and chief blogger, is a regular Liberal Drinker.

Living Liberally. While our main focus is bringing people into face-to-face communities, we blog as well. "Screening Liberally Big Picture" and "Reading Liberally Page Turner" columns offer cultural reviews through a liberal lens. "Laughing Liberally to Keep From Crying" gives you the comedic turn on the day, "Drinking Liberally Shot of Truth" talks about the strength of social bonds in the progressive movement, and "Eating Liberally Food for Thought" connects food and politics.

There are two features of blogs that far surpass traditional news. One, they actively reference each other. In the blogosphere, any one blog is stronger because so many other blogs exist. That's how they generate audiences and build stories. Blogs look out for each other.

Second, readers can participate. Letters to the editor are an established way to voice opinion, but there are inherent limits to how many can be published. On many blogs—like Eschaton—the commentary is often longer than the original posts, and the empowered readers come to know and trust each other as a community.

Don't just read blogs—join them. Add your voice, challenge the assumptions, and share your knowledge. You will discover entire online communities where you feel at home.

Then, share what you learn. An advantage of electronic media: you don't need a lending library to pass along your findings. Send an e-mail. Friends may read what you forward them because

they trust you. Send them interesting posts, and you'll become
their trusted source.

Television

TV has obvious imperfections as a source of good information.
Commercial pressures get in the way of important discussions.
News shows that are more entertaining—with bright lights,
dramatic music, attractive anchors, and conjured controversy—
make more money. Fox News proves that point.

However, for many people, TV is going to shape how they view
the world. So how do you engage someone who is learning
televisedly, to encourage them to learn liberally?

Encourage them to change the channel. Unless they're PBS
junkies, they're probably not absorbing too much "must-
see" television. Channel surfing is a good way to shake up
perspectives. You see that CNN covers something differently
than MSNBC, or that the shrill urgency of cable news is a
different tone than the comparable calm of the network evening
news. People should have more than one source of news, and
suggesting that someone switch around is an easy way to shake
them up.

Ask them to identify the channel's bias. If bias is too strong a
word, ask what the "angle" is. People pretty much accept that
very few reports are totally objective. Urging friends to think
about the subjectivity of news coverage—who the channels
may be protecting, why some industries are targets and others
are not, whether the station has interests other than telling
the news—is a good way to subtly challenge the information
they're getting.

Give them a magazine. You're not going to break their TV habit,
but you can work around it. Give them a week-old magazine,

highlight a story of interest, and make it easy for them to get more than one perspective.

Talking Liberally

Where you gather your news is important, but real learning happens through interaction. Who do you speak with? Who are you influencing? How are you influencing them? Are you making the most of each opportunity?

Often the people most comfortable discussing politics are the people most confident in their views. That's unfortunate. Those people may be overconfident because they see the world in black-and-white and don't tolerate nuance. This may make them short-tempered with people who are still discovering their views. This may make them especially loud, and have a silencing effect on those around them. This doesn't lead to good discussion.

While these overbearing folks tend to be blustery, demagogic right-wingers, we on the left have our share of shouters. They're not out to discuss, engage, or convince; they lecture and rant. While I can respect the passion of such voices on both sides, this is not the best way to draw new people into political discussion, much less persuade them.

Studies show the greatest determinant of your likelihood to vote is whether someone has asked you to. Someone personally inviting you into a process is more effective than ads and news stories declaring that an election is important. Similarly, young people vote for the first time because somebody took the time to ask their opinion. Young people are often topics of political conversations, but less frequently participants in those same debates. When someone asks them about their views and connects the issues they care about with the political process, they do vote. Furthermore, if you vote once, you're more likely to vote regularly and develop a lifelong voting habit.

Therefore, it is important to talk politics with regular voters and new ones. Old dogs can learn new tricks. Conservatives can change their minds. They are not going to switch stripes because of a *New York Times* editorial. They are going to do it because personal experiences and appeals ask them to view the world in a new light. So if we want to liberalize the country, we have to start locally, by liberalizing those around us.

The responsibility is yours. You have to bring politics to the dinner table. You have to question your friends. You have to engage your conservative relatives.

Talk Liberally With Non-liberals.

It can be fun to talk with people who agree with you and, honestly, we do that at Drinking Liberally. Ultimately, those conversations should lead to you having the confidence to engage non-liberals as well. No conservative is ever going to change his mind if all he hears is what other conservatives have to say. We are the side of inclusion, engagement, and the belief that we're all in this together—that means we have to live those values in our own conversations. If we believe in a foreign policy of engaging hostile nations, then certainly we can engage ornery conservatives.

Don't shout. We get that you might be right and they might be wrong, but starting a conversation with that is the surest route to ending it right away.

Respect them. You may not agree with their opinions, but if you are engaging someone, you probably have some respect for them. Express that respect: listen to them, don't condescend, and let them know that your respect is why you're having this discussion.

Be willing to disagree. Friends and family do not always feel comfortable contradicting each other too blatantly. This can lead to a lot of "No, no, I agree," and "I think we're saying the same thing." If you were really saying the same thing, you wouldn't be having the discussion. Make clear that it is not a crime to disagree. You may want the same end, or share values, but you may differ nonetheless. Only by pointing out those differences will there be room to learn and convince.

Make it personal. Your conservative friend is listening to you. They are not watching Rachel Maddow or reading *The Nation*. There is a personal bond that has drawn them into the conversation, and some amount of trust. Don't quote statistics that you're regurgitating from an online poll. Talk to them about your values, feelings, and experiences. Share anecdotes from the lives of your friends to demonstrate points about rights for gays and lesbians, the need for health care, the challenges faced by working families. Antigay discrimination will cease someday not because we legislate against it or because celebrities challenge it but because everyone will eventually know and love a gay friend or family member. In issue after issue, if you can make it personal, you can at least budge people from their lockstep conservatism.

Do it at a dinner table. "No talk of politics, religion, or sex at the table" seems to be a rule for polite company. Like the rule against ending sentences with prepositions, it's a rule I refuse to subscribe to. First of all, what's left to talk about—the weather? Second, if you don't talk politics with people with whom you're willing to break bread, then you'll only get it dished out by professional reporters and commentators, and that's just not good enough. At a dinner table, people are together long enough to have a real conversation. This should give you time to talk and to listen.

At Drinking Liberally, sharing a pint—or even better, a pitcher—ensures the conversation continues until the drinks are drained.

Parenting Liberally

There are some audiences who have no choice but to dine with you: your children. If you are a parent, you are making choices that influence your kids all the time, and those choices teach them liberal attitudes from an early age.

There is no question that I learned liberal values from my family. I went to a cooperative preschool where parents volunteered one day a week. We all came to know each other's moms and dads from an early age and called them all by first names, creating an egalitarian spirit that made it easier to question them, learn from them, and, as I got older, debate with them.

We had a closet full of costumes in my house, inviting me to be creative and invent my own stories. From theater games to a video camera, there was always incentive to improvise, to become comfortable speaking and sharing. There was also ample opportunity to "produce"—live productions, videos, elaborate adventures. I quickly learned that I couldn't produce alone and discovered the joys of collaboration.

There were no rules limiting the number of friends who could come over after school. So while some friends had to choose two or three playmates when they invited us over, I was allowed to invite anyone and everyone, a lesson in inclusion.

When my friends weren't around, my parents were, and they were playmates to me as well. We read more than a dozen *Wizard of Oz* books aloud as long as I would write down every word I didn't know the meaning of and promise to look it up or ask what it meant.

In addition to storytelling, Mom and Dad included us in conversations of all kinds. I remember talking politics at the dinner table, learning from my parents about what was happening in the world. It was never as formal as a lesson-of-the night. They would simply ask us what was going on in our lives and share what was happening in theirs. They believed children should be seen and heard.

I am not yet able to speak from the perspective of a parent about raising a child with liberal values . . . fortunately, I was able to turn to the two best experts I know: my parents. They brought me to a Walter Mondale rally at age six, encouraged my student activism in middle school and high school, and taught me that I had a responsibility to care about the world. And it turns out they have a few ideas about parenting.

Tips for Parenting Liberally

Written with guest contributors Suzanne Karp Krebs and Eric Krebs (Mom and Dad)

Create a participatory home. If you want to raise children with the belief that we all are in this world together, then you need to reflect that lesson in your home. Have your children participate in family discussions and decisions, whether that's planning a vacation or deciding what charities to support. The process does not need to be pure democracy, but ask their views and explain your decisions. Additionally, include them in family responsibilities, setting up chores so they understand how they contribute to the common good of the household. Bring them to your office, and share your hobbies, so they are familiar with your life.

As you involve them in the household, in return you need to participate in their lives. Meet their friends and friends' parents; attend their sporting events, school productions, and group activities; and offer to coach, drive, and support them when you can. Be involved in their education at school and at home by meeting their teachers, joining the Parent-Teacher Association at school, and helping them with their homework. You should give your kids room to learn and play on their own, but by encouraging everyone to participate in each other's lives, you teach them how you hope they will engage with the world.

One more great example of this participatory spirit is collective child care. For people who can't afford preschool, setting up a child care collective is another way to build a supportive network around your children. As Hillary Clinton wrote, "It takes a village . . ."

While inclusive, group experiences are great, don't forget to spend quality one-on-one time with your child as well. Find activities you and she share, just the two of you.

Encourage exploration. John Dewey was an educator and philosopher who laid out a vision for what a liberal education should look like. Children needed to be given opportunities to try, fail, and learn from failure; they needed to be encouraged to think creatively, not memorize by rote; they needed experiences that challenged them and left them with a sense of navigating the complexity of the real world, not simply academic tasks.

This is more than theory. It plays out in some of the best schools and childhood experiences you can imagine. As federal funding pushes more schools to put pressure on test scores, it can be harder to create these alternative, authentic assessments in the classroom, making it even more important that such creative, risk-taking exploration happen outside the school day.

Giving children freedom does not mean always saying yes.

372 Children need boundaries and structure (one wishes that the titans of Wall Street who tossed our economy into crisis knew a little more about "boundaries"). Limiting television time will teach a child to make choices and will keep him from becoming an addict. When you say "no" to your children, explain why. They might resent the decision, but, over time, they will feel respected.

373 **Tell stories.** Storytelling excites the imagination and encourages expression. It also can be a way to cultivate compassion, empathy, and community spirit at an early age. The stories we tell have morals. They teach us to trust, to help one another, to build community, to develop values other than love of money, and to sacrifice for a common good.

374 **Share your values.** If you want your children to embrace values of inclusion, diversity, charity, compassion, and free expression,
375 you need to lead by example and demonstrate those values. However, it's not enough to do good. Take a moment to discuss
376 your choices. Talk to your kids about the environment, and what you all can do as a family to conserve energy and reduce waste. When you participate in community service, give to a charity,
377 or vote, explain why these causes are important.

378 Furthermore, do not hesitate to discuss the values you see your children demonstrating in their behavior. If you do not like how they are treating other children, tell them. Being honest with your children about their behavior is still a way of showing your

love, and will educate them on how to be kind and inclusive to others.

Encourage play. . . . and fair play. Being playful is a virtue in itself, and a generation that grows up joyful is a generation that will spread its joy to others around the world. What and how we play also teach us values. It's common to say that sports encourage teamwork, discipline, strategic thinking. All games teach some lessons, some more profound than others. Think about what those lessons are. 379

Choose games that teach inclusion, where every kid has a role and kids with different skills can contribute. The activities can still be competitive, and teams can win and lose, but you want to make sure everyone is learning from those experiences. 380

Encourage collaborative activities where kids can work together. Whether these are puzzles, scavenger hunts, or competitive team-based games like Capture the Flag or charades, they teach children to work together and trust each other. Find games that inspire creative thinking . . . after all, we need liberals to be able to creatively solve the problems we're inheriting from the right wing. 381 382

Start early. It's never too early in a child's life to learn love, compassion, and inclusion, or to learn that reading is more thought-provoking than watching television, or to understand that waste isn't a virtue. And as soon as your kid talks, ask what she's thinking and feeling. Listen. Respect. Share. Engage. It's easier to do now than to have to wait and engage a conservative uncle at the Thanksgiving table. 383

And the Liberal Moral of the Story Is . . .

If you want to raise little liberals, encourage them to pick up books that will cultivate a sense of inquiry and independence, compassion and wonder. Here are a few suggestions for their recommended reading list . . . or to read out loud with them.

384

The Lorax. This Dr. Seuss fable tells the story of the ultimate environmentalist—the Lorax, who speaks for the trees. An unfortunate fate meets the forest and its inhabitants when nobody listens to his message. The result is a basic lesson in conservation, tucked into a colorful, comical, creative tale.

The Harry Potter Books. One of the most successful series of all time, these books are thick with liberal lessons. In these tales— which are addictive, watch out—you learn to trust people who aren't like you, to believe that people of mixed backgrounds can embody the best of both worlds, and that everyone—even a house elf—deserves to pursue his dreams. A few avid readers even turned activist and formed an organization called "The HP Alliance" that has created social action around the morals of the story: they have conducted campaigns against genocide in Darfur and for tolerance and diversity in America.

385

Free to Be You and Me. "I find everyone I know who was raised on this book is well adjusted," observes Eating Liberally founder Kerry Trueman. This book-album tag-team teaches you about embracing differences, encourages you to love yourself, and prepares you to love others.

386

The poetry of Shel Silverstein. Whether creating a band out of playing your belly, or telling the story of Hector the Collector's lovely junk collection, poems from *Where the Sidewalk Ends* and *A Light in the Attic* cultivate a sense of whimsy, playfulness, and the belief that anything is possible. They create a beautiful world, made magical by exploration, collaboration, and appreciation.

387

The Encyclopedia Brown series about a reality-based boy detective who investigates, exposes irrational inconsistencies, and beats bad guys with logic.

388

Blubber, by Judy Blume, is a classic coming-of-age story that makes a case for ignoring the mob and learning empathy.

389

The Lord of the Rings trilogy. A fellowship of underdogs, across race, sets aside differences to topple totalitarianism.

390

The Little Prince. The children's book for all ages, that simply, thoughtfully, and creatively reminds us to be good in the world, to take responsibility, and to open our hearts.

Religion

I grew up in a Reform Jewish household, and there are some proud liberal elements to that religion. Israel literally means "one who wrestles with God," and Jews are encouraged to wrestle with ideas and authority. Even traditional Judaism encourages debate, and more modern strains assume that today's Jews will be finding their own ways to continue traditions in a modern world.

Most faiths have liberal traditions within them. Catholicism has often been a major force in caring for the poor. Unitarianism, the church in which Ralph Waldo Emerson practiced, was a voice for abolitionism in the mid-1800s, and has been a model of tolerance for people of different faiths throughout its history. Quakers are leaders in antiwar activities. Islam has been an engine of science and learning and has an emphasis on charity and hospitality. Even religions that seem more conservative are never monolithic. Increasingly, younger evangelicals are participating in the environmental movement. More Protestant faiths are accepting gay and lesbian ministers.

Furthermore, even within conservative religious contexts, people find ways to be faithful to their church and to their political beliefs. There are Catholic churches that embrace their homosexual members openly. There are conservative synagogues that welcome their interfaith congregants with open arms. You just have to know how to look for the right congregations.

Take It from a Rabbi . . .

I do not participate in organized religion in an everyday way . . . so I turned to an expert for her advice: Hayley Siegel, a friend and rabbinic student at the Academy for Jewish Religion, a pluralistic, nondenominational seminary. Hayley suggests a few areas where a congregation can live up to its responsibilities in an interdependent, inclusive world. While these questions are posed to Jewish synagogues, you can easily translate to other faiths and congregations.

Environmental

★   Does the synagogue serve as a site for a CSA? Increasingly, synagogue members are even organizing their own food co-ops for kosher/organic meat, veggies, and fruit.

★   What kind of "green" initiatives does the synagogue implement? Do they provide members with bike racks? Does the shul have energy-efficient appliances? Are they planning any initiatives to reduce waste/pollution?

★   Do they procure foods or materials for holidays, bat and bar mitzvahs, and weddings from local vendors?

Liturgical/Prayer

★   Do their prayer books use gender-neutral pronouns in the liturgy? Do they not refer to "God" as "King" or "He"?

★ Do they accept women and gay/lesbian congregants on the bimah as rabbis and cantors?

Economic

397 ★ Does the synagogue pay all its workers a living wage?

Social

398 ★ Does the synagogue organize service projects that might help a broader community outside their neighborhood, such as travel to New Orleans?

399 ★ Do they have an usher volunteer exchange program with a church, through which Christian ushers help out during the Jewish High Holidays, and Jews help out during Christmas?

Intermarriage

400 ★ Does the synagogue have an inclusive policy and attitude toward intermarriage and non-Jewish spouses? What kind of a role does the non-Jewish spouse play within the synagogue? Can he/she vote in synagogue-wide elections? May he/she participate during the child's bar/t mitzvah? Will the rabbi officiate at an intermarriage and, if so, what are the terms?

Many people find in their religion the type of community I find in liberalism—so it's important to find the places where religion promotes liberal values and where today's liberal lifestyle can be incorporated into traditional religious institutions. Whatever your religion, here are a few general questions you can ask to decide if your liberal and religious life can coexist.

Does the congregation respect non-congregants? It almost seems obvious in today's world that religions respect one another, but that isn't always the case. Some churches will discourage you from fraternizing with people outside the faith, or will continue to condemn those who aren't believers. There isn't room for that anymore. Churches that actively participate in interfaith dialogues have more to offer to our modern America.

401

Does the congregation respect gender equality? Our government finally gave women the right to vote ninety years ago, but we're still fighting for equal wages and other equal protections. Religion is a moral leader in the cause for equality. Any church that doesn't fully respect its women is far behind the times.

402

Does the congregation respect gay and lesbian members? It's heartbreaking to hear stories of men and women who grow up in a religion, who consider it their community and core to their values, and then are told they're not welcome anymore. While not every religion yet recognizes full marriage equality, every faith has more progressive denominations that clearly embrace their gay and lesbian brothers and sisters.

403

Does the congregation invest in the neighboring community? Churches have long been leaders in efforts to run shelters, feed and clothe the poor, protect the environment, and provide educational and athletic opportunities. These activities build community in the neighborhood of the congregation, lending important credibility to local efforts.

404

405   **Does the congregation celebrate?** Again, we look back to *Footloose* and the idea of a minister against dancing. As famed progressive leader Emma Goldman once said, "If I can't dance, I don't want to be part of your revolution." The same should be said of religion. Churches are meant to appeal to the highest elements of our soul, to reveal the beauty of the world. This should occur through song and dance, community meals and festivals. If not, then what's the point?

Finally, there are ways to participate in faith outside a congregation. Many of us celebrate holidays outside formal services. We gather with our families, exchange gifts, and leisurely enjoy the day. You don't need a congregation to be liberal on your behalf. Holidays are great opportunities to live the belief that we are all living for each other and not for ourselves alone. **406 407 408** Donate to food and clothing drives. Consider giving to charities in your loved one's name rather than giving him or her a gift. Volunteer at soup kitchens or shelters on holidays, when the needy may **409** be feeling particularly lonely. Shop consciously for gifts that support local craftspeople and artists and cut down on waste. **410** And make sure to show goodwill to all. That's the most liberal and religious action you can take.

CHAPTER 6
SPENDING LIBERALLY

Liberals feel unworthy of their possessions. Conservatives feel they deserve everything they've stolen.
—MORT SAHL

Recently, the "No Impact Family" sought to bring their environmental impact as close to zero as possible, while still living a full life in New York City. They gave up take-out, bought from the local farmers' market, and skipped items that had unnecessary wrapping. They reused bags, stopped riding cars and subways, and turned off their electricity. What this experiment, and the book and movie that document it, proved was not that it's easy or even possible to eliminate all impact—but that you can find ways in which every facet of your life can be made healthier, more sustainable, and less commercial.

"No Impact Man" conducted an extreme and exciting experiment, but you don't need to live at an extreme to live liberally. You may start by spending less and by spending more consciously.

We only vote on Election Day. Daily we endorse elements of the world around us by voting with our dollars. Let's spend that money on businesses and industries that invest in the community. Spend in ways that green our planet, rather than blacken it, and that reward trust and compassion, not commercialism and greed.

Are you ready to spend liberally?

Conservation, not consumption, should be a goal. However, we're all going to consume. Being conscientious doesn't have to mean practicing ascetic self-denial. A progressive life should be abundant with meals, adventures, and everyday joys. Let's ensure that we spend in communitarian, socially conscious, green, creative, diverse ways . . . and that will be Spending Liberally.

Buying Liberally: Purchase Politics

You've heard of "purchasing power," right? They call it power for a reason. Where you spend your money symbolizes what you're investing in. Businesses will compete for those dollars, even if it means they have to become better businesses. You don't even need to appeal to their better angels, if their lesser angels can get the job done.

Think about where you spend your money each month: clothing and transportation, electric bills and your cell phone, gifts and games, nightlife and necessities. What if every time you spent money, you also created social capital?

Stores get that you have an incredible amount of freedom in where and how you spend, which is why they spend so much time creating incentive programs such as frequent shopper cards. Credit cards also offer you points or miles or rebates because they get power from your purchases.

It would be terrific if you accrued karma points the way you collect credit card points. While there may not be a formal program (yet) for such a system, there are ways you can spend that will give and get more than just a commercial exchange.

The Mom-and-Pop vs. The Big Box. There are words for businesses that swoop into communities, undercut local businesses, shut out the competition, then jack up prices, limit selection, and undervalue workers. Pirates? Monopolies?

Big box stores.

I understand the appeal of the big box store: they can be convenient. Everything in one place. They offer low prices.

But what's the real cost of this abundance? It's not factored into the price, which is why the consumer is spared thinking about it. There are costs to the environment in the footprints of these mega-chains. There are costs to the workforce, small businesses, and the community. Big box stores put local stores out of business, reduce jobs, and devastate downtowns. When one big box store replaces dozens of smaller establishments, there's no incentive for employers to compete for labor; workers just accept what they can get: often minimum wage jobs, rarely with benefits.

The most famous culprit is Walmart. Walmart regularly promoted men over women. Walmart has a record of locking overnight workers in the store. Walmart has long fought any unionization effort. At one point, it was documented that Walmart's human resources department was helping full-time workers apply for food stamps because they did not earn enough to support their families.

Walmart, and other large scale chains, are capable of positive impact. When they agree to stock energy-efficient products, they boost the industry that produces them; and when they switch to more sustainable practices, that has a big impact across their chain. Walmart is the country's largest food retailer, so they have the ability to transform the market. They are also a company deeply invested in efficiency, as it affects their bottom line. The result is that they have instituted policies demanding less packaging for their items, and this has caused many manufacturers to reduce their waste. See, even Walmart can learn to spend liberally.

Some people have no choice but to shop at Walmart. There are ways to shop consciously within a big box, and the suggestions throughout this chapter about intentional purchasing can be applied anywhere.

411 First and foremost, though, if you have the opportunity, shop at the mom-and-pop stores.

They are the stabilizing staples of a community, the establishments where it's in the business's interest to know customers by name and keep employees in real jobs over time. They are more responsive to customer concerns and invested in community projects. A range of small stores employs more people at better wages than a single large store, creates more middle-class jobs, and supports stable families . . . who keep investing their money into the communities as well.

These neighborhood establishments add texture to your life. People are shaped by the memories they have from their local shops. These stores are where many of us learned lessons about trust and social interaction.

412 **Buy union.** If you want your money to support overall prosperity, make a point of spending on products that carry the union bug. By doing so, you support institutions that continue to raise working conditions across the country. You can be sure that the workers are benefiting from the purchase: paid a living wage,

given benefits for their families, and working in conditions that meet ethical and environmental standards.

If you don't buy strictly from union shops, you can ask where your products are made. You've heard about sweatshops, and there's a reason our country is proud that our history includes replacing sweatshops with decent jobs. Yet sweatshops exist around the world where workers are paid pennies, where their days are long and they are given no breaks, where they have no rights to complain and no job guarantees, and are discarded when they can't work anymore. In many sweatshops, child labor continues to be part of the workforce.

There are other brands in America that may not be union, but are sweatshop free, or guarantee (and publicize) their workers' wages and conditions. Once, it might have been hard to get this information. Now, there are resources all over the internet that make it easy. Surf through the "Green Pages" for a search engine to businesses that take their environmental impact seriously, or visit "The Responsible Shopper" to view the profiles of companies you might patronize.

Be a conscientious customer—Whatever your purchases, through your actions and questions push businesses to be better:

a. Learn the conditions of the workers that produced your purchase.

b. Check on the environmental record of a business.

c. Check on the politics of the business. Do they lobby? Do they donate to political causes?

d. Ask friends for recommendations and offer your own.

e. Choose items with less packaging.

f. Get a sense of the work environment in the store.

g. If an item is disposable, choose one that is recyclable or biodegradable.

h. Support independent producers and crafts-people.

i. Give feedback (praise *and* flack).

j. Ask yourself: Do I really need this?

In addition to acting individually, you always get more bang for your liberal buck when you act together. That's one thing the big box stores have right: by amassing a significant share of a market, they can move that market. That's true for you and your fellow shoppers.

There are many examples of collective consumerism that have allowed progressive purchasing power to flourish.

Boycott. If you don't like the practices of a particular business, stop shopping there. Make sure to tell the owner why, and make sure to take a lot of friends away from the business with you.

Buycott. Why only oppose what we're against? Let's also reward good behavior. Denying dollars may hurt a business, but collective spending can help one you like. The Buycott is a push to encourage people to spend their dollars on businesses making the right decisions.

Create new markets. Many people now get the opportunity on their energy bill to check off if they'd prefer their electricity come from alternative sources of energy. Eventually, enough people will make this choice, and there will be even more investment in those sources of energy. Organize people to demand something of a business, and build that incentive for the business. As more people purchase hybrid cars, the market for repairing and outfitting those cars will grow.

Create alternatives. If you can't get a business to behave the way you want, can you work around it? If what you want isn't sold in your local businesses, could it be created through collective creativity and ingenuity? 430

One company that decided to be an alternative and provides a model of living liberally is Working Assets. A San Francisco business, it's a do-gooder save-the-planet enterprise disguised as a series of for-profit ventures, most notably the CREDO Mobile phone company. I worked with Working Assets/CREDO a few years ago, and saw firsthand how they work and play liberally. But I wasn't just an employee; I'm also a member—a proud subscriber to CREDO cell service, and carrier of the Working Assets credit card. 431 432

The founders of Working Assets recognized a problem in the progressive movement. Nonprofits and political organizations were always scrounging for money. They didn't possess a reliable, respectable revenue stream to conduct their work. The creators of Working Assets saw a solution: progressives had plenty of funds they spent regularly on services like their telephone. Was there a way to funnel that money, which people willingly and regularly paid, through the progressive movement?

Working Assets got into the long-distance business, an area where people didn't feel great loyalty to their provider so would switch to an equivalent service if given a reason, such as a good cause and some coupons for free Ben & Jerry's ice cream. The company invested a portion of every phone bill into a pot of money that went to progressive nonprofit causes. Working Assets expanded into cellular service with CREDO Mobile.

If you're going to send your money some direction, you might as well give it to a company that:

433 **Donates profits.** A very transparent process pools money from the phone bills paid year-round and dedicates it to fifty national progressive nonprofits, across sectors like human rights and the environment. Members (the customers) nominate causes and vote for where their money goes.

434 **Respects its customers.** Working Assets is in constant communication with customers about both their service and their politics, inviting members to be partners in business and activism.

435 **Treats workers with respect.** CREDO employees have the ability to offer creativity and feedback, dress as they like, and enjoy kitchen facilities and common areas.

436 **Embodies ethical practices.** CREDO invests in environmental improvements in their office. They print phone bills on recycled paper and offer electronic alternatives. They are fair and proactive with customers (I've been late more than a few times) and they communicate about major decisions with their community. They also didn't help the Bush administration's illegal domestic spying program, unlike other major phone companies.

437 **Markets less.** A large cost of doing business in America is marketing, which drives up the price of products, and drives us crazy with an ad-infused culture. CREDO has much narrower, targeted outreach, relying on partners, word of mouth, and awareness among progressives.

Lobbies for the public good. Most telecommunications companies take stances to consolidate power and monopolize the market. In particular, Verizon and AT&T back efforts to create tiers of internet service to justify charging people for faster access to different websites. Working Assets could benefit from moves that hurt the public, but they put consumer rights first.

438

Takes action. CREDO invests money in progressive infrastructure, not only through donations but also supporting innovation and building tools and web applications the movement needs. They created a widget that allowed any website to become a hub of voter registration. They funded nonpartisan get-out-the-vote efforts. They support blogging and independent journalism. They run an activist e-mail list with which they rally for health care and energy reform and against war and cronyism.

439

They also find creative ways to do this activism with their actual phones. They've invested in text technology, and will text action alerts that call upon their customers to use their phones to call Congress. On Election Day, they gave everyone free outbound calls to encourage us to contact voters. They don't just want you to Spend Liberally by subscribing to them. They want you to Call Liberally as well.

I became a customer of their phone service in December 2006. More than three years later, my phone still works. I can't complain about that.

Working Assets obviously isn't the only company that lives its values. There are plenty of businesses working to earn our trust and improve our planet. Here are just a few that offer you alternatives:

Better World Club. An alternative to AAA, which has a history of lobbying against public transit and promotes a car-crazed culture. Gives you the automotive support you need without sacrificing your politics. As they say: improve your car-ma.

Organic Valley. A collective of family farmers that created a big enough business model to reach wider distribution than any individual farmer could achieve.

3R Living. A provider of environmentally friendly gifts and household items, such as a backpack with solar panels that charges your computer or phone as you go about your day.

Etsy. A website that allows independent artists and craftspeople to reach a far wider audience and allows buyers to support local creators.

Progressive Book Club. A bookseller that features progressive authors and publishers and builds up a base of members so left-leaning voices get wider circulation and are pushed into the public discourse.

Beware vs. Buy Now

Wherever you shop, there are a few easy guides that provide a green light or red light for your purchases.

Beware: Plastic. We're all going to own plastic items in our lives, but that's all the more reason to think twice before you purchase it. It feeds our petroleum-based economy, and it doesn't go away. 445

Buy now: Used goods. If you can find what you need secondhand, you help reduce the carbon footprint of your consumerism. 446

Beware: Made in China. Yes, the Chinese need to work, too—but their government doesn't do a whole lot to protect its workers or the world we all live in. 447

Buy now: Local, handmade. Get to know the people behind the product. 448

Beware: Unaccountability. If the store clerk can't tell you where an item is from, who produced it, or who takes responsibility for it, you may want to think twice. 449

Buy Now: Anything from a lemonade stand. Because it's always nice to support kids. 450

Eating Liberally

As much as you reduce your purchases, you will still need to eat. Every day, you have three opportunities to "vote with your fork." Making a few relatively simple improvements to your diet can put your politics on your plate.

Until recently, this idea was pretty foreign to me.

I was a "growing boy" through my teenage years. That is, I ate ceaselessly. I loved all-you-can-eat buffets. I loved the endless meals in my college dining hall. I cared more about how big the portions were than what I was consuming.

Then *Fast Food Nation* opened my eyes to a wider view about the connections between what I ate and its impact on the larger world. Eric Schlosser's tremendous work details the detrimental impact the fast food industry has on public health, labor, and the environment and the industry's masterful manipulation of marketing, addiction, and market forces. The book made me question how my own eating habits related to those issues. I used to regularly purchase from McDonald's magical ninety-nine-cent menu. Since reading *Fast Food Nation*, I've completely cut fast food burgers from my diet.

Overall, I was not yet a food advocate when friends suggested Drinking Liberally needed to branch out. Kerry Trueman and Matt Rosenberg were avid blog readers and frustrated liberals. They suggested Eating Liberally, so they wouldn't have to talk politics on an empty stomach. Eating Liberally hosts gatherings about politics over food and about the politics *of* food.

A Glossary on Gustatory Goodness

Loads of labels are attached to the food you eat. How do you know what you're spending your limited liberal dollars on? Look for:

★ **Organic.** Describes more natural approaches to farming, which is not reliant on chemical support, especially pesticides.

- ★ **Locally grown.** Food that comes from nearby sources, appealing to people who wish to reduce environmental impact of shipping food, avoid big agribusiness, and know more about their sources of food. Locavores believe that fresher local food is also healthier and tastier. 453

- ★ **Grass-fed.** Attributed to meat or products from animals that are raised on pasture, rather than grain, which is usually associated with mass production and adverse ecological impact. 454

- ★ **Fair Trade.** An approach to purchasing ingredients directly from farmers who often work together in co-ops and reinvest funds in their communities. 455

- ★ **Biodynamic.** A farming technique that works to find more balance in the use of the farmland, seeing the soil, animals, and produce as part of a unified ecosystem. 456

- ★ **Retrovore.** One who favors conservation over consumption. One who forages for food that's fresh, local, minimally processed, and grown with care. One who aspires to live in harmony with nature rather than pummel it into submission. 457

There is a large, diverse, passionate, informed, activist community engaged in every niche of food policy. Sadly, they too infrequently overlap with activists engaged in progressive electoral politics or more conventional issue advocacy. Many "foodies" see politics as messy, and few politicians speak to their issues meaningfully. Many progressive politicos place food in a personal sphere and ignore how much political decision-making goes into what we eat. That divide is slowly changing. Popular authors like Marion Nestle, Michael Pollan, and Eric Schlosser and films like *Food, Inc.* are promoting food issues in a new light. An increasing number of bloggers straddle the food movement and progressive organizing. They two communities are collaborating around farm subsidies, school lunches, and the drive to include food issues in public health, energy, and sustainability policies.

The politics of food is substantial; just as important, the food can be delicious. Many of us mistakenly assume that eating smartly may mean eating blandly. Eating Liberally proves you could eat well and eat good.

You don't need to be a food expert, or become consumed about what you consume, to make a few small changes that lead to much smarter choices.

Six Steps to Start Eating Liberally

by guest contributor Kerry Trueman, cofounder of Eating Liberally

458

I.   **Eat less meat.** Livestock production is a significant source of greenhouse gas emissions. Think of plant-based foods—beans, grains, fruits, veggies, nuts—as your own personal source of solar power.

459

2.   **Cut back on industrially produced eggs and dairy.** All factory-farmed foods rely heavily on fos-

---

sil fuels. Opt for grass-fed animal products whenever possible.

3. **Support your local food producers.** They're your best source for sustainably grown foods, whether or not they're officially certified "organic." Save your "food miles" to splurge on things that don't grow in your region: spices, coffee, or chocolate (Fair Trade, of course!).

460

4. **Limit your consumption of processed convenience foods,** which create tons of excess packaging and don't do your body (or soul) any favors.

461

5. **Reduce food waste** by buying only what you're really going to eat. A whopping 40 percent of the food we produce goes to waste, generating massive amounts of methane. Convert your kitchen scraps to black gold by composting them yourself or taking them to a composting facility in your community.

462

463

6. **Take the time to make a meal from scratch** now and then, or grow even just a little of your own food. It will reconnect you with the seasons and the pleasures of fresh, homemade meals. Not a born chef or gardener? Find some folks who are, and hang out with them! They'll be happy to share the weeding and the feeding with you.

464

Living—or eating—like a liberal is never just about making politics personal, but about making personal politics public. When it comes to eating habits, start with *what* to buy. Next, think about *how* to buy. The "how" takes you from living sustainably, healthily, and intentionally to living liberally: spending and eating in a way that connects to a community.

Buy Local. In addition to the health and environmental reasons, there's a classic community reason to buy local. The local farmer and grocer are going to be more invested in your community, more responsive to neighborhood needs, and more interested in being a local partner over the long haul.

My mother remembers from her childhood in Brooklyn when her mother sent her to the butcher. Grandma instructed her: "Tell him you're Mrs. Karp's daughter . . . he'll give you a good cut."

Would the butcher really have given a substandard piece of meat to a stranger? Regardless, he knew Mrs. Karp. He would see her again. He knew she talked to other neighbors. He didn't want her to take her business elsewhere. Knowing each other's names established a relationship that was good for both of them.

Supporting local stores makes it more likely that they will support your local interests. They may stock particular items you request, donate to neighborhood charities, or promote election efforts and community events.

Buy local, and you are investing in your community.

Shop at farmers' markets. Once upon a time, people grew their own food, or purchased from neighboring farmers or from a local store supplied by area farmers. With mass distribution, we began to patronize larger stores with more options, and consequently we had less sense of who produced the food we ate. Bigger and bigger companies got into the business of mass-producing food to supply the bigger and bigger stores. Eventually, fewer family farms could compete.

The wave of the future is sometimes a return to the past. Farmers' markets connect consumers directly to the producers again. They give local and independent farmers a chance and give consumers fresher produce and a stronger connection to their food.

Join CSAs/farm-shares. If you like farmers' markets, take the next step. Community-supported agriculture (or CSA) is a collective way of supporting local farms in return for consistent, reliable produce. Members pay a fixed fee for a season, guaranteeing farmers a reliable income. Members receive a weekly harvest. The exchange is made more affordable because of how many members are involved, demonstrating that a little teamwork goes a long way.

Join a food co-op. Supermarkets often have national or regional deals with food distributors. Thus, their shelves may be full of products that offend your politics, and their management may not be as interested in diversifying its offerings. In many cities, food co-ops offer an alternative. Co-ops specialize in purchasing from independent producers and distributors, often stocking healthier, more lifestyle-conscious items. They stock in bulk to serve the cooperative membership, which drives the price down from what you might find at a specialty store.

Many co-ops also expect members to work shifts. You may not be part of a farm or a community garden, yet you can contribute your labor to improving your food selection.

Push your supermarkets. Not every town has a food cooperative or farmers' market. You rely on A&P or ShopRite to provide for you. They work on a large scale, and many of their partners are big industry producers. There's very little way to avoid that. What can you do?

You can organize. Ask supermarket managers to make local arrangements with area farmers and producers. Suggest items you would like the store to stock. Prove to them that there would be a market for your requests by asking neighbors to sign letters. These supermarkets may not be as concerned about community opinion, but they care about their bottom lines. If they know you'll buy, they'd be foolish not to sell.

Also, show them the success of Wegmans, New Seasons, Whole Foods, Trader Joe's, and other establishments that successfully market more green-conscious food options. Whole Foods' premium prices may not work for all of us, but your supermarket can find affordable options to create healthy alternatives.

Advocate for food access. In many urban areas, there are more McDonald's than there are providers of fresh fruit. In sprawling exurbs, there may be large consolidated supermarkets with little access to farm produce, because so many independent farmers were pushed out of business. When that's the case, it's difficult to make change through your spending habits, because there are no options to spend differently. That's when you need to advocate.

Talk to your elected officials about public health and access to food. This issue is growing in visibility, and more local city governments are coming to understand it. They also realize the health costs of limited food access and the detrimental impact poor diet has on youth. Give them reason to engage in the issue. Encourage them to look to other areas that already subsidize green markets or have begun to map "community foodprints." That way everyone can Eat Liberally.

Drinking More Liberally: Politics in Every Pint

As you eat well, wash it down by drinking well. Ask about what you're imbibing, and you'll quench your thirst to drink your way into a more liberal life.

Ask your bartender:

★ Who brewed this? A large company or an independent brewery?

★ What are their labor practices?

★ How do they account for their environmental impact?

★ Do they confront the ills associated with alcohol?

★ What are their politics?

You may not hold every drink up to this level of scrutiny. However, it is useful to know that there are breweries and distilleries that reflect your values while they refresh your spirit. You don't want a moral hangover following a binge of bad booze.

471
472
Drink locally. We all know the big names in brewing, including Anheuser-Busch and Coors. The alternative: microbrews. These independent breweries frequently have less negative impact on the environment, more connection to the communities in which they are based, and great-tasting beers. While they rarely have national reach, microbrews can be found in most cities.

473
Often, microbrews are examples of craft beer. This movement breaks away from brewing as a mass-market competition. Craft beers focus more on the art of brewing and the taste of their product, using traditional brewing methods that rely less on rice and corn.

Because there's no way any one independent brewery can compete with the incessant marketing for the "King of Beers" or the "Taste of the Rockies," many microbrews are working together. They see each other as collaborators more than rivals as they promote a vision of drinking locally.

474
Toast labor. Yuengling, the nation's oldest brewery, recently engaged in a public effort to break its union. Why would a beer that wants to appeal to the workingman try to crush the workingman? After the Yuengling news spread on Daily Kos, hundreds of comments expressed disbelief and regret, as many readers announced they'd stop drinking it.

I hadn't planned on boycotting Yuengling, but I find myself more frequently choosing alternatives. Over Labor Day weekend, my friends brought a case of Yuengling to our holiday barbecue. I must have looked stricken; they asked me if I were ill. I explained my dilemma: Though it is inappropriate to reject a gift, I could not stomach Yuengling on Labor Day. Once I explained it, my friends understood. I returned the beer to the liquor store, explained the reasons to the clerk, and traded up for tastier and more conscientious Magic Hat.

Yuengling is losing loyal drinkers, one liberal liver at a time.

Drink green. I had the chance to tour the Magic Hat Brewery 475 476 with the founder and owner Alan Newman. He spoke extensively about how they used less energy and produced less waste than their competitors. It didn't surprise me: Magic Hat has a cool, liberal feel, and Alan was a cool, liberal guy. If anyone were going to make green brewing its modus operandi, it would be a quirky Vermont-based brand.

The real motivation was the bottom line. These were cost-saving measures. As a small brand, Magic Hat carefully watched their use of resources.

Another brewery that famously makes its energy policy part of its marketing is the New Belgium Brewery in Colorado. The 477 makers of Fat Tire generate their electricity from wind energy. They use a renewable resource to brew a drink that renews many grateful drinkers each day.

Maker's Mark is a brown drink with a green spirit. The distillery 478 of this bourbon has reduced its environmental impact and recycles the by-products of distillation. As a loyal drinker of that whiskey, I felt my heart warm when I learned this (and no, I hadn't just done a shot). Now I tell everyone they can drink Maker's with a clean and green conscience.

There are Fair Trade vodka brands that support their suppliers from indigenous communities with fair wages and community investment. Other booze companies support the arts, live music, and community radio.

Saving the world is in the self-interest of the liquor lover. Global warming has hurt hops production. We need a healthy planet to keep our pint glasses filled.

479 **Confront the ills of alcohol.** Most big companies give to charity. Magic Hat targets causes related to the abuse of alcohol. They donate to domestic violence shelters and invest in sex education, family planning, and contraception. The tobacco industry has always tried to deny any of the deleterious effects of smoking. It's commendable to see a business that acknowledges the potential dangers of its own product and engages the issue, rather than ignores it.

480 **Drink politically.** Coors beer is a national institution, a well-known brand, a ubiquitous option. It's also the source of wealth that has helped fund the right-wing movement for the past decades.

Several large families have underwritten much of the conservative infrastructure that has been waging a concerted effort against a progressive agenda, functional government, and the American way of life. They finance organizations that push the our court system to the right; create right-wing message machines, think tanks, and echo chambers; support young conservatives; and distort the role of social welfare and government programs.

481 Every Coors six-pack you buy helps fund that movement. If you want to drink your politics, go dry on Coors. Honestly, you won't be missing much.

Sadly, they're not alone in putting their politics before their potential customers.

Anheuser-Busch, now part of the international InBev, is the maker of Budweiser, Beck's, and many other brands. This company sits on the board of the United States Chamber of Commerce, an organization that outspokenly denies global warming. We should tell Bud: we like the King of Beers, but we love Mother Earth more, and ask them to take a stand against the Chamber. [482]

As the health care battle heated up, a handful of liquor companies decided to become involved. Guinness, Johnnie Walker, Bacardi, Baileys, and others wrote to their customers to ask them to oppose health care reform due to a phantom threat of "luxury taxes."

These companies that can have harmful effects on people's health were working against making health care affordable. Furthermore, many people who work in nightlife as waiters, bartenders, bar backs, and bouncers are rarely provided with medical benefits. They are often part-time, hourly workers, earning a lower minimum wage. Yet their own industry lobbies against their interests.

You might want to send Guinness and Johnnie Walker, frequent favorites of mine, the way of Yuengling. With all these bad-faith brewers, I'd worry that soon I'd be completely dry but fortunately with the growth of craft beer, that there's no doubt I'll keep drinking liberally. [483]

Investing Liberally

You can earn liberally. You can spend liberally. Now, invest liberally.

Despite the stereotype of being "tax and spend liberals," we're more often "earn and invest liberals"—we create the stable societal structures that allow people to earn more for themselves, their businesses, and their families. We invest that wealth in an America that produces for everyone. We share the benefits of our prosperity and produce dividends for the future:

an educated next generation, old age with dignity, a habitable planet, and resources that stretch further because we share them consciously.

Saving money and establishing wealth is not the purview of conservatives alone. As with all aspects of life, we liberals do it a little differently.

484

Switch to a credit union. You may break free of the Agricultural Industrial Complex and the grip of Big Telecom. What can we do about the Big Banks?

Few people actually like their banks. Once upon a time, people did. They had neighborhood banks. Kids got lessons in financial education by starting junior savings accounts. Loan officers knew their communities, and people were proud to pay back loans because they knew their bankers.

But the bank of my childhood was bought. Then it was bought again. It became Fleet, which became Bank of America, and somehow I went from a neighborhood bank to having an account at one of the biggest, most heartless financial monoliths in the country.

They change fee structures and charge exorbitant fines. They battle against unions. They overcompensate executives who take massive risks and bring our financial system to the brink of insolvency.

While I politically differ with Bank of America, it has always appeared easier to stay put. I did not see an obvious alternative.

Credit unions offer a way out. Much like the neighborhood banks of old, these are localized establishments that hold and protect your money. They invest their holdings and yield interest, but unlike Big Banks, they invest in their communities. Quite the opposite of "too big to fail," these are often "too small to notice." They rarely market themselves or put their names on ballpark marquees.

Credit unions are governed by cooperative principles. Their members participate in decision making and democratically decide how to invest their shared capital. Credit unions spend resources to educate their members, allies, and stakeholders.

Bank of America, Chase, Citi, and Wells Fargo donate to good causes and offer resources on financial literacy, but I know my personal experience with them has never felt cooperative, democratic, or community-invested.

Visit the Credit Union Co-op, a site that explains credit unions and helps you find your local options. Many have debit/credit cards, participate in ATM networks, and give you all the familiar comforts of banking. Plus, we've never had to bail them out. `485`

Take part in socially responsible investment. If you're not just looking to save, but looking to invest, you don't have to hand your money to UBS and call it a day. Nor do you have to place your bets on Exxon Mobil. `486`

Research socially responsible funds. These funds consider the labor and environmental standards of the companies they invest in. They track the community practices of their investments and publish reports on how these businesses behave. While you're not necessarily investing in "good" business, like solar power or microgrants, at least you will be certain that you are not investing in companies that do bad.

Keep in mind that this isn't always easy or obvious. Many companies may make improvements in one area, like environmental awareness, while falling short on human rights practices. This is where it becomes tricky for a liberal. Do you support only companies that have already achieved a high level of progressive credibility, or would you invest in a company that is in the process of improving but has not reached its socially responsible goals?

Furthermore, there are plenty of big companies that take part in "greenwashing." They showcase very specific environmental improvements, but are not transforming their practices. Even Exxon runs ads about saving the planet.

In the end, you'll need to do your own research and decide your own priorities. Check out the Social Investment Forum for studies on this type of investment, or look to a group like Social Funds that investigates many of the socially responsible investment vehicles available. Consider a firm like Domini, which has an explicit social aim in how it manages individual and institutional investments.

No need to rely on brokers. You can run your own investments. It can be daunting to research all the possibilities and track each business that interests you, so do what any good liberal does: do it with others. Start your own investment club.

This tried-and-true concept empowers people to try their hand at investment, pool knowledge, and tie their financial fates to those of friends and neighbors. The Tucson chapter of Drinking Liberally took it further, creating an Investing Liberally club. It makes sense: you share values with each other; now create value with one another as well.

Be a conscious shareholder. It's not enough in a democracy to vote, then wait four years to see how things play out. You need to remain involved to hold your elected officials accountable; they need to hear from you to know how they are doing, and you need to organize with other voters to threaten your representatives when they're not getting the job done.

We accept that notion with politics, but very few of us apply it to corporate governance. Many of us own stocks, yet few of us take seriously our rights and responsibilities as owners. We tend to look at our shareholder status as a bet. We let the people we're betting on make the decisions. Then we're surprised when the companies don't behave as sustainably, diversely, and intentionally as we'd like.

Think of the word: "shareholders." We are sharing something, and like any communitarian enterprise, it's only going to be as good as we all make it. We share responsibility, share decision making, and share the fortunes. So get involved.

Shareholder actions have increased in recent years so much that white-shoe law firms have been advising corporate boards on how to prepare for them. Why should they be scared of their shareholders? Well, shareholders often are the engine behind changing the management. They can also become the impetus for making a company behave better to the world around it.

There are several ways to become an active shareholder:

Use those proxy votes. If you own stock, you get voting power. That's the easiest place to start.

492

Organize a shareholder resolution. If you don't like what you're voting on, create new choices. Similar to organizing a workplace, this is a matter of finding other shareholders who share your concerns. Social Funds, which advocates for socially responsible investment, offers a clear guide on who can create a resolution and how to do it.

493

494 **Sell.** Personally divesting from a company, getting a group of shareholders to sell, or even causing an institutional investor to back away is a big decision. Is it better to remain involved in a company in order to change it? Or is there a time when you want to have nothing to do with it? You will need to decide for yourself where that line is drawn.

495
496
497
498 Use your shareholder power to ask about the distribution of wealth within the company. Ask how the business behaves in new communities. Ask for a plan to reduce the company's carbon footprint. Recruit others to ask with you if you want to get answers or, even better, shape solutions.

CHAPTER 7
ACTING
LIBERALLY

> *What is conservatism?*
> *Is it not adherence to the old and tried,*
> *against the new and untried?*
> —ABRAHAM LINCOLN

> *I'm not a member of any organized*
> *political party, I'm a Democrat!*
> —WILL ROGERS

You rise and shine and start your day liberally. You're conscientious about what you buy and what you use, you greet your neighbors, lead by example with your family, engage your coworkers. You now think twice about the movies you go to and the sites you surf. You are already changing the world.

Now do more.

It's great to internalize liberal lessons in your everyday life, and even better to share that lifestyle with those around you. Real change, though, requires a step deeper into politics. Ultimately, we need to make systemic change, which comes from banding together around our ideals and electing representatives who will live up to our values. We need to push those in power and not only involve ourselves in the issues we face in our neighborhoods but also get involved in the issues we face as a society.

Drinking Liberally has been a gateway into this type of political activism for many. Our vision was that you would start by becoming more aware and confident in your views by gathering at the bar. Then your drinking buddy would convince you to come make some phone calls for a campaign. Before you knew it, your new social circle would lead you into the field on Election Day.

In 2004, a dozen of us rented a van and drove out to Pennsylvania to knock on swing-state doors in an effort to prevent Bush's second term. We spent four days together, culminating in a late drive home on Tuesday, November 2nd. As we drove, the news coming over the radio got worse and worse. We had spent four days waking up early and staying up late. We had knocked on doors in the cold and made more phone calls from the office at night. We had lived on floors, traveled in a cramped vehicle, and even wore matching shirts. We must have been best friends.

The funny thing: only a couple of us had even known each other before the launch of Drinking Liberally. Most of us had become friends over the six months prior to this election road trip. But the strength of our bonds that formed through our weekly social gatherings, galvanized by the intensity of a critical election, led us from Drinking Liberally to Acting Liberally.

Taking action shouldn't be a chore separate from the tips listed throughout this book. It should be an extension of your life and integrated with the values of the liberal lifestyle: it should be rooted in community, it should be an easy and accessible activity that meets you where you are in life, it should be communal and expressive, and, yes, it should even be fun.

Acting Liberally isn't something you do instead of going to the movies, creating community dinners, or improving your workplace with your colleagues. Your social networks give you the strength and resolve to look beyond your community and take action to reshape our government and our society.

Fortunately, great organizations are doing this work, threading social life with political action in ways that are enjoyable and politically potent. Maybe one of these examples will inspire you to Act Liberally ... and maybe you will become an inspiration to others.

Beating the Red State Blues: The Snake River Freedom Coalition

In 2006, several high school students in the conservative town of Idaho Falls decided to protest the war. Maybe they had read stories in the news and said enough was enough. Maybe they knew people who had been sent to Iraq. Maybe they were fearful, as teenagers would rightfully be, that perpetual war would bring back a draft.

They engaged in a creative protest. They wrote the word "WAR" under the word "STOP" on traffic signs around town, thus turning street corners into "STOP WAR" billboards.

Unfortunately, that's also vandalizing public property, and anything that interferes with traffic signs jeopardizes public safety. So they were arrested and punished for their actions. They were fined for the cost of replacing the signs and assigned community service hours. More than the penalties, they suffered as their conservative community ostracized them. They worried whether this would affect their ability to attend college.

The members of Idaho Falls Drinking Liberally followed the story and decided to take action. This club is more than a group of beer drinkers. As with many of our chapters in red towns in red states, the Liberal Drinkers become a tight-knit community. They lean on each other for political information and for moral support. In each other's company, they no longer feel isolated in their beliefs. In some areas, Drinking Liberally the only event that uses the word "liberal," and many chapters serve as organizing hubs for local progressive causes.

The Idaho Falls members have marched in the town's Fourth of July Parade as a Drinking Liberally cadre. They host community barbecues and guest speakers. They arrange political comedians and musicians to tour their conservative area. Talk about Putnam-style social capital: they helped paint one member's new home.

This group decided to act on behalf of the antiwar high school students. They began the Snake River Freedom Coalition, a new organization, and committed to three actions:

1) The group wanted to raise money to cover the youths' fines. They auctioned off the vandalized stop signs, which had become the possessions of the students, and made shirts and stickers with the STOP WAR image.

2) The Coalition joined the teens for their community service. The teens were no longer alone. Instead of feeling isolated and ashamed, they now had the support of others literally standing by their side.

Additionally, it turned community service from a punishment into a public good. This action sent a different message about community involvement and made the teens feel less criminalized by their punishment.

3) The Coalition wanted to ensure that high schoolers could express their opposition to the war legally. Protest should not have to destroy public property or jeopardize college applications. The group began working with high school peace activists, supporting their efforts to engage in creative, effective, and safe protest.

507

What began as a way for a community of social peers to take action has grown into a community of its own. The Snake River Freedom Coalition now hosts the Loving Day celebration, marking the Supreme Court decision to strike down laws against interracial marriage. Last year they honored local organizers, labor leaders, and businesses. They did so at an awards dinner: a potluck barbecue at their local park.

508

Party Politics

While Drinking Liberally was promoting political involvement one pint at a time in New York City, a kindred spirit was hitting the road on the West Coast. The Oregon Bus Project worked to engage young people in political action in fun, social ways. They created actions around education, the environment, health care, and the economy. And they had a bus.

The bus became a physical manifestation of the liberal spirit: people who were part of a movement together were able to move together. The bus would make a social event out of a day of canvassing, driving forty people on an adventure. It was a field trip for politics.

509

They hosted events like <u>Candidates Gone Wild</u>, a night that brought local candidates to speak to packed houses of young voters. Rather than creating a night of stump speeches and stiff forums, the Bus Project engaged the candidates in talent show/talk show style events that loosened up the politicians and opened up politics for new audiences. In New York, our

511 version was <u>Mayoroke</u>—any candidate in the 2005 municipal race could stump . . . but first they had to sing.

512 The Bus Project will best be known for <u>Trick or Vote</u>. What do you need to do to get people to vote? You talk on them. You knock on their doors. What day do people willingly open their doors to strangers? Halloween. It only took two centuries of American elections for some folks in Portland, Oregon, to figure out that Halloween always falls within a week or so of Election Day.

Young progressives, attired in costumes that range from the politically satirical to the straight-up ridiculous, hit the streets, a couple feet taller than most trick-or-treaters, and with a taller order: engage people in politics and remind them to vote.

This activity is spreading across the country. It's localized, it's social, it's fun; it allows you to take a holiday and invest it with more meaning; it creates a shared experience for the activists and the residents and builds on an existing shared occasion. And it's goofy. People don't get annoyed. They take notice, which means it is effective. At the end of a night of Trick or Vote you will have spoken to more people than on your usual canvass.

In Durham, North Carolina, good works are mixed with good vibes by another group of "Tractivists." They're part of Traction, which spices up politics and brings younger North Carolinians into progressive action—through kickball, movies, bike rides, and art openings. This is not your usual political fare.

Much like Drinking Liberally, Traction is a gateway. They host purely social events to draw you in. They create other events that mix social and political impulses. Then they organize outings that are particularly activist. On cold weekends before Election Day, they throw field day parties, which draw people out for games and chili and use the opportunity to energize them to vote. They invite you out to pick blueberries, then teach you to become advocates for local agriculture. They bring you on a bike ride and end up engaging you about the area's green spaces. [513] [514] [515]

Other groups put the party into politics on Election Day. People always wonder how to turn out voters in low-turnout areas: knock on more doors? Send more fliers? What if you invite the community out to a party? [516]

From this notion, Party at the Polls was born. These parties take place near polling sites on Election Day and are nonpartisan and open to the public. They don't require you to vote in order to get your burger. Rather they made it convenient, desirable, and community-oriented to come out and vote. Local businesses donate food and drink, performers and community leaders come speak, and local radio helps promote.

Researchers at Yale University demonstrated that it worked. Per dollar spent on nonpartisan get-out-the-vote activities, inviting neighbors to a community party or barbecue near the polling site turned out more voters than any other investment of the same resources. In 2006, Working Assets promoted these Parties at the Polls in conjunction with partners like the League of Young Voters, Young People For, and Democracy Matters. Each election, new organizations continue to employ this idea.

You have to connect to people in ways that work with their lives. Not everyone is ready to step beyond his or her comfort zone. If you can create a community impulse to vote, you're strengthening democracy and strengthening your community.

We should reinforce positive political habits by associating political involvement with fun activities. If "participation" means standing in line in a school cafeteria to vote, it's not going to bring a smile to your face. What if you associated political participation with music? <u>HeadCount</u> brings issue advocacy messaging and voter registration to concerts. Politics becomes part of a hip experience.

What if you created a memory that connected politics and baseball? Baseball is America's pastime, and ballparks love to swell with shows of patriotic pride. It makes you love your country, love your team, . . . and love your vote? That's in part what inspired <u>Get In The Game</u>, a nonprofit that registers voters at baseball games and other sporting events around the country.

My sister started this organization in the summer of 2004. After Major League Baseball said that nonpartisan voter registration was "too political" for a league-wide partnership, Arielle contacted each team for permission to register voters at their stadiums. The Yankees were the first team to sign on. The Yankees may not always be good neighbors, but they know good PR when they see it.

Arielle is a die-hard Democrat and even more die-hard Yankee fan. However, she puts both loyalties away when she puts on her nonpartisan Get In The Game T-shirt. She has registered Republicans . . . and even Red Sox Fans. Hey, everyone deserves a vote.

Making the Call

A feature of every political campaign is phone-banking. You call potential voters to identify their leanings, persuade them, or remind them to vote. Volunteers gather in large rooms with dozens of phone lines. Smart volunteer coordinators order pizza to give the event a social feel. Usually the gatherings are in big offices—at union halls or law firms—and the scene is not particularly fun.

In 2004, organizers realized that technology could free campaigns from the staid office environment. We had cell phones. Many of us had more nighttime and weekend minutes than we knew what to do with. Why not burn those minutes calling voters?

Democracy in the Park innovated a new vision for phone banks: come out to Central Park on a weekend afternoon, lounge on a picnic blanket, snack, laugh, and call voters. Soon, there was Democracy in the Quad, a college expansion that encouraged students to organize in their campus commons. [519]

Two years later, in the 2006 election, MoveOn had developed the tools to allow people all across the country to organize house parties around swing-state calls. MoveOn would give you access to the call lists online and track the calls you and other volunteers were making at countless events. When you come to someone's home, you feel more connected to the host and other volunteers than you might at a phone bank in an office. Those calling parties have led people to join other group actions such as letter-writing campaigns and rallies. They also introduce volunteers to new political friends with whom they go the movies or out for a drink. These house parties made a political act into a community act. [520]

Old School

Twenty-somethings in and around 2004 did not reinvent politics. While a young generation brought fresh energy and new technology to the political landscape, making socializing part of politics is the tried-and-true approach of the Democratic Club. At their core, these clubs were all about getting votes. Club leaders could deliver votes on Election Day, which made them influential in electing public offices and party positions.

However, these clubs weren't simply lists of voters and groups of reliable volunteers. Year-round activities made the clubs a center of community life that kept members involved beyond Election Day. The activities were more than political. The clubs were more than debate societies. They were active in the whole lives of their members: where they lived and worked, their fortunes and misfortunes.

The best existing model of this old school club is the McManus Democratic Association, which for over a century has held sway in the Democratic Party on the west side of Manhattan. The club was founded by Thomas "The" McManus in the 1890s when he defeated famed Tammany Hall ward-heeler George Washington Plunkitt in the race for district rep. McManus had no intention of overturning the power structure. He just wanted his piece of it. His club became an independent piece of the Tammany machine. For the next eleven decades, as sons and nephews took on his role, a man named McManus has been the district leader of Hell's Kitchen. As Tammany lost power and the subsequent generations of power brokers emerged, McManus endured.

How'd they pull off surviving the sea change in city politics? They acted as more than a political force. The McManus Club was always first to welcome immigrants to the neighborhood. Without question, they tapped into this new bloc of voters by registering them to vote, teaching them to use voting machines, and telling them who to vote for. They really cultivated loyalty by doing more: they helped all members, including immigrants, find apartments and jobs; they arranged legal advice when necessary; and consoled community members when they lost loved ones.

As Reformers replaced old-school Democrats in neighborhood after neighborhood throughout New York, the new clubs focused on organizing endorsement meetings and circulating petitions to add candidates to ballots. The McManus Club still hosts office hours with volunteer lawyers two nights a week. They still make calls for people behind on their rent. They attend community board meetings to speak for local establishments. They realized that to be successful in the political business, you should be in the community business.

Jim McManus is the current district leader, a post he's held for forty years. He throws a birthday party every year on the Sunday before the Democratic primary. You celebrate Jim, eat free sandwiches and drink cold beers, see your neighbors, share long tables in a large church basement . . . and you get introduced to the candidates you're expected to vote for two days later. Traction and Party at the Polls have nothing on these guys.

521

While the McManus office may be decorated with artifacts dating back decades, and many of their regular members are well into their senior years, this club is more than a holdover from the past. It has remained politically relevant because it has changed with its community. A century ago, it was a club of Irish immigrants; now Columbian and South Asian immigrants are part of the membership. The McManus Club did not find its strength in a particular culture or ethnicity. It has adjusted to include whoever makes up the cultural landscape of New York.

The Club is also open to new politics. In 2003, as the Democratic presidential primary heated up, the newly formed Drinking Liberally wanted to watch the debates together. The McManus Club opened its doors to us, bought us beers, and made us feel right at home. Jim was delighted to have a crew of twenty-somethings in the old building, hearing old stories and bringing new life to the club. Over the years, the Club has consistently welcomed new political groups to use their space.

522 The McManus Club's crowning annual event is a St. Patrick's Day Breakfast. More than 500 people crowd a T.G.I. Friday's before the St. Pat's parade. Every local politician shows up. The party begins at 7 AM. The senior citizens from the Club start lining up at 6:30 AM outside the restaurant. I was not invested in St. Patrick's Day before I first attended the breakfast. Now I would not dream of missing it. It is clearly a political event, but without stump speeches, debates, or petitions. It is nothing more than people sharing drinks and food and finding cause to be together. That's politics enough.

523 I've attended one event that has rivaled the McManus St. Patrick's Day breakfast as the epitome of social politics: the Tom Harkin Steak Fry. The long-serving Iowa senator knows his crowd. They want to support him, and they like a good party. Senator Harkin he throws a field day—a regional festival with vendors and booths, a grandstand stage, and 15,000 people in a balloon field in Indianola.

At the 2006 Steak Fry, then–freshman senator Barack Obama's speech fueled speculation about his presidential ambitions. In 2007, all the Democratic candidates attended and took turns addressing the first-in-the-nation caucus-goers. Everyone watched as though listening to an outdoor music festival: leaning back on lawn chairs and picnic blankets, eating meat and corn from Styrofoam plates, and drinking cheap beer.

It was Drinking Liberally on steroids.

This is more than a social outing. It is a major fundraiser for the senator. Your fee to join the party is a donation to his reelection effort. He has become such an institution that supporting 524 him politically feels like a donation to your community. Every contribution is a way of taking action. Every small donation gives politicians the financial and moral boost to push ahead. You might have thought you were hitting a field day, but in fact you were Giving Liberally. Which counts as Acting Liberally.

Activism 101

Not all action needs to be a party. Political involvement can take the form of working with disenfranchised communities 525 and learning the challenges others face in their lives. It can be the tedious act of testifying at City Council, where you might 526 wait hours for your five minutes at the podium. Your political participation may cause doors to be slammed in your face, and as you get closer to November, the rain gets icier.

When you engage liberally with a social spirit and act as a community, those difficulties become manageable. You share the frustration with your friends, who have experienced the same, and soon it becomes a common bond or a mark of honor, rather than a source of weariness. You grab a drink after a day in the field and replenish your commitment to the cause. You see the change in the community in which you work and

---

What if you were Acting Conservatively?

You'd be part of a campaign that traded on fear and division, that wanted to dial back progress and ignore the course of history, and you'd probably end up ashamed of what the people around you were up to: like attacking abortion doctors or screaming that our president was born in Kenya.

---

witness the results of your efforts. There are just three tricks to any good activism: make it easy, make it social, make it rewarding.

527 **Make it easy.** The challenges will not be easy to overcome. The work itself will not be painless. But it should be simple for people to get involved.

528 **Organize it for the volunteers.** Don't make newcomers do a lot of guesswork about the task. Be clear about when and where to show up and what to expect there. Arrange car pools, sign folks up in advance, and follow up to confirm.

529 **Bring it to the volunteers.** Could the project be done close to home? Could people participate in their natural habitat: a home, park, or café? When volunteers can engage in their familiar settings, it becomes easier for them and reaffirms that politics can fit into your life.

530 **Remember to translate!** Entering a situation and not knowing the jargon is frustrating and isolating. Don't assume that everyone knows the terms of the trade, or even that they are as familiar with all the issues. Provide a primer, a basic introduction to each activity. When everyone has the same tools and terms, you will have a stronger team.

531 **Make it social.** When you do an action together, you have the joy of common purpose, and you become involved more deeply. Acting liberally gives you the chance to learn from each other and support each other.

532 **Make it easy to invite friends.** Ask people if they'd like to bring a buddy. Make it easy for them to do so. Your volunteer might feel more confident, you get an extra participant, and you start the project with a social rapport.

Keep it casual. Even if you have a lot of work to do, make sure people know they can chat and laugh. Introduce everyone at the start. They'll be sharing an experience—empower them to have a dialogue about it by knowing who else is with them. Make sure folks take breaks to keep their spirits up.

533

Host an after party. Every good action should have a social event after it. This may be a chance to decompress and debrief. It could be an opportunity to connect with others who didn't participate in the action and for them to see what they missed. It's a way to recharge your batteries and strengthen your community. If people have a beer when the day is done, they're more likely to come back again, because they will have bonded with other folks as well.

534

Make it rewarding. There are frequent occasions when volunteering can feel fruitless. You don't see results, or see the bigger picture. I remember being asked by volunteers once why they were calling voters and not persuading them. They were told just to ask questions about preferences but not to offer more information or engage in conversation. It was my first campaign, and I didn't know why. It turns out that campaigns have phases. In some phases you just identify whether voters are likely to support your candidate. You do this so in later phases you can target the voters that support you and not waste limited time calling the voters who don't. The bigger picture makes sense. However, if nobody explains the strategy, you'll feel like you're wasting your time. From the perspective of the campaign staff, it may seem like a burden to explain the strategy, but it always pays off if it keeps people involved.

535

536 **Lay out the big picture.** People will often do very minute tasks if they see how it fits into a grand scheme. Laying out the road map keeps people from feeling like they're just engaged in busywork.

537 **Mark progress and celebrate victories.** Talk to people about what they've accomplished. Demonstrate how their role contributes to a pattern of real change. One of the most inspiring moments I've experienced was in New Hampshire in the fall of 2008. We were heading out to knock on doors and we knew many people would not be home or would refuse to talk to us. The volunteer coordinator reminded us that in 2000, Al Gore had lost New Hampshire by a few thousand votes. There were a few thousand of us going into the field that day. If each of us connected with three voters, that would be the margin that would have changed the course of America. That got us motivated.

Many campaigns forget to celebrate their accomplishments. The staff gets caught in the burden of the longer battle. For activists, it's important to note when progress has been made. It keeps people energized and engaged.

538 **Saying thank you.** Thank you to the hosts in every state around the country, and increasingly around the world, who decided they were proud of the word "liberal "and willing to mix their political and social lives, and volunteer to help others do so as well.

A toast to the tens of thousands of Liberal Drinkers who want to improve our world, promote a progressive agenda, and have decided to do so one pint at a time.

I raise a glass to all the folks that have steered, shaped, and led Living Liberally: co-founder of the original DL, Matt O'Neill; our partner, Katrina Baker; David Alpert, who saw something much larger in this little club; Katie Halper, who kicked off the first Laughing Liberally; Wendy Cohen and Leigh Wolinsky who envisioned Screening Liberally; Kerry Trueman and Matt Rosenberg who cooked up Eating Liberally; our fellow national leaders in New York: Greg Rae, Claire Silberman, and Mary Bruch; and our leadership team, past and present, around the country: Adam Bartel of Cincinnati, Chris Blazejewski of Providence, Mark Campbell of Charlotte, Cass Chulick of Spartanburg, Amy Clinton of Winston-Salem, Heather Culligan of Salt Lake City, John Erhardt of Denver, Susan Harrison of San Francisco, Dan Henry of Idaho Falls, Tom Holland of Oklahoma City, Amie Hollis of Nashville, Greg Leding of Fayetteville, Robin Marty of Minneapolis, John McClelland of Addison, Bill Nothstine of Portland, Bill Poorman of Peoria, Amanda Mittlestadt Riordan of Des Moines, Jeremiah Roth of Salt Lake City, Jesse Rubin of San Diego, Vicki Sansbury of Louisville, McKay Schwalbach, Marcus Williams of Charlotte. And of course to Josh Bolotsky, our National Program Coordinator of three years, who kept it all going and growing.

Three cheers to our organization's creative inspirations along the way: Owen Roth, who created the name; Daniel Greenfeld who gave us a logo; Johnny Dirt of Rudy's for opening his backyard; Danny DePamphilis of Rudy's for being the consummate host; Andrew Hoppin, the first person to export Drinking Liberally beyond New York City.

Special acknowledgment to guest contributors: Katie Halper, Josh Bolotsky, Franz Hartl, and Hayley Siegel. Many friends and fellow schemers contributed the ideas throughout the book, especially to the group project of developing the lists of literature, music, and other cultural offerings. In addition to the leaders and hosts listed before, these brainstormers include Fred Gooltz, Jen Johnson, Allison Kilkenny, Elana Levin, Dave Levy, Leah Plunkett, Bede Sheppard, Brian Sonenstein, Shaunna Thomas, Alex Urevick-Ackelsberg, Josh Wojcik; and Laughing Liberally regulars Lee Camp, Matthew Filipowicz, Jamie Kilstein, Negin Farsad, Baratunde Thurston who contributed ideas and humor. And thank you for the support and inspiration I've received from Governor Howard Dean, Markos Moulitsas, Matt Stoller, and the good people at CREDO, MoveOn, Music For America, ActBlue, Advomatic, Netroots Nation, Open Left, The Tank, and our many allies who are building political culture in our country.

The book itself would not have happened without Ann Treistman of Skyhorse Publishing insisting that there was, in fact, a book to be written. The book would not have been beautiful without designer Paul Pierson, who has offered his inspired talent to Living Liberally through the years. The book benefitted from the edits of Katrina, Matt, Kerry, Josh, Julie Hilimire, my father and sister, and of Anne Jump, whose understanding of how to support and steer an author helped me in ways I could not have improvised on my own.

Finally, of course, a toast to the liberals closest to me. One grandmother insisted until her final day that we donate to the ACLU; one grandmother showed me that everything I needed was walking distance from home; Casey Selzer, with whom I live liberally each day; my sister Arielle, who took time off the campaign trail to read and re-read every sentence; and my parents, Suzanne and Eric, who brought me to a Mondale rally when I was six years old.

Cheers.

CONCLUSION

A Day in Holland, Michigan

During the writing of this book, I went to Holland, Michigan, to officiate a friend's wedding. It was an intimate affair, mostly family. I was invited because the bride and groom had different religious backgrounds and they wanted a neutral officiant. I had been ordained by an organization that certifies laypeople to perform rites reserved, in many states, for the clergy.

I had never been to Holland, but I was warned that it was "very conservative." The groom alluded to it. Other friends laughed and cautioned me that it would be one of the most conservative towns I'd ever been to.

What would that look like. A dry town? Confederate flags? Angry anti-Obama signs in every window? Having spent most of my life in a liberal areas in central New Jersey, Cambridge, and New York City, I was a little nervous. The bride and groom lived in Chicago, but how would their families, from these conservative towns, react to a long-haired East Coast Jewish liberal arriving to marry their children?

When I got there, I found a small city with a tidy, walkable downtown. There were establishments for locals and for the college campus near the town's center. There were pocket parks and courtyards dotting the streets, with public benches every block down the main strip.

Maybe conservative towns aren't so bad.

There were churches everywhere as well, in a greater density than where I grew up. They were classic, stately buildings, with proud facades and well-manicured lawns. The churches even outnumbered the banks, which also embodied a municipal bravado with public fountains, tall doors, and strong brick frames.

Together, these banks, churches, downtown improvements, and open spaces created a heart of the town that felt very welcoming and communal. I could imagine these features encouraging interaction with your neighbors and pride in your town identity.

Then I met the people.

The two families mingling around the nuptials were white, unpretentious, and had northern Midwestern accents. I was prepared to be viewed as an outsider, ready to tiptoe through a few political debates. So when, the bride and groom's parents and grandparents inquired about the nature of my ordination, I was hesitant, almost apologetic, in explaining what certified me for this affair.

I explained how the Church of Universal Life serves to democratize the clergy. Then the bride's grandmother spoke up. "We have a gal who does that in Elk Rapids," she announced. "She does weddings and funerals, down by the bay." It became clear that the "gal" was in her sixties. Grandma thought it was great that people were taking ownership of their own services and inviting loved ones to play a role. She was curious how I had prepared, and was delighted to learn I had spoken with the happy couple about their relationship, their hopes and fears, the language and images that most reflected their feelings, and their future together.

"It's just wonderful that you take all that into consideration," she said. "The best weddings do. And I've seen a lot of weddings." That's when she revealed that for twenty-eight years, she'd worked at the local Catholic church, where she was a devoted parishioner.

This warm, welcoming woman who had set me completely at ease was the "religious" grandmother we had been concerned about upsetting with our unconventional service. Far from being upset, she was enthusiastic.

Far from being scrutinized, I felt embraced.

Later, I met the bride's grandfather, an old, slightly portly, kindly looking gentleman. Since he was the oldest white male there, I thought for sure he would be the more conservative voice. Instead he shared his wish that a poem he wrote about living in peace would be translated into all languages and brought to every country in the world. He also sang "Only You" a cappella for the newlyweds' first dance.

I wasn't debating with the man as I expected. I was singing along with him.

The groom's father told me about the excitement he had seen around the state for Obama. The groom's childhood friends, who still lived in the right-leaning upstate towns of their youth, told me how infuriating it was to combat the talking points of Fox News. The groom's brother-in-law, who ran a local auto dealership, talked with me about how the government program "cash for clunkers" was working for him.

He and his wife, the groom's sister, live in Holland. He said Holland was a place where people ask you what church you belong to as a way to get to know you. She said it was the kind of town where people ask her what her husband does rather than what she does. Yet they were both Holland residents and neither of them fit their own stereotypes of the town.

Despite warnings from East Coast friends and these Holland natives, I experienced a very different town. In my short time there, I found the locally brewed craft beer. I visited the hotel, which boasted of its LEED Certification for environmental sustainability. I saw signs of the regional farmers' market the town promoted. I walked past the independent cinema on Main Street advertising a season of socially conscious documentaries and art-house flicks.

I found the local independent coffee shop that served Fair Trade coffee, offered free Internet service, and charged you less if you used a reusable mug. With fliers for concerts plastered across its walls, snarky satire mags for free on its shelves, and a mix of alternative high school patrons and college kids with laptops propped open, it looked exactly like what you'd expect at the edge of a campus in a town of 30,000.

What made this surprising was that I'd internalized the idea that Holland would be a different world. And here I was, drinking from a big yellow mug (the place also has an honor policy if you're in a rush; you just drop money in a cup and go), feeling very much like I was among my people. I found a free monthly paper about sustainability in western Michigan, replete with condemnations of big box stores and Walmart's environmental practices. I found photocopied signs for Holland's ninth annual Tulipanes Latino Cultural Festival.

I found one pinup advertising "a church as liberal as Jesus." If you're going to be a liberal in a religious town, that's one way to do it.

The day after the wedding, I attended part of the Tulipanes Festival: a worship service in Centennial Park. The prayer service was fully bilingual. The youthful, rocking, God-loving musical medleys had verses in both English and Spanish.

Families of different ages and hues along with a good showing of senior citizens filled the lawn, and young kids sang and danced along. The sermon was on needing to accept change when we seek to build something strong together: a house, a community, a country.

Holland is not a liberal town. There are probably many people in that town who would express their fear of immigrants. There are also people prepared to embrace another culture. There are residents who complain about big government, high taxes, and Democrats wanting to take their guns away. Other residents want to make the town greener, increase public transportation, and support the arts.

Despite my presumptions—my prejudices—going in, I would not have known what typical Hollanders believed without talking to every one of them. Maybe there was no such person as a typical Hollander.

Even in that "conservative" town, there are liberals. Some broadcast it proudly, others hold their beliefs more quietly, and some find ways to meld liberal values with the town's more religious, traditional character. There are probably many Hollanders who would never use the word "liberal" to describe themselves and would be astonished by the characterization. Yet they were living freely, diversely, compassionately, and sustainably. They were living for one another, not for themselves alone.

From the publicly funded parks and community spaces to the embrace of multiculturalism, Holland is doing plenty to be proud of. That might not be left or right on the political spectrum. That might win praise from as many Republicans as Democrats.

In my view, it's just more evidence that in every corner of the country, Americans are living liberally.

APPENDIX
THE COMPLETE
538 WAYS
TO LIVE WORK AND PLAY LIKE A
LIBERAL
CHECK THEM ALL OFF!

- [✓] Read this book

- [1] Drink liberally

- [2] Choose your morning news

- [3] Listen to public radio

- [4] Cover your television

- [5] Leave magazines out and open around your house

- [6] Choose local stations

- [7] Watch public television

- [8] Switch off Fox News in the mornings

| 9 | Read the morning paper or online news |

| 10 | Make your lunch |

| 11 | Use a reusable lunch bag |

| 12 | Compost |

| 13 | Know your recycling rules |

| 14 | Shut down your house when you're out |

| 15 | Turn off the AC or turn down the thermostat |

| 16 | Turn off lights |

| 17 | Unplug electronics |

| 18 | Use surge protectors and power strips |

| 19 | Use an Energy Hub |

| 20 | Monitor your energy use |

| 21 | Switch to compact fluorescents |

| 22 | Switch to low-flow showerheads |

| 23 | Ask your power company about alternative energy |

| 24 | Get a solar-panel backpack |

| 25 | Telecommute |

| 26 | Bicycle to work |

27   Use public transportation

28   Drive a hybrid

29   Carpool to work

30   Use HOV or carpool lanes

31   Brew your own coffee

32   Use a travel mug

33   Lobby coffee shops for discounts for mug users

34   Know your brew

35   Support Fair Trade coffee

36   Buy shade-grown coffee

37   Brew coffee for carpoolers

38   Bring a travel mug to your carpool-mate

39   Check out Energy Star efficiency ideas

40   Read *50 Simple Things You Can Do to Save the Earth*

41   Turn off the water while brushing your teeth

42   Know your neighbors

43   Smile at your neighbors

44   Keep an eye out for your neighbors and their kids

| 45 | Read *The Death and Life of Great American Cities* |

| 46 | Visit your neighborhood parks |

| 47 | Use your local playgrounds |

| 48 | Support the Play Cities agenda to bring playgrounds to all children |

| 49 | Remind elected officials about the importance of open space |

| 50 | Start a community garden |

| 51 | Create a local play street |

| 52 | Participate in "Won't You Be My Neighbor" Day |

| 53 | Sit on your porch |

| 54 | Say hi to your neighbors |

| 55 | Invite your neighbors into your home |

| 56 | Host neighbors for game nights |

| 57 | Invite neighbors over for TV night |

| 58 | Buy a projector to create big-screen experiences |

| 59 | Make enough food to share |

| 60 | Share an internet connection |

| 61 | Leave your wi-fi network unlocked |

62	Think public
63	Get vaccinations
64	Don't smoke
65	Pick up trash
66	Don't go to work when you're sick
67	Advocate for paid sick days
68	Reduce your carbon footprint
69	Reduce your foodprint
70	Shrink your 'hoodprint
71	Read the website Greater Greater Washington
72	Serve on a Block Association
73	Help a neighbor with a chore
74	Take climate change seriously
75	Work for the expansion of health coverage
76	Support immigrant rights
77	Advocate for the expansion of the estate tax
78	Speak up for progressive taxation
79	Use our national parks

| 80 | Cheer on our public fire department |

| 81 | Volunteer for the fire department |

| 82 | Promote our public police force |

| 83 | Enjoy your local library |

| 84 | Volunteer at and donate to your local library |

| 85 | Use public schools |

| 86 | Join a PTA |

| 87 | Be a guest speaker at your local school |

| 88 | Open your business to a school trip |

| 89 | Support food pantries |

| 90 | Volunteer at soup kitchens |

| 91 | Talk to a homeless person over a meal |

| 92 | Celebrate public access television |

| 93 | Support a seed bank |

| 94 | Drive on public roads |

| 95 | Use the post office |

| 96 | Get your office recycling |

| 97 | Make energy-saving improvements in your office |

| 98 | Switch your workplace to energy-efficient bulbs |

| 99 | Install motion-activated lights at work |

| 100 | Turn off office lights at night |

| 101 | Install low-flush toilets and urinals in your office restrooms |

| 102 | Install hand driers at work restrooms |

| 103 | Install timed faucets at work |

| 104 | Turn off work computers at night |

| 105 | Improve the office kitchen |

| 106 | Stock dishware and utensils in your office kitchen |

| 107 | Have clear cleaning duties in your office kitchen |

| 108 | Provide common condiments and often-used items in your office kitchen |

| 109 | Have a coffeemaker at work |

| 110 | Get rid of the water cooler |

| 111 | Fight the bottled-water business |

| 112 | Relax the office dress code |

| 113 | Relax the office climate control |

| 114 | Create avenues for staff feedback |

115 Provide flex time

116 Dedicate a staff lounge

117 Allow independent time at work

118 Organize staff outings

119 Build community with your coworkers

120 Take a green graduation pledge

121 Advocate for workplace change

122 Research better business practices

123 Visit Business.gov for workplace ideas

124 Anticipate objections to workplace improvements

125 Invest yourself in workplace improvements

126 Engage your coworkers about their lives

127 Make coffee for everyone at work

128 Start a lunch co-op

129 Host work socials

130 Spike the water cooler conversation

131 Find some common ground

132 Make sure coworkers are registered to vote

133   Organize your coworkers

134   Thank labor unions

135   Join Working America

136   Talk with your coworkers about what's important to them

137   Delegate organizing tasks to your coworkers

138   Circulate a petition in your workplace

139   Have a letter-writing campaign at work

140   Identify targets and allies in your workplace

141   "Just do it" to make change at work

142   Say yes to employee ideas to work liberally

143   Understand your business's landscape of workers and community

144   Read *Fast Food Nation*

145   Pay higher than the mimimum wage

146   Offer health benefits

147   Subsidize child care

148   Compensate employees for continuing education

149   Open your business venue for community meetings

| 150 | Donate profits to nonprofits |

| 151 | Respect work |

| 152 | Listen to your workers |

| 153 | Share the wealth |

| 154 | Know your community |

| 155 | Have a longer—and larger—view |

| 156 | Join Net Impact |

| 157 | Join the Social Venture Network |

| 158 | Shorten, or eliminate, your commute |

| 159 | Eliminate office rent and utilities costs |

| 160 | Waste less paper |

| 161 | Cut down office costs |

| 162 | Make your work schedule fit your family schedule |

| 163 | Share costly resources with other freelancers |

| 164 | Get involved with coworking |

| 165 | Join the Freelancers Union |

| 166 | Volunteer your professional skills |

| 167 | Order beer by the pitcher |

| 168 | Read *Bowling Alone* |

| 169 | Use Meetup.com |

| 170 | Join Green Drinks |

| 171 | Join Slow Food USA |

| 172 | Love liberally |

| 173 | Watch *The Daily Show* |

| 174 | Watch the *Colbert Report* |

| 175 | Laugh liberally |

| 176 | Cheer on Al Franken |

| 177 | Watch Mort Sahl routines |

| 178 | Check out Lenny Bruce |

| 179 | Find old Dick Gregory sets |

| 180 | View George Carlin clips |

| 181 | Watch Smothers Brothers videos |

| 182 | Enjoy Richard Pryor comedy |

| 183 | Catch old Ellen DeGeneres material |

| 184 | Laugh along with Tina Fey |

| 185 | Watch *Guess Who's Coming to Dinner* |

186 Rent *Philadelphia*

187 Check out *Superbad*

188 Support Ron Howard films

189 Learn about Participant Films

190 Watch *An Inconvenient Truth*

191 Judge films for their portrayal of women

192 Judge films for their portrayal of people of color

193 Judge films for their portrayal of gay and lesbian characters

194 Judge films for their messages of deference to authority

195 Watch *One Flew Over the Cuckoo's Nest*

196 Ask whether a film trades on love or on violence

197 Check film reviews for liberal themes

198 Look at how movie posters treat women

199 Let your friends see films through your liberal lens

200 Screen liberally

201 Host Brave New Films screenings

202 Support independent movie theaters

203 Research films you want shown

204 Organize friends to request films

205 Approach your local theater to show films

206 Watch *The Grapes of Wrath*

207 Watch *Footloose*

208 For Martin Luther King Jr. Day, watch *4 Little Girls*

209 For Valentine's Day, watch *But I'm a Cheerleader*

210 For Presidents' Day, watch *Dave*

211 For Earth Day, watch *The Age of Stupid*

212 For Memorial Day, watch *The Great Dictator*

213 For the Fourth of July, watch *Good Night, and Good Luck*

214 For Labor Day, watch *Norma Rae*

215 For Halloween, watch *The Last Supper*

216 For Columbus Day, watch *Smoke Signals*

217 For Christmas, watch *It's a Wonderful Life*

218 Play a State of the Union drinking game

219 Host primary night parties

220 Join debate night parties

221 Celebrate with election night parties

222 Host a screening for presidential press conferences

223 Join a screening of premium political comedy

224 Watch HBO documentaries

225 Participate in a Screening Liberally Oscar Night

226 Share your favorite liberal shows

227 Check out *Battlestar Galactica*

228 Catch up on *The Wire*

229 Watch *P.O.V.*

230 Create a gathering for the State of the Union

231 Watch Keith Olbermann

232 Watch Rachel Maddow

233 Check out old episodes of *All in the Family*

234 Check out old episodes of *Murphy Brown*

235 Check out old episodes of *The West Wing*

236 Check out old episodes of *Maude*

237 Check out old episodes of *Family Ties*

238 Check out old episodes of *The Simpsons*

239 Check out old episodes of *Saturday Night Live*

240 Check out old episodes of *Sesame Street*

241 Attend a show at The Tank

242 Pay a visit to the Des Moines Social Club

243 Read, see, or stage a production of *Lysistrata*

244 Read, see, or stage a production of *Inherit the Wind*

245 Read, see, or stage a production of *Mother Courage and Her Children*

246 Read, see, or stage a production of *The Cradle Will Rock*

247 Read, see, or stage a production of *Waiting for Lefty*

248 Read, see, or stage a production of *Twelve Angry Men*

249 Read, see, or stage of production of *Master Harold and the Boys*

250 Read, see, or stage a production of *Hair*

251 Read, see, or stage a production of *Les Misérables*

252 Read, see, or stage a production of *Rent*

253 Listen to Public Enemy

254 Listen to Black Star

255 Listen to Le Tigre

256	Listen to Outkast
257	Listen to Radiohead
258	Listen to The Clash
259	Listen to Discount
260	Listen to Marvin Gaye
261	Listen to Fela Kuti
262	Listen to TV on the Radio
263	Listen to Dar Williams
264	Listen to Rage Against the Machine
265	Listen to Bruce Springsteen
266	Listen to Ani DiFranco
267	Take a road trip to historical sites
268	Take a vacation building homes
269	Find tips for environmentally friendly hiking
270	Learn about socially conscious hunting
271	Join Karma Krew
272	Visit minor league ballparks
273	Eat at a local diner

274 Read the local paper

275 Reuse and recycle while traveling

276 Take part in CouchSurfing

277 Tip well

278 Wear sunscreen

279 Join a flash mob

280 Follow Improv Everywhere

281 Carry the spirit of Billionaires for Bush

282 Discredit conservative tropes

283 Honestly assess where we, as a country, fall short

284 Hold up America's liberal themes as an ideal

285 Reread the Declaration of Independence with a liberal lens

286 Reconsider the liberal message of the Revolution of 1800

287 Learn the lessons of abolition

288 Learn the lessons of breaking up the trusts

289 Learn the lessons of women's suffrage

290 Learn the lessons of the New Deal

291 Learn the lessons of our entrance into World War II

292 Learn the lessons of the Marshall Plan and GI Bill

293 Learn the lessons of the struggle for civil rights

294 Reconsider the liberal message of the moon landing

295 Applaud Thoreau's political protest

296 Study the achievements of Frances Perkins

297 Celebrate Repeal of Prohibition

298 Embrace *Loving vs. Virginia*

299 Highlight the importance of the resignation of Richard Nixon

300 Refute that our founders were all slave owners

301 Reconsider whether the yeoman farmer was the ideal American

302 Challenge the idea that baseball was born in the countryside

303 Deny that the 1950s were a time of peace and prosperity

304 Know that Ronald Reagan did not end the Cold War

305 Read *1984*

306 Read *Catch-22*

307 Read *The Grapes of Wrath*

308   Read *Slaughterhouse-Five*

309   Read *No Name in the Street*

310   Read *To Kill a Mockingbird*

311   Read *Fahrenheit 451*

312   Read *Beloved*

313   Read *The Shock Doctrine*

314   Read *A People's History of the United States*

315   Read the poetry of Walt Whitman

316   Talk out your thoughts or confusion with others

317   Read more

318   Read magazines

319   Explore a newsstand

320   Check out *Mother Jones*

321   Subscribe to *The Nation*

322   Read *The New Yorker*

323   Pick up some conservative magazines to know their arguments

324   Read *50 Simple Things You Can Do to Fight the Right*

325   Leave a magazine out and open on a library table

326	Organize your library's purchasing power
327	Become your own library
328	Include your name and contact info on books you share
329	Start a reading group
330	Choose something from the library stocks
331	Support liberal publishers
332	Don't make your book club too dry
333	Make everyone in the book club a decider
334	Mix in some living authors with your book selection
335	Read the writings of Frederick Douglass
336	Read the writings of John Steinbeck
337	Read the writings of Elizabeth Cady Stanton
338	Read the writings of Upton Sinclair
339	Host your book club as a potluck
340	Host an author
341	Check out Daily Kos
342	Check out Think Progress
343	Check out Talking Points Memo

344 Check out FireDogLake

345 Check out Jack & Jill Politics

346 Check out Empty Wheel

347 Check out Feministing

348 Check out Open Left

349 Check out FiveThirtyEight

350 Check out Crooks and Liars

351 Check out Eschaton

352 Check out Living Liberally

353 Join the discussion on blogs

354 Share what you learn from blogs

355 Encourage friends to change the channel

356 Ask friends to identify every news channel's bias

357 Give friends a magazine to get them off television

358 Bring politics to the dinner table

359 Question your friends

360 Engage your conservative relatives

361 Talk liberally with non-liberals

362 Create a participatory home

363 Include your children in family decisions

364 Include children in household chores

365 Bring children to your work and your social activities

366 Meet your children's friends and their parents

367 Participate in your kids' activities

368 Be involved in your kids' education

369 Participate in collective childcare

370 Spend one-on-one time with your children

371 Encourage your children to explore

372 Create boundaries and structure for your children

373 Tell stories with your children

374 Share your values with your children

375 Lead by example and demonstrate values to your children

376 Talk to your kids about the environment

377 Explain to your kids the causes you support

378 Discuss the values you see in your children's behavior

379 Be playful

380 Teach inclusion through children's games

381 Encourage games that ask kids to collaborate

382 Play games that inspire creative thinking

383 Start early as you parent liberally

384 Add *The Lorax* to your children's reading list, or read it aloud

385 Add the Harry Potter books to your children's reading list, or read the novels aloud

386 Add *Free to Be You and Me* to your children's reading list, or read it aloud

387 Add Shel Silverstein to your children's reading list, or read his poetry aloud

388 Add Encyclopedia Brown books to your children's reading list, or read them aloud

389 Add *Blubber* to your children's reading list, or read it aloud

390 Add the Lord of the Rings trilogy to your children's reading list, or read the novels aloud

391 Add *The Little Prince* to your children's reading list, or read it aloud

392 Choose a congregation that hosts a CSA

393 Make sure your congregation is taking green steps

394   Ask your congregation to buy food from local vendors

395   Choose a congregation that uses gender-neutral liturgy

396   Choose a congregation that accepts female and gay officiants

397   Choose a congregation that pays workers a living wage

398   Choose a congregation that organizes service trips

399   Choose a congregation that has usher-exchange programs with other congregations

400   Choose a congregation that allows interfaith spouses to participate

401   Choose a congregation that respects non-congregants

402   Choose a congregation that respects gender equality

403   Choose a congregation that respects its gay members

404   Choose a congregation that invests in community

405   Choose a congregation that celebrates

406   Donate to food and clothing drives over the holidays

407   Give to charity rather than give gifts

408   Volunteer on holidays

409   Shop consciously for the holidays

410   Show goodwill to all

| 411 | Shop at mom-and-pop stores |

| 412 | Buy union |

| 413 | Ask where your products are made |

| 414 | Check out the Green Pages |

| 415 | Check out The Responsible Shopper |

| 416 | Learn about the conditions in which workers produce items you buy |

| 417 | Check on the environmental record of a business |

| 418 | Check on the politics of a business |

| 419 | Ask friends for recommendations on conscientious shopping |

| 420 | Offer your own advice on conscientious shopping |

| 421 | Choose items with less packaging |

| 422 | Get a sense of the work environment in the store |

| 423 | Choose items that are biodegradable |

| 424 | Support independent producers and craftspeople |

| 425 | Give feedback to stores |

| 426 | Ask yourself: Do I really need this? |

| 427 | Boycott |

428 Buycott

429 Create new markets

430 Create alternatives

431 Subscribe to CREDO cell service

432 Carry a Working Assets credit card

433 Choose a business that donates profits to good causes

434 Choose a business that respects its customers

435 Choose a business that treats workers with respect

436 Choose a business that embodies ethical practices

437 Choose a business that markets less

438 Choose a business that lobbies for the public good

439 Choose a business that takes action

440 Patronize the Better World Club

441 Patronize Organic Valley

442 Patronize 3R Living

443 Patronize Etsy

444 Patronize the Progressive Book Club

445 Beware: plastic

446 Buy now: used goods

447 Beware: made in China

448 Buy now: local, handmade

449 Beware: unaccountability

450 Buy now: anything from a lemonade stand

451 Eat liberally

452 Purchase food that is organic

453 Purchase food that is locally grown

454 Purchase food that is grass-fed

455 Purchase food that is Fair Trade

456 Purchase food that is biodynamic

457 Consider a retrovore lifestyle

458 Eat less meat

459 Cut back on industrially produced eggs and dairy

460 Support your local food producers

461 Limit your consumption of processed, convenience foods

462 Reduce food waste

463 Convert kitchen scraps into black gold by composting

464 Take the time to make a meal from scratch

465 Buy food from local shops

466 Shop at farmers' markets

467 Join CSAs/Farm-Shares

468 Join a food co-op

469 Push your supermarkets

470 Advocate for food access

471 Drink locally

472 Support microbrews

473 Try craft beer

474 Toast labor

475 Drink green

476 Drink Magic Hat

477 Drink New Belgium Brewery

478 Drink Maker's Mark

479 Confront the ills of alcohol

480 Drink politically

481 Go dry on Coors

482 Tell Anheuser-Busch to stand against the Chamber

483 Stop drinking Guinness and Johnnie Walker

484 Switch to a credit union

485 Visit the Credit Union Co-op

486 Learn about socially responsible investment

487 Check out the Social Investment Forum

488 Look to Social Funds for ideas on socially responsible investment

489 Learn about Domini for socially responsible investment

490 Start your own investment club

491 Be a conscious shareholder

492 Use those proxy votes

493 Organize a shareholder resolution

494 Sell shares to send a message

495 Ask about distribution of wealth in businesses in which you invest

496 Ask how the business behaves in new communities

497 Ask for a plan to reduce your carbon footprint from businesses in which you invest

498 Get others joining you in asking for better practices from businesses in which you invest

499 Elect representatives who reflect our ideals

500 Push those people who are in power

501 Involve ourselves in issues we face as society

502 March in the Fourth of July parade as a liberal

503 Host community barbecues

504 Paint a friend's home with fellow liberals

505 Raise money to pay fines incurred by antiwar activists

506 Do community service along with teens punished for antiwar activism

507 Organize safe, legal protests for teens

508 Host a Loving Day celebration

509 Make a social event out of canvassing

510 Host Candidates Gone Wild

511 Host Mayoroke

512 Participate in Trick or Vote

513 Throw a field day party the weekend before Election Day

514 Organize blueberry picking to teach agricultural education

515 Take a bike trip to teach open-space advocacy

516 Invite your community to an election day party

517 Support HeadCount

518 Get involved with Get In The Game

519 Make political calls from a park

520 Organize house parties around swing-state calls

521 Throw a party the Sunday before the primary

522 Host a political St. Patrick's Day breakfast

523 Attend the Tom Harkin Steak Fry

524 Contribute to campaigns

525 Work with disenfranchised communities

526 Testify at City Council

527 Make volunteering easy

528 Organize volunteer activities in ways convenient to the volunteers

529 Bring actions to the volunteers

530 Remember to translate for volunteers

531 Make volunteering social

532 Make it easy to invite friends to volunteer

533 Keep volunteering casual

534 Host an after party for volunteers

535 Make volunteering rewarding

536 Lay out the big picture to volunteers

537 Mark progress and celebrate victories with volunteers

538 Say thank you

Who *REALLY* Killed Martin Luther King Jr.?

The Case Against Lyndon B. Johnson
and J. Edgar Hoover

Phillip F. Nelson

New Foreword by Edgar F. Tatro
New Afterword by Phillip F. Nelson

Skyhorse Publishing

Library of Congress Cataloging-in-Publication Data is available on file.

Cover design by Brian Peterson

Print ISBN: 978-1-5107-5014-2
Ebook ISBN: 978-1-5107-3107-3

Printed in the United States of America

CONTENTS

ACKNOWLEDGMENTS

As improbable as it seems in this, my fourth and final book on the life and times of Lyndon B. Johnson, I want to put in a word of posthumous thanks to none other than . . . Lyndon B. Johnson. Though quite indirect and inadvertent, possibly even cosmic—with no knowledge on his part of how he provided the best incentive for me to be the first in my family to graduate from college through the draft deferment given to college students in the 1960s—I had, from about July 1960 on, felt an intrinsic distrust of him, just from reading contemporaneous news articles about his involvement in various scandals and other subtle signs of what seemed to be chronic criminal conduct. Without that distrust, I would never have worked so hard in my "retirement" to pursue these works, which I felt were necessary to counteract the many fawning and obsequious paeans that have been written about him— initially at his personal direction, now perpetuated by servile, uninformed lackeys. One such essay, by Leo Janos, was published in the July 1973 issue of the *Atlantic Monthly*, shortly after Johnson's death. It reads in part:

> His first year in retirement was crowded with projects. He supervised nearly every construction detail of the massive LBJ Library complex on the University of Texas campus, which houses not only thirty-one million documents acquired over thirty-eight years in Washington, but also the LBJ School of Public Affairs. At one point, university regent Frank Erwin approached Johnson about an Indiana educator who was interested in running the LBJ School. Johnson frowned at the mention of the state which sent to the Senate one of Johnson's least favorite persons, and among the most vocal of his war critics, Vance Hartke. "Frank," Johnson responded, "I never met a man from Indiana who was worth a shit."

As a Hoosier by birth, I take this presidential assessment of Indiana natives as the ultimate compliment and treasure it wholeheartedly. Like most of his pronouncements, the truth is the exact opposite of his assertion.

One of my earliest contacts in the JFK research community was a lady from Dallas named Betty Windsor, who had always preferred to stay far in the background because of her many extended connections to others who wished to protect their confidential relationships. She has now consented to allow me to reference her here, after the passing in May 2013 of her close friend Billie Sol Estes, whom she got to know after his release from prison. Estes had been rehabilitated by that experience—and his disassociation with Lyndon Johnson—through the efforts of US Marshal Clint Peoples, the former Texas Ranger who guided him onto a path of atonement for his past sins. Betty eventually became Estes's close friend and knew that he had become much more trustworthy in the final decades of his life. Despite that, people who did not know him well continued to portray him as a villain in books as recently as 2016. Betty's stellar reputation, recognized by dozens of the most prominent longtime researchers in that community, vouches for the turnaround in Estes's credibility as nothing else could. When he died, he was at peace with himself, knowing that in his final decades he had redeemed himself by admitting the sins of his past and revealing the truth about his long-term criminal conduct as a facilitator of Lyndon Johnson's nefarious schemes. Estes realized, while Johnson was still alive, that he could never separate himself from Johnson—that was guaranteed by the five associates of his who had been "suicided"—but after he had done his time, he redeemed himself by exposing the secrets related to their joint crimes.

During the last several years, as I became more and more involved in the research of Johnson's treacheries, fortunately I got to know the widely respected researcher Edgar Tatro, who generously provided his thoughtful assistance to me during the development of the previous books, and again for this one. He was one of the earliest of the many JFK assassination researchers, a man who could truly be considered as the finest exemplar of that iconoclastic group doggedly following the evidence as it unfolded, wherever it led. Tatro's involvement began immediately after JFK's assassination, and then Oswald's two days later, when his father told him there was something very "wrong" about what was happening. He subsequently examined the anomalies and cover-ups related to the other 1960s assassinations and the Jim Garrison investigation and trial that followed, when Ed drove through a major blizzard to attend some of that event. Coming onto the scene as a recent college graduate, he amazingly became friends with the judge in that trial. Ed described how the judge invited him into his chambers to discuss the progress of the trial:

> When I first met Judge Edward Haggerty, I told him I had driven all the way from Boston to reach his court and that I had been studying the JFK assassination since it had occurred. He

asked me a series of questions about the case and I knew the answers. He replied, "You know your stuff, don't you boy?" I said, "Yes sir," and he wrote out a pass for me to attend the trial. He also instructed me to tell the bailiff that he wanted to see me before I returned home because I only had the week off due to the February school vacation.

On my last day, a Friday, when I told the bailiff that the judge wanted to see me in his chambers, the press had all left the courtroom. Only Clay Shaw and his lawyers were still present. I think it would be safe to say that Shaw and his lawyers seemed stunned and concerned when I looked at their faces as the bailiff invited me to come to the entrance door to Judge Haggerty's chambers, especially since I had sat behind Mr. Shaw and we had interacted occasionally during the proceedings, particularly when the judge had decided to deny a directed verdict, which would have freed the defendant right then and there.

The judge allowed me to look at all the court exhibits on display in his chambers including still color frames of the Zapruder film. The judge made it clear to me that he was impressed with the testimony of Dr. John Nichols, a medical expert in forensic pathology, who asserted that the film confirmed that a shot had originated from the right front due to JFK's head movement to the back and left. (Eventually, I corresponded with Dr. Nichols prior to his untimely death.) There was no doubt that Judge Edward Haggerty believed there was a conspiracy to assassinate President Kennedy. I was only twenty-two years old then, but in retrospect, I can say with certainty that if I had exited his chambers and talked to the press outside the courthouse about what the judge had just admitted, there would have been a mistrial and my name and photo would have been plastered all across the world on television and newspapers, but that thought never even occurred to me.

At that point, Ed had just begun his first teaching job, at a high school in Quincy, Massachusetts. He continued on, through the Watergate episode of the early 1970s and then the HSCA investigation, as he prodded various congressmen to pursue unresolved anomalies, despite the inevitable failure of that effort as the political axes fell, crushing what remained of that fleeting awakening. Ed's incisive analysis of unfolding political scandals and crises since then have helped many others, especially his high school students, in developing the critical thinking skills required to fully understand current events. In all, his legacy is that of a truth-seeking, iconoclastic researcher/ historian and erudite philosopher who has few genuine peers.

In 2016, Ed introduced me to Victoria Powell Sulzer, who, coincidentally, had been a student in a lower-age class at Beauregard Jr. High School, at the same time that Lee Harvey Oswald had attended there. Later she became an acquaintance and neighbor of Dr. Mary Sherman, a prominent orthopedic specialist and surgeon, then working at the famed Oschner Clinic in New Orleans. They lived as neighbors at the Patio Apartments in New Orleans in 1963 and the first half of 1964, until Sherman's mysterious and truly gruesome murder in July of that year, a case still open and unresolved.* For the ensuing five decades, she has devoted herself to being a mother of six children while pursuing her career as an educator and becoming a self-taught artist, practicing her lifelong philosophy of what many New Orleanians call "savoir-faire," being gracious and respectful through kindness and gratitude to others. In that spirit, Victoria graciously provided me with information about the existence, and importance, of Judge William H. Williams's files from the Tennessee Court of Appeals, which he had gifted to the University of North Carolina—Chapel Hill, where I reviewed them. His position on that court put Judge Williams in a nearly-unique position from which to witness and chronicle the adjudication process involving the state's case against James Earl Ray. I doubt that I would ever have made that discovery without her having informed me about them, and those files turned out to be essential to my understanding of their pertinence relative to the state's frail and tenuous "case" against James Earl Ray. Judge Williams's collection consolidates most of Ray's attorney-related correspondence and legal documents associated with the case into a single location and is a valuable resource for researchers.

Another longtime researcher and author who has been helpful to me for nearly a decade is Dr. Gerald D. McKnight, Professor Emeritus at Hood College in Frederick, Maryland. His book *The Last Crusade: Martin Luther King Jr., the FBI, and the Poor People's Campaign* proved to be one of the key sources for me regarding Dr. King's last campaign, which was clearly hijacked by many of the powers that be in Washington, all of whom were furious with King for having the temerity to plan to bring his followers right into the center of the city, where they were to set up a long-term camp of ramshackle tents and shanties on the Washington Mall. To say that many people—led

---

* For more information on Dr. Sherman, see *Dr. Mary's Monkey* (TrineDay Publishing, 2007, 2015) by Edward T. Haslam.

in large part by an enraged Senator Robert C. Byrd of West Virginia—were highly agitated by this turn of events is a definite understatement. As Dr. McKnight described it, the scene was that of a "siege mentality settling over Washington" that allowed the plotters "to exploit it for their own political ends."

Gary Revel was yet another researcher who worked on the case over many years and provided me with a number of important insights. He began his involvement in the mid-1970s as an investigator for James Earl Ray's attorneys, Jack Kershaw and Mary Noel-Kershaw. His name can be found in the HSCA volumes in the National Archives. A song entitled "They Slew the Dreamer" was later written by Revel and Mary Noel-Kershaw as an elegiac reflection of the trauma and long-term damage done to America as a consequence of the murder of Martin Luther King Jr. The song, available on iTunes and other music venues, recently marked its fortieth anniversary; it includes segments of the real-time police recording made in the immediate aftermath of the assassination.

Saint John Hunt, son of CIA official E. Howard Hunt, was also helpful in sorting through the "wilderness of windows" left behind by his father's friends and associates. Having seen much of the 1960s cloak-and-dagger capers from his front-row seat as a teenager, he developed a natural instinct for knowing where the bodies were buried and the critical thinking skills for evaluating long-buried secrets.

Another consistent supporter of my work, Professor David Denton, has allowed me the opportunity to present this book at the Washington, DC, conference titled "THE BIG EVENT: New Revelations in the JFK Assassination and the Forces Behind His Death" in March, 2018. Though seemingly unrelated to that subject, there were a number of parallels and connections between the two, as will be revealed in the latter chapters of this book, and to the fact that certain records pertaining only to the Martin Luther King Jr. murder—to be cited within this book—were inexplicably released as part of the opening of previously classified files from the JFK assassination.

Finally, and of utmost importance, I am indebted to the many other researchers and authors of books, news articles, and other publications cited within the narrative that were devoted to uncovering the truths that have been revealed. It should be noted that the sources I've named within the narrative that were *not* written with this objective—although they are listed in the bibliography, since they have been cited repeatedly—still helped to frame this story, albeit indirectly. They formed the contrast relief, the construct that portrayed a myth created in real time and extended practically every decade since, a fable of a man falsely accused of being a "vicious Southern racist and stalker-murderer" of Dr. Martin Luther King Jr. We know now that Ray was actually none of those five adjectives originally created by William Bradford Huie—he was not even a "Southerner"—and that will be proved within the pages to follow. In the five ensuing decades, numerous other books, also to be examined in detail, were written to sustain the original myths and—to this day, unfortunately—continue to form the widely-held, but now proven false, public perception of James Earl Ray.

Huie was the original author contracted by the plotters to create that myth and earned the infamy that is now being exposed more clearly than ever previously presented. It should become self-evident, by the end of this book, that Huie had been recruited—based upon his decades-long associations with both J. Edgar Hoover and Clyde Tolson—to create both that meme about Ray as well as the numerous lies he planted that became the basis of the myth we will examine that successfully, but falsely, convinced an entire nation that James Earl Ray was the assassin of Martin Luther King Jr.

A partial list of some of the most important truth-telling books would start with Dr. William F. Pepper, whose tireless efforts spanned nearly the entire five decades since Dr. King's death. His latest book, *The Plot to Kill King: The Truth Behind the Assassination of Martin Luther King Jr.*, can be considered as the keystone around which this work was built. Several other books, without which this book would not exist, were similarly very valuable. Among the many other books listed in the bibliography, those by the following authors are in this factually accurate category: Taylor Branch, John Avery Emison, Mark Lane and Dick Gregory, Dr. Philip H. Melanson, Athan Theoharis, and Harold Weisberg. The books by James Earl Ray himself, and those by his two brothers, Jerry Ray (with Tamara Carter) and John Larry Ray (with Lyndon Barsten), were also critically important in completing a mosaic of what I believe is the truest and most complete account of the real story behind the murder of Dr. Martin Luther King Jr.

Whether or not this book succeeds in its goal of deconstructing the original myths related to the murder of Martin Luther King Jr., the promise of Shakespeare that eventually ". . . the truth will out" is enough to have us believe that it might help future generations to learn the complete truth of Dr. King's murder.

FOREWORD
LYNDON BAINES JOHNSON: THE CHARLATAN LIBERAL

BY EDGAR F. TATRO

Having spent a major portion of my adult life investigating the criminal history of Lyndon Baines Johnson, a documented sexist, sexual predator, hypocrite, liar, cheapskate, narcissist, thief, blackmailer, bully, and conspirator in multiple murders, it is LBJ the racist whom figures most prominently in Phil Nelson's *Who Really Killed Martin Luther King Jr.?*

Phil's meticulously detailed prologue exposes the shameless and Machiavellian macrocosm central to Johnson's political agenda—the clever ploy to pass civil rights legislation in a devious attempt to create a facade to falsely show his presidency in a liberal and historic light—and that bigotry in overdrive helped give birth to political assassination.

Herein, it is my intention to expose the microcosm of LBJ's amoral inner core: a brief, succinct behind-the-scenes peek at a more up-close-and-personal racism inherent in the man. Brevity is mandatory in a foreword, but the following vignettes and quotes unearthed by diverse historians and researchers and courageous whistleblowers should convince the reader to digest Phil Nelson's insightful and scholarly tome with an open mind.

Are you ready?

***

During the 1964 Democratic Convention, a top official of a major television network picked up the phone to hear Lyndon Johnson, the president of the United States, growl, "Get your God damn cameras off the niggers out front, (civil rights protesters from Mississippi), and back on the speaker's stand inside, Goddamn it!"[1]

***

When he was a youngster, Johnson would throw rocks at black kids to scatter them in all directions away from the local swimming hole. As a congressman, when he would return to Texas, he would place snakes in his car trunk, then ask a black gas station attendant to check his spare tire and laugh with glee as the poor guy would react in horror and fear at the snakes.[2]

******

In January of 1964, he told a friend from Texas—"I'm gonna try to teach these nigras that don't know anything how to work for themselves instead of just breedin'. I'm gonna try to teach these Mexicans who can't talk English to learn it so they can work for themselves...and get off our taxpayers' back."[3]

***

In his 2005 autobiography, Billie Sol Estes, the notorious convicted Texas wheeler-dealer, wrote, "One of (Lyndon's) most annoying faults was his dislike for blacks. In private, he used the 'N' word, but as a politician, he courted their votes." Estes admitted that LBJ's racism and hypocrisy were some of the reasons that he testified before a grand jury in 1984 about Johnson's ordering the "hit" of agricultural official, Henry Marshall.[4]

***

During his presidency, Johnson asked Larry Temple, an attorney for LBJ's best friend, Texas Governor John Connally, his thoughts regarding the appointment of a black man to the Supreme Court. Temple recommended Judge A. Leon Higginbotham, a federal district judge from Pennsylvania. Johnson told Temple, "The only two people who ever heard of Judge Higginbotham are you and his momma. When I appoint a nigger to the bench, I want everyone to know he's a nigger."[5]

***

Warren Trammell, the son of Seymore Trammell, who was a primary adviser to Alabama's George Wallace during Wallace's tenure as governor, sent an email to a Texas JFK researcher on August 28, 2013 about his 1965 visit to the White House Oval Office with his father and Lyndon Johnson. The key discussion centered around the civil rights protests in Alabama. According to Seymore Trammell, LBJ ranted, "Now you boys, you gotta get your God damned asses back down to Alabama and make those God damned niggers act right and calm the hell down! I am God damned tired of hearing 'bout those God damned niggers on the God damned news every night...."

* * *

Even Johnson's political pawn, Bill Moyers, offered another glimpse of LBJ's exploitation of racial divides in the Washington Post on November 13, 1988. One night after drinking in a hotel in Tennessee, Johnson commented on the racially-charged signs they had seen earlier in the day during a political motorcade. He told Moyers, "I'll tell you what's at the bottom of it. If you can convince the lowest white man he's better than the best colored man, he won't notice you're picking his pocket. Hell, give him somebody to look down on, and he'll empty his pockets for you."

* * *

The most eye-opening and truly despicable anecdotes corroborating Lyndon Johnson as a racist were documented by an unlikely source: a black insider, Robert Parker Jr., who was a waiter, cook, messenger, and chauffeur for LBJ and other Washington politicians. Parker's ability to tolerate abuse and obey orders for the sake of a paycheck and his family's wellbeing eventually led him to the position of maître' d of the United States Senate Dining Room from 1964 until his retirement in 1975.

Parker admitted that Johnson never called him by his name. He was always called "Boy," "Nigger," or "Chief". When Johnson, as a senator, asked him in the back seat of his car once if it bothered him when people didn't call him by name, the black chauffeur cautiously responded, "Well, sir, I do wonder. My name is Robert Parker."

Johnson shouted, "Let me tell you one thing, nigger. As long as you are black, and you're gonna be black 'til the day you die, no one's gonna call you by your God damn name. So no matter what you are called, nigger, you just let it roll off your back like water, and you'll make it. Just pretend you're a God damn piece of furniture."[6]

Whenever Parker was late picking Johnson up from an event, Johnson would call him a lazy, good-for-nothing nigger. Parker wrote, "He especially like to call me 'Nigger' in front of southerners and racists like Richard Russell. It was, I soon learned, LBJ's way of being one of the boys." In private, Johnson would soften a bit and say, "I can't be too good on you. I don't want to be called a 'nigger lover.'"[7]

* * *

In 1954, Johnson missed an important senate vote because he was stuck between floors on a broken elevator. A black waiter named Lamb was stuck with him and Johnson was kind and considerate during the wait. The two men sat together on the floor while mechanics corrected the problem. The next morning, a reelection year in the balance, Johnson issued orders that, from now on, colored waiters would deliver food only by way of the stairs. The Texas newspapers loved it and Johnson won the 1954 election in a landslide unlike his stolen victory in 1948. One of LBJ's friends commented later, "Lyndon, you shoulda had a nigger on the elevator in 1948." Johnson agreed and replied, "Yeah, it's always good to have a nigger in the woodpile."[8]

***

Having established the basics confirming LBJ as an unmitigated bigot, it also seems fitting to substantiate his total disdain for human beings, his dark void of empathy for anyone but himself. Bill Gulley, the director of the White House Military Office, became a whistle blower extraordinaire in 1980 with his book, *Breaking Cover*. The book detailed a wide array of illicit financial abuses by LBJ of the Military Office Secret Fund and the White House Communication Agency for his own personal use and to enhance many areas of the LBJ Ranch in Texas, but it was one singular quote from LBJ which stayed with Gulley permanently: "Just you remember this: there's only two kinds at the White House. There's elephants and there's pissants. And I'm the only elephant."[9]

***

Air Force One steward Robert MacMillan's recollections are strikingly similar to those of Robert Parker and Bill Gulley. McMillan said LBJ often referred to staff members as "You damn fools" or "Boy," but he noted Johnson's contempt was also directed at the American public. MacMillan said, "Johnson would come on the plane, and the minute he got out of sight of the crowds, he would stand in the doorway and grin from ear to ear, and say, 'You dumb sons of bitches. I piss on all of you.'" MacMillan's overview of Johnson was profoundly sobering: "I doubt that there was a day in Johnson's life in the White House that he didn't do something that was dishonest."[10]

***

Senator Barry Goldwater summarized the essence of Lyndon Johnson as well as any politician who had dealt with him: "The last thing Lyndon Johnson wanted to do in life was talk political principles or beliefs. He wouldn't do it. LBJ never believed in either. His only political dogma was expediency. Things were never right or wrong. Most problems in the country could be fixed with cunning and craftiness. He never cleaned that crap off his boots. It trailed him from the senate to the vice presidency and into the Oval Office itself. There's an old saying out in Arizona: If you get down in the manure, you come up smelling like it."[11]

***

LBJ's press secretary, George Reedy, a brilliant writer and an astute analyst of Johnson's psyche, wrote, "As a human being, he was a miserable person—a bully, sadist, lout, and an egotist. He had no sense of loyalty (despite his protestations that it was the quality he valued above all others) and he enjoyed tormenting those who had done the most for him. He seemed to take a special delight in humiliating those who had cast in their lot with him. It may well be that this was the result of a form of self-loathing in which he concluded that there had to be something wrong with anyone who would associate with him."[12]

***

Jerry Bruno, the primary advance man for JFK's Texas trip in 1963 and a devout and patriotic loyalist to President Kennedy, knew that LBJ's key henchmen were responsible for setting up the Dealey Plaza deathtrap, which included tall unsecured buildings, extreme right angle motorcade turns, and plenty of potential sniper lairs by forcing the motorcade to travel to the Trade Mart instead of his choice, the Women's Building.[13]

In Bruno's memoirs, he perceived a metaphorical parallel to Adolph Hitler: "There's a story that's told about Hitler.....Hitler was reviewing the troops one day, and somewhere in the ranks, a man sneezed.

"'Who sneezed?' Hitler says. No answer.

"'Who sneezed?' Hitler shouts. Nothing. So he orders the whole front row of troops mowed down with a machine gun.

"'Now who sneezed?' Hitler says.

"And from way in the back comes this voice, 'I did, Mein Fuhrer.'

"'Oh,' says Hitler, 'Gesundheit.'

"There's something about that in Lyndon Johnson."[14]

***

Please realize that these examples cited are the proverbial tip of the amoral Johnson glacier, but, hopefully, my brief primer has offered the reader at least a sobering snapshot at Lyndon Baines Johnson, a true master of amoral, outrageous acts and racist beliefs, the "Mr. Hyde" of his generation. Now it is time to read Phil Nelson's book to judge for yourself *Who Really Killed Martin Luther King Jr.!*

ENDNOTES

1. Robert Sherrill, *The Accidental President*, (New York: Grossman Publishers, 1967), p. 19.
2. Robert A. Caro, *The Years of Lyndon Johnson: Master of the Senate*, (New York; Alfred A. Knopf, 2002), p. 715. D. Jablow Hershmann, *Power Beyond Reason: The Mental Collapse of Lyndon Johnson*, (Fort Lee, New Jersey: Barricade, 2002), p. 30.
3. Robert Dallek, *Flawed Giant*, (New York: Oxford University Press, 1998), pp. 111-112.
4. Billie Sol Estes, *Billie Sol Estes, A Texas Legend*, (Granbury, Texas: BS Productions, 2005). For more information regarding the murder of Henry Marshall, go to *Youtube* and type "The Guilty Men," Part IX of "The Men Who Killed Kennedy' series, broadcast on The History Channel in November, 2003.
5. Dallek, *Flawed Giant, p. 441*.
6. Robert Parker, *Capitol Hill in Black and White*, (New York: Dodd, Mead and Company, 1986), P. V.
7. ibid. p. 16.
8. ibid. p. 77.
9. Bill Gulley with Mary Ellen Reese, *Breaking Cover*, (New York; Simon and Schuster, 1980), pp. 44-45.
10. Ronald Kessler, *Inside The White House*, (New York: Pocket Books, 1995), pp. 25-27.
11. Barry Goldwater, *With No Apologies*,(New York: Berkley Books, 1979), pp. 51-52.
12. George Reedy, *Lyndon B. Johnson: A Memoir*, (New York: Andrews and McMeel Inc., 1982), p. 127.
13. Personal papers of Jerry Bruno at the JFK Library, Boston, Massachusetts. House Select Committee on Assassinations: Jerry Bruno file at the National Archives in College Park, Maryland. Jerry Bruno and Jeff Greenfield, *The Advance Man*, (New York: Bantam Books, 1971).
14. Bruno and Greenfield, pp. 97-98.

PROLOGUE

"For the habitual truth-teller and truth-seeker, indeed, the world has very little liking. He is always unpopular, and not infrequently his unpopularity is so excessive that it endangers his life . . . In no field can he count upon a friendly audience, and freedom from assault. Especially in the United States is his whole enterprise viewed with bilious eye. The men the American people admire most extravagantly are the most daring liars; the men they detest most violently are those who try to tell them the truth."

—H. L. Mencken (1880–1956),
American journalist, editor, and satirist

Of the three major political assassinations of the 1960s, only the murder of Dr. Martin Luther King Jr. is considered by many people as having been solved shortly afterwards, with the alleged assassin's plea of "guilty." Yet that presumption is just as erroneous as the government's "official" verdicts in the case of JFK's assassination (that Lee Harvey Oswald was the sole assassin) and RFK's murder (that Sirhan B. Sirhan was the sole assassin). The premise of James Earl Ray's guilt is based upon a provably false narrative constructed of lies and deceit that was designed years in advance by the same plotters who organized Dr. King's murder.

By the time of Ray's aborted "trial" in March 1969, the primary chronicler of the government's "official" account, William Bradford Huie, had already written two articles in *Look* magazine (November 12 and 26, 1968) to begin setting the primary themes. Just a few weeks after the plea bargain hearing—the intentionally flawed, final legal proceeding Ray would ever receive—Huie wrote a third installment (April 15, 1969), effectively "proving" Ray's guilt to everyone in the country. Huie then published his 1970 book, *He Slew the Dreamer* (a title that was changed from what he originally promised Ray: "They" was replaced with "He"), which was considered the basis for the government's official account by the FBI and Department of Justice and, in 1976–79, the House Select Committee on Assassinations (HSCA), which referenced it repeatedly.

Two subsequent books—Gerold Frank's *An American Death: The True Story of the Assassination of Dr. Martin Luther King, Jr. and the Greatest Manhunt of Our Time* in 1972 and George McMillan's *The Making of an Assassin: The Life of James Earl Ray* in 1976—added more finality to the presumption of Ray's guilt. A decade later, the US House Select Committee on Assassinations (HSCA) would use these combined works as the baseline for its report.

Interestingly, the HSCA investigators—basing their "investigation" on those works of fiction—would ignore the more factual and scholarly accounts by such early researchers as Clay Blair Jr., Harold Weisberg, and Mark Lane in their focus on the Huie, Frank, and McMillan books, as will be conclusively demonstrated in this book. Furthermore, as I will examine in detail in Chapter 11, the HSCA set out to brazenly and brutally attack Mark Lane, an effort that was derailed only because one staffer alerted him to it and he was able to turn it around, exposing the scurrilous plot that was traced back to the highest-level federal officials, the same ones who were supposedly attempting to find the truths behind JFK's and MLK's assassinations.

This book will methodically deconstruct the thesis presented by these earliest authors and governmental authorities, as well as the books of subsequent popular authors (read: "novelists") that were based upon those first books: Gerald Posner's 1998 *Killing the Dream: James Earl Ray and the Assassination of Martin Luther King Jr.* and the 2010 *Hellhound on His Trail: The Electrifying Account of the Largest Manhunt in American History* by Hampton Sides. Other similarly tainted, lesser-known books, such as those by Lamar Waldron, Stuart Wexler, Larry Hancock, and Pate McMichael, will also be noted—and their premises similarly debunked.

Lessons from History

Winston Churchill famously said, "History is written by the victors." Truth is often the first casualty in the aftermath of conflict. The creation of mythological stories about real-life historical figures has become entrenched in every facet of American culture for a very long time. It can be argued that the legacies of many of the founders and early presidents—from Thomas Jefferson to Abraham Lincoln—have been written in such a way as to hide or minimize their less noble acts and highlight their most glorious accomplishments.

Likewise, the same phenomenon has prevailed with modern-day politicians fortunate enough to succeed to the highest offices. In the case of mid-twentieth-century leaders, it has taken nearly five decades for truth-seekers to sift out the myths—composed of subtle deceits and brazen lies—from the basest pure truths. President Lyndon Johnson and FBI Director J. Edgar Hoover are the clearest examples of how the tension between myths and truths is still being wrought, in a continuing cultural movement that has no end in sight.

Three days before the opening of the movie *Selma*,* the self-described "historian" Mark Updegrove (the previous director—and recently named president—of the taxpayer-financed Lyndon Baines Johnson Presidential Library), having seen a preview, then wrote a critical review, as if to prove Churchill's original point. His article, published in Politico ("What 'Selma' Gets Wrong," December 22, 2014), stated that the movie distorted the relationship between President Johnson and the civil rights leader. Ironically, Updegrove claimed that the movie misrepresented historical truth when in fact it is Updegrove's narrative that repeats the sanitized, mythical "history" of what was, in reality, a highly fractured, poisoned, and extremely short relationship between LBJ and MLK as their narrow mutual goals briefly intersected with their individual pursuits. Updegrove wrote:

> *Selma* misses mightily in faithfully capturing the pivotal relationship—contentious, the film would have you believe— between King and President Lyndon Baines Johnson. In the film, President Johnson resists King's pressure to sign a voting rights bill, which—according to the movie's take—is getting in the way of dozens of other Great Society legislative priorities. Indeed, *Selma*'s obstructionist LBJ is devoid of any palpable conviction on voting rights. Vainglorious and power hungry, he unleashes his zealous pit bull, FBI chief J. Edgar Hoover, on King, who is determined to march in protest from Selma to Montgomery despite LBJ's warning that it will be "open season" on the protesters. This characterization of the 36th president flies in the face of history. In truth, the partnership between LBJ and MLK on civil rights is one of the most productive and consequential in American history.

Mr. Updegrove went on to describe how Johnson then instructed King on what steps he needed to take with his followers to inform the public about the worst cases of voter discrimination (as if King's many followers had not already thought of that, and in fact had already spent much time informing the national public of such bigotry, widely and repeatedly). Throughout his article, Updegrove portrayed the Johnson-King relationship as uniformly friendly and positive, as when he quoted President Obama on that point: "Like Dr. King, like Abraham Lincoln, like countless citizens who have

---

* Paramount Pictures, 2014. Directed by Ava DuVernay—starring David Oyelowo as Martin Luther King and Tom Wilkinson as Lyndon B. Johnson, with Oprah Winfrey and Cuba Gooding Jr.

driven this country inexorably forward, President Johnson knew that ours in the end is a story of optimism, a story of achievement and constant striving that is unique upon this earth . . ." President Obama, a gifted wordsmith, can only emulate some of his predecessors, including the master debater himself, Lyndon Baines Johnson.

As with so many other "historical" stories, the narrative of the Johnson-King relationship has been twisted, parsed, and skewed over the years from what was originally described by the actual participants. One account of that came from Andrew Young, then working side by side with King, as described by Dr. Gerald McKnight in his book *The Last Crusade*: ". . . there were ugly scenes in the Oval Office late in the war-ruined Johnson administration when the president, in one of his Texas-sized towering rages, referred to King as that 'goddamn nigger preacher.' Young recalled the deceptive signals emanating from the Johnson White House: *'on the surface we were being smiled at and granted grudging support; below the surface we were distrusted, resented and undercut.'*[1] (Emphasis added.)

Preeminent King biographer Taylor Branch, in his last book of a trilogy, *At Canaan's Edge: America in the King Years 1965–68*, compared Martin Luther King Jr. to Moses, who saw the promised land, Canaan, from Mount Nebo looking across the Jordan River; Moses died there, as King died in Memphis, in both cases just after having "seen" the promised land.[2] Branch stated that Johnson's treatment of King was "unpredictable," often going from "shared dreams" to a "towering, wounded snit."[3] Branch described the tension between them in August 1965, after a telephone conversation about the Watts race riot the previous week. Each recognized that the other man could not be relied on to achieve their own goals, yet to accomplish their narrow immediate objective, they had to get along and not let their distrust of the other become public: "Their skittish, intimate consultation left few clues that it would seal the last words on record between King and Lyndon Johnson. Unwittingly, they were saying goodbye."[4]

The fact that the period of their "collaboration" came to an end only months after it had begun, according to Branch, has not been widely reported, but it is essential for an understanding of the larger point regarding the short length of time that transpired before the "partnership" that Mr. Updegrove overly extolled came to an end. It had started in March 1965, shortly before King led the fifty-four-mile march from Selma to Montgomery; it quickly chilled a few weeks later and was effectively over after only five months of existence in August, 1965, after the Watts Riots in Los Angeles.

Moreover, Branch wrote, after Johnson hung up the phone at the end of their last conversation in 1965, he and the aides who had attended and overheard all of it laughed about King's refusal to back the presidential call for patriotic loyalty in the face of wartime conditions (the point had been discussed only briefly, as both seemed to walk on eggshells around that subject). They mocked King for "wobbly judgment and dubious political loyalty," which, combined with the 1965 riots that had just occurred in the Los Angeles ghetto of Watts, had raised the specter in their minds of an outrageous betrayal by the very group that should have been praising Johnson's policies. In the days after that telephone call, White House aides leaked false stories to news reporters about how strongly the president confronted Dr. King on his Vietnam position.[5] This narrative from Branch reveals more of the true nature of that "collaborative" period: it was one of distrust, derision, and mockery on the part of Johnson, whose real agenda was highly personal and selfish, never at all consonant with the noble aspirations of Dr. King.

On April 4, 1967, precisely one year before his murder in Memphis, when Dr. King delivered his speech at New York's Riverside Church about LBJ's Vietnam misadventure, they officially became bitter enemies. By that point, Johnson wouldn't even talk to him and often referred to him in the most vulgar and derisive language imaginable, as referenced in the previous paragraphs.

Taylor Branch's account, based upon his scholarly work that includes references to contemporaneous comments of Andrew Young as noted above, accurately portrays the real context of the Johnson/King relationship throughout the brief period of their collaboration to achieve their narrow and temporary mutual goals, but for opposite reasons. King's motives were noble, pure, and righteous. Johnson's goal was driven by his habitual cunning and guile, his basest instincts, which were anything but sincere or noble—because LBJ's motive was derived merely from his desire to create a contrived "presidential legacy" that would hide his deepest secrets. It was the natural result of his single greatest trait, as described by his own preeminent biographer, Robert Caro, who wrote that Johnson hungered for power ". . . in its most naked form, for power not to improve the lives of others, but to manipulate and dominate them, to bend them to his will . . . it was a hunger so fierce and consuming that no consideration of morality or ethics, no cost to himself—or to anyone else—could stand before it."[6]

Furthermore, Caro was told by a former aide to Johnson that there was never anything altruistic about Johnson's motives and that he had no real empathy for any of the causes he espoused, certainly not the civil rights of minorities, whom he disparaged and ridiculed. That aide (who spoke to Caro on condition of anonymity) stated that above all else, Johnson was a pragmatist who would do whatever was required to accomplish his own highly personal agenda of the moment. The aide then added: "There's nothing wrong with being pragmatic. Hell, a lot of us were pragmatic. But you have to believe in *something*. Lyndon Johnson believed in *nothing*, nothing but his own ambition."[7]

The actual, and historically accurate, Johnson/King relationship can only be understood if it is considered in the context of Lyndon Johnson's lifelong record of being a racist and segregationist. Throughout his career, he had aggressively resisted numerous attempts to eliminate the poll tax and literacy tests during the twenty-three-year period he served in the House and Senate. He then blocked every piece of meaningful civil rights legislation that had found its way into the Senate when he was its powerful majority leader. It was Lyndon Johnson who neutered the 1957 Civil Rights Act with a poison pill amendment that required violators of the act to be tried before state (all white), not federal, juries.

Many contemporary liberals such as Joseph Rauh, the president of Americans for Democratic Action, and A. Philip Randolph, a black vice president of the AFL-CIO, called the bill worthless, and "worse than no bill at all." As vice president, Johnson orchestrated southern congressional opposition to JFK's civil rights agenda and repeatedly warned JFK to go slow on the civil rights, voting rights, and open housing legislation that Kennedy had promised in his 1960 campaign. There was a reason that Johnson had resisted this overdue reform all those years: he was reserving these initiatives for himself, as he repeatedly cautioned President Kennedy to wait "until the time is right."

On Capitol Hill, throughout the years of his vice presidency, Johnson continued to lobby his "establishment" friends to stall that same legislation. This point was validated, ironically, in the November 22, 1963, issue of the *Dallas Times Herald*. The headline read: "Senior Senators Shrug off Attack—Thwarting JFK, Liberal Charges." The article stated, in part: "Sen. Joseph S. Clark's new charge that the 'Senate establishment' [of which Johnson was still in control, having upstaged the shy and professorial Mike Mansfield] is staging a sit-down strike against major Kennedy legislation left the targets of his attack unruffled today. *The Pennsylvania liberal told the Senate that Democratic Leader Mike Mansfield, Mont. was not responsible for so many key bills still being in committees. Clark said the impasse should be blamed on a 'Senate establishment' of senior, conservative senators.*" (Emphasis added.)

Immediately upon JFK's assassination, Lyndon Johnson made a 180-degree turn the moment he became president, as he began pressing his Senate "establishment" friends to finally pass the Kennedy slate of legislation that he had previously impeded. He did it because now that he was president, finally, "the time was right." A record number of 104 bills had by then been stalled in Congress, some as long as twenty years in the case of Medicare for the elderly.[8] As president, Johnson knew that his eventual "legacy" would require that his reputation be reframed with a visage similar to that of the "great presidents" like Washington, Lincoln, and his personal idol, Franklin Roosevelt; he wanted to be seen as a man of vision, whose name would reflect a character known for his brilliance, and as a generous, magnanimous, erudite leader of all American citizens. In other words, he wanted future generations to think of him as being a person who was opposite of his real attributes.

Yet in fact, Johnson only pressed Congress remotely and did none of the personal arm-twisting for the 1964 Civil Rights Act himself; he left it to Sen. Hubert Humphrey—then the putative vice-presidential candidate-in-waiting—to round up the votes, but he did give him detailed lobbying instructions by going through a list of every congressman and senator, explaining their strengths, weaknesses, and personal vulnerabilities.[9] Hugh Sidey, the syndicated *Time* magazine columnist, had gotten the story from Humphrey and wrote about what he had been told: "'Johnson knew how to woo people,' remembered Humphrey . . . 'He was sort of like a cowboy making love . . . He knew how to massage the senators.' Johnson knew whom to nurture, whom to threaten, and whom to push aside. The whole chamber seemed subject to his manipulation. *He played it like an organ. Goddamn, it was beautiful! It was just marvelous.*'"[10] (Emphasis added.)

Even though they tried, neither Johnson nor Humphrey could deliver all Democrats to vote for the 1964 Civil Rights Act, arguably the most important legislation of the twentieth century. In fact, some of the most famed liberals of their day voted against it, including Tennessee senator Al Gore Sr., Arkansas senator J. William Fulbright, and West Virginia senator Robert Byrd (Byrd even filibustered the bill on June 10, 1964, for over fourteen hours in his passionate attempt to derail it). It only passed because of the vigorous support of Senate Minority Leader Everett Dirksen and twenty-seven Senate Republicans; in the House, only 59 percent of Democrats voted in favor of the legislation, while 78 percent of Republicans supported it. Johnson had stripped the voting rights section—which had been in Kennedy's original bill—out of the 1964 bill, saving it for still another bill in 1965 so it would add yet another "bullet" for his legacy.

Of the many statements that demonstrate incontrovertible evidence of Johnson's true attitudes, none can match a comment he made to visiting governors, in explaining why the civil rights bill had become so important for him: "I'll have them niggers voting Democratic for two hundred years."[11]

One other pertinent Johnson maxim—contained in an otherwise obsequious account of Johnson's presidency—was noted by Doris Kearns Goodwin:

These Negroes, they're getting pretty uppity these days and that's a problem for us since they've got something now they never had before, the political pull to back up their uppityness. Now we've got to do something about this, we've got to give them a little something, just enough to quiet them down, not enough to make a difference. For if we don't move at all . . . we'll lose the filibuster and there'll be no way of putting a brake on all sorts of wild legislation.[12]

From Operation Mockingbird to Politically Correct Groupthink

President Johnson's real "greatest" legacy was the nascent phenomenon that George Orwell had warned the world about two decades earlier: "groupthink." Orwell was still writing his prescient novel, *1984*, at the time of the CIA's birth in 1947, but he could already foresee much of what the world could expect to look like in the decades ahead. The ravaged remains of World War II were still smoldering but were about to become the foundation of what would be called the Cold War, which would be fought with words. One of the early manifestations of this was the CIA's Operation Mockingbird.

In the 1950s, CIA director Allen Dulles put Frank Wisner in charge of establishing direct contacts between the agency and the Fourth Estate— the American press—journalists and book publishers who would willingly help the CIA communicate their view on any national or international political or military issue in a favorable light. The principal responsibility of the CIA's Office of Policy Coordination (OPC) and the Plans Division was conducting secret political operations, in contrast to the other agency functions of gathering intelligence and making analysis. In 1951, Wisner established Operation Mockingbird, a program to influence the American media. "Wisner recruited Philip Graham (*Washington Post*) to run the project within the industry," according to Deborah Davis in her 1979 biography of *Post* owner Katharine Graham, *Katharine the Great*: "By the early 1950s, Wisner 'owned' respected members of the *New York Times, Newsweek, CBS* and other communications vehicles."[13] These journalists sometimes wrote articles that were unofficially commissioned by Cord Meyer, based on leaked classified information from the CIA.

In the aftermath of the JFK assassination, the program was running at full tilt in the clamor to inject governmental propaganda into the news stream to replace the facts being brought to bear by the early researchers who were discovering multiple cases of official "disinformation" and outright fabrications. To combat this, by 1967, after the publication of at least a half dozen books by Warren Commission critics, the CIA decided to act. This was also simultaneous with a large segment of the public becoming highly aware of the governmental lies about the rationale of the Vietnam War. High-level CIA officials issued a memorandum that was intended for all of its agents and other operatives, but specifically targeted to its "media assets," originally part of Operation Mockingbird. Through their direct conduit to numerous publishers, newspaper columnists, and reporters, they fed a steady stream of propagandized "news" that they wanted to become accepted as the "official" news.

In April 1967, when their dispatch was issued, Mockingbird was still a secret and would not become widely known until decades later; even now, that code name is not recognized by many people, as one could easily prove by conducting "man on the street" interviews with one hundred randomly selected adults. Within that document (which can be viewed in Appendix D) the term "conspiracy theories" was coined. The message conferred a negative characterization and denigrating attitude onto whoever would critique the government on anything it might say or do. The memo also made suggestions of how their operatives might discredit such "theories." The dispatch was marked "psych"—short for "psychological operations," which would include disinformation and schemes to manipulate the public with propagandized, "fake" news.[14]

A Few Words About the Primary Sources for This Book

Many books have been written on the murder of Martin Luther King Jr., including three by Dr. William F. Pepper: *Orders to Kill: The Truth Behind the Murder of Martin Luther King* (1995); *An Act of State: The Execution of Martin Luther King* (2008); and *The Plot to Kill King: The Truth Behind the Assassination of Martin Luther King Jr.* (2016). The last two books essentially updated the earlier work as new research brought additional information into play. His website summarizes the latest book thusly:

> This myth-shattering exposé is a revised, updated, and heavily
> expanded volume of Pepper's original bestselling and critically
> acclaimed book *Orders to Kill*, with twenty-six years of addi-
> tional research included. The result reveals dramatic new details
> of the night of the murder, the trial, and why Ray was chosen
> to take the fall for an evil conspiracy—a government-sanctioned
> assassination of our nation's greatest leader. The plan, according

to Pepper, was for a team of United States Army Special Forces snipers to kill King, but just as they were taking aim, a backup civilian assassin pulled the trigger.

Among the dozens of other books, websites, original documents in library collections, and periodicals referenced within this book, Dr. Pepper's latest, *The Plot to Kill King*, stands apart from all others, as the singular tour de force of his four-decade-long investigative reportage. It succinctly captures the essence of the people, events, and timeline of a plot that began its development four years before the actual murder of Dr. King and has then continued on as a still-active cover-up operation for the last five decades. Dr. Pepper has devoted more than half his life to solving the enigma of Martin Luther King's murder. In addition to representing the accused assassin, James Earl Ray, in seeking the justice that he had been cruelly denied, he has courageously—and nearly singlehandedly—completed the investigation that should have been done by the FBI nearly half a century ago. But as he has amply demonstrated, since that was the organization primarily behind the setup for MLK's murder and cover-up, the reason for their failure to conduct that inquiry becomes painfully obvious.

Dr. William Pepper's book examines and reconstructs the plot to murder Dr. King, generally in the context of a "bottom-up" examination of forensic, ballistic, and pathological evidence; interviews with key witnesses; and extensive insights from Ray, the accused patsy, himself. It exposes the threads that connect all of these persons, places, and events to the men who gave the street-level orders, and from them to others higher up the ladder, right into the executive offices of the FBI. Dr. Pepper's conclusions may be summarized as (1) James Earl Ray did not kill Martin Luther King Jr., and (2) the murder of Dr. King was the result of a conspiracy by various federal and local law enforcement agencies, with assistance from the "Dixie Mafia,"* to eliminate him as a potential future political leader.

These claims are supported by ballistics tests (done nearly thirty years after the fact by Judge Joe Brown, as we will detail in Chapter 10) that

---

* The "Dixie Mafia" was and is a loosely-tied Southern U.S. manifestation of criminal enterprises ranging from illegal alcohol and drug and gun smuggling to fencing stolen merchandise, usually through money laundering facitilites such as pawn shops, strip clubs, and other "front" organizations, as well as other more deadly ventures when circumstances require(d). Mostly run by local, Southern-born white men whose small-time crimes led them into state-wide organizations at such small towns as Dothan, Alabama, Biloxi, Mississippi, and Caruthersville, Missouri, although most of their operations are conducted in the larger cities of the South. Ties between the heads of these organizations with the Italian Mafiaosi, particularly Carlos Marcello of New Orleans, were numerous, either in direct form (as with Joseph Campisi of Dallas or Frank Liberto of Memphis) or indirect, vicariously invoked as needed.

proved that Ray's gun was not involved in the shooting, as well as Ray's claims that he had been set up as a "patsy," just like Lee Harvey Oswald had been five years earlier. The evidence that Pepper assembled is persuasive and compelling proof of his assertions and conclusions. It proves, for example, that the shooter's location could not have been above Dr. King and to his right; the bullet taken from King did not match Ray's gun; there was evidence of another rifle and other clearly planted evidence; neither normal ballistics tests of the alleged weapon nor an autopsy of King was performed, as would be the normal procedure for any murder. Many other similarities to JFK's assassination were established by contemporary investigators and later by independent researchers, such as the fact that policemen and other officials destroyed the crime scene through mishandling and contaminating it, rendering it impossible to use for reliable forensic testing.

While Pepper's book is a primary source, it is just one of many that have been referenced in a narrative that blends the findings of practically all of the original researchers into a single coherent story line. Another important book listed in the bibliography, which was also a key source for these findings, is the 2008 book by John Larry Ray (James Earl Ray's brother) and Lyndon Barsten, *Truth at Last: The Untold Story Behind James Earl Ray and the Assassination of Martin Luther King*. Mr. Barsten interviewed scores of witnesses, investigators, and other researchers and reviewed over four thousand Freedom of Information Act (FOIA) records, including James Earl Ray's Army documents. His findings exposed a number of otherwise shadowy associates of Ray's, as well as accounts of how Ray was being repeatedly "sheep-dipped" by clandestine operatives and hypnotists, from Montreal to New Orleans and Los Angeles. While much of this background has not been repeated here, it has nevertheless been of great influence to me in understanding, thus describing, the complexity of how Ray had been managed, monitored, and controlled during his year of "freedom."

Among the numerous other primary sources are the 2015 *Murder in Memphis* by Mark Lane and Dick Gregory—an updated version of the 1977 original, previously titled *Code Name "Zorro"*; the 2014 *The Martin Luther King Congressional Cover-Up: The Railroading of James Earl Ray*, by John Avery Emison; Dr. Gerald D. McKnight's 1998 *The Last Crusade: Martin Luther King, Jr., the FBI, and the Poor People's Campaign*; Harold Weisberg's 1970 classic *Frame-Up*; and the book by James Earl Ray himself, *Who Killed Martin Luther King? The True Story by The Alleged Assassin*. These were all used as important primary references in the construction of a blended narrative that describes one of the greatest unsolved 1960s assassinations.

All of the key points include citations to the original sources for anyone wishing to validate them with further detail directly from those sources, all based upon nearly five decades of meticulous original research.

It is an extremely troubling story of government gone awry, plotting deadly retribution to a charismatic leader it viewed as a threat and then mounting a massive cover-up in order to protect the guilty. As we examine the details of the plot in the chapters to follow, it will become clear that the misuse of governmental power by a relatively few powerful key men was sufficient to accomplish high crimes and treasons. The crimes—committed, paradoxically, by the governmental entity originally created to investigate and bring law-breakers to justice during the nearly half-century tenure of J. Edgar Hoover—are legend, having been kept secret for as long as he was alive before the truths were slowly exposed. Many of them are now finally known to most reasonably informed citizens.

Yet the exposed crimes are only those closest to the surface. Many others were buried much deeper, and were kept hidden, but are now finally unraveled. Primary among them is the fact that the FBI's already well-known attacks on Dr. King, its attempts to "neutralize" him in the eyes of the public, were only the beginning. In the following pages, we will show that the plot to kill King was put into motion by the highest-level officials of the FBI, with help from certain Tennessee and Memphis politicians, a few key members of the Memphis police, units of the army's military intelligence, the CIA, and the leaders of the Dixie Mafia.

Connecting the people and entities directly involved in Dr. King's assassination are threads that led to the highest federal officials in Washington during this time frame. Those threads were partially revealed within the aforementioned books and many others cited within the narrative. This book will further expose those threads and connect them to others from yet other credible sources that were not included in any of the previous books. Those facts will then be distilled and presented from another prism, from the top down, tracing the plot from where it originated in the highest echelons of the federal government, and examine how the plot was hatched, planned, monitored, executed, and covered up. This view of the people, places, and events will be from the perspective of the plotters' seats, within the Oval Office of the White House and in the "Seat of Government" (SOG), the term coined by J. Edgar Hoover to describe himself at FBI headquarters, a few blocks down Pennsylvania Avenue.

In the context of the many other traumatic events that occurred throughout the 1960s, it is not hyperbole to stipulate what should now be obvious to anyone who has studied these events: that there was a reason for the repeating patterns of how they were executed—especially the commonalities of the cover-ups. It was because they were all done with either the instigation, the blessing, and/or the acquiescence of President Lyndon B. Johnson, using essentially the same resources that were uniquely available to him in his all-powerful position as president of the United States.

Some of the books referenced above have been viciously attacked by people and organizations who would prefer that certain lines not be crossed in the course of the investigation of this abominable crime, as though the paradigm they present allows only low-level hardened criminals to be eligible for scrutiny as the perpetrators of this and other murders of high-level leaders. That constraint, unfortunately, gives criminals in high places the "license to kill" their adversaries and might explain why the 1960s assassinations, for example—among other criminal acts committed through officials of the federal government—have never been solved to anyone's satisfaction. Except, of course, by those who actually facilitated them, or systematically covered them up, or those who carried them out through orders issued by their superiors in the military chain of command.

One of those attacks was directed to Dr. Pepper's latest work, *The Plot to Kill King*, in a review written by Martin Hay dated August 1, 2016, and published at the website of the organization known, paradoxically, as the CTKA (mistitled as "Citizens for Truth of the Kennedy Assassination"). That entity has recently been replaced by another site representing itself as being interested in solving the 1960s assassinations under the anonym "Kennedys and King," even though the same blinders are still being worn by the administrators of the new venue: their rules forbid any references to certain areas that they have deemed "out of bounds" (these include, but are not limited to, any suggestion that JFK's personal life might have compromised his security, or any assertion that Lyndon Johnson had direct involvement in JFK's assassination). A full point-by-point critique of that review, exposing the lengths to which some go in their efforts to hide real attempts to seek truths, is presented in Appendix A.

Ed Tatro, the iconoclastic long-term JFK assassination researcher, has described the reader's dilemma created by such propagandized, cherry-picked, and factually incorrect book reviews written with a preestablished—but hidden and unstated—objective of disparagement thusly:

> One must not only evaluate the credibility of the witness telling the event. One must also question the integrity of those who are judging the aforesaid witness. There is a fallacy entitled "selected preference," the selecting of evidence or testimony

which supports a previously determined answer or desired result. If the "Judge" harbors a hidden agenda or possesses a belief contrary to the testimony of the witness, the "Judge" will seek all kinds of rhetoric, all kinds of spin, and all kinds of manipulation to attempt to discredit the witness and the account which would, otherwise, undermine the "Judge's" previous beliefs or conclusions.

The Warren Commission and the 9/11 Commission are ideal government case studies for avoiding the truth and anyone or anything providing glimpses of it. Many lawyers are the masters of fallacies and misdirection and red herrings. Their job is to win, not necessarily determine truth or justice. The same can be said for many individuals who will never admit they are wrong about a particular issue. Henry Winkler's "The Fonz" could only utter, "I was wron . . . I was wron . . ." he could never finish the phrase. There are plenty of organizations and political writers and "talking heads" who are guilty of Fonzie's tragic flaw, but please be assured that fallacies, although illogical in some fashion, are very effective unless the audience is very well educated and possesses the acumen of a critical thinker.

Unfortunately, I am reminded of a quote attributed to Winston Churchill who once said, "The best argument against democracy is a five-minute conversation with the average voter." I am also reminded of a quote in the brilliant who-done-it murder mystery, *Sea of Love*, in which the homicide detective (played by Al Pacino) concludes, "People are a lot of work." Alas, selected preference and the employment of other fallacious machinations can misdirect the populace from seeing the truth in a very complex and messy world.

For the same reasons, many other researchers and authors have also come to distrust a significant number of so-called "JFK Truth" websites and blogs, suspecting that many of them are beholden to persons and entities intent on protecting their own narrow interests, ready to insert disinformation into the marketplace of ideas. Even the venerated Mary Ferrell website, despite its quasi-hallowed name, has a interesting past of which most people are unaware. One such researcher—John Kirsch, on his website "JFK: Researching the Researchers"—summed up his study of the Ferrell organization thusly: "Writing about the Ferrell foundation (or trying to) makes me feel like Lewis Carroll. I keep leaping down rabbit holes and staring into the looking glass."[15]

Researcher Harrison Edward Livingstone described Mary Ferrell's apparent objectives at length in his 1993 book *Killing the Truth: Deceit and Deception in the JFK Case*, summarizing all of it by calling her the "gatekeeper" and the head of a "sophisticated private intelligence operation . . . a *de facto* secret society in Texas, run by powerful people there, to protect the name and reputation of Texas and to protect those who were involved in the murder of John Kennedy."[16] Other organizations purporting to be in favor of finding the truth about the Kennedy and King assassinations have memberships so varied that they include not only people who are sincerely interested in finding the truth, but a number of members who openly oppose it, even some who support the most ludicrous forms of disinformation originally concocted by the Warren Commission—which should have been named after the man who had more to do with managing it, Allen Dulles.

Authors of Books Supporting the Original Myth: Government-Paid Shills?

Dr. Pepper devoted the entire twenty-eight-page epilogue—titled "DISINFORMATION"—of his latest book, *The Plot to Kill King*, to a critique of the multiple books published in the first decades after the assassination that were filled with lies and deceit; those books led to Pepper's systematic destruction of the fault-riddled HSCA "investigation." Clearly, the early books were created to establish a false narrative of the long-discredited official so-called "history" (more accurately called "mythology") of how the plotters themselves had portrayed the story.

It has been well documented by a number of authors, including James Earl Ray himself, that the story line for all of the original books on Martin Luther King Jr.'s assassination was being managed by Assistant FBI Director Cartha DeLoach to show—incorrectly—how Ray had purportedly denigrated blacks as a means of creating a motive. Indeed, DeLoach suggested to Hoover two days after Ray's purported "trial" that the Bureau "quietly sponsor a book that would tell the 'true story' of the King case."[17] DeLoach wrote a memorandum to Clyde Tolson on March 11, 1969 (a point originally discovered by Dr. Philip H. Melanson and presented in his 1991 book, *The Martin Luther King Assassination: New Revelations on the Conspiracy and Cover-Up*):

> Now that Ray has been convicted and is serving a 99-year sentence, I would like to suggest that the Director allow us to choose a friendly, capable author, or *The Reader's Digest*, and

proceed with a book based on this case. A carefully written factual book would do much to preserve the true history of this case. While it will not dispel or put down future rumors, it would certainly help to have a book of this nature on college and high school library shelves so that the future would be protected.

I would also like to suggest that consideration be given to advising a friendly newspaper contact, on a strictly confidential basis, that Coretta King and Reverend Abernathy are deliberately plotting to keep King's assassination in the news by pulling the ruse of maintaining that King's murder was definitely a conspiracy and not committed by one man. This, of course is obviously a rank trick in order to keep the money coming in to Mrs. King, Abernathy, and the Southern Christian Leadership Conference. We can do this without any attribution to the FBI and without anyone knowing that the information came from a wiretap.

It didn't take long for the FBI's top level officials to select the ideal authors of the several such books—the ones that would set the baseline for all future "official story" news accounts and books—on the purported assassin. Both Gerold Frank and George E. McMillan were mentioned in the FBI's subsequent 1969 correspondence. The memoranda were noted in handwriting at the bottom with an "O.K." and initialed with an "H," as Hoover always signed in the margins or the bottom of correspondence to indicate his approval (or disapproval) of such requests.

The Loathsome Ethics of William Bradford Huie and His Legend as the "Checkbook Journalist"

The actions taken by DeLoach in 1969 to relaunch the FBI campaign to create, promote, and sustain falsely premised books were not the first time that the power and authority of the FBI was directed to myth building. By then, the misallocation of those resources on behalf of President Johnson was an entrenched, continuing practice, beginning in the aftermath of the JFK assassination. In this case, their mission was to enlist the assistance of willing authors for the purpose of reframing the King murder to ensure the guilt would be put on the selected patsy, James Earl Ray. By 1969, the first two books on that subject had already been written.

The first book, *The Strange Case of James Earl Ray: The Man Who Murdered Martin Luther King*, was written shortly after the 1969 "mini-trial" and was mostly an honest attempt by a little-known author, Clay Blaire Jr. His book was published shortly after Ray's "minitrial" and based upon early facts, though it was contaminated by his apparent presumption that Huie's first two magazine articles (in November 1968) were similarly untainted. Obviously, that was not the case; thus, his belief that the judicial system correctly determined that Ray was guilty of the murder was invalid.

The second book, by William Bradford Huie, *He Slew the Dreamer*, appeared in 1970, but it was based largely on his two 1968 articles in *Look* magazine, followed by another in April 1969. It will be shown in the chapters to follow that, in Huie's case, the die was clearly cast for a preset plotline even before the assassination, with a lot of discreet help from the FBI.[18] His book can best be described as an artfully done "Trojan Horse," personally directed by a very conflicted author who has been widely described—and acknowledged by himself—as a "checkbook journalist" whose writing skills were honed as a novelist (i.e., gifted in the art of elegantly describing things, people, and events that never were). But the worst of his conflicts related to his long-term association with J. Edgar Hoover.

Huie had gained fame for his books and articles dating from the 1940–50s. Before he began his mission to destroy James Earl Ray, his magnum opus—once famed, but now exposed as infamous—work was a lengthy article for *Look* magazine in January 1956, and another follow-up piece a year later, about how two Mississippi half-brothers (Roy Bryant and J. W. Milam) purportedly murdered a fourteen-year-old black boy from Chicago, Emmett Till, who had gone south for the summer of 1955 and committed a crime. Allegedly, it was merely flirting with a white woman.* Actually, it was nothing of the sort, according to the confessions of the woman who had made the claim, when she recently recanted her original testimony sixty years after the fact, as we will review below.

The already sensationalized story—complete with published news photos of Till's brutally battered face, drawing over half a million mourners to the week-long viewing and funeral in Chicago—was further embellished by William Bradford Huie in his January 1956 *Look* magazine story. Huie was one of hundreds of reporters who gathered in the tiny town of Sumner in Tallahatchie County, Mississippi, to attend the nationally sensational trial that summer. The nature of that event can best be understood by considering

---

* The complete story of the Emmett Till murder, as reported contemporaneously in a series of articles published in *Jet* magazine, can be found at http://jetcityorange.com/emmett-till/index.html.

two unusual statements. First, the prosecutor stated in his summation that there had been no need to kill Till: "The most he needed was a whipping . . ." Then, the defense lawyer said in his summation that "Your ancestors will turn over in their graves if [the accused murderers] are found guilty and I'm sure every last Anglo-Saxon one of you has the courage to free these men in the face of that (outside) pressure." It took the all-white, all-male jury only sixty-seven minutes to decide against a guilty verdict, but it would have been even less time if they had not deliberately stalled the decision "to make it look better to outsiders."[19]

In the immediate aftermath of the murder there were reports that the "lynching party" actually consisted of three men and a woman (Carolyn Bryant—Roy's wife), though the third man was never identified. It was Carolyn's story about the alleged "flirtation"—which started with a "wolf whistle" and later supposedly included Till's having "touched" her—that caused her husband to seek vengeance on Till. Though the deputy sheriff, John A. Cothran, stated, "We will get him [the third man] before we are through," that was never done, and the third man's identity was never established. The county sheriff, H. C. Strider, decided not to arrest Mrs. Bryant for her involvement since "She has two youngsters to take care of."[20]

The Huie stories of the Emmett Till murder were tainted by his methods of getting the accused murderers—both white Klansmen— to admit their guilt after their release by the jury. He paid them four thousand dollars each to sign a contract giving him all rights to publish the magazine article, books, and/or a movie. The deal was struck based on the premise that they were free from ever being charged again for that murder. Their greed overrode any personal embarrassment they might have had, since the murder of a black boy for such a heinous act—flirting with a white woman—was not unheard of in that time and place. Huie called the payment an "advance libel settlement" since they would be called "murderers," so it was not technically a payment for their story, at least as Huie rationalized it. David Halberstam called it one of "the most intriguing examples of checkbook journalism on record, and many people were appalled." Even Huie admitted it was "distasteful and I have not found it particularly pleasant." Yet he boasted to his editors about "drinking out of the same jug [with the murderer] and letting him drink first."[21]

That landmark event was one of the most egregious and notorious civil rights crimes of the twentieth century and, combined with all the other crimes, finally set off the thunderous demonstrations and protests of the late 1950s and early 1960s. Now, sixty-three years after the event, the already-horrid story has just turned into an even more shameful spectacle. The accused men were recently pronounced innocent by the original purported "victim," who—by her own admission—turned out to have been one of the protagonists. As reported in a February 6, 2017, news article titled "Could lies about Emmett Till lead to prosecution?" in the Jackson, Mississippi, *Clarion-Ledger* by Jerry Mitchell, Carolyn Bryant Donham, her conscience getting the better of her over sixty years later, "has admitted she lied when she testified in 1955—that Emmett Till had touched her — a lie she repeated to the FBI [as recently as] a decade ago."

Furthermore, according to Tim Tyson, the author of a 2017 book titled *The Blood of Emmett Till*, Mrs. Donham (having divorced Roy Bryant and remarried) said that neither of the men who had been tried and acquitted—and who then actually confessed to the murder, *evidently, merely for the "paycheck" from Huie*—had actually pulled the trigger. She finally confessed that "her then-brother-in-law, Melvin Campbell, was the one who shot Till."[22] Campbell, now deceased, lived out his life—if Donham's latest story is true—as the real killer, despite never having been accused of the murder while he was alive, much less prosecuted for it. The doubled—now tripled—miscarriage of justice, still never adequately captured in book or film at this point, will lamentably be another lost lesson for future generations.

This shameful decades-long series of events puts the odious ethics of the "checkbook journalist" William Bradford Huie in an even more bizarre and monstrous context than had been previously understood. Were it not for Huie's promises of financial rewards, would these men have confessed to something that the "victim" now claims they did not do? But this sordid episode—a massive, multiple breakdown in journalism ethics—does help to illustrate how "acclaimed" writers such as Huie can demolish truth by replacing facts with lies so thoroughly that the actual true stories are replaced by a myth made nearly impenetrable by delayed pathological reportage and finally written as revisionist history. Half a century after the fact, we can finally see how the use of financial awards to produce miscarriages of justice—suppressing the truth and validating the lies—produce long-standing myths that were believed by millions to be the unvarnished truth. But this was not the last time that Huie's manipulative skills would be used to reframe events to impede justice for the guilty parties while freeing those actually behind the most horrid of crimes, nor would it be the most egregious example.

To be sure, there were numerous other instances of Huie's chronic state of confusion between "fact vs. fiction." One additional example will suffice for now—as others will also be noted throughout the narrative—related to an injunction he filed in 1960 against NBC television for a television show called "The American," which Huie claimed infringed on his copyright for a story titled "The Hero of Iwo-Jima." While he had claimed that the story was true within the book, to the court he demonstrated that numerous episodes previously stated to be factual were actually "the product of his imagination." He lost the case in this litigation because of his confusion between "historical facts," which are not subject to copyright protection, and fiction, which is.[23] He apparently had still not learned those distinctions during 1968–1970, as he wrote three magazine articles, then a book on James Earl Ray. As we will establish within the chapters to follow, his articles and book were filled with carefully crafted lies sprinkled with enough truths to make the tales believable, at least in the early years before they could be completely debunked.

Furthermore, these examples reveal how the FBI specifically selected famed novelists to tell their story, assignments based upon their ability to transform fantasy into fabricated "facts." We will show how Huie, the hijacker of the Emmett Till murder case, was used by the FBI to write the first widely read account of King's murder and how two others, Gerold Frank and George McMillan, would follow the same path a few years later as a means of strengthening the myths by embellishing the original lies with even more fabricated "context." Huie's obvious assignment was to establish the foundation of myths for many other future authors assigned the task of firming up their "official story."

More FBI-Selected Authors Add to Huie's Original James Earl Ray Legend as "Vicious Southern Racist"

As noted above, in *The Plot to Kill King*, Dr. Pepper meticulously deconstructs several early books. One of these, the 1972 *An American Death* by Gerold Frank, was seemingly determined to restate practically everything Huie had written with additional newly created fiction. Among the other worst books (after Huie's) was the 1976 *The Making of an Assassin* by George McMillan. Over half that book—arguably 60 percent of it—consisted of a psychic-historical review of Ray's dysfunctional family by a man with no apparent credentials to conduct such a study. Most authors of this genre (books written to create, and then support, the "official version" of MLK's assassination) attempted to portray Ray as a southern racist; McMillan assigns a more abstruse motive than that, one based in the deepest recesses of Ray's psyche, caused by his alleged deprivation of psychic needs from a childhood spent on the edges of the same Mississippi River (the other, eastern, side of it) that, paradoxically, also produced the antithesis of the character profile he worked so hard to create, the fictional, happy-go-lucky Mark Twain characters, Tom Sawyer and Huckleberry Finn, from Hannibal, Missouri.

McMillan hypothesized that the reason for Ray's purported hatred of Dr. King was King's popularity as a great leader, "who offered love and warmth to thousands of people." According to this thesis, King reminded Ray, in a pointedly bitter way, of "how *he* had not been taken care of."[24] One of McMillan's more interesting, albeit confusing, sentences was this: "It is an axiom of behavior that every murder is a suicide, and every suicide is a murder."[25] If that is indeed an "axiom," one might question why it is not widely known, or even understandable. He explained it by proffering the notion that Ray, in allegedly taking King's life, would—emotionally—be taking his own.

McMillan never met Ray, and he had no discernible background in social sciences or anything else other than his skill at spying, thanks to his long association with the CIA (and its predecessors, the OSS [Office of Strategic Services] and OWI [Office of War Information]). Eventually his association extended to the FBI as well, where he participated in the "by invitation only" National Academy, a training and indoctrination program for high-profile citizens—and authors-in-training—which helps to prove his long-term ties to the officials of that organization. In 1965, he also married Priscilla Johnson, who had worked extensively for the CIA and had famously been placed in Moscow in advance of the arrival of Lee Harvey Oswald, whom she would interview within days of his arrival.[26] As George worked on his 1976 book on James Earl Ray, she worked simultaneously on a book, published in 1977, about Marina Oswald; unfortunately for Marina, she did not realize until it was published that it too was filled with fabrications. (That book, and another by Norman Mailer, caused Marina to turn away from any further interviews; and, unfortunately for her and for the rest of us, the real story of her experiences may never be told.)

Thanks to George McMillan, James Earl Ray was forever painted as one of the most horrid people who ever lived. Ray as a "stalker" and vicious hard-core racist full of hatred for Martin Luther King Jr.; a jailhouse drug dealer, homophobe, George Wallace supporter, pro-KKK, ultra-right-wing nutjob, and practically every other invective one can imagine, became the pervasive theme of his book. Ray was far from perfect, but he never truly fit any of those descriptions, as we will also demonstrate.

Astonishingly, McMillan also pinned his profile of Ray's entire family on an alleged "great-grandfather" who happened to have the same surname— despite offering absolutely no evidence of an actual genealogical connection to Ray's forefathers—who was an outlaw from the Old West, hanged by a Montana posse in 1865. Compelled to come up with "interesting angles" to use in his portrayal of the entire Ray clan as being the most evil, conniving, cutthroat barbarians in the world, McMillan was willing to use the smallest sliver of "evidence" to connect all of them—James, his father, brothers John and Jerry, his sister, and his grandfather—back to one of the worst desperadoes the Wild West ever produced. He must have visited dozens of libraries in search of someone with that same surname, in his quest to satisfy the specifications he had undoubtedly been handed by the FBI (a continuing project of DeLoach's, based on his memos, which we will shortly examine in detail).

One of McMillan's other (arguably) "assigned objectives" was to tie Ray's motives to other world-class scoundrels, including not only Adolf Hitler, but the contemporaneous American racist George Wallace, neither of which "connections" had any basis in fact (modern-day authors, such as Sides in 2010 and McMichael in 2015, picked up on this and added even more illusions to that hoax). To do this—and to attempt to show Ray's purported racism and hatred for King—he relied on a notorious liar, prison inmate-snitch Ray Curtis, who was willing to say anything for gullible authors to gain fame (or points for an early release) for himself. McMillan even admitted that he had to track Curtis down to a jailhouse in Dalton, Georgia, for his interview, where he awaited trial for "the murder of one man and the gunning down [wounding] of three others in a dispute over a poker game."[27] Here McMillan was, interviewing a man he apparently found to be very credible, perhaps even erudite, honest, and forthcoming; a man purporting to put his reputation on the line for faux "justice" for James Earl Ray. Clearly, McMillan was an author on a mission, ready to believe anything Curtis uttered (after taking numerous obligatory swipes at the "local yokels" in that town, about how the lot of them were poor, miserable "mountain" people who always voted to keep the county dry while partaking in the local business enterprises known colloquially as moonshining).[28]

Another one of Curtis's lies that McMillan accepted hook, line, and sinker was that James Earl Ray was "a narcotics addict and peddler," which was completely debunked by Missouri Corrections Department Chief George M. Camp, who called the charges "totally unsubstantiated." Furthermore, Chief Camp stated that during Ray's six-year incarceration there, "he kept primarily to himself and, other than for the fact that he attempted to escape on more than one occasion, he had only one conduct violation during that entire time and that was the possession of three packages of cigarettes, a ballpoint pen and one pound of coffee." When Camp asked McMillan for specific details about his charges, the famed author "responded that it was common knowledge."[29] Aside from a news report of this development from the *St. Louis Post-Dispatch*, nothing else was ever announced about this salient point by the mainstream media.[30]

Then, of course, there was the clearly deceitful 1998 book *Killing the Dream* by Gerald Posner. Among his many deceptions was repeating the earlier lies by Huie, Frank, and McMillan (i.e., the fabricated Hitler and Wallace associations noted above) and reselling them to a public hungry for reinterpreted "truth" two decades later. William Pepper devoted over nine pages of *The Plot to Kill King* to the thorough dissection of Posner's dreadful book. Numerous other critics—too many to mention but easy for anyone to Google—have similarly exposed the lies, the fabricated testimony he claimed to have gotten from witnesses whom he never interviewed, and the numerous other forms of deception that were used throughout his books. Yet one would never know it looking at the dust jacket of *Killing the Dream*, with praise heaped upon it by the denizens of propaganda at the formerly credible primary organs of the mainstream media: "His work is painstakingly honest journalism," concluded the *Washington Post*. The *New York Times* lauded his "exhaustive research techniques," and the *Boston Globe* determined that Posner is "an investigative journalist whose work is marked by his thorough and meticulous research." "A resourceful investigator and skillful writer," says the *Dallas Morning News*. All of which proves that there really is a parallel universe, in their case one populated by mythmakers and anyone who still believes any of them.

Posner's earlier book *Case Closed: Lee Harvey Oswald and the Assassination of JFK*, written specifically to prop up the picked-over, discarded remains of the Warren Report on the thirtieth anniversary of JFK's assassination, has also been thoroughly debunked by numerous reviewers in ways that extend to any and all of his other works, because the same methodologies were used in all of them. Dr. Peter Dale Scott, professor of English at the University of California, Berkeley, in the November/December 1993 issue of the *San Francisco Review of Books*, stated in his review of *Case Closed* that "some of the weakest sections of the Warren Commission argument have been strengthened by suspect methodologies and even falsehoods, so systematic they call into question the good faith of the entire project." The late Harrison Edward Livingstone devoted fifty-two pages—the entire Chapter 7—of his 1995 book, *Killing Kennedy*, to a destruction of Posner's clearly deceptive methodology and a point-by-point refutation of his conclusions.

But even that dissection did not stop Posner from repeating the same techniques in *Killing the Dream*, his book on Dr. King's murder. Despite his having been called out for his deceptions by critics, Posner doubled down and used the same methods to write his 1998 tome on Dr. King's assassination as he had used five years earlier on JFK's. A summary of those deceptions follows.

Gerald Posner's Lies in *Killing the Dream* (Also see Dr. William F. Pepper, *The Plot to Kill King*, pp. 299–306)

Posner has regurgitated much of the official story previously discredited by researchers Harold Weisberg, Mark Lane, Dr. William Pepper, Professor Philip Melanson, and numerous others. That "official" story (never disproved in criminal court, thanks to Ray never being given a fair trial, but completely discredited in civil court) relied heavily on the testimony of Reverend Billy Kyles, who created numerous lies, even to the point of betraying his supposed "friend," Dr. King. Kyles was a paid Memphis Police Department informer. Moreover, Posner's own history of plagiarism—yet another deceitful practice—should be sufficient to end his publishing career and further discredit everything he has previously written:

- Posner claims the discredited Kyles went from the balcony into King's room at the Lorraine Motel, room 306, at 5:30 p.m. and then accompanied King back onto the balcony at 6:00 p.m. *In fact, according to Patrolman Willie Richmond's surveillance notes, Kyles merely knocked on King's door at 5:50 p.m. and then walked away, down the balcony walkway, and stood thirty to forty feet away. Richmond's report and testimony made clear that King stood alone on the balcony at 6:01 p.m. when he was shot.*

- Posner stated that James Earl Ray would have known where Dr. King was staying in Memphis from "the front-page photograph in the *Commercial Appeal* on the morning of April 4." *But there was no such photo!* (See copy of newspaper below) *Furthermore, the only article in it did NOT say that King was staying there, only that his group had had lunch there the day before.*

- Posner denied that Kyles was an FBI informant: "[In] *Orders to Kill*, William Pepper raises the strong inference [sic: implication] that Kyles might have been an *FBI informant.* 'It's degrading and insulting,' Kyles says about author Pepper's accusations." *But Dr. Pepper had actually said that Kyles was an "MPD [Memphis Police Department] informant."* (Emphasis added.) By clearly intentionally misquoting, Posner introduces a technical error, allowing Kyles an opening to deny the assertion, and thereby reframes the entire story, sowing confusion in those who did not go back and recheck the book to see the trickery for themselves (including the many mainstream critics who lauded his book for

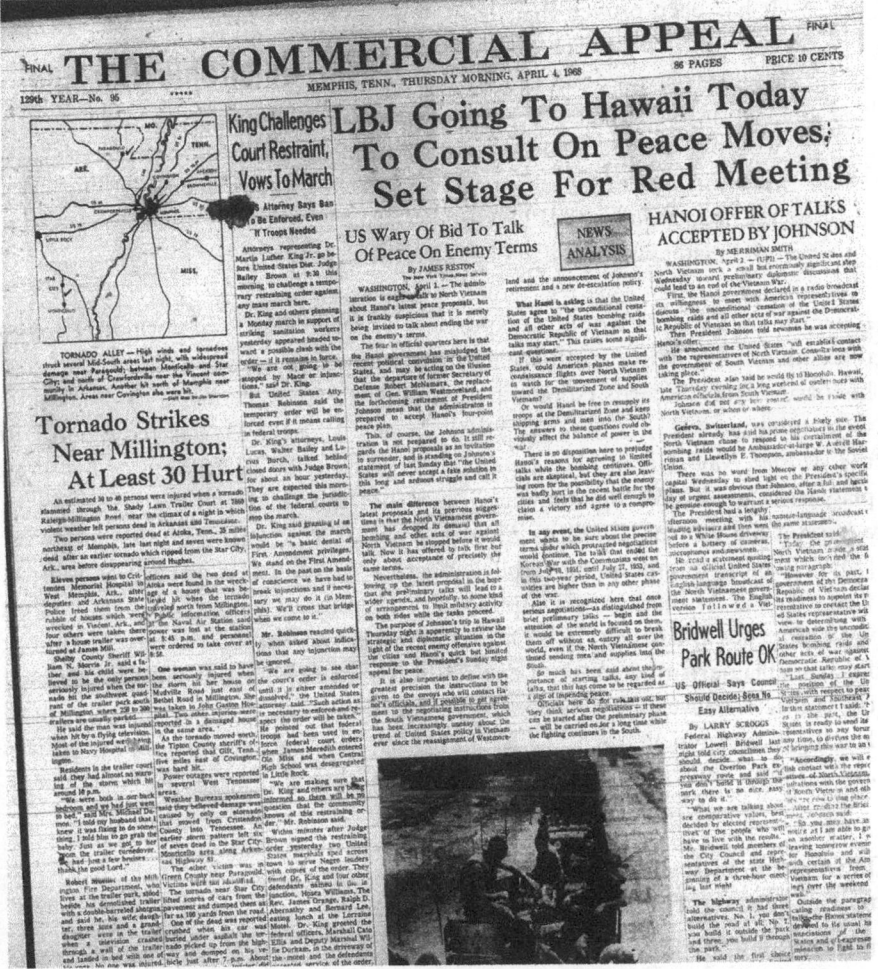

Memphis *Commercial Appeal* April 4, 1968.

"his fine investigative reporting techniques," as noted on the dust jacket of Posner's wretched book).

- Posner ignored the well-established fact that the morning after the assassination, the Memphis Public Works Department (as testified by the department head, Maynard Stiles) cut down all the trees and bushes behind the rooming house—*which not only would have prevented a shot from the rooming-house bathroom, but in fact provided the "cover" for the actual shooter, who had hidden himself in those bushes. This was one of his biggest "dual deceits."*

- It has been proven that the state's key witness, Charlie Stephens (who claimed to have seen Ray run down the hallway after the shooting), was dead drunk at that time. MPD homicide detective Tommy Smith stated he was incoherent; taxi driver James McCraw would not even allow him to ride in his cab; and Stephens's roommate, Grace Walden, insisted that he hadn't seen anything. Yet Posner quoted MPD officer Roy Davis, who only saw Stephens hours later, after he had been filled with black coffee.

A decade later, Posner would be exposed as a serial plagiarizer, normally the kiss of death for any writer (with notable exceptions, including such luminaries as historians Doris Kearns Goodwin and the late Stephen Ambrose). His thefts were summarized in a May 10, 2010, article, "Posner Plagiarizes Again," in the *Miami New Times*: "He apparently whitewashed an account of his serial plagiarism on his Wikipedia page, then threatened *Miami New Times* with a lawsuit for writing about it. And now he's retained an 83-year-old lawyer [Mark Lane], infamous for publicizing the 'grassy knoll' theory of John F. Kennedy's assassination, a conspiracy Posner refuted [or rather attempted to, with more lies and deceit] in his most famous book."[31] When questioned about Posner's plagiarism, attorney Lane refused to comment but quickly changed the subject: "Have you guys done anything about the fact . . . that the Central Intelligence Agency and the FBI and other intelligence organizations have assets in the news media and agents posing and working as reporters?"[32]

Hampton Sides's (and Others') Attempts to Perpetuate the Fictional Accounts

Finally, another more recent disingenuous book, *Hellhound on His Trail*, by Hampton Sides—which should have been more properly labeled as lightweight fiction—and a CNN "documentary" with Soledad O'Brien were also categorically dismissed by Pepper. These latter entries were both error-filled and short on facts, a seeming continuation of the original myths as dictated by the unindicted criminals then running the FBI, to ensure that the aphorism first uttered by Joseph Goebbels (paraphrased as "lies told often, and with authority, will eventually become truth") would be faithfully strengthened and carried directly into the new millennium.

Hampton Sides even acknowledged his loose interpretation of events, citing the Memphis historian Shelby Foote, the author of a Civil War trilogy who stated that "he had 'employed the novelist's methods without his license,' and that's a good rule of thumb for what I've attempted here."[33] He really should have left it at that, but he went on to say that his book "is a work of nonfiction. Every scene is supported by the historical record."[34] Throughout much of this book, that assertion will be examined in detail and ultimately proven to be quite incorrect.

At the Memphis civil trial (see Chapter 12) in 1999, defense attorney Lewis Garrison—representing the man accused by the King family of complicity in Dr. King's murder, Loyd Jowers—requested Gerald Posner to be an expert witness and give testimony. But Posner chose not to put himself under oath and be subject to questioning by William Pepper (Hampton Sides similarly ducked a request—a subpoena in his case—to appear for questioning).

Despite all of these now-exposed blemishes on his history as a plagiarist and prevaricator, Posner is still often cited as a credible source for these clearly bogus works of "nonfiction," a term that should be considered an oxymoron when used in the context of his works.

Together, the books written by William Bradford Huie, Gerold Frank, George McMillan, Lamar Waldron, Gerald Posner, and Hampton Sides—and to a lesser extent by others such as Pate McMichael, Stuart Wexler, and Larry Hancock—have formed the foundation upon which the "official" government account now rests. Unfortunately, that case can be metaphorically compared to a rotting block of aged Swiss cheese, where all the voids represent missing pieces, but the rest of the mass is so contaminated with lies and deceit that it is spoiled beyond redemption.

Throughout this book, we will present passages or descriptions from these books and put them under a virtual microscope, examining them in context and determining the purpose of each deception. The key lies will be proven beyond a shadow of a doubt, for they were originally linked to alleged newspaper articles that either never existed or did not state what they were claimed to have stated. The deceptions worked because they relied on the presumption that no one would go to the trouble of finding those old articles in an era before the Internet made them available to anyone with an interest in researching them.

Through rigorous deductive reasoning and critical analysis, we will incrementally lay bare the roots of many of the core deceptions used by these authors (largely planted originally by the FBI handlers they were subordinate to, and subsequently adopted by the HSCA investigators) and demonstrate how they were separately used to reframe the entire event to support the overarching story line laid out by high-level FBI officials into the pre-established official solution: yet another murder by a poor, slovenly, ignorant malcontent, in this case one whose intense racial hatred, and purported goal of achieving lifetime notoriety by becoming the No. 1 name on the FBI's

Ten Most Wanted list of wanted criminals, led him to murder Martin Luther King Jr. This was the precise profile specially created for James Earl Ray.

Much of that process will be focused on the linchpin of the plot, the enigmatic person named "Raul"* who could not be considered by the FBI as being real and therefore was deemed not to be by all of the books written by these six authors and by the House Select Committee on Assassinations (HSCA) investigators. Dr. William Pepper was able to conclusively prove that Raul did exist, and one FBI agent, Donald Wilson, provided additional physical evidence in 1998 that further proved his existence. Wilson's testimony was criticized greatly by the FBI, but if he had not presciently withheld that evidence in 1968, it would have certainly been "lost" or destroyed immediately, just as so many other pieces of exculpatory evidence have disappeared. The FBI of that era, led by the same men who originally created the plot to kill King, was of course never seriously interested in actually solving the case, as will be demonstrated in this book.

Truman Capote, celebrity author of both fiction and nonfiction books, screenplays, short stories, poems, and an autobiography, made twenty-one appearances on *The Tonight Show Starring Johnny Carson*. On one appearance in 1968, he became probably the first person to describe, in general terms, the themes of this book. He stated that it was inconceivable that James Earl Ray, Lee Harvey Oswald, and Sirhan B. Sirhan were not well-prepared triggermen who were set up in highly sophisticated operations akin to those described by novelist Richard Condon in *The Manchurian Candidate*. The only difference between them, he ventured, was that—unlike Oswald—Ray and Sirhan were allowed to live because they had no inside knowledge of the preparations behind the assassinations for which they were set up. Capote argued that Ray's petty-criminal past would not have sufficiently prepared him for his actions and travels during the nearly year-long period of freedom he enjoyed between his escape from prison and April 4, 1968.[35] Without considerable help from others who financed his travels, his new car, cameras, shelter, food, and funds to pursue his personal interests (plastic surgery, dance lessons, bartending, and locksmith courses), along with the promise of meeting his future goals of obtaining what Raul had promised to him once his "smuggling job" was complete—$12,000, a passport, and passage to Europe or Africa, to gain and secure his independence—none of it would have been realistically possible. This book merely adds more detail to Capote's prescient vision from fifty years ago.

---

* "Raoul" as spelled by James Earl Ray, who apparently used a phonetic interpretation because the Hispanic name "Raul" has two syllables, unlike the single syllable Anglican "Paul."

Part I

Malevolent Background (1950s through 1963)

Chapter 1

LBJ AND JEH: FRIENDS AND NEIGHBORS

"Dick, you will come to depend on Edgar. He is a pillar of strength in a city of weak men. You will rely on him time and again to maintain security. He's the only one you can put your complete trust in."
—President Johnson to President-elect Richard Nixon, 1968

In the wake of the Teapot Dome scandal of Warren Harding's administration, a furor arose about the covert extralegal activities of the Justice Department's Bureau of Investigation (the forerunner of what would become the FBI, when Hoover added "Federal" to its title a decade later). The Bureau had experienced previous scandals related to its ill-defined charter since its unilateral formation in 1909, when it began to stray from its original purposes of enforcing antitrust and interstate commerce laws and started monitoring political dissent or the personal activities of congressmen, usually at the request of high-level officials in the executive branch. It had compiled dossiers on American residents and organizations, among others, such as antiwar senators like Robert LaFollette of Wisconsin, pacifists like Jane Addams, and civil libertarians like Roger Baldwin.[36] In his attempt to calm the furor, Attorney General Harlan Fiske Stone began a major housecleaning of the Bureau and appointed twenty-nine-year-old investigator J. Edgar Hoover to replace the previous discredited director, William J. Burns. Hoover was put on temporary "probation" until December 1924. By his thirtieth birthday on January 1, 1925, he had achieved—through his well-practiced political blackmail of future presidents, in LBJ's case the result of multiple, mutually-executed treasons—what would become a lifelong position as the head of a major federal agency. That is a stunning assertion, but it will be vindicated in the pages ahead.

Realizing that he would have to please Attorney General Stone, and knowing that his actions would be closely monitored by him, Hoover mounted a public relations program to portray the Bureau as an honest, efficient, and important government agency run by "God-fearing professionals," who looked and acted accordingly.[37] But it was these public relations programs that Hoover became the most devoted to, always intent on creating the *perception* of professionalism, efficiency, dynamism, and productivity, not necessarily the reality of those characteristics. In fact, despite Stone's ban against surveillance of personal and political activities, Hoover pursued those aspects even more vigorously, but always subject to his direct monitoring, and only when he believed their secrecy would not be jeopardized. To further ensure his ultimate control, Hoover required Bureau officials to obtain his written approval before undertaking sensitive investigations, then provide written reports regarding their discoveries. To protect against other government officials (such as the attorney general), congressional subpoenas, or court-ordered discovery requests from ever accessing these records, he required all such files be maintained in his own office in his "personal and confidential" file drawers.[38]

This enabled him to maintain secret files on practically all the politicians in Washington. They were voluminous and included much noncriminal information, yet also included all the information he—or others whom he personally designated to have access—might find useful for more effective negotiations. Things like "obscene or indecent" information, including sexual dalliances and proclivities, especially those of a homosexual nature. His even more exclusive subset of those files, which he designated "Official and Confidential," held some of the most sensitive records. These provided the best insight into his private agendas. One folder in that set was labeled "'Black Bag' Jobs." Within it were summaries of the procedures Hoover had instituted in 1942 to ensure that FBI agents could conduct break-ins with no risk of discovery; by 1966, they were changed to reflect the restrictions he had put on those methods to ensure that they would not be used to force his early retirement. By 1970, those files were set up to protect himself even further, by documenting the fact that his verbal approval for agents in New York City to conduct break-ins in their investigation of the radical Weather Underground organization was due to pressure he had received from the Nixon White House.

Hoover's PR campaigns were based on projecting images of the Bureau that were based upon images of the agents themselves. Until forced to admit minorities in the early 1970s, all agents were white males, and all were required to dress and act like Hoover, Tolson, and their high-level assistants. His own preferences for work attire were expected to be followed by all agents, as well: a dark solid gray or blue suit with handkerchief; white shirt; conservative tie; dark, well-polished shoes; and jewelry limited to tie pin, watch, cufflinks, and wedding ring (if applicable, otherwise a blue sapphire ring on the wedding finger). Agents were instructed on expected demeanor as well, to convey an image of strength, moral rectitude, and calmness.[39] The basic rules for all special agents were "Never embarrass the Bureau" and "Look like an agent."[40] Making a good first impression was the highest priority on hiring special agents, and one unstated criterion was that applicants have a full head of hair; bald-headed men were not eligible because Hoover felt that they could not make a good first impression. Once Hoover saw a young man in the office who not only had pimples but had also committed the horrible mistake of wearing a red vest under his suit coat; he immediately ordered that the man be fired and that whoever had recommended him for employment be disciplined.[41]

Hoover felt that many people were "communist dupes" and could not be trusted, especially anyone with a weak handshake or sweaty palms. To portray himself as a regular guy for his bachelor friends, his club room was papered with "nude photos and foldouts of women" in various stages of undress.[42] Hoover was a man of many contradictions, whose own persona was, by many accounts, conflicted due to his own confusion over his sexual identity, which he tried to keep hidden and beyond the reach of public scrutiny. Hoover had lived with his mother until she died in 1938, when he was forty-three. His father, Dickerson Hoover, was never a role model for Edgar as a boy; that role was fulfilled exclusively by his mother, Annie. When he was born, his parents were still mourning the death of his infant sister, Sadie. As a result, Edgar became the single object of his mother's affection, having lost not only her daughter, but effectively any feelings she had ever had for her husband, as well. In giving all her attention to Edgar, she made him understand that she expected much from him in return, which led him to becoming rather neurotic and concerned only with achieving his own goals, to satisfy her objectives, thereby cutting himself off from all others, including the rest of his own family. His childhood dependence on only his mother's influence left him unable to establish close and meaningful relationships with anyone else.[43]

In due course, his amalgamation of psychic disorders was manifested in notable actions, as attested to by a number of psychiatrists. One of them was Dr. Harold Lief, Professor Emeritus of Psychiatry at the University of Pennsylvania: "There is no doubt that Hoover had a personality disorder, a narcissistic disorder with mixed obsessive features. I picked up some paranoid elements, undue suspiciousness and some sadism. A combination of narcissism and paranoia produces what is known as an Authoritarian Personality. Hoover would have made a perfect high-level Nazi."[44] This was only one of the disorders that other psychiatrists would later affirm Lyndon Johnson shared with Hoover. They were far more than neighbors and friends; they were "birds of a feather" in many other ways, as well.

It would be difficult for anyone, especially a layman, to pinpoint any of the disorders described by Dr. Lief and link it, or them, to Hoover's known homosexuality, much less the transvestitism described by Anthony Summers in *Official and Confidential: The Secret Life of J. Edgar Hoover*.[45] Authors Summers and Gentry noted his devotion to his mother throughout his life with her that might have had an influence, as well as his estrangement from his father. Gentry quoted one of his nieces, who stated that he never married because "there was no room in the house for another woman and he simply did not have the money to run two [homes]," thus suggesting that he used his mother, while she was alive, as an excuse to not marry.[46] According to Hoover's friend George Allen, "he never spent another Christmas in Washington after [his mother] died."[47] After she died, Hoover and his only true friend, associate FBI director Clyde Tolson, would spend nearly every weekend in New York, where they stayed in a complimentary suite at the Waldorf Astoria. Hoover feigned the excuse that the trips were necessary to tend to business in the largest FBI field office, which he rarely actually visited unless he wanted to make a press release. The year after she died, he bought a house near Rock Creek Park, which then became a shrine of sorts to his mother, with pictures of her in every room.[48] But for our purposes here, whatever the basis of his strong relationship his mother might have been, it is sufficient to say it was what it was and may not be related to his homosexuality.

For whatever reason, J. Edgar Hoover had been immediately impressed by Clyde Tolson's application for employment to the Bureau in 1928. Most biographies reference Hoover's serendipitous review of Tolson's application, especially "his first glimpse of an exceptionally handsome young man"[49] in the photograph attached to the application. But according to Curt Gentry's account in *J. Edgar Hoover: The Man and the Secrets*, Hoover already knew Tolson even before receiving the application,[50] which suggests that there was nothing serendipitous at all about his seeing it; furthermore, it raises the suspicion that Hoover may have even invited Tolson to apply for a position that Edgar had created just for him.

Hoover immediately hired Tolson and then ensured that he was promoted at a rate unheard of within any federal bureaucracy, let alone the FBI. He was sent to Boston for four months to gain some quick field experience before coming back to Washington to work under Hoover's own tutelage. So that he could gain more experience as an Agent in Charge, Hoover sent him to Buffalo, New York, for only two weeks before bringing him back and promoting him again to inspector in 1930. Even more astonishing was Tolson's rapid rise after that to become, in 1931, within three years of being a trainee, one of only two assistant directors of the Bureau.[51] He remained in that position until the most senior assistant retired in 1947; Hoover then created a new position, called associate director, and Tolson was promoted to that, officially becoming the "number-two" man of the FBI.[52]

Tolson's real job was not only to cater to and flatter Hoover, but, more important, to communicate his boss's brilliance, leadership, and technical law enforcement expertise to everyone else in or out of government, especially journalists.[53] It extended even beyond that, to making sure that the others extended that message to the public, which was expected to also flatter Tolson as well, especially those employed as columnists, reporters, editors, publishers, or television network anchors, whom he carefully maneuvered such that they would repeat the accolades to the public at large. The fawningly obsequious statements nearly always got back to Hoover, thanks to Tolson's efforts.

Syndicated gossip columnist and radio show host Walter Winchell was the dean of this group from the 1940s into the early 1960s, with a readership estimated at forty-eight million, while his Sunday night radio show was said to have reached almost 90 percent of US adults.[54] As Hoover's biographer Curt Gentry wrote, "It was Winchell, more than any other journalist, who sold the G-man image to America; while Hoover . . . supplied Winchell with 'inside information' that led to some of his biggest 'scoops.' Hoover denied this. 'The truth is that Winchell got no tips from me of a confidential nature, I cannot afford to play favorites.'"[55] Hoover's remark, with its ever-present ambiguous qualifier, hid the actual truth, but there was never any question that Winchell got favorable treatment in exchange for his lavishing praise on the FBI in general and Hoover in particular. William C. Sullivan, one of Hoover's high-level assistants, confirmed Winchell's role with the FBI: "We sent Winchell information regularly. He was our mouthpiece."[56]

Winchell's radio voice even sounded similar to Hoover's, with the flat, monotone, rapid staccato delivery style that both of them employed. Winchell's voice became familiar to television viewers as the announcer who introduced new scenes in *The Untouchables* (1959–63), the TV series about 1930s Prohibition gang busts led by Eliot Ness (Robert Stack). But several controversies caused Winchell's popularity to wane. Those controversies started with his previous backing of Joseph McCarthy's witch hunt, mounted when he denounced Adlai Stevenson for being a homosexual, and crashed when he engaged *Tonight Show* host Jack Paar in a public feud, with each taking on-air potshots at the other.[57] Winchell faded from the limelight after his anchor newspaper, the *New York Mirror*, went bankrupt in 1963 and his broadcasting sponsors abandoned him.

Hoover's routine—a pattern well established and practiced for decades—started every morning at the same time when his chauffeur-driven, bullet-proof Cadillac picked him up (it was replaced annually and was so heavy with armor plate that it was equipped with a truck chassis and engine). Hoover was the only government official to have such a car—even the president's cars were not so equipped (until after JFK was assassinated in such a vehicle), which speaks volumes about his rarefied government position. Clyde Tolson was already in the car by the time it got to Hoover's home, only a few blocks away. The chauffeur, James Crawford, was a black man who worked for Hoover for decades and was used by Hoover and Tolson several times to "impersonate" a black FBI agent, as proof of their not having any racial hiring biases.[58] They had also used another black man, an office clerk named Sam Noisette, to do the same thing.[59] They had to resort to that kind of trickery because they had no real black agents on the payroll.

Hoover and Tolson lunched together every day at Harvey's, at a table well hidden and surrounded by empty tables, thanks to the owner or manager blocking access with a large serving cart. They also went to either Harvey's or the Jockey Club inside the Mayflower Hotel for dinner on most evenings. The owners comped them every day, at great expense, which of course was never reported to the IRS as income (until the owner of Harvey's sold the business to another man, who did not get the memo that their food and drinks were supposed to be "on the house"—they stopped dining there).

Their hotels were also comped when they took their winter vacations at the Gulf Stream Hotel in Miami or their summer vacations at the Hotel Del Charro in California, and always at the Waldorf Astoria in New York. All travel, either by rail to New York or by air, was billed to their government expense account under the lie that they were on official business, "inspecting FBI field offices."[60] Of course they had never intended to do anything of the kind, instead spending all of their time either at the Murchison/Richardson Del Mar racetrack or lounging around their hotel pool sipping cocktails and eating thick steaks, also "comped" by Clint Murchison and Sid Richardson, the oil-billionaire owners.

There is no doubt that Hoover and Tolson were long-term committed homosexuals, but that was not consistent with the myths they had built around their lives. Their real lives remained an official secret, their homosexuality was always closeted. Anyone suggesting otherwise would be vilified as "public rats, gutter-snipes and degenerate pseudo-intellectuals."[61]

In 1963, FBI Director J. Edgar Hoover was sixty-eight years old and had held that position for thirty-eight years. He was five feet eleven, weighing well over two hundred pounds, with a pugilistic bearing, jutting jaw, bulldog face, piercing and hooded dark brown eyes usually fixed with an unblinking glare, and pugnacious expression. He always spoke plainly, with a minimum of words and a gruff, staccato voice in a manner that never invited a reply; anyone tempted to reply innately understood that to do so might trigger a raging response. Hoover disliked most people generally, even white people if they were of "French, British, Dutch [or] Australian [descent] and felt that many people from all walks of life were 'communist dupes.'" Of course, he had no empathy for minorities of any color, despite the hushed rumors of his own father's real genealogy.[62]

Hoover's hatefulness and obsession with blacks was well known.and is mentioned in practically every biography of him (except the most obsequious and distorted ones, such as "Deke" DeLoach's servile hagiography[63]). DeLoach (who was known as "Roachie") had replaced Courtney Evans as the FBI liaison to the president because Johnson had taken a liking to Deke when both he and Hoover realized what an outstanding sycophant he could be, becoming almost a son—to both of them. Hoover finally became a bit chagrined with DeLoach when Johnson started inviting Deke and his family to come to Camp David and the LBJ Ranch with him and the First Family, and when DeLoach was given his own direct telephone line to Johnson's bedroom in the White House. One of William Sullivan's anecdotes reveals how much DeLoach was like Johnson, in how "perceptions" were much more important than essential truths: Deke knew that Sullivan liked to browse around bookstores, adding to his own personal library, so he asked him to pick out a few books for him as well. When asked what kind of books— biographies, history, or novels—Deke said "all of them." His wish was only for books that looked serious and important, to create the perception of sophistication and look nice on a bookshelf, to impress his guests, not that he would ever read any of them.[64]

Cartha DeLoach was hated by most of his peers for his unctuousness,[65] but not by the servile Hampton Sides, who held him in the highest esteem as he quoted Deke triumphantly stating that he "could not have been prouder of his field agents," who had followed Ray across the country: "Nothing Ray did threw us off the path . . . From the time we found that photograph at the bartender's school, his fate was sealed."[66] This was a rather surreal comment, considering that it took the FBI over two weeks to identify the fingerprints from the gun and other items found in the bundle outside the doorway of Canipe's or in the Mustang found in Atlanta. In the meantime, they were still looking for a man named "Eric Galt," with only a sketchy physical description of the wanted man, not even an artist's drawing. According to Harold Weisberg, a Memphis police official complained two weeks after the murder about the absence of artist sketches or photos; the FBI had even denied having one, though they had prepared a composite sketch. The police in Memphis, Atlanta, Birmingham, and Los Angeles complained of numerous discrepancies in the descriptions of "Galt" and how the FBI had frozen out the local police, saying "they didn't know what to look for."[67]

They didn't identify who was wandering around the Northern Hemisphere using the Galt name for over two weeks despite having a plethora of fingerprints and other physical evidence regarding the items found immediately after the murder in a bundle of carefully packed items including the rifle and ammunition, a transistor radio with Ray's inmate number scratched onto it, the recently purchased binoculars and their receipt from a nearby sporting goods store, and an assortment of clothing. How they "followed him across the country" was difficult to understand too because within three days he was in Canada, well before the FBI knew his name.

That statement about the indefatigability of the FBI was not only exceedingly overstated, excessively boastful, and a bit defensive on DeLoach's part—a reflection of the fact of widespread criticism over the ten weeks it took for Ray to be arrested in England—it was offensive. The FBI had gone to great lengths to claim credit for the arrest when the reality was they had virtually nothing to do with it. William Sullivan gave the credit to the Royal Canadian Mounted Police—who had carefully reviewed 250,000 passport applications, checking photos and handwriting until they came up with Ray's new travel alias—and the British police who arrested him. But Hoover could never allow anyone other than the FBI to take the credit for Ray's capture and refused to give any of them even partial credit.[68]

A Possible Source of J. Edgar Hoover's Demons: His Family Secrets?

While most people outside Washington and its environs were unaware of them, within the city there were whispered rumors that Edgar had "black blood in his veins." They had been ubiquitous in Washington for well over two decades—rumors of which "he was certainly aware" according to Anthony Summers—and were confirmed by the famed novelist Gore Vidal, who grew up in Washington during the 1930s: "Hoover was becoming famous, and it was always said of him—in my family and around the city—that he was mulatto. People said he came from a family that had 'passed.' It was the word they used for people of black origin who, after generations of interbreeding, have enough white blood to pass themselves off as white. That's what was always said about Hoover."[69]

Vidal also stated that Hoover himself must have known his past was the subject of widespread rumors around Washington. "There were two things that were taken for granted in my youth," Vidal would say, "that he was a faggot and that he was black. Washington was and is a very racist town, and I can tell you that in those days the black blood part was very much the worst. People were known to commit suicide if it was discovered that they had passed." Most white people of that era, even in cosmopolitan Washington, were condescending to anyone thought to have black blood in them. Summers also reported that even Helen Gandy, Hoover's longtime personal secretary, mentioned the rumors in interviews but then decided to drop the subject,[70] undoubtedly remembering that it was among her boss's deepest secrets, of the "personal and confidential" type.

One of the most compelling pieces of evidence that Hoover's legendary animus toward African Americans was due to his paranoia about the possibility that his own genealogy being discovered comes from Millie McGhee-Morris, a Mississippi lady whose ancestors were slaves, and whose grandfather told her as a child that she was related to J. Edgar Hoover. She told that story to M. Wesley Swearingen, the former FBI agent who wrote the 1995 book *FBI Secrets: An Agent's Exposé* and later the 2008 book *To Kill A President.* In that second book, Swearingen describes "Millie McGhee-Morris, Hoover's Black Cousin" in Chapter 61. Swearingen explains how he had come to believe her story after working with her, encouraging her to keep researching the story further, to make a solid case of her story's accuracy. She did and wrote her first book in 2000, *Secrets Uncovered: J. Edgar Hoover—Passing For White?* In 2005, she created a DVD titled *What's Done in The Dark.*[71] According to the highly credible Swearingen, "Millie has done an excellent job of uncovering the facts surrounding her childhood and developing the oral history to document and to prove J. Edgar Hoover's linage. Millie has even received the backing of Hoover's white relatives." From Ms. McGhee-Morris's book cover: "Mrs. McGhee reveals to the world the shocking truth of how her own African American lineage intersected with that of the former FBI Director J. Edgar Hoover."[72]

Ms. McGhee stated that as a child in the 1950s, she mentioned Hoover's name to her grandfather, whom she called "Big Daddy," and he asked her what she knew about him. She told him that she learned that he was the head of the FBI and had a lot of power, maybe even more than the president. "Well, that could be true," her grandfather responded. "He does have a lot of power." Then he shrugged, and said, "That old goat is related to me, he is my second cousin." Then he warned her not to tell anyone: "This is a family secret." Her grandfather said that Hoover was "passing," and that he could have them all killed if he discovered that they were the source of rumors. "He doesn't want the secret out, and he is a powerful man!" the trembling young girl was told. When asked about records such as birth certificates or court documents, her grandfather responded, "J. Edgar Hoover has a lot of power. He can destroy files, and he's already done it."[73]

McGhee hired professional genealogist George Ott of Salt Lake City to sort through archives at the Mormon Family History Center. While he did not find definitive evidence of a centuries-old illicit sexual encounter somewhere in rural Mississippi involving Hoover's ancestors, according to William J. Maxwell in his book *F.B. Eyes: How J. Edgar Hoover's Ghostreaders Framed African American Literature*, Ott did discover the next best thing: "courthouse evidence that several of Hoover's ancestors were Pike County, Mississippi, slave owners who lived in proximity to several of McGhee's maternal relations, opening the option that Hoover men formed relationships with a contemporaneous female slave, Emily Allen, a foremother of the modern McGhees . . . Ott conjectures that John T. Hoover, J. Edgar's grandfather, may have been the mulatto son of Hoover's great-grandfather William: a son who snatched the advantages of passing as white, but who was aware of his mothering by Allen, a trusted household slave who may also have slept with Williams's father, Christian."[74] Maxwell also noted that although John Hoover died before J. Edgar was born, his wife Celia survived until J. Edgar was fourteen years old, long enough to possibly inform him about the family's "darker" secrets. Based upon Ms. McGhee's passionate research into her family history and her earned credibility, it is reasonable to conclude that her assertions are valid.

Millie McGhee also recounted a different possibility that had been passed down through her family; either one might have been accurate: "[The other one] was that J. Edgar himself was not the son of Dickerson N. Hoover of Washington, as officially reported, but that he was actually the son of one Ivy (Ivery) Hoover [being of mixed race], and was born in the South, probably New Orleans, and then taken to Washington, DC at a very young age, and raised by the Hoovers in Washington."[75] Either of these possibilities—both of which caused him to be self-conscious—might account for his enmity toward African Americans, suggesting that it might have been a form of self-hatred, which might have been the source of a number of Hoover's other behavior patterns. For example, according to Anthony Summers, "Edgar never discussed his father at all, not even with his closest friends."[76] Dickerson Hoover Sr., Edgar's father, was resented by his wife Annie for his low-paying government job as a printer, and according to a niece of Edgar's, he was ashamed of his father because of his history of mental illness, which required Dickerson to spend lengthy periods in an "asylum" in Laurel, Maryland, about twenty miles northeast of Washington. That niece, Dorothy Davy, thought the whole Hoover family was "a little off in the head." His 1921 death certificate stated that Dickerson died of "melancholia" and "inanition." The first condition is now described as clinical depression; the second one is described as "the patient loses the will to live, stops eating and dies."[77]

Regardless of who slept with whom over a century before he was born—or to what extent, even whether or not he might have had a mixed racial genealogy—it was Hoover's negative attitudes, his obsessiveness about racial matters, his own conflicted sexuality, and his many other contradictions and peculiar traits that indicate he was deeply troubled by his own persona. His deep embarrassment about his racial lineage can be presumed to be a causal link to his attitudes, neuroses, and paranoia about the liberals, Communists, and "niggers" (to use his favored term) that seemed to occupy his mind to a great extent.

These personal traits, fueled by his narcissism and megalomania, combined to produce an all-powerful dictator-director of the FBI who unabashedly referred to the bureau, and himself, being inseparably and vicariously attached to it, as the "Seat of Government." (With his passing, that term lost its meaning, and the bureau was never referred to again as such). Running his empire like his private fiefdom, he came to believe he could do anything he wanted, since he was beholden to no one and had by 1950 amassed so much power that no one else in Washington could threaten his position, even any of the presidents who came and went during his reign. The level of his power can be seen in those annual bulletproof limousines for his personal use—a perquisite not even enjoyed by any of the presidents whom he served. It was this power that led him to believe that he could violate every law that got in his way, from routinely defrauding the government to conducting unconstitutional search and seizure actions—using "black bag trespass break-ins" to do it—in short, every imaginable illegal act up to and including multiple murders. Ultimately, he rationalized it as justifiable, even his patriotic duty, to conspire with others to murder multiple American leaders with whom he disagreed due to their political views.

Washington, DC, stayed segregated into most of the twentieth century, which began when Hoover was five. According to Tim Weiner, "In his world, blacks knew their place: they were servants, valets, and shoeshine boys. He feared the rise of a black 'messiah,' to quote a COINTELPRO mission statement. He presided over an Anglo-Saxon America, and he aimed to preserve and defend it."[78] His provincial—"plantation" is not too strong a word—attitudes about the lack of need for civil rights reform surfaced as early as 1955, after the Supreme Court's decision in *Brown vs. Board of Education* in 1954.

It was shortly after that, in 1955, when Martin Luther King Jr.'s activism began in the black communities of Georgia and Alabama, then expanded throughout the South over the next two years. On May 17, 1957, King took his message north to Washington, where he delivered his first major address to white America on the steps of the Lincoln Memorial.[79] Stanley Levison, a New York lawyer who had helped found the Southern Christian Leadership Conference in 1956—who had previously been thought by the FBI to be a key member of the US Communist Party—had been taken off the Bureau's list of top American Communists just seven weeks before King's speech. But six weeks after King's speech, the FBI noted in his file that he "was a CP member with no official title, who performs his CP work through mass organization activity. He appeared to have left his leading role in the Communist underground to devote himself to civil rights."[80]

The single time that Hoover had a major disagreement with Eisenhower's attorney general Herbert Brownell was related to the AG's proposals for new civil rights laws and enforcement provisions. On March 9, 1956, Brownell took Hoover along for a meeting with congressional leaders to advance a proposal for a new independent Civil Rights Commission, for establishing a civil rights section within the Justice Department "and the power to bring suits in federal courts to enforce voting rights." Hoover proceeded to "pull the rug right out from under him."[81] Fearing that the specter of racial intermarriage would become inevitable once the court's mandate for "mixed schooling" was implemented around the country, Hoover, Brownell's subordinate, argued against his boss, using that opportunity to accuse the NAACP and other civil rights advocates of preaching "racial hatred" and of being guided by Communists, while the White Citizens Councils were composed of "bankers, lawyers, doctors, state legislators and industrialists . . . some of the leading citizens of the South."[82] It was during the same period that Hoover casually implemented the outrageously illegal COINTELPRO program, targeting civil rights groups and their leaders, specifically Martin Luther King Jr., whom he would famously announce in November 1964 as "the most notorious liar in America."

J. Edgar Hoover: A Star Among Stars

Hoover was a master of promotion and public relations. That was important in 1968–70, because the public had still not been exposed to Hoover's nefarious, darker side and would not be until decades after he died. He was still held in high esteem by most people, a paragon of virtue and fairness in the administration of justice and the establishment of national policing standards. That was evidenced by the fact that forty million Americans tuned in faithfully, in the late 1960s and early 1970s, to watch the widely acclaimed television series *The F.B.I.* every Sunday evening.[83] The program was directly controlled by Hoover and Tolson, who, among their other duties, had placed an agent in Hollywood whose only function was to oversee the production of each episode. A major problem arose when Tolson and Hoover objected to the story line in the premiere episode, in which the "bad guy" had a strange personality disorder that caused him to murder women when he touched their hair; from that point on, there were no more hair fetishists allowed in any scripts.[84]

Casting was one of Hoover's highest priorities, and he personally approved the choice of Efrem Zimbalist Jr. as the star of the show, after meeting with him for two hours and giving him one of his famous monologues on subjects ranging from Soviet premier Nikita Khrushchev to Shirley Temple. After that meeting, Zimbalist called Hoover "the ideal . . . benevolent ruler"[85] and spoke glowingly of Hoover's formal and genial character: "He was a gentleman of the old school. He had that marvelous slight Virginia accent—it was a gentility, really, that he had—and I enjoyed watching him talk because he had this little dialect, those little ways the Virginians have of saying words. Very charming. And, as I said, he spoke with complete candor. That's why he was such a Godsend in Washington, where everybody is creeping around and pussyfooting and foggy-bottoming and all that kind of thing, and Hoover was a breath of fresh air . . . I really think if history is fairly told in the years to come—which is a big question—I think his importance is going to be enormous in this country. He's going to rank as one of the great figures. But it depends on who writes the history and God knows what our future is going to be."[86]

That description generally reflects what typical Americans thought of J. Edgar Hoover at the time Zimbalist gave that interview in the late 1960s, before Hoover's true nature—one of the most demented, high-level criminals without peer, except possibly in Nazi Germany—that only became known long after his death. Hoover and Tolson personally ensured that they were seen by the country as the good guys, and it would not be until five to seven years after their deaths that the true stories began to be revealed, ever so slowly, trickling out over the next three decades. But even after nearly five decades, some of the ugly truth is only now beginning to be revealed.

Birds of a Feather Flock Together

President Johnson and Hoover were very much alike, in many ways. It would be difficult to determine which had a greater dislike for the Kennedy brothers, since in both cases the hatred was profoundly visceral. Some historians and biographers believe that Johnson did not hate John as much as Robert, and there was probably a small margin of truth to that. However, Johnson was much more careful about allowing anyone—especially reporters—to see it, in John's case, for fear that it might reflect badly upon their relationship. Johnson attempted to portray himself as an admirer of JFK, at least before JFK's eventual murder. But he loosened his circumspection about his real feelings about John Kennedy in a September 1965 interview with historian William E. Leuchtenburg, when he slowly worked up to a mean-spirited diatribe that startled the history professor from the University of North Carolina at Chapel Hill as he quoted LBJ:

> "No man knew less about Congress than John Kennedy. He never even knew enough to know how to get recognized. When he was young, he was always off to Boston or Florida for long weekends. I never saw him in the cloakroom once. [Speaker Sam] Rayburn never knew him. The only way Rayburn thought of him at all was as a very young-looking man who might be going to die of malaria. He was a Joe College man. He didn't have rapport with Congress. He didn't have affection for Congress. And Congress felt that he didn't know where the ball was. Then, when he became president, all Kennedy had was leftover programs from Roosevelt, Truman and Eisenhower."
>
> I sat there on the green settee getting this all down on paper, but I could not believe what I was hearing. How could he be so careless as to say that about John F. Kennedy at a time when, less than two years after his assassination, grief at his murder was still raw?[87]

At the end of that interview, Leuchtenburg described his unusual ninety-minute interview as one in which Johnson felt compelled to compare himself not only to Kennedy, but to every other previous incumbent of that office: "The President had been comparing himself with others, past and present, and finding no peer . . . I managed a good-bye and a thank-you and departed, profoundly disquieted by what I had just seen and heard. I was reminded of something Barry Goldwater had said: that LBJ had so much power the Democrats could plug him in."[88]

Hoover and Johnson were also both extremely narcissistic, self-centered men with very large but fragile egos who could not handle criticism from others. Indeed, they would not condone anyone who might have the temerity to disagree with their policies. Both of them surrounded themselves with subordinates, all of whom were expected to give them unquestioned, blind devotion, never disagreeing with them on any substantive issues, always showering them with fawning adoration and love, either pure or feigned. When they met others, as part of their screening process both Johnson and Hoover would categorize them in multiple ways, but first and foremost was their weaknesses, how these might make them susceptible to future manipulation. They looked for men who had a strong need to belong to a greater cause: in Hoover's case a powerful and famed law enforcement agency admired around the country and the world, in Johnson's case to work for a very powerful politician on his way up the political ladder and, after 1963, the leader of the free world.

The most appropriate term to describe these men and women was, and is, "sycophant." David Halberstam described this characteristic of Johnson:

> [He] could catalogue the strengths and weaknesses of every man [in Congress]. The strength of a man put him off, but his weaknesses attracted him; it meant a man could be used. Whereas Kennedy had been uneasy in the face of another man's weakness, it embarrassed him and he tended to back off when a man showed frailty, to Johnson there was a smell of blood, more could come of this.[89]

Johnson would have used the same technique on people outside of Congress, as well. It can be reasonably deduced that, as he watched the FBI's success in the 1930s, and how the Bureau was universally well regarded then—owing to Hoover's promotional efforts—by the time he became a congressman in 1937, he had already established a personal long-term goal of ingratiating himself with Hoover as a means to accomplish his own agenda.

Thus it was undoubtedly no coincidence that Lyndon Johnson's home for nineteen years, at 4921 30th Place NW in Washington, was in the same block and across the street, about two houses away, from that of J. Edgar Hoover, who had moved into his home at 4936 30th Place in 1939.[90] Johnson's decision to buy that particular house in 1942—out of all the other ones then available in Washington—was undoubtedly one of his most meticulously planned decisions, knowing that opportunities to insinuate himself close to the famed director of the FBI would routinely come for many years thereafter. The homes in the area were certainly nice custom-designed homes, but they were not much larger than average for the area, not nearly the size of the mansions that were built nearby, along Massachusetts Avenue.

But for nineteen years, throughout his Senate majority leader tenure, Johnson continued living in that quiet, well-established, stable neighborhood in Northwest Washington, nestled in the four blocks between Connecticut Avenue and Rock Creek Park. Among Johnson's neighbors there, besides Hoover, were lobbyist Fred Black (next door), his acolyte Bobby Baker (a block away), and the "king" of Washington lobbyists, Irving Davidson (around the block on an adjoining street). All three were later indicted on various fraud charges; Black and Baker would serve time in prison. Davidson's indictment involved his association with Jimmy Hoffa and the Teamsters Union, but those charges were later dropped—coincidentally, after Hoffa disappeared in July 1975. Davidson also had extensive contacts and contracts with many foreign dictators, such as Fulgencio Batista of Cuba and his successor, Fidel Castro; "Papa Doc" Duvalier of Haiti; the other family dictatorships of Nicaragua (the Samozas) and the Dominican Republic (the Trujillos); and a number of mafiosi, including Carlos Marcello. One of Davidson's primary clients was Clint Murchison, a major Dallas oil baron connected closely to Johnson and Baker.[91]

Coincidentally, another neighbor (around the corner) was Louella Parsons, the movie columnist and screenwriter. According to Wikipedia, "She was retained and promoted by William Randolph Hearst—soon thereafter her columns would be read by twenty million people in four hundred newspapers worldwide."[92] She was also a regular guest and friend of both Johnson and Hoover, providing them access to news outlets around the country and world, to feed the news-hungry masses whatever propaganda they needed to dispense.

In 1961, having established a long-term friendship with Hoover that he knew would endure for as long as they both lived, Johnson moved on, buying a mansion called "The Elms" at 4040 52nd Street NW—just three miles away—when he became vice president.[93] That house had previously been owned by Washington socialite Pearl Mesta, known as "the hostess with the mostess" for her lavish parties featuring artists, entertainers, and Washington political figures. It is noteworthy that shortly after Johnson moved, Bobby Baker and Fred Black both sold their houses and moved next to the Johnsons so they could continue to be neighbors. As Mark North wrote about Baker's new house: "On one side was [Baker's] friend and business partner Fred

Black. On the other side was his longtime mentor, Lyndon B. Johnson."[94] Yet when they both got caught up in their respective scandals, Johnson would deny ever knowing them very closely at all, just as he had done when Billie Sol Estes was indicted for his frauds against the government—which Johnson himself had facilitated for many years: he would say about all three of them, "I may have met him once or twice, but I don't know him."

Possibly LBJ's Least Prevarication: Giving "Lady Bird" Her Nickname

Lyndon B. Johnson had begun using "LBJ" in the early 1930s, according to *Safire's Political Dictionary*. According to the legend, his wife, known previously as Claudia Alta Taylor, was conveniently given the nickname "Lady Bird" when she was two (in 1914) by a Negro nurse because "She's purty as a lady bird."[95] It is difficult to know which parts of this "family legend" were real or contrived, since much of LBJ's family lore was made up, such as Lyndon's repeated claim that one of his grandfathers was killed at the Battle of the Alamo, a story he had fabricated years before and had repeated so often that he apparently came to believe it, despite none of his forebears having been among those known to have been there.

When Lady Bird met Lyndon in 1934, his mania to pursue a political career, and achieve his life-long goal of becoming president,[96] was in full stride, and according to Caro, "he first showered her with questions ('I never heard so many questions; he really wanted to find out all about me'), and then—this man whose 'mind could follow another mind around and get there before it did'—with answers, answers, as she puts it, to 'questions that hadn't been asked . . . He told me all sorts of things I thought were extraordinarily direct for a first conversation'—about 'his ambitions,' how he was determined to become somebody."[97] It is admittedly conjecture, but it is not a stretch, given his manic manipulative skills, to suggest that he would eventually use that expression sometime during their courting, saying in his familiar Texas drawl, "You're as purty as a lady bird," and then immediately rechristening her for the exact purpose of giving her his initials, just as he did with his daughters, his dog "Little Beagle Johnson," his ranch, and his belt buckles (even having "LBJ" printed on ballpoint pens, cigarette lighters, and other trinkets that he gave away). It was consistent with how, throughout the entirety of his life, he had created the conditions around which his eventual legacy would be framed.

Chapter 2

PREVIOUS CRIMES
AND TREASONS

"[Hoover] was a brilliant chameleon . . . He had a very cunning, crafty, shrewd mind and he could make fools out of [intellectuals, and] . . . some senators and congressmen. He was one of the greatest con men the country ever produced, and that takes intelligence of a certain kind, an astuteness, a shrewdness." [98]

—William C. Sullivan, Former FBI Assistant Director

FBI's Illegal Placement of "Bugs" and Telephone Wiretapping

According to Tim Weiner, "The FBI had spied on every prominent black political figure in America since World War I . . . . Hoover spent his career convinced that communism was behind the civil rights movement in the United States from the start. Hoover gave special attention to William Edward Burghardt Du Bois. Born in 1868, the venerable Du Bois had become the head of the NAACP in 1910." [99] Hoover had begun his government career as head of the FBI during the Ku Klux Klan's heyday in the first half of the twentieth century, as they burned black churches and Jewish synagogues. The uniquely American terrorist organization was virtually ignored by Hoover and the FBI. This was confirmed by one of the FBI's Georgia agents, Fletcher D. Thompson: "Headquarters came out with instructions that we were not to develop any high-level Klan informants because it might appear that we were guiding and directing the operations of the Klan." [100] As Weiner stated, "This was a rationalization for racism." [101]

Eisenhower's attorney general, Herbert Brownell, in a May 20, 1954, memorandum to Hoover, gave him full carte blanche authority to conduct microphone surveillance and to bug whomever he chose, for whatever reason he might conjure up, using his "unrestricted" use of any methods he chose. Brownell even later testified that "[t]here never was any definition of the methods that were to be used in carrying out the directive . . . The methods were left to the discretion of the FBI." [102] As soon as Martin Luther King

Jr.'s name came to national prominence in December 1955, J. Edgar Hoover began monitoring his activities, even as King and his closest associates mistakenly presumed, according to Andrew Young, that "we thought of the FBI as our friends, the only hope we had."[103]

During the five years of Hoover's surveillance of Martin Luther King before JFK was sworn in, Hoover had become obsessed with destroying him, and he required his Special Agents in Charge (SACs) of his field offices to cull their files for all the "subversive" information they could gather and send it to him. Hoover's assistant, Cartha "Deke" DeLoach, was put in charge of compiling this assortment of innuendo, half-truths, and whole lies, sprinkled with sufficient "facts" to make it salable.[104]

During this period, Hoover had decided to order his agents to burglarize the Southern Christian Leadership Conference offices to obtain personal information about Dr. King and to install telephone wiretaps as well as "bugs" to record nontelephonic conversations and assorted other noises. Hoover did this on his own and without higher authorization. Those bugs were, by definition, contrary to the Constitution's Fourth Amendment: "The right of the people to be secure in their persons, houses, papers and effects, against unreasonable searches and seizures, shall not be violated."

Massive violations of that cherished tenet had gone on for decades before it was extended to King's surveillance, and it had been done with no authorizations from the judicial branch of government, or any other agency or department. Former FBI agent Wesley Swearingen, just one of thousands of agents around the country, stated that "[d]uring the 1950s, I was involved in hundreds of Black Bag Jobs in Chicago along with the late William F. Roemer Jr., who has written several books about his exploits with the Chicago Mafia." They were so commonly done, and numerous, that Swearingen said that he sometimes did two of them in a single day. Other former FBI agents confirmed that point, including William Turner, who stated that some agents were kept so busy doing these illegal break-ins that they were given special incentives—cash awards—and that all of this was kept top secret "and no one outside was privy to it." [105]

This well-established, brazenly illegal activity continued without pause when the Kennedy administration came into office in 1961, despite their initial ignorance of it pertaining to King. When he did become aware of it, Attorney General Robert Kennedy attempted to bring the wiretapping under some semblance of control. However, by that time the SCLC and King had already begun fighting back, with the issuance of a special report attacking the FBI on January 8, 1962. By then, the freedom rides that had begun in 1961 revealed which side the FBI was really on, and it was not

King's. The FBI's illegal wiretaps had provided evidence that two people in King's entourage, Stanley Levison and Jack O'Dell, had ties to the American Communist Party. This knowledge compromised the Kennedys' ability to cooperate with King until that issue was dealt with and impeded them from ending the illegal surveillance because of Hoover's brazen use of his powerful position as he exercised subtle blackmail to achieve his goals.[106]

By the summer of 1963—thanks largely to the congressional gridlock created and sustained by Lyndon Johnson as he cautioned Kennedy against moving too quickly on his civil rights initiative—the pent-up frustrations of African Americans had reached the boiling point. The tensions extended to civil rights leaders, including Dr. King, and was compounded by the enmity that had materialized between King and the Kennedys, which emanated from the FBI's investigation related to King's supposed Communist leanings. The situation between the Kennedys and Martin Luther King just before JFK's assassination was described in an article by John Meroney in the November 11, 2011, issue of the *Atlantic*:

> President Kennedy didn't worry about an espionage leak, or that the men would necessarily insert propaganda into King's speeches . . . Rather, the president feared the political fall-out that would come if it were revealed that the nation's foremost civil rights leader had advisers with ties to the Soviet Union . . . . by June, the president had grown weary of the risks King was causing him and decided to have a come-to-Jesus meeting with the minister in Washington. In the Rose Garden, he exhorted King that Levison was, as Kennedy described him, a "Kremlin agent." Get rid of him, demanded the president.[107]

Everyone of the political class in Washington knew the extensive nature of Hoover's files, and Robert Kennedy had constant reminders of it from the director himself: Hoover regularly sent updates to RFK on the files of Sam Giancana and his mistress Judith Campbell (whose talents the gangster shared with the president) as well as the president's favorite party girl, Ellen Rometsch, newly arrived from Communist East Germany and courtesy of the Quorum Club, run by Bobby Baker and Lyndon B. Johnson.

On August 28, 1963, Dr. Martin Luther King Jr. gave his most famous speech to a crowd of more than a quarter million people at the Lincoln Monument in Washington, DC: "I Have a Dream." It was inspirational to millions of Americans, black and white and all shades in between, yet others viewed it as a radical idea and a threat to their very existence.

Unfortunately, those "others" were also among the most powerful and richly arrogant, "very important" people, who believed that King's "dream" would become their nightmare. Thus, while he captured the imaginations and interest of people the world over, his speech also galvanized the powerful forces that feared him the most: the paranoid and reactionary leadership at the White House and the FBI, who subsequently undertook one of their biggest surveillance operations ever. Richard Nixon's misuse of governmental power paled in comparison to that of his predecessor, yet it ignited a reaction that led to the exposure of high-level crimes that had gone on for decades. The worst of Nixon's offenses related to various crimes that were conducted under the aegis of Lyndon B. Johnson but were not exposed until after Johnson's death, too late for a full accounting and atonement. Thus, they quietly slipped into oblivion.

Finally, some of the least critical governmental misdeeds (which spooks call a "limited hangout"*) became public a few years later, when in 1976 the Senate convened a special committee to investigate intelligence activities, popularly called the "Church Committee," for its chairman, Idaho Democrat Frank Church. There was a reason why this committee was so successful in uncovering much of the dirt left in the governmental "laundry" of the previous decade: both of the then-all-powerful men who created it were then dead. Hoover passed in 1972, then Johnson in 1973. Moreover, Richard Helms and James Angleton of the CIA were retired, and their successors were more circumscribed by the congressional sweeping process that had finally begun to calm a very disgruntled public. Despite the release of a limited amount of information, the highest secrets of government involvement in the 1960s assassinations were successfully kept hidden from the public.

The Church Report concluded that "the FBI's program to destroy Dr. King as the leader of the civil rights movement entailed efforts to discredit him with churches, universities and the press . . . through an extensive surveillance program, employing nearly every intelligence gathering technique at the Bureau's disposal."

---

* Per Wikipedia: A **limited hangout** or **partial hangout** is, according to former special assistant to the Deputy Director of the Central Intelligence Agency Victor Marchetti, "spy jargon for a favorite and frequently used gimmick of the clandestine professionals. When their veil of secrecy is shredded and they can no longer rely on a phony cover story to misinform the public, they resort to admitting—sometimes even volunteering—some of the truth while still managing to withhold the key and damaging facts in the case. The public, however, is usually so intrigued by the new information that it never thinks to pursue the matter further." Citations to: Victor Marchetti (August 14, 1978), *The Spotlight*, and "720 F2d 631 Hunt v. Liberty Lobby Dc." OpenJurist. 1983-11-28. Retrieved 2016-07-13.

Robert F. Kennedy: Fall, 1963—Squeezed from Both Sides

All summer long, the pressures on JFK and his attorney general brother had continued to mount, and by September they were manifest: the congressional gridlock; Hoover's insistence for more aggressive action against Martin Luther King Jr.; the steadily increasing publicity of Lyndon Johnson's unraveling scandals (both the TFX Air Force contract being wrestled away from Boeing to reaward it to General Dynamics and the myriad scandals in which Bobby Baker had become embroiled); and, among the worst, JFK's own secrets regarding his involvement with a number of ladies who had been procured on his behalf by none other than that same Bobby Baker who had been put into the position of pimping call-girls for the president by his mentor, Lyndon B. Johnson. By early October, the scandals had already produced the forced resignations of two of Johnson's highest-level appointees, Secretary of the Navy Fred Korth and Secretary of the Senate Robert G. "Bobby" Baker. The pressures on the Kennedys paled in comparison to the pressures on Lyndon Johnson, which were being applied to him directly by the Kennedys.

Protecting JFK was always Robert Kennedy's highest priority, and to do that he decided to stop any investigation into the Rometsch affair by having her deported. To keep her under the radar, he then tried to stop the Senate from investigating the sex angle of the multifaceted Bobby Baker scandals any further. Those actions immediately hit the newspapers (the October 28, 1963, headline of the *Des Moines Register* was "U.S. Expels Girl Linked to Officials—Is Sent to Germany After FBI Probe"; this article was subsequently read into the Congressional Record). Although RFK steered the investigations away from the sex angle, he continued for a time to feed Senator Williams information on the financial frauds being committed and was conducting his own investigation on Baker for tax evasion.[108] Meanwhile, Kennedy had collected more information regarding the party girls and which members of Congress had been involved with the girls. The numbers and parties involved were going to be difficult to sweep under the rug.

Johnson and Hoover knew that the Kennedy brothers were aching to replace them both in their second term. They also knew that they had to tread very carefully around the breaking news stories and rumors that were then quickly spreading about Capitol Hill's sex scandal because it was so closely related to the concurrent Bobby Baker financial scandals, which included Johnson's procurement and acceptance of a $100,000 payoff for the TFX contract and numerous other related financial payoff schemes developed over many years.[109] As Burton Hersh noted:

According to Justice Department insiders . . . Hoover had been tapping his attorney general's line, and he had heard Bobby laughingly assure his friends that, as big a pain in the ass as the Director had become, it really would not matter for a whole lot longer because he was on his way out. At worst, he would be seventy in 1965 and Jack would dump him then . . . Hoover—to whom his position and his existence were interchangeable—panicked. The stage was set for that very grim executive-mansion lunch. Watching both autocrats, Courtney Evans could imagine a head-on collision that would obliterate them both. "I figured I had one mission," Evans maintains with all the conviction his ninety years can muster. "Just keep the Kennedys from firing J. Edgar Hoover. I thought that was a blow they'd never recover from politically."[110]

At this point, Robert Kennedy faced the delicate task of dealing with not just one devil but three, simultaneously: Hoover, Johnson, and Baker. Hoover had insisted on expanding the FBI wiretaps on King, which RFK wanted to end completely; yet they had yielded the information about the Communist connections to two of King's associates and his own need to obtain Hoover's assistance. At that point in time, RFK's position over FBI Director Hoover had been severely compromised, and he needed to defer to him—in desperation—for his help in quashing the breaking presidential sex stories, to avoid their bringing down the entire administration. Obviously, Robert Kennedy couldn't go to Johnson for help, so he was forced to appeal to Hoover, hat in hand. Hoover's intense hatred of both Kennedy brothers put him into a quandary over how far he would go to help them, but he finally decided that he would use it as an opportunity to exploit their anxiety, using it as his ace in the hole to obtain another waiver from mandatory retirement. Undoubtedly this only worked because it gave the director added leverage with Bobby, to be used as an IOU and a guarantee of his extended tenure.

Hoover reluctantly agreed to Robert Kennedy's request of him, even though it didn't appeal to him, but he decided that he would go along with it since it would also bring a collateral benefit for his friend, Vice President Johnson, by removing the sex scandals Johnson had ties to that would otherwise result from congressional inquiry. But Hoover had a high price for his service: assurance from both the attorney general and the president (with whom he lunched on October 31, 1963) that he would not only not be forced to retire, but would also be given approval for four new wiretaps on Martin Luther King Jr., "a man both Kennedys, but particularly Bobby, had come to admire and respect."[111] Yet, while Bobby gave in to Hoover's demand a month before JFK's assassination, he limited it to a thirty-day period, whereby in the absence of compelling reasons to extend it further, it would end on November 21, 1963. It was a net cast widely, and it included the customary telephone taps that did not require on-site presence at King's residence, his offices and hotel rooms, and also extended to include bugs that required agents to conduct "black bag" operations involving illegal trespass to record nontelephonic audio to capture all other sound waves on the premises.

Keeping his end of the bargain, Hoover met secretly with Senate Majority Leader Mansfield and Senate Minority Leader Dirksen on October 28, 1963, at Mansfield's apartment.[112] His request to them, to limit the Senate's investigation, produced immediate results: by that afternoon, the Senate's plans to discuss Rometsch had been canceled. As noted by Richard Mahoney, "There was no more private discussion, much less public debate, of the Rometsch affair by the 'world's greatest deliberative body.'"[113]

Just a week after RFK reluctantly gave the nod for what he thought would be temporary wiretaps on King, his efforts to remove the sex angle from further publicity hit another snag: The Long Island tabloid *Newsday* printed an article on October 29, 1963, titled "Baker Scandal Quiz Opens Today," beginning with these words: "Already liberally spiced with sex, scandal, and intrigue, the tantalizing case of Robert G. (Bobby) Baker comes under official scrutiny today. And what everyone wants to know is: Who is going to get caught?" The article continued: "A report, from those who claim 'inside information,' is that the Justice Department started an investigation of Baker as a means of embarrassing Johnson and eliminating him from the Democratic ticket next year . . ."

A week after that, the pressure escalated again, for both Robert Kennedy and Lyndon Johnson, when the November 8, 1963, issue of *Life* magazine was published featuring a cover with a picture of Bobby Baker at a masquerade party with a bold headline: "Capital buzzes over stories of misconduct in high places: the Bobby Baker bombshell." The article (page 36) asked the rhetorical question: "How had a simple, hardworking majority secretary, earning $19,612 a year, struck it so rich in so short a time?"

November 22, 1963: Everything Changes

After JFK's assassination, Robert F. Kennedy became ineffectual in his position as attorney general, cut off from above by Johnson and from below by Hoover, both of whom hated him with a passion. Thus, his shock and grief in the aftermath of his brother's death ended his control over the King wiretaps and even over Hoover himself, when the FBI director immediately had the direct telephone line to the attorney general's office disconnected. Hoover ignored the thirty-day termination date of RFK's condition and did nothing to seek a renewal of that authority, while continuing the King wiretaps that Robert Kennedy had tried to limit. Athan Theoharis, in his 1991 book *From the Secret Files of J. Edgar Hoover*, explained that "Hoover did not comply with Kennedy's conditional requirement of a reevaluation in thirty days. Preoccupied with the assassination of his brother on November 22, 1963, the attorney general failed to request an evaluative report—nor did Hoover remind him of the condition."[114]

One month after the JFK assassination, on December 23, 1963, the FBI conducted a major conference involving the highest Bureau officials and a number of people from the larger field offices, including Atlanta and Memphis. As we will examine in more detail in later chapters, the conference was intended to identity all the avenues to intimidate and delegitimize Martin Luther King Jr. to his own followers as well as the country at large. Among them came the idea of enlarging the electronic surveillance that had already been conducted to include the planting of bugs in his hotel rooms, necessarily planted by illegal black bag operations. It is highly likely, according to Hoover biographer Curt Gentry, that the FBI already knew that *Time* magazine was planning to name Dr. King their Man of the Year, which indeed occurred on January 3, 1964. Two days after that, on January 5, FBI agents installed a bug at the Willard Hotel in Washington, which would produce audiotapes that would eventually be heard by dozens, perhaps hundreds of high officials, journalists, and newspaper publishers, television anchors, and others on Capitol Hill.[115]

Within weeks of becoming president, Lyndon Johnson personally began receiving the FBI tapes and transcripts for his personal listening and reading pleasure. The first Willard Hotel tapes were delivered to him on January 14, when DeLoach brought him eight pages of "Top Secret" FBI expert analysis of all of it. J. Edgar Hoover, upset about *Time*'s action, had vowed that the tapes "will destroy the burrhead."[116] Both Hoover and DeLoach, the newly appointed FBI liaison with the White House and Congress, quickly realized that the new president particularly enjoyed this special perquisite, including tales of other prominent people's personal lives direct from the FBI files. By early 1964, just as Johnson began his entreaties of cooperation to Martin Luther King Jr., he was enjoying a steady flow of FBI files and audiotapes at a rate that far exceeded anything in previous administrations. Hoover's exploitation of his direct relationship with the new president in the weeks and months following JFK's assassination, as part of his long-standing plan to destroy King, couldn't have been more clear.

On March 9, 1964, Hoover and DeLoach spent an entire afternoon discussing the King file with the new president, giving him a number of the latest illegally obtained audiotapes. According to Curt Gentry, "It was the longest period of time the FBI director had held a president's attention since his secret meeting with JFK about the Judith Campbell matter."[117]

Shortly afterward, Johnson began using the tapes to entertain certain of his guests, as some of them later confirmed. One of them, his longtime Texas crony, then lieutenant governor Ben Barnes, even described in his memoirs how Johnson played them for the purpose of sharing information. Barnes then stated that Johnson greeted him and said, "I want you to hear something, Barnes . . . You're not going to believe this":

> We walked into his bedroom, sat down, and he punched the "play" button on a tape recorder. And he was right—I couldn't believe what I was hearing. It was a recording, obviously made in secret, of Martin Luther King Jr. in what I will only describe as a very compromising situation. There were voices of a couple of women on the tape, as well as that of another man. I literally could not believe that I was sitting in the White House, in the company of the president of the United States, listening to an embarrassingly intimate tape of the greatest civil rights leader in our history. [118]

Afterwards, Barnes stated—apparently believing the president for whom the term "credibility gap" was created—that Johnson then told him that he was going to ask Hoover to destroy the tape and all copies of it. Still carrying his longtime tradition as one of LBJ's top apologists/protectors, Barnes tried to frame it as though the president weren't really using it for personal entertainment, writing that "Johnson wasn't playing the tape for prurient reasons."[119]

The truth was that Johnson's glee in playing those tapes became a semisecret legend among Washington politicos. There were numerous other reports (only a few selected samples follow below) affirming how President Johnson relished getting the FBI tapes, and how he took great delight in listening to all of them, but especially those featuring King's sexual exploits. One recent account was a 2011 article in *Atlantic* magazine, which stated: "He listened to the tapes that even had the noises of the bedsprings." This story was originally reported back in 1975 by *Time* correspondent Hugh

Sidey, who also stated that Johnson would say to anyone having nice things to say about Dr. King, "Goddammit, if you could only hear what that hypocritical preacher does sexually."[120]

Harold Weisberg noted in his 1970 book *Frame-Up* that Carl Rowan, a notable syndicated African American columnist and television pundit of the era, who had also served as head of the United States Information Agency, acknowledged that, as "a ranking government official," the FBI had sent him some of their sleaziest King reports; furthermore, he also confirmed that the reports had been "widely disseminated throughout the government."[121]

Benjamin Bradlee, editor of the *Washington Post*, said that he had been offered all of the transcripts but stated that he had declined them because he found all of it to be "offensive." Bradlee went further, stating that "they showed them to plenty of people. They showed them to Gene Patterson when he was editor of the *Atlanta Constitution*. But I'm sure they were not printable, I mean, I have the substance of them; they had to do with his sexual exploits . . . one that I particularly remember was King watching the televised funeral of Kennedy in some hotel room, I don't remember which, and he made some reference to the sexual habits of the President and Mrs. Kennedy." Demaris asked Bradlee, "And DeLoach would be peddling this?" Bradlee replied, "Peddling, smeddling. They [the FBI] were trying to discredit King."[122]

Jack Anderson (who was hated by Hoover) was never offered the tapes or transcripts directly but had obtained copies of some of the material from another source and published some of it after confirming it with the woman who had been identified within the documents.[123]

The real purpose of the tapes was thus revealed: the fact that the first tapes quickly produced the second set, then the third, and so on, proved the real intent of the taping, that by the time that Lyndon Johnson had become president, these tapes were not for the purpose of investigating the accused "communist" Stanley Levison; one need only look at what then occurred with the recordings. They were all immediately played for Hoover to screen, and then have transcripts prepared, after which DeLoach was quickly dispatched to the White House to present them directly to the president or his chief of staff (Bill Moyers), as though they contained special state secrets or wartime strategy freshly purloined from the Russians. As soon as each crop of new tapes was harvested, processed, and the fruits immediately sent to the president, agents were then ordered to the next city where King was to visit, to make sure no "intelligence" was missed. All of the requisitions were prepared, assignments given to the designated special agents, airline and hotel reservations secured, bugging equipment ordered and installed, the taping of the subjects completed and copies made, in a continuing process that worked like a well-oiled machine so that they could keep the pipeline filled and fresh tapes dispatched regularly to the president, all for his personal entertainment.

David J. Garrow noted in his 1981 book *The FBI and Martin Luther King, Jr.: From "Solo" to Memphis* that Hoover had a strong obsession with the sexual lives of others generally, but in no case was it stronger than in relation to King's.[124] Hoover, according to Garrow, had attempted to portray his interest not as a voyeur—unlike Johnson, "who took perverse pleasure" from it—but wanted others to believe that he was offended by it, as though he looked at it as a puritan might. Yet while uttering "denunciations of virtually every possible sort of sexual conduct, his relentless collecting of such material revealed that his professed offense . . . was rhetoric rather than fact . . . the performances always had an air of 'isn't it awful; please show me more.'"[125]

The playing of those tapes was not confined to the White House, and it went well beyond being merely a source of amusement for President Johnson and his chief of staff, Bill Moyers. It had become a favorite party gag enjoyed by other high-level government officials in those heady days of the mid-1960s, even for FBI officials customarily thought of as a bit haughty. In addition to Hoover and Tolson, DeLoach had even played them for the amusement of his Bureau friends in Congress.[126] Garrow also noted that many others in the FBI shared the obsessions of those at the highest level, such that they "were so fascinated by King's activities they could not stop talking about them in extensive detail . . . the voyeurs saw him as an animal too, but one in a circus, one to be watched in performance."[127]

Robert Sherrill, author of *The Accidental President*, writing contemporaneously in 1967, said that Bill Moyers had "expressly approved" circulating, within the executive branch, a secret FBI report intended to discredit Dr. Martin Luther King.[128] An entire section of this report was devoted to the details of King's personal life and sexual preferences, according to a Senate Intelligence Committee report in 1976. Moyers admitted under questioning that he understood that the FBI reports dealt with personal information, that he never questioned the propriety of it, that he never considered it inappropriate, and that neither did anyone else in the White House. As the *New York Times* later reported, "Johnson found gossip about other men's weaknesses a delicious hiatus from work."[129] It is interesting that a decade later, Moyers admitted that some of the taping the FBI did on behalf of Johnson was excessive, but it took even longer for him to admit that they were constitutional violations.[130] He has never been held to account for his own actions, nor was Johnson ever held to account for his abuse of illegal bugs and wiretapping, as eventually happened to Richard Nixon under much less egregious circumstances.

Still another such reference to how the tapes had become a kind of party-time ritual at the White House during LBJ's reign was made by the late CBS News reporter Morley Safer in his 1990 memoirs. Safer's characterization of Bill Moyers's involvement with Johnson in the bugging of King's private life was summarized as being "not only a good soldier but a gleeful retainer feeding the appetites of Lyndon Johnson . . . Moyers, the sometimes overly pious public defender of liberal virtue, the First Amendment, and the rights of minorities, playing the role of Iago."[131]

Jack Anderson and Drew Pearson teamed up to reveal much of the salacious material, not just to more government officials and layers of bureaucrats toiling away in the cubicles of scores of government buildings around Washington, but at long last to the public at large (to men, anyway, to minimize the possibility of embarrassment to ladies) when it was published "in the men's magazine *True,* dated January 1969 [but] written months earlier":

> LBJ has always had a fine appreciation for a story about a leader's extracurricular love life. A typical backstairs report, passed on to the White House by Hoover, dealt with an alleged affair of a prominent civil-rights leader. The secret FBI memo quoted a confidential informant as reporting that the man "has been having an illicit love affair with [a Los Angeles woman] since 1962." A love affair, no matter how sordid, is no business of the FBI—unless, perhaps, one of the parties happens to be a spy. There is no evidence that the leader and the lady, if the story is true at all, were plotting between tendernesses to overthrow the government. Yet J. Edgar Hoover solemnly informed the President: "[He] calls this woman every Wednesday and meets her in various cities throughout the country. The source related an incident which occurred some time ago in a New York City hotel, where [the leader] was intoxicated at a small gathering. [He] threatened to leap from the 13th floor window of the hotel if this woman would not say she loved him . . ."[132]

Six months later, the story went even more widely public, when Richard Harwood and Lawrence Stern wrote about it in the June 11, 1969, *Washington Post*, as these excerpts show:

> For several years a piece of Washington apocrypha known as "the Martin Luther King tape" was the subject of sly and ugly surmise among certain journalistic insiders. There are those who claim to have had The Tape played for them by obliging law enforcement officials. Others are said to have been given transcripts of a gathering, bugged by Government [*sic*] investigators, at which Dr. King and friends were present.
>
> It was one of those repugnant but enduring stories that cling to controversial public figures. The FBI and Justice Department steadfastly denied knowing anything specific about electronic surveillance of Dr. King. Shoulders would shrug, eyebrows would arch knowingly, fingers would point discreetly in other directions. And FBI Director J. Edgar Hoover contented himself with attacking the civil rights leader as "the most notorious liar in the country."
>
> [. . .]
>
> The gist of the testimony was that a group of men—one of them a 22-year-old FBI clerk—sat in air-conditioned rooms and listened to the private conversations of this prominent American without the faintest shred of legitimacy or sufficient cause . . .

Ironically, it was President Johnson, in late 1965, who finally ordered that the practice be restricted, due to pressures that had started to mount from the newly appointed Solicitor General Thurgood Marshall. Johnson had already begun planning to eventually appoint Marshall to the Supreme Court, as another move on his political chessboard. Marshall had asked the Supreme Court to vacate convictions due to illegally obtained evidence after receiving three such complaints.[133] According to ex-FBI agent William Turner, as a result of Marshall's action regarding the Bureau's "promiscuous bugging without the attorney general's authorization . . . scores of important prosecutions would have to be dropped (one beneficiary was Bobby Baker, LBJ's political crony, who had been found guilty of influence peddling)."[134] That parenthetical point might be one reason why LBJ did nothing to intercede in Marshall's action. Although Johnson had often expressed his opposition to electronic surveillance generally, that sentiment was exposed as a ruse when he was the recipient of the FBI files, tapes, and transcripts, especially those pertaining to King's personal life.[135]

Johnson had always enjoyed listening to the tapes of others, especially those of King, but he decided to concede the point to Marshall, probably due in part to his own paranoia about being caught on tape himself in a discussion with someone else being targeted, unbeknownst to him. Hoover resisted compliance with the new restrictions for months, at one point giving advance authorization without first getting the attorney general's approval, according to Taylor Branch, "implying that Katzenbach would have approved it if there had been time, [so] he sent notice afterward in an unprecedented sort of post-facto request." This happened in October 1965 and was one of several incidents that led to Katzenbach requesting reassignment to the State Department one year later, mostly due to his inability to effectively control Hoover.[136]

The first evidence that the Bureau was finally (almost) on board with the new restriction against all forms of this surveillance was contained in a memo dated July 19, 1966, from Assistant Director William Sullivan[137] to his peer Cartha DeLoach, which stated: "We do not obtain authorization for 'black bag' jobs outside the Bureau . . . Such a technique involves trespass and is clearly illegal; therefore, it would be impossible to obtain any legal sanction for it,"[138] despite then admitting that these burglaries had been very effective in the past. Six months later, Hoover wrote to both Sullivan and DeLoach in response to continued requests from field offices for such authorizations: "I note that requests are still being made by Bureau officials for the use of 'black bag' techniques. This practice, which includes also surreptitious entrance upon premises of any kind, will not meet with my approval in the future."[139]

The reason the requests continued to be received for several months after the policy had finally been suspended was clearly because it had long been a customary and routine practice of the field offices and an entrenched policy at the "SOG" for about four decades, interrupted only briefly by Robert Kennedy's valiant attempt to bring them under reasonable control—which Hoover and his acolytes firmly resisted—then resumed again for another two and a half years after RFK's failed attempts.

The pertinent point in this study of the FBI's use of electronic surveillance on Martin Luther King is that in his case it continued nearly unabated for at least ten years. Hoover had quickly reverted to the pre-Kennedy surveillance rules and gave carte-blanche approval to the FBI to continue monitoring King throughout that period, and then, when that news became public, he cunningly attempted to place the blame back on Robert Kennedy and cited RFK's temporary thirty-day approval to do that.

Repeatedly using RFK's authorization (which had been temporary, originally expiring on November 21, 1963) throughout 1964–65 and early 1966 to justify the practice, Hoover again reverted to using it for months, even *after* the 1966 suspensions went into effect for new surveillance. According to King biographer Taylor Branch, author of a three-volume set subtitled *America in the King Years,* during December 1966 and into early 1967, "Hoover authorized 'Deke' DeLoach to launch preemptive sabotage. Agents discreetly monitored results over the consolation wiretaps on Stanley Levison . . . ."[140] Upon receiving the bounty produced by this continued illegal action, "Hoover scrawled 'Excellent' on a report that stated, 'our counterintelligence aim to thwart King in receiving money from the Teamsters has been quite successful to date.'"[141]

Yet Hoover had the temerity, in December 1966, to inveigle one of his congressional sycophants, Iowa Republican H. R. Gross, into releasing a statement to newspapers that predictably showed up on the front page of the *New York Times* on Sunday, December 11, under the headline "Hoover Asserts Robert Kennedy Aided Buggings."[142] This despite the fact that it was Robert F. Kennedy who, upon finding out about the outrageously illegal, long-term FBI practice, had attempted to finally bring it under control but failed to overcome Hoover's efforts to resist it. This news story spread like wildfire to newspapers across the country, under subheadlines such as "Which Do You Believe?"

Robert Kennedy remained as attorney general until he won election as a New York senator and took office in January 1965. The newly appointed attorney general, Nicholas Katzenbach, discovered the existence of the electronic surveillance programs when he took office.[143] Even then, though he was appointed in February 1965, according to the previously noted King biographer Taylor Branch, it took him over a year to make much headway: "By July of 1966, Katzenbach had managed to trace and shut down not only shadowy [and much more intrusive] bugs but also many wiretaps."[144] But he still had not managed to overcome Hoover's intransigence. As Katzenbach explained in a 1968 oral history interview with Paige E. Mulhollan, he had to deal with a threat on the part of the FBI "to stop organized crime investigations if they couldn't have this technique."[145]

MULHOLLAN: It got down to that?
KATZENBACH: They said without this your whole program will collapse.
M: Is this the period in which you got into this public misunderstanding with Hoover which made the papers several times when he said things were one way and you—
K: No, this was really subsequent to that when he was doing it with respect to Kennedy, and I succeeded in getting both Hoover and Kennedy mad at me.
M: That's what happens to the man in the middle.

K: By my statement which I honestly believed to have been true, I said Mr. Kennedy did not know about it but Mr. Hoover thought he did.

M: So both of them in effect were right.

K: And I thought you couldn't sit calling one or the other a liar, which is the way they tended to do with each other.

Ramsey Clark, the new attorney general (after Katzenbach had left for the State Department, finally realizing that Hoover's power and ruthlessness were uncontrollable), advised the president that Hoover had coerced his agents—reportedly between forty and fifty of them—who had witnessed RFK reviewing or becoming aware of illicit bugs, to sign affidavits to the effect that he was complicit in their installation.[146] Of course, they did that for fear of being fired if they hadn't. It was worse than a pot calling a kettle black; it was more akin to a burglar, after decades of plying his criminal craft, then blaming a property owner for a burglary he committed that went undetected because of an alarm system that he had jimmied. Kennedy admitted his prior approvals of limited wiretaps of telephones to aid FBI investigations but stated that he had never approved the highly intrusive and illegal practice of trespassing for the purpose of planting electronic bugs.[147]

President Johnson's apologists have attempted to portray his relationship to Martin Luther King Jr. as a magnanimous and friendly collaboration fueled by a common desire to spring the nation into a newly desegregated "great society" where all people were suddenly equals. They were only half-right, as that was clearly not among Johnson's dearest dreams, though it was King's singular lifelong goal.

Part II

The PLOT Timeline (1964–1967)

Chapter 3

THE BACKGROUND OF RACIAL VIOLENCE IN THE EARLY 1960S AND THE LBJ/MLK "COLLABORATION"

(Elapsed Time: Three Months)

"We believe the highest patriotism demands the ending of the war and the opening of a bloodless war to final victory over racism and poverty."

—*Martin Luther King Jr.*

One Week After Selma:
The FBI's Hand in the Murder of Viola Liuzzo

In the wake of the March 1965 "Bloody Sunday" attempt in Selma, Alabama, to march across the Edmund Pettus Bridge, many people from northern states decided to respond to Martin Luther King Jr.'s call to participate in a new attempt the following week. Detroit activist Viola Liuzzo, a thirty-nine-year-old housewife and mother of five, was one of them. Heeding Dr. King's call, she drove the family Oldsmobile from Detroit, Michigan, to Selma, Alabama, and participated in the successful Selma-to-Montgomery march. She also actively helped with coordination and logistics, even loaning her Oldsmobile to the cause, allowing other volunteers to use it to pick up and drop off fresh recruits at the airport and, in the interim, to shuffle the marchers about. On March 25, she had been looking around for her car and saw it at the St. Jude staging area in Montgomery, with a nineteen-year-old volunteer, Leroy Moton, at the wheel.

Liuzzo had heard that Moton did not have a driver's license, so she took his place behind the wheel, first dropping someone off at the airport before heading back to Selma with others. After being harassed by Klansmen, then evading them by speeding up and slowing down, she drove one black man from Selma to the airport and returned with three white females from

Pennsylvania to Selma. After resting for a short time, she and Moton began the trip back to Montgomery to pick up others who were stranded there. On the way back, they encountered an "action team" of four Birmingham Klansmen, who were restless and brooding over their anticlimactic day after their failed attempts to harass Negro marchers, then being stopped by an Alabama trooper for having a loud muffler. After that, they had been frightened off from harassing another targeted group of pedestrians by a National Guard jeep with a machine gun mounted on its rear.[148]

At a stoplight on Broad Street in Selma, the Klansmen spotted the Oldsmobile with Michigan plates being driven by a white woman with a black male passenger. They speculated on what kinds of lewd acts this racially mixed couple might have been up to, deciding that their day was not to be wasted after all. Following them as they left the city, one of the Klansmen in the back promised the other a souvenir trophy: "the nigger's sport coat." After they had traveled well into the country, the windows were lowered on the right side of the Klansmen's car as they began to pass the Oldsmobile; as they pulled up alongside Mrs. Liuzzo, three guns were pointed at her car when they began firing, killing her instantly. Moton had been busy fiddling with the radio dial and had not noticed that they were being followed. Realizing that Liuzzo was now dead, he grabbed the wheel, hit the brake, and turned off the ignition, which safely stopped the car.[149]

A few hours after the ambush, after midnight, reacting to the bulletins coming across the newswires, Lyndon Johnson called Attorney General Katzenbach, saying, "I didn't wake you up, did I?" Then he asked, "The woman is from Michigan?" and Katzenbach replied that she was but explained that they still didn't have many details about the incident. Not satisfied with his attorney general's promise to have more information to him "before breakfast," Johnson called the overnight duty officer's desk at FBI headquarters, asking for an update at 1:07 a.m., then again four minutes later. The only information available, he was told, was that the victim was dead, an autopsy was being performed, bullet fragments were recovered, and her clipboard, headed "transportation committee," had also been recovered from the car. That was all they knew, at least at FBI headquarters, but the night supervisor, Harold Swanson, following the president's instruction, called Inspector Joe Sullivan in Selma to tell him, "The president just called me and said you should work all night."[150]

Some of the news had not yet reached Washington: in Selma, the police had already arrested the nineteen-year-old volunteer who had survived the attack, Leroy Moton. As the only known witness to the attack, in a town now seething with emotion on both sides, he was in grave danger of being handed off to policemen from Lowndes County—the scene of the crime—who might have had their own customized white sheets hanging in their closets. Another activist, Diane Nash, who managed to complete a telephone call to FBI headquarters sometime during the night to alert them to Moton's predicament, was assured that Inspector Joe Sullivan and other FBI agents were interviewing Moton, and that he was merely in protective custody.[151]

But FBI Director J. Edgar Hoover knew much more about that crime scene in the wee hours of Friday morning, March 26, 1965. He called President Johnson before breakfast, assuring him that everything was under control, in fact nearly solved, because "one of our men [was] *in* the car" (emphasis in original). He then incorrectly stated that "of course [he] had no gun and did no shooting."[152] Johnson thanked his friend Hoover, saying, "As usual, you're right on top of it," and asked him the difference between an infiltrator and an informant. "We only go to someone . . . who is in the Klan, and persuade him to work for the government. Uh, we pay him for it. Sometimes they demand a pretty high price, and sometimes they don't. Now, for instance, in those three bodies we found in Mississippi, we had to pay thirty thousand dollars for that," Hoover replied. Regarding the incident in Alabama the previous night, he said the informant was "not a regular agent of the Bureau," but "fortunately he happened to be in on this thing last night."[153]

Taylor Branch noted, "President Johnson hung up the telephone and looked blankly at his aides. 'Do you know Hoover had a guy, an informer, in that car that shot her?'"[154] Branch, using the plural, did not identify all of the aides who were there, only Katzenbach; it is highly likely that his highest-level aide at that time, Bill Moyers (famously designated as being "in charge of everything"), was there as well, among others. Hoover's "radioactive secret" about having an FBI informant, Gary Thomas Rowe, in the backseat of the car and being one of the three shooters would haunt the Bureau for three decades. At the time, the only people who knew about Hoover's secret—other than President Johnson and an unknown number of his aides—were a few of Hoover's top level aides (at a minimum, Tolson, DeLoach, and Sullivan, possibly others) and the local agents who had made contact with him.[155]

Assistant FBI Director William C. Sullivan, who had been in charge of these hooligans, wrote: "When I got hold of Rowe, I really gave him hell. Why hadn't he grabbed the gun, or hit the killer's arm and deflected his aim? 'I couldn't,' he told me. 'There were five [*sic*—lying to protect himself] of us in the car. I was in the back seat behind the driver. We were driving along very slowly when suddenly the guy sitting in the front passenger's seat, way out of my reach, drew his gun and fired. I knew he had a gun, and I knew that the others had guns too, but there was no reason to think anyone would use one.'"[156] Sullivan's account portrays the informant as being caught up unwittingly in an attack he could not have anticipated, which is a bit unbelievable given the context. For what other purpose were they chasing the car, then? It is also notably different than the account by the Pulitzer Prize–winning Taylor Branch, including the number of men in the car and how many guns were being used; clearly, Sullivan's account was slanted toward a version of events to portray the FBI in a better light.

Despite the fact that their informant's "intelligence" led the FBI to close the case very quickly, with an arrest of all four Klansmen the next day, the fact that Gary Thomas Rowe wound up in the back of the Klansmen's car would prove to be an immediate, and nearly endless, embarrassment for the Bureau. That very afternoon, Rowe was not present when the other three suspects appeared, and of course the news reporters wanted to know why. It was because he went with his trusted FBI handlers back to the crime scene and told them where they could find the shell casings that were thrown out the window. He was certainly aware that his fellow Klansmen would be quick to suspect him as being a turncoat, so he claimed that the FBI had given him a severe grilling, keeping him in isolation all day, and then, when he appeared for his arraignment, he did so with a snarling and surly look on his face to the reporters and everyone else as he portrayed himself as gallantly resisting all the pressure being put on him. Meanwhile, the FBI lowered the cloak of secrecy over the entire city, county, state, and finally the country, with an edict from Director Hoover: "All agents must keep their mouths shut." He added in longhand, "I want no comments nor amplifications made in Ala. or here, as President has made his statement & it ends there."[157]

By April, President Johnson began wondering if he had offended Dr. King in some way because he had heard nothing further from him. It was probably an early sign that their short-term "collaborative period" would soon end, when he said to an aide: "Normally they're tellin' you that you are either playin' hell, or you're doin' a good job, and we just haven't heard anything."[158]

By the time the first trial in the Liuzzo case began for defendant Collie LeRoy Wilkins, Robert Shelton, the Imperial Wizard of the Alabama Ku Klux Klan, joined him at the defense table. FBI Inspector Joe Sullivan accompanied the informer Gary Thomas Rowe, who by then had been "outed" and had been given a protective guard to dissuade other Klansmen from harming him. The attorney for Wilkins was referred to as "Klan Klonsel" Matt Murphy, who performed like a showman himself, denouncing the victim, Mrs. Liuzzo, as a "white nigger who turned her car over to a black nigger for the purpose of hauling niggers and communists back and forth." He also accused Leroy Moton of shooting Liuzzo himself after interracial sex and then verbally attacked the informer/star witness Rowe "as a liar— 'treacherous as a rattlesnake . . . a traitor and a pimp and an agent of Castro and I don't know what all'—for violating his membership oath to guard Klan secrets." "Klonsel" Murphy later sued Rowe for legal fees before Rowe defected from the Klan, acknowledging his role as an informer; after that, he could no longer find any lawyer in the state willing to represent him.[159]

The *New York Times* reported that "No one, prosecutor or defense lawyer, had a kind word for the dead woman." Finally, on May 7, the jury deadlocked on a guilty verdict by a vote of 10–2 for manslaughter, which caused the case to be put back onto the court calendar for a new trial. Several jurors complained that Rowe was escaping justice for his own involvement and felt that the jury would have concluded matters with a guilty verdict had he been forced to stand trial himself.[160]

At this point, Rowe's role had become something of a national controversy, thanks in part to nationally syndicated newspaper columnist Inez Robb, who wrote: "What sorely troubles me, if we accept the prosecution's account of the slaying, is the moral aspect of Rowe's presence in the car . . . Under what kind of secret orders did Rowe work? It is one woman's opinion that the FBI owes the nation an explanation of its action in the Liuzzo case."[161]

Five months later, another dramatic trial commenced for Klansman Collie Wilkins in the murder of Viola Liuzzo, with the defense counsel, Arthur Hanes, taking over, having replaced "Klan Klonsel" Murphy, who had died in the interim. Hanes was an attorney then known throughout Alabama as the "gentleman segregationist." Upon deliberating an hour and a half, the new jury voted to acquit the accused trigger-man of all charges on October 22, 1965, a Friday. By Monday, the national outrage prompted the Justice Department to announce support for an ACLU initiative banning all-white juries in Alabama. Dr. King, with Coretta in Paris, decided to cancel his trip to Britain to return home and participate in protests of that cruelly unjust verdict, fearing that to do otherwise would be tantamount to accepting "the beginning of vigilante justice."[162] Hanes later defended both Wilkins and another Klansman involved in the attack, Eugene Thomas, against federal charges of violating Mrs. Liuzzo's civil rights, but he lost that case, and the two men were sentenced to ten years in prison. Arthur Hanes had previously been the mayor of Birmingham and had accused King of being behind the city's racial unrest that led to the Public Safety Commissioner Eugene "Bull" Connor's use of German Shepherds and fire hoses to control that "unrest."[163]

Hanes and his son, Arthur Hanes Jr., were also the first attorneys for James Earl Ray after his arrest and will reappear later in this book.

The FBI, courtesy of Director Hoover, paid Gary Thomas Rowe $10,000 in January 1966 and obtained a release from any further liabilities for his "service." In inducing Rowe to testify against his old friends, he was given dispensation by Katzenbach for his own acts, and, in return, he would be given a new identity and moved far away, in the US Federal Witness Protection Program. That new identity turned out to be as a deputy US marshal based in California. However, even in his new life, he hadn't given up his taste for liquor in large quantities, which caused him to be quick to display his badge and revolver whenever he overindulged. In the meantime, a decade later, Attorney General Griffin Bell discovered that back in Alabama, even up to five years before the Liuzzo murder, Rowe had involved the FBI in other crimes: he had first warned the FBI in advance of a Klan-police agreement to beat Freedom Riders in Birmingham in 1961, then participated in the attack, becoming directly "involved in the violence."[164] The numerous other legal minefields Rowe had left in his wake allowed DeLoach and Hoover to escape accountability for all their related misdeeds pertaining to Rowe because of the open-ended commitment given by Katzenbach, who had never known about any of his prior activities—having incorrectly presumed he had become an informant just before the Selma incident in March 1965.[165] Rowe eventually died in 1998 under the pseudonym of Thomas Neil Moore."[166]

The Real Relationship between MLK and the FBI . . . and LBJ

One of Dr. King's associates at the Southern Christian Leadership Conference, Ralph Abernathy, said, "We looked upon the President as our friend, and we really didn't hold him responsible"[167] for what the FBI had been doing to undermine King. But as David Garrow noted, the FBI was deliberately running afoul of its own guidelines not only from within, but with the active prodding of the president. The question of how much the sharing of those audio files—not only with Johnson, but with other high-ranking officials—might have undermined the support King and the SCLC otherwise would have had was incalculable.[168] This statement affirms the one noted earlier, from Andy Young, who stated the actual White House attitude was that "on the surface we were being smiled at and granted grudging support; below the surface we were distrusted, resented and undercut."

In his book *The Last Crusade*, Gerald McKnight affirmed that the FBI did everything it could to disrupt the Poor People's Campaign, aided and abetted by local police agencies as well as other agencies of the federal government, including military intelligence.[169] McKnight wrote that "it was the president's [Johnson's] politically convenient pet thesis that the ghetto rebellions of the 1960s were the work of small cadres of black conspirators. Johnson believed that the community surveillance and intelligence-gathering program coordinated by operatives from the Justice Department, military intelligence, and the FBI would give the government the inside track on when the next ghetto would 'blow,' allowing the government to take preemptive action. Although the whole concept was spectacularly wrongheaded, it reflected the hold the mystique of counterinsurgency had on official Washington."[170]

What numerous other authors have documented—each of the individual facts being scattered pell-mell among dozens of other books—collectively proves, beyond a shadow of a doubt, that the very short period of "collaboration" between Dr. King and Lyndon Johnson was even less of a collaborative venture than the movie *Selma* depicted as only three months. It was in fact merely a temporary joint venture, nearly forced upon two principals having no real or substantive, long-term mutual goals; they combined their efforts together in a torturous relationship to accomplish a single mission, though their motives were diametrically opposed. As previously noted, Dr. King's goals were noble and clear; Johnson's were murky and self-serving, merely a part of his eternal cunning quest to leave a trail of legislative accomplishments in his wake, all designed for the purpose of creating a faux "legacy" to distract future generations from his real imprint on America. He knew that having a noble cause would create the legacy he craved, even if that was merely the public perception of his motive.

As referenced in the Prologue, King's primary biographer, Taylor Branch, confirmed that the end of King's working relationship with Johnson occurred only two weeks after the Voting Rights Act was signed into law on August 6, 1965.[171] In their last conversation, the shadow of the escalating Vietnam War had already begun to create a chasm that would never be bridged. In the ensuing period of nearly two years, their short-term "collaborative" period went into a kind of dormancy before it crashed for good: On April 4, 1967, the chasm became official, dramatic, and irreversible. Dr. King's speech at the Riverside Church in New York City on that day created a figurative line in the sand that Lyndon Johnson viewed as a threat to his presidency. Precisely one year later, on April 4, 1968, that threat was eliminated when King was murdered. The late Dr. Martin Luther King Jr. would never be in a position to threaten Johnson's own presidency, or his eventual contrived "legacy."

Many stories have been previously reported about Johnson's real attitudes about minorities, all of which affirm his lifelong racism. His preeminent biographer, Robert Caro, wrote an entire chapter ("The Compassion of

Lyndon Johnson") in his third volume, *The Master of the Senate*, explaining how Johnson portrayed himself "for the record" to his friends (those with whom he "talked liberal") and aides who earnestly testified that he had no "bigotry" or "prejudice"—yet according to his true friends and those who were being more honest and candid, the exact opposite adjectives would be used. In the latter case, the descriptors came from the wheeler-dealers he socialized with in Suite 8F of the Lamar Hotel in Houston. These were "men who felt that Negroes and Mexican-Americans were inherently dumb, dirty, lazy, stupid, looking only for handouts ('gimmes,' as 8F's presiding spirit, Herman Brown, called black Americans) and talked to them, too, so passionately that they believed he shared *those* feelings, shared them fully."[172] Within that lengthy chapter, Caro repeated a continuing chain of paragraphs beginning with "To take Lyndon Johnson at his word—his word that 'I never had any bigotry in me'—it is necessary to ignore other words of Lyndon Johnson's—his own words, written, in his handwriting, in a private diary he kept . . . words spoken in his own voice, and preserved on a tape recording[s] . . . it is necessary to ignore notes taken by reporters on statements he made in off-the-record conversations . . . it is necessary to ignore certain phrases in his early speeches."[173]

After each of these, Mr. Caro noted the specifics, all of which provided irrefutable citations to back up the claim that Lyndon Johnson had conflated and conflicted his prevarications and attempted to use them to replace the more solid, actual instances of his true sentiments. The entirety of that chapter was a reflection of Johnson's desultory attitudes toward all minorities, whether black, brown, or yellow. But Caro tempered it, as he had done with so many other conflicted stories of Johnson's mythological official record. All of the real and objective criteria morphed into a more gilded, subjectively wrought narrative. Now he portrayed Johnson as being empathetic to other people, capable of being able to "read people so deeply, to look so deeply into their hearts and see so truly what they were feeling that he could feel what they were feeling—and could therefore put himself in their place."[174] Here, Caro created a Johnson attribute, "empathy" for others, a character trait that was nowhere to be found by most of his contemporaries, even by Caro in his earlier works.

As with so many other Johnson biographers, this was another chronicle of Johnson's legendary attempts, throughout his career and on every level, to replace truth with lies; actual conceit with stories based in deceit. He seemingly trained his contemporary biographers, and then others who picked up and repeated those stories, to perpetuate the myths at the expense of the truth.

Lyndon Johnson's description of King was the same in 1967 as it had been three years earlier, despite how they had "collaborated" on the passage of the legislation in between. This is because Johnson used King to help accomplish his own personal goals in 1964–65, yet despite Johnson's own legendary womanizing, he had the temerity to call Dr. King "hypocritical."

One year after the assassination of John F. Kennedy, the FBI, under the direction of J. Edgar Hoover, sent a letter to Martin Luther King Jr., essentially asking him to do the right thing and kill himself. According to the Letters of Note website, "In November of 1964, fearful of his connection to the Communist Party through Stanley Levison, the FBI anonymously sent Martin Luther King the following threatening letter, along with a cassette that contained allegedly incriminating audio recordings of King with women in various hotel rooms—the fruits of a 9 month surveillance project headed by William C. Sullivan. Unsurprisingly, King saw the strongly worded letter as an invitation for him to take his own life, as did an official investigation in 1976 which concluded that the letter 'clearly implied that suicide would be a suitable course of action for Dr. King.'" Three days after Hoover branded Dr. King "the most notorious liar in the country," the following letter was sent to King:

> In view of your low grade . . . I will not dignify your name with either a Mr. or a Reverend or a Dr. And, your last name calls to mind only the type of King such as King Henry the VIII . . . King, look into your heart. You know you are a complete fraud and a great liability to all of us Negroes. White people in this country have enough frauds of their own but I am sure they don't have one at this time anywhere near your equal. You are no clergyman and you know it. I repeat you are a colossal fraud and an evil, vicious one at that. You could not believe in God . . . Clearly you don't believe in any personal moral principles.
>
> King, like all frauds your end is approaching. You could have been our greatest leader. You, even at an early age have turned out to be not a leader but a dissolute, abnormal moral imbecile. We will now have to depend on our older leaders like Wilkins, a man of character and thank God we have others like him. But you are done. Your "honorary" degrees, your Nobel Prize (what a grim farce) and other awards will not save you. King, I repeat you are done.
>
> No person can overcome facts, not even a fraud like yourself . . . I repeat—no person can argue successfully against facts . . .

Satan could not do more. What incredible evilness . . . King you are done. The American public, the church organizations that have been helping—Protestant, Catholic and Jews will know you for what you are—an evil, abnormal beast. So will others who have backed you. You are done.

King, there is only one thing left for you to do. You know what it is. You have just 34 days in which to do it (this exact number has been selected for a specific reason, it has definite practical significance). You are done. There is but one way out for you. You better take it before your filthy, abnormal fraudulent self is bared to the nation.[175]

It is still unclear who actually wrote that letter; many have suggested it was written by Assistant Director William Sullivan, but he wrote in his memoirs: "Enclosed in the box with the tape, I learned later, was an unsigned note to Dr. King warning him, 'your end is approaching' . . . "[176] The letter could have been written by either Sullivan or DeLoach, or their subordinates, or any of numerous other officials, but in any case it was clearly at the direction of J. Edgar Hoover. It was sent exactly thirty-four days before he was scheduled to receive the Nobel Peace Prize in Stockholm, thus the reference to the deadline he was given to commit suicide.

On November 3, 2017, another release of previously classified government documents—purported to be only related to the JFK assassination—included a twenty-page file pertaining only to the FBI's surveillance of Dr. King. In announcing this news, the *Washington Post* framed the story around this headline: "In the latest JFK files: The FBI's ugly analysis on Martin Luther King Jr., filled with falsehoods."[177] Among the falsehoods referenced were additional unsubstantiated assertions of King's infidelities, his supposed involvement with "black nationalists advocating violence," and his alleged influence by a number of members of the Communist Party USA (CPUSA) and their associations with foreign operatives. Some of the assertions reference unnamed sources, such as "a very responsible Los Angeles individual in a position to know."[178] Since the document was intended to be provocative (though clearly not substantiated), it is noted here only for the fact that it might have been an important part of the plot we are examining because of the date on its cover: March 12, 1968, three weeks before King was assassinated. Was it the final piece of the lengthy course of events that marked a high-level "go-no go" touchstone decision on whether to proceed to execute the plot?

In not accepting that demand to kill himself in 1964, Dr. King effectively signed his death warrant just as surely as if he had swallowed a poison pill on the date requested by Hoover, but he gained over three more years of life as the plot to kill him was planned and executed at the highest levels of the federal government.

Two of Hoover's highest-level aides, DeLoach and Sullivan, possibly others, even had the temerity, in 1964, to pick a successor to King to recommend to the NAACP, should their recommendation that King kill himself be accepted. The official candidate recommended by the top FBI officials was Dr. Samuel Riley Pierce, a man, according to Sullivan, who "had a fine reputation . . . high character, ability and the capacity for leadership."[179] The idea originated with Sullivan, but he noted that his recommendation to Hoover to pick Dr. Pierce for recommendation to the NAACP was first approved by DeLoach, and Tolson, before being submitted to Hoover.[180] Since King did not act on the FBI's advice, the recommendation for his successor was never sent to the NAACP leadership.

It wouldn't have mattered anyway, because Hoover (and probably DeLoach, and undoubtedly Tolson, too) had already picked another candidate among some others whom they selected through their own highly trusted field personnel, all men whose skills did not necessarily have anything in common with those listed above for Dr. Pierce: The strongest, most audacious of the possible candidates would become obvious within hours of King's assassination: Jesse Louis Jackson, a man whom Dr. King neither trusted nor liked, according to some of King's associates. The statements of his associates regarding King's attitudes toward Jackson will be described in later chapters.

Attorneys general Kennedy and Katzenbach's repeated attempts during the period of 1962 to 1966 to first install reasonable controls on the use of all forms of electronic surveillance (telephone taps and the more intrusive bugs) all failed. Even after all of it was supposedly stopped completely, Hoover never stopped trying to get the program restarted. In 1968, Hoover asked Attorney General Ramsey Clark for permission to install telephone surveillance on the national headquarters of the Southern Christian Leadership Conference in Atlanta because of Dr. King's announcement of plans for a protest in Washington, DC, in April of that year. Hoover's first request was made on January 2, 1968, and was quickly declined by AG Clark. He then made another request on April 2, 1968, two days before King was murdered.[181] At that point, his request was probably made for appearances, and to "paper the file." It, too, was rejected.

By 1970, with the election of Richard M. Nixon to replace Johnson, and the appointment of Attorney General John Mitchell, the restrictions were once again removed. The White House had broken the previous rules in demanding that the FBI wiretap certain of their own aides and National Security Council staff, as well as "four leading Washington reporters," in their efforts to control people they had identified as enemies.[182] Those requests were sufficient to cause Hoover to revert, once again, to the uncontrolled surveillance procedures he was most comfortable with, which led him to "verbally approve FBI agents in New York City to conduct break-ins during an investigation of the radical Weather Underground."[183] It was this clearly illegal action that led to the decision of the Justice Department to waive prosecution of certain suspects in multiple acts of domestic terrorism, including the bombings of the Capitol and Pentagon buildings.

According to investigative reporter William Turner, "A particular target was the elusive Weather Underground, a small radical band violently opposed to the Vietnam War. The Bureau was frustrated because it couldn't locate Weather members, so it burglarized the homes of relatives and friends in the hope of picking up some clues."[184] The Church Committee investigated the FBI's practices in 1975, and the new director, Clarence Kelley, who had been on record stating that the break-ins stopped in 1966, then had to subsequently admit that he had been "lied to" and conceded that he could not even affirm that they were not *still* being conducted, even as he spoke.[185] (As noted below, they *had still not been stopped*.)

The mid-1970s congressional investigations into the FBI's abuses, specifically the Church Committee, accomplished many reforms while identifying the most onerous instances of governmental overreach. The final report of that committee stated: "Many of the techniques used would be intolerable in a democratic society even if all of the targets had been involved in violent activity, but COINTELPRO went far beyond that . . . the Bureau conducted a sophisticated vigilante operation aimed squarely at preventing the exercise of First Amendment rights of speech and association, on the theory that preventing the growth of dangerous groups and the propogation [*sic*] of dangerous ideas would protect the national security and deter violence."[186] The Church Committee erred in stating that the COINTELPRO program "ended in 1971 with the threat of public exposure." As reported on publiceye. org, "According to Nat Hentoff, writing in the *Village Voice* in 1981"[187] . . . the illegal activities continued for two more years, and had been directed by Mark Felt, then working as the acting associate director, *the second-highest level of the Bureau*:

> W. Mark Felt and Edward S. Miller "supervised break-ins, without a warrant, of the homes of 'friends and acquaintances' of the Weather Underground in 1972 and 1973." Felt was Acting

Associate Director of the FBI; and Miller was Assistant Director of the Domestic Intelligence Division. The DC Grand Jury indicted Felt and Miller. Among the charges: "On or about October 6, 1972, in Quantico, Virginia, FBI agents attending a Weatherman in-service training course were given a lecture on how to conduct surreptitious entries."

Not only had the illegal activities not been stopped in 1971–72, or even 1973–1974, according to former FBI agent M. Wesley Swearingen, these activities only disappeared further under the surface and were carefully executed by far fewer agents, all very tightly controlled. Swearingen stated that the activities even extended to far more maleficent crimes. He cited a 1990 attempt to murder a lady named Judy Bari when the FBI was involved in bombing her car; Bari subsequently died seven years later from complications of her injuries from that incident. Furthermore, according to Athan Theoharis in his book *The FBI and American History*, a number of incidents in the more recent history of the Bureau suggest that "an insular culture of secrecy" continued to shape the darker side of its reputation. One of the largest hits to its reputation came in 1995, when a whistleblower named Frederick Whitehurst issued a scathing report attacking the mismanagement of the FBI laboratory, which until then had been erroneously thought of as a high-quality operation. According to Whitehurst, it used "sloppy laboratory procedures and mishandling of evidence by lab employees and inadequate supervision by career employees having no scientific training or expertise." In 1997, the Justice Department's inspector general confirmed Whitehurst's charges and even went further, stating that "laboratory findings had at times been 'tilted' to support prosecution and incriminate defendants."[188]

The inspector general's report didn't say as much, but it can be presumed that this sloppiness and tilting had to have begun much earlier than that and undoubtedly had its genesis during Hoover's long reign, with his personal instigation; it was the kind of cancerous growth that would have evolved over decades.

In 1980, ex-Acting Associate Director Mark Felt became the highest-ranking FBI official to ever be convicted of criminal charges. Without Felt's ever requesting clemency, within three months of being elected president, Ronald Reagan pardoned both him and Edwin S. Miller, the assistant director of the Domestic Intelligence Division, for their crimes. As the *New York Times* reported at the time, "Mr. Reagan said that W. Mark Felt . . . and Miller . . . had served the bureau and the nation 'with great distinction.' To punish them further—after three years of criminal prosecution proceedings—would not serve the ends of justice."[189] That finding was at odds with what the government's own prosecutors had stated during the trial: that Felt's actions were a "violation of the rights of all people of this country, violations that cannot and will not be tolerated as long as we have a Bill of Rights."

But it wasn't only Mark Felt and Edwin Miller who were let off the hook in this sordid chapter of American history. William Ayers, the head of the Weather Underground who had led his followers to commit acts of violence, would eventually become a friend and collaborator of President Barack H. Obama. According to the Wikipedia entry for Ayers, "Due to the illegal tactics of FBI agents involved with the program, including conducting wiretaps and property searches without warrants, government attorneys requested all weapons-related and bomb-related charges be dropped against the Weather Underground, including charges against Ayers."[190] The FBI's egregious conduct effectively negated the equally unlawful acts that they had been attempting to investigate and prosecute, thus both sets of perpetrators got off clean.

The failure to bring these domestic terrorists to justice is because throughout the FBI regime of J. Edgar Hoover, a brazenly illegal eighteen-year campaign of surveillance and neutralization of political groups was carried out; that program had been nearly out of control the entire time, except for brief periods of feckless attempts by his overseers to control Director Hoover. These actions were taken against such organizations as the Black Panthers, the American Indian Movement, Students for a Democratic Society (SDS), Weather Underground, the Young Lords, and Vietnam Veterans Against the War, among others.[191]

But none of it compared to the decade-long constant surveillance and harassment leading, finally, to the assassination of Martin Luther King Jr.

J. Edgar's Legacy

The wholesale, essentially uncontrolled long-term conduct of illegal acts by the primary federal "law enforcement" agency was a curious paradox, considering that the man who ran this major piece of the federal bureaucracy as his personal fiefdom was fundamentally a consummate control freak who had always prized complete organizational discipline and a by-the-book mentality in all his underlings. Yet he had personally directed the creation of an organization that had become a gigantic, amorphous, lawless leviathan, the exact opposite of every precept that he professed to hold most dear. As conflicted as he was in other more personal, less dangerous ways, this was one of the greatest threats ever dealt to the real national security of America, for it compromised—practically destroyed—the very pillars of democratic governance and the rule of law that his agency was created to protect.

Ironically, when Hoover was first appointed to the office that he would run, essentially unsupervised, for forty-eight years—virtually untouchable, thanks to his secret files, by either the executive or legislative branches—he swore that he would never engage in the kinds of practices that had destroyed the career of his predecessor. Yet he only paid lip service to that promise, as he betrayed it almost immediately, after his probationary period ended on January 1, 1925, on his thirtieth birthday. It was his failure to abide by his word that ultimately cost him the grand legacy that he believed he had attained before he died in 1972. It is an abomination that the current FBI headquarters building in Washington is still named for him. Worse than that, even its replacement, according to current news reports,[192] may carry on that disgrace for many more decades.

Chapter 4

THE POSTCOLLABORATION CHASM

"I believe we can continue the Great Society while we fight in Vietnam."
—Lyndon B. Johnson

"If America's soul becomes totally poisoned, part of the autopsy must read: Vietnam."
—Dr. Martin Luther King Jr.

"[Martin Luther King Jr.] is the most notorious liar in the country."
—J. Edgar Hoover

The Brief Trial Run of Presidential Collaboration

A little over three months after the Selma march—and just one month before the 1965 Voting Rights Act was signed by President Johnson—at 8:05 p.m. on July 7, 1965, the White House logged the first telephone call initiated by Martin Luther King Jr. to President Johnson. After ten minutes discussing pleasantries and the progress of an effort to finally repeal the poll tax (an initiative Johnson had never previously supported—in fact, he had voted against the repeal numerous times during his congressional career), they briefly discussed the Vietnam situation. King nervously sought to clear up some previous statements he had made on it, backpedaling to save face with the president, with whom he was supposed to be collaborating. He said that he had been "speaking really as a minister of the gospel" about the problem of war in general. Johnson responded by saying that he had never wanted to be a warmonger, but "Now I don't want to pull down the flag and come home runnin' with my tail between my legs." As King's biographer Taylor Branch further described it, "Johnson had minimized his war motive to the point of apology, just as King circumscribed his criticism."[193]

Six weeks later, they would have their last conversation together. After that, neither of them would have to watch their words so carefully; by then, King's true feelings about Vietnam had been expressed on a number of occasions, including his statement just a few weeks after his first call to the White House, on August 13, that "Few events in my lifetime have stirred my conscience and pained my heart as the present conflict which is raging in Vietnam . . . The true enemy is war itself."[194]

By 1965, the United States was being subjected to two enormous competing cultural movements, both set in motion by actions taken by the new president within days of ascending to that office. The US involvement in Vietnam was set in motion by actions Johnson took at his first cabinet meeting, even before John Kennedy's body was buried. The civil rights movement, after Johnson's having impeded it for decades, was suddenly being pushed through Congress the same week he became president, in his address to Congress where it had suddenly become his highest domestic priority. Whereas he had previously sustained this cultural divide as a senator and vice president, he now reversed himself and sought to unite as president; his clear intent in doing so was to ensure himself a durable legacy while simultaneously using the opportunity to take public focus off the bloody scene in Dallas that had brought him into the Oval Office.[195]

On September 10, 1965, Dr. King and a group of key advisers—Bayard Rustin, Andrew Young, Bernard Lee, and Harry Wachtel—met with the newly appointed UN ambassador, Arthur Goldberg, to discuss the history and present state of affairs in US–Vietnam relations. As King explained his views on Vietnamese history in considerable detail, the group quickly noticed how most of his extemporaneous comments appeared to be received by Goldberg: it was information of which he had not previously been aware.[196] The purpose of the meeting was not to argue with Goldberg, but merely an attempt to make sure that he understood that Ho Chi Minh was not really a part of any Eastern Communist movement so much as that of an age-old nationalistic resistance to external colonialist and Chinese efforts to control Vietnamese interests.[197] They were there to remind Goldberg that the United States, while not committing troops to fight alongside French soldiers, had nevertheless played a major role in financing their debacle, which killed 74,000 of their soldiers, with about a million casualties in all, including a quarter of a million civilians.

Dr. King was simply attempting to educate Ambassador Goldberg about the downside of following the futile French effort to fight the "international communist conspiracy" by committing more American resources to the same objective. Shortly after their seventy-minute meeting, Goldberg acknowledged to reporters that he had met with King but would not respond to his requests, stating that "we do not covet any bases there. We do not seek any territory." Then LBJ's friend Senator Thomas Dodd jumped into the fray to further rebuke Dr. King's "intrusion" into foreign affairs and his "intemperate alignment with the forces of appeasement." The unctuous and duplicitous Senator Dodd—later censured by the Senate for double-billing expenses and other instances of campaign fund mishandling—then announced that King possessed "absolutely no competence to speak about complex matters of foreign policy. And it is nothing short of arrogance when Dr. King takes it upon himself to thus undermine the policies of the president." King remarked to his advisers that "I am convinced that Lyndon Johnson got Dodd to say this." Taylor Branch summed it up by stating that King believed the meeting had been a "trap" to provoke him into making his true feelings known and put into the record.[198]

The chasm that divided Johnson and King was a reflection of the widening crevasse that suddenly split the country, one popularly characterized by birds of peace, doves, versus birds of prey, hawks. Families and fraternities, congregations and political parties—cultural subgroups of every kind— were split apart to some degree. It was illustrated by the popular 1970s sitcom *All in the Family*, in which the head of the family, Archie Bunker (Carroll O'Connor), most definitely a "hawk," and his son-in-law, Michael Stivic (Rob Reiner), who represented the family "dove," argued every week. Brothers fought with brothers and cousins argued with cousins—or, in some cases, they simply stopped communicating at all—forever afterwards. Starting in early 1965 and extending through the next ten years into the presidencies of Nixon and Ford, the fissures started by Johnson deepened, and widened, as they led the country deeper and deeper into a war that could not be understood, much less rationalized, by most citizens—whether they considered themselves doves or hawks, despite the certitude of their arguments.

Even the highest-level military leaders couldn't agree on the merits of the war. Generals Douglas MacArthur, Matthew Ridgway, and James Gavin, among others, all strongly advised against committing ground troops in Southeast Asia. Ridgway had thoroughly studied the issue as early as 1954, when the French forces were still fighting that war, and concluded that it would take a minimum of ten divisions—at least one million combat troops, and up to twice that—to attain victory. As David Halberstam observed, "When Ridgway briefed Eisenhower on what the cost would be, a groan seemed to come from the President. Ike was, Ridgway noted laconically years later, a much better listener than Lyndon Johnson."[199]

Others, like William Westmoreland, not as well schooled in the historical, political, socioeconomic, demographic, and geographic milieu of the region, were wildly supportive of the notion of "saving" the population there from the "falling dominoes" theory of allowing the "international Communist conspiracy" to take control of that area, a view that most people came to realize was a quaint, primordial, and patronizing attitude. But that position was aggressively advanced as being the patriotic, "America right or wrong" attitude, as President Johnson had framed it. Johnson's long-planned trap for sending Navy destroyers into the Tonkin Gulf to provoke an attack from North Vietnamese gunboats (which turned out to be a phantom attack by imaginary forces) succeeded in fooling a nearly unanimous Congress into giving him the carte blanche authority that he needed to "Americanize" that civil war.

As the split between Johnson's attempts to reframe the decision he had made to create his own war on the other side of the globe—to enrich himself and his closest friends, based upon their "insider" knowledge,* and to gild his legacy with the trappings of being a wartime president—and his putative efforts to build a "Great Society" on the home front continued to grow, he succeeded only in leaving a legacy with a schizophrenic imprint. His interviews with Walter Cronkite of CBS News had been blasted by critics, which he blamed on Cronkite: "Cronkite came down here all sweetness and light, telling me how he'd love to teach journalism at Texas someday, then he does this to me," he fumed.[200] Shortly after Johnson's death in 1973, the journalist Leo Janos wrote, in the *Atlantic,* of his interviews with Johnson in his retirement years:

> His publishers talked him out of separate books, and Johnson cautiously began unfolding his version of his presidential years. Assisted by two trusted staff writers, Robert Hardesty and William Jorden, he issued only one firm guideline, that not one word should appear in the book that could not be corroborated by documentation. To aid in this effort, Johnson threw open to his writers every file and document from his White House years, including telephone conversations he had held as President, which were recorded and transcribed for history.[201]

The contradictory double-talk of Johnson is reflected in this excerpt of the article. First, it notes the two men who are identified as "staff writers" but

* As Colonel John Downie admitted, in his last session with Johnson in 1966, after he had repeatedly "urged him to get out of Vietnam, a frustrated LBJ pounded the table and exclaimed, 'I cannot get out of Vietnam, John, my friends are making too much money.'" (See Pepper, p. xxxiv.) It was during this same time frame that Johnson repeatedly explained to the American people how well things were going there, though he admitted that they would have to carry "perhaps for a long time the burden of a confusing and costly war in Vietnam."

nothing whatsoever of the real ghostwriter, Doris Kearns, who was given the task of actually writing his autobiography. And it states that his only desire was to require that "not one word should appear in the book" that could not be *corroborated* from his own files, *not* that there should not be one *inaccurate* word, since there were plenty of those. For example, Johnson's memoir (written by Ms. Kearns), *Vantage Point*, states that only ten men were killed and 100 injured in the 1967 Israeli attack on the USS *Liberty*. It was known immediately that many more men were killed and over 100 men injured, but these statistics were withheld from the public, which were initially told the numbers were four dead and fifty-three wounded. Despite the fact that the book was written four years after the attack, such a distortion was still possible only because of the tightness of the cover-up put into effect by Johnson: all sailors who survived were threatened with prison time ("or worse") if they uttered a word to anyone else about the attack. Yet within a few days of the attack, when it was finally put into dry dock in Malta, it was established that thirty-four men were killed and 171 injured (later revised to 174 injured). The enormity of that lie—allegedly a "corroborated fact"— illustrates how such an instruction from Lyndon Johnson was ultimately meaningless.

President Johnson, still trying to minimize the actual results from this attack on his own ship, four years later, still fudged the numbers because he had ordered the navy—invoking absolute secrecy for all the sailors and officers who survived that incident or had anything to do with it—to cover up the facts, so he assumed that the lie would remain undiscovered. That was only one of the numerous deceits contained in the Janos article, and in Johnson's memoirs, the book that bore his name.

Martin Luther King Jr. Gives Up All Pretenses of Collaboration with the Deluded President

Dr. King had understood that Lyndon Johnson was primarily concerned with public perception of any political issue, rather than their details and realities. After the Civil Rights and Voting Rights Acts were passed in 1964 and 1965, King watched the president boasting about his successes in getting the legislation passed, even though the Justice Department had only deployed a fraction of the federal officials needed to enforce the new laws. There were many flagrant violations still occurring, and unresolved complaints had been filed in hundreds of southern counties, which required that King's own time and that of others working in the field now be focused on holding the ground already won, rather than making progress in other arenas.[202]

After over two years of denouncing the Vietnam War, on April 4, 1967, Martin Luther King Jr. delivered his most notable, critical speech, "Beyond Vietnam," condemning the Vietnam War in front of over 3,000 people at Riverside Church in New York City. King described the war's crushing effects on both America's poor and—obviously, to an even greater extent—Vietnamese peasants and insisted that it was morally imperative for the US to take radical steps to halt the war through nonviolent means. King noted the progress finally made just three years earlier, when he recalled the "real promise of hope for the poor, both black and white, through the poverty program." Then, drawing the sharp contrast between hope and reality, he declared:

> And then came the buildup in Vietnam, and I watched this program broken and eviscerated as if it were some idle political plaything of a society gone mad on war, and I knew that America would never invest the necessary funds or energies in rehabilitation of its poor, so long as adventures like Vietnam continued to draw men and skills and money like some demonic destructive suction tube.
> Somehow this madness must cease. We must stop now![203]

King literally shook the country's collective conscience when he stated that the devastation to the Vietnamese population was being conducted against all of them (implicitly irrespective of the borders separating the south and north sections of the same country), due to "deadly Western arrogance" and that America was acting "on the side of the wealthy and secure, [while creating] a hell for the poor." He portrayed the underlying cause as "American colonialism," which made "peaceful resolution impossible by refusing to give up the . . . immense profits of overseas investments." King appeared as much more of a radical when he asserted that what was needed was "a radical revolution of values."[204]

Clearly, Dr. King had become more radical at that point. That opinion was shared by Johnson and Hoover, others in the highest-level governmental offices throughout the rest of Washington, and at the leading newspapers throughout the country. The negative reactions in the *Washington Post* and the *New York Times* appeared over the next two days, with the *Post* noting that King's speech had "diminished his usefulness to his cause, to his country, and to his people."[205] Henry Luce's *Life* magazine called it a "demagogic slander that sounded like a script for Radio Hanoi."[206]

Over the next three months, preparations would begin to eliminate the problem that Dr. King presented because of his increasing popularity with urban blacks, his reinvigorated efforts to bring attention to the growing disaster of Vietnam, and his determination to bring masses of protesters into Washington. Polls began to show that support for the Vietnam War had fallen below 50 percent in July 1967 for the first time, and the people who were against it had become much more vocal than in previous years. It was then that plans for a large protest of Johnson's war policies began to take shape. Three months later, on October 21, a group conservatively estimated at 100,000 (possibly twice that, according to other estimates) gathered in Washington to register their objections. Over 50,000 marched across the 14th Street Bridge to the Pentagon. Four months after that, even greater numbers of Americans had joined those who realized that the Johnson administration had lied about having seen the "light at the end of the tunnel." It was the Tet Offensive of February 1968 that proved that point, as the following excerpt from History.com affirms:

> When the Johnson administration announced that it would ask for a 10 percent increase in taxes to fund the war, the public's skepticism increased. The peace movement began to push harder for an end to the war—the march on Washington was the most powerful sign of their commitment to this cause. The Johnson administration responded by launching a vigorous propaganda campaign to restore public confidence in its handling of the war. The president even went so far as to call General William Westmoreland, commander of U.S. forces in Vietnam, back to the United States to address Congress and the public. The effort was somewhat successful in tempering criticisms of the war. However, the Tet Offensive of early 1968 destroyed much of the Johnson Administration's credibility concerning the Vietnam War.[207]

The Ultimate "Nightmare"— An RFK/MLK Presidential Ticket

Dr. William F. Pepper eventually came to the conclusion that Johnson's decision on March 31, 1968, to withdraw from the 1968 presidential election was indeed related to the plot to murder King.[208] He stated that he learned sometime later that J. Edgar Hoover had advised Johnson that Robert Kennedy had been trying to contact Dr. King to tell him of his decision and seek his support. No one knows if Kennedy might have had other plans to ask King to consider accepting an offer to become RFK's nominee for the vice presidency of the United States, but that was widely rumored to have happened. The very idea of that possibility must have kept Johnson up at night before he made his stunning announcement. Within four days—after April 4, 1968—that part of it would no longer be a worry, and two months after that, by June 6, 1968, he would be able to sleep well again, no longer worried about Robert Kennedy's aspirations.

One year before that, as part of the fallout over Dr. King's long-simmering revulsion at Johnson's Vietnam policies and his final break with him in his April 4, 1967, Riverside Church speech, rumors began surfacing about King possibly making a run for the presidency in 1968. They soon even included a proposed vice presidential candidate, the famed pediatrician Dr. Benjamin Spock, who had also become a strong antiwar proponent. In September 1967, five thousand delegates from around the country met in Detroit for the National Conference for New Politics (NCNP) to initiate action to begin this movement but met such fierce opposition in Washington that it collapsed before it could get underway. Dr. Pepper, then executive director of NCNP, stated that by then, the "siege mentality" of Washington was at full strength throughout the federal government, especially in the FBI, CIA, and all military branches. He stated that like other such organizations that were involved in antiwar demonstrations or social change, they were "infiltrated, subjected to surveillance, and/or subverted."[209]

In an ironic reaction to those rumors, Stanley Levison had begun urging Dr. King to repudiate the rumors of his political ambitions, probably knowing any attempt by King to run for president would have little chance of success while carrying a very great risk of violent reprisals. The Bureau became aware of these developments and kept Johnson apprised of them, while soliciting field offices around the country for ideas on how to subvert such a campaign should it become a reality.[210] Within weeks, Dr. King acted to squelch that idea, but not before the issue had been raised directly into President Johnson's consciousness. And once there—as with all of his major concerns throughout his career brought about by his long and sordid history of scandals (TFX, Estes, Baker, et al.)—it would have remained as one of his greatest manic worries until he could be satisfied that it had been eliminated with preemptive planning.

Predictably, Lyndon Johnson would become very concerned that King's nascent popularity might eventually catapult him into the presidency. He undoubtedly considered the fact that King was a very young man—in 1967 he was only thirty-eight years old; if he didn't run in 1968, he would still have many years to run for the presidency, long after Johnson knew his time on earth would be over. David Garrow acknowledged this point, writing that Johnson's concerns about King's actions to lead protests on his Vietnam policies led him to seek more information about his political plans, specifically on any plans he might have for running as an antiwar candidate.[211]

That idea must have become a nightmare for Johnson, along with the other continuing nightmare that Robert F. Kennedy might also decide to run. What if the two of them ran together, he must have asked himself during that period, setting up King to run at the top of the ticket after first serving as RFK's vice president? The very thought of such a potentially winning ticket must have been terrifying. Such a nightmare must have been extremely detrimental to the amount of sleep Johnson was getting in the latter half of that fateful year, 1967.

It is speculative, of course, to suggest that either Johnson or Hoover had such nightmares. But it can be reasonably presumed that Hoover would share what were probably Johnson's very real fears: that either Kennedy or King—hated equally now by Johnson and Hoover—might someday, possibly even in the upcoming 1968 election, become potential aspirants to the Oval Office. That fear would extend well into future elections, possibly even many years after they—Johnson and Hoover—were dead and no longer able to control the outcome. Their shared worst possible scenario, while admittedly conjecture now—yet undoubtedly real to them then—was probably as certain as the question of which direction the sun would always set.

In their most nefarious planning scenarios, the anticipation of possible outcomes and what steps might be needed to mitigate them would have been a basic part of their skill sets. Together, these old friends and secretive collaborators would have not thought twice about the need to prevent that potential occurrence. Their planning to eliminate such an outcome would undoubtedly begin with each repeating a mutual understanding that it must ultimately be as discreet and secretive as all of their previous immoral, unethical, illegal, and/or unconstitutional actions. Nothing committed to paper, all participants vetted and approved by both of them, nearly all conversations done face to face if possible, telephone conversations limited only to secure lines that they both knew to be free of wiretaps (of which only they could be completely confident).

It is not speculative to point now to the evidence that supports the assertion that specific, tangible evidence exists to connect the actions of Lyndon Johnson and J. Edgar Hoover to people and events that can be directly tied to the murder of Martin Luther King Jr. on April 4, 1968. Likewise, there is an abundance of other evidence that connects the highest echelons of the federal government (the Johnson administration, the FBI, and the CIA) to the assassination of Robert F. Kennedy two months later, but that is outside the limited scope of this book.

Chapter 5

TRACES OF THE PLOT DIRECTION: FROM WASHINGTON TO MEMPHIS

"The further a society drifts from truth, the more it will hate those who speak it."

—George Orwell

A Summary of the Actual "Murkin"* Plotline

In the pages ahead, we will examine the many linkages of President Johnson and Director Hoover to a number of political leaders in the state of Tennessee, the city of Memphis, and the county of Shelby. Before we begin putting meat on the skeleton—factually supported evidence added to the core framework and plotline, as it was conceived by the Washington sponsor-planners—let us begin by outlining what will be shown as the development of a very elaborate assassination plan. Throughout the remaining narrative of the book, sufficient evidence will be presented as circumstantial proof of high crimes and misdemeanors by the highest levels of Washington officials, executed by local people operating within their normal scope of operations:

- On November 22, 1963, immediately upon becoming the newly installed president, Lyndon B. Johnson began planning for his eventual legacy, pulling scores of congressional bills off the shelves, after having previously stalled them for months, years, or in some cases, decades. Chief among them was the Civil Rights Act that JFK had submitted to Congress five months before he was murdered. Johnson extracted the voting rights section from Kennedy's original bill to save it as another separate "bullet" of

---

* "Murkin" was the FBI code name for the "MURder of KINg" investigation, paradoxically named for what was anything but an honest and thorough "investigation." This book represents what that report should have contained.

his legislative achievement, to be passed in 1965. He knew that both bills would require that he exploit Martin Luther King Jr.'s certain support for quick passage. He would need to court Dr. King for as long as it took to accomplish their passage, despite already having misgivings about King's ultimate objectives.

- FBI Director J. Edgar Hoover knew that his long-held position was no longer assured by the passive acquiescence of the president: previously, it depended on the president simply not firing him, but as of January 1, 1965, it became subject to Johnson's active annual approval of a waiver of the institutional rule of mandatory retirement at age seventy (he had turned sixty-nine on January 1, 1964). Therefore, he also knew that he would have to be cooperative, even solicitous, toward Johnson to continue in his position. But doing so for a few years, having accomplished Johnson's primary goal of becoming president, meant he would have to actively assist Johnson to achieve his legislative agenda, even if it meant temporarily, albeit minimally, assisting their two mutual nemeses, Martin Luther King Jr. and Robert F. Kennedy.

- On December 23, 1963—one month after JFK's assassination— Hoover was ready to move on from investigating that crime. He called in his top lieutenants and select key senior agents from field offices around the nation to attend a nine-hour meeting at FBI headquarters to explore "avenues of approach at neutralizing King as an effective Negro leader." A list of twenty-one proposals was agreed on, including such disparate ideas as the question of whether adding black agents to certain offices such as Atlanta might be advantageous and the possibilities of "placing a good-looking female plant in King's office."[212] David Garrow called this meeting a "major planning session." An FBI memo sent to Assistant Director Alan Belmont the next day summarized the "desired results" of that conference as ensuring the "neutralization of King as an effective Negro leader" and listed twenty-one action items to accomplish that, including the possibilities of recruiting King's housekeeper and various ways to use Mrs. King.[213]

- After the Great Society legislation was completed, the two of them could finish the plans that Hoover had started to conceive a decade earlier, when he first jotted down the initials "JFK, RFK, MLK" on a notepad preprinted with the label MY PERSONAL PRAYER LIST.[214] By 1964, there were two names left on that list; the time had finally come to finish the plans.

- Until mid-1966, the plans had remained in a tentative state, but—according to the meticulous, four-decade period of active investigation and research of Dr. William F. Pepper—it became an "official decision to take [Dr. King] out."[215] It can be reasonably presumed that such a plot, involving multiple governmental entities, could have only been made at the very highest senior level of government, which could only mean within the White House.
- Under J. Edgar Hoover's direction, Clyde Tolson personally delivered to Russell Lee Adkins a $25,000 payoff, which Adkins then conveyed to Harold Swenson, the warden of the Missouri State Prison, in November or December of 1966, to facilitate the escape of James Earl Ray, a transaction that was witnessed by Adkins's fifteen-year-old son, Ron.[216]
- Instead of aggressively pursuing Ray after he escaped from Missouri State Prison, prison officials were not convinced he had even gone over the walls and for several days did not actively pursue him as an escapee. When they finally put out a circular, the fingerprints used were not even Ray's, but some other prisoner's, evidently as part of a plot to avoid capturing him, not an inadvertent "error" (which, given the payoff to the warden, would have been expected).

In this chapter, the context of these linkages will be developed, which will set the stage for the remainder of the book as we examine how the "patsy," James Earl Ray, was manipulated by a man named Raul ("Raoul" as spelled by Ray). Ray was then led, through promises of protection and financial rewards, to return from Canada to the United States, first into the deep South, then extended trips to Mexico, then Los Angeles, then back to Atlanta, Birmingham, and finally on to Memphis. The purpose of routing him to these US cities, where FBI informants knew Dr. King would visit in similar sequence, was to fulfill a part of the plan that would purport to show that Ray had stalked King for several weeks, leading up to his alleged attempt to kill King. The manipulation of Ray during this period is itself proof of the extensive behind-the-scenes manipulation by the FBI and CIA as they finished the planning for King's murder in Memphis.

Ray's journey would become the central thesis and the primary proof of his guilt, picked up by the earliest (and even several of the latest) FBI-picked fiction writers, the FBI "task force" itself, and, a decade later, the HSCA congressional "investigation." The continuity of that theme—begun months before the assassination, through the lengthy manipulation of Ray—was no accident. The confusion and obfuscation thus produced continues even today to draw a veil of secrecy over the murder of one of America's greatest twentieth-century leaders. More context of how this well-planned but thinly fabricated frame-up will be closely examined in the next chapter.

Secrets Between Friends—Required Elements of Covert Ops

Essential to understanding the dynamics that played out in the months before Martin Luther King Jr.'s assassination is the fact that covert operations require close and trusting personal relationships between the highest-level sponsors. In this case, as in the other 1960s political murders by those who were behind the successful coup d'état of 1963, it was the major players back in Washington and their personal relationships to the key local operators who would be orchestrating all the moves in the streets and alleys of Memphis, Tennessee.

First, there was the closeness of President Lyndon B. Johnson to Tennessee Governor Buford Ellington, both of whom were also united by their respective long-term ties to the Dixie Mafia.[217] According to Ellington's press secretary, Hudley Crockett, the closeness of their relationship was "something to behold."[218] A former speaker in the Tennessee House of Representatives, William L. "Dick" Barry, who also served as Buford's attorney, said that "they talked on the phone quite often, [and] went hunting out in Texas . . ."[219] It is that kind of personal closeness between the two that implicitly suggests that their relationship was one of confidential trust, and mutual knowledge of the other's foibles, concerns, and pet peeves. In LBJ's case, he would have made mental notes of such traits on Buford during these escapades for later use. As Hubert Humphrey, a Minnesota senator who became Johnson's vice president, once said, "He knew all the little things that people did. I used to say he had his own private FBI" (unbeknownst to Humphrey, Johnson had the entire FBI's files available to him through his friend Hoover). "It was just incredible! I don't know how he was able to get all that information, but he lived and breathed and walked and talked politics . . . He was just totally immersed in it."[220] Johnson liked to say, "Give me a man's balls, and his heart and mind will follow."

Johnson's use of other men's weaknesses for his own purposes was vividly described by David Halberstam. Johnson methodically analyzed other men, categorizing all of them according to their strengths and weaknesses, always much more interested in the latter as a way to exploit them for some future scheme: "To Johnson there was a smell of blood, more could come of this."[221] Exploiting others' weaknesses, whether through blackmail or bullying, mimicry or bribery, pleading or threats, was arguably one of his strongest traits. Whatever weaknesses Buford Ellington might have had—possibly merely intrinsic sycophancy, which many men automatically proffered to Johnson for their own career purposes—Johnson would have exploited them, as evidenced by the governor's complete obedience to a number of obvious concessions. Arguably the most important was the fact that Tennessee authorities did everything possible to ensure that James Earl Ray never receive a criminal trial—as we will examine in Chapter 10—yet he was kept in prison for three decades, until the day he died.

Another Ellington associate, Samuel "Bo" Roberts Jr., reported that Ellington always stayed at the White House (as a guest in the Lincoln bedroom) whenever he visited Washington.[222] Moreover, Ellington was Johnson's floor manager at the 1960 Democratic National Convention in Los Angeles and dutifully delivered the Tennessee delegation to his mentor. Between his terms as governor (1959–1963 and 1967–71), Johnson appointed him to be the director of the federal Office of Emergency Preparedness, which conveniently put him into a power position in Washington for nearly four years, just as the plot to murder King was in its early planning stages.[223]

Johnson's political ties in Texas also connected him tightly to Houston attorney Percy Foreman, who would become a key figure in assuring that the patsy was denied a fair trial and would remain in prison for the rest of his life. As John Avery Emison put it, "The last thing President Johnson wanted—thus, the last thing Governor Ellington wanted—was for weak evidence to be revealed in court that could suggest the involvement of a person or persons other than [James Earl] Ray."[224] It was essential to the entire operation that all of it be the work of a single patsy, just as it was in Dallas in 1963.

Emison included an example of how such close and personal relationships were able to keep things moving when hurdles appeared to have blocked the road to success. When US Attorney General Nicholas Katzenbach became frustrated with his inability to make contact with Alabama governor George Wallace in the 1965 Selma civil rights imbroglio, a taped telephone call on March 8, 1965, of Johnson speaking to Katzenbach revealed how that was resolved, and how it was done through using those same close personal relationships, one of Johnson's primary manipulative tools:

> [Johnson said] "This would have to be mighty quiet, but Buford Ellington . . . was born in Mississippi, raised there, and then identified with the rural elements of Tennessee . . . It could be that he knows Wallace. It could be that he could sit

down with you, and you could give him some leadership and
direction. Might be [Wallace] won't talk to him. I'll ask him
if he knows him and how well he knows him, and if it looks
like there's any . . . he has any confidence—Wallace has any
confidence in him—he might be a go-between . . . [Ellington]
knows both sides of the coin, and I guess he's been on both
sides."[225]

As Emison noted, the result of this intervention by the president was that after
Katzenbach called Ellington, Governor Ellington called Governor Wallace
later that very day and, using the southern charm approach as prescribed by
the president, established a good rapport, paving the way for Katzenbach to
proceed with his communications. That LBJ gave Ellington the authority
to make statements and commitments to Wallace in his name, according to
Emison, "speaks volumes about the trusting relationship between Buford
Ellington and Lyndon Johnson."[226]

Another of those trusting relationships that "speaks volumes" was the
one between Hoover and Memphis Police and Fire Department Director
Frank C. Holloman, who before he was appointed to that office had been a
twenty-five-year veteran of the FBI and for nearly eight of those years (1952–
59) had worked directly under J. Edgar Hoover.[227] That would indubitably
extend further to include Associate Director Clyde Tolson, also working side
by side with both of them on a daily basis for the better part of a decade. After
that, they remained in close contact for several more years when Holloman
was appointed as the senior agent in charge of the Memphis branch office,
working there six more years until 1965, when he retired. He stayed in
Memphis, working briefly as director of development of Memphis State
University before being appointed to the position of director of the Memphis
Police and Fire Department just a few months before the assassination team
began their final preparations. He started in that position on January 1, 1968,
and left there November 1, 1970.[228] One of Holloman's stated objectives
upon assuming the office of director of MPD/MFD, according to his own
words, was to ensure that "the FBI's intelligence techniques and political
standards [would] serve as a model for the police force [. . .] his first priority
[. . .] was to push 'for a good, efficient intelligence bureau' and *to ensure
there was always 'a two-way street in terms of the flow of information' between
the MPD and the FBI.*"[229] (Emphasis added.)

As we will demonstrate, Hoover personally directed the overall operation
of the assassination plot, through his closest, most intimate associate and
frequent travel companion, Clyde Tolson, directly to their mutual friend,

Frank Holloman. There can be no question that they would have regularly communicated throughout this period, probably on a daily basis. This was undoubtedly the key element that ensured close coordination of every move made during the planning and execution of the plot. Holloman's role in the plot undoubtedly started well before his appointment four months before its execution on April 4, probably as much as two years before, after he left his position at Memphis State University, considering it was being planned at least four years before the assassination occurred, as noted elsewhere.

Why Memphis Was Selected

Brief reference has been made to the lengthy two-part deposition of witness Ron Tyler Adkins in December 2009, conducted by Dr. William F. Pepper. Ron Adkins's father, Russell, worked for the city of Memphis in the engineering division. He was a personable and popular Mason and Klansman, whose work led him to know many high-level city officials, including Mayor Henry Loeb and Memphis Police and Fire Department Director Frank Holloman. Mayor Loeb's grandfather had founded the largest laundry and dry-cleaning company in Memphis, an industry noted for its low pay. Like his father and gradfather, Mayor Loeb was paternalistic to blacks and all had the reputation, common among the post-colonial plantation class, of being subtly condescending to them.

Henry Loeb was a self-described segregationist holding the nice-sounding "separate but equal" attitudes of many white leaders of that era. He was elected to his first term—1960 through 1963—and again in 1968 through 1971, despite intense opposition from Memphis's black community. Their opinion of him was reflected in the 1968 polling results, which he won entirely by white votes, while blacks opposed him 98–2. One primary cause of the 1968 Memphis sanitation strike was the harshness of Loeb's electioneering rhetoric and the miserly wages he proffered for their contract negotiations.[230] As with the family business, to sustain prosperity he kept wages and overhead low, and he also set out to run the city with an iron fist, beginning with the first challenge: demands by the sanitation workers for higher wages, improved working conditions, and recognition for their labor union. The national union had attempted to unionize the sanitation workers, and Mayor Loeb had determined to make a stand against them on "principles" about unions in the public sphere, but possibly also for the purpose of gaining national attention for himself.

The catalyst for getting the attention of Dr. King and the world came on February 1, 1968, when two sanitation workers, Echol Cole and Robert

Walker, working on the back of a garbage truck, took temporary shelter from a hard rain by kneeling inside the back of the truck, as they had apparently done routinely under similar conditions. Unfortunately for them, Cole and Walker were crushed to death in the back. It was this tragic "accident," as reported in all the news media, and the paltry assistance the city gave to the families of the victims, that prompted Dr. King to travel to Memphis and join a citywide march in support of the striking sanitation workers. But according to Ron Adkins, the witness whom Dr. William F. Pepper interviewed decades later, it was no accident: "Somebody pulled the hammer, pulled the lever on the truck and mashed them up in there."[231]

Russell Adkins's original hometown was Gates, Tennessee, on the eastern bank of the Mississippi River, about seventy-five miles north of Memphis. Growing up there, at some point—it isn't clear exactly when—he became a friend of Clyde Tolson, Hoover's deputy in the FBI, who grew up in Missouri, on the western bank of the Mississippi River. Russell and his brothers, Carl and Morris, got to know many others who were involved in bootlegging operations and other postprohibition, assorted mob-controlled businesses in the early 1930s. From his family's connections, back in western Tennessee and southeast Missouri, Russell Adkins, a gregarious and helpful man to those he liked, developed a very large network of connections to men in the political and underground realms. Ron said that people in power and politics liked his father because "he would do what he said he'd do. If Daddy told you he would do something, he would do that. Win, lose or draw, even if it cost him money, he would do that."[232]

When Russell was very young, he had gone to work learning to run and maintain heavy equipment, which then led him to a job with Mallory Depots in Memphis, which were government-owned military bases and staging areas used during World War II and the Korean War. Russell Adkins eventually ran the Mallory Depot in South Memphis, and that led him, in 1944 or 1945, to a job with the city of Memphis as supervisor of plant utilities in the engineering department, which, among other duties, oversaw the operations of the city dump. Ron's father ran the dump, supervising other employees but also working the bulldozers. Even when Ron was only five, he would be with his daddy riding around the dump in bulldozers. He was known to all the truck drivers and other city employees, who called him "little Russell."[233] Russell Adkins's boss was a man named Maynard Stiles, whose name will come up in later chapters.

Both Ron and his older brother, Russell Adkins Jr., served in the Marine Corps, in Ron's case for six years, 1969–75, after he was thrown out of school for shooting off a revolver (the judge gave him a choice of prison or the Marine

Corps). His brother served for thirty-three years, much of it in intelligence operations in a division called CID COMPAC (Central Intelligence Division of the Department of Defense).[234] Ron was always aware of the connections his father had to many other men who were active in the Dixie Mafia, including Frank and Charles Liberto, wholesalers of produce in Memphis, who were closely connected to New Orleans Mafia don Carlos Marcello. As a teenager, he knew many of them only by their surname because he would address them as "Mr." rather than their given names. Some of those names will also appear in later chapters.

Ron Adkins was only sixteen years old in 1968, but he was very close to his father, who allowed him to be included in many of his discussions with others. Adkins spent hours with Dr. Pepper and others explaining, in a highly detailed factual account, many specific actions—naming many names, places, events, and dates, with nothing to gain but his interest in coming clean. He provided details known only to him about how his father, Russell Lee Adkins, and his older brother, Russell Lee Adkins Jr., were directly connected to a lengthy and widespread conspiracy to murder Dr. Martin Luther King Jr. He described the origins of the plot, how it had begun with an ocean cruise in 1964.[235]

Adkins explained that by the time he was eight years old (about 1960), "I started getting privy to a lot of business as far as being able to . . . sit and listen. My job was to bring the coffee and the doughnuts . . . cornbread and buttermilk . . . [The meetings were held] down at Berclair Baptist Church, I can't ever remember seeing either one of my granddaddies in church or my daddy, but they all had a key to Berclair Baptist. There was a lot of meetings in there. We'd go around in the back door . . . We'd go in and go up the staircase . . . They'd have their ["prayer"] meetings up there . . . Mainly I sat outside the door, you know, and more or less just watched. Daddy would tell me if you see anybody coming up through there, you let me know . . . So I guess I was the birddog . . . "[236]

Adkins's credibility as a witness—some people whose own motives are questionable have attacked him as an "easy mark" (See Appendix A)—must be considered highly credible due to the fact that he was vetted by the highly respected Dr. William F. Pepper, whose intense examination of him solidly imbues his testimony as being honest and truthful.

Political Connections: Washington, DC, to Nashville to Memphis

Adkins went on to explain that in addition to the regular attendees— Klansmen, Masons, Outlaws, and specifically a Klan member named Chester

"Chess" Butler were regulars at their "prayer meetings"—many other city and state and even some national officials would also attend the meetings from time to time, including Memphis Mayor Henry Loeb and "Governor Wilder, before he became lieutenant governor."* Adkins stated that "I know John Wilder from top to bottom, damn near inside and out . . . I know he is a crook."[237] Moreover, Adkins stated that his father's relationship with Wilder was "Tight . . . Real close."[238]

The result of these close connections of the FBI to the Memphis Police Department (MPD) through Frank Holloman, according to the research of Dr. Gerald McKnight, "resembled a textbook version of cooperation between local and federal law enforcement agencies. There appeared to be none of the instances of paranoia revolving around issues of control, refusal to share file resources, or attempts by the Bureau to shove aside the local police and grab the headlines that historically marred relations between Hoover's agency and local police functionaries. Frank Holloman, the Memphis director of public safety, characterized this relationship as 'unique.'"[239] Within the MPD, a special unit was organized, called the Domestic Intelligence Unit, headed by Lieutenant Ely H. Arkin Jr., that consisted of a four-man "red squad," tasked with "collecting, evaluating and acting on political intelligence."[240]

Ron Adkins also stated in his 2009 deposition that "I know Senator Byrd [presumably US Senator Robert C. Byrd, D-WV] was there once at the church. I don't know what his status was. I think he was in the Klan back then. I think he was, but I'm not sure when he got out." He also stated that "Marcello came up for meetings. But hell, so did Clyde Tolson."[241] It was a well-established fact that Senator Byrd had led congressional efforts to recast Dr. King—widely known for his insistence that his followers remain nonviolent in words and deeds—as, in Byrd's words, a "self-seeking rabble-rouser" who was planning to bring "violence, destruction, looting and bloodshed" to Washington in April with his Poor People's Campaign.[242]

What is not so widely known is that Hoover's emissary to President Lyndon Johnson, Cartha DeLoach, told Clyde Tolson on January 19, 1968, that he had just met with Senator Byrd, who expressed concern about King's plans to come to Washington and requested the FBI's help in preparing an appropriate speech for him to deliver on the floor of the US Senate. That would have made it a "special" speech, not one of the routine, shorter speeches he commonly made in the Senate. There was only one speech Byrd gave on the subject of King's Poor People's Campaign that would be memorialized in

---

* John Shelton Wilder, a Tennessee state senator, upon becoming speaker of the State Senate in 1971, was automatically made lieutenant governor and served for thirty-six years in that capacity.

a Senate speech, even though it is now somewhat hard to find on an Internet brimming with all sorts of other historical trivia (see Appendix C). But that speech was not delivered until over two months later—just one day after Dr. King went to Memphis to march with the sanitation workers, which quickly turned violent and was immediately canceled by him—and it was stunning for its level of hyperbolic racist invective of the kind for which the FBI's scribes were famous. But worse, Byrd's speech now raises—in a context apparently never seen before—some curious questions as to its timing in relation to the occurrence of certain other events.[243] These issues will be examined shortly, after a brief review of selected excerpts of the FBI's speech delivered by their Senate mole:

> Senator Robert Byrd (D-WV): "The nation was given a pre-view of what may be in store for this city [Washington, DC] by the outrageous and despicable riot that Martin Luther King helped bring about in Memphis . . . it was a shameful and to-tal uncalled for outburst of lawlessness undoubtedly encour-aged to some considerable degree, at least by his [Dr. King's] words and actions and his presence. There is no reason for us to believe that the same destructive rioting and violence cannot, or that it will not, happen here if King attempts his so-called Poor People's March, for what he plans in Washington appears to be something on a far greater scale than what he had indi-cated he planned to do in Memphis . . . what occurred yester-day in Memphis was totally uncalled for—just as Martin Luther King's proposed march on Washington is totally uncalled for and totally unnecessary."[244]

The entire speech, approximately 2,500 words, is filled with the same vindictive "I told you so" warnings about the danger of allowing King's "Poor People's Campaign" to come to Washington the following month. But the nexus of this speech with the following series of other coincidental facts begs the question posed by novelist Ian Fleming: "Once is happenstance, twice is coincidence, but three times is enemy action":

- The fact that Senator Byrd—according to Ron Adkins, who stated he had seen him there—attended a "prayer" meeting with the Memphis plotters,[245] along with Clyde Tolson, who attended many of them,[246] indicates he had also been part of the planning for the lead-up to King's murder. Since Adkins was unclear about exactly when Byrd attended that meeting, the only conjecture is whether he attended the meeting before or after he gave a major Senate speech condemning Dr. King.

- The elapsed time between the DeLoach memorandum (reporting on a meeting he had just attended with Senator Byrd) and the day Byrd finally gave the speech was seventy days. That was more than enough time to have such a speech drafted, circulated to at least Tolson and Hoover and probably other assistants including Sullivan, reedited, and approved. Why else would Byrd have waited so long to give a speech that he had asked the FBI to write for him? Could it have been because it was written in the context of a march that had not yet occurred, one that they already knew would turn violent in Memphis? As Mark Lane pointed out, there were earmarks of the FBI's tutelage within Byrd's speech, including the reference to King as the "Messiah," who would be "conducting a lay-in at a posh Washington hotel," all of which resembled other FBI memos eventually uncovered by the Church Committee in 1975–76.[247]

- The Memphis march-turned-riot, to be examined more closely in Chapter 7, was not only triggered by an FBI informant who had infiltrated himself into the Invaders,* but the riot, as will be shown, was planned and instigated by the FBI themselves. If that seems far-fetched at this point, it will be conclusively demonstrated that it was all an extension of the FBI's (ergo Hoover's) COINTELPRO program to "neutralize and destroy" Dr. King. They were long suspected by many researchers to have been behind the violence that occurred in Memphis on March 28; by now it seems even superfluous to prove it, but that will be done in the following chapters.

- Senator Byrd's speech was delivered the day following the sanitation workers' march that turned violent as soon as it started. The entire speech was built around the events from the

---

* The Invaders group was comprised mostly of young (18–20-year-old) black men who had been described by reporters and the police as presenting themselves as an organization whose purpose was to protest racial injustice. Led by John B. Smith and Charles Cabbage, they attempted to recruit younger men from local high schools to become activitists. There were a number of men who infiltrated their ranks who had connections to the MPD and/or the FBI, however, intent on using the group to sabotage Dr. King's goals. This will be the subject of more scrutiny in the remaining chapters. The Invaders (and certain infiltrators to the group) were primarily responsible for starting the riot that disrupted the protest march on March 28, 1968.

day before, and it was given at 9:00 a.m. on March 29 as the first order of business. Could Senator Byrd have realistically written this quite lengthy speech overnight and been prepared to read it the next day? Given the timing issues outlined above, the length and depth of the speech itself, the earmarks of FBI origin, and the unlikelihood of Sen. Byrd writing it overnight, the most realistic explanation of the provenance of Sen. Byrd's speech was that it became the product of his meeting with Cartha DeLoach over two months previous to the date he delivered it on the Senate floor. That means it was written in accordance with the scheduled plotline by persons having full knowledge of a well-planned riot in Memphis that would be portrayed as a spontaneous event caused by the reckless leader Martin Luther King Jr.

- Finally, just thirteen days after the meeting of Byrd and DeLoach, on February 1, the strange "accident" that Ron Adkins stated was no accident occurred. The two sanitation workers had been crushed to death in what was described as an "accident" but which, according to Ron Adkins, who was in a position to know, was done to inflame the garbage workers and bring the attention of the country—and Dr. King specifically—to their demands. To the plotters, it was just another task on the timeline to ensure that Dr. King would respond to the calls to come to Memphis.

Regarding Ron Adkins, it is important to understand that his testimony was based upon memories from his teenage years, rendered over forty years after these events. While he had excellent recall of the aspects that he knew about, his knowledge base was limited to those specific names, dates, events, and actions. For that reason, his knowledge was almost entirely related to the narrow prism of his father's interface with his Memphis contacts and their connections to others in the Dixie Mafia. But it did include his memories of visits by his father's longtime friend and confidant, Clyde Tolson, whom Ron called "Uncle Clyde," a central figure in organizing the plot beginning in 1964, having started conceiving it seven years before that, as explained elsewhere.

Ron Adkins knew nothing about the internal machinations going on at the CIA, FBI, Memphis Police Department, or army military intelligence; moreover, while he knew minute details of his father's and his older brother's involvement, he had no reason to have ever been aware of the involvement of certain others, like "Raul," the FBI handler of James Earl Ray, or even of Ray himself. Thus, critics who find fault in his testimony because of his lack of knowledge of these other aspects—which he had no reason to have ever been aware of—only reveal their own ignorance and lack of understanding of the importance of his testimony, which reflects an insight that would have otherwise been lost in history.

In the underbelly of Memphis mob operations where streetwise criminals thrived, Russell L. Adkins Sr. was known as a fixer, someone who could bring trusted specialists together to achieve the objectives of those who needed something done. Asked how his father's position with the city was the basis for his widespread influence, Ron Adkins said:

> "Daddy was just always an old boy. Him and both the grand-daddies was [*sic*] just always old boys. They could make stuff happen. They just would fix stuff, I hate to use that word 'fixer,' but for lack of a better term, that's what they did . . . He knew so many people and so many people trusted him."[248] [Asked if the Klansmen and Masons, with whom his father was involved in their "activities," interacted with organized crime, Ron Adkins's response was:] "They *were* organized crime. The whole bunch *was* organized crime . . . if you [can] call them organized." (Emphasis added.)[249]

But the connections went beyond penny-ante local crimes to direct links with Mafia operations, through the Libertos of Memphis, who were connected to Carlos Marcello of New Orleans and through him not only to other national mafiosi, but also to high-level Washington officials, including Clyde Tolson and thereby J. Edgar Hoover, through his own associates as previously described. It was through this apparatus that Adkins had been operating for several decades as the fixer to whom high-level figures would turn to make things happen in Memphis.[250]

Honor Among Thieves and Murderers, Too: The Value of Friends in High Places

These combined relationships were clearly one of the primary reasons that Tennessee was chosen as the ideal state and Memphis was chosen as the city within which the plan would be executed. This would only become clear over four decades later when Dr. Pepper's witness, Ron Adkins, decided to come clean and swore under oath that Clyde Tolson had told his Dixie Mafia contacts to make sure that King would be murdered in Memphis for that very reason. It ensured the highest-level plotters in the White House and the

"SOG" that the murder of Dr. King would be firmly under the local control of the men whom Hoover knew best, men that he would implicitly trust. Those close friendships—especially between Hoover and Holloman, and President Johnson and Tennessee Governor Buford Ellington—are essential to a complete understanding of how this abominable crime was carried out.

Governor Ellington's loyalty—or rather his sycophantic subservience—to Lyndon Johnson was demonstrated when he fired the state's commissioner of corrections, Harry S. Avery, for having the temerity to believe that Dr. King was murdered as the result of a conspiracy, although he attempted to blame it on what he said was Avery's plan to write a book about his own knowledge of the case based upon his position.[251] As the director of all of Tennessee's penitentiaries since 1963, he was responsible for every prisoner in the state. Previously, when Governor Ellington announced that he had reappointed Avery to his position in December 1966, he had praised him for his accomplishments in effecting improvements throughout the system, including specifically the program to rehabilitate youthful prisoners. But when Avery began discussing plans to meet with Ray in conversations with the warden of the main prison, Lake F. Russell, Russell decided that he could use this information to ingratiate himself with the governor. He also realized, of course, that doing so might also result in getting Avery an early retirement in order to make way for Russell's own career advancement.[252]

Avery's plan evolved into something more when he began reviewing letters flowing in from around the world to the new inmate. One in particular caught his attention that was typed on the letterhead of McGill University in Canada, which Avery believed might have been related to how Ray was able to obtain many of the aliases, and some Canadian passports, that were used in his escape; another came from Birmingham, Alabama, and indicated that the author had a previous association with Ray. Instead of merely using the Ray information for a "prison management" methodology document, it appears to have become more of an investigation into what he believed was James Earl Ray's still-untold story. After Avery's first meeting with Ray on March 12, 1969, Russell tipped off the governor and Ellington ordered Avery to drop the investigation. In the following weeks, negative news stories began appearing in Nashville newspapers—including details that had been circulated by Russell, and reported to Ellington but evidently leaked originally by his press secretary, Hudley Crockett. The circle clearly started, and ended, with Governor Ellington himself and was done merely to paper the file as justification for his decision to terminate Avery.

According to Emison, Governor Ellington had his staff manipulate Avery into a vulnerable position, having the appearance of official misconduct, and then ordered the director of the Tennessee Bureau of Investigation, W. E. "Bud" Hopton, to question Avery "at length," after which he reviewed the notes and files Avery had accumulated during his interviews with Ray. Ellington's order for Hopton to investigate Harry Avery was based on the presumption that Avery had allegedly coerced Ray to state that there was in fact a conspiracy to murder Martin Luther King and that Ray had unwittingly become involved in it as the fall guy. Ellington—indubitably under pressure by Johnson and Hoover to get this maverick under control—went to great lengths to derail Avery's attempts to discover the truth of how Martin Luther King Jr. was murdered.

On May 29, the *Nashville Banner*'s page-wide headline read, "ELLINGTON BOOTS AVERY" with a subheadline that read, "Lake Russell Named Commissioner."[253] By the following day, the story had grown in scope and geographic coverage. Newspapers from Hartford, Connecticut; Pittsburgh, Pennsylvania; Dubuque, Iowa; and many other cities around the country carried articles that conveyed the real story: that Governor Ellington had fired Harry Avery "because he was getting too close to unraveling the conspiracy."[254]

Hopton's TBI investigative report was referenced by the HSCA's Final Report (in a footnote on page 658), but it mysteriously disappeared from the Tennessee state archives at about the same time. Inexplicably, all of the HSCA evidence files were sealed for fifty years (until 2029), possibly due to the contents of that document, according to Emison: "The memorandum may have contained information embarrassing to the Ellington or even LBJ administrations . . . [and might be] the only remaining record of key pieces of evidence."[255]

Proof: Injustice in the Justice Department

During the same period of time (1968–69)—according to John Avery Emison, a nephew of Harry S. Avery—Avery overheard a telephone conversation between certain persons in the governor's office and "high officials in the US Justice Department that there would be no trial for James Earl Ray and there would be no evidence tested in open court."[256] This meant to Emison that the governor's office had entered into an agreement with federal authorities to ensure that justice for James Earl Ray would be subverted, and that he would be jailed for the rest of his life and the case closed with no possible avenues for ever reopening it. Emison, moreover, stated that one of Governor Ellington's senior staff members confirmed to him that there were many such conversations, not just the single one that his uncle Harry had overheard.[257]

The "federal authorities" to which Emison referred, with whom the governor talked "many" times, would have undoubtedly included the man he was closest to, Lyndon B. Johnson, and his highest-level aides. Others would have included J. Edgar Hoover and his highest-level associate, Clyde Tolson—along with the FBI liaison to the White House, Cartha DeLoach, acting as the chief of operations of the entire project to "neutralize" Martin Luther King Jr. that had started at least a decade earlier.

If Dr. Pepper's book can be criticized at all, it would only be that he did not adequately stress this point—the intensely personal nature of the mostly secret relationships of the key people, and the reason the plot to murder King "had to be in Memphis"—as much as he might have. We are stressing it here because it is such a critically important theme, just as it was the glue that held the plot together in real time.

How the FBI's Campaign to Destroy MLK Began: December 1963

The intense surveillance of Dr. King—electronic and otherwise—during the period before JFK was assassinated was of two types, broadly defined: (1) salacious "entertainment" for Washington bureaucrats up to and including President Lyndon Johnson; and (2) directed toward "proving" that Dr. King was a secret Communist, aided and abetted by a known Communist, Stanley Levison.

But right after the assassination of JFK, the new strategy of Dr. King's surveillance and persecution kicked in, when the FBI redirected and fundamentally transformed its investigation of King. As explained by David Garrow in *The FBI and Martin Luther King*, beginning in December 1963, it was as the senior officials of the FBI discussed the content of the new audiotapes they had just received that it was decided to transition their case away from the focus on Levison toward destroying King in the eyes of his supporters.[258]

In his attempt to question the Bureau's motives for the change, Garrow put forth several hypotheses but then cited their weaknesses: One, that it was simply a matter of the "intensification of hostility" previously conducted; two, that it was merely the racism of Hoover, or the FBI generally, much of that gleaned from the writings of William Sullivan and David Wise. The third possibility, and according to Garrow's thesis the most likely, was that it was all purely an ideological dilemma or the inherent conservatism of the Bureau, which came up against the liberalism of the administration. He cited Attorney General Ramsey Clark (although he had not been named to that position until 1967) and lawyer Charles Morgan, who wrote that "it had to be ideology that made King numbers one through ten on Hoover's personal enemies list."[259]

All of these listed possibilities are wide of the mark. Since Garrow himself ruled out the first two, we'll limit our rebuttal to the third: the ideological argument fails because that did not really change with JFK's assassination. In some ways (foreign policy is the most compelling, but not the only one), the Johnson administration became much more conservative. In fact, it could be argued that in practically every way Johnson himself was much more conservative, at least up until that point; in the next few years, his "Great Society" program was more liberal than he had ever been, but it must be understood that that program was merely his ticket to a grand legacy for himself. It was something he had planned for decades, as he had stalled much of that same legislation in order to pull it off the shelf and push it through Congress when the time was right (i.e., when he became president).

The Medicare bill, the best illustration of that, had been sitting on the congressional shelf since at least 1945, when Truman had attempted to get it passed. To buttress the point that he had always craved the notion of his eventual legacy, Johnson even bullied George Wallace to reverse his negative image as a segregationist when he issued this challenge to him in 1965: "What do you want left when you die?" Johnson intoned. "Do you want a great big marble monument that reads, 'George Wallace—He Built,' or do you want a little piece of scrawny pine board that reads, 'George Wallace—He Hated'?"[260] Johnson's daily mantra for decades was that he would one day become president, and not just any president but one in the pantheon of greatest presidents, which he believed to be Washington, Lincoln, and Roosevelt (the latter). He wanted his own name to be added to that shortened list and would do anything to ensure it would happen.

Garrow then made the stunning assertion that "Just as the December 23 conference *was the first significant event after the wiretaps went on . . .*"[261] He went on to make the point that the only other "important development after the conference" was the bug installed in King's room at the Willard Hotel, and therefore, he concluded, the decision to destroy King was caused by the Bureau officials' reaction to their feelings about King's personal life.[262]

Evidently Garrow, in failing to note the far more momentous other significant event that had occurred in that time frame (*after the wiretaps went on in October*)—the assassination of President John F. Kennedy one month before that December meeting—misidentified the real reason for the decision to simultaneously "up the ante" by deciding to "destroy King." It was because he, like so many other authors, prognosticators, news reporters, and their broadcasting or newspaper superiors, failed to realize the significance of that event, misled as they were by the new president and the government as a whole into thinking it was merely the result of the actions of a "lone nut."

The only realistic explanation for the sea change in the FBI's campaign against Dr. Martin Luther King Jr. starting in December 1963—after evaluating all of the possible reasons presented by Garrow—is that it was all due to the only material thing that had changed, *dramatically changed*, in the weeks before that fundamental revision in FBI policy: the assassination of the president. That stupendous change had automatically reordered the priorities of much of the government, not least of which was its primary investigative agency, the FBI. And just as it became refocused (from one of facilitation of the executive change to one of leading its cover-up), so too did it modify its long list of other action items. The focus became, as Mr. Garrow correctly discerned, the destruction of Dr. Martin Luther King Jr.

From January on, throughout 1964, Bureau memoranda show that Hoover and Sullivan, and all his men in the Domestic Intelligence Division (or "Division Five"), had become obsessed with Dr. King's sexual behavior and the apparent need to record more of it, as well as the need to circulate all of it to the White House (i.e., Johnson) and selected other men in Congress or other federal agencies and journalists. The focus was reflected by the extensive efforts to get bugs installed before King's trips to different locations, such as Hawaii, then Los Angeles, and afterwards, in their reports of a lack of "developments," in Hawaii.[263]

But that failure was quickly restored by their success in the reports from Los Angeles, with the communications then reflecting "unconcealed joy" and the gloating pleasure that several agents expressed about the notion of Robert Kennedy reading the files and reports of the surveillance. The references to "communist subversives" had nearly disappeared from these reports, except for a handwritten afterthought, "in view of his association with Communists," that had been inserted into a July 1964 memo indicating that more information on King's personal activities was needed; as biographer Garrow noted, it "was only the most sadly amusing example of this veneer."[264]

As the events of 1964–67 continued to play out—the temporary forced collaboration between King and Johnson; the repeated incidents of race riots throughout that period in many major city's ghettos; Dr. King's receipt of the Nobel Peace Prize and the angst that created throughout the FBI, thanks to its leadership; and the diametrically opposed courses that King and Johnson were to take during that period—the increasing talk that King might one day run for the presidency became one of Johnson's and Hoover's worst nightmares.

It might have started out for Hoover and Johnson to be a choice of whether to "'discredit,' 'neutralize,' or 'expose' King," as posited by Garrow, but given their combined histories of criminal conduct and increasingly brazen and diabolical plotting to bend the arc of history to conform to their respective agendas, it is much more realistic to deduce that they had reached a mutual conclusion: that their only choice was to physically "destroy" their nemesis, Martin Luther King Jr. Or, as Johnson liked to euphemistically put it when he pegged someone for murder, according to his closest criminal partners, "He has to go."

Let the Planning Begin

Discreet word of the need to begin sketching a plot began in 1956, when J. Edgar Hoover first scribbled three sets of initials onto his "prayer list": JFK, RFK, and MLK.[265] But nothing beyond such wish lists and talk among friends and colleagues had been cast in concrete because nothing in the way of planning could be started on the remaining subjects until the first priority was complete, the assassination of President Kennedy. Only when that was done could the remaining actions be put into the gristmill of street-level planning. After the first target was eliminated in November 1963, the next two were moved up to the top of the list, and the two men whose cooperation in many hidden areas that had been underway for two decades reached a common goal. Johnson and Hoover undoubtedly agreed that the next subjects would be planned jointly and simultaneously, because they both knew that time was limited and the plans for each would both require long lead times. For obvious reasons, only one of the two prongs of this double-duality can be covered within a single book; thus, we will focus on the plot to kill Dr. King.

Seven years before, when Hoover wrote the three sets of initials on his prayer list and had Clyde Tolson send it, via Senator Joe McCarthy, to Russell Adkins in Memphis, the decision had been made as to how that operation would be conducted.[266] Now that Johnson was secure in his position, in early 1964 reservations were booked at a facility that would guarantee the two highest-level planners—Tolson and Adkins—maximum privacy and minimal interruptions. It was a meeting that would last nearly four months, on the ocean liner SS *United States*, on a cruise from New York to Southampton, England, via Le Havre in France and back, from May 27, 1964, to September 16, 1964.[267] Clearly, there were stopovers in one or both ports, which would explain the lengthy trip on what was the fastest ocean liner of its day; it still holds the record for transatlantic cruises, a little more than three days on its maiden voyage. The two primary designated plotters made this trip—Russell Adkins Sr. and Hoover's "right-hand man," Clyde Tolson.

Upon their return from that trip, the word was "The coon had to go. The coon has got to go." The "coon" was Martin Luther King Jr., who was also referred to derisively as "HNIC" (i.e., "Head N****r In Charge"). These expressions were said to have emanated from the highest ranks of the White House and the FBI. They were repeatedly used by Russell Adkins Sr. during the meetings held in the ensuing years, beginning in the latter half of 1964. It was a continuing series of meetings, at least weekly, sometimes on Sunday at Adkins's home, other times during weekday evenings at the Berclair Baptist Church, among other places. The ones conducted at the church were called "prayer meetings."[268]

Through these early meetings, different ideas for how to entice Dr. King to eventually come to Memphis were discussed, in accordance with the instruction from Clyde Tolson to "make it happen in Memphis," to ensure complete control over all facets of the operation. With Mayor Loeb's concurrence, it was decided to use the city's garbage workers—who were always kept in a state of submissive obedience, living from paycheck to paycheck at poverty-level wages, unorganized, in accordance with city rules— to create a catalytic moment that would guarantee King's appearance.[269] It had to be carefully designed to ensure the target was exactly where they wanted him to be, at the point when the plans and logistics, the men and their equipment, would all be in place. Every contingency would have to be anticipated, down to the point of having the patsy, James Earl Ray, on site and ready to be shot and killed, but with a backup plan in place if he wasn't; and what would have to be done to ensure the target, Dr. King, be killed—if not by the shooter, then by someone ready to do that in the hospital where he would be taken. The plotters did not expect anything to go wrong, but it did, in both of those scenarios, as we will see in Chapter 8.

The story that Ron Adkins got directly from his father was that J. Edgar Hoover would routinely give Clyde Tolson money to perform various criminal deeds with his contacts around the country, including arranging "local-area killings." We will never know all the other cases around the country commissioned in this manner, but a number of likely victims of this ad hoc execution program (similar pogroms run by the CIA, even by Johnson himself through his personal hit-man, Mac Wallace, might overlap) were very well known, which leaves the question of how many more there were.

After his father's return from the ocean cruise in late 1964, many meetings would take place in and around Memphis, involving high-level Memphis city and Tennessee state officials and key men from Washington, DC, to develop a master plan to accomplish the goal set during that ocean cruise. Among those identified as requiring the longest lead times was planning for the right men to be put into certain jobs, such as the Memphis police commissioner, who—uniquely—doubled as the fire department commissioner, a very convenient arrangement since a single person could control both of these important roles. Frank Holloman fulfilled that requirement to a tee. According to Ron Adkins, Mayor Henry Loeb brought up the need to appoint Holloman to his position at one of the meetings at Berclair Baptist Church.[270]

But another, even greater lead-time requirement undoubtedly related to the identification of candidates to become the "patsy," who would be tagged to take the blame, and then the selection of the single best candidate. Like the others used before him, he would be selected by the same officials who had conducted previous "experiments" to ensure their man was a good subject for manipulation; the nominee would come from the field of those who had been used for previous experimentation in Operation MKULTRA, the psychological warfare program that developed myriad mind-control techniques and drugs. Other qualifications were no doubt related to the subject's background. Probably someone coming from a poverty-level, lower-class dysfunctional family would be favored for the role, preferably one who could be portrayed as a slovenly ex-con and hateful southern racist. He didn't need to actually meet all those criteria; he just needed to be vulnerable enough to be portrayed that way. Probably months, even a few years were devoted to this preparatory work.

Clearly the field of candidates was winnowed down by mid-1966, because in November or early December 1966, Tolson arrived in Memphis with envelopes of money to be paid to informants and to the warden of Missouri State Prison to arrange for the escape of James Earl Ray.[271] That plan would come to fruition on April 23, 1967, when Ray, the designated patsy, took the bait and, with a lot of help from his "friends," made his escape amid confusion and indifference on the part of prison authorities, who, when they finally released "wanted" posters and background information on the escapee, put the wrong fingerprints on the documents, clear evidence that they were not interested in recapturing him. His brother John wrote that after James's escape, "they had been switched by [bureau of corrections commissioner] Wilkinson and [warden] Swenson with another man's prints."[272] So, even if someone had recognized his photo on the "wanted" poster, the police would have freed him again because of the fingerprint mismatch.

When Russell Adkins Sr. died, in 1967, Ron's older brother Russell Adkins Jr. picked up the pieces of the plot that his father had left and kept its momentum going, alongside the other key participants including Mayor

Loeb and Director Holloman. While Russell Jr. attempted to take over his father's role after his death, he became frustrated at times that Commissioner Holloman interceded and began personally running the operation, according to Ron Adkins in his deposition to Dr. Pepper.[273]

President Johnson's "Other" Legacy: Operation CHAOS Overriding the Constitution to Spy on Whomever the CIA Chose

Johnson must have felt very frustrated with his lack of access to wiretaps and bugs after being forced to order the FBI to cease using them in 1965 (although they didn't end until his attorney general, Nicholas Katzenbach, finally closed the remaining one down in 1966). Even though there were still exceptions being made, as noted in Chapter 2, they were very few, as Johnson became squeezed between Thurgood Marshall, then his solicitor general, later Supreme Court justice, and Attorneys General Katzenbach and Ramsey Clark in the Justice Department, all of whom took his order seriously. By 1967, Johnson decided to subvert his own rule by moving such operations to the CIA, where they could be conducted much more discreetly.

In August 1967, a series of meetings took place at the White House; Fort Holabird, Maryland; Langley, Virginia (CIA HQ); and the Pentagon, which, at Lyndon Johnson's order, led to the formation of a "Special Operations Group" developed—clearly in defiance of the statute that created the CIA, as well as constitutional limitations—to penetrate and undermine the domestic protest movement. It consisted of three divisions:[274]

1. OPERATION MHCHAOS, which eventually spied on over 7,500 US citizens;
2. PROJECT MERRIMAC, to infiltrate ten major peace and civil rights organizations; and
3. OPERATION MUDHEN, dedicated to spying on syndicated columnist Jack Anderson.

The brazenly illegal operation MHCHAOS (the "MH" designation signified its worldwide area of operations, even though it was primarily directed to domestic operations) became commonly known as Operation CHAOS. The Johnson-appointed Director of Central Intelligence (DCI), Richard Helms, went along with it, setting up the program to detect and monitor foreign influences within the student antiwar movement despite the fact that there weren't any, as they would eventually determine. It was all done to assuage Johnson's paranoia. Helms certainly knew that it was outside the scope of the CIA's charter, and anyone should have known it was highly illegal and unconstitutional, yet he directed his chief of counterintelligence, James Jesus Angleton, to establish the program, which Richard Ober was chosen to head. Ober had worked directly for Angleton for over twenty-five years at that point and was the number-two man in the CIA's Office of Counterintelligence.[275]

President Johnson's orders to DCI Helms that created Operation CHAOS gave the CIA's Richard Ober (and thereby the FBI's liaison to the CIA, Sam Papich) the tools to monitor any US citizen they chose to deem a "person of interest" and allowed them to examine every detail of that person's life. No limitations were made to their quest for information, including "personal, medical, financial, political, social, religious, educational, sexual or business information," because the CIA decided that they needed every single detail they could find to perform their presidentially decreed function.[276] The FBI, in their secret COINTELPRO operation, had already been doing that kind of surveillance on certain people for years, persons selected by J. Edgar Hoover (Dr. King, for example), but Johnson's order effectively extended the same kind of intrusive harassment previously focused on a few dozen to, potentially, the entire population; it was limited only by the resources available to Ober's and Papich's crew, and at their whim it could be directed at whoever might come into their radar. Ultimately, the program raised the number of people under intense surveillance from a handful to at least 7,500 citizens,[277] in what can only be described as a major assault on the Constitution and the statutory limitations on the CIA's restricted authority.

The CIA and its sister intelligence agencies within the US Army, Navy, and the FBI took an interest in James Earl Ray after the assassination when a "Person of Interest" 201 file was opened first on Eric S. Galt on April 18, 1968, then changed on April 22 to Ray's name. Interestingly, when the CIA's 201 file on Ray was declassified and released in 1994, it was annotated: *"MATERIAL REVIEWED AT CIA HEADQUARTERS BY HOUSE SELECT COMMITTEE ON ASSASSINATIONS STAFF MEMBERS,"* although nothing about that—or whether the full file, or a redacted file, was reviewed—had been included in the HSCA's Final Report.[278] It also stated that no written request had been made by the FBI, but that Mr. Ober had "a number of conversations with Mr. [Special Agent Sam J.] Papich of the FBI."[279] Clearly, they were following the standard that Lyndon Johnson had always used: the most illegal, or outrageously unethical, operations would never be put into writing on the premise that "if there is no physical record of the crime, then it could never be proven, therefore it didn't happen."[280]

As Emison adroitly noted, Ober was very concerned that someone's cover—undoubtedly Raul's—could be exposed if Ray ever got a real, fair trial, where actual evidence was revealed and witnesses subjected to cross-examination in a court without a controlled judge overseeing the process.[281] That concern would certainly have been shared in Ober's numerous conversations with the FBI's Papich, possibly even being first voiced by him. Emison also observed that this same concern—the risk of James Earl Ray ever being allowed a fair trial in any court where unfiltered facts might be exposed—had also been the subject of conversations expressed by Tennessee Governor Buford Ellington's staff that were overheard by Tennessee Commissioner of Correction Harry S. Avery while he was in the governor's office, as previously noted.[282] LBJ's personal friend Ellington fired Avery shortly after that incident.

Given the fact that the CIA, the FBI, the related military intelligence officials, and the Tennessee governor (and, through him, key judges within the Tennessee judiciary system) were all brought into play to ensure that James Earl Ray was never given a trial—least of all a "fair" one—it becomes clear that the course was set by someone who was in control of all of these entities. That person could only have been President Lyndon B. Johnson, whose reach extended across all political and geographical boundaries to all of them. It is not written anywhere, but the result—how James Earl Ray was railroaded into prison for the rest of his life without ever getting anything resembling a trial—is as clear as if there were fingerprints labeled "LBJ" on every facet of the operation, from start to finish.

According to the *Dictionary of American History* regarding the 1967 riots: "Beginning in April and continuing through the rest of the year, 159 race riots erupted across the United States. The first occurred in Cleveland, but by far the most devastating were those that took place in Newark, New Jersey, and Detroit, Michigan. The former took twenty-six lives and injured fifteen hundred; the latter resulted in forty deaths and two thousand injuries. Large swaths of ghetto in both places went up in flames. Television showed burning buildings and looted stores, with both National Guardsmen and paratroopers on the scenes."[283] The total for all the riots around the country, according to a report that Major General William P. Yarborough received on August 23, was 122 deaths (including ninety-nine blacks and seven policemen).[284]

In October 1967, 200,000 antiwar demonstrators gathered in Washington, much to the consternation of the nation's political, law enforcement, and military leadership. They viewed it as an invasion by the enemy, a major counterinsurgency that, if they'd had their druthers, would have been met with fierce resistance and heavy artillery. A description of that comes from an article in the March 21, 1993, edition of the Memphis

Commercial Appeal, by Stephen Tompkins, titled "Top spy feared current below surface unrest," which stated that one of General Yarborough's top aides said that he was obsessed about "radicals and subversion":

> "He was always saying that we knew how to deal with subversion in other countries but not at home." Yarborough's opinion of antiwar protesters comes across clearly in this excerpt from an interview conducted by two Army historians shortly after his retirement in 1975. The general described "the burning of Washington, the siege of the Pentagon" during an October 1967 antiwar march on the Pentagon. "What some people don't remember was the terror that all this struck into the hearts of the people that thought the empire was coming apart at the seams." Yarborough said he stood on the Pentagon roof: "It looked like a castle where the Huns had gathered around: as far as the eye could reach, there they were, shaking their bony fists. There were American Nazis. There were Communists. There were hippies . . . I can assure you it was a sight to make you stop to think," he said. Army Chief of Staff Harold Johnson and Defense Secretary Robert McNamara also were on the roof, Yarborough remembered.
>
> "As we looked at this great horde below us, waving their battering rams, so to speak . . . the Secretary of Defense [McNamara] turned to the Chief of Staff of the Army [Harold Johnson] and said. 'Johnny, what are we going to do about this?' Johnny said, 'I'm damned if I know.'"
>
> Yarborough knew: He doubled his intelligence-gathering efforts against King and his supporters.
>
> [. . .]
>
> "To dig it out," Yarborough said, " *a jettisoning of certain civil rights must take place. One has to resort occasionally to curfews, to search and seizure, to mail monitoring, to telephone tapping, in order to get to that vast (guerrilla) underground.*" (Emphasis added.)[285]

Despite his actual words that belied what he claimed in public—that he was attempting to advance "law and order" in behalf of his fellow Americans—and while denying that they were totalitarians, Yarborough claimed that that "jettisoning certain civil liberties" was necessary to accomplish that objective.

These men, looking at the mostly nonviolent antiwar protesters as their mortal enemies, had still not understood the deeper currents that were reshaping attitudes of blacks and whites alike. Instead, the military leadership looked upon the protesters as enemies gaining ground, while the protesters had simply come to believe that the war was based upon lies and deceit, that young draftees were being treated merely as bodies to be used as fodder by Washington politicians. The protesters had no attachments to foreign powers; they simply wanted to get their own brothers, and country, out of a war that lacked a raison d'être.

The Emergence of Military Intelligence in Surveilling, then Plotting Against, Dr. Martin Luther King Jr.

High-level military officers had also been surveilling Martin Luther King Jr. for many years. In fact, the US Army had started a file on him in 1947, ten years before he became a well-known civil rights activist and twenty-one years before his assassination. That was because he had become a member of the Intercollegiate Council at Morehouse College, which was headed by Mrs. Dorothy Lilley, a suspected Communist, according to army intelligence.[286] In January 1963, the 113th Military Intelligence Group (MIG) filed a report on King's activities at a dinner at the Edgewater Beach Hotel, when he was overheard telling others that "Project C" (to disrupt government and businesses in Birmingham that spring) was about to be deployed.[287]

But their focus on him was greatly increased when he began his antiwar speeches in the two years before his April 4, 1967, Riverside Church speech. His speeches from late 1965 to early 1967 had already caused great backlash and sporadic protests and demonstrations throughout the country. One short excerpt from the Riverside Church speech illustrates the heightened tone of his oratory:

> Now it should be incandescently clear that no one who has any concern for the integrity and life of America today can ignore the present war. If America's soul becomes totally poisoned, part of the autopsy must read "Vietnam." It can never be saved so long as it destroys the hopes of men the world over. So it is that those of us who are yet determined that "America will be" are led down the path of protest and dissent, working for the health of our land.

The following day, as if choreographed from afar, 168 newspapers around the country expressed their outrage at King's remarks. The *New York Times* attacked him for linking the war to the struggle for basic civil rights, saying it was "too facile a connection" and that he was doing a "disservice" to both causes. Moreover, it asserted that there "are no simple answers to the war in Vietnam or to racial injustice in this country." The *Washington Post* stated that King had "diminished his usefulness to his cause, his country and his people." President Johnson discontinued all contact with King. "What is that goddamned nigger preacher doing to me?" Johnson was said to have uttered to an aide. "We gave him the Civil Rights Act of 1964, we gave him the Voting Rights Act of 1965, we gave him the War on Poverty. What more does he want?"[288]

After the Riverside Church speech, the reverberations became ever more violent, the rhetoric more strident, while the numbers of protesters grew exponentially. And from Vietnam, dispatches from the 525th MIG "reported that 'Negro troops are unsettled' by articles on King's speech in *Pacific Stars & Stripes* and their hometown newspapers."[289] As the ambient temperatures of the continent increased that spring, over the next two months, so did the emotional heat level in the nation's inner cities, as more and more of the inhabitants became aware of the young men who were being drafted into a confusing war against peasants on the other side of the world—a war that seemed wholly unrelated to US interests—and the haunting fact that many of them would never return alive.

From the first to the last of 1967, nothing had been done to assuage the domestic turbulence being caused by the conduct of the war by the president; he dealt with it by turning up the heat and came close to putting major cities in the United States under martial law. In a Yarborough staff meeting at the Pentagon on July 28, just as riots had broken out in many of the major cities, the minutes indicate that he was told by his staff that there was no foreign or domestic enemy involved in the Detroit riots; yet the minutes were noted that he "REJECTS" this information and stated that "they will find either HAVANA or PEKING behind this conspiracy," obviously references to the previous reports and strangely similar to rants being made in the White House by President Johnson at about the same time.[290] Furthermore, the minutes noted that he stated, "There are indications weapons have been stolen from a number of military posts including Dugway Proving Grounds where there are some pretty sophisticated weapons. There are indications Negroes have been trucked from one scene of activity to another—indicating an organization."[291]

Shortly after the Detroit riots, in July 1967, the plot to kill Dr. King in Memphis had passed the initial planning phases; a meeting took place in the

Pentagon that included Colonel John Downie of the 902nd MIG, General Yarborough, and others.[292] Downie (or possibly an impersonator who claimed to be him, but nevertheless very familiar with his activities as a colonel with the 902nd MIG) would admit in 1996 to Dr. Pepper's investigator Stephen Tompkins that the "Memphis operation seemed to have been put in motion following a meeting that took place about a week after the riot in Detroit."[293]

Dr. William F. Pepper's magnum opus, *The Plot to Kill King*, details the many meetings held during 1967 and 1968 between various military, FBI, White House, and CIA officials as they discussed plans for surveilling and undermining Dr. King and his associates and the extreme methods— including suspending constitutional impediments to facilitate their actions— that they believed would restore "law and order." One early example related to a meeting early in the new year, held in J. Edgar Hoover's office on January 18, 1967, with General Yarborough and Colonel F. E. Van Tassell for a discussion of plans to deal with the "antiwar movement."[294]

Toward the end of that year, another instance report, distributed during a December 12, 1967, conference at the Pentagon, described King's plans for the march on Washington as "a devastating civil disturbance whose sole purpose is to shut down the United States government." It described King as "a Negro who repeatedly has preached the message of Hanoi and Peking."[295] Any military leader sitting in on that meeting would have understood implicitly that aggressive reaction to that message would be inevitable, and anyone caring about their own career longevity should be prepared to respond accordingly.

Dr. Pepper's extensive investigation and research, merely summarized here, proved that a military presence in Memphis was authorized within the Pentagon and subsequently planned and deployed in advance of the King assassination. Units of military intelligence were sent to Memphis as a backup to ensure the desired outcome would be successful. It proved to be unnecessary and was not used, but it is important to examine the "who, what, where, and how" aspects of it, in addition to the "why" (the motivations). There are some names noted below, but some of the key others—to ensure their protection and security—were presented by Dr. Pepper and others as pseudonyms; the reasons need not be explained, as they should become obvious. This brief summary of those events is intended as a recap of the much more detailed investigation Dr. Pepper conducted over many years, as presented in *The Plot to Kill King*, supplemented by numerous other complementary books, articles, and documents from new proceedings and old archives.

Stephen Tompkins, previously an investigative reporter for the Memphis *Commercial Appeal*, had an extensive background in all phases of the King murder investigation. His experience brought more expertise and credibility to Dr. Pepper's investigation, including his involvement with the man who came forward and identified himself as Colonel John Downie.[296] He had also validated the statements of two ex-Special Forces men (whom Pepper only identified through the pseudonyms "Warren and Murphy"), each of whom gave Tompkins detailed accounts that implicated the army and other government agencies in the assassination of Dr. King, "one of our nation's deepest, darkest secrets."[297] Their perspective was formed through their own participation in a sniper team backup as Special Forces Alpha 184, but never called upon to fire a shot, since that was done through another nonmilitary team, described elsewhere.

Tompkins had spent nearly eighteen months researching the role of military intelligence units in surveilling and infiltrating black organizations and civil rights groups, finally publishing a front-page story in the Memphis *Commercial Appeal* titled "Army feared King, secretly watched him" on Sunday, March 21, 1993, with the subtitle "Spying on blacks started 75 years ago."[298] The article began, "The intelligence branch of the United States Army spied on the family of Dr. Martin Luther King Jr. for three generations," which would indicate that the government's domestic spying practice had begun even much earlier than previously indicated, or anyone suspected. That point continued into the next two paragraphs of Tompkins's article, where it was asserted that the intrusions were often focused on black churches in the South and their ministers, caused by the conviction of top army intelligence officers that black Americans were "ripe for subversion— first by agents of the German Kaiser, then by Communists, later by the Japanese and eventually by those opposed to the Vietnam War." The article stated, furthermore, that the program included the use of "infiltrators, wiretaps and aerial photography by U2 spy planes."[299]

Tompkins's disturbing article also stated that in the late 1960s, some of the units began "supplying sniper rifles and other weapons to civilian police departments" as they began planning for a possible "armed rebellion." While much of the story was revealed in the congressional hearings conducted in the early to mid-1970s, the key officials who knew the most about the program did not testify, thereby leaving the worst of the secrets secret.[300]

Downie's purpose in meeting with Tompkins, he explained, was to proffer corrections to Dr. Pepper's previous statements—which, he stated, were mostly "remarkably accurate"—and also to correct the impression left of his own role, which he felt was given more responsibility than had actually been the case. He did confirm that he had played a "key role" in coordinating the task force of military intelligence units during the first week of April

1968. While conceding that he had met personally with General Yarborough, the founder of the units known as the Green Berets (whom Steve Tompkins called "the army's top spy") on a regular basis, Downie stated that his orders were routed through one of Yarborough's previous subordinates who was, in 1968, playing the role of a trusted emissary, outside of the normal chain of command. Downie confirmed that his role was one of coordinating the several military units brought to Memphis during March, in preparation for the events that had been planned over several months and to film or photograph the run-up, the execution of the plan, and the aftermath, so that military intelligence officers would be able to identify everyone in the vicinity and be able to ascertain what their respective roles had been. Clearly, this meant that they knew precisely who the shooter really was and who else had been put there to facilitate his role and assist in his exit from the scene.[301]

One month after Dr. King's December 1967 announcement of his plans for the April Poor People's Campaign, General Yarborough and his fellow high-level army officers were preparing for major protests in Washington for that event. Suddenly, just as the Tet Offensive broke out in Vietnam, which resulted in further calls for more combat troops, the Pentagon realized that the Vietnam sinkhole had swallowed up so many troops that there weren't enough left in the United States to control a national emergency should the protests become a more violent armed revolution. Beyond the April event, contingencies were also under way for another possible large-scale antiwar demonstration again in October, and another contingency had to be added to the mix: being "on call" for what was expected to be yet another major event in Chicago, when the Democratic National Convention was planning to meet there in August.

"We knew the whole country was a tinderbox," said Ralph M. Stein, a Pace University law professor who in 1968 was the top army intelligence analyst in the Counterintelligence Analysis Bureau at the Pentagon. "Once we recognized the magnitude of actual civil disturbances, based on our worst possible scenarios, we didn't have enough combat-type troops to react to widespread riots," Stein said. "At one point, we even considered pulling troops out of Vietnam or withdrawing units from the Seventh Army (in Europe)." Upon his return from the MacDill meeting, Yarborough told a top aide: "I can't believe what sorry shape we're in."[302] Evidently, the need for reordering priorities from the top down—a far more effective and needed option—had never occurred to him or anyone else higher in the chain of command.

Although MHCHAOS was established originally by President Johnson, it was later expanded by President Nixon, who eventually took most of the blame for it under the same Watergate umbrella of his other offenses—all of which pale in comparison to Johnson's. In the aftermath of the Watergate break-in, which two CIA officers had participated in, the public finally awoke to the agency's overreach, which forced the closure of Operation CHAOS. The full account of the secretive, illegal nature of the program was revealed by Seymour Hersh in a 1974 article in the *New York Times* titled "Huge CIA Operation Reported in US Against Antiwar Forces, Other Dissidents in Nixon Years." It was this article that led to Angleton's forced retirement and Ober's transfer to the National Security Agency.[303]

In the face of the severe public reaction to these revelations, Congress created the Rockefeller Commission, led by then-Vice President Nelson Rockefeller, to investigate the surveillance. The real purpose, though—according to Richard "Dick" Cheney, then-Deputy White House Chief of Staff—was to avoid "congressional efforts to further encroach on the executive branch."[304] Following the revelations by the Rockefeller Commission, then-DCI George H. W. Bush admitted that "the operation in practice resulted in some improper accumulation of material on legitimate [*sic*] domestic activities."[305]

Chapter 6

MANIPULATION
OF THE PATSY

"Like the Mafia, the Agency [CIA] forms a true brotherhood—one for all and all for one—except that, in the clutch, alas, everyone is expendable. But up to that final point, the members of the Company will do anything for each other—lie, cheat, steal, kidnap, suborn perjury, bribe, corrupt, subvert, kill and kill again."
—Harrison Salisbury (award-winning *New York Times* reporter)

James Earl Ray's Induction into the World of "Intelligence"

This chapter will present a thorough account of how the patsy was selected and groomed to play his part in the elaborate scheme to murder Dr. King, and how he was kept out of the loop as an unwitting accomplice completely unaware of the intended objective in a plan set up by Hoover and Tolson, with help from the Dixie Mafia and others in the CIA and military intelligence. It will trace his escape from the Missouri State Prison, followed by his wanderings around Illinois, then on to Canada. Questions will be raised about why he went all the way to Montreal, rather than the much shorter trip to Toronto, and why he reentered the US after vowing never to return. We will review how the man named "Raoul" was able to maneuver him around three countries over a period of nine months and then, just as everything else was in place, have him make his grand appearance in Memphis just in time to unwittingly participate in the scheduled execution of Martin Luther King Jr.

In 1944, James Earl Ray had dropped out of school at age sixteen and found a job with the International Shoe Company in Hartford, Illinois, about ten miles south of Alton, where he lived with his grandmother and uncle. During the two years he worked there in the dye shop, his wage was sixty cents an hour plus overtime, but by living frugally, neither drinking, smoking, nor partying, and saving his money, he had accumulated a few thousand dollars in cash and war bonds. His younger brothers looked up to him as a role model. After the war, the shoe company went bankrupt since their primary sales were boots for soldiers. Ray, suddenly unemployed, decided to enlist in the army. For the rest of his life, Ray would say that his time in the army put him on the "road to ruin."[306]

In February 1946, at age seventeen, James Earl Ray enlisted in the US Army; the following month he turned eighteen and after basic training was stationed at a base near Nuremberg, Germany. He was initially assigned to a trucking company; as a military policeman (MP), he drove a jeep, mostly shuttling guards back and forth to their posts.[307] In April 1948, according to researcher Lyndon Barsten, the twenty-year-old Ray was reassigned to a unit that carried a four-digit designation, the 7892nd Infantry Regiment, which was said to be an "unusual" situation that military experts thought indicated that "someone did not like the idea of this unit's formation in the first place."[308] The unusual things did not end there, as Barsten also discovered, including the fact that James was given two serial numbers, the official one (#16163129) as well as an encoded one (#16242515). When he questioned a former army covert operative why something like this was done, Barsten was told, "He was doing something the army didn't want attributed to him."[309]

Another officer told Barsten that the four-digit army unit numbers were used for intelligence work, as cover. Since Ray had joined a new organization formed out of the old OSS, he had unwittingly joined the CIA at that point. James would subsequently tell his brother, John Larry Ray, "When you join the OSS [ergo, the CIA], it's like joining the Mafia: you never leave."[310] Mr. Barsten's research into this area has not been widely recognized previously by other authors, but it is arguably one of the most important pieces of the mosaic, which might explain a lot about how Ray came to be picked for the role he was being groomed for even before he broke out of prison in April 1967 at the age of thirty-nine. The fact that he had been chosen by someone at the highest levels of the FBI—J. Edgar Hoover's consort and number-two man in charge, Clyde Tolson—had set the stage for the prison break, unbeknownst to Ray. That point is the most compelling argument indicating that he had been pegged for eventual use in a covert role as much as two decades earlier, by someone in James Angleton's Counterespionage Division of the CIA, who was running those programs when Ray became a one of the soldiers being studied.

During his time in this unit—while working as an MP—army records show that James was administered two lumbar punctures (spinal taps), one on March 25, 1948 (labeled "headache, lumbar puncture"), and the second on October 28, 1948 (spinal puncture), which apparently contributed to him becoming ill, leading him to miss his shift (those records have since been lost by the government, apparently incinerated, along with millions of others, at a massive fire at the National Personnel Records Center, near St. Louis, in July 1973).[311]

Based upon Barsten's research and the data still available, it appears that Ray was given experimental drug treatments by the army, in cooperation with the CIA, which were being conducted with the goal of creating thousands of mind-numbed robots performing as killing machines, the product of the "Black Sorcerer" Sidney Gottlieb, who was put in place by CIA Director Allen Dulles. Ray's brother, John Larry Ray, and researcher Lyndon Barsten believed that the drugs given to James Earl Ray led to his shooting of an African American soldier from Tennessee named Washington, as he resisted being arrested by Ray and another MP. Ray felt extreme guilt for wounding this soldier for the rest of his life, knowing that his injury had crippled the soldier permanently, having severed his spinal cord.[312]

A CIA document released through the Freedom of Information Act (titled "MORI 428311") indicated that various narcotics were used in their experiments to induce hypnosis, including barbiturates, chloroform phenobarbital, sodium amytal, and sodium pentothal, which, according to the CIA statements, all "show great promise and may be adaptable to clandestine use." The paper then presents a rhetorical question: "Can a subject be hypnotized against his will? Excepting the use of drugs, the answer must be 'no' if he understands what is going on. However, if the question can be rewritten to read, 'Can a subject be hypnotized without his knowledge?' the answer appears to be 'yes' under favorable circumstances: disguised induction and a good subject."[313] There can be little doubt that it was the latter premise under which Sidney Gottlieb practiced his cunning plot to create mindless robots to inhabit the bodies of unwitting soldiers.[314]

Barsten and John Ray then posed the question: "Was the shooting of the soldier Washington part of a drugging operation; and was James's psychological makeup the reason he was chosen to be the patsy years later, in the murder of Martin Luther King? Was my brother a 'good subject,' as the document describes?"[315] This intriguing question, of whether James's psychological profile had been the object of studies by military intelligence—and their documented collaboration with the CIA's MKULTRA experiments in the late 1940s—gives rise to the hypothetical possibility that Ray's military records might have been annotated with the results of secret studies of his psychological makeup for possible future use. The parallels with how Lee Harvey Oswald was similarly channeled might be yet another in a long series of replicated patterns carried out by the same men, and similar resources, used in the assassination of John F. Kennedy.

The larger question was, besides Sidney Gottlieb, who else was closely watching the mind-control programs back in Langley, keeping tabs on various candidates who might be tagged as "adaptable for clandestine" future projects? Possibly the head of the Counterintelligence Division, James Jesus Angleton himself, and others at a high level who reported to him, such as his longtime associate Richard Ober, put in charge of Operation CHAOS?

John Larry Ray wrote that "My brother was a changed man when he returned from Germany. To be frank, he seemed drugged, even though I never saw him take anything . . . Also, he seemed easily persuaded to do things he never would have done before. This was never truer than his involvement in criminal activities."[316]

According to Barsten and John Larry Ray, before going on to Canada, James had stopped in Chicago to meet with someone from the Chicago Mafia, with which he had previously become involved, apparently related to setting him up with contacts in Canada. As John Larry observed, "Once you become involved in the Mafia's operations and they pay you, you are indebted to them for life; you don't really have any choice."[317] That sentiment was very similar to what J. Edgar Hoover would always say about the FBI: "Once you're FBI, you're always FBI." The same precept certainly applied to the CIA as well, undoubtedly in even greater strength.

James Earl Ray's Earlier Crimes and His Aliases

Until he was charged with the murder of an internationally acclaimed icon, James Earl Ray's history of petty crime read like the rap sheet of many of his fellow street thugs who also became prisoners: stealing a typewriter in 1949, holding up a Chicago cabbie in 1952, repeated bootlegging of moonshine, and finally cashing in postal money orders, stolen by another ex-con named Walter Rife, while on a trip to Florida in 1955. After serving prison time for that, he was arrested for a supermarket robbery in 1959 that netted him $120.00 and put him back into prison in Jefferson City.[318] All of his run-ins had been for punk street crimes, none of them of a particularly violent nature.

Among the many deceits planted by the fiction writers—e.g., Gerold Frank, George McMillan, Gerald Posner, and Hampton Sides[319]—was to portray the Ray/Rife crimes as the opposite of what really happened: all four of these authors' books state either that Ray robbed the post office and had Rife help him pass the money orders or that they had both robbed the post office. In fact, according to the far more accurate and credible books by Dr. Pepper, James Earl Ray, and his brother John's book with Lyndon Barsten,

James was not involved in, nor was he ever charged or convicted of, stealing the money orders, only of helping Rife pass them.[320] John Ray and Barsten wrote that Rife had already stolen the money orders before Ray had even met him.[321] The HSCA—evidently aware of the disreputable provenance of this lie—skirted the point by referencing an FBI report that stated the same point in a roundabout way: "both had been charged with possession of stolen money orders from a Post Office at Kellerville, Illinois, in a burglary and that he [Rife] and JAMES EARL RAY had then traveled throughout the United States cashing these postal money orders."[322]

John Ray explained how Walter Rife became "a gift to the feds and the press, who were busy reinventing James Earl Ray."[323] Rife helped them, and William Bradford Huie—who was the indirect beneficiary of all the lies—create numerous legends by planting various stories that would be repeated, over and over, by other authors. Rife started telling his yarns about their hell-raising days in the early 1940s, when they were both only ten or twelve years old, but the truth was that they never even met until James was twenty-seven years old, soon after James was released from the Pontiac prison and Walter had just stolen the money orders from the post office in Kellerville, his hometown. Rife even lied about James's uncle, Earl Ray, having supposedly taken James to whorehouses when he was only thirteen or fourteen years old, which, John Ray said, had that really happened, his father might have killed Earl.[324]

The legend of James Earl Ray, as orchestrated by the high-level FBI plotters, was created by hand-picked authors gifted with the kind of fiction-writing skills that do not require careful attention to factual accuracy, publishing books carrying a false "nonfiction" label. Together, they launched a set of massive distortions of fact in the wake of Martin Luther King's assassination that still stand today. One of the worst instances of this was illustrated by a lie originally started by the completely unscrupulous, well-known liar and repeat prisoner, Walter Rife: that "Ray hated Negroes intensely." Rife told reporter Daniel Greene of the *National Observer* that "He was prejudiced to the point that he hated to see a colored person breathe," a quote that Gerold Frank first referenced in his 1972 book; the lie was later repeated by Posner, Sides, and some of the lesser-known books as well, most of them never noting the lack of credibility of the person who first uttered the outrageously untrue assertion.[325]

The oleaginous Hampton Sides—though naming two fellow prisoners, Rife and Raymond Curtis, both known to be proven liars as detailed within these pages—then proceeded to repeat their lies while conceding that prisoners "were notorious for telling authorities just about anything." Then he claimed that the lies had a "consistency" (undoubtedly because they had been repeated so many times) that could not be ignored as he piled on more, including Curtis's alleged comment about Ray calling "Martin Luther Coon" his "retirement plan."[326]

Walter Rife liked being quoted in newspapers, magazines, and books; however, he never stated that he believed Ray had killed King, because he apparently knew that Ray did not have that kind of hatred within him. But the detestable lies about Ray's alleged racism have been categorically debunked elsewhere and are contradicted in the many more factual and truthful books that, among many other proofs, note the number of black girlfriends James had during his travels. Moreover, King's son Dexter King has also stated on numerous occasions that not only he did not believe Ray killed his father, but that Ray was never a racist.

Ray was finally arrested for a crime that some of his friends had committed while using his car, a 1949 black Lincoln; the police linked him to an armed robbery in which he claims he did not participate. He did admit to robbing a couple of grocery stores, however, and the appeal for the other robbery was never resolved. It was after being arrested for those robberies that he was tried and sentenced to prison in Jefferson City, Missouri, in 1960. He began planning his first escape from that prison after only seven months and attempted to do that in November 1961. His attempt failed, and he wound up in solitary confinement for six months. In 1965, he made his second attempt, which also failed, but instead of another six months in solitary, he decided to refuse to plead guilty and demanded a trial. The judge had him transferred to the Missouri Hospital for the Criminally Insane in Fulton to be tested for mental competence to stand trial. After seeing another prisoner being given electric shock therapy, he "instantly lost interest" in claiming that he was mentally ill and wound up back in prison in Jefferson City.[327]

It was in early 1967 that Ray met another prisoner, John Paul Spica, who had heavy mob connections and was reputed to be an "informer." It appears that he had deeper connections than Ray even knew, as discovered by Dr. William Pepper in his interviews. It can be imputed that those connections were put to work by men in Washington who were engaged in carrying out the early stages of the plot to kill Dr. King. Either Spica or Ronnie Westberg (according to J. J. Maloney, another prisoner who later became an accomplished journalist)[328] appears to have been given the task of assisting Ray with a new escape plan that Ray described in his book, using a routine procedure for transporting a large crate of freshly baked bread out to the facility that was used for the prison farm's crews.

This development was probably the end result of secret and stealthy meetings at the highest levels of the Washington circle at which the meticulous planning was conducted in the last weeks of 1966. It was then that, at J. Edgar Hoover's instigation, Clyde Tolson made a delivery of $25,000 in cash to their Dixie Mafia collaborator, Russell Adkins Sr., for the purpose of arranging Ray's eventual escape, with assurances that minimal efforts would be made toward his recapture.[329]

An elaborate plan had been created—one that Ray believed a fellow prisoner had hatched on his own—for Ray to hide in a small room near the bake shop where the bread was stored, after working hours, from which he would slip into the box while someone else filled it with loaves of bread on top. An accomplice (presumably either Westberg or Spica) would then take the box down an elevator and onto the shipping dock, where he would wheel it onto the delivery truck. Ray would then break the bread box open after a few miles, before it reached the prison farm, jump off the truck, and sneak away. Ray stated in his book, "The prisoner who'd thought up the plan decided not to try it himself, but he was willing to let me in on it because I had more seniority."[330]

Based upon Dr. Pepper's findings as noted elsewhere, there were clearly other parts of that plan and it did not originate with another prisoner, but the prison warden himself, who had been paid off to look the other way after Ray escaped. It appears that after the escape, the warden was still not very worried about the whereabouts of his soon-to-be-famous prisoner, consistent with Dr. Pepper's findings that the warden's interests were not related to recapturing the prisoner. A news article appeared the next day in the *St. Louis Post-Dispatch*, datelined Jefferson City, indicating the warden still wasn't convinced that Ray had even escaped:

> James Earl Ray, St. Louis, has made his third attempt to escape from the state penitentiary here, but it still was not clear this morning whether he had finally succeeded. He has been missing since 5 p.m. yesterday when inmates returned to their cells after the evening meal.
>
> "Frankly we don't know whether he is outside the walls or inside," Warden Harold R. Swenson said. "He is a hide-out guy. Last year, he hid out inside the prison and it took us more than a day to find him."
>
> In that attempt, Ray was found hiding in a ventilation shaft. He tried to escape in 1961, but was discovered hiding in

the dry-cleaning plant after a makeshift ladder he had built to scale the walls apparently collapsed under his weight.[331]

According to four-decade MLK Jr. investigator Gary Revel, Warden Swenson had the prison staff and inmates search for Ray within the prison walls for two days before even taking the search beyond the walls, a decision based on his belief that Ray was still hiding inside. This delaying tactic would provide ample time for Ray to get far away from Jefferson City, Missouri. Additionally, Mr. Revel revealed more about this point to me in an email message:

> [Warden Swenson] released 3 contact names and addresses, 2 of which were bogus, and the other was for his brother, Jerry Ray. He also released a false set of fingerprints to police and federal authorities after James Earl Ray's escape. What that did was give Mr. Ray time to get to where he was going without fear of being discovered as being an escaped prisoner. The false fingerprints were not discovered by authorities until 2 weeks after the escape, which gave Mr. Ray plenty of time to make arrangements for safe passage to where he needed to go.

Ray's escape was successful, and with the food he took from the prison kitchen, he managed to hike through the forests and farmland, and within a week he wound up in New Franklin, a town about fifty miles northwest of Jefferson City; after hitching a ride on a railcar, he made it to safe haven in St. Louis. From there, he took a bus to Chicago and rented a room in a rooming house and, just two weeks after escaping from prison, found a job as a dishwasher at the Indian Trails Restaurant in Winnetka, Illinois, under his alias "James R. Rayns," making $100 per week, with a rent of only $11.00 per week. After a month, he had accumulated enough money to buy a seven-year-old Chrysler, which he brush-painted a dark blue.[332] With his new car he would decide, after working there only about six weeks, to move on—afraid of being caught by the authorities—toward finding a safer place for a wanted fugitive, by starting life all over again as a resident citizen of Canada.

A year later, after King's assassination, Missouri Prison officials were "stunned, unwilling to believe that Ray was capable of the crime."[333] Warden Swenson himself said he was very surprised to hear of Ray's alleged role when he exclaimed, "Once a guy is gone they'll talk. We've got 2,000 prisoners in here and none of them recognized him. I was floored. This guy's penny ante. It doesn't shape up. He's innocuous. Penny ante."[334]

According to George McMillan (who can sometimes be considered credible on the mundane, minor points for background context), Swenson also said, "If James Earl Ray had amounted to a hill of beans here, I would have a card on him in this pack of Big Shots and Bad Actors. And Ray isn't in here," he added, shuffling through a bundle of three-by-five index cards.[335] Furthermore, Fred Wilkinson, the Missouri corrections commissioner, affirmed that point, asserting that "Ray was just a *nothing* here." Wilkinson also labeled the drug charges as "nonsense," saying, "No one seems to have wondered where Ray would have gotten his drugs. Do you know of any supplier who would risk sending drugs into prison when the outside market has nowhere near the same dangers?" As Weisberg also noted, drugs are generally smuggled into prisons not by the usual suspects, but by friends and relatives of the prisoners.[336]

Here, McMillan—just like Huie had done six years earlier and Frank had done two years after that—inadvertently included truthful information from witnesses that contradicted the most incredible main themes of his own book, in this case, undermining his assertions that Ray was running his own little commissary out of his prison cell. Despite what these prison officials had stated, McMillan reframed those descriptions, asserting the contradictory story that Ray was anything but a nobody, in his attempt to remake him into a kingpin of the underground economy of the prison, a popular, back-slapping "merchant" widely known throughout the prison as someone who controlled sales of prison contraband—everything from razor blades and toilet paper to cigarettes and drugs.

The similarities between McMillan, Frank, and Huie—remarkable for how they all reveal their own intrinsic lies through such obvious contradictions—show how each one was evidently given specific assignments that required them to go to great lengths to create a public image of Ray that was provably untrue. The operative aphorism is "The proof is in the pudding."

The elaborate plot was hatched only one month after JFK's assassination, when J. Edgar Hoover convened a meeting at FBI headquarters on December 23, 1963, of the top FBI officials around the nation. That conference was dedicated to a discussion of the different methods the Bureau could take to "neutralize" King's stature and effectiveness as a popular black leader.[337] Not that the plot itself was ever discussed at that time, of course, but a list of twenty-one other "avenues" were. Senator Walter Mondale described that well-known conference during the 1975 Church Committee hearings: "So this meeting was called to bring together FBI agents to explore every possibility of spying upon and intimidating Dr. Martin Luther King."[338]

That meeting was merely evidence of the "new agenda," and the plot was undoubtedly an outgrowth discreetly added sometime thereafter. The proof is how the first major task on the plotline was initiated just five months later, after the arrangements had been completed in the meantime for Clyde Tolson and Russell Adkins Sr. to begin a nearly four-month ocean cruise with stopovers in Britain and France to develop the broad outline and task list for the plot.

One of the key tasks was the identification of the best candidates for the patsy role. Another was the identification of the best candidate to write the original story that would quickly set the official narrative—well before the niceties of due process—of a fair trial for the patsy (a contingency plan B, if he was not killed in the immediate aftermath, according to Plan A). It would be a trial designed to assure his "conviction," and the story would need to be written so compellingly that it would be sustained for decades, even forever. Yet another contingency would be to prepare an ideal attorney to represent the chosen patsy, one who would ensure that the officially wrought narrative would be provided to the chosen author of the contingency narrative. Clearly, having these actors in place and prepared in advance to assume their respective roles—together as one—was indubitably the key task on the critical path.

Given the proofs already cited, or to be disclosed in the chapters to come, it can be imputed that these were among the major items discussed during the long hours dedicated to that purpose as the two men created the plan to permanently neutralize Martin Luther King Jr. That they gave themselves ample opportunity to develop the grand plan—in the confines of a stateroom, and hotel rooms in England and France, for nearly four months on the SS *United States* as it crossed the Atlantic Ocean, twice, during the summer of 1964—should be self-evident.

The Mystery of Ray's Selection of His First Attorney, Arthur Hanes

For the above reasons, it was no surprise that one of the FBI's former agents—who had *also* been a CIA operative[339]—then became Ray's first attorney. Arthur Hanes Sr., from the start, was acting in a dual capacity, being putatively responsible for representing Ray's legal interests while taking his instructions from the famed novelist William Bradford Huie. Even before either of them had ever met James Earl Ray, Hanes and Huie were double-teaming Ray, acting in concert to undermine him, while giving Huie exclusive "insider" rights as a direct source to Ray's supposedly confidential statements to his attorney. As the astute early researcher Harold Weisberg originally stated it, "Huie and Hanes, we will see, cooked up this deal and sold Ray on the need for it."[340]

It will also be shown, at multiple points in the narrative to follow, that both William Bradford Huie and Arthur Hanes had long-time connections to the FBI generally and specifically J. Edgar Hoover and his high-level assistants for many years, suggesting that their sudden appearances in the immediate aftermath of Ray's capture was not happenstance.[341] Hanes even finally acknowledged that he believed that Ray had been advised, even before King's murder, to contact him if he needed a lawyer.[342]

The puzzling manner of how Arthur Hanes—a long-term segregationist and virulently anti-Communist lawyer, whose career started out under the tutelage of the same organization, and men, that became the primary sponsor of Dr. King's murder—had been selected by Ray was, and for many still is, a mystery. Yet somehow, when James Earl Ray was arrested in London, he quickly picked an attorney in Birmingham, Alabama, who stated that he had "no idea whatsoever" how Ray had decided to pick him, and then consistently refused to discuss his fees, or the source of any funds, for that purpose.[343] The answer to that enigma, according to one of Ray's later attorneys, the researcher Mark Lane, was that Huie took it upon himself to set up the arrangement, when he *"immediately contacted Hanes"* after Ray's arrest and offered to pay him a "substantial sum" indirectly, through Ray, if as part of the deal he got the exclusive rights to Ray's story.[344] (Emphasis added.) As noted previously, both Arthur Hanes and William Bradford Huie had long associations with the FBI; it doesn't take a long, audited paper trail (which, of course, does not exist) to connect them, but it could probably have been done directly through Clyde Tolson's telephone records for 1968, had they been accessible.

Arthur Hanes Sr. was a former FBI agent who resigned from that position because, he said, "I felt I couldn't express myself about the growing Communist influence in our country as an agent."[345] Upon becoming mayor of Birmingham in the early 1960s, he always defended his public safety commissioner, Eugene "Bull" Connor, who often appeared on the nightly television news reports using police dogs and fire hoses as his unique way of calming the protesting citizenry—demonstrators who merely wanted to ride in any of the available seats on city buses, or maybe be able to have a ham sandwich at certain lunch counters in Birmingham. That was even before some of them had even thought about the fanciful notion of attending college at the nearby state-supported universities, or freely casting their vote at election time.

In its June 28, 1968, edition, *Time* magazine stated, "In 1963, though just out of office as a bitterly anti-integration mayor, [Hanes] continued to fight against Martin Luther King's Birmingham campaign," and the Associated Press reported him saying about the protests that they "were not spontaneous but had been carefully plotted at a Communist-inspired workshop." One of the original 1960s researchers of the JFK assassination and then the MLK assassination, Harold Weisberg, framed the Arthur Hanes mindset this way: "any black protest is Communist, King was a Communist, and—here we take a small jump—anyone who did anything to or against King thus became a true patriot."[346] The impression one gets is that ex-FBI agent Arthur Hanes had a lot in common with J. Edgar Hoover and perhaps learned these basic principles directly from him.

Hanes would make three trips to London to meet with Ray (except the first trip, ten days after the arrest, when he was refused permission, thanks to the efforts of Ray's British solicitor, Michael Eugene, who thought that Ray's choice of Hanes would be "unwise"), but Hanes wouldn't divulge who paid for them either, always saying that he "had faith that I'll get by" and that he "understands that this man has funds." In an interview with the *New York Times*, he was quoted as saying, "I work for money, but I will not tell you who will pay. I cannot discuss the fees. I have the faith I'll get by and I'll meet expenses."[347]

Among the files strangely released by the FBI on the JFK assassination on October 26, 2017, was a 395-page file with some of their records pertaining to the Martin Luther King Jr. assassination.[348] Within those pages, we find that the first hearing after Ray's capture on June 8, 1968, was conducted on June 19, where the date of July 2 was established for Ray's extradition hearing. At that hearing, as Ray denied his involvement in King's murder, his British solicitor argued that the crime he was being accused of was political in nature, therefore it was not subject to extradition. The chief magistrate, Frank Milton, dismissed that argument and ordered the extradition but stated that the statutory period of eighteen days must be provided first, during which the order might be appealed. On July 3, Arthur Hanes—having tried two weeks earlier to visit James Earl Ray to arrange his appointment Ray's attorney but failed due to miscommunications with the British authorities—arrived on his second trip and was finally able to meet his new client. They spent thirty-five minutes together the first day and seventy minutes the next day. Hanes left the following day but returned on a third trip on July 15, and the following day it was announced that Ray had decided not to pursue an appeal of the extradition order. Hanes told the press that his client "was anxious to prove his innocence and combat 'an unprecedented, vicious and libelous press campaign portraying my client as a convicted murderer, monster, degenerate and dope addict.'"[349] Had Hanes been more interested in his role as a protector of Ray's rights, he would not have immediately begun by waiving his rights to avoid extradition.

Arthur Hanes was already—from the start of his representation of Ray, in Britain—clearly acting against the interests of his new client and in step with the FBI's urgent pressure to get Ray back on American soil to begin the process of ensuring he would be incarcerated for the rest of his life. A US Embassy official made a statement on how Ray would be returned: "Ray will disappear out of Wadsworth Prison and appear in Memphis before the public even knows about it." Hanes, apparently wanting to show that there was some level of enmity between him and the federal government, announced that he was not being allowed to return on the same airplane with his client and "denounced this refusal as dangerous, wrong and out of step with recent US Supreme Court decisions."[350]

Ray indicated that the only substantive thing he discussed with Hanes while incarcerated in Britain was the contracts for his representation as well as giving him a power of attorney to sign publishing contracts with William Bradford Huie, who wanted to write a series of articles about the case prior to the trial. Hanes, against Ray's doubts about giving away all his own rights to royalties, convinced Ray to do so anyway, because it was necessary to finance his defense. Hanes also advised Ray to waive his rights to appeal an extradition order, which Ray agreed to do.[351]

Moreover, Ray stated in his book that he had contacted both Arthur Hanes and the well-known Boston lawyer, F. Lee Bailey (the latter of whom, Ray wrote, "said he had a conflict of interest [in later years, he'd serve as an attorney for the King case prosecution]).[352] But, even taking Ray at his word, it is still unclear about how he would have known about Hanes, since Ray had been in prison during the period when Hanes had gained notoriety as the defender of the murderers of Viola Liuzzo; as noted elsewhere, he had no access to televisions there. There is no valid reason to believe that James Earl Ray would have ever been a fan of Hanes because of the lawyer's fame for defending those Klansmen; to do so would imply that Ray was a rabid racist, which he was certainly not. Despite the concerted efforts of the FBI and their mouthpieces (Huie, Frank, McMillan, and later authors), Ray was not the racist he had been depicted to be.

Huie, famous for his reputation as a "checkbook journalist," was described by David Halberstam as a "somewhat roguish journalist . . . considered more talented than respectable by many of his peers."* Moreover,

---

* Huie's book on James Earl Ray, *He Slew The Dreamer*, reads like a novel and looks like a novel—sans footnotes, endnotes, index, or bibliography. It appears to have been written more on the basis of the author's preconceptions than factually based statements as documented herein. Even though he portrayed it as having been published in 1968, it did not appear in bookstores until the summer of 1970 (Weisberg, p. xi).

Halberstam noted, "Huie specialized in eccentric journalism, was from Alabama. Shrewd, iconoclastic, proud . . . not [to be] a liberal."[353] By January 30, 1969, according to an article in the *Washington Post* on that date, Huie had paid his final $5,000 installment of a series of payments totaling "over $30,000" to Arthur Hanes, then Percy Foreman (who wanted $150,000 for his "services"), for Ray's handwritten 20,000-word manuscript recounting his travels and activities.[354] Huie used that as the basis for his three articles in *Look* and his book; however, the story he wrote became less and less consistent with what Ray wrote over the time period in which they appeared. The following week, Huie was arrested and charged with contempt of court for violating a ban on pretrial publicity that had started with his two November 1968 magazine articles; he later continued with his request, through Ray's new lawyer Foreman, to obtain photographs showing Ray in his jail cell, which Huie planned to publish in his third *Look* article.[355]

By May, after Judge Preston Battle died, his successor, Criminal Court Judge Arthur Faquin Jr., dismissed the charges against Huie, along with other pending contempt charges against attorney Hanes and a number of reporters, investigators, and others. That was about the same time that Judge Faquin also summarily rejected Ray's appeal for a new trial—despite the fact that he never really had the first one, only a "minitrial" where the "facts" were not argued,[356] and despite the Tennessee statutes, which mandated a new trial under the exact prevalent circumstances, when a judge died during that period of time after the motion was made and before it had been decided.

William Bradford Huie's name appears prominently throughout this book because of his original role in framing James Earl Ray, actually reinventing his persona in every way imaginable. It will be conclusively demonstrated that he was commissioned to transform a very common man of average intelligence, low self-esteem, nominal education, and limited ambition into one whose putative, now-obsessive ambition, and all-consuming need for recognition, would make him the most fearsome criminal in the world. It was a commission that apparently existed well in advance of the assassination of Dr. King, one awarded to Huie by the highest-level officials of the FBI. That it was assuredly meticulously planned long before King's execution should be considered as axiomatic.

The success of the FBI's faux legend of James Earl Ray was based on the determined efforts of Huie, Ray's first "biographer," to dutifully report—but purposefully downplay and ignore—the descriptions he was getting from everyone who had actually met James during this period, while playing up the mythological fables that the FBI had constructed for public consumption. He met their expectations by crafting a folklore story line that remains today and is still referenced as the mythos of James Earl Ray: "A lone-nut racist loser fighting against the world, on the side of his friends in the Klan." But the man that William Bradford Huie used fiction to build—as only a novelist could—never existed.

Huie's book set the theme from the start, and thereafter he consistently portrayed James as a slovenly and forlorn soul who had the misfortune of being [purportedly] born in the "southern" part of Illinois, ergo he would axiomatically fulfill a caricature that his readers would forever remember, and one that nearly all future authors supporting the official line would repeat ad nauseam. The nexus of Ray's recast psychological profile portrayed by Huie in 1968–69 undoubtedly had its origins in the psychological studies and MKULTRA experiments conducted two decades earlier, when Ray was subjected to intensive study during his army service, as previously noted.[357]

Gerold Frank and George McMillan Carry the Baton Forward—Just in Time for the 1977–78 HSCA "Investigation"

Gerold Frank's 1972 book, *An American Death*, was largely an attempt to take Huie's screed to another, albeit lower, level through more fantasizing, for example when he wrote, as though he had personally witnessed it, that Ray drove off Highway 78, between Birmingham and Memphis, on April 3, 1968, to a "secluded spot" off a dirt road, then "walked into a glen hidden by trees and, aiming carefully through a telescopic sight fixed on the barrel, fired about a dozen shots."[358] His only caveat to the pretense of that description of Ray taking a few practice shots with his new gun was his qualification of the number of shots Ray fired: "about." As we will note, that citation is representative of the contents of the rest of the book, a succession of artfully formed suppositions, unlikely leaps of logic, and deliberately crafted, false negative accusations about James Earl Ray's essential character traits; all of the stories he wrote contained these commonalities that rendered the entirety of it unbelievable.

George McMillan, in his previously cited 1976 book—anxious to prove that Ray was never a "nothing" and was really a majordomo while in prison at Jefferson City, Missouri—contended that he was a popular "merchant" who banked many thousands of dollars by trading in such commodities as cigarettes, instant coffee, cans of soup, razor blades, and eggs, all "very negotiable items inside Jeff City." He used that pretense to explain the answer to the question he posed, "Where did that little punk criminal get the money?" to pay for all his subsequent travels, to buy a year-old Mustang for $2,000 cash and all the cameras and other goods he bought during the year after his escape from prison.[359] McMillan made this point a central thesis of his book, calling it:

"[A] matter of crucial historical importance. On it hinges the central mystery and uncertainty about the Martin Luther King assassination. If Ray was paid, as he has alleged, by a man named 'Raoul,' who was an agent of a *foreign* government [*sic*—nice try, though] then that is where the money came from and there was a conspiracy in the assassination." [Conversely, he asserted, if Ray made] "several thousand dollars in the seven years he was in there, then the question of where Ray got the money . . . is answered."[360]

Against everything we know about James Earl Ray at this point, McMillan's premise about where Ray's funds came from is as weak as his perfunctory efforts to psychoanalyze Ray. Equally obtuse was how he attempted to prove that Ray's reason for declining a chance in 1957 to be transferred to the honor farm, when he served time in Leavenworth prison, was because it was integrated, and he didn't want to be housed with blacks.[361] Ray stated that the real reason he did not want to take advantage of the offer to transfer to the honor farm was because it was generally known that drugs were being traded there, and if caught, prisoners were being put into solitary confinement, and he did not want to take the chance of becoming involved in that environment.

Like Huie, McMillan included within his book contradictory statements of credible people who told him the opposite of many of his main themes, but instead of adjusting his thesis accordingly, he persisted in using disinformation fed by noncredible ex-cons like Raymond Curtis, who was trying to sell a story and (according to the FBI) "had the mind of a child."[362] According to Curtis, and accepted without question by McMillan, the rap on Ray was that James Earl Ray was a "merchant," making untold thousands of dollars as a prisoner; Ray was a violent racist; Ray was an abuser of drugs and liquor; and to top it all off, Ray was a Nazi sympathizer—despite being told by numerous other witnesses that none of those things were true. One example was a black prisoner who had known Ray well: Malik Hakim, who had also escaped from Jefferson City Prison. McMillan was surprised to find that Hakim did not hate Ray; rather he seemed to like him, calling him a "*concrete* con," which meant that at his core he was solid and trustworthy.[363] (Emphasis in original.) As the HSCA investigators found, many of the people they interviewed confirmed that Ray had a number of black friends, including two of his favorite prostitutes, one of whom he even proposed to, twice.[364]

Another former prisoner—one who successfully reformed himself so completely that he became an award-winning journalist and book reviewer for the *Kansas City Star* newspaper—was J. J. Maloney, who admitted that he had abused drugs during his time at Jeff City. He told Jerry Ray that "never at any time did he see my brother purchase, use, or sell amphetamines . . . [and] during the nearly seven years that he was around Jimmy at Jeff City, he never witnessed Jimmy conduct himself in any way that would have indicated he was a racist of any kind."[365]

To ensure that McMillan's book was given maximum promotion, TIME magazine featured it in two major articles (four full pages) in its January 26, 1976 issue. One of the articles had the title, "I'm Gonna Kill That Nigger King," which is what McMillan stated that James told his brother Jerry in a telephone call on the morning of the assassination (both of whom vehemently deny even having such a call). But this was only one of dozens of bald-faced lies excerpted from his book and printed in this national news magazine, all the product of George McMillan's wildest imaginations, as directed by the same handlers who guided Ray's movements for an entire year.

As if to illustrate the breadth of their license to concoct the most outlandish story possible, facts be damned, a drawing was included, which brazenly portrayed Ray aiming his rifle in the opposite direction from what would have been required, had he actually made such a shot. In order to show the ease of making a shot from there, the artist pivoted the bathtub, such that the long side was up against the wall under the window, eliminating the problem of the slanted end of the tub interfering with the sniper's comfort. Even more bizarre was how the other wall—extending outwards from the left edge of the window—was left out completely. The result was to render what Harold Weisberg had declared was "impossible" for a shooter's ability to fire an accurate shot to be a very comfortable position for any shooter, even one with such little "sharpshooter" skills as James Earl Ray.

Playing the "George Wallace Supporter" Card: Over and Over Again

An illustration of the growth of these canards originally planted by Huie was his not-so-subtle reference in his book to what he said was Ray's interest in the 1968 presidential campaign of Alabama governor George Wallace, whose racial antipathy toward blacks appealed to people who shared that sentiment. That unsupported assertion (which became indirectly supported essentially as the result of Huie's original creation) was passed on through other books until—over four decades later—Hampton Sides made repeated references to it, including dedicating the entire Chapter 5, "Dixie West," to reinforcing the premise by making it a cornerstone of his argument of Ray's alleged inherent racism.

Before the Posner and Sides books were written, Ray had told Mark Lane that this was one of the "many statements in the McMillan book that are not true."[366] Moreover, according to the research of John Avery Emison, Ray was never even interested in politics, as demonstrated by the fact that "Ray never registered to vote at any time in his life."[367]

Furthermore, as Ray himself explained, it was ridiculous for Huie, then McMillan, Foreman, and the FBI to make false statements about him becoming a "political activist" working in George Wallace's presidential campaign since he was a fugitive, desperately afraid of being discovered and arrested. That was the reason he had never even registered to vote, even though he admitted considering doing that under an assumed name since voter registration cards were good IDs for entering Canada. He also said the only time he was ever around a registration place was when he took a woman to register, while in Los Angeles. He stated that the reason for encouraging her to do that was that her boyfriend was doing a five-year term for marijuana possession, and that she needed "influential friends." His advice to her was to join an organization that had influence to meet people who might be able to assist her in getting his term reduced, so she registered as a Republican (in the 1960s, Orange County was heavily Republican). Ray claimed "that was the extent of my political work."[368]

Throughout all of the more credible books on James Earl Ray, it becomes quite clear that he was, if anything, apolitical, not one who gave George Wallace or anyone else from the political world much attention and least of all because of any racial animus, as finally acknowledged by the HSCA. The fact that Hampton Sides attempted to make the case that practically all white Southerners in the 1960s wanted King dead—especially those who backed George Wallace (ergo, presumptive proof positive of Ray's guilt)—it should instead be considered proof of Sides's monumental work of fictional disinformation: James Earl Ray was neither southern nor a Wallace supporter; he was simply an apolitical northerner who had unfortunately been subjected, arbitrarily, to secret mind-control experiments through the CIA's MKULTRA program in the early 1950s, thanks to Allen Dulles and the "Black Sorcerer," Sidney Gottlieb.

As another illustration of how the earliest authors attempted to portray Ray as a southern racist, McMillan made allegations that a former cellmate of Ray's, Raymond Curtis, had stated that whenever James saw Martin Luther King on television, he would derisively call him derogatory names in his presence.[369] McMillan also asserted that whenever Ray saw Dr. King on television, he would fly into a rage and shout "somebody's got to get him." In *The Making of an Assassin*, McMillan wrote that Ray watched Dr.

King on television in 1963–64, where he was often shown talking about the injustices faced by black people, and insisting that nonviolent resistance would eventually overcome their suffering. McMillan repeated the lies he had been told by Curtis, about how Ray avidly watched the news on the cellblock television just so he could get angry and trigger outbursts such as calling him "Martin Lucifer Coon." McMillan would also assert in his turgid book that "the very sight of King would *galvanize* Ray. 'Somebody's gotta get him,' Ray would say, his face drawn with tension, his fists clinched. 'Somebody's gotta get him'" (Emphasis in original).[370]

It has been well established that Curtis (and/or McMillan) made up all of that. According to James Earl Ray's own book, "*there were no television sets in the cells or on the cellblocks.* Prisoners didn't have such access to TV until 1970, three years after my escape."[371] (Emphasis added.) Ray's brother Jerry wrote that the aforementioned reformed prisoner, Pulitzer Prize nominee J. J. Maloney, confirmed the point about no televisions in Jeff City cellblocks until 1970 and the fact that James never did anything that would indicate he was ever a racist.[372] Mark Lane also validated that fact in February 1977, when he questioned the associate warden at the Jefferson City penitentiary, Bill Armontrout, who confirmed that television sets were introduced in the cellblocks "for the first time in early 1970," three years after Ray had escaped.[373]

There were numerous other instances of McMillan's lies and deceits, but in most cases it came down to his assertions of a number of incriminating statements allegedly made by James's brother Jerry, which Jerry denied ever saying. Therefore, unlike the one above, which has been debunked by Mark Lane and other authors, the others are reduced to a "George said/Jerry denied" conundrum that weighs heavily against George McMillan and favorably to Jerry Ray, who wrote this about his interactions with McMillan, whom he described as:

> [A] writer in the service of official government agencies . . . I became deeply familiar with his distortions and outright fabrications. He tried to portray my family as a bunch of whiskey-guzzling, cross-burning racists who hated everybody who wasn't white—blacks, Jews, Latinos, anybody. Although these bogus allegations had no basis in fact, they were hatched by certain writers to convince the gullible public that "Jimmy" [as they called James Earl Ray] had been raised in a bigoted environment, had evolved into a racist because of it, and had killed King because of those racist views.[374]

Throughout these early, supposedly nonfictional books, we see embedded traces of truthful contradictions to their own themes, though none of them reappear in the later volumes by Posner and Sides, who preferred not to contaminate their works with contrary, truthful, or factual evidence. Despite the books' themes of Ray as a racist, laid by Huie in 1968 and reinforced by Frank in 1972 and again by McMillan in 1976, those traces tell us that Ray had known and become friends with many blacks, and run counter to the overall theme of Ray they attempted to portray. The racist theme was finally rejected by the 1978 HSCA investigation report, as will be examined in Chapter 11. But the contrast between what most of the men who knew Ray best said about him—his fellow prisoners, and the men who ran the prison—and the profile wrought by Huie, Frank, and McMillan could not be more dissonant.

The HSCA sent their investigators to the prison to determine whether there was any merit to that argument, as noted in the following excerpt:

> The committee then interviewed approximately 30 prison associates of Ray. While some recalled that Ray had demonstrated anti-Black feelings, *the majority said he was not a racist.* On balance, therefore, the committee viewed the inmate testimony as essentially inconclusive. *It could not be relied on as proof that Ray harbored the kind of deep-seated, racial animosity that might, on its own, trigger the assassination of Dr. King.*[375] (Emphasis added.)

Even Ray's 1977 interview in *Playboy* magazine fit that pattern, as when he was asked about why he had refused to be transferred to the prison's honor farm, for which he had been approved; his reply to that question was that "he did not want to go to the honor farm [because] whenever marijuana was found in the dormitory, extra time was handed out to all prisoners in the vicinity even if they were not involved. When *Playboy* [pointedly] asked if Ray meant that blacks smoked dope and he was worried about getting punished for it, he answered, 'Maybe.'"[376]

The HSCA investigation noted that Ray had voluntarily worked with blacks in 1967 after his prison escape, at the Indian Trails Restaurant, but even then, the committee could not overcome the tendency to leave the cloak of racism on Ray's faux "legend":

> The committee was unable to determine whether Ray's response to *Playboy* was the truth or simply an attempt to draw attention away from the documented evidence concerning this issue. Even accepting—on face value—Ray's stated reasons for resisting the

> transfer, they nevertheless reflected a tendency to engage in racially oriented generalization on human behavior. The incident did not, however, indicate fanatical racism on the part of the assassin . . . The incident was viewed, therefore, as simply one more example of general lack of empathy for blacks.[377]

As John Avery Emison put it, "This was another attempt to stigmatize Ray and transform him into the image of a racist."[378] As the far more truthful authors Emison and William F. Pepper have proven with meticulous detail, Ray was never the dyed-in-the-wool southern racist, as he had been portrayed.

Ray wasn't even southern, unless one considers someone born in Alton, Illinois, qualifies for that description. Alton is "20 miles upriver from St. Louis," as Ray himself noted in the first paragraph of his book, but at age six his family moved 120 miles farther north to Ewing, Illinois. He spent much of his youth even a little farther north, in Quincy, Illinois, with his grandparents, uncles, aunts, and cousins.[379] To put that into context, Quincy is actually farther north than Springfield, Illinois, Indianapolis, Indiana, or Columbus, Ohio. Since Huie repeatedly attempted to describe Ray as "southern," it should be further pointed out that the towns of Ewing and Quincy are almost exactly in the center (latitudinally) of Illinois, which is approximately 420 miles from its boundary with Wisconsin to the north, to its most southern point on the Ohio River border with Kentucky. The towns where he grew up are roughly 200 miles from both of these borders, yet Huie demonstrably skewed everything he wrote to portray the southern racist meme, which is itself based upon the false notion that racism exists wholly in the South.

This technique—repeatedly retelling the lie—was used to instill the image of George Wallace into the reader's mind as being representative of the mindset of James Earl Ray: a magician's trick akin to using blue smoke and mirrors to hide reality while inserting a false image to replace it. Evidently, Huie was following the Goebbels maxim noted in the Prologue.

How Readers—As Reviewers—Of Fiction Perpetuate the Myths

The reviews for each book spread the disinformation even further, when read by many more people who would acquire their notion of the content of the book, without ever having read it. Nonetheless, the readers of the reviews inevitably become conditioned by the repeated lies. An example of this was manifested in a review by Laura Miller of the Hampton Sides book on *Salon*, dated April 18, 2010:

> The people Ray associated with ("knew" seems an overstatement) during the year between his escape and the assassination were a sundry assortment of misfits and kooks . . . He most likely supported himself with petty crime: stickups and low-level drug deals. But he also became passionately involved in the presidential campaign of segregationist, and former Alabama governor, George Wallace.
>
> Ray's enthusiasm for Wallace—a trailblazer for Sarah Palin and similar demagogues capitalizing on white working-class resentment—is what makes his story more than just the tale of a hate-fueled creep who struck down a great man (though it's that, too). Sides notes that Ray must have had help on two or three occasions, probably from his brothers, but perhaps also from equally racist wingnuts who shared his so-called values, whether or not they actively collaborated on his one major crime.

That Ms. Miller makes such assertions—that Ray could only relate to other "sundry assortment of misfits and kooks," that his financial support "most likely" came from penny-ante street crimes, that he was a "hate-filled creep" and "passionate" supporter of George Wallace—only demonstrates that this reviewer is obviously unaware of the numerous more factual books that tell the true story of Dr. King's murder, and thereby accepted the fictionalized, syrupy, quasi novel, Sides's book *Hellhound on His Trail*, as though it were the unvarnished truth. Clearly, she got this bit of disinformation from Sides's twisted account that took the seeds of the lie planted by Huie in 1968, replanted them, and nourished them again through other authors seemingly intent on strengthening the myths, and finally gave them over completely to the imagination of a novelist to polish into the national shrine of mythology.

As noted elsewhere, Huie originally—one might even say facetiously and farcically—also made the case of Ray being a loner who was putatively incapable of sustaining deep relationships with others, *despite his having repeatedly documented the opposite of that fabrication*. One example of that came within a few weeks after Ray escaped from prison, when he secured a job as a dishwasher in a large restaurant in suburban Chicago. He immediately became so well liked by the owners of that establishment that they quickly promoted him to higher-level duties before he voluntarily left that job, to keep "on the move," at which point they practically begged him to stay.

This was one of the actual truths that were, sparingly, included in Huie's original book; he knew that to lie about what they said might come back to haunt him. Another one referenced a lady whom Ray met in Montreal, whose testimony finally belied the Huie account and convinced the HSCA that Ray was not the racist as portrayed by Huie and all the other subsequent books noted above. Huie located that woman, only to be surprised when she turned out to be a beautiful, well-educated, and very intelligent person who quickly became very close to Ray. But she was only one of many who contradicted that meme. How do all of these credible witnesses—whose affirmation of Ray as essentially a nice guy in the books by far more credible authors[380] than Mr. Sides, and his predecessors named above—possibly merit the description of such a deplorable and horrid person as described by Ms. Miller? Her description mimicked the straw man described by Sides, Posner, McMillan, and Frank, all of whom used a devolved description of James Earl Ray that originated from the original fiction writer William B. Huie. Her review—ironically more sophistic than sophisticated—illustrates the larger point about the multiple examples of disinformation purveyed by books written by authors offering more politically correct entertainment than disturbing reality.

The latest, and slickest, "nonfiction" thriller (by novelist Sides) not only sidesteps the existence of Raul as a possible source of Ray's funds, it merely states that "Ray must have pulled off several robberies while he was in flight,"[381] which was supposed to resolve the question. Moreover, Sides also cites (with zero acknowledgement that it was always a canard that was completely discredited) the July 13, 1967, bank robbery in Alton, Illinois, that netted the bandits (whoever they were) over $27,000 in cash. His only other explanatory comment about it was that though it remains unsolved, the FBI had always believed the Ray brothers were involved somehow.[382] It doesn't help his case to point out that the FBI had their reasons for trying to pin the blame on the Rays, since actually solving the crime was never their objective.

McMillan Extends His Portrayal of James Earl Ray: His Entire Family—From 100 Years Back—Purportedly Hard-Core Criminals

The fact that McMillan's portrayal is so dissimilar to practically everything else ever written about James Earl Ray suggests that he was given certain objectives to fulfill in rendering a story that would "fill the void" to explain a lot of missing pieces in the official story, including such enigmas as the source of Ray's funds as well as his life history of flimflam schemes netting only enough cash to get from one day to the next, usually conducted in dusty prairie towns and the honky-tonk areas of larger cities.

But it was not just James's life story; McMillan presented an epic psychic examination of his entire family, going back to 1865, starting with his purported great-grandfather, one Ned Ray, who had been deputized by a notorious cutthroat sheriff named Henry Plummer, who used his position to conduct a reign of terror for prospectors trying to take their gold-laden saddlebags out of the mining town of Bannack, Montana, to the safety of a bank in a larger city. According to this bizarre story in the second chapter of McMillan's book, Ned Ray was captured, with Plummer and a man called Buck Stinson, by a vigilante posse, and the threesome were all hanged in makeshift gallows, their corpses left hanging in the nooses until they were frozen solid.[383] It should be noted that McMillan did hedge a bit on this story—uncertain that there was an actual genealogical connection—by explaining that "people like the Rays don't keep family trees, perhaps for the very reason that they might find nooses on them."[384]

In other words, with nothing other than the common surname, McMillan made a series of wholly unsupported assertions of lineage—and the required leaps of logic to complete the circle—that led to this apocryphal conclusion, one that he then qualified as possibly not true at all: that the Ray family's tendency toward violence was at least a hundred years old by the time of Martin Luther King Jr.'s assassination, but then declaring all of it as merely his own conjecture.

The disconnect he ignored in the process was that James Earl Ray was never actually violent (other than using a pistol to scare people during armed robberies as a threat) and never physically harmed anyone—despite all the prevarications by McMillan and his predecessors—much less murdered anyone. And yet, he had stood accused of that, and to top it all off, it was supposedly done merely for the sake of gaining recognition as the fabricated plotline required.

James Earl Ray Meets "Raul"

James was rather cagey with his attorneys and Huie, whom he never met face to face and communicated with only through his attorney, Arthur Hanes Sr. Within three months, Ray came to distrust them all due to the confusion related to whose interests they were most interested in protecting. Despite being deliberately obtuse on matters that would put himself, or anyone else, at risk (e.g., identifying the prisoner who had helped him escape, or his lady friends), there were some points on which he never wavered. Most important was the story he had always maintained, which was that he had met a man named "Raoul" in Montreal, who guided him into different locations throughout the North American continent that finally put him into a rooming house in Memphis, Tennessee, on April 4, 1968.

The "serendipitous" meeting between Ray and Raul at the Neptune Bar was clearly planned, and it may not have even been the first meeting between Ray and unknown others that prepared him in advance for such a meeting. In fact, his brother John Larry stated that "[t]he meeting of Raul C. in Canada was not a chance meeting, as he [James] would later state. He had to make that claim, since it would have been fatal to cross the Chicago Mafia."[385] That same point explains why James was so circumspect in much of his later testimony regarding his time in Montreal and New Orleans in particular; it was as if those places, and nearly everything connected to them—especially some of the people he came into contact with—were off limits because he had been thoroughly warned to avoid disclosing too much about either.

Based on the indications of Raul and others keeping Ray in their sights throughout his secretly facilitated "escape" and movements in the three months before he showed up in Montreal, it was just a matter of arranging for the right moment for Ray to meet Raul as the unit monitoring his movements kept their superiors informed in their daily reports.

Like many other small-time criminals, prior to the King assassination Ray had used such varied aliases as James McBride, James Walton, W. C. Herron, and James O'Conner. After escaping from prison in April 1967, he briefly used the name John Larry Raynes, which is similar to the name of one of his brothers, John Larry Ray. According to the early research of Harold Weisberg, and corroborated by Dr. Philip H. Melanson, Ray tended to select aliases based on names of people he knew, at least up until the time he went to Canada and became entangled with the man he referred to as "Raoul" in July 1967.[386]

Before furnishing Ray the names and other vital data for his aliases, it is highly likely that Raul first gave him certain drugs—ones for which he had previously registered closely monitored reactions—that impeded his memory, similar to the experiments he had been subjected to when he had served in the mysterious 7892nd Infantry Regiment of the Army in Germany. In that story, described above, his brother John Larry Ray and researcher Lyndon Barsten presented some of James's long-hidden history. It led up to the point where John L. Ray asked, laconically, if his brother James had turned out to be a submissive "good subject" for the army/CIA experiments in the psychological warfare program involving various drugs to create Manchurian-type robots to do things they would not normally consider doing. In that netherworld "Matrix," anything was, and is, possible.

Throughout his US and Mexico travels, Ray had used his Eric Galt alias, and at Bessie Brewer's boarding house in Memphis, he used the name of another

Canadian, John Willard, evidently using it only on that single occasion. It is interesting that both of these aliases were used in the period *before* King's murder, and in both cases, he used names of Toronto-area men, despite the fact that he had not gone there in his first Canadian trip after his prison escape. He had driven right past Toronto on Highway 401, on his way to the Montreal and Ottawa areas in the summer of 1967, according to his own book.

When he returned to Canada—in April 1968, in the aftermath of King's assassination—he rented a room in Toronto under the name of Paul E. Bridgeman, and later, a second room in that city under the name Ramon George Sneyd. He also obtained a false Canadian passport using the Sneyd name and took flights to London and Lisbon under that name (and would later get caught carrying the original passport issued, incorrectly, as "Sneya"). These aliases were names of actual Canadians living near Toronto in 1968. Four of the five names he had used during the period between July 1967 and April 1968 (Galt, Sneyd, Bridgeman, and Willard) all lived within a few miles of one another in a town called Scarborough.[387]

But the geographic area and methodology used by Ray—or someone else on his behalf—to acquire these names was not the most stunning of the similarities. Three of those four Canadian aliases (Galt, Bridgeman, and Sneyd) were closely similar to Ray's own physical characteristics (forty years old, five feet ten inches tall, brown hair, approximately 170–175 lbs.). None of these men had ever met Ray, or had even been aware that their names had been used by him until they were contacted by police. Bridgeman had been questioned about it by the Royal Canadian Mounted Police, but they did not explain why they were investigating him, so he was caught by surprise the following day when he heard his name broadcast on the radio after Ray was arrested in London. Sneyd was similarly caught unawares, finally learning about it during the broadcast of Robert F. Kennedy's funeral, when the first announcement of Ray's capture was made. Moreover, just as Ray had a small scar on his face, above the right eyebrow, so did the real Eric Galt. The real Willard had a two-inch scar just below his right eye These issues were explored further in the three-minute video titled "The Assassination of Martin Luther King—Another CIA-LBJ-Hoover Production," in which the real Eric Galt was interviewed; the ex-Air Force Colonel L. Fletcher Prouty also appears in the referenced video at about the 2:13 point, commenting on the unlikelihood of Ray obtaining the aliases without help from someone high up in the intelligence organizations of the US in collaboration with their Canadian counterparts.[388]

Another enigma was created when the real Eric St. Vincent Galt (whose signature "Eric St.V. Galt," written cursively with little "o"s instead of dots, looked very similar to "Starvo") changed his signature to be simply Eric S.

Galt in 1966; later, Ray also dropped the "Starvo" and switched to a simple "S." abbreviation in his signature. When Ray bought the Mustang, he used "Starvo," but eight months later, when he checked into the New Rebel Motel, he signed in with only the "S." For such minor transactions, Ray would sometimes use names he made up on the fly, especially in the fleabag motels he often used, where the clerks never asked for IDs anyway, only the tag number of the customer's automobile. But where it was likely that he would be asked for an ID, he generally used the Galt name throughout this period of his travels through the US, Canada, and Mexico. Even that rule of thumb would be broken, however, when he used the alias "Harvey Lowmeyer" and a fake address to buy the rifle(s) in Birmingham.

Even more curious than any of that was the fact that the real Galt had obtained security clearances for his work with Union Carbide, which operated the nuclear facility at Oak Ridge National Laboratory in Tennessee. Galt's security clearances put him into a position in which he also worked with the highly secret 902nd MIG (the presence in Memphis of which will be noted in the following chapter) on covert operations projects.[389] Ray had written to the Canadian Department of Veterans Affairs under Galt's name to obtain credentials. An investigator for the HSCA asked him why he had written it. His response started with "Well, I didn't . . . it was something insignificant. I was just trying to get an answer from them so I would have the Galt on the identification in case I had to . . ."[390]

Before he caught himself at the start of that sentence, it appears that he decided against candor, possibly afraid of getting too close to verboten areas that he had been cautioned about. Unfortunately, his voice trailed off and the interviewer changed the subject before getting a complete answer to this question, possibly because he had suddenly realized that he was getting too close to issues that he had also been previously warned to avoid.

Later, HSCA Chief Counsel Richard Sprague asked him how he began using the Galt name:

Sprague: How did it come about that you used the Galt name?
Ray: I have no idea. I just, just a name. I might have seen it in the phone book or something.
Sprague: Where were you when you saw this name in the phone book?
Ray: I don't know if I saw it in a phone book. I just, I'm just trying to explain to you where I could have gotten these various names from.[391]

Melanson referenced several other similar interviews with Ray, none of which produced coherent answers to the puzzle of where those names originated. Dr. Melanson also noted the close relationship throughout the 1960s between James Angleton, the chief of counterintelligence of the CIA, and the Canadian counterintelligence chief, Leslie "Jim" Bennett, and the distinct possibility that the two had worked together to pass certain files back and forth to provide these covers for Ray through his trusted friend "Raoul."[392]

The aliases discussed here, of course, were all acquired prior to the murder of Dr. King (except possibly Sneyd and Bridgeman, which Ray claimed were obtained only after he returned to Canada and never used until then), apparently by someone using methods only available to people having access to classified documents and covert means, given to either Raul or others with whom he worked through the guidance of his (or their) own superiors. If that were the case, it might also explain not only the physical similarities previously noted, but possibly Ray's faulty memory of—and his obvious reticence to describe—how he came across all of those names and that the reason he refused to divulge it was really because he knew it would be a fatal mistake. If the provenance of those aliases was as posited here, then the quick issuance of the Canadian passport—with the name "error" noted above—was not an inadvertent happenstance after all. That would also mean that Ray was being tracked for much of that time, even as the FBI dithered for weeks, seemingly unable to connect the dots on "Galt's" real identity.

A prison psychiatrist who had examined Ray in 1966 later told a reporter for the *New York Post* that he was "a habitual criminal, [but] all of whose crimes were associated with money. 'We didn't find anything to indicate he was a killer or had tendencies to kill.'" The article also stated that there was "growing concern that when Ray is tracked down he might be shot by his captors" because the FBI had used the provocative word "killer" and stated that he was "armed and extremely dangerous" despite the opposite descriptions of him from the prison warden and psychiatrist and the fact that he was virtually unknown by any of his fellow prisoners.[393]

But a professional's opinion of James Earl Ray's psyche was woefully inadequate to describe the designated patsy of the murder of Martin Luther King Jr. That was left to a succession of inventive novelists as outlined above. William Bradford Huie, Gerold Frank, and George E. McMillan in the late 1960s, 1970s, and 1980s were then joined in 1998 by Gerald Posner and in 2010 by Hampton Sides. All had made up assertions to repaint the same contrived portrait of James Earl Ray. The germ planted originally by Huie in his first magazine articles and book was then replanted in the books by the others, becoming an organic linkage between them and the future books designed as additional boosts for the original myths that reblossomed each time with ever more flagrant deceits and distortion.

It suggests that the earliest authors were brought in to FBI headquarters in Washington and put in a conference room with Hoover, Tolson, DeLoach, Sullivan, and Papich, where they were told to make up as many stories as they could and write them up as convincingly as possible, to reframe the narrative to paint the most derogatory profile they could of James Earl Ray. Based on the results, it would appear that they were competing with one another for the winning entry, probably even a grand prize for the winner, who could come up with the most absurdly outrageous fiction, and sell it to the public: whoever's book sold the most in the first production run would be declared the "winner."

Part III
APPOINTMENT
IN MEMPHIS (1968)

Chapter 7

PREPARATIONS COMPLETE

"I learned more about the art of deception from [Lyndon Johnson] than I did from my father . . . he was a man who understood the art of misdirection—of making the eye watch 'A' when the dirty work was going on at 'B.'"
—Harry Blackstone Jr. (announcer for LBJ's radio station and son of magician the Great Blackstone)

A Study in Contrasts: Comparing Ray's Movements with Huie's Account

Like Mr. Blackstone's description of Lyndon Johnson, there were many charlatans and sorcerers at work in 1968 to create actions and events—within shell games—to completely change the true story of Dr. King's assassination, by drawing the public's attention to "A" when the real truth was far removed from there. But truth was not even in shells B or C. It was not even on the table when the story appeared in the first articles and books that were written.

In this chapter, we will demonstrate how William Bradford Huie had drawn the attention of his readers—and the police, FBI, and other government investigators—into examining stalker theories that were nothing more than figments of his imagination. This point will be examined in detail in the pages ahead and is arguably the game-changing revelation of this book. For once and for all, it will prove conclusively how the lies that Huie put into his book—complete fabrications made for the singular purpose of railroading James Earl Ray—became the accepted meme of an entire American culture.

Practically everyone in the country, and the world, who has an opinion about Martin Luther King Jr.'s murder believes that the "killer," Ray, was a vicious southern racist and stalker of Dr. King. *Nothing* about that is accurate—not only was he not the killer, he wasn't vicious, he was never a racist, he wasn't even a southerner, and Ray was certainly not a stalker. This myth will be thoroughly deconstructed in this chapter. Huie, and later the numerous other authors repeating his fiction, made a series of bald-faced lies, even referencing a series of news articles that purportedly stated things that they did not. These were not inadvertent mistakes; they were coldly calculated untruths, meant to transform a common man capable of relatively minor unlawful acts into a vicious murderer and stalker, which he was not. We will show not only how the original distortions were accomplished, and why, but demolish the foundation upon which they were constructed, thus dismantling the larger fallacies they were intended to establish for posterity.

On November 19, 1967, Ray left Mexico, having been "ordered" to do so by Raul, driving to Los Angeles and expecting to stay there for several months, until April 1968. There he began a number of self-improvement activities: beginning a correspondence course in locksmithing—saying that he had an affinity for that kind of work—starting dance lessons (apparently an effort to become more sociable), and signing up for a bartending class, evidently another effort to both improve his skill set and the related social savvy.[394] Meanwhile, he also visited a plastic surgeon to have his nose reshaped, to reduce the noticeable point on the end. According to Huie, Ray also consulted eight different psychiatrists, hypnotists, and Scientologists in his attempt to correct what Huie portrayed as his "feelings of inadequacy."[395] He also hung out around an area near Hollywood Boulevard, where he rented an apartment on Serrano Avenue and frequented the Sultan Club, a bar in the old St. Francis Hotel, three blocks from his apartment. There he became friends with a barmaid named Marie Martin.

It was at this point in his book that Huie began repeatedly framing his novelette around an unsupported premise of Ray's allegedly burning desire to become a notorious criminal. His completely groundless assertions included such statements as: "*Most certainly* he was obsessed with the idea that the FBI would soon put him in the Top Ten and give him his yearned-for status as a criminal." (Emphasis added.) Huie averred that he did not believe that Ray had selected Dr. King as his target, to achieve the infamy he supposedly coveted, until he went to Los Angeles. By then, Huie concluded, Ray had come to believe that it was the only way he could, purportedly, rid himself of his "depressed feelings."[396] Huie wrote that until Ray went to Los Angeles, he was simply a drifter, and it was not until then that he came to decide that he must give his life a strong purpose in order to overcome his feelings of inadequacy (as if Huie's interviews with all of those "psychiatrists, hypnotists and Scientologists" whom he postulated that Ray consulted had imbued to Huie himself his own supernatural powers of clairvoyance).

During all this time, Ray's own actions contradicted this alleged obsession, as he kept switching to new aliases and went to great lengths to change his physical appearance—buying new horn-rimmed glasses he didn't need, the plastic surgery to reform his nose, nearly always being dressed in suit and tie—all done to ensure that he would escape identification and capture. It is difficult to reconcile his supposed obsession to be recognized with his numerous actual behaviors, all opposite those alleged intentions. Huie must have known that he would have to use his creative wordsmithing skills like never before to overcome this contradiction, because he did just that: in creating his fictional account, he had to invent a series of subtle deceits and outright lies to portray Ray—always the penny-ante, small-time, streetwise punk—as a vicious, hate-filled racist with a violent and murderous core, which was nothing more than a fake profile none of his credible associates had ever seen. Despite Huie's epiphany about Ray's suddenly acquired intense need for "recognition," his innate traits, and real interests, had always been about making himself as invisible as possible, given that he was a wanted fugitive, on the run from the law.

Huie's search for a plausible explanation for Ray's sudden decision to stalk and kill Dr. King inevitably led him to create an answer to the puzzle that would conform to his own mission: to establish the earliest possible description of Ray's persona that would eventually become the default public perception. The disconnect between what Huie had stated was his intention—his commitment to tell Ray's story of how he had been unwittingly manipulated into being framed for King's murder—and what he had cunningly decided would be his actual objective—of proving that Ray was the sole assassin of King—could not be more stark. It could not be clearer that that goal was planned; it could not have been something that Huie would have gravitated to if he had simply followed the real leads, all of which he consistently ignored. To the contrary, Huie actively created leads that did not exist, including the false motives for Ray, to support his own claims of a stalking theme—an illusion entirely created by Huie—that became the centerpiece of his frame-up.

Huie's epiphany came with the decision to portray the shy and backward James Earl Ray as essentially the opposite of how his intrinsic personal characteristics—traits he was born with, or acquired over forty years—defined his true persona. That enabled him to project onto Ray's psyche a previously unknown, recondite need to perform a shocking crime in order to resolve his inner conflicts, obtain status and worldwide recognition as an infamous fugitive, and thereby find peace of mind.

Huie knew that his book would need to have a powerfully profound revelation such as this if it were to create the same indelible impression within his readers' minds as had existed in his own. Only something acutely momentous could eventually become—following Goebbels's maxim—

the accepted conventional wisdom of Ray's permanent legacy. Huie would need to show how Ray was so desperate to transform himself, by becoming a worldwide, well-known criminal, that he would have naturally begun to devote hours daily to create a plan to achieve that putative goal. His task was to show that—despite Ray's actions in taking several concurrent self-improvement initiatives—he was simultaneously acting to become a cunning vicious stalker of a national civil rights leader. Huie had to paint him as a Jekyll and Hyde character, which he simply was not.

Huie, and later the numerous other authors repeating his fiction, made a series of bald-faced lies, even inventing news articles that he claimed stated things that they did not. To create his illusive tale of Ray's stalking of Dr. King, he decided to use these made-up stories, claiming they were supposedly supported in specific newspaper articles, assuming that no one would go to the bother of looking them up since—by the time they read his book—they would be at least two years old. That artifice worked successfully at the time, and for the five decades since then, but its premise finally failed because he never thought that eventually something called the Internet would make such a verification quite simple. Until now, no other author thought to recheck the basics.

Thus, Huie's completely false account was propped up by contrived "facts" that, he claimed, were reported in specific newspapers in New Orleans, in Selma, Alabama, and finally in Memphis, completely untrue assertions, as we will shortly prove. He made this cunning decision shortly after Ray's first attorney, Arthur Hanes, fed him a story about how Ray had made a wrong turn on his way to Birmingham to meet Raoul, on a stormy night after dark, when he randomly decided to get a room at the Flamingo Motel in Selma and continue on to Birmingham the next day. Huie decided to make that Selma sleepover stop the centerpiece of his stalking meme, one concocted to prove that King's expected presence there was the reason for Ray's long journey from Los Angeles. This demonstrably false, devious, and brazenly intentional deception was created by Huie despite the fact that Dr. King had never planned to be there in the first place. In fact, he had been scheduled to be in Memphis on that very day.

It all started in early December 1967, when Raul sent word to Ray that he needed to meet him in New Orleans so they could begin planning their next "job," which was, coincidentally, just when Ray was in need of an infusion of cash to keep himself solvent. Marie Martin asked him to take her hippy cousin, Charles "Charlie" Stein, with him on the trip so they could pick up her two young nieces there and bring them back on the return trip.[397] Ray made the trip, sharing driving duty with Stein. Once there, Raul paid him another $500 to keep him on a sort of retainer for a few more months, promising him that after their next smuggling job, he would help him obtain a passport and pay him a sum of $10,000–$12,000. After two nights in the Crescent City, they returned to Los Angeles with the young girls as planned.[398]

Huie's account of this first New Orleans trip was based on a conversation he had at a hotel in the French Quarter with a "friendly, white-haired woman" who told him that he should try to associate Ray's time there with the fact that Lee Harvey Oswald had stayed in that very area. She felt that there was a connection between Oswald and Ray, that they had both been managed by certain men there who were behind all three of the 1960s political assassinations (she was obviously a very perceptive lady). Huie thought that made sense, saying that in New Orleans, living "with the ghosts of assassins, you find it easy to believe in conspiracy. You feel surrounded by criminal intent."[399]

With that, Huie concluded that Ray had made that trip—not at Raul's request to plan more smuggling operations, as Ray had always insisted, but because Ray "*might* have been plotting to murder Martin Luther King on April 4, 1968!"[400] (Emphasis added.) He then stated that this was the reason, when he wrote his first articles in *Look* magazine, why he believed that Ray made that trip to meet with men who wanted Ray to murder King for his own financial rewards, and to assist them in fulfilling their purpose of inciting racial rioting in order to aid the campaign of George Wallace for the presidency. But Huie later rejected all of that, because, he then claimed, the "conspiracy thesis" was merely what "Ray wanted him to believe."[401]

Of course, Ray had never told him that, since he had always maintained his own innocence; nevertheless, Huie stated that he began to reject it by October 1968, now saying that it was because Ray told him he traveled there at his own initiative, that he was never actually *summoned* there; it was just another twist in his tangled tale.[402] But Huie, as ever, made up all sorts of things to fill in the blanks. This was merely one more instance of the novelist's methods of creativity.

Having spent the rest of December and the first two and a half months of 1968 in Los Angeles, Ray left on March 17 after stopping by the post office to file a change-of-address form to forward his mail to "general delivery" in Atlanta. He had received a letter from Raul a few days earlier to proceed to New Orleans, moving up the April date that had originally been scheduled.[403]

Before Ray left Los Angeles, Marie Martin asked him to deliver a package to her daughter in New Orleans, which he did. On that point, Huie asked a rhetorical question as to whether such an action would be taken by a criminal on a lengthy trip for the purpose of murdering someone.[404] Answering his own question, Huie stated, "not necessarily no," then ventured the explanation that such a person would not need to hide his movements if "*he expected to escape!*" after the murder.[405] (Emphasis in original.)

An epiphany—a stunningly cold, hard truth—should by now be clear to readers: It was the creative literary license of William Bradford Huie—heretofore presumed by his readers to be merely a scribe charged with digging out facts and chronicling an accurate account of an assassin's motives—that should by now begin to reveal how James Earl Ray's "legacy" was created. It is proof that he was on a mission to accomplish another preestablished objective, which had no basis, reason, or room for truths.

Ray Becomes the "Stalker" of MLK—According to Huie

Huie's original book's influence on so many subsequent authors—even the chairman of the House Select Committee on Assassinations (HSCA), Louis Stokes, a decade later—makes it essential to examine all the ways he planted unsubstantiated suppositions or made-up "facts" within his book, and before that in the three articles in *Look* magazine.

His multiple deceits—to be conclusively proven below—were used to paint James Earl Ray as a southern racist vagabond who somehow secretly financed his travels and lifestyle with small-time criminal activity as he mounted a "stalking" campaign against Martin Luther King Jr. A thorough examination of Huie's premise will reveal how he constructed a grand myth about Ray that still lives on and has now become engrained into the minds of practically everyone who has ever read, or heard from others who have read, about the murder of Dr. King.

Huie stated that he had become convinced that Ray decided to set a goal to have his name on the FBI's Ten Most Wanted poster back in late 1967, when he was living in Los Angeles. This revelation, Huie claimed, did not occur to him until October 1968—coincidentally, just as Ray was becoming disenchanted with both Huie and his lawyer, Arthur Hanes. But it is more likely that it was Huie's own duplicity that was beginning to show, since the publication of his *Look* articles, in which that would become clear, was then imminent.

Furthermore, according to Huie's apocryphal account, to ensure that Ray would become famous in the process of killing Martin Luther King, he imputed to Ray a plan to deliberately leave evidence at the murder scene, ensuring that he would be quickly identified. It was part of his supposed sudden new desire to ensure his own fame and notoriety, while intending to evade capture by escaping to Portuguese West Africa, from where he could never be extradited. Huie proudly proclaimed that his prognostications were later proven to be correct and that his readers would also eventually be convinced,[406] as if to acknowledge the shaky, unproven, and notional nature of his own conjecture. But to people who knew Ray, the incongruity of him—and his unassuming, submissive, and introverted personality type— never quite fit Huie's new portrait of him as suddenly having a desire to become infamous on a worldwide scale.

The one thing Huie got right was that it did become the faux legend that still persists, at least for the credulous people who read his articles and book as though they were really the "nonfiction" genre as marketed—the same being true of all the subsequent authors who carried the myth forward into the new millennium. But Huie wrote his invented theories about Ray's motives despite the lack of any evidence that James Earl Ray had ever contemplated the need to escape justice for a murder that he had never planned, nor was even aware of before it happened, and certainly did not commit. Despite his claim that the two articles he wrote for *Look* magazine in November 1968 were merely benign "pretrial" background information that supposedly did not yet point to Ray's guilt, it is clear from reading them that they were highly prejudicial. For one thing—despite still claiming to be telling Ray's story—he had already begun to describe Ray erroneously as a stalker of Dr. King, something that Ray would have never stated, since he had never had a conscious awareness of King's itinerary.

The real catalyst for Ray's alleged stalking undoubtedly arose from the FBI's need for a reason to explain Ray's purported motives and justify the charge of his guilt. To do that, Huie needed to hide, create, or modify evidence early on, to prove that Ray was the stalker/murderer of Dr. King. This idea was clearly manifested within Huie's book, actually becoming its primary theme. Those first two articles in *Look* magazine in November 1968 were a reflection of Huie's conflicted position: On the one hand, he needed to delicately avoid outright assertions of Ray's guilt, in order to keep him tethered to his puppeteer's strings and willing to continue as Huie's source; while on the other hand his handlers needed him to begin paving the way for a complete betrayal of Ray, eventually showing him as a lone-wolf stalker and murderer. All of these actions—beginning with the magazine articles and leading into the book—indirectly point to the real source of Huie's allegiance, and it definitely was not James Earl Ray.

In those *Look* articles, Huie had already begun laying out the blueprint for the FBI's investigation, which would be designed to prove that Ray had gone to Selma for the primary purpose of stalking King. Huie had counted on Ray not being smart enough to realize the real direction those earliest articles portended; it was a mistake that nearly destroyed his insider status, were it not for the inventive new lawyer, Percy Foreman, who, as we will show shortly, had been waiting in the wings, ready and willing to help him resecure his position after Ray saw those articles and became so upset with him that he fired his attorney Arthur Hanes and, he thought, Huie, as well. With the change of lawyers, Huie's relationship with Ray went from one of an openly overt status to a secret and covert basis: he was operating in the shadows, behind Ray's back. The worst part of Ray's dilemma was how he had been put into the position of being the source of funding his own demise; it was that realization that finally caused him to fire both Hanes and Huie.

Huie's narrative in the first *Look* article generally conformed to Ray's claims of having met "Raoul" on the Montreal waterfront in July/August 1967—and over the course of a total of eight meetings with him that summer (at least six of which were in the Neptune bar, according to Harold Weisberg)—but his portrayal of Ray had already begun to show signs of negativity toward Ray. By the end of it, Huie posited that Ray had finally agreed to Raul's proposition: dropping his quest to obtain a Canadian passport in order to escape to a country from which he could not be extradited back to the United States. Huie's first article even allowed that the proposal from Raul was so lucrative for Ray that it actually ensured he would return, almost immediately, to the United States. Furthermore, Huie explained that in exchange for Ray's agreeing to that, Raul promised to pay his living expenses, buy him a new car, and later give him $12,000 in cash and a counterfeit passport if Ray would merely "establish himself in Birmingham and be 'available' [for future services]."[407]

But after that first *Look* article, Ray caught on to Huie's real mission, and he immediately fired his attorney Arthur Hanes, and Huie as well, just two days before his original trial was about to begin. This resulted in a sudden need to find a new attorney and begin the entire process all over again, without the encumbrance of Huie calling the shots from the back rooms—at least Ray thought that would be the case. But his new lawyer— suddenly making himself available out of the blue, Houston attorney Percy Foreman, a longtime friend of Lyndon Johnson and their mutual friend George Parr, the "Duke of Duval"[408] whose various fraudulent schemes had benefited both of them—went behind Ray's back and enlisted Huie to continue his work under virtually the same arrangement he had previously had with Hanes.[409]

After the November articles, no longer working with Hanes but now secretly working through Foreman, Huie reversed course completely, and beginning in mid-March 1969, he started telling reporters that he had changed his mind and now believed Ray had acted completely on his own. An *Associated Press* article was printed on March 17 in newspapers nationally under the headline "RAY'S BIOGRAPHER NOW HAS DOUBTS OF CONSPIRACY." Quoting Huie, the article referenced his previous articles, which hinted at a conspiracy but noted that he told reporters in "an NBC television interview that he concluded early this year that Ray made the decision to kill King himself." He then admitted that: "But I do not know this and Ray insists otherwise. Ray has a strange mind and a sharp one. He takes great satisfaction out of the fact that we still have doubts. That we still have unanswered questions. He wants continuing drama in his life." That phrase was to become the new meme about Ray that he would repeat many more times.

This fundamental change of course actually started in the last half of his second *Look* article. For example, instead of stating that Ray had been summoned by Raul from Los Angeles to New Orleans on March 13, Huie wrote in the last parts of the *Look* article dated November 26, 1968, that "Ray drove from California to Selma, Ala., in March 1968, and registered on March 22 at the Flamingo Motel," *completely omitting his primary destination: the stopover in New Orleans.* That was done for two purposes: to begin disassociating him from Raul specifically, but any and all other possible "coconspirators," as well; and to begin the meme that Ray had really acted alone throughout his travels, while simultaneously creating the faux "stalker" theme that would ultimately become the primary motive for Ray's purported actions. Henceforth, Huie would conflate Ray's two brothers— interchangeably, as individuals, or together as though there was only one brother—into the narrative as being the contact Ray consistently claimed was the mysterious "Raoul."

In his third *Look* article, on April 15, 1969, he acknowledged only that Ray "stopped in New Orleans; then on March 22, he was at the Flamingo Motel in Selma, Ala., when Dr. King was 40 miles away [*sic*] recruiting for the Poor People's March."[410] Now, instead of merely stating that Dr. King had *planned* to be near Selma (which he never had), Huie asserted the blatant lie that King was actually *there*; as we will prove below, Dr. King was in Atlanta that entire day, having canceled a planned trip to Memphis— while *never having been scheduled to be in or near Selma.*

By the time he wrote his subsequent book in 1970, Huie stated that Ray had really wanted to go to Selma and Birmingham, despite the fact that neither had been in his plans when he left Los Angeles; Huie noted, almost as an afterthought, that he did stop briefly in New Orleans* before continuing on to Selma, where he registered at the Flamingo Motel on Friday, March 22.[411] But by then, in Huie's narrative, Ray was not associated with Raul anymore: now it was a mysterious group of white southern racists who had allegedly put a bounty on King's head. It becomes obvious that by the time he wrote the book, Huie realized that he had to include at least a stopover in New Orleans, since he would reference—blatantly inaccurately—a purported New Orleans newspaper article that would become the centerpiece of both his argument and, ironically, now its destruction. This article will be examined closely below, as it was a shameless lie that Huie invented to help him sell his book fifty years ago. Its exposure now will destroy not only his entire premise, but those of all the other fiction writers who later attempted to prop it up.

The New Orleans newspaper article was only one of several brazen deceptions by Huie. He also inaccurately described another news article in a Memphis newspaper (to be examined in the next chapter) and misrepresented still another one, dated March 21, in a Selma newspaper—one that Ray could not possibly have seen until he had arrived in Selma the evening of the *following day*—that was purported to have stated that Dr. King would be in Camden, Alabama, just thirty-three miles away from Selma, on that very day, March 22, which could not possibly have influenced Ray's decision to stop there for the night (presuming it even existed, it would have been clearly incorrect, since King was actually scheduled to be in Memphis). Huie—as if to try to synchronize their travels—stated that Ray then left Selma for Atlanta (again purposely misstating his true initial destination of Birmingham, where he would meet with Raul before both of them continued on to Atlanta). By minimizing Ray's primary destination of New Orleans, and completely omitting his next one, Birmingham, replacing both with Selma, Huie was able to create, in the minds of his misinformed readers, a coherent tale of the stalking of Martin Luther King where it would otherwise not exist. The mention of either of those cities would risk his conceding the possible presence of Raul, which, he had apparently been advised by his handlers, was verboten.

---

* By acknowledging that Ray had driven "through" New Orleans, he skirted the larger point, that it was initially his primary destination, allowing him to put emphasis on Selma, as though it had always been his real destination. And the mention of Birmingham was the single reference he made to it in this context, before dropping it afterward in his narrative. The people who had supposedly "wanted" Ray were not identified by Huie, nor even supported by any evidence, but, apparently, they were simply the shady racists offering to pay him for the murder of King.

In framing Ray's travels as he did, Huie clearly ignored what Ray had told him about his travels in order to begin an alternative that Huie had already concocted, to incriminate Ray before the trial began. He (or, more plausibly, his FBI handlers) had already decided that Raul would have to be dismissed from the get-go, and additional references to him were thereby stricken from the book. The lack of even a mere mention of either of Ray's true destinations—first New Orleans, then replaced by the handlers to Birmingham—was only the most obvious of a series of similar deceits.

The far more credible story was Ray's own account, that after leaving Los Angeles on March 17, he arrived, as directed by "Raoul," in New Orleans on March 21. This nearly 2,000-mile trip, even with today's interstate highways, would take approximately thirty hours of solid driving—a minimum of four days of at least nine to ten-hour segments depending on length of stops—at five hundred miles per day. It was virtually impossible for him to have left Los Angeles any later than March 17, yet that is exactly what Huie (and, a decade later, the HSCA) tried to portray, claiming he only left *after* Dr. King did on the 18th, again obviously to fit the stalking narrative: what rational stalker would leave town a day before the stalkee?

Ray stated that he delivered the package to Marie Martin's daughter, as requested, on March 21, then called Raul's number and was told, by an unidentified intermediary, to make his way to Birmingham and plan to meet Raul on the morning of March 23. So he left New Orleans on March 22 on his drive to Birmingham, a day of stormy weather throughout the South, but he only made it as far as Selma, Alabama, about three hundred miles or at least six to seven hours of driving, with short rest/refueling stops on state highways. It is reasonable to believe that this was simply an unplanned stop—in bad weather and on top of the long drive just completed from Los Angeles—for the reasons Ray claimed: that the trip had been so tiring that he simply decided to find a motel to stay for the night, planning to leave early for the last hundred-mile sprint to Birmingham the following morning to meet Raul.

Yet Huie used this impromptu overnight stay in Selma as a cornerstone event in his yarn about how Ray had allegedly stalked King. As we will examine next, he made up numerous false premises and claimed support for them in false newspaper articles that he apparently believed were so innocuous that no one would ever figure out that they were fabrications. He realized that most readers would presume their accuracy, because to doubt them would require a diligent reader to go to great lengths to dig up old newspapers to ferret out what was true and what was not. Evidently, he counted on the fact that finding these old articles would require too much time for anyone to bother ever rechecking these "facts," and that over time the chances would continue decreasing until eventually it would become all but impossible to discover that they were all lies. In 1968, he had no reason to fear that such a presumption would eventually collapse, when the Internet would make checking such assertions very easy, indeed so easy that practically anyone could do it within minutes if they chose to.

Huie was obviously on a mission, and evidently following the orders of someone who had planned the actual scheme to "prove" that Ray was Dr. King's assassin. Thus it became imperative to prove Ray was stalking him, no matter how ridiculous the lies became. Had Huie been interested in being a careful journalist, he would have never gone to all the trouble to lie to prove a point in such complete contradiction of Ray's real intent, because going so far out of the way—not only to avoid revealing truths, but in the cunning creation of bald-faced lies—would run the risk, eventually, of proving that he was given a mission by very powerful people to do just that in their efforts to cover up one of the most heinous crimes of the twentieth century. No legitimate journalist—nor an author of serious nonfiction, being of right mind and pure intent—would have that kind of deceitful motive; ergo, it could only have been done by a gifted novelist driven by such character traits as avarice, brutishness, cunning, deceit, evasiveness, fraud, and guile (and perhaps nineteen similar others, not to put too fine a point on it). William Bradford Huie—long before this mission was created for him—had proven that he possessed all of those attributes twelve years earlier—with his deceitful articles on the Emmett Till murder—in the same *Look* magazine that he would use to create a new profile for James Earl Ray beginning in November 1968.

The Rosetta Stone: Proof of Huie's Big Lie About Ray as a "Stalker"

Huie had taken yet another liberty with his supposedly nonfiction book that was intended to reframe history forever, to make James Earl Ray out to be the stalking killer that he never was, because Dr. Martin Luther King was not in or near Selma that evening and had never planned to be there, having returned home to Atlanta on March 21. Reverend James Lawson called him from Memphis early in the morning of Friday, March 22, to inform him that a freak blizzard the night before had left seventeen inches of snow on the ground.[412] Dr. King had been scheduled to fly to Memphis that morning—*not* Selma—for a march in support of the strike of the sanitation workers, but he had to cancel that trip and reschedule it for the following week.[413]

As a central part of the frame-up of Ray, Huie devoted over half of Chapter 7 to "prove" that Ray had deliberately gone to Selma as part of his alleged stalking of King. He wrote that on March 22, "*Dr. King was within a few miles of Selma recruiting for the Poor People's March*," and that this information about King's planned trip was reported in newspapers in New Orleans on March 21.[414] (Emphasis added.)

Huie's presumption that he could make such a baseless assertion—when Dr. King spent the entire day in Atlanta—rested on the fact that by the time anyone read his book (two years after the fact), no one would bother to double-check such a seemingly innocuous point. Even the early researcher Harold Weisberg missed that point,[415] and Dr. Pepper in his most recent book accepted the assertion without objection[416]—possibly the one significant error in his book—having not closely reexamined what he undoubtedly presumed to be a benign point, just as every other reader of that book has for the forty-eight years of its existence, until now. Yet it was anything but benign; it was clearly the result of an elaborate, cunning effort to frame James Earl Ray as a vicious, racist stalker of Dr. King that had no basis in fact. The exposure of this key lie is arguably the Rosetta Stone of the Martin Luther King Jr. assassination cover-up.

In the critically important context that was missed by so many others, it absolutely proves that the premise of James Earl Ray being the "mad racist stalker and assassin of Dr. Martin Luther King" was a sham, then, now, and forever—for as long as it continues to stand in the official record and in the public's mind. The fact that Huie went to such great lengths to make this shrewd point, based entirely on his portrayal of James Earl Ray in a false and deviously biased manner—one that completely reframed his persona as the opposite of what it was—could only mean that he had been assigned that duty as his primary objective, a key point in his overall mission. Axiomatically—with the absence of any other realistic motive—this is conclusive proof that Huie's entire mission had to have been conceived by the same powerful forces in Washington that had worked for at least ten years to neutralize King; it is a track record they had created and unwittingly documented themselves, which exposes their evil intent, beyond a shadow of a doubt.

Thanks to digital archives and the Internet, anyone with a computer can now ascertain that the only mention of Dr. King in the New Orleans *Times-Picayune* (the morning newspaper Huie cited) on Thursday, March 21, 1968, was an article on page 58, headlined "Negroes Plan Capital March: Army of Poor Will Move in April." It was an AP article by John Pearce, datelined Jackson, Mississippi, about the planned "Poor People's Campaign" in Washington the following month, *which made no mention whatsoever of any plans for Dr. King being in or around Selma, Alabama, the next day.*[417]

It did mention that "King wound up a two-day speechmaking tour [March 19–20] of Mississippi with a rally in a Masonic temple near the campus of all-Negro Jackson State College."

A brief review of Dr. King's itinerary that week helps to set the context. According to his preeminent biographer, Taylor Branch, after leaving Los Angeles on a flight to Memphis on March 18, upon arriving there that evening, Dr. King announced to a packed crowd of supporters of the sanitation strike that he would return there on Friday, March 22: "I want to tell you that I am coming back to Memphis on Friday, to lead you in a march through the center of Memphis."[418] That became a definite commitment of Dr. King's, and it was known to anyone who read actual news stories or tuned into television broadcasts that evening.

Upon leaving Memphis the next day, Tuesday, March 19, King and his party drove into Mississippi and stayed there that evening. On Wednesday, March 20, after making other stops, they finished the Mississippi tour with the Jackson stop noted above in the news article. From there, King's entourage drove to Bessemer, Alabama (near Birmingham), to spend the night.[419] The few stops in Alabama planned for the next day (March 21) were all canceled due to bad weather, and he returned to Atlanta that morning—Thursday, March 21, instead of the late afternoon, as planned—to rest and prepare for a trip to Memphis the next morning, Friday, March 22.[420]

That was the exact same day that Huie purposely lied to his readers about, to support his clearly invented "stalking" thesis: he knowingly wrote, incorrectly, that Dr. King planned to be in Selma that day and that was the reason James Earl Ray purportedly drove there in his supposedly desperate attempt to begin his stalking obsession. The fact is, King was in Atlanta, about 225 miles away from Selma, the evening of March 21 and would remain that far away the entire next day—unable to fly to Memphis, where he had intended to be—but regardless, still very far away from Selma, where Huie repeatedly stated he planned to be.

Huie cannot be excused for this error, as if it had been an inadvertent mistake. It was a calculated deceit to purposely reframe the most innocuous event of Ray's journey across the South, when he became so tired after driving six hours in stormy weather that he spontaneously decided to stop and get some rest at the closest motel. Huie took that opportunity to reframe the Selma sleepover—exploiting the name of the infamous town to satisfy his nefarious plot—to be the centerpiece of the entire trip from Los Angeles to Atlanta.

It is important to understand that the *only* change in King's itinerary was that he had returned to Atlanta in the morning rather than the afternoon of March 21. He had never planned to stay overnight in Selma, Alabama, the night of March 21 or be there at any time on the 22nd. These were deceits planted by a novelist who was used to spinning yarns with a predetermined result, not the skills of a careful researcher, journalist, or historian who is constrained by actual facts, provable motives, and plainly written narrative. Huie wasn't the last of the authors of this genre to have written this type of book; it suggests that they were all carefully selected and given special perquisites for their efforts to create and/or sustain official myths.

This single cunningly fabricated story is at the heart of what Huie presented as the primary foundation of his grand, epic saga about how James Earl Ray stealthily made his way there—all the way from Los Angeles, for his purported plan of stalking his prey—even well before he had bought a gun to complete this dastardly deed. The fact that Huie lied about a news report that had supposedly stated King would be in Selma in the March 21 edition of the *Times-Picayune* is clear and incontrovertible and can be confirmed by reading the article itself, as available at the newspaper's archives (New Orleans *Times-Picayune*, March 21, 1968 [p. 58]).

Huie wrote over 2,500 words in his effort to reframe Dr. King's plans for the singular purpose of misinforming his readers about King's plans for that key date. It was his intent to make that the key argument of his own diabolical plot to portray James Earl Ray in a theme repeated throughout his book, one that can be reduced to this: "James Earl Ray was a conniving, lone-nut stalker, obsessed with making the Top Ten Wanted criminals of the FBI, who chose to murder Dr. King in order to achieve that rarefied status of the most brutal criminals."

The cornerstone of Huie's elaborate lie written fifty years ago now becomes the focal point of its complete destruction: Even if Dr. King had made it to Camden, Alabama, forty miles from Selma as Huie posited, on the morning of March 21, it is clear—based upon Taylor Branch's much more veritable research—that his plans were to leave by the afternoon of that day to return to his home in Atlanta. He had never intended to go to Selma to spend the night either March 21 or 22. But even if the "surly stalker" James Earl Ray had somehow thought King might be there anyway, and was so intent on beginning his stalking in Selma, one would have thought that he might have made it a point to get there at least by the evening of the 21st, instead of the 22nd. The simple, incontrovertible fact is that Ray missed King by *more than a full day and 100 miles.* So much for his stalking abilities.

Evidently, this key lie by Huie was unnoticed by all the other authors who have repeated parts of it since then, together with the FBI and HSCA investigators who relied on it to construct the official history of the Martin Luther King Jr. assassination. The worst part of Huie's elaborate hoax is that it formed the "violent racist" baseline of the frame-up that caused James Earl Ray to spend the rest of his life in prison for a crime for which he had literally nothing (wittingly) to do with. His only real instance of ever being in close proximity to King was for about three hours in Memphis, thanks to an FBI and/or CIA handler named Raul who the FBI and CIA always denied existed for obvious reasons, since any acknowledgement would only lead back to themselves. Clearly, a decade after the crime, this fact was then communicated to the new leadership (after Richard Sprague was removed) of the HSCA, to ensure that certain leads would continue to be ignored.

After waking up in his own bedroom in Atlanta the morning of Friday, March 22, Dr. King got the news about the record-breaking freak snowstorm that had fallen overnight in Memphis, which caused a disruption of flights in and out of the area. King abruptly changed his travel plans, finally deciding instead to spend a few days in New York to recruit people for the April Poor People's Campaign in Washington, while rescheduling the Memphis stop for Thursday, March 28.[421] Just as King was finally able to return to Memphis on that Thursday, James Earl Ray prepared to leave Atlanta the next morning, with Raul, to go to Birmingham. Yet somehow Huie even turned those itineraries—entirely different journeys, from and to different cities—into further evidence of Ray's stalking King, through skillful use of contrived events and deceitfully parsed words, again obviously fulfilling a preestablished mission.

As he did in so many other areas, William Bradford Huie, followed by at least a half-dozen other authors, let nothing stand in his way of framing James Earl Ray for the murder of Martin Luther King Jr. Many other authors have helped to accomplish this, piling on many other deceits in the process. But special attention should now be paid to the latest one in this lineup, given the accolades he has received by many people who have evidently not noticed the craftiness of his distortions or the brazenness of his deceits in his supporting narrative.

How Hampton Sides Further Distorted Reality

Four decades later, in 2010, Hampton Sides would further clone Huie's (et al.) lies in *Hellhound on His Trail,* his dogged attempt to continue portraying Ray as a racist stalker of Dr. King, and to up the ante by attempting to portray Ray's alleged ties to "Galt's beloved Governor Wallace." He then went on to remind his vast readership how the 1965 Selma march had prompted President Johnson to sign the historic Voting Rights Act of 1965, in his attempt to solidify LBJ's exalted status as the hero of civil rights legislation, ignoring the fact that he was its primary impediment for twenty-six years during his reign in Congress and as vice president, even being a stalwart defender of such measures as poll taxes and literacy tests to keep blacks from voting.

Then Sides explained to his readers: "One didn't easily wander into Selma on the way to someplace else."[422] Yet, looking at a map of Alabama, one can easily discern that it is actually located, geographically, directly in line between New Orleans and Birmingham. It wasn't exactly the detour that Sides claimed—again repeating Huie's forty-three-year-old deceit—to pass through Selma on a such a trip, yet he must have felt the need to repeat the story left by Huie so many years ago to sustain the stalking myth. The fact that Selma lies directly between New Orleans and Birmingham is as true today as it was fifty years ago, and whether it was on the main road or not does not merit the contrived argument that to have stopped there, on a trip between those cities, was such a purportedly drastic sixty-mile detour. This concoction stretches credulity beyond reason.

But the real point of this detour canard was always to evoke the memory of Selma—with the attendant reminder of the despicable obstructionist people gathered there, whom he wanted to bring into the narrative in order to associate them with the supposedly abhorrent racist and stalker James Earl Ray—as another distraction for readers of their contemptible books, otherwise they might begin to connect the dots.

Sides began his Selma treatise on the bottom of page 95 of his book, describing "Galt" as having "swung" his Mustang into town on March 22, exhausted from his "four day" trip from Los Angeles: he then proceeded to describe Selma as having been Ray's primary destination all along, not New Orleans (the destination that even Huie had reluctantly noted, only because he alleged that Ray bought a paper there). After waxing on for two full pages about how "Galt" continued "stalking" Martin Luther King,[423] he then repeated the lie about the purported article in the New Orleans *Times-Picayune* (and added more deceit to the mix when he asserted that "Other newspapers and TV stations across the South reported King's plans as well") about how Dr. King was scheduled to make an appearance in Selma.[424] To be clear, there was *nothing* in the *Times-Picayune* on either March 21 or 22 about King being, or having ever been scheduled to appear, in Selma that day, because he hadn't—he actually planned to be in Atlanta the first day, Memphis the second.

These contradictory statements came, inexplicably, despite the fact that on the very next page, further confusing and contradictory assertions were made, even though he finally got one correct when he actually noted that King had been scheduled to be in Memphis that same day, but it had to be canceled because Memphis was hit with the "seventeen inches of *snow*" (emphasis in original).

It is interesting to point out that even the editors of his book, apparently used to his works of fiction, missed that contradiction of where King was supposed to be that particular day. Even famed novelists understand the need to tie their fictional stories to actual historic events, but to give them the aura of credibility, they should at least recognize the fact that no one can be in two places at the same time. Dr. King was back home in Atlanta that day, not in Memphis, where he had been scheduled to appear, nor in Selma, where he had *never* been scheduled to appear.

Even More Confusion and Distortions Materialize in 2015

Even worse than Sides, another fiction writer named Pate McMichael, *Klandestine: How a Klan Lawyer and a Checkbook Journalist Helped James Earl Ray Cover Up His Crime,* took the lie to new heights when he stated that "King planned to recruit in neighboring Eutaw the following day" (the context meant March 23), despite then noting that the alleged newspaper article from the previous day (in context, March 21) had stated that King was supposed to be in Camden that day—March 21—but then fly back to Atlanta (which he did, that morning, after canceling his midday stops because of inclement weather).[425] In other words, McMichael—like Sides before him, except using different cities, also apparently believing a man can simultaneously be in two different places—asserted that King would be in both Eutaw, Mississippi, and Atlanta, Georgia, at the same time, March 23, even after having stated unequivocally that he went from one to the other only two days before that.

The simple fact of King's actual itinerary during this period, according to the eminent King biographer Taylor Branch, was that he flew home to Atlanta in the morning of March 21. After canceling the March 22 trip to Memphis, he stayed in Atlanta that day and then, on March 23, took his young sons Dexter and Martin III on a quick trip to Macon and Waycross, Georgia, on a chartered Cessna. After that, he went to New York City to give a sermon at a church in Harlem on March 24, remaining in the New York area until the following Wednesday.[426] Against the factual record of King's itinerary, the series of glaring errors made by these three authors (among others) proves once and for all how lies can be converted to long-standing myths just as Joseph Goebbels stated in his most famous dictum previously noted. Fiction writers especially, used to having the freedom to write with such abandon, must remain vigilant to keep their worst lies well hidden. In this case, not only has the Rosetta Stone of all lies been exposed, but also how two of them attempted to violate such mundane rules as how one man cannot be said to have been in two different places at the same time.

These are only a few of the many errors in books that borrow heavily from other works by authors gifted in the novelist's esoteric art of wordsmanship, while not using any references from the many factually accurate books by discerning researchers listed in the bibliography of this book. Space does not permit a detailed review of McMichael's rather incoherent book, other than noting that its underlying premise, like the Wexler-Hancock book *The Awful Grace of God* before it—that Ray's putative motive of racism was alleged to be driving a whole series of actions he had nothing to do with—was destroyed through the only significant accomplishment of the HSCA committee, in finding that Ray was not the racist he was alleged to be by a series of authors, beginning with Huie.

Despite that finding, the committee's biggest failures were (1) not giving it sufficient emphasis, and (2) not taking that conclusion one step further, to nullify everything else that had been built upon that false premise: the stalking meme—a lie begun by Huie and repeated ad nauseam by every other fiction writer since then—was based upon the racism premise, just as his alleged Klan connections were, as well as the invalid assertion that he was ever an active supporter of George Wallace. It does not take a genius to understand that without racism as a genuine premise, none of the other related claims can possibly make sense.

The stalking scenario originally concocted by Huie—which eventually made it into a number of other books as well and finally even the HSCA hearings initially as unquestioned gospel—was so critical to the myth that Huie used the first ten pages of Chapter 7, plus two more at the end of it, for this single aspect of Ray's alleged stalking. Many more pages were devoted to other invented events—from Los Angeles, New Orleans, Birmingham, Atlanta, and of course Memphis, all to present fabricated, fragmented evidence supporting his stalking scenario, one that he simply made up as he crafted his novelette.

Huie even put his myth into the record, when he wrote to Ray in October 1968, just before Ray's trial was supposed to begin: "Remember this: when you were in Selma on March 22 you were stalking Dr. King. That is truth already admitted by you [*sic*] and to be published by me." [427] Just as Ray never admitted to killing King, he never admitted anything resembling a stalking theme; in fact, it had never even occurred to him, since he was always oblivious to King's whereabouts. Furthermore, Huie stated that it was also Ray's purpose in going on to Atlanta from March 24–28 (without informing his readers that King was actually in New York then), before Ray traveled back to Birmingham with Raul on March 29 to buy the rifle(s), the very same day that King returned to Atlanta.

Huie was evidently given a firm instruction to use his editorial license as a fiction writer to do whatever was necessary to make this specious stalking argument sound plausible. The proof is in the result, an elaborate lie by a master storyteller that lives on even now. The fact that he tried to portray his original intent as being supportive of Ray's story—but then slowly deciding that Ray was not so innocent after all, and finally deciding that he really was the murderer acting alone—reveals his true mission all along: he consciously made up all of it, as will be further proven within these pages, and that gives him away. His deception was not inadvertent missteps—he went to great lengths to create an elaborate, cunning plot—it was purposeful and it had no basis in fact. His largest mistake was related to his one attempt at honesty—where he actually admitted that numerous credible witnesses actually liked Ray, and spoke highly of him as a fair-minded, reasonably intelligent though not well-educated man bearing no hatred of blacks—but he then turned around and made up hateful comments that he claimed they said about Ray, undermining his own account, which the HSCA members finally established were untrue.

In the *Look* magazine article of November 26, 1968, published at a time when Huie was supposedly trying to be impartial so as not to contaminate a potential jury with information injurious to his client (in effect, he was vicariously connected to Ray, through the attorneys Arthur Hanes Sr. and Jr., then, after their services were terminated, unbeknownst to Ray, Percy Foreman), Huie stated the following not-so-benign conclusions as to the potential guilt of the accused:

> The outline of the plot to murder Dr. King now begins to become visible to me. It may not be visible to my readers because, until Ray has been tried, I cannot reveal all that I have found to be true. But from what I know, from what I have learned from Ray, and from my investigative research, some of the features of the plot were:
> - Dr. King was to be murdered for effect. His murder was planned, not by impulsive men who hated him personally, though they probably did hate him, but by calculating men who wanted to use his murder to trigger violent conflict between white and Negro citizens.
> - He was to be murdered during the election year of 1968.
> - Since he was to be murdered for maximum bloody effect, he was to be murdered, not while he was living quietly in

his home in Atlanta, but at some dramatic moment, at some dramatic place where controversy was raging.

Those conclusions do not directly name James Earl Ray as the murderer of Dr. King, but they implicitly, and artfully, lead the reader in that direction, at a point before he was ever tried (which never actually happened, at least not a fair trial in any sense). But the assertions made by Huie clearly implicate Ray, erroneously, as having been the source for these insights, the only one with a very specific knowledge of the overall context of the origins of the assassination.

The Culmination of Months of Planning: Dr. King Takes the Bait

Spending most of the remaining week—after having to cancel his snowed-out Memphis visit—in New York recruiting volunteers for his Washington Poor People's Campaign scheduled for the following month, Dr. King returned to Atlanta Wednesday evening and then flew on to Memphis Thursday morning, March 28, accompanied only by traveling aide Bernard Lee. Flight delays caused their arrival to be pushed back to 10:30 a.m. In anticipation of his arrival, thousands of people had gathered around Clayborn Temple, where pandemonium reigned by the time Dr. King arrived at nearly 11:00 a.m. Ralph Abernathy was there to greet them as they arrived, though due to the crowds surrounding his car, it took almost ten minutes to extricate King and get him placed at the head of the march line, locking arms with Abernathy and H. Ralph Jackson in the process.[428]

Among the crowds were many young black high school students who had cut classes for the day, encouraged by older youths, most of whom the leaders, including Reverend James M. Lawson, the chief marshal of the parade, had never seen before in any of the planning meetings. Some of them, it was later determined, had come from as far away as St. Louis and Chicago.[429] Among them were members of a black activist group of a more militant mindset, most of them wearing jackets printed with INVADERS on the back. Those blue denim jackets, with sewn letters, were easy to make, so many were turning up on men and boys not actually associated with the organization. Lawson did recognize some of young men from the planning meetings and he realized that certain of their tactics were not compatible with the "nonviolent" theme Dr. King had always maintained, but at this point, there was little that could be done about that.

The march finally started, but when they had advanced only a few blocks, to Second and Main Streets, they began to hear the sound of breaking glass behind them. Dr. King recognized the sounds of trouble and exclaimed, "We can't have that!" He called for Lawson to stop the march, and it was quickly agreed that King must leave immediately. His aide and bodyguard Bernard Lee saw a black lady driving her car across Main Street and stopped her, explaining that Dr. King needed to borrow her car. Lee took the wheel and King and Abernathy got into the backseat, and a police escort took them to the Rivermont Holiday Inn, where they took a room on the eighth floor. By the end of the day, a teenage black boy was dead (twenty witnesses claimed he died after being shot while his hands were raised in submission), sixty other blacks had been roughed up, and nearly three hundred more were arrested. According to Taylor Branch, sixty demonstrators, mostly young males—but including females ranging in age from twelve to seventy-five—would be hospitalized for emergency care. Governor Ellington ordered four thousand National Guardsmen to the scene, and Mayor Loeb declared the entire city in a state of emergency and ordered a curfew of 7:00 p.m. to 5:00 a.m.[430]

The police call logs from that incident state that at 11:32, "Mr. Holloman talked to Mayor Henry Loeb. 'You call the Governor [*sic*] and I'll call in the Guard,' he said." Holloman, evidently already having that level of authority, would indicate that it had been delegated to him in advance by the governor; had it not, then the call logs indicate that he had usurped it at that point. According to Special Investigator Gary Revel, the police call logs "are evidence of multiplicity in a conspiracy to kill Martin Luther King Jr. and derail the following investigation with the singular purpose of putting James Earl Ray in prison for the crime. Frank Holloman is the man who oversaw the operation and the only man who could have done it and gotten away with it due to his unique appointed position of 'Director of the Police and Fire Department.' It just so happens that he also was a close friend of FBI Director J. Edgar Hoover and had worked closely with him on other assignments."[431]

Under the direction of Frank Holloman, the massive use of weapons, clubs, tear gas, and mace by the police was obviously a carefully planned response to what had been purported to be a "spontaneous" eruption, cunningly provoked through numerous infiltrators and informants. It was done for the primary purpose of discrediting Dr. King, by making a shambles of his commitment to nonviolent, legally sanctioned protest. It was a setup that went beyond simply discrediting him in the eyes of a public that had become increasingly attracted to the movement he had led. More important, it fulfilled the plotter's agenda as the means to draw him back to Memphis a week later—knowing that he would have to quickly make amends if he wanted to proceed with his campaign in Washington the following month with proof that he could conduct a major, nonviolent demonstration. They used what they knew he would have to do as the ultimate "hook" to bring him back to the city on their schedule, one designed to have all of the logistics in place: men, money, equipment, artillery, and, most critically important to the mission: a designated patsy.[432]

"The Violence in Memphis was a Godsend to the FBI"

(MLK scholar Adam Fairclough)[433]

A memorandum was drafted—immediately after the violence erupted—back in the Washington DC FBI headquarters, in a cubicle on the lower floors, by a man named Theron D. Rushing, the supervisor of a group known as the Racial Intelligence Section. Rushing reported to Section Chief George C. Moore, who was indicated to be the author of the memo, addressed to his superior, Assistant Director William Sullivan, head of counterintelligence of the Bureau. In addition to Sullivan, Rushing stated that "I dictated the cover memorandum and letters of transmittal to . . . Mrs. [Mildred] Stegall." Stegall was the presidential secretary most trusted by President Johnson for all of his most secretive communications, both outgoing and incoming. To send anything to her was effectively the same as if he had addressed it directly to Johnson himself. But, curiously, when an HSCA staffer first read the memo to Rushing, then asked, "Had you seen this?" Mr. Rushing first denied that he had ever seen it, then quickly reversed himself and corrected the record by admitting, "Yes, I dictated it."

The memorandum, as replicated in the HSCA report, stated in part:

> A sanitation workers' strike has been going on in Memphis for some time. Martin Luther King Jr., today led a march composed of 5,000 to 6,000 people through the streets of Memphis. King was in an automobile [*sic*] preceding the marchers. As the march developed, acts of violence and vandalism broke out, including the breaking of windows in stores and some looting. This clearly demonstrates that acts of so-called non-violence advocated by King cannot be controlled. The same thing could happen in his planned massive civil disobedience for Washington in April.
>
> Under "Action Suggested" it states that: "The attached is a blind memoranda [*sic*] pointing out the above which if you approve should be made available by the Crime Records Division to cooperative news media sources."

The blind memorandum reads as follows:

"Martin Luther King, Jr., president of the Southern Christian Leadership Conference, injected himself into the sanitation worker's strike in Memphis, Tennessee, and the result of King's famous espousal of non-violence was vandalism, looting and rioting. Previously King involved himself in the strike, called for a general strike and called for a mass march. *Today he led the mass march in an automobile at the head of the line* [*sic*]." (Emphasis added.)

"Negroes began shouting 'Black Power' and trouble began. King, apparently unable or unwilling to control the marchers, absented himself from the scene. Window breaking and looting broke out. Police officers were forced to use gas to break up the march and to control the crowd. It was necessary to activate the National Guard. Martin Luther King claims his much-heralded march on Washington, scheduled for April 22, 1968, will also be 'non-violent.' He says he has persuaded militants and black nationalists to abandon violent extremism in Washington, D.C., during the march. Memphis can only be the prelude to civil strife in our nation's capital." [434]

As expected, the memorandum provoked the desired result the following day, when front-page articles and editorial page hyperbole appeared in newspapers around the country. The *New York Times*, for example, printed an editorial titled "Mini Riot in Memphis" that picked up on all of the points laid out originally by Mr. Rushing, the scribe toiling away in the back rooms of FBI headquarters, who, following orders, had produced the germ of a new theme for Dr. King: that of a fomenter of unbridled chaos and violence.

Fortunately for America, that was a temporary diversion. Even President Ronald Reagan capitulated to the juggernaut of support for a national atonement of the injustices Dr. King endured and fought against when, fifteen years after King's murder, he signed into law the legislation passed by Congress to establish King's birthday as a national holiday. Hoover and Johnson probably turned over in their graves when that happened.

In the aftermath of it all—including the planned plethora of furious editorials in newspapers around the country condemning King for letting it happen, and the speech on the Senate floor (delivered at 9:00 a.m. the next day as described in Chapter 5, is reproduced in its entirety in Appendix C) by Senator Byrd—President Johnson joined the chorus in two speeches, pledging to "stand behind local law enforcement agencies to the full extent of our

Constitutional authority." He also had one of his aides look up an appropriate Abraham Lincoln quote, which he repeated, something about no grievance ever being fit for "redress by mob rule." On Sunday, March 31, 1968, at 10 a.m., he left to work on changes in his speech scheduled for that night regarding revisions being made in his Vietnam strategy. There was another item to be revealed in that speech, one he had not shared with even his top aides, about his own personal plan to not run for reelection the following year.[435]

It wasn't in the news right away—the very important point about the real catalyst behind the outbreak of violence that morning—but it dribbled out later that the Invaders were behind the breakup of the march. King and Abernathy found out shortly afterward, but for others it leaked out slowly, over months, years, and even decades later. One of the leaders of the Invaders in Memphis that day was a twenty-three-year-old man named Charles Cabbage. He was a recent graduate of Dr. King's alma mater, Morehouse College in Atlanta, and was linked to the leadership of the militant Student Nonviolent Coordinating Committee (SNCC) and the Black Panthers.[436] Cabbage, along with Calvin Taylor and Charles Carrington, met with Dr. King and Reverend Abernathy the following morning and denied that they had anything to do with it, saying they had left the area at 10:30 a.m., before the march started. They pressed King to give them a role in the sanitation strike and for substantial financial support and then blamed King's associates for causing the violence because they had not included them in the planning sessions.[437]

Evidently, by 10:30 a.m., assured that their previous work to incite the younger students to do what they had been led to do was complete, they decided to leave early so their claims of noninvolvement would ring true. The following day, however, their requested meeting with King did not go well, as they presented him a list of their demands, which included—for their acceptance of his nonviolence standard—for him to accept their doctrine of "tactical violence" and specific approval of a financial commitment to support their budget. King rejected all of it, saying, "I don't negotiate with brothers," and subsequently admonished Hosea Williams for having let the Invaders ingratiate themselves into the SCLC's business.[438]

According to a black reporter for *Newsday*, Les Payne, in an article titled "FBI Tied to King's Return to Memphis," there were several FBI informants and one Memphis police undercover agent who were among the most active members of the Invaders, put there to incite the violence as a means of discrediting Dr. King among his followers and the editorial boards of newspapers across the country. It was all according to the FBI's COINTELPRO program that had been provoking King for nearly a decade by that point. Payne wrote: "One of the informants [in the Invaders] reportedly planned a large portion of the group's violent confrontations." One of the members of the group said that the undercover policeman was "at the scene of the violence on the day of the riot. He was a very active and vocal member of the group . . . He was always suggesting actions that we should take; I never saw him physically attack anyone. But he was one of the most provocative members of the Invaders."[439]

Ed Redditt, a black policeman who had been on the surveillance detail for Dr. King before being relieved of that duty by Police and Fire Commissioner Frank Holloman, revealed that the black undercover cop who had infiltrated the Invaders was named Marrell McCollough. He would remain close to Dr. King from the moment he arrived at 11:00 a.m. on April 3 until the moment he was shot on April 4 at 6:01 p.m., and he would be one of the first to check on his condition. Unbeknownst to practically anyone else at the time, however, McCollough was also a military intelligence agent who had been assigned to the Memphis Police Department to work as a provocateur and infiltrator of the Invaders activist group.[440] He had been in the army in 1964–66, but had been reactivated for this assignment ten months earlier in June 1967 and hired as a military intelligence informant at the 111th MIG in Camp McPherson, Georgia.[441] After his stint in Memphis, he eventually joined the CIA and spent the rest of his career with the Company. Redditt had gotten to know McCollough well in 1968 and ran into him a few years later; he stopped him on the street to confront him because he pretended not to recognize Redditt:

> He left the police department . . . and the word was that he went to Washington, D.C. Then a couple of years after the King slaying I ran face to face with him in downtown Memphis. He was wearing a disguise. He acted very mysterious, saying that he was now with the Central Intelligence Agency, and begged me not to blow his cover.[442]

The cofounder of the Invaders, Cobey Smith, testified in the 1999 civil trial that a number of the mysterious outsiders came from Chicago. He didn't draw the connection in his testimony, but the fact was that the group he referenced, the "Blackstone Rangers," was connected through Jesse Jackson's Operation Breadbasket, also known as the "Black P Stone Rangers street gang":[443]

> A: Our people started to report the influx of other individuals who were coming in with Illinois license plates who were seen

about town, who were seen on Beale Street by our affiliates on Beale Street, and who were members of several organizations, some the Black Egyptians out of East St. Louis, some reported to have been Blackstone Rangers out of Chicago.

Q: So these were strangers that came to Memphis just prior to this march. Is that what you are saying?

A: That's right.

Q: Why would they have come to Memphis?

A: We have no idea, because usually when organizations came to town, they would contact us. The Black Egyptians did. Chuck Cohen and some other people did in fact contact our people in an appropriate fashion. The ones we were concerned about were unidentified. This is very unusual, because the nature of the movement was such that people relied on each other for housing, for accommodations, for transportation, for information, for all kinds of things. The nature of the movement was a very communal kind of thing. Everybody helped everybody if we could. [444]

The "outsiders" who appeared, including the Blackstone Rangers from Chicago, were apparently brought in by unidentified others, possibly some of the informers noted elsewhere. In addition to the several FBI informants noted by Payne within the Invaders, there were others within Dr. King's own organization and the Memphis counterpart-hosts as noted elsewhere. They allegedly included (as noted here and in subsequent chapters) King's young associate Reverend Jesse Jackson and his aide/chauffeur Solomon Jones.[445] Another was the famed black photographer and reporter Ernest C. Withers, who was considered by the FBI as a "superinformant" because he could get into any meetings of King's associates as well as other civil rights activists with his camera and report his findings directly back to the FBI. He regularly reported to the FBI details about King's schedule, the people he met with, what they talked about, the license plate numbers and cars for his entourage, even the hotel room numbers where he was to stay, in advance of his arrival.[446]

Another informant to the Memphis Police Department was the Memphis-based Reverend Samuel "Billy" Kyles. They were all paid from money provided by J. Edgar Hoover, delivered to Memphis through his close associate Clyde Tolson, who funneled it through Russell Adkins Sr. (and, after his death, his son Jr.) to O. Z. Evers, also a paid informer since the early 1960s, often providing information on the comings and goings of Martin Luther King Jr.

Tolson would come to Memphis "four or five times a year" for the purpose of attending the meetings of the steering committee (originally led by Russell Adkins Sr.) of the plot, to make sure everything was proceeding on schedule, and to pay this cash to O. Z., ensuring the continuity of the information flow.[447] This evidence, compiled by Dr. Pepper over many years, finally reveals the real nature of a very elaborate plot to kill Dr. King: one that was personally and closely managed by Hoover's highest-level associate.

More Inexplicable Anomalies in James Earl Ray's "Stalker" Legend

After Ray spent the stormy night of March 22 in Selma, completely oblivious to the whereabouts of Dr. King, the next morning he got behind the wheel of the Mustang and continued his drive to Birmingham to meet Raul at the Starlight Club there. Later that day, they drove on together to Atlanta, arriving there that evening, where they found a room just off Peachtree Street, at 113 14th Street NE. The next day, Raul went on, alone, to Miami— purportedly to arrange more gun-smuggling operations to Mexico—and returned to Atlanta to Ray's apartment on March 28, the exact same day that the FBI bushwacked Dr. King in Memphis. With tragic irony, they did that by instigating the very acts of violence for which they would quickly put the blame back on him by getting their press release—disguised as a news article—printed in newspapers the next day across the country.

On that same day, March 29, as King returned to Atlanta, the alleged stalker Ray left Atlanta with Raul, driving back to Birmingham, where Raul had instructed Ray to buy a rifle. Evidently, Raul had already planned, regardless of what brand or caliber it was, that it would be unacceptable and have to be returned for another in order to ensure that Ray would be remembered there. Upon their arrival in Birmingham, Ray went to a large sporting goods store called Aeromarine Supply to purchase a .243 Winchester under the name of "Harvey Lowmeyer." He took it back to the motel but Raul didn't like it, saying the bore was too small, so Raul picked out another model from a sales brochure that Ray had picked up, as instructed, and the next day, March 30, Ray exchanged it for a Remington Model 760, 30.06 caliber. Raul then left for New Orleans but instructed Ray to meet him in Memphis, where they would be meeting with "some prospective gun buyers" on April 3.[448]

After exchanging the rifle on March 30, according to his memoir, Ray began a leisurely drive north toward Memphis, stopping at a motel near Decatur, Alabama, the first night; on March 31 he stayed in a motel close to Florence, Alabama; on April 1 he stayed at a motel "near Corinth, Mississippi."[449] The HSCA investigators, ten years later, identified a particular Corinth motel—the Southern Motel—which James thought might be the same one where he stayed, even though he could not remember precisely the name of it since it had been, by 1978, a distant memory from ten years before. His brother Jerry Ray also believed that James had stayed at that hotel, but that the FBI had seized the hotel's records, according to the HSCA report, "to prevent exculpatory evidence pertaining to James from being divulged."[450]

Given the lengths that the FBI went to in their quest to prove that James had returned to Atlanta after buying the rifle, Jerry's assertion about the hotel's records is probably much closer to the truth of the matter. Through questioning the coowner of the motel, Freddie Phillips, the HSCA investigators attempted to show that this was not the hotel he stayed in, because neither Ray's name nor any of the aliases that he was known to have used were listed in the motel's registration log. That he might have used another alias (as he would often do, making one up on the fly, especially for such mundane purposes as renting a motel room[451]) seems to have never occurred to them, nor that he might have misidentified the point on the map that he used of Corinth, Mississippi, ten years after the fact to attempt to identify the motel he had stayed in that night. In their interview with Mr. Phillips—conducted in 1978, exactly a decade after the incident—the HSCA investigator asked him, "Have you ever seen that man (James, shown in a newspaper photograph from 1968) on or about the motel in April of 1968?" His answer was unequivocal, suggesting that he had an amazing recall for everyone he had seen, or not seen, that otherwise nondescript evening so very long ago: "No, sir, I have not."[452] Phillips did acknowledge that there were three motels along that road in 1968, but the others were apparently never investigated, and he claimed that his would have been the "closest to fitting that general description," and that was accepted into the record with no further commentary. The abrupt and perfunctory manner by which the committee "settled" this matter should be considered as being merely one example of how their entire mission was completed.

For the HSCA lawyers, it was critically important to establish, for the record, that Ray had not stayed where he said he might have slept that night. Their purpose, evidently, was to discredit his account, and thereby eliminate the notion that he was in Corinth at all. This exercise was done for the purpose of "proving" to themselves that he had gone to Atlanta on March 31, as posited by Huie for the purpose of stalking Dr. King, and that would have meant that he had to have rushed back to Memphis instead of making a series of stops in his trip. This was done despite the fact that they did not produce evidence that he had stayed overnight in any other specific place on any night during that period, including the Atlanta apartment for which he had previously paid rent in advance, as a contingency, should he have needed to return there.[453]

Today, the approximately 400-mile drive between Atlanta and Memphis on I-20 and I-22 is a six- to seven-hour trip with no stops. In 1968, however, those interstates were still in the planning and earliest construction phases, so to make that trip on the state highways then in existence, in much slower traffic, and with stops, would have probably been closer to an eight- or nine-hour drive, no easy feat to accomplish in a single day, though still technically possible. But in Ray's case, his consistent story was that he had no reason to return to Atlanta first, so he decided to take a leisurely drive from Birmingham, north and west to Memphis, the destination, by April 3, as instructed by Raul. Raul had already carefully selected the motel in Memphis where they would spend the first night. The Rebel Motel—it had a nice ring to it, Raul undoubtedly thought.

At this point, based on the evidence already presented—with even more to come—we can conclude that the entire stalking theory has been completely discredited, thus giving credence to the inescapable fact that Ray was completely unaware of, even oblivious to, Dr. King's whereabouts. The fact that Raul did exist, as demonstrated most persuasively by Dr. Pepper in his latest work, gives Ray's account the credibility of being the most veritable one available. Moreover, he had no reason to drive 150 miles east to Atlanta for a day before turning around and retracing the same path in the opposite direction, on his way to Memphis. Indeed, the single reason given by Huie and the other fiction writers, the FBI, and the HSCA investigators was to stalk Dr. King (who had been scheduled to go to Washington that very day, March 31st), which we have shown was always fiction. That, and to go to a laundromat, according to these same sources—a ridiculous argument for a 300-mile round trip merely to drop off laundry.

All of the FBI's (and later the HSCA's) efforts to prove that Ray had returned to Atlanta were focused on a laundry ticket from an Atlanta laundry, purportedly dated April 1, that putatively proved Ray had returned there, allegedly stalking Dr. King. It was essential to the case they were trying to make, one that was centered on the need to prove that Ray's motive was based upon Huie's invented tale of his becoming a stalker of King, whose far-fetched goal was to make the FBI's Ten Most Wanted list, just as the fiction writer had originally posited. There were other reasons, to be closely examined in Chapter 11, that will further discredit this key FBI/HSCA premise. At this point, however, the possibility that the FBI had used extralegal measures to modify the laundry ticket (which Ray had actually received on March 28, before he and Raul went to Birmingham) and the hotel records previously noted—given all the rest of the evidence of official misconduct presented throughout this book—should not be minimized.

On April 2, according to Ray's account, he stayed overnight at the DeSota Motel near the Tennessee border outside the Memphis city limits. The following day, April 3, as violent storms raked the entire Delta region, Ray crossed the state line and, as instructed by Raul, checked into the Rebel Motel in Memphis. Raul also arrived there, in a drenched trench coat looking like the spook that he was, and he told James: "We're staying for a few days in Memphis. There's a place located near the waterfront where we will rent a room." He gave Ray the address where they would meet at 3:00 p.m. the following day: 422 ½ S. Main Street.[454] As always, Ray was under the long-standing admonition to avoid asking questions of Raul; he was only told that the rifle was purchased as a model to be shown to the putative buyers whom Raul would be meeting there. Ray's constant instruction was to stay in the background.

All of this part of Ray's travels was parlayed in the earliest books— by Huie, Frank, McMillan, and of course the 1978 HSCA report based on those books, and then the later books by Posner, Sides, and others—as a lengthy attempt by him to surveil and stalk Dr. King, in preparation for a supposed long-held wish to murder him. The motive contrived to explain that was that Ray was a "violent, sadistic, racist, worst-case criminal," who supposedly sought recognition and therefore, he had purportedly reasoned, his legacy would require that he murder the iconic civil rights leader known throughout the world, so that his face would be pictured at the top of the FBI's "Ten Most Wanted" criminals poster.

The first problem with the multiple, repeated attempts to portray Ray's travels as being timed to track Dr. King to various cities is the plain and irrefutable fact that—other than Memphis, which we will examine further in the next chapter—he was only in the same town or city as King on a single day in Los Angeles, March 16, due entirely to the coincidental fact that Dr. King had arrived there that day, where Ray had already resided for the better part of four months. By the time Dr. King arrived, Ray was already preparing to leave the next day, which he did, more than a day before Dr. King left to fly to Memphis on March 18. Then, instead of heading straight to Atlanta to pursue his alleged stalking in King's hometown, Ray headed for New Orleans, as Raul had asked, then on to Birmingham, where Raul had subsequently asked him to go after he had changed his own travel plans.

Huie's reframed account, in his third article in *Look* (April 15, 1969), stated confidently that "The final decision to kill Dr. King, made by Ray or someone else, appears to have been reached on March 16 or 17. Dr. King was in Los Angeles on those days, his movements and statements reported by newspapers, radio and television."[455] While he did not specifically assert that Ray had actually made an effort to stalk King at his speaking engagements (on Saturday the 16th to the California Democratic Council in Anaheim, or Sunday the 17th at the Second Baptist Church in Los Angeles), by stating that on Monday the 18th, "Dr. King left Los Angeles for Mississippi, and Ray left too,"[456] he deceptively left the point for readers to infer such a conclusion. This despite the fact that Ray stated that he left on the 17th immediately after filing the change-of-address form at the post office, to allow himself four days for the 2,000-mile trip to New Orleans. Huie's conflated account left only three days for Ray to travel that distance, which would have required an average of 667 miles per day, over eleven hours of driving without stops.

By the time that Ray and Raul met in Birmingham on March 23, then traveled on to Atlanta together, King had gone to New York to recruit people to participate in his planned Poor People's Campaign. Then, when King returned to Atlanta on March 29, Ray left the same day to return to Birmingham. On March 30, while King stayed in Atlanta, Ray remained in Birmingham, trading the first gun for a second, much more powerful—unnecessarily powerful—rifle, as instructed by Raul for reasons that Ray did not even understand. The real reasons had nothing to do with the choice of one gun or another, but everything to do with the necessity of having Ray make a firm impression on the salesman at Aeromarine Supply, who later remembered Ray as someone who knew absolutely nothing about rifles.

The next day, March 31, while Ray was traveling in Alabama on his leisurely trip from Birmingham to Memphis, Dr. King had flown to Washington, DC, to speak to 3,000 people at the Washington Cathedral on April 1, after which he then returned to Atlanta and attended a SCLC staff meeting there. It was only then that King's itinerary was publicly announced, and the world learned that he would return to Memphis on April 3. But that plan was already known to the FBI and CIA, through their paid informants; ergo, their employee—or agent provocateur—Raul would have known it, as well. But since that schedule had not previously become public, it would be embarrassing for the FBI then, and the HSCA later, to disclose the fact that Ray was already on his way to Memphis. And of course, for the same reason, it might also expose their operative Raul's existence; therefore his instruction to Ray could not be allowed into the record.

For all of these reasons, it became extremely necessary for the FBI to go to great lengths to prove that Ray was in Atlanta on April 1. We will examine this issue further in Chapter 11, in reference to the HSCA "investigation" ten years later, and their attempt to validate the myth, rather than seek out the truth. Yet Ray had no reason to return to Atlanta when his handler Raul had told him to be in Memphis on April 3 for their supposed next meeting with the putative "gun buyers."

It is well past time that Huie's account—and all its subsequent iterations that form what has been presumed to be the official record—be completely discarded for once and for all. If Ray had really been stalking Dr. King, why would he have waited until less than three weeks before he killed him to begin that obsession, according to the theory posited by the man who created it, William Bradford Huie? And if he had really been that obsessed with stalking Dr. King —remotely, from a distance, in other cities and states, maybe even telepathically during the months he spent in Los Angeles during the winter of 1967–68, up to March 17—one would think that he would have had plenty of time to have at least bought a rifle—even practice with it, in order to learn its nuances—well before his attempt to do his dirty deed.

Why would a man who had never had the slightest interest in becoming skilled in the use of firearms have waited until five days before the big day he selected to kill King to finally purchase a rifle to perform the act without even having test-fired that model? And then waiting until a couple of days before the big event to purportedly even try it out, but just once, and only once. Had he bought it at least a month—even two or three months—in advance, he could have practiced with it, which is the only possible method for anyone to learn and perfect a shooting skill. This was especially true for a novice who had never demonstrated the least interest in becoming a sharpshooter; it would have been essential that he practice it repeatedly, with the specifically unique gun and telescope that he had chosen.

Ray's lack of interest in shooting long rifles was affirmed by the salesman who sold the Remington GameMaster—by its very name, designed to take down big game such as elk, buffalo, or bear—to Ray on March 30. The salesman later told HSCA investigators, "He did not seem to know anything at all about firearms, I mean nothing."[457] Yet, having purchased one precision rifle, Ray then returned it the next day, using the excuse that his brother-in-law didn't like it and wanted one with a bigger bore, because the deer were supposedly bigger in Wisconsin, which, though possibly true, should still be considered a distinction without a difference; it would have been quite adequate for the task in any case. Had he been interested in a rifle more suited to a 206-foot shot across a parking lot,[458] he should have kept the first gun, as the higher caliber rifle he bought was designed for longer distances and bigger game than Dr. King.

There was only one purpose for his handlers wanting to have Ray return the first gun and replace it with the larger gun: to ensure that the salesman had an indelible impression of this man. But the impression would have the opposite effect: that this man was no marksman. That point should have raised a lot of red flags for every one of those investigators, and their supervisors, and on up the chain to the HSCA congressional members who were supposedly interested in finding the truth, especially the committee's chairman, Representative Louis Stokes. But in their haste to close the case, they all seemed to miss that point.

These are all rhetorical questions because, as examined above, the record now revealed shows that James Earl Ray never actually did any such stalking. It was all part of the grand fictional account dictated by the highest-echelon government administrators in the FBI, headed by a man suffering severe delusions resulting from his acquisition of unchecked power over nearly five decades in what he referred to as the Seat of Government, his personal fiefdom. That gun was not even the one used in the murder, as we will examine closely.

These points have been glossed over in nearly every book—to a greater or lesser degree—ever written about this event, many of which don't mention them at all; though some note them with passing interest, none make them the major issue that they should have always been. It is confounding that so many leads like these were never pursued and suggests that the HSCA seemed to have been instructed to purposely ignore any exculpatory evidence that they might stumble across. In Chapter 11, we will endeavor to establish that that was, unfortunately, clearly the unstated mission.

How Mr. Hoover Lured Dr. King to the Lorraine Motel

Without using the word, Huie implicitly divined unto James Earl Ray a kind of clairvoyance that no one, not even Ray himself, had ever noticed previously. Ignoring the fact that Dr. King had always stayed at other hotels, notably the Holiday Inn Rivermont Hotel,[459] Huie incorrectly asserted that "Dr. King had stayed at the Lorraine before, always in one of the new, more comfortable rooms fronting on Mulberry Street . . ." According to Dr. William F. Pepper, who was a friend of Dr. King's, he had *never* stayed overnight there previously, although he had held meetings with local leaders there in the meeting rooms.[460] Pepper also noted that one of his black police bodyguards confirmed that he usually stayed in either of the two Holiday Inns. Furthermore, Huie would incorrectly state that all the rooms are in full view of the second-floor rooms along the back of the rooming house run by Bessie Brewer.[461] As will be explained in the next chapter, only a few of the rooms at the Lorraine were visible from Ray's room 5-B, and there were many other Lorraine Motel rooms that were not at all visible from any part of the rooming house, including the one originally reserved for Dr. King (Room 202).

Gerald Posner picked up on that deception too, writing: "For Ray, it was fortunate that King's favorite Memphis motel, the black-run Lorraine . . . ."[462] Posner then went on to identify the reason for Ray's good fortune, noting that the motel was located in a "seedy area frequented by transients and drunks. The witnesses to the day's events would be of poor quality."[463] Much has been revealed about Posner's character traits, but his tendency to stereotype, to make sweeping statements to denigrate everyone residing in an entire community, speaks volumes about where he is on the snarkiness gamut.

The plotters knew that Dr. King, absent a compelling reason to change his hotel from the more elegant Holiday Inn Rivermont, his favorite Memphis hostelry, to the Lorraine Motel, would undoubtedly return to that one unless he was given a compelling reason to do otherwise. That was one of the multiple objectives they had planned to achieve on his first trip to Memphis, in addition to the other, equally imperative, one: to ensure that he would return a second time, according to their schedule, to prove that he could control his supporters to remain nonviolent. That meant that his first visit to march with the sanitation workers would fail that test, requiring him to return, and when he did, he would be placed not only in the Lorraine Motel, but specifically in Room 306. All of their other planning required it.

On March 29, following the disastrous attempt to conduct a march with the sanitation workers the day before, the FBI's Domestic Intelligence Division (Racial Intelligence Section) drafted a "news article" that it distributed to "cooperative news sources," denigrating King for his choice of hotels:[464]

[Suggested Headline]: "Do As I Say, Not As I Do"

Martin Luther King, during the sanitation workers' strike in Memphis, Tennessee, has urged Negroes to boycott downtown white merchants to achieve Negro demands. On 3/29/68 King led a march for the sanitation workers. Like Judas leading lambs to slaughter [sic], King led the marchers to violence, and when the violence broke out, King disappeared.

The fine Hotel Lorraine in Memphis is owned and patronized exclusively by Negroes, but King didn't go there for his hasty exit. Instead, King decided the plush Holiday Inn Motel, white owned, operated and almost exclusively patronized, was the place to "cool it." There will be no boycott of white merchants for King, only for his followers.

That article was circulated by the "SOG" as an attachment to an internal FBI memorandum to senior officials explaining the purpose, which was to publicize King's alleged hypocrisy, but the real purpose was to shame Dr. King into using the Lorraine Motel on his next trip by having it printed in newspapers around the country. The document was personally approved by J. Edgar Hoover, who noted, "O.K., 'H'."[465] The file copy had also been noted "handled" by someone whom the investigators for the Church Committee questioned, but he said that he did not recall whether or not he disseminated it as the note implied. The fact that King obviously acted on it suggests that it worked very effectively, since he did in fact move, as authors Lane and Gregory noted, "from the relative safety of the imposing and isolated Rivermont Holiday Inn to a very vulnerable location at which he was, in fact, killed . . ."[466]

Their close proximity to Fire Station #2 (a.k.a. Butler Street Fire Station), where the tactical team (Alpha 184) photographers and snipers were stationed on the roof, showed that the term "vulnerable location," used by Lane and Gregory, was not only an accurate description, but arguably an understatement. The fact that it was purposefully chosen as the location by the plotters underscores that it was the objective of all of their actions to get Dr. King to commit to returning to Memphis in the first place, secondly to ensure that he would stay at the Lorraine, and thirdly that he would be assigned Room 306, of all the rooms available there.

According to the sworn testimony of Ron Adkins, whom Dr. Pepper considered credible, it was a plan being directly controlled by the Memphis Police and Fire Department Commissioner Frank Holloman, who, as noted previously, was a man with direct connections to Tolson and Hoover in the executive suite of FBI headquarters.[467] Holloman gave the instruction to Russell Adkins Jr. to make sure that King's room at the Lorraine would be changed from 202, in the isolated interior section, to 306, which had a large balcony that faced directly to the back brushy area and the back of Bessie Brewer's rooming house. Russell Jr. had his mother contact O. Z. Evers to make a telephone call to the Lorraine's owner, Walter Bailey, to set it up and to have Jesse Jackson ensure that it was done.[468]

Military Intelligence Groups (MIGs) Join Their Brethren

We previously noted how military intelligence units had responded to a series of domestic disorders throughout the Johnson administration, mostly in reaction to his policies related to the Americanization of the Vietnam civil war and the long-delayed reformations on civil and voting rights issues. Those delays had still not caught up with the direction and speed at which the American culture had already moved, thanks to his previous twenty-six-year effort to impede that same legislation. Of course, that was before he became president—at which point he suddenly became the biggest supporter of reform—but by then it was too late to avoid the inevitable backlash from the previous dithering.

In the mid-1960s, the US Army had become very concerned with the increasingly vitriolic rhetoric coming from civil rights activists as more black Americans began resisting the Vietnam policies of the Johnson administration. The fears of the military leaders and other high-level political officials emanated largely from Dr. King's pronouncements regarding the immorality of the war, which they feared might cause black soldiers to begin laying down their rifles and resisting orders they might believe to be too high risk and intrinsically immoral. Leaders were also concerned with the question of whether black teenagers would continue their legally required obligation to register for the draft at age eighteen, should public opinion against Johnson's policies rise to too high a level.

Knowing that the CIA had illegally accepted President Johnson's unconstitutional order to begin spying on American citizens through Operation CHAOS, just as the FBI was engaged in their longer-term unconstitutional program, COINTELPRO, the army decided it must prepare to address its own internal ability to sustain its operations.

Major General Creighton Abrams Jr. wrote an eleven-page letter to Army Chief of Staff General Earle G. Wheeler in May 1963 recommending actions aimed, curiously, to "obtain equal rights and opportunities for Negro citizens and how the Army can best organize and accomplish that mission." The previous experiences of getting troops involved in restoring domestic order—at that point Abrams was in Oxford, Mississippi, engaged in just such an action—were always done as an "ad hoc organization, hastily improvised" without adequate preparation. With that, Abrams proceeded to implement his own recommendation, despite the lack of either approval or disapproval from General Wheeler. As noted by Emison, the surveillance program that Abrams implemented was similar to those of the CIA and FBI, in that all three treated Dr. King, the civil rights movement, black activists, and white reactionaries such as the Ku Klux Klan as "suspects."[469] For five years, every summer from 1963 on had brought new violence on a seemingly increasing arc through the deadly riots in many cities in 1967. There were many indications that the summer of 1968 would be worse than the previous summers, but no one could have predicted how much greater.

Chapter 8

THE HIT

"Like anybody, I would like to live a long life. Longevity has its place. But I'm not concerned about that now. I just want to do God's will. And He's allowed me to go up to the mountain. And I've looked over. And I've seen the promised land. I may not get there with you. But I want you to know tonight, that we, as a people will get to the promised land. And I'm happy, tonight. I'm not worried about anything. I'm not fearing any man. Mine eyes have seen the glory of the coming of the Lord."

—Martin Luther King Jr., April 3, 1968
Among his last public words, spoken at Mason Temple,
Memphis, Tennessee

More Huie Lies and Deceits Twist the Truth About the Memphis Murder

The trap was set, the very lengthy plot to have the logistics in place in Memphis was ready to launch—including shooters from the Dixie Mafia and military intelligence units. Coordinated secretly by carefully selected men at the highest levels of the FBI, CIA, and Pentagon, each responsible for specific "compartments," nothing was left to chance. Raul, MPD, CIA, MI and FBI informants and operatives (a number of whom, as we will see in Chapter 12, were reputedly retired FBI agents) were prepared to execute all of it—and most important of all, James Earl Ray was just about to arrive on the scene at center stage. Ray was the perfect unwitting patsy, feeling very confident now in his new Mustang, driving into town like the world was his oyster; even as an escaped fugitive, he had traveled all over North America on Raoul's dime. His thoughts now were about getting a new passport and a big payoff after this last gun-running job, which would allow him to escape to Europe or Africa and live out his life free of worries of ever returning to prison. As he drove into Memphis with his fingerprints on a newly bought rifle in the trunk (a demo for the prospective buyers), he was ready for action but unaware of the plot, and, as always, completely oblivious to the whereabouts of Dr. King.

But this was not the story that eventually was told in the first lengthy articles and book by William Bradford Huie. The famed novelist's hallucinations had created a completely different script, which would become the official story written to assuage the public's alarm about another assassination of a preeminent national leader of the mid-1960s. As instructed, Huie had fashioned a completely different account of the pending assassination of Dr. King—arguably even before King was murdered—a set of lies that still remains in the official account, to be examined below, exposed now for all the world to discover. The first was the result of another devious Huie scheme to create news articles that never were. He had to come up with an answer to the puzzle of how James Earl Ray—having never been to Memphis before in his life—would drive into town just three hours before the murder and try to figure out where Dr. King was staying, without help from anyone else, since Huie had portrayed him as a sole assassin: a contradiction to his own fleeting premise of how Ray had expected a bounty.

Security for MLK Jr. Removed, Replaced by Military Intelligence, Special Forces, National Guard

In previous chapters, we reviewed the extreme measures begun in 1967 to intensify surveillance of all the men and women who were considered as threats to national security, at President Johnson's behest, by the FBI, the CIA, and the heads of the MIG through Operation CHAOS. At the heart of all of their concerns stood Dr. Martin Luther King Jr.—their single most feared threat, they were convinced, emanating from his purported "Communist connections." They attributed all other protests and demonstrations against their policies (which they had convinced themselves were invincible) to that source: from racial rioting in major cities and undermining the morale of military troops in Vietnam, to the spread of political dissension on college campuses. By 1967, King was feared more than any other single person and was considered a direct and immediate threat to the very fabric of America. He was, in their minds, a dangerous man who had to be stopped without delay.

Frank Holloman had been selected to become the first director of fire and police under the new mayor and council form of city government, implemented on January 1, 1968. As a political appointee, his FBI background and network of influential local contacts in the city of Memphis, the state government in Nashville, and of course his many years in Washington would have been the deciding factors in his propitious selection. Of course, the main decider would have been the newly elected mayor, Henry Loeb, a self-described segregationist determined to hold the line against demands by the sanitation workers for higher wages, improved working conditions, and recognition for their labor union. He viewed their plaintive pleas for a measure of improvement in their dangerous and horrid working conditions and menial wages as outrageously greedy and a threat to the maintenance of his proudly lean city budget. That Mayor Loeb would select Holloman to become the police chief could be justified by the ex-FBI man's background, but for him to decide to consolidate the two major municipal functions and—uniquely, for the first time ever—choose this particular individual to head both of them is curious indeed, considering the central roles both would assume during the period leading up to the murder of Dr. King.

The confrontation between the sanitation workers and the new city administration seemed to erupt spontaneously, but there were many indications that it had been a well-planned, highly controlled event that was part of a preordained schedule. Even the "accident" noted earlier, one month after the new government took effect, on February 1 when the sanitation workers Echol Cole and Robert Walker were killed, has been said to have been a part of the larger plot to entice Dr. King to come to Memphis, as noted in Chapter 5. Throughout 1967 and into 1968, the plot was unfolding in the background, on many levels. The focal point of the surveillance and operational planning had become trained on "the Memphis Operation" well in advance of Dr. King's appearances there, based upon the plot foreknowledge of the intelligence leaders. By March 1968, the MIGs were preparing for another deadly summer, and this one would begin in Memphis with the arrival of Dr. King's march with the sanitation workers. These assertions will be proven in the later chapters of this book, but for now it is sufficient to lay the context for how multiple forces were put to work in a very elaborate plot.

By April 3, everything was in place. Most important, the patsy was in town and would be in position the next day by midafternoon; the real shooters, their backups, and the shooters of the patsy were also locked and loaded. When Dr. King returned to Memphis on that day, he was shadowed—unbeknownst to him—by men attached to the 111th MIG. All of his movements were monitored from a vehicle loaded with electronic bugging equipment. Eight special service soldiers from a unit called "Alpha 184 Team" were also moved into Memphis assigned to an unknown mission.[470]

As noted in Chapter 5, through Dr. Pepper's associate, ex-reporter Stephen Tompkins, interviews were conducted with two men who agreed to confide their stories under condition of anonymity. They opened up to Dr. Pepper because of his long-term involvement in researching and solving the MLK murder but were identified only by their pseudonyms, "Warren and Murphy." They told the story of how they had become involved in "one of our nation's deepest, darkest secrets."[471] Their stories are merely summarized here; readers are encouraged to reference *The Plot to Kill King* for much greater insight into these events.

"Warren and Murphy" were part of an eight-man "Operation Detachment Alpha 184 Team" consisting of a Special Forces field training team in civilian clothes. On February 22, a two-man reconnaissance unit entered Memphis to map egress routes from the city. The team was assembled at Camp Shelby at 4:30 a.m. April 4, 1968, and briefed on its mission: the order that they were to shoot to kill Dr. Martin Luther King Jr. and Reverend Andrew Young. They left in cars, carrying M-16 sniper rifles with 8-power scopes—equivalent to the Remington 760 rifle that James Earl Ray had been instructed to buy. When they arrived in the city, they met with Lieutenant Eli Arkin from the Memphis Police Department, who had also been the department's liaison with FBI Special Agent William Lawrence from the Memphis FBI field office.[472]

In the afternoon, Warren and Murphy met their CIA contact, who took them to the top of the Illinois Central Railroad Building, a tall building from which they could see most of downtown Memphis. They remained there for the rest of the afternoon, more than five hours. Their two-man sniper unit consisted of Murphy as the spotter and radio operator and Warren as the shooter. They spent the afternoon studying photos of the targets, their associates, their automobiles, details of the Lorraine layout, and other items on the checklist, such as the fact that "friendlies" would not have ties on. (It is notable that, unlike King and Young, Jesse Jackson did not have a tie on and actually refused Abernathy's request that he put one on, as noted elsewhere.)

At the TTH point (the "top of the hour"), 6:00 p.m., as scheduled by some of his own staff, Dr. King came out of his room and walked onto the balcony, just as Andy Young appeared, putting on his coat. As Warren and Murphy awaited the order to shoot, both prepared and ready to respond, they heard the report of another rifle, knowing that another sniper team was in place but surprised that they never received the order to shoot, since they were expecting a simultaneous shot with the other team. Warren never took the shot because he never received the order. After a long silence, the team leader came to them and ordered them to disengage and leave in an orderly fashion. They went across Riverside Drive and down to the river to a waiting boat that took them down the river to a point where cars were waiting for them.[473]

Apparently unbeknownst to Warren, the second sniper team had not made the shot as he had presumed was the case. It became clear later that it was one of the two other teams on-site, either a "wacko civilian" who had jumped the gun and made the shot, or a third assassin team, which would have meant a triple redundancy.

James Earl Ray's Impossible Legend of Stalking Dr. King in Memphis

As previously noted, within the earliest quasi-fictional "nonfiction" books from authors Huie, Frank, and McMillan—and the more recent books by Posner, Waldron, Sides, and others—a common theme was planted, then transplanted over and over again,* to the effect that James Earl Ray had been stalking Dr. King as he traveled around the country. This premise has already been rendered preposterous; however, it is pertinent to address a few more details of that issue, in reference to a point where he actually did enter a city (finally) where Dr. King was widely known to be visiting: Memphis, on April 4, 1968.

Ray did not check out of the Rebel Motel until about noon on April 4, and when he went to the car he noticed that one of the tires was nearly flat, so he removed it and mounted the spare tire.[474] When he drove into Memphis in the afternoon, Ray stated that he had mistakenly gone to another nearby bar, named Jim's Belmont Cafe, instead of Jim's Grill, where he was supposed to meet Raul, at 3 p.m. After he walked a few blocks to the correct one, he noticed that two men were there whom he had just seen at the first bar; he noticed that they seemed to be taking an unusual interest in him.[475]

Those two men, according to a man who claimed to have been one of them, noticed Ray from a photo that had been shown to him by a man named "Paul" (apparently, Raul). This man, James Cooper ("Jim") Green, had been placed there as a "backup shooter"—not of King, but of James Earl Ray, who was supposed to be shot by a policeman as he made his "escape," but if the policeman failed to kill him, it was Green's task to do so. (As the shot was made at 6:01 p.m., Ray was no longer at the scene, having decided at the spur of the moment to have his flat tire fixed and fill up the gasoline tank, clearly saving his own life.) Green had been accompanied there by a man

---

* Even in the obscure 2012 book *The Awful Grace of God* by Larry Hancock and Stuart Wexler, while not directly using the term "stalk" outright, an Amazon reviewer stated, "While they are agnostic as to whether Ray actually shot King, it is quite clear from the evidence they assemble that Ray was stalking him in the lead-up to the murder."

named Butch Collier, who had been the designated backup shooter of King, in case the primary shooter (identified by Dr. Pepper as Frank Strausser) missed his shot. Green is now deceased, but his story was found credible by veteran researcher Lyndon Barsten, who claimed that he checked it against FBI documents he obtained through FOIA requests and that his story "fit" everything else.[476]

After seeing the two men in the bar, but not Raul, Ray then decided to return to the first bar to retrieve his car, bring it back, and park it directly outside the door to Jim's Grill.[477] Jim's Grill was in an old brick two-story building at 418 South Main Street, alongside a series of similar buildings, including one next to it that was separated by a four-to-five-foot passageway and staircase to the second floor (where the buildings were connected through a walkway on their upper floors). Above Jim's Grill on the second floor of those two buildings was Bessie Brewer's rooming house, whose address was 422 S. Main Street at the street level, and 422 ½ S. Main Street at the upper level. The first floor of the building to the south was occupied by Canipe's Amusement Company, at 424 S. Main Street, which sold and serviced pinball and jukebox machines. Beyond Canipe's was a mostly vacant lot that was partially paved and served as a parking lot for Fire Station No. 2 (also referred to as the Butler Street Fire Station). Behind all of it stretched the Lorraine Hotel (older section) and Motel (newer section, where Dr. King's Room 306 was located). In between the two were unkempt, overgrown brushy areas on both sides along Mulberry Street.

When James returned, the two strangers he had seen before were gone, but Raul was there. Raul told him to rent a room in the flophouse upstairs and kill some time because his business with the gunrunners might take a little longer than expected. James did that, choosing, rather arbitrarily, one out of the two rooms offered to him, as if either would do, although he preferred the second, cheaper one because the first one included a kitchenette, which he didn't need. He had not indicated to Ms. Brewer that he had an interest in a "room with a view."

Most of the fiction writers attempt to show that he picked that room because it had a direct view of King's balcony; however, this point will be disproven. How he would have known that King was even staying at the Lorraine—more important, which room he was staying in—remains a mystery. It was this premise that some of the early authors used as the basis for some of the most reckless assertions of Ray's supposed stalking of Dr. King.

Huie began this canard in his original work of fiction, intimating that every room had the common "characteristic that proved fatal to Dr. King," that when going in or out of any door, the guest would be in "full view" of anyone looking out the windows of the building in back.[478] That was potentially true only of those along the portion of the Lorraine's second floor for rooms with balconies, but it was also possible to obtain a room (as had originally been reserved for King) in the interior of the building, without such a balcony, or on the lower floor, under the balconies. Only the MPD and FBI informants knew that Dr. King's room reservation would be changed at the last minute, from the second-floor interior to Room 306. Moreover, as noted earlier, the HSCA would state in its report that "room 306, [was] the only room to which a marksman in the rooming-house bathroom would have had an unobstructed view."[479]

Huie noted that the rooms along the back of the rooming house were already rented when Ray arrived, despite the fact that there was no indication in the record (Bessie Brewer's testimony) that Ray had even asked for one of those rooms. Ray introduced himself as "John Willard" to Bessie Brewer and merely said he wanted a room, and Mrs. Brewer showed him two, according to her statement as quoted by a reporter with the Memphis *Commercial Appeal*:

> I showed him Room 8 [in the front part of the building], a $10-a-week kitchenette, but he said, "I only want a sleeping room." I showed him Room 5 and he said, "This will be fine." We went back to the office . . . and I wrote him out a receipt. He paid with a $20.00 bill . . . He spoke like any other Memphian.[480]

Harold Weisberg, who worked with Ray's legal team and became a "friend" to him, pointedly observed that Ray did not speak "like any other Memphian" because Ray had no southern accent, that he was from the north. But the meme about him being a southern racist had quickly become the standard buzzword among journalists of the era, clearly because it was dyed into the fabric of most news stories; it was repeated so often that it became the accepted shorthand to succinctly explain the whole story. It was part and parcel of the plot that began well before the assassination, when Ray's handler, Raul, directed him to get rid of his old Plymouth (which he gave to one of his brothers in Chicago), then take a train to Birmingham and buy a newer car there; obtaining an apartment there would also establish an official residence, needed to support an address for his new Alabama driver's license. It was all part of the cunning plan designed to begin typecasting him.

Ray acceded to Raul very hesitatingly; after all, going to Canada in the first place was for the purpose of gaining more distance from US police and the FBI, and he had vowed to himself that he would never return to the US.

By capitulating to Raul's request, he set himself up to acquire a Birmingham address and drive a newer Mustang equipped with Alabama license plates. It was plenty enough for the eventual fiction writers to depict him forever as a southerner who had the stereotypical mid-1960s attitudes of a fortyish white man from Birmingham. That it worked, and continues to into the twenty-first century, is undeniable.

Gerold Frank, in his 1972 book meant to reinforce Huie's original story, stated that by merely driving down Mulberry Street, on his right side, "he would see all the motel rooms, ground and balcony level. To his left, he would see the rear windows of buildings on South Main Street. He had only to drive around to the front of these buildings" to find the sign for the rooms-for-rent. Then, as if to prove he had never been there, and didn't know that there were many other rooms at the Lorraine that could *not* be seen from that view, he summarily dismissed all the "talk that King had been deliberately assigned a motel room facing the bathroom window of 422 ½ South Main Street."[481]

Huie stated that Ray watched for Dr. King to emerge onto the balcony from his Room 5, on the north side of the building. That window looked out to another building (about four to five feet away), which would have impeded his rearward view of the balcony of King's room. Then Huie asserted that "I sat in this window: the fatal shot could have been fired from it."[482] If that were true, it would seem that Ray (as Huie alleged him to be the shooter) would have stayed there to fire the shot, rather than—as he was purported to have done—going into the shared bathroom. Four decades after Huie's book, Hampton Sides expanded on the lie, stating that Ray (whom he referred to throughout most of the book as "Galt" for literary effect) liked the view from room 5: "with just a glance he could see the Lorraine Motel through the smudged windowpanes."[483]

But what authors Huie, Frank, McMillan, Posner, and Sides said must be reconciled with what first-generation researcher Harold Weisberg, who inspected that room in 1969, stated, that "it is obvious the window of Room 5-B faces onto the narrow areaway between the two parts of the rooming house. To see any part of the motel at all is 'awkward' in the least. This room is far from the back end of the building; the passageway is narrow . . . this room *does not give a view of the King room*."[484] (Italics in original.) Weisberg did acknowledge that, by leaning out of the window, one could see some of the hotel.[485] I visited the old Lorraine Motel in 2017, which is now the home of the National Civil Rights Museum, and can state that Sides's comment is not accurate. The only way the motel could be seen from that room would be to lean out of the window far enough to have one's head and shoulders completely outside of the window, which is set at least 6" from the exterior wall surface.

It was because of this fact that the original plotters, thus Huie, had to use the canard of a shot from the bathroom, instead of Ray's room as the supposed sniper's lair, to connect him to the shooting. But the real shot did not come from either of these rooms—it was made from the brushy area in back of the building, which someone decided early the next morning had to be cleaned up, immediately destroying the crime scene. That area today is a very well-groomed lawn, in contrast to a 1968 photo taken just before the brush was cleared.

These distortions and inconsistencies, originally created by Huie, should be considered as some of the most obvious, clearly contrived examples of the series of outrageous lies originally presented by him and subsequently repeated (and usually further amped up) by the numerous other authors and later investigators. This point alone should be sufficient to force the case to be reopened for a complete and honest reinvestigation, since both the original 1968 FBI investigation and the HSCA inquiry a decade later relied on that book to perform their own faulty "studies."

James Earl Ray as the Unlikely Sharpshooter

On April 4, 1968, in Ray's room at Bessie Brewer's rooming house in Memphis—having only purportedly fired the gun a few times on a country road outside Corinth, Mississippi, en route to Memphis on April 1 or 2, to merely try it out—Ray had allegedly prepared to use it, though he had never taken the time to sight-in the rifle scope,[486] an essential act for firing accuracy. Ray allegedly then proceeded to load the Remington GameMaster, with one bullet cartridge, and *only* one, before taking his shot.

To illustrate how the myths were extended by the 2010 novelette previously referenced by Hampton Sides, he described how filthy the bathroom was, down to the streaks in the toilet and the "scuzzy" bathtub with a knot of hair plugging the drain—no detail too irrelevant to include in the watercolor portrait he set out to paint, even noting that the walls had long ago been painted the "color of a robin's egg." To set the stage for that purported but nearly impossible act, we will quote from the prattling narrative of Mr. Sides's book, apparently written for people who prefer to read only the most effusive forms of syrupy novels, to illustrate the point that fiction writers should really stay within their natural genre:

> Squinting through the Redfield scope, he found King, still standing there on the Lorraine balcony . . . . A television murmured somewhere down the hall; a ventilation fan thumped

in a nearby window. The smell of charred burgers tendriled up from Jim's Grill, where happy-hour Budweiser was flowing and intense games of barroom shuffleboard were in session.[487]

What Sides left out in that otherwise highly detailed, factitious narrative was how Ray, supposedly sitting with a rifle in a public bathroom shared by other roomers who might try to burst in on him at any time, might have known whether, and when, Dr. King would even show up on that balcony. How would he—while being simultaneously portrayed as a lone-nut vagabond who had just arrived in town the very day he had supposedly planned for weeks for the dastardly deed—have even known that King was staying in that motel, much less the room number, and where that room was from the outside, as distinct from all the other adjacent rooms? Had he really been the crazed killer he was accused of being, one would expect that he would have shown up in Memphis several days earlier and secured a better room with a clear line of sight to the balcony; but then, he would still have to have been clairvoyant to know where King's room was located.

Whether unintentionally or not, all of the billowy language in Hampton Sides's description of the purported sniper's nest fails to describe how difficult it would have been for any shooter—much less an inexperienced one (having only allegedly shot a few practice rounds with his brand-new rifle) who had never had the inclination to become an expert sharpshooter—to aim a long-range rifle from that very small, cramped bathroom and accurately hit a target 206 feet away with a mounted telescope that had never been sighted. To better explain that, we have included a summary of how one of the earliest real researchers, Harold Weisberg, described it:

> [One of the prosecutors, Assistant Attorney General James W.] Beasley was . . . careful to avoid description of the bathtub and the window. [In a photo published by the French magazine *Paris-Match* on April 20, 1968] we see that both the tub and the window are as close to the north wall as possible . . . This picture makes it apparent the last thing the assassin could have done was to use that rifle in the required trajectory and rest it on the windowsill. The posed man could not stand in the tub, the sloping back keeping him too far away from the window, so he stood on the rim in the back. This raised him too high, and the wall kept him from the end of the window, away from King. It was then impossible for him even to contort himself into a position which would enable him to use the rifle at all. He had

to get his head almost on its right ear even to see the sights . . . And unless, after the murder, when the tub should have been under police guard, it was traversed like Grand Central Station, the visible marks on it are so numerous—all over it—they cast doubt on any meaning the prosecution could have attributed to them and on the honesty of any effort to do so.[488]

Diagram of Bessie Brewer's Rooming House

Miscellaneous Material

"A report of a second Mustang (B) added a new angle yesterday to investigation of the slaying of Dr. Martin Luther King, Jr. Earlier theories had indicated that a man being sought in the murder entered a flight of stairs at 422½ South Main, went to the second floor where he rented a room (line of black dots) and crossed a passageway to 418½ South Main to Room 5. Sometime before 6 pm the night of the murder, it is believed that he went to the bathroom of the rooming house and from the window of that room shot Dr. King as he stood on the second floor balcony of the Lorraine Motel in front of Room 306. He then went out the hallway (broken line) and down steps between the two buildings. Reports indicate the same man dropped a rifle and a suitcase in front of the Canipe Amusement Co. at 424 South Main (cross). The second Mustang reportedly bearing Arkansas license plates, was seen leaving shortly after 6:01 pm. Customers in Jim's Grill at 418 South Main said the other Mustang (A) was seen leaving the area about 6:15 pm."

The drawing (by John Jacobs) is from *The Commercial-Appeal* (Memphis, Tennessee), Thursday, April 11, 1968. The explanatory material appeared under the picture.

Diagram of Crime Scene

An Official Story: Lies Piled upon Lies

The point of this trip deep into the weeds—in this case, the tiny, dirty bathroom in the rooming house—is to illustrate how the prosecution, and the numerous credulous authors who readily accepted the unlikely notion, created a story based on an outline designed by the FBI from the start. Even as recently as the Sides book, that fable has grown further, morphing finally into an overwrought yarn untethered to reality. Meanwhile, the more critically minded, plain-speaking researchers and authors, who have attempted to ferret out the real truth, must spend (as proven by this very paragraph) considerable time deconstructing the untruths with explanations of all the reasons that the official story was and still is a fabrication.

Huie, the first of the fiction writers who set the paradigm, stated that "The *Memphis Commercial Appeal* of the morning of April 4 [reported] that Dr. King was at the Lorraine Motel." [489] However, as John Avery Emison established, that edition of the paper only stated that he was *"eating lunch at the Lorraine Hotel"* and that no room number was included. He also established that before the assassination, *"there was no mention in any paper where King was staying."* [490] (Emphasis added.) Moreover, he also determined that the *Memphis Press-Scimitar*, on the *afternoon* of April 4, did note that King had stayed at the Lorraine the previous day (*but had not included his room number*), yet by the time that story was published in this evening paper, Ray had already rented his room at Bessie Brewer's rooming house. [491]

Gerald Posner took Huie's inaccurate account and added more errors to it when he incorrectly stated: "Ray knew that King was at the Lorraine from either television or radio news on the night of April 3 *or the front-page photograph* in the *Commercial Appeal* on the morning of April 4." [492] The lie was further repeated, and egregiously compounded, by Hampton Sides—citing Posner as the source—in his own fictional account, when he stated that Ray saw in the morning copy of the Memphis *Commercial Appeal* a front-page photograph of "King *standing in front of room 306* at the Lorraine." [493] (Emphasis added.) The only thing true about any of this was that there was a front-page article titled "King Challenges Court Restraint, Vows to March." But the only mention of the Lorraine Motel in the article was the statement that the US marshals who took the judge's restraining order to him found Dr. King with several of his associates having lunch there; there was nothing about his having stayed overnight or a plan to be there the next night. And there was *no* photograph of Martin Luther King Jr. anywhere on that page (or any other page within that newspaper), as the following photograph of the front page shows.

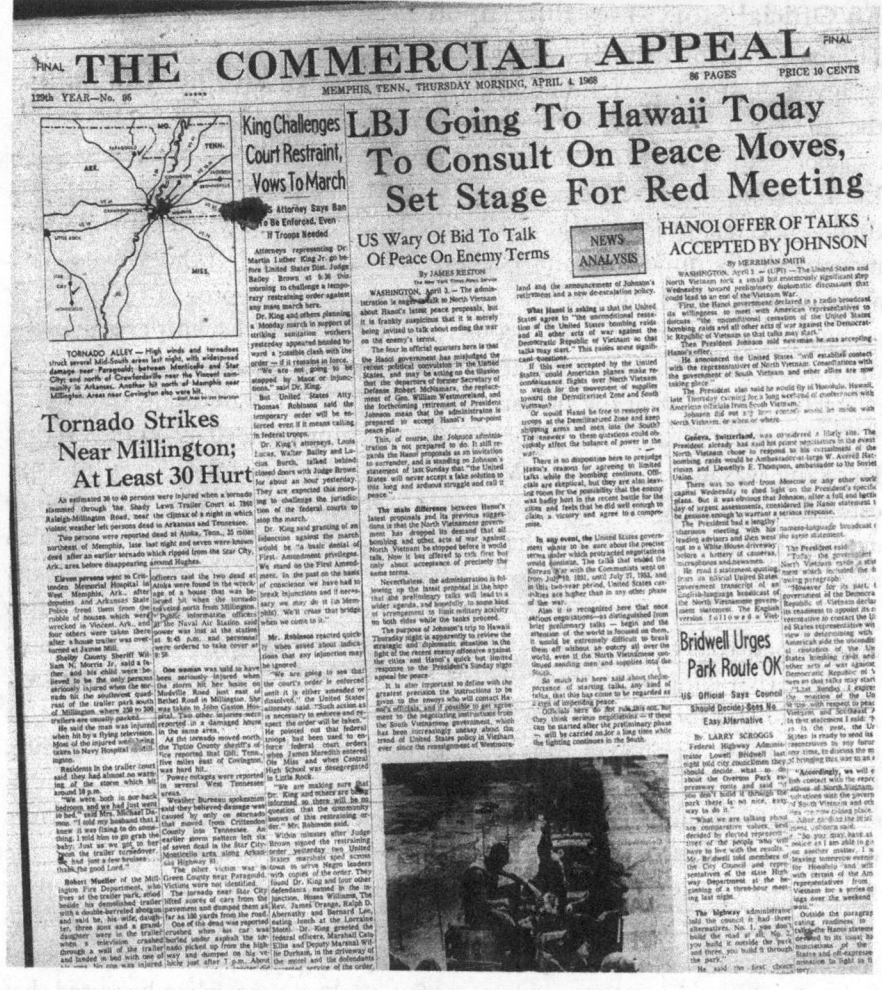

Memphis *Commercial Appeal* April 4, 1968.

Sides probably picked that untruth from Gerold Frank's book, which stated—with no proof or any citations to the assertion—that photographers had taken a picture of Dr. King on the balcony, standing in front of the door to his room, "with the numerals 306 showing behind him."[494] But that photo was never published anywhere before King was assassinated.

These writers of fiction were at the top of their game when they ventured into the nonfiction book market and went to this length—of inserting a series of unsupported assertions or flat-out lies into their books for posterity—to convince the public that James Earl Ray was the stalker/murderer that they

King Challenges Court Restraint, Vows To March

...S Attorney Says Ban To Be Enforced, Even If Troops Needed

Attorneys representing Dr. Martin Luther King Jr. go before United States Dist. Judge Bailey Brown at 9:30 this morning to challenge a temporary restraining order against any mass march here.

Dr. King and others planning a Monday march in support of striking sanitation workers yesterday appeared headed toward a possible clash with the order — if it remains in force.

"We are not going to be stopped by Mace or injunctions," said Dr. King.

But United States Atty. Thomas Robinson said the temporary order will be enforced even if it means calling in federal troops.

Dr. King's attorneys, Louis Lucas, Walter Bailey and Lucius Burch, talked behind closed doors with Judge Brown for about an hour yesterday. They are expected this morning to challenge the jurisdiction of the federal courts to stop the march.

Dr. King said granting of an injunction against the march would be "a basic denial of First Amendment privileges. We stand on the First Amendment. In the past on the basis of conscience we have had to break injunctions and if necessary we may do it (in Memphis). We'll cross that bridge when we come to it."

But United States Atty. Thomas Robinson said the temporary order will be enforced even if it means calling federal troops.

Dr. King's attorneys, Louis Lucas, Walter Bailey and Lucius Burch, talked behind closed doors with Judge Brown for about an hour yesterday. They are expected this morning to challenge the jurisdiction of the federal courts to stop the march.

Dr. King said granting of an injunction against the march would be "a basic denial of First Amendment privileges. We stand on the First Amendment. In the past on the basis of conscience we have had to break injunctions and if necessary we may do it (in Memphis). We'll cross that bridge when we come to it."

Mr. Robinson reacted quickly when asked about indications that any injunction may be ignored.

"We are going to see that the court's order is enforced until it is either amended or dissolved," the United States attorney said. "Such action as is necessary to enforce and respect the order will be taken." He pointed out that federal troops had been used to enforce federal court orders when James Meredith entered Ole Miss and when Central High School was desegregated in Little Rock.

"We are making sure that Dr. King and others are being informed so there will be no question that the community knows of this restraining order," Mr. Robinson said.

Within minutes after Judge Brown signed the restraining order yesterday two United States marshals sped across town to serve Negro leaders with copies of the order. They found Dr. King and four other defendants named in the injunction, Hosea Williams, The Rev. James Orange, Ralph D. Abernathy and Bernard Lee, eating lunch at the Lorraine Motel. Dr. King greeted the federal officers, Marshall Cato Ellis and Deputy Marshal Willie Durham, in the driveway of the motel and the defendants accepted service of the order.

News Article regarding Dr. King's Receipt of Court Ruling

claimed he was. But just for the sake of argument, and assuming for a half-moment that there was a scintilla of truth to the possibility that Ray was clairvoyant, and had seen an ephemeral broadcast of a photo that no one else saw, which told him King's room number, such a stalking premise still fails the smell test because the fictional scenario rests ultimately on a number of other weak assumptions:

- The first of these started with the preposterous assertion by Huie that somehow Ray, the former "nice guy," as he himself inadvertently established, according to a number of people who got to know him intimately, somehow later transformed—albeit ironically and unwittingly—into a stone-cold killer. Huie was told point-blank by a number of people he interviewed that they had found Ray to be likable, submissive, tolerant of others. Huie had to have been sent on a mission to turn those descriptions upside down to write the opposite, characterizing him as a violent, horrid racist with no redeeming virtues.

- Ray then, having morphed himself so completely, also acted on a suddenly acquired need for worldwide recognition, a trait that no one who knew him had ever seen before, which then suddenly manifested into a devious plan to begin stalking Dr. King. Unfortunately, as we previously demonstrated, that premise was based upon another series of untruthful statements based upon no concrete evidence, only deceitful statements by a succession of fiction writers.

- According to the various versions of the official story, James Earl Ray then decided, five days before his murderous act, to acquire a new rifle. But a day later he changed his mind and determined that it wasn't what he needed and exchanged it for another one for inexplicable reasons that even he could not describe to the gun salesman who sold him both guns, other than the preposterous story about bigger deer.

- Then he practiced, but only once, on how to shoot his new rifle, despite never having sighted in the telescope,[495] a task that only an experienced shooter could approximate manually and would require a specially designed machine to do accurately.

- The fiction writers have portrayed Ray as an exceptionally fast learner of guns and the associated sharpshooting skills: as Gerold Frank divined that story, having found a "glen" off the highway on his way to Memphis, as previously noted, he wrote that Ray "was obviously trying his skill at various distances on such objects as tree branches, leaves, and rocks. Then he returned to his car, packed his rifle in its box, drove back to Highway 78, and continued toward Memphis."[496] Obviously, Mr. Frank was no sharpshooter himself, as evidenced by his apparent conclusion that that experience would have been sufficient to so qualify Ray as one—extending the benefit of a doubt that it had even occurred.

- Supposedly, after firing the gun on that single occasion—in a field, at "tree branches, leaves and rocks"—without having done so in a shooting gallery, using a standard target annotated with specific measured distances from which he could analyze the results, Ray had mystically acquired the skillset of a great sharpshooter (the real shooter, and his backups, would have already had the expertise to begin with but would nonetheless spend the entire previous day— or days—at a practice range firing hundreds of rounds as he [they] worked to master that skill on the chosen weapon).

- With that single purported experience of firing his brand-new rifle with its "fixed telescopic sight" that had never been properly installed, he would then set out to kill Dr. King, so confident of his newly acquired skill that he only loaded it with a single bullet, when he could have loaded five.[497]
- After going to Memphis, a city he had never been to (apparently after having seen a "vision" of King standing before Room 306 of the Lorraine), he quickly cased the location on the very same day that he had chosen for his hit.
- Finally, seeing the windows of the rooming house opposite Mulberry Street from the Lorraine Motel, he then drove around the block and entered Bessie Brewer's rooming house, requesting, according to these authors, a "room with a view" of the Lorraine.

Clearly, this ridiculous story, as originally told by fiction writers in collaboration with officials in the FBI headquarters, was constructed on a foundation of outright lies and then repeated and expanded, from one book to the next. One of the best examples of that is the fact that Hampton Sides asserted that "Galt"* watched the balcony in front of Room 306, with the binoculars he had just purchased, from his own Room 5-B in the rooming house, clearly a very difficult if not impossible task; at best, he would have had to lean out the window so far that he would risk being spotted by the many men then moving about the parking lot and motel balconies, as demonstrated by the photos, diagrams, and Weisberg's narrative noted above.

Yet Hampton Sides piled on again, now incorrectly describing the view from Room 5-B as having a "mostly unobstructed view of the Lorraine . . . the same balcony where King stood in the photo Galt had seen in the *Commercial Appeal*,"[498] doubling down on the same demonstrable lie examined above.

---

* Sides had taken a partial cue from Gerold Frank, whose book also referred to Ray using his aliases, but instead of sticking with the same one throughout most of the narrative, he switched them up based upon the last one used. When he was in Birmingham, he was "Lowmeyer," then he reverted to "Galt" again, then "Willard" after registering at Bessie Brewer's flophouse, then he became "Galt" yet again, adding to the confusion already present in that book.

What Really Happened? The More Plausible Story Summarized

Dr. William F. Pepper's 2016 book *The Plot to Kill King*, referenced throughout these pages, lays out in considerable detail, within its Chapter 22, the complete, reconstructed factual account of what his forty-plus years of research has proven to have occurred on April 4 in Memphis, and the related events in the days leading up to and following Dr. King's murder. His account, based upon his unique and peerless lifetime work, should be considered the last word on the matter.

It should therefore be understood that any attempt to summarize it will necessarily lack the depth of his monumental research toward resolving the case with finality. Our mission, on the other hand, is simply to expand and reframe his work—and those of the numerous other researchers and authors who have also made great contributions—to solving the mystery left by the original plotters. It requires that the massive details found in all of the *legitimate* books, newspapers, and public records be sorted, collated, distilled, and summarized in a way that allows an average reader to easily understand the complexities of a very sophisticated plot.

In that context, what follows next is this author's interpretation of what really happened in Memphis fifty years ago during the period after 4:00 p.m. on April 4, 1968. Citations, therefore, are sparingly used to denote only those facts that appear in sources not otherwise previously referenced.

Examining the Government's Belief that Ray Threw Down the Gun with Other Belongings in Front of Canipe's Amusement Company Doorway

James Earl Ray claimed that he last saw the Remington GameMaster pump-action rifle when Raul took it with him on the morning of April 4, under the pretext of showing it to the "gun buyers" whom he was to meet in downtown Memphis. By then, of course, it had Ray's fingerprints on it and they would become the most important piece of evidence against him, irrespective of whether there was any real proof that he had shot it that day; which of course he always maintained he didn't.

Over time, two disparate, mutually exclusive, fundamentally conflicting stories developed about how the murder of Dr. King occurred. The single compatible point of them was that Martin Luther King Jr. was hit in the right side of his jaw with a bullet fired from a rifle at 6:01 p.m. on April 4, 1968, as he stood on the balcony in front of his Room 306 of the Lorraine Motel in Memphis, Tennessee.

Those stories can be summarized thusly:

- The official story adopted by the Memphis Police Department, the FBI, the Justice Department, and various judges whose opinions were derived therefrom was that the shooter was James Earl Ray and the shot came from the bathroom window in the back of the rooming house across Mulberry Street, where Ray had rented a room just hours before. The only witness who allegedly saw Ray within those premises at the time was one Charles Quitman Stephens, who became the star witness for the prosecution, but whose veracity as a competent witness was less than stellar, as we will examine further. The primary evidence for Ray's guilt was a bundle, consisting of a green bedspread wrapped around a blue briefcase (containing extra ammunition, the binoculars purchased earlier that day, and Ray's transistor radio, with his prisoner number conveniently engraved on its back) and a box containing a rifle, with Ray's fingerprints on some of the articles, including the rifle. That bundle had been dropped in front of the doorway leading into a store called Canipe's Amusement Company, owned by Mr. Guy Canipe. However, Mr. Canipe told Ray's original lawyer, Arthur Hanes, that the bundle had been dropped there about ten minutes before the shot was fired.[499]

- The alternative story, fleshed out incrementally by a number of independent researchers, was developed one piece at a time to explain the numerous gaps and anomalies left by the government's cobbled rendition. In large part, Dr. Pepper's magnum opus *The Plot to Kill King* is a consolidation of much of that as well as his own decades-long work of discovery. It includes the testimonies of many more credible witnesses, whose statements are consistent with those of others, all of which are more realistic than that of Charles Quitman Stephens, the one eyewitness proffered by the officials. In its most basic essentials, the shot came not from the rooming-house window, but from within the brushy back lot of the row of buildings across Mulberry Street, specifically that portion of lot directly behind Jim's Grill, as several eyewitnesses would testify. Several of them stated that they saw the aftereffects of the shot moments later: two men had positioned themselves there, one the shooter and the other a man given the responsibility of taking the rifle from the shooter as he made his escape. The other man then carried it to the back door of Jim's Grill, passing it on to grill owner Loyd Jowers. While Jowers denied his involvement for many years, he eventually came forward to tell about how he had participated in the murder of Dr. King.

In the pages to follow—and throughout the remaining chapters—elements of both versions will be examined in some detail, but in pieces at a time, to make the story more readable and understandable and less intimidating. The fullness of the overall story will thus become revealed piece by piece and fit into a mosaic that will be complete by the final chapters.

Which Account is More Believable? Evaluating the Merits

The original story—complete with blemishes that should have been obvious from the start—would be repeated again and again in the books written by the fiction writers as well as news articles in the mainstream press, all written for the purpose of supporting the government's fabrications.

One of those appeared in April 2013 in an award-winning article, "Six:01," by Marc Perrusquia in a special edition of the Memphis *Commercial Appeal*, complete with "facts" taken from the Sides book. That article stated that "*Room 5-B, with a window looking out the back of the rooming house onto the Lorraine Motel . . .*" was rented by James Earl Ray.[500] In another section of the article, the point is repeated: "*A second-story room on the back gives him a clear view of the Lorraine.*"[501] (Emphasis added in both sentences.)

Clearly, the reliance of numerous authors on the "facts" presented by the earliest prevaricator (Huie) and embellished with more deceptions by each of the successors has contaminated the truth so completely that even those who aspire to correct the record often repeat those same mistakes, some of which are critical to the story, while others are seemingly innocuous.[502] It is especially troubling in the Perrusquia article, since as a reporter for the Memphis newspaper, he presumably could have determined that the description he used was incorrect simply by visiting the building site, as demonstrated multiple times above.

Finally, according to Sides, Dr. King came out onto the balcony at about 5:55 p.m. Then, despite having such a purportedly perfect view, Sides at least acknowledged that Ray would have to lean out the windowsill to fire the rifle.[503] But then he stated that Ray ("Galt") ran down to the bathroom to check the view from there and then ran back to his room to grab the rifle (and his other belongings) before returning to the bathroom to fire the only bullet he loaded into the gun. Sides explained that Ray apparently was in a hurry to take his shot because he only loaded the gun with one bullet; otherwise, he would have put more bullets in the clip—a rather odd explanation for a man long obsessed with killing his target, which would make his task much riskier than it needed to be.[504] After making that astonishingly accurate shot with a gun he barely knew—equipped with a misaligned scope—he then purportedly put the rifle back in its box, bundled it up with other items within the bedcover, and quickly ran from the building and then down the street to the front of Canipe's storefront, where he tossed all of it down, a complete and convenient bundle full of incriminating evidence, seemingly guaranteed to be quickly discovered.

If that scenario were true, one might ask, "Why wouldn't he have just taken the rifle and bundle with him, and tossed them into the Mustang before taking off to make his escape?" Because then, according to Huie, he might never be found and thus never achieve his goal to make the FBI's Ten Most Wanted list. But if that were his primary intention, why would Ray have bothered to take the bundle of evidence out of the rooming house in the first place? If that notoriety was his intended goal, he could have saved himself the trouble and just left it there in the bathroom or his Room 5-B, where it would have inevitably produced the same result.

A more likely answer to that puzzle (one that would also explain Mr. Canipe's claim that the bundle was dropped even before the shot was fired) was that it was Raul who took the bundle there but then discovered that Ray had taken off in the Mustang fifteen minutes before the shooting. Raul had probably intended to put it into the car's trunk as incriminating evidence guaranteed to link Ray to the crime—whether or not Ray made his escape or was shot on his way out, either by the policeman assigned that task or the backup shooter noted elsewhere.

Another reason required by the official story is that its premise was based on only one Mustang, and it had supposedly been parked approximately sixty feet south of Canipe's. That was required by the official story, to explain why Ray allegedly dropped the bundle in the doorway before reaching his car, when he purportedly saw a MPD TAC (Tactical Area Cruisers) Unit station wagon in the parking lot just beyond Canipe's, panicked, and dropped the bundle in the doorway before proceeding on to the Mustang. But that explanation does not take into account that there had been (until 5:45 p.m.) two white Mustangs parked along that block, one just south of Canipe's (with Arkansas red-on-white plates)[505] and James's car (with Alabama white-on-red plates). Ray's car had earlier been parked directly in front of Jim's Grill until he left at 5:45 p.m. and never returned, because the streets were blocked by police when he attempted to do that.[506]

A witness, Charles Hurley, distinctly remembered seeing a white Mustang parked there (south of Canipe's) and consistently stated that it had Arkansas license plates.[507] But ignoring his repeated claims, the fiction writers would write it off as mere confusion on his part because the plate designs were so similar. Gerold Frank, for one, wrote simply that "[Hurley] was to remember it as an Arkansas plate, because Arkansas, like Alabama, had red and white plates."[508] Unfortunately, this is only one specific instance of how the facts have been twisted: readers were (and are still) supposed to believe that "red on white" and "white on red" are "similar," rather than what they really are: opposite. Of course, in each case, the name of the state would also serve to clarify the point, especially for a man observing the tag from his car parked for several minutes directly behind the Mustang. Moreover, unlike the Arkansas tags, which had at least two alphabetic characters, the Alabama tags were all numeric (Ray's tag number was 1–38993).[509] The official story is only true in relation to the fact that there really was only one Mustang on the scene at 6:01 p.m., and it was parked about sixty feet south of Canipe's—but it wasn't James Earl Ray's.

A tactical team of twelve Memphis police officers and county detectives had been ensconced at the Butler Street Fire Department (a.k.a. Fire Station No. 2), and another Memphis police officer was also there conducting surveillance on Dr. King and his party. After the shooting, those officers quickly converged on the scene, both at the Lorraine Motel on Mulberry Street (which required them to cross the parking lot and jump down from the top of the retaining wall to the street) and the buildings facing Main Street, both of which were visible from the fire station. Those officers were there within about a minute of the shot. The fact that none of them saw James, or anyone else, run out of the rooming house and drop the bundle suggests that Mr. Canipe was correct about the bundle being placed there even before the shot was fired. In the process, some of the officers quickly located that bundle in front of Canipe's Amusement Store, which included a 30.06 hunting rifle with one spent cartridge casing in its chamber, with a mounted rifle scope and a partial box of unfired ammunition.

To change the subject, and add a little more bravado to his own legend, Huie segued out of that scenario and proceeded to claim that he had acquired a rifle and scope of the same model as Ray's and proceeded to fire ten shots into a two-inch circle from the same distance as Ray's shot and, to add emphasis to the ease with which this could be done, averred that a preteen boy could have done the same.[510] But what Huie conveniently avoided mentioning was that he would have undoubtedly taken the time to have the telescope sighted in, and he was not standing in an antique bathtub, trying to balance himself at the sloped end of it and twisting himself into a window firing sideways at a target that he had only one bullet to hit, using a rifle with which he had not become familiar.

Which Witness is More Credible: Charles Quitman Stephens or Loyd Jowers?

Charlie Stephens was the only person to place James Earl Ray at the scene, stating that he "heard the shot coming apparently through this wall from the bathroom" and then "got up, went through [his] room out into the corridor in time to see the left profile of the Defendant as he turned down this passageway." As Harold Weisberg noted, Stephens's affidavit was first used in the extradition hearing from England, and his statement said that the profile "was very much like the man he had seen," which was not exactly an unequivocal statement that he was in fact the same man. [511]

Moreover, according to Weisberg, Stephens "was a well-known drunk," and in the period immediately after the murder, he "was picked up by the police twice for public drunkenness." Charles Stephens lived with his common-law wife Grace Walden Stephens in the room next to the one Ray rented in the rooming house. Grace Stephens was quoted as saying that Charlie was so "drunk [he] saw nothing" but that she saw a man running down the hallway who "wore an Army jacket and was much shorter and lighter than Ray, weighing no more than 125 pounds" (a description that was a much closer match to the description of Raul). Evidently, that was among the several other contradictory statements made by Grace that the police and FBI could not let into the public's awareness, so they put both Charlie and Grace under close surveillance in the immediate aftermath, even escorting them around Memphis.

On June 28, 1968, the *Washington Post* reported a UPI article under the headline "3 Witnesses Against Ray Vanish From Memphis." [512] Charlie Stephens, the rooming-house manager Bessie Brewer, and another occupant-witness, Willie Anchutz, were all reported to have "dropped from sight and may be in protective custody." Both Frank Holloman, the fire and police director, and FBI Special Agent Robert Jennings refused to comment on where they were. Moreover, it was reported: "A fourth witness has been confined to a mental hospital, authoritative sources said. The witness was not identified." [513]

It was later revealed that the Memphis police had taken Grace Walden Stephens to the John Gaston Hospital to have a leg injury looked at, but while she was there, a psychiatrist had appeared unannounced and decided her problem was of a mental nature. On July 31, she was taken before a Memphis probate judge, Harry Pierotti, who declared her mentally incompetent and had her committed to Western State Psychiatric Hospital in Bolivar, Tennessee, essentially rendering her testimony ever after meaningless. Mark Lane discovered that a series of illegal actions by the police and hospital administrators was the basis of her confinement and that the real reason, according to her attorney, C. M. Murphy, was "to safeguard their case against Ray," meaning that it was all about forcibly preventing exculpatory evidence that would point to Ray's innocence. After spending *over ten years* there, Lane eventually obtained her release with the assistance of Reverend James Lawson. [514]

But Charlie Stephens's condition on April 4 was far worse than simply being a little drunk, as Dr. Pepper later discovered from other witnesses. A taxi driver whom Stephens had called to pick him up, James McCraw, arrived there a few minutes before 6:00 p.m. and found that Stephens was so drunk at that point that he had actually passed out. McCraw refused to carry him anywhere in his cab. Moreover, McCraw stated that when he walked by the bathroom he noticed the bathroom door open, the light on, and the fact that it was then empty.[515]

The lead homicide detective of the Memphis Police Department, Thomas H. Smith, would later testify under oath at the 1999 *King v. Jowers* trial that shortly after the murder of Dr. King, he questioned Mr. Stephens and found that "he had been drinking heavily." Detective Smith further stated that he had been aware of the fact that Stephens had later made statements that had been used in the hearing on Ray's extradition from London and in the legal case put together by the state prosecutors against him, but those statements were not the ones he had put into the record. When asked whether Stephens would have been capable of making an identification of James Earl Ray, his response was: "No sir. No way . . . I don't think he could. I didn't think enough of his statement that I took to take him downstairs, downtown and take a formal statement from him and so put it in my arrest report that he was intoxicated to the point there was no sense in bringing him downtown." When asked if he knew whether his report was included in the final MPD report of the investigation, he volunteered the information that, before he had a chance to read that report, MPD chief John Moore took the copy of the final report from him and never returned it.[516]

These points were either minimized or completely evaded by the fiction writers. For example, in Gerold Frank's case, he portrayed Stephens as a very alert and reliable witness, one who had not missed a sound—*even the absence of sound*—from the bathroom next door. He stated that Stephens was even aware of the fact that, despite the purported nearly constant presence of his new neighbor in the bathroom, the toilet had never been flushed.[517] Not to put too fine a point on it, but this level of divergence from what credible witnesses reported to impartial and authentic researchers and authors—compared to those on an obvious, preestablished mission—could not be more stark. That the consistent use of their work product was subsequently referenced by other authors, and used by government investigators, in lieu of the works by the truth-seeking journalists and researchers should by now be just as conspicuous.

Contrasted to Stephens—the prosecution's star witness—it must be acknowledged that some of the other witnesses supporting the alternate scenario were also not above reproach; however, the degree of difference and the rationale for that is another matter. An analogy used by the witness Ron Tyler Adkins is useful here to put this point into perspective: "If you get into bed with those snakes . . . you got to snuggle up to work with them."[518] That simply meant that the witnesses to be used were not selected from groups of followers of either Mahatma Gandhi or the new saint, Mother Teresa. They were generally people who were, either directly or indirectly, connected to the criminals involved in this treacherous plot—men and women who happened to have intimate knowledge of many details related to the murder of Dr. Martin Luther King Jr.

In other words, to use a common maxim, you have to play the hand you're dealt. But in witness Ron Adkins's case, the analogy was actually used in the context of the "snakes" being the Feds with whom they (the local Dixie Mafia thugs, certain state and Memphis officials including the mayor, the director of the police and fire departments, certain police officers, highway patrol officers, paid FBI informers, and agents) had conspired with, specifically, J. Edgar Hoover and Clyde Tolson: "He [Russell Adkins] knew the 'Feds' were using him. He knew they were getting him to work with the Libertos and the likes of Holloman . . ."[519] Some of these people had lived their lives one paycheck to the next, always scraping by. When offered great sums of money to perform relatively minor tasks, especially those who were kept in the dark about the full dimensions of the plot, compartmentalized under the precepts of "need to know," it was clearly very tempting for them to participate.

Such was the case with the man who came forward near the end of his life to confess his own involvement after years of denial. For twenty-five years, Loyd Jowers, the owner of the tavern called Jim's Grill—the epicenter for the plot to kill Dr. King—had, for obvious reasons, refused to talk about his real role in the assassination. But when Jowers did confide to his closest personal friend, cabbie James McCraw, about the secrets he tried to keep hidden from the rest of the world, he was not above embellishing his stories with detours into events that were not always entirely accurate.

On December 16, 1993, the ABC television program *Primetime Live* aired a special show on the King assassination in which Loyd Jowers finally admitted to the world that he had been indirectly involved in a conspiracy led by Frank Liberto. He stated that "Liberto had done me a large favor. I owed him a favor." Moreover, he admitted to ABC's Sam Donaldson that Liberto paid him $100,000 for his role and assistance in facilitating the removal and destruction of the rifle that had been used to murder Dr. King. Donaldson, in a voice-over, stated, "*Primetime* has been told there was approximately $100,000 delivered to Jowers in a produce box, but that's not all he received. Jowers says another man came to see him, a man whose name sounded something like Raul." Donaldson asked him about both Raul and Liberto in this exchange: [520]

Jowers: "And he [Raul] looked like he was part Mexican, possibly part Indian, because he didn't have a heavy beard, talked with an accent."

Donaldson: "Did he bring a rifle with him?"

Jowers: "Yes, sir. He brought a rifle in a box."

Donaldson: "What did he ask you to do with this rifle?"

Jowers: "He asked me to hold the rifle until we made—he made arrangements or we made arrangements, one or the other of us, for the killing."

[. . .]

Donaldson: "Did he talk about the police?"

Jowers: "Liberto? Yes, sir."

Donaldson: "What did he say?"

Jowers: "He said they wouldn't be there. Said they wouldn't be there that night."

Donaldson: "Did he say there would be a decoy there?"

Jowers: "Yes, sir. Said he had set it up where it looked like somebody else did the killing?"

Donaldson: "Enter James Earl Ray. Was he part of the conspiracy?"

Jowers: "He was part of it, but I don't believe he knew he was part of it."

Donaldson: "Well, Mr. Jowers, did you find someone to do the killing?"

Jowers: "Yes, sir."

Donaldson: "Why would a person participate in a conspiracy to kill Dr. King?"

Jowers: "A portion of it, naturally, was for money. Any involvement I might have had in it was doing a friend—doing a friend a favor."

Donaldson: "Would it have been because you hated Dr. King?"

Jowers: "No, I didn't hate Dr. King."

Donaldson: "Or hated black people?"

Jowers: "No, sir. It was for a friend, doing a friend a favor that I owed him, a large favor."

Donaldson: "Well, is doing a friend a favor called murder the kind of favor you would do?"

Jowers: "Depends on how good a friend it is and what you owed the friend."[521]

William Hamblin, another taxi driver and good friend and roommate of James McCraw, recounted a story he had been told many times by McCraw—but only when he was intoxicated—about how Loyd Jowers had admitted that he received the "smoking gun" at the back door of his tavern. In fact, Jowers gave McCraw the rifle and told him to get rid of it for him, which he did by tossing it off the Memphis-Arkansas bridge. Hamblin and McCraw lived in an apartment owned by an FBI agent named Purdy, who promptly evicted both of them after the murder. Purdy came into the barbershop where Hamblin also worked, two weeks after the murder, for a haircut by the owner, Vernon Jones. Jones asked Purdy who really killed King and later told Hamblin that Purdy, the FBI agent, had said that it was done by the CIA.[522] A lot of people who seem to suffer from chronic "perseverance deficit" syndrome—never knowing the names of CIA personnel, or even if they know a name, whether it is only a moniker—prefer to leave such questions with that final acronym, "CIA," knowing its implicit finality.

Dr. Pepper acknowledged that there were inconsistencies over time in Loyd Jowers's testimony. However, on balance, the overall story was essentially truthful, and therefore the whole story should not be dismissed entirely. Jowers certainly had legitimate reasons to be circumspect, after all, not the least being the fact of his self-incrimination in a murder, for which there is no statute of limitations; added to that was the lengthy period that had already elapsed, which impeded clear memory; and there was the potential of retaliation by those who preferred that their involvement remain secret. Dr. Pepper therefore used careful professional judgment in stating that Jowers's story—in the whole—was valid, and he denied that Jowers had a motive for anticipating a book or movie deal: "Jowers lost everything. Even his wife left him. There was no book or movie deal, and he was, for the most part, telling the truth."[523] The point his other witness, Ron Adkins, made about being in bed with snakes remains pertinent. To get to the bottom of a fifty-year-old unsolved murder of a national leader, one must carefully cull through all of the evidence and testimony and choose carefully in the selection of only that which is true, exactly what Dr. William F. Pepper has done.

The Real Story of James Earl Ray's Tethered Travels to and within Memphis

After getting lunch and going on an errand to buy binoculars for Raul—as he had been instructed—Ray then went back to the room, where he tossed them on the bed, telling Raul that he would need to get the infrared attachments elsewhere, because the store did not carry them. In his book, Ray wrote that he left the rooming house again at about 4:00 p.m. and went to the grill downstairs for a hamburger, then went for a walk and got an ice cream. Around 5:00 p.m. he returned to the hotel again, finding that Raul was still in the room, but he told Ray that he wanted to meet with the gun buyers alone, suggesting that Ray take in a movie, but to do it on foot since he would be needing the Mustang. Ignoring that request, Ray went back to the Mustang and sat in it as he contemplated what to do next before meeting Raul again later, unaware of the murder agenda he had never known about. Then he suddenly remembered that he needed to get his flat spare tire fixed, thinking that Raul would be even more upset if he did drive it and had another flat tire and no spare.

He stated that he left in the Mustang around 5:45 p.m. and drove a few blocks up the street to a service station to inquire about getting the tire fixed and getting the gasoline tank filled. He stopped briefly at one service station, only to be told that they would not be able to get it done immediately, so he left that one and attempted to have it done elsewhere, again finding that it would have to be left for later repair, so he decided to refill the gas tank and take his chances with the tire until he could have it fixed.[524]

The Missing Witnesses: At the Bottom of an FBI File Drawer for Three Decades

Two witnesses to Ray's driving the car away from its parking spot in front of Jim's Grill came forward shortly thereafter and gave statements to the FBI, which were then promptly hidden away and suppressed for the next several decades. Those witnesses, Ray Hendrix, of the Corps of Engineers, and

William (Bill) Reed, a photographic supply salesman, had noticed James's Mustang parked in the front of Jim's Grill around 5:35 p.m. They stated that they had coincidentally examined it closely as they exited the bar, before walking north on Main Street. In separate statements (on FBI 302 forms), they both stated that at about 5:45 p.m. they saw that same car turning the corner onto Vance Street just as they were preparing to cross the street and that they saw a male driver inside, thus providing validation of James Earl Ray's account. Those documents were hidden from both the defense and the guilty-plea jury the following year. It would have remained a secret forever if Dr. Pepper had not discovered those documents, decades later, at the bottom of a file cabinet drawer within the District Attorney General's office.[525] This became another one of many pieces of exculpatory evidence of Ray's guilt, but, even more important, it was prima facie evidence of the massive cover-up orchestrated by the FBI, directed from the very top to eliminate, hide, or minimize any traces of incongruent documents existing within their own files.

Also Missing From the Crime Scene: The "Alleged Shooter"

Just as the drunken Charlie Stephens would become the prosecution's star witness, many highly credible, sober and alert witnesses would be ignored by police and the FBI, and therefore by the prosecutors, HSCA and Justice Department investigators, and early authors. A number of them would not get an opportunity to tell their stories for three decades until, finally, they would give their testimony at the 1999 civil trial *King v. Jowers*. That trial will be examined in more depth in Chapter 12; however, the fact that certain key eyewitnesses should have testified in 1968–69, but did not, is noted here to put their later testimony into proper context.[526]

- One such witness was Carthel Weeden, who had been the fire department captain in charge of Fire Station No. 2. For thirty years, he had never been interviewed by any local, state, or federal government law enforcement officer but finally testified in detail about how he had been approached the morning of the assassination by two men who wore civilian clothes but presented their army credentials to him. They asked him to show them to the roof of the building so that they could prepare to surveil the area and take photographs during the day of everyone coming and going into buildings in that area. After he escorted them to the roof, he left them to do their work and did not see them again after that, assuming that they finished their tasks and left. Dr. Pepper presented evidence that those men actually photographed the shooter and that one of the men stated it was *not* James Earl Ray.

- Another "new" witness was Olivia Catling, whose house on Mulberry Street was only one block away from the Lorraine; she testified that she saw a man leave the rooming house across from the Lorraine, get into a parked 1965 green Chevrolet, and speed away so quickly that the tires spun on the pavement, burning rubber, despite the presence of several policemen in cruisers who ignored all of it.

- A prominent witness (in videotaped testimony) who had never been asked by the police or FBI what he had seen was *New York Times* reporter Earl Caldwell, who was told by his national editor, Claude Sitton, to "go to Memphis and nail Dr. King." Dr. Pepper introduced a deposition from Caldwell that stated that when he heard the shot, he walked out of his room, onto the balcony, and noticed a figure in the bushes behind Jim's Grill, next to the parking lot; furthermore, he stated that the fatal shot came from that area, not the window of the rooming house. He also reported that he saw policemen running from the bushes.

- Still more witnesses (in affidavits) had also reported stories similar to the testimony of Caldwell: Solomon Jones (Dr. King's chauffeur) and Chauncey Eskridge (King's attorney) saw a hooded figure in the bushes across Mulberry Street. The highly credible Reverend James Orange had also just arrived at the parking lot in back of the motel minutes before the shot and happened to be looking toward the fire station close by when he noticed either smoke or possibly kicked-up dust rise from bushes next to the fire station just as he heard the shot. He stated, "From that day to this time I have never had any doubt that the fatal shot, the bullet which ended Dr. King's life, was fired by a sniper concealed in the brush area behind the derelict buildings."[527] Yet another contemporaneous witness, Harold "Cornbread" Carter, since deceased, had also reported seeing someone running from the bushes moments after the shot.

That all of these key witnesses were intentionally overlooked in 1968—and still ignored for thirty more years after that—is arguably proof enough of how the so-called "investigation" was managed from the start to pin the blame squarely on one vulnerable and malleable man and never on the possibility of anyone else. Accepting that single, simple premise leads inexorably to the fact that this was not normal police protocol and could not possibly be a series of multiple inadvertent omissions, which in turn leads to the logical, inescapable conclusion that Martin Luther King Jr.'s murder could have only been executed by the forces arrayed against him in a very sophisticated plot.

John McFerren, Tennessee Civil Rights Pioneer, Hears Frank Liberto's Order to Kill King

John McFerren grew up in Fayette County (the next county east of Memphis's Shelby County). Upon his return from World War II, where he had met many other American men, he had gotten a taste of the freedom of other cultures. He came to believe that "the battle for African American rights was 'just as important as World War II'" according to his biography on the Tennessee Encyclopedia of History and Culture website. He and his wife, Viola, would become civil rights activists, helping to found the Freedom Village of Fayette County, known locally as "Tent City," which provided minimal housing for hundreds of African American tenant farmers left homeless when the white farm owners evicted them because they had registered to vote.[528]

McFerren also became a founder of the Original Fayette County Civic and Welfare League in 1959, which was formed to register African Americans to vote and had to sue the county's Democratic Executive Committee to allow them to cast ballots, since they had attempted to bar all black voters from the polls. Although they eventually earned the right to vote, the county's white leaders retaliated against McFerren's small businesses, a gas station and small grocery store in Fayette County. He had previously relied on suppliers to deliver his grocery and gas station inventories, which they had done up until that point, November 1959. The Ku Klux Klan and the White Citizens Council pressured companies like Coca-Cola Bottling Company, Gulf Oil Company, and wholesale grocery operators to put all black-owned stores, especially those active in civil rights activities, on embargo lists, to discontinue deliveries to his country store. That caused McFerren to have to drive fifty miles every week to buy stock for his store.[529]

Every Thursday, McFerren would make his grocery run to Memphis, to restock his shelves and produce cooler in preparation for the weekend sales. On Thursday, April 4, 1968, he made his last stop for the day at 5:15 p.m. at the wholesale grocery Liberto, Liberto and Latch Produce Company. He was in the back of the store picking out the produce he would purchase, unnoticed by either Mr. Liberto or Mr. Latch. The telephone rang and Liberto nearly shouted, "I told you not to call me here. Shoot the son of a bitch when he comes on the balcony." He then told the caller to pick up his payment of $5,000 from his brother in New Orleans.[530] McFerren didn't know what to think about that immediately—it could have been referring to anything from shooting a varmint to the caller being a photographer—but after the assassination was described on the radio, he decided that all the rumors of Liberto's underground connections meant that he had been talking to the assassin.

McFerren told the executive director of the Tennessee Council on Human Rights about what he had witnessed. The director urged him to tell his story to the FBI, which he agreed to do on a promise of secrecy. On April 8, he did tell his story to FBI agent O. B. Johnson, MPD Homicide Chief N. E. Zachary, and Frank Holloman, the Director of the Memphis Police and Fire Departments. Within three days, the three of them decided that either McFerren had misheard the conversation or that it was about something other than the assassination, and chose not to follow the lead. This made McFerren feel like they believed he had given false testimony, so he then decided to not discuss it any further, which was what he did for the next decade. In 1978, the HSCA committee also dismissed it; again, he suppressed further discussion of it for two more decades, until he finally came forward to testify at the 1999 civil trial described in Chapter 12.[531]

For the first time, he was treated with a modicum of respect and his sworn testimony was properly considered. In separate testimony by several other witnesses, sufficient details were added that, combined, showed conclusively that Liberto was a central figure in the assassination plot. Also, both former UN ambassador Andrew Young and Dexter King—Martin Luther King Jr.'s youngest son—testified that Loyd Jowers confirmed to them that Liberto had been present in the planning meetings and had told Jowers that he would be given $100,000 in a vegetable delivery box that was to be turned over to the man named "Raul," whom none of the investigators cared enough about to investigate.[532]

The Scene at St. Joseph's Hospital

Johnton Shelby came forward after more than four decades to tell the story that he had withheld during that entire period, too afraid of the potential consequences: first as to his mother's safety and secondarily as to his own, should those who were keeping the cover-up viable seek retaliation. Shelby claimed that his mother, Lula Mae—who was a surgical aide at St. Joseph's Hospital in Memphis and took part in Dr. King's emergency treatment—gathered the family together the morning after the assassination to tell them about what she had experienced the prior evening.

Lulu Mae Shelby was still recovering from the traumatic events that began as soon as Dr. King was brought into the emergency room and throughout the attempt by the doctors to treat his injury and possibly save his life. After working for twenty to thirty minutes to do that, one of the other orderlies, John Billings, following a doctor's instruction, left the room for several minutes to "find the men in charge." By the time he returned with these men, the doctors said that there was nothing further they could do, and that they were going to stop their efforts to save him, after which the entire staff was instructed to leave the room and to not talk about what had occurred. After most of the staff had left the room, according to Lula Mae's son Johnton Shelby, his mother was the last one to leave. Billings made no mention of anything that might have occurred after that, evidently because he had left the room earlier than Lula Mae Shelby and did not witness what she claimed happened next.[533]

But the new witness whom Dr. Pepper deposed, Lula Mae's son Johnton, said that there was more to the story, that Dr. King had not yet passed at that point. What he told Dr. Pepper over forty years after the fact was about the final incident that only his mother had seen, which had so upset her; it was one that she could not hold within her and chose to reveal to her family the following morning. She told them that as she made her way out of the room, she had heard the head of surgery and a couple of "men in suits" tell the doctors to "Stop working on that nigger and let him die." She had also heard spitting sounds and turned around just in time to see doctors spitting on King and removing his ventilator tube, while putting a pillow over his face to ensure that he died.[534]

It can be reasonably assumed that since she was the last to leave, Lula Mae Shelby would have been the only one of the departing staff to have witnessed what she said she saw, and what she then described to her family when she returned home. This was despite the order not to say anything about what they had witnessed;[535] however, given human nature, eventually people occasionally ignore such orders, especially when they see a beloved hero figure treated so contemptuously. Johnton Shelby stated that his mother had also confided her secret to a few of her friends, some of whom had since died, but one in particular still refused to discuss it, for fear of losing her pension.[536] Johnton Shelby, out of fear for his life if he talked, had waited forty-five years to tell his mother's story, the first time by calling a radio talk show in 2013; at Dr. Pepper's request, he submitted to a detailed deposition in July 2014.

Last, it should be noted that given the sophistication of the plot, it would have been axiomatic that such a contingency would have been included in case King was not killed by the shot; that would explain why he was taken to that particular hospital, St. Joseph's, where the original chief plotter's (Russell Adkins Sr.) own longtime family doctor, Dr. Breen Bland, was also the head surgeon. Dr. Pepper confirmed that point by writing, "preparations were in place to ensure that Dr. King would never leave that hospital alive."[537] Ron Adkins, under oath, stated that he had been with his father (and later, after his father died, with his older brother, Russell Adkins Jr., who took over his father's role) when they discussed the plan with Dr. Bland and Police Chief Frank Holloman regarding the need to take King to that particular hospital if he had not been killed. "Ron recalls that Dr. Bland was prepared to give him a certain lethal injection if it became necessary."[538]

Meanwhile, FBI Agents in Atlanta Celebrate the News of MLK's Demise

When the news of Martin Luther King's assassination reached the FBI's Atlanta office, it was greeted with shouts of *"They got Zorro! They finally got the SOB!"* (Emphasis added.) As noted in the HSCA's MLK report, one agent even "literally jumped with joy."[539]

The retired FBI agent who came forward and revealed those statements, Arthur L. Murtagh, further stated that as an agent who had been involved in the investigation of Dr. King's assassination, he did not believe it was completed thoroughly or effectively:

> I think it was incomplete, mainly because I think that the Bureau was so heavily weighted against King that it affected its ability to rationally and fairly carry out the investigation. They went through the motions of carrying it out, and I recall that the question of conspiracy was pooh-poohed from the very beginning, that any mention of it was looked upon as being the workings of some crazy imagination.
>
> I recall having been told . . . that the Bureau had decided sometime within 24 hours after the killing that it wasn't a conspiracy; and I worked on the file A, Mississippi killings of the civil rights workers, and it took us 2 ½ months of concentrated

investigation before we could establish and prove the conspiracy in that case; and the difference between the way the two cases were worked is as different as night and day.

The file A, Mississippi case, was pushed by President Johnson. He called the office in Washington every day and asked about the progress of the investigation, and the Bureau conducted a full field investigation, going to the extent of getting U-2 flights over the area to take pictures and all of that sort of thing. They pulled out all the stops, because the President was pushing the investigation; and we solved that case, and we came up with a conspiracy.

We solved several cases along about that time, and in all of them there was pressure from the White House to get them solved. In the King case, as soon as we identified Ray, for all practical purposes you couldn't tell that there was any special investigation going on . . . it was handled like a fugitive case instead of an intelligence case, although our original interference with Dr. King was an intelligence matter; it was handled as a simple fugitive case [i.e., the focus was only on finding and capturing the "fugitive," James Earl Ray, as the single assassin, as though the case had already been solved].

[. . .]

I just think that it defies and assaults reason to think that people who have been engaged in a 10-year-long vendetta against Dr. King are the ones who should be investigating his death . . .[540]

Clearly, President Johnson was very interested, for his personal political reasons, in solving those other cases, and not so much interested in solving the King case for some (not so) mysterious reason. In fact, truth be known, Johnson was arguably not only disinterested in solving it, he was instrumental in covering it up, as will be demonstrated.

The questioning of Arthur Murtagh continued. At one point Representative Devine of Ohio asked him if he thought that Mr. Hoover was a "maniac, as someone described him to you?" He replied that he didn't know him personally, but that, "he was a person who had arrogated to himself great power over a period of forty years, and I believe in the adage that power corrupts and absolute power corrupts absolutely. I think he was corrupted."[541]

A little while later, Representative Fauntroy of the District of Columbia, noting the "allegations that have been made about the possible direct role of the FBI in the assassination of Dr. King," then asked Murtagh a question: "Do you have any reason to believe that FBI agents could have been involved in any way in the assassination of Dr. King? " Murtagh responded thusly: "No reason whatsoever, except the sum total of my testimony is that if that raises implications in some people's minds, they are raised; if it doesn't, it doesn't. I have no evidence of a first-hand nature, no."[542]

Mr. Murtagh was then asked by Representative Fithian of Indiana to state in what ways the FBI investigation should have been conducted. He contrasted the FBI's perfunctory and shallow investigation to the very aggressive, intensive investigation of the three murdered civil rights workers in Mississippi:

> [We talked to] nearly everybody in the county in two weeks. We had 70 agents in there interviewing people. My attitude was that if there is truth somewhere, if you stay at it long enough you will find it. I encouraged the inspector to push forward, I made suggestions as to things that could be investigated, and I don't mean to claim credit for the solution of the case—a lot of other agents did a lot of good work on the case also—but we pushed forward in doing a lot of things.
>
> Now as to just what needed to be done in the King case, I think that there was enough evidence in my mind to raise some suspicion as to how far the Klan might have been involved. I think there was a cursory kind of an inquiry through informants as to whether anybody could come up with any information, whether the Klan had assisted in the killing. If that had been [investigated like] the Philadelphia [MS] thing, we would have interviewed every Klansman and some of them five and six times, and ultimately, we would have developed informants as we did in Philadelphia [MS]; we would have gone into an informant development stage that would have probably taken 2 or 3 months, and at the end of 2 or 3 months we would have some informants in some of the client groups.
>
> I think I would have gone into, because of the violent attitude of some of the right-wing groups that were never very thoroughly investigated by the Bureau, we should have gone into them in an effort to uncover a conspiracy if it existed. I think if it existed it is going to be very deep and going to be hidden, and I don't think any of that was done. *In fact, I know it wasn't.* (Emphasis added.)[543]

Representative Fithian then asked Murtagh whether he had made "any specific recommendations then of the nature that you are now making ex post facto?"

[Murtagh responded] No, because I know it was hopeless. I did suggest the idea of a conspiracy, and I got shot down as if I was some kind of a nut by [his boss] Hardy . . . I wouldn't [press it] in the circumstances that existed in the Bureau at that time. I was aware of the fact that the Bureau had made up its mind there was no conspiracy, and I had been told in 1958 you don't try to tell them anything. I had experience going way back to 1958, when there was a cover-up on an investigation in which we were told by the boss not to do specific investigations because it might develop something and we would get into more investigation than we wanted in the office at that time. I knew that was the attitude, and I didn't want to fight it. I know it wouldn't do any good to fight it.

Fithian: I must say that it seems to me—I have never been in the Bureau, but it seems to me—there would have been dozens of things that you might have done as an individual that you did not do then.

Murtagh: That is because you were never in the Bureau, sir.

Fithian: Did you ever talk to anybody outside the Bureau, like newspaper people? There was such a—

Murtagh: I thought of talking to news people outside the Bureau but I knew what happened to some agents that did and I didn't intend to go that route. Those agents aren't here testifying. They didn't find out what went on in the Bureau.

Fithian: I understand that. I am just suggesting that my general impression here is that you are coming on pretty strong many years later, but you really had quite an opportunity then confidentially to share your views.

Murtagh: I had no opportunity whatsoever, sir. I know it is very difficult for a person who has never lived in a dictatorship to understand it, but I would have had no more chance I think than "Hogan's Heroes" and the scare that they put into everybody when they speak of the Gestapo. When you were in the Bureau under Hoover, you were [in] an organization which was for all intents and purposes modeled on the same mold as the Gestapo, and to even raise the issue that anything was wrong would mean instant discipline.[544]

After further comments from Representative Fithian—e.g., "there must have been fifty different ways that you would develop contacts [to go outside the Bureau and reveal to others], [t]o what extent do you believe that what you are now taking as such a strong position is in some way to make up for not acting in the past?"

> [Murtagh] ". . . sir, I laid awake all night last night thinking about how I could best, in the time allowed, impress upon this committee, upon Congress, upon the press, the drastic need for reform in these areas before it is too late. I am horribly afraid of what might happen if we went this route again and developed another J. Edgar Hoover and all the trappings that went with it.
>
> We have got to plug the leak in the dike and we have got to do it now, or our kids aren't going to live in a free society, and I really feel that. I feel it when I think it out. I feel it when you ask me the question the way you just asked it.
>
> I am deeply concerned about our freedoms, and I think that the Bureau has to be reformed, and I am saying so very strongly. I realize that. I don't think it has anything to do with the past [i.e., his own limited ability to expose the "Hoover problem" from his position as a lowly agent].
>
> I can tell you that from our own personal experience that the battle is getting old with me. When I was called and asked to come down, I toyed with the idea of trying to get out of it because it upsets my wife, it upsets my family, it upsets—it has upset our lives since 1958 in so many ways [i.e., his entire career with the FBI].
>
> Does that help answer your question, sir?[545]

Mr. Murtagh is an excellent example of the fact that all FBI agents of that era were not mind-deadened, robotic, sycophantic enablers of the criminals running that organization. Unfortunately, he seemed to have been a very rare exemplar of that point.

The contrast between Murtagh and DeLoach reveals how they were polar opposites. In his obsequious "Hoover was beyond reproach" book, DeLoach said about Murtagh: "[He was] a man we called 'the crying agent,' because he was forever making emotional proclamations that the bureau had engaged in illegal activities and that the truth must out."[546] The pronoun "we" implicitly meant, besides himself, Hoover, Tolson, Sullivan, and undoubtedly every other high-level FBI official at the "SOG."

MLK Jr.'s Most Passionate Assassination Researchers: Dick Gregory and Steve Cokely

Much of this story began to be revealed in the 1980s and 1990s by a Chicago activist, the late Steve Cokely, who was a staff member of Chicago mayor Harold Washington's administration and an assistant to former mayor Eugene Sawyer. Cokely was a futurologist who lectured on conservation matters and the history of various political movements such as the Black Panthers. Of all these topics, arguably the single greatest one of interest to him was the research of the hidden secrets related to the assassination of Martin Luther King Jr. It was his research and study of this still-unresolved mystery that led him to passionately believe that James Earl Ray was set up and managed by the combined efforts of the CIA, the FBI, certain officials in military intelligence and local Memphis police, and a few "insiders" at Dr. King's own organization, the SCLC.

The late Mr. Cokely's several videotaped presentations on the subject document his passion and his lengthy research into Dr. King's murder; one such is presently available (at the time of this writing) on YouTube, titled "JESSE JACKSON KILLED MARTIN LUTHER KING JR."[547] Within this presentation, Cokely made a number of startling observations as he wove a story that connected numerous provocative but factual assertions, which, combined, came to the inescapable conclusion that the most truthful stories coming out of Memphis proved Ray's innocence. By the same token, they proved that Martin Luther King Jr. was assassinated by a widely based, well-orchestrated conspiracy, one having forensically provable traces of being thoroughly planned.

In fact, Cokely believed that the murder itself was not only designed and then choreographed by people from afar, but managed by people on the scene at the Lorraine Motel as proven by their presence inside Room 306, which they had caused to be reassigned to King shortly before he and his party registered there on April 3, 1968. The request for that change, to move him from an inside room without a balcony to that specific room with a large balcony, according to the motel manager, Walter Bailey, supposedly came from someone at the SCLC headquarters in Atlanta earlier in the afternoon. Moreover, Cokely stated that it was Jesse Jackson's assignment, as the designated man on the ground, to ensure that all of the plan's arrangements were completed on schedule. This was also—independently of Cokely's conclusions—the gist of the sworn testimony of Dr. William Pepper's aforementioned witness, Ron Tyler Adkins, to ensure that the plan's objective—the murder of Martin Luther King Jr.—was successfully executed.[548]

Several key points that Mr. Cokely made in that video may be summarized as follows:

- That Reverend Billy Kyles—a Memphis preacher who also became a local functionary for King— knowing that "friendlies" would not be wearing ties, was given the task of making sure that Dr. King *did* have a tie on.[549]
- That Jesse Jackson had chosen to stand in the parking lot ("chickened out," according to Cokely) below the balcony, without a tie, and had been talking ("arguing" might be a better descriptor) with Dr. King, emphatically stating that he would not wear a tie to dinner, and while this was going on, Reverend Kyles stepped back away from King "to clear the way for the shooter to have a clear shot."[550]
- That Andrew Young (appearing on the video) stated that immediately after the shooting, Jackson then went up to the balcony to Dr. King and put his hands into King's blood and wiped it onto his sweater.[551]
- A few minutes after that, Jackson would say that he held King's head, repeatedly asking, "Dr. King, can you hear me?" But he had not even touched him, other than to put his blood into his hands.[552]
- That Jackson took control over everyone there shortly after the shooting, ordering that no one else was permitted to talk to the press, other than himself.[553]
- That after Dr. King was loaded into an ambulance, and as the other staff members all got into the available vehicles to follow in a procession to the hospital, Jackson called around asking for a ride to the hospital yet made no effort to leave.
- That Jackson then waited until everyone else had gone and began his first press conference as the heir apparent, telling all the reporters there that he was the last person to talk to King, as he pled with him to answer, "Dr. King, can you hear me?"[554] This was only the beginning of Jackson's efforts to establish himself as King's successor, repeatedly using the word "resurrection" to describe his rise into that role.
- That it was Ralph Abernathy who had actually been with King, in person and spirit, before, during, and after of the shooting, inside the room and subsequently on the balcony, then in the ambulance, and in the hospital emergency room.

- That Jackson was never close to King until the balcony scene, where he decided that he would prove his closeness by wiping Dr. King's blood all over his own sweater as proof, then repeatedly tell the lie about his closeness to the murdered martyr.[555]
- That in the immediate aftermath of the assassination—as traffic was closed down on the major roads and highways leading out of the city and to the airport—somehow Jesse Jackson was cleared to leave the city and board an airplane to Chicago. Cokely asked rhetorically, "How did [Jackson] get out of Memphis when the trains, planes, buses, cars, and boats were all cut off?" Then he answered his own question, quoting what he had been told by Dick Gregory, "Well, you know what happened, don't you? The FBI called the airport and told them to let one plane out, one plane with one Negro man on it . . . Jesse Jackson had claimed he was sick and needed to return to Chicago." There could be only one reason that the FBI had treated him so specially, Cokely continued, and that would be due to his being the "chosen one."[556] The choice, it soon became apparent, was made—not by the SCLC leadership in Atlanta in the aftermath, but by the FBI leadership in Washington, in the weeks and months before the mayhem in Memphis.
- That the following morning, just twelve hours after the murder of Dr. King, Jackson appeared on NBC's *Today Show*, emotionally announcing a series of lies about how Dr. King had "died in my arms," that he been beside him when he was shot, had cradled King's head and "was the last person on earth" to have spoken with King.[557]
- That a white, Jewish man, a "fixer," Don Rose, was put in charge of assisting Jackson to take the mantle left by Dr. King;[558] it was Rose who cleared the path for him to leave Memphis, to be booked on the *Today Show,* to meet with the Chicago City Council later that day in a special meeting convened by Mayor Daley as a memorial service to commemorate King as a means to calm the anger of the African American population, who generally resided on the south side of the city.
- That in his book, Gerald Posner, in one of his numerous and infamous lies and non sequiturs, cunningly denied that Reverend Samuel "Billy" Kyles was an "*FBI*" informant, writing: "'[In] *Orders to Kill*, William Pepper raises the strong inference that Kyles might have been an *FBI informant*. It's degrading and

insulting,' Kyles says about Pepper's accusations. 'It casts an aspersion on my forty years in the civil rights movement. I saw how Pepper operates.'"[559] But Dr. Pepper had actually said that Kyles was a Memphis Police Department informant. (Emphasis added.) By making that clearly intentional misquote, Posner reframes the entire story, sowing confusion in those who did not go back and recheck the book to see the trickery for themselves.

- That at the time of King's assassination, "the Secretary of the Army was Cyrus Vance, his military attaché was Alexander Haig, and his legal counsel was Joseph Califano. *Not one single book on [the]King assassination or the [Robert] Kennedy assassination appropriately brings up the role of Vance, Haig, and Califano.*"[560] (Emphasis added. It should be acknowledged here that they may not have known anything in advance about the plot despite what others, under their purview, have now been accused of by a number of people, not only the late Mr. Cokely, but Dick Gregory, as well.)

- That nine years later, in 1977, when Jesse Jackson asked Joseph Califano, then secretary of Health, Education, and Welfare (HEW) under President Jimmy Carter, for a $25,000 grant to help educate inner-city youths, Califano told him no, that he really needed "a million."[561] (Dick Gregory noted the irony by asking his audience, "Now how many white people that you have ever met, you ask them for a quarter, and they give you a hundred dollars? You ever met a white person who would do that?") Califano then proceeded to give Jackson a series of grants between 1978 and 1981 totaling $3,280,000 from HEW. Combined with more grants from the Department of Labor ($3,072,704), the Department of Commerce ($250,000), and Housing and Urban Development (HUD) ($75,000), the total grant awards given Jackson's PUSH-Excel program during the Carter administration was $6,677,704.[562]

- Related to the above point, Cokely then states: "Of the six million dollars, [Jackson] misappropriated one million dollars. Now the feds got him for misappropriation of funds. He's one million dollars missing [*sic*]. Reagan becomes the president; Jesse gets scared. Jesse asks [famed DC attorney] Edward Bennett Williams to talk to Reagan to cut him a deal on the million. Edward Bennett Williams says, 'When federal auditors asked to look at Jackson's books early in the Reagan administration, they found chaos. Jackson's organization, Push-Excel [was unable to account for over $1 million of the money. The matter was referred to the Justice Department.]'"[563] Cokely continued, "You saw that other thing called Rainbow Coalition. When PUSH had to pay back the money, he left the liened organization, 'L-I-E-N' like 'lien'; he left the organization that had a lien on it and went to Washington to set up another organization. When PUSH paid back the lien, he leaves Washington and sets up PUSH/Rainbow coalition. Check? OK, 'cause you gotta watch him, 'cause he's a magician. But white people was his Merlin."[564]

According to the Evan Thomas biography of Edward Bennett Williams, *The Man to See*, Williams found that the Justice Department "had no intention of prosecuting Jackson or his organization," saying they had "no evidence of fraud." But despite that finding, in settlement of the $1 million of missing funds, they agreed to a payback of only half that amount, leaving Jackson with the other half that was never accounted for: $500,000 of free money, according to our math.[565]

The plot, according to Ron Adkins, called for Reverend Jesse Jackson to make sure that Dr. King would be moved from the original room booked for him to Room 306 with the large balcony.[566] By the intervention of these paid informers, the room change was completed even before the King party arrived to check in at the motel. The assignment given to Reverend Billy Kyles was to get Dr. King out of that room and onto the balcony at 6:00 p.m. and be certain that he (King) had his tie on, so the marksman hiding in the bushes would have no doubt about which man to shoot.

Dr. Pepper's 2016 book, *The Plot to Kill King*, includes a transcript of a videotape that had been played in the 1999 civil trial by his associate, a young black lawyer named Juliet Hill-Akines. She played the videotape three times to ensure that the jury became very aware that Kyles had, obviously inadvertently and subconsciously, admitted his complicity in the shooting by actually verbalizing—thereby implicitly acknowledging—that he had stepped aside so that a shooter would have a clear shot at Dr. King after they had talked:[567]

> Reverend Kyles: What preachers talk about when they get together, revivals and all the like. About a quarter of six we walked on the balcony, and he was talking to people in the courtyard. He stood here and I stood there. Only as I moved away so he could have a clear shot, the shot rang out.

Steve Cokely died in 2012 of heart failure at age fifty-nine; his friend, comedian Dick Gregory, stated that he does not believe it was due to natural causes.

Many people besides Steve Cokely and Dick Gregory have raised a most provocative question about Jesse Jackson's possible background involvement in the planning, execution, and cover-up of the Martin Luther King Jr. assassination: does he have an extra measure of leverage with the federal government, with which he is able to thwart certain rules and regulations that apply to everyone else, in exchange for his silence? It might explain much about the power he has managed to accrue, as though he were in some way above many others, which allows him to enjoy a double standard by which different rules seem to apply to him.

The Reverend Jesse Jackson's Claims: Was He the Last Person to Speak with Dr. Martin Luther King?

In the immediate aftermath, Jesse Jackson would claim—over and again—that he "was the last man King spoke to before he was shot in Memphis. Jesse ran to the balcony, held King's head, but it was too late." The *Chicago Defender* newspaper reported on April 8, 1968, that "Jackson, whose face appeared drawn, talked briefly with newsmen about the moments just before and after the shooting occurred. He said he rushed to Dr. King's side immediately, but got no response when he asked, 'Doc, can you hear me?'"[568]

Practically everyone—except, notably, the men who were there—assumed Jackson's statements were true. However, the Reverend Ralph D. Abernathy, then vice-president and treasurer of SCLC, stated: "I am sure Reverend Jackson would not say to *me* that he cradled Dr. King. I am sure that Reverend Jackson would realize that *I* was the person on the balcony with Dr. King and did not leave his side until he was pronounced dead at St. Joseph's Hospital in Memphis. I am sure that he would not say to *me* that he even came near Dr. King after Doc was shot."[569] (Italics in original.)

In a major article in the January 6, 1984, *Des Moines Register* by reporter Dennis Farney titled "What makes Jackson run? Fears that cut deep from his childhood," Ralph Abernathy was quoted in reference to a heated argument about strategy for the Poor People's Campaign. He said that when Jackson began arguing with Dr. King, a few days before his assassination, Dr. King became fed up with him and walked out of the meeting, saying to Jackson on the way out: "Jesse, it may be necessary for you to carve your own individual niche in society. But don't bother me. Don't bother me."[570] Farney wrote, "Then Martin Luther King was dead. What Jackson did after the assassination remains confused and controversial today." Farney also noted a number of points that illustrate the resulting confusion:[571]

- Farney observed that Hosea Williams, a top King aide, stated that "Andy (Young) and Ralph (Abernathy) came back from the hospital and said, 'Martin is dead,' and . . . it was no time before Jesse was down in that courtyard, holding a press conference."
- While everyone else gathered together in prayers and somber reactions to the tragedy, not realizing that Jackson had disappeared, the next morning when they turned their televisions on, they were astonished to see him appearing on NBC's *Today Show*, and later that day addressing the Chicago City Council, still wearing the clothes stained with Dr. King's blood.
- "That was the start of a Jackson publicity juggernaut," wrote Mr. Farney.[572] In the following months, Jackson would appear in *Playboy* and *Time* magazines, and dozens of others in the five decades since.
- Chauncey Eskridge, attorney for Dr. King, stated: "If anyone could have gotten blood on their clothes, other than Abernathy, it must have come from the balcony after King's body was removed. Jackson's appearance at Chicago's City Council with that blood on his shirt was not only deception, but sacrilege. The City Council meeting offered him a public forum to be seen and heard, and that was what prompted him to appear."[573]
- Hosea Williams, another SCLC official, said that "the only person who cradled Dr. King was Abernathy. The last man King spoke to was Solomon Jones. It's a helluva thing to capitalize on a man's death, especially one you professed to love."[574]
- Andy Young, executive director of SCLC at the time, later mayor of Atlanta, Georgia congressman, and UN ambassador, stated that "the blood, the cradling, were all things I read in the newspaper and they are all mysteries to me."[575]
- Ben Branch, leader of Operation Breadbasket's band, said, "My guess is Jesse smeared the blood on his shirt after getting it off the balcony. But who knows where he got it from. All I can say is that Jesse didn't touch him. I think that should answer it all."[576]

Other Prominent Voices Calling Out the FBI and CIA

Carl T. Rowan, a famed black journalist and television personality, called for an independent investigation of the FBI's complicity in the assassination, stating, "Very clearly the FBI is suspect. We may never know the truth—but we must search for it."[577] He also asserted that within four hours of King's murder—despite having possession of Ray's rifle and binoculars with his fingerprints on them—the FBI was trying to put out a "spurious lie that Russians had killed King because of some hitch in his relations with 'Soviet spies.'"[578]

A video posted on YouTube in 2012 featured—among many others who have previously been involved in the investigation—Dr. King's son, Dexter King, who stated that "I believe, and my family believes, that this man [James Earl Ray] is innocent."[579]

G. Robert Blakey, a former Justice Department official who also served as staff director to the House Select Committee on Assassinations (HSCA) from 1977 to 1979, appeared in this video and stated, "The government, did they have anything to do with it? I've seen what the FBI did, I've seen what the CIA did, *I wouldn't trust them at all.*"[580] (Emphasis added.) That statement represents a major change in his attitude, which stemmed from his 2003 discovery that the CIA had deceived him during the HSCA investigation, as described on John Simkin's website Spartacus Educational:

> Blakey was furious when he discovered this information. He is-
> sued a statement where he said: "I am no longer confident that
> the Central Intelligence Agency co-operated with the commit-
> tee . . . . I was not told of Joannides' background with the DRE
> [the Cuban exile group Directorio Revolucionario Estudiantil],
> a focal point of the investigation. Had I known who he was, he
> would have been a witness who would have been interrogated
> under oath by the staff or by the committee. He would never
> have been acceptable as a point of contact with us to retrieve
> documents."[581]

Blakey was also quoted, in 2013, in an article appearing in the Jackson, Mississippi, *Clarion-Ledger,* stating that "Thoughtful people today, not just nuts, think that more people than James Earl Ray were involved."[582] But the *most* thoughtful people, those who have studied the case at any length, including the King family, don't believe Ray was even involved, at least not wittingly. He was simply a small-time swindler and burglar who escaped prison with help from the warden, unbeknownst to him, then made his way around the country and into Canada, intent on never returning to the United States—that is, until he ran into a man in a bar named Raul, who offered him money, cover, a nearly new Mustang, and fake identity cards, all for helping him smuggle guns and drugs across the Canadian and Mexican borders; it was a dream job, for as long as it lasted, or so he thought at the time. Unfortunately, he did not put two and two together, until he turned on the radio in the Mustang on his way out of Memphis and heard what had just happened back at the Lorraine Motel.

Dr. King had great confidence in the advice given him by his "strategist-philosopher," Reverend James Bevel, and after the assassination he stood out prominently as one of King's advisers who never believed that James Earl Ray was the assassin. Bevel stated his concerns clearly when he said, "We should not let this country give us a poor, defenseless goat in sacrifice for the body of our lamb. I don't believe Ray was capable of killing Dr. King . . . Ray's execution would not take us one step further in recognizing Dr. King's dream. It would furnish our enemies with a scapegoat. They could wash their hands of guilt."[583]

Chapter 9

THE AFTERMATH AND CAPTURE OF THE PATSY

"The central factor of what happens is that, after the assassination, this assassin rushes out of the rooming house and what does he do? He does a very amazing thing. He takes a suitcase and very carefully drops it in front of a store."

—Truman Capote

Escape From Memphis: Ray's Two-Month Escape From the "Jaws of Justice"

In the following pages, we will trace Ray's harrowing escape from Memphis amid police roadblocks of the main arteries and sirens sounding throughout the city, as he finally figured out that he had been had. After refueling the Mustang, Ray had attempted to return to the area of Jim's Grill to find a parking place and noticed uniformed policemen diverting vehicles away from there. Anxious to depart that scene, he turned on the radio and heard a report about a CB operator announcing that he was following a speeding white Mustang in the northeast sector of the city, which he believed was involved in a shooting. Several police cruisers were dispatched into that area as the radio operator claimed that he was being shot at by the driver of the Mustang. As Ray drove south out of Memphis and into Mississippi, he heard the news about Martin Luther King Jr. being shot. Soon after that—well after the report about the CB driver and a second report about MLK being shot—he heard that the police were now looking for a white male in a white Mustang, a clear description of himself. It was only then that he began suspecting that he had been had by Raul and immediately decided not to call the intermediary contact in New Orleans, but head straight for Atlanta instead.[584]

Despite a massive diversion of resources and considerable confusion for many future researchers and authors, the matter was never fully resolved, except for a tentative finding by the 1978 HSCA's "Findings on the MLK Assassination," which eventually recorded that incident as follows:

"Investigative records of the Memphis police and the FBI indicated that an eighteen-year-old CB enthusiast, Edward L. Montedonico Jr., was considered the most likely perpetrator of the hoax, although prosecution was not recommended. Memphis police officers chiefly responsible for the investigation told the committee that Montedonico was considered the prime suspect."[585]

The presumption was that the boy had heard a police report over the CB radio that described the getaway car even before that information was released to the radio stations; since the description matched the car that Ray was known to be driving, well before he had been identified as the possible shooter, it is curious as to who described the alleged shooter's car to the police. At that early point, such an incriminating detail could have only come from either Raul himself, still on the scene, or other police officials who had advance knowledge of the entire plan.

As he left the chaos in Memphis, Ray first drove south into Mississippi and then east to Alabama, finally stopping in the middle of the night to dump all his camera gear in a ditch, thinking not that it would incriminate him, but that he would not have time or opportunity to dispose of it later and he needed to prepare to travel light. He also decided on getting an early start to wiping the car's exterior of fingerprints, knowing that he would eventually abandon it in Atlanta and would need to get away from it as quickly as possible. He continued on into Georgia and reached Atlanta about 8:00 a.m., parking the car in an apartment complex known as Capitol Homes. There he finished wiping down the car's interior and took a taxi to the rooming house, where he dug up the .38 caliber pistol he had buried in the cellar and collected his remaining belongings.[586]

He left only his television set and a few unnecessary items, including a map that he'd marked up to indicate the apartment location in relation to other sections of the city. He said that four circles he put on the map had been to help him orient himself to the area, marking "[p]laces I came in, the highway I came in off of Peachtree Street, where I went to the bank one time to cash in some money [convert Canadian currency]. I marked a restaurant on there and I think I glanced at it a few times to get my bearings on it, and that was it."[587] Huie wrote in his third *Look* article that Ray had marked the map to indicate the locations of Dr. King's home, office, and church.[588] Led on by Huie's imagination, the police and FBI would interpret more sinister meanings of Ray's scribbles and add that to their "stalking theme" concoction.

This incident, as it was portrayed in Posner's book, illustrated beyond question his unparalleled canny ability to cherry-pick sentences out of official documents and parse them into his deceitful series of lies. He stated that "Ray himself realized that the markings were highly incriminating" and then, quoting the HSCA report Vol. IX, p. 224, cited these quotations from Ray: "I could never explain that away to the jury . . . I gave it a lot of thought and that's the best I could come up with." Those statements were not only taken completely out of context, but they were reframed into an opposing, incriminating, context. The following excerpt is what is stated on the page that Posner cited:

> I don't particularly recall marking, I don't even, the Atlanta map. I don't particularly recall marking that except that they made a big issue about it and I started to thinking [*sic*] about it. I would probably never recall all the details on that if I hadn't have tried to—let me explain why. I don't know if you have read all these books or not. William Bradford Huie said he found the map in Atlanta somewhere in my suitcase— It had circles of Dr. King's church, his house, his office and his ministry, his church or something [as he had been told by Huie, most likely the result of Huie's own distortions], and I knew that was all false. I mean, I knew—I started thinking and I knew I marked a map, but I knew that would have been a coincidence if I had marked all these places that would have been too big a coincidence. *I could never explain that to a jury.* So, I got to thinking about it, and *I gave it a lot of thought and that's the best I could come up with* [i.e., his best recollection of what was otherwise a hazy memory from ten years before]. Now, if you can look at that map get it from the FBI. I think that would settle that once and for all, if I marked anyone's church. [Italics added to note the cherry-picked sentences Posner used.]
>
> [When the HSCA attorney asked him for clarification, whether the markings were "where you lived, the highway you came in on, where the bank is, and where the restaurant is, or is it that you think that is what must have happened just from trying to recreate the incident after reading about Huie's explanation . . . Why [*sic*] was your reason for circling that highway then?" (p. 226), Ray elaborated: "That was just to get the bearings, no other reason."]

Clearly, the juxtaposition of Ray's faint memory of doing something so innocuous—in marking up a map for his own reference about navigating around a city he had never been to before—was no match for the professional, world-class fiction writers whose vivid imaginations were called upon to reframe his "scribblings." Their own scribblings would be used to reinterpret (and possibly even augment the original, in the case of Huie and his FBI friends) what was never intended to be reinterpreted by anyone else. Ray's testimony to the HSCA was easy pickings for Gerald Posner, two decades after that round of further obfuscation.

Cover-Up Operations Begin the Morning after the Assassination

A reporter from the *Memphis Press-Scimitar*, Kay Black, stated that the former mayor, William Ingram, called her the morning after Dr. King's murder to report that the brush and trees behind the rooming house—from which several witnesses claimed the shot was made—were being cut down and cleaned up. She immediately went there after receiving this call, about 1:00 p.m., and found that they had already completed most of it, and when she contacted the Public Works Department about it, she was told that it had been a "routine cleanup."[589] The sinister aspects of this matter were never vigorously pursued until decades later, when Dr. Pepper eventually determined that there was nothing routine about it.

Maynard Stiles was a senior administrator of the Memphis Department of Public Works in 1968. Thirty years later, he testified in the civil trial Dr. Pepper had labored hard to bring about, *King v. Jowers*. Stiles explained his role in getting an order to clean up the brush behind the rooming house early the next morning after the assassination. He stated that MPD inspector Sam Evans called him at 7:00 a.m. the morning of April 5, 1968, requesting a crew to clean up the area behind the rooming house on South Main Street. The job entailed cutting down all the thick brush, trees, and bushes to ground level and have it raked into piles and then loaded onto trucks and hauled away. He stated that the crew started later that morning and "went to that site and *under the direction of the police department*, whoever was in charge there, proceeded with the cleanup in a slow, methodical, meticulous manner."[590] (Emphasis added.)

As noted in chapter 8, Reverend James Orange had noticed smoke, or possibly kicked-up dust, coming from those bushes. The next morning, he was shocked when he returned to the crime scene and found the bushes had already been removed.[591]

Contrary to what Ms. Black stated she had been told—that it was a "routine cleanup"—what Mr. Stiles testified to was clearly not a routine procedure. Such projects are not generally supervised by the police while they are conducting a major criminal investigation within the scene of the crime they are evaluating, obviously involving the destruction of the crime scene itself. Even though it involved substantial alteration of the crime scene, Stiles's belief was that he was simply cooperating with the police, for the purpose of clearing the area in order to help them examine it more closely. Furthermore, Stiles also testified, when asked if he had personally gone there to check on the progress, that "I didn't go by to see how it was progressing. I went by to see if I could give them any assistance in any other way. Because it wasn't up to any of us as to how it was progressing. *That was up to the police department.*" [592] (Emphasis added.) Stiles stated that no authors had ever interviewed him about this subject (until Dr. Pepper, who was then preparing for the civil trial).

For three decades, this point had been covered over as a result of the statement Ms. Black had received from her call to the Public Works Department, that it had been a "routine" coincidence that the work just happened to be on their schedule for that day. It was just another one of many undiscovered lies that took thirty years to materialize as such, even though it had been known by several people at the time: at least those mentioned above, Ms. Black, Reverend Orange, and Mr. Stiles. This testimony from Mr. Stiles should be considered as another absolute proof that the cover-up operation—of a planned murder at dusk on Thursday—was in full gear at dawn on Friday, when Stiles got the 7:00 a.m. telephone call from MPD inspector Sam Evans; likewise, it should be considered obvious that the telephone operator at the Public Works Department had been instructed in advance about what to say to any inquirers.

It is also understandable, in a sense, that the early books did not cover this story for the above reason. But it is also troubling that something so obvious to the policemen and other people, who must have been on the scene the next day as observers of this traumatic historic event, apparently did not talk about it to reporters and first-generation authors. Moreover, one might naturally expect that the authors of all books on this subject written since that 1999 trial that exposed this clearly salient issue should have also noted it. But Hampton Sides's 2010 book, Hancock and Wexler's 2012 book, and Pate McMichael's 2015 book all ignore it completely, as if it had no real pertinence in getting to a full understanding of what happened to Dr. King; all—in one way or another—merely repeat the tired old lies originally planted by original novelist Huie (which is not to say there weren't other ones that missed it, as well).

The Fugitive Ray Returns to Canada: Without Raul

After abandoning the cleaned-up Mustang, Ray went to downtown Atlanta to the Greyhound bus terminal and took a bus to Cincinnati and Detroit. From there he took a taxi to Windsor, Ontario, and a train to Toronto. His thoughts at that point related to the steps he would need to obtain a new identity and then to acquire the documents necessary to apply for a Canadian passport. According to Ray, after renting a room, he then went to the reading room of the Toronto *Evening Telegram* to look up back issues of 1932 newspapers, looking up birth notices. He noted two names that he would use, Ramon George Sneyd and Paul Bridgeman, both of whom were approximately the same age as Ray. He subsequently called both of them, pretending to be a government official conducting an investigation into passport irregularities. Mr. Sneyd told him that he had never applied for a passport, which meant to Ray that his photograph would not have been on file. Ray did apply for a passport under that name, not realizing that Sneyd was a Toronto policeman, whose photo would most certainly be on file. By May 2, less than a month after Dr. King's assassination, Ray had received the passport and had purchased a round-trip ticket from Toronto to London on BOAC, now known as British Airways. On May 6, he flew to London and then exchanged the return ticket for a ticket to Lisbon, Portugal. By May 7, he was trying to act like an average tourist wandering around Lisbon.[593]

After making a few attempts to immigrate elsewhere, he flew back to London on May 17 and stayed in the Heathrow House at the edge of downtown London through May 28. He read a newspaper article about organizations that helped people leave Europe to join a military unit in the Nigerian war that was then building up steam. In the meantime, he tried to keep moving to different hotels, worried that the law was closing in on him. On June 5, he purchased a copy of the May 3 *Life* magazine with a cover story titled: "The Accused Killer: RAY alias GALT, the Revealing Story of a Mean Kid." Ray wrote: "Looking at the cover, I got a preview of the lynch party the American press was readying for me."

Ray explained that the photo used by *Life* was a grainy black-and-white enlargement from the class photograph taken when he was ten years old and a student at Ewing School, and that the red arrow actually appeared as very dark red printed against a black background, which had very little contrast, making it nearly unnoticeable. Had they used a brighter color, such as yellow or white, it would have been more apparent that the "mean-looking" boy (a childhood friend of Ray's named Robey Peacock) in the center of the photo was not the accused killer of Martin Luther King Jr. He also said that *Life* had a choice of two photos and that the other one was much better, since all of the kids' faces showed and no one's eyes were closed, as in the photo they decided to use. The other difference was that Ray's face appeared in it unhidden, with a smiling, friendly look, very similar to the 1950s television character Beaver Cleaver, an average American boy.[594]

But the misleading front cover—distorted to portray what a boy later accused of the murder of a martyr looked like at ten—was not the worst part of an intentionally deceptive assault on this "innocent until found guilty" accused man. The article itself portrayed the fugitive's character as having been shaped by his "mean life," asserting that the numerous aberrations and illnesses all through his life and that of his family were related to their dysfunctional, bleak existence. It also stated, incorrectly, that Ray's father had died in 1951 from his addiction to hard liquor, which left James "an anti-social loner."[595] The fact that his father was still alive, and would remain so until 1985 when he died of natural causes at age 86, was somehow missed by the fact-checkers at that magazine. Ray also noted that the rest of the article was similarly filled with "error and innuendo, all designed to convict me of Dr. King's murder long before I ever saw the inside of a courtroom."[596]

The plain, simple fact is that a lot of people were incentivized to go out of their way to distort Ray's public image. That fact leads inexorably to the deduction that such incentives could only originate at the highest, most powerful level, one that had complete control of the unfolding scheme. There can be little doubt about the source of the lies and deceit, and how it had been choreographed from the same Washington offices on Pennsylvania Avenue that had directed William B. Huie and his *Look* magazine articles and subsequent book and the other 1970s books by Gerold Frank and George McMillan that were demonstrably commissioned by the highest officials of the FBI.

Was the Real James Earl Ray a Vicious Racist, or Merely Fictionalized as One by a Succession of Novelists—One per Decade for Fifty Years?

Between the assassination of Dr. King on April 4, 1968—possibly even before that—and the capture of James Earl Ray on June 9, William Bradford Huie had already been recruited to write magazine articles and a book to set forth the FBI's "official" account of the murder and the investigation, but more important, all of the reasons the designated suspect was guilty of the crime.

James Earl Ray's first lawyer, Arthur Hanes, a former FBI agent and CIA informant, was instrumental in arranging the Huie contract to accomplish his scheme to make money on the deal to pay for his services. According to

Harry Avery, who worked directly for Governor Ellington and was head of all state prisons, *"one of the things that interested me about that contract was that it was signed and acknowledged by Huie and Hanes a long time before James Earl Ray signed it.* He acknowledged it after he got back to the United States before a notary in Shelby County in jail down there and this thing was gotten up in Birmingham . . . *a long time before Ray signed it."*[597] (Emphasis added.) Since it was the first thing on Hanes's agenda to talk to Ray about, Avery's comment indicates it was done almost immediately after the assassination (which suggests that the idea was possibly germinated even before April 4, 1968).

On September 1, 1968, two FBI officials went to Huie's home in Harselle, Alabama, to discuss the contract that had already been made between Huie and Ray. According to Ray's own book, at his first meeting with attorney Hanes the only thing discussed was his contract and the related Huie contract. Ray signed the Hanes contract and also executed a power of attorney for Hanes to proceed with another contract between Ray and Huie. The FBI memorandum on this arrangement stated: "While JAMES EARL RAY was incarcerated in London, England, he (Huie) entered into a contract with RAY to write the true account of RAY's activities and background concerning the assassination of Reverend Martin Luther King. This contract is also of interest to RAY's attorney, ART HANES, inasmuch as the cost of the trial, including attorney fees is dependent upon the commercial success of the contract . . ."[598]

The memo from the SAC Birmingham to the FBI director also confirmed to Hoover the "understanding" reached with Huie: "HUIE further advised he would be most willing to divulge all information he has received to date to the Bureau on a confidential basis, as well as all information he may receive in the future on a current basis, provided the two above requests (that this relationship between himself and the FBI be kept confidential and that he be furnished certain confidential information and current non-publicized photographs of RAY of character type [i.e., not mug shots]) could be met."[599] Months later, Ray realized that the Huie-Hanes relationship had led to wholesale leaks to the FBI and even to the public, resulting in a horrible conflict of interest. Ray had even lost his ability to argue with his attorney over whether he could testify because that had been seized by Huie, under his threat to cut off funds for Hanes. Now that Huie had been put into control of the basic decisions governing the conduct of Ray's defense, he decided that he had no choice but to fire Hanes, and with him Huie, as well. Little did he know that by replacing Arthur Hanes with Percy Foreman, things would go from bad to worse.

Unfortunately for Ray, he wound up in a far worse position. Hanes was at least trying to put on a defense, unlike the attorney Ray was coerced to replace him with—LBJ's Houston friend, Percy Foreman. But behind Ray's back, Foreman continued that same agreement with Huie for his own profit-making schemes. The worst part of the deal was that Foreman's efforts, despite his big promises to work on Ray's behalf, were really to ensure that Ray would remain in prison for the rest of his life. Obviously, Foreman's relentless obsession to make Ray give up his few residual rights to a fair trial clearly shows that he was very successful in achieving that objective.

Huie Lays the Foundation of Ray's Vile Legend

Huie started the "James Earl Ray as a violent southern racist" meme in his very first *Look* magazine article, published on November 12, 1968, which was supposed to be the scheduled beginning of Ray's trial. In the first sentence of the fourth paragraph of his narrative, he wrote, "Born in 1928 in dirt-poor poverty in *southwest* Illinois, he was a *miserable, hungry, defiant* youth, embarrassed by his *ignorance*, his *appearance* and his *odor*." (Emphasis added.) Huie not only misstated where Ray had lived within Illinois, he offered no evidence to support the subjective and offensive assertions of Mr. Ray's personal characteristics, apparently because he was used to the kind of literary license generally found in fiction. Huie described an alleged racist comment that he claimed Ray had made to a Canadian woman. Ray had met her after his prison escape in the summer of 1967, in a resort north of Montreal called Greyrocks. Huie could only have gotten her name from Ray's attorney, Arthur Hanes, even though Huie claimed that Ray himself had informed him of the story.[600] Moreover, Ray himself stated that "anything I told Hanes would show up in *Look* magazine before the trial, courtesy of Huie, who kept nagging Hanes to nag me for details."[601]

Ray stated that he had consistently attempted to keep the Canadian lady's name out of any magazine articles and books and had revealed her identity only to his attorneys and investigators.[602] To this day, many books still refer to her as the "Canadian woman"; however, John Avery Emison did name her in his book as Claire Keating.[603] Keating declined to cooperate with HSCA investigators in 1977, but she had already given a statement to the Royal Canadian Mounted Police in October 1968, which stated, "*He never mentioned the name Martin Luther King and never indicated any hatred towards Negroes.*"[604] (Emphasis added.) Moreover, the RCMP officer who conducted that interview said that "the subject of race never came up during her meetings with Ray." He also stated that Keating "seemed honest and truthful throughout the interview."[605]

But according to Huie's hallucinations, the Canadian woman supposedly said that Ray had told her, "You got to live near niggers to know 'em" and "all people who 'know niggers' hate them."[606] This false statement by Huie (among others) was cunningly created for the single purpose of creating the legend of James Earl Ray as a vicious racist, a baseless charge that was more than merely inaccurate: it is further proof of Huie's own devious mission. After the American public had long ago accepted that notion of Ray as a vicious racist—too little and too late to change that perception—ten years later the HSCA finally stepped back from that original lie. In one of their few significant contributions toward discovering actual truths buried within the myths, their Final Report concluded:

> During her RCMP interview, the woman said Ray never indicated any hatred of Blacks and never mentioned Dr. King in her presence. Once more, therefore, the committee's evidence tended to pull in opposite directions . . . The committee saw a need to scrutinize closely the evidence bearing on Ray's racial attitudes. In light of the contradictory evidence, *the committee was unwilling to conclude that deep-seated hatred of Blacks was the sole or even the primary motivating factor* in Ray's decision to murder Dr. King. While the committee was satisfied that Ray's lack of sympathy toward Blacks and the civil rights movement permitted him to undertake the assassination, *it was equally convinced that the murder did not stem from racism alone.*[607] (Emphasis added.)

The contrast between what Huie said Ms. Keating told him and what the investigators stated she actually reported is as different as night and day. There can be no question that Huie made it all up, and the reason for that could only be that he was attempting to reframe Ray's real persona with a false profile intended to incriminate him for Dr. King's murder. The difference in how Huie decided he could posit a bald-faced lie about what Ms. Keating had told him (which was clearly his own lie) and how he did not convey such untruths from most of the other people he had interviewed was that he knew that she would never publicly call him out on it, as it would be too much of an embarrassment to her; that was also the reason he did not name her, so that it could not even be proven that she was the person behind the lie. This incident, more than any other, demonstrates Huie's intrinsic dishonesty as well as the methods he used to create the false legend of James Earl Ray as a racist, and thus the prop for his further accusations of him being a stalker of Dr. King.

Another incident with which Huie attempted to portray Ray as a racist had allegedly occurred in a bar in Puerto Vallarta, Mexico, in October 1967. A prostitute whom Ray met, who used the professional name of Irma Morales, purportedly told Huie of an incident involving Ray (actually, his alias "Galt"). They were in the bar one evening, drinking together. A group of four black sailors, the crew of a private yacht, were drinking nearby. According to the story rendered by Huie—clearly hyped by him, as will be shown below— Morales said that "Galt" had become angry at them because they were making too much noise. As the HSCA report (1978) described the situation:*

> He told Morales he hated Blacks, and he went over to their table and insulted one of them. Then, he went to his car, returned, and stopped to berate the Blacks again. When he got back to his own table, he asked Morales to feel his pocket. She noted he was carrying a pistol. Galt said he intended to kill the Blacks. When one of them came over to Galt's table to try to make peace, Galt muttered another insult. When the Blacks left, Galt appeared to want to go after them, but Morales told him it was about time for the police to pay a 10 p.m. visit. Galt said he wanted nothing to do with the police. *This incident had since been reported in the writings of popular authors and was often cited as support for the proposition that Ray harbored racial hatred toward Blacks.*
>
> When investigated by the committee, the evidence was contradictory. With the assistance of the Mexican authorities, the committee reinterviewed Morales in Puerto Vallarta. Her recollection of her association with Ray and of her period of employment at the Casa Susana seemed clear and exact; further, her memory on many subjects was corroborated by other evidence and testimony taken by the committee. Yet her description of the alleged incident varied significantly from the published reports.

---

* NOTE: As the authors of this report indicated in the last [italicized] sentence of the first paragraph, below, all assertions came directly from the articles or books by either Huie [1968–1970], Frank [1972], or McMillan [1976].

Morales explained that she and "Galt" had been seated in the club when a Black sailor from a nearby table of both black and white sailors touched her as he was attempting to maneuver past them. She recalled thinking that the sailor was drunk, causing him to stumble as he passed her. He reached out and touched her, she explained, in an effort to break his fall. Morales added that the sailor was escorted out by another sailor and that Galt did become angry. Nevertheless, it was her opinion that *Galt's anger was prompted by the sailor touching her, and not because of his race.* She said further that *Ray never mentioned his feelings about Blacks to her.* Indeed, she said that conversation had been quite limited because of the language barrier. (Emphasis added.)

The committee found that Morales was a reliable witness on this point, who was certain of her recollections of the Casa Susana incident. *It would appear, therefore, that the racial overtones of this incident were seriously distorted, both in the original reports and in subsequent popularized versions of the event.*[608] (Emphasis added.)

What we have here, as confirmed by the actual people whom Huie interviewed—proving that he would have known these true stories—is a complete bald-faced set of lies, written to support a theme of a violent racist for which he deliberately misstated the facts in a way to conform to the distorted meme, which he clearly concocted and sold to the public. To this day, that description of James Earl Ray still resonates, not only throughout the North American continent—from the testimony of these women from Mexico and Canada and others from the United States—but throughout the world, thanks largely to these same completely false but best-selling books.

When the first article of Huie's three-part *Look* series was published, on November 12, 1968, it finally became clear to Ray that Huie was actually writing the story according to the FBI's rendering, not Ray's, though there was still ambiguity in the portrayal of Ray's involvement. By the time of the last article, on April 15, 1969, Huie had completely eliminated any residual confusion when he stated that there was no conspiracy because *only* Ray had murdered Dr. King and no one else had anything to do with it. When his book was published in 1970, Huie had even changed the title to *He Slew the Dreamer*, with "He" replacing "They," as it had been originally set when he initially pretended to write Ray's account. Now Ray was portrayed according to the myth created by Huie and laid for future researchers and authors: a lone-nut racist and murderous stalker of Martin Luther King Jr.[609]

William Bradford Huie Exposed: A Man on a Mission

The HSCA report concluded not only that Ray was not motivated by a streak of inherent racism, but that the stories that made him out to be such a deplorable human being were "seriously distorted" by the authors who had gone to great lengths to portray him as such an individual. In its decision to reject the racism canard that Huie had created, the HSCA implicitly concluded that he had just made it up—exposing his agenda to create an abhorrent character trait, and with it, a legend for James Earl Ray—right out of thin air.

What the HSCA report did not say was that once the premise of Ray's racism was removed as a motive, everything else that had been attributed to him based upon that canard would also be undermined and therefore should have been explicitly rejected. That includes, of course, the related theme of an intrinsic hatred of Dr. King and with it the never-proved supposed need for recognition posited by Huie—whose vivid imagination had always been the only real basis for it—and thus, the entire related premise of Ray's stalking of Dr. King. Nevertheless, that faux legend will be thoroughly examined and debunked in the pages to follow.

In addition to Huie's obvious attempt to frame James Earl Ray as a racist, he also made numerous attempts to portray him as a chronic liar, an antisocial misfit, using such other words as "creep, loner, stalker," which were taken from the FBI's fabricated profile of him, accepted as fact by not only Huie, but most everyone else who read it either directly or from the numerous news articles then being written.[610] Huie had convinced himself that the FBI's legend of James Earl Ray was true and had already repeated it at length in his *Look* articles.

Huie also described Ray as being afraid of women, due to having been in prison for thirteen years, and as having avoided women, being unable to have a normal relationship with them, and even stating to the Canadian woman, Ms. Keating, "You must have seemed overwhelming to him. Yet you say he is perfectly normal."[611] Huie even admitted that he had expected to find her to be "a shapeless frump" but was "flabbergasted" to find that she was "most attractive," and a "tastefully dressed and coiffured mature woman." Ms. Keating explained to him that she had been at the end of a marriage with an aggressive man and was attracted to Ray because he seemed to be a lonely man who was "neat and well-dressed and shy," and "a man she felt comfortable with."[612]

Despite being surprised to hear this woman's description of Ray as a down-to-earth regular guy, Huie continued to frame him as being an irredeemable misfit who was unable to associate with women, or even normal men for that matter. But Claire Keating was not the only person who had met Ray during the course of the period after his escape from prison who had "surprised" Huie. He heard repeated descriptions of a man far different from what he had been expecting to hear, and how he had continued to describe him, per the FBI's contrived profile. Several other people whom Huie interviewed said essentially the same thing as Ms. Keating (including two couples, plus other employees of the second couple, below, as well as the proprietor of the Birmingham rooming house, for a total of at least eight people):

- The first couple that Ray met after escaping from the Missouri State Prison on April 23, 1967, were a Mr. and Mrs. Donnelly, the managers of a rooming house on the north side of Chicago. They described James (living under his first alias, John Larry Rayns) as a "nice, quiet fellow, neat and clean . . . always paid promptly . . . tidy and careful about his garbage . . . He stayed here six or eight weeks, got mail several times; and when he left, he said he had to go to Canada on business. I sure hope nothing has happened to him."[613]

  In the November 12 *Look* article, Huie noted, after that same piece, "I didn't tell Mrs. Donnelly what had happened to the nice, quiet fellow named John Rayns. When she reads this, she'll know."[614]

- Using the same alias, Ray then went farther north, to the Chicago suburb of Winnetka, Illinois, where he got a job at a well-established eatery called Indian Trail Restaurant, which had been in business for thirty-four years at that time, owned by the Klingeman family. Huie met the family's patriarch and matriarch, the latter of whom first surprised Huie with this description: "Such a nice man. He was here for two or three months and we so regretted to see him go. He came here as a dishwasher. But during his first week we saw that he could be more than a dishwasher. So we promoted him to the steam table and raised his wages. He was quiet, neat, efficient, and so dependable. He was never late a minute, though he had to ride the buses for perhaps 15 miles each way . . . I hope he is well. We wrote him after he left and told him how much we valued him."[615] After Huie explained to her that his real name was James Earl Ray and that he was a suspect in Dr. King's murder, he described her reaction: "I'll never forget the astonishment, followed quickly by anguish, in Mrs. Klingeman's eyes . . ." Then she asked: "Are you sure? It seems impossible. You mean he is the man we have read so much about? So cruel? So senseless? So shameful? . . . I would have trusted John Rayns in my home to babysit with my grandchildren . . ."[616] Evidently, this wasn't stunning enough to make Huie soften his profile of Mr. Ray. He rationalized it to Mrs. Klingeman by stating: "Maybe you weren't so mistaken about the man you knew. Maybe he was reliable while he worked for you,"[617] implicitly suggesting that he had since changed his whole persona and had only now become a deplorable specimen of the human race.

When Mr. Klingeman mailed Ray his last paycheck, he enclosed a letter that restated their regrets and further stated that Mrs. Klingeman had "hope[d] that you would stay and learn all she knows. She was also most willing to go along (if given the opportunity) to do all possible to make you feel more and more happy working here. She and I both wish you well. Please know you are always welcome [to return to the restaurant]."[618] Moreover, the Klingemans stated to Huie that, of their seventy-eight employees, about 25 to 30 percent were ordinarily "Negroes," and that *no reports of any problems between them and Rayns (Ray) were reported by anyone and that he was never discourteous to anyone.* Finally, Mrs. Klingeman stated that "whatever he is and whatever he has done, while he was here, we saw a little spark of dignity in John Rayns."[619] (Emphasis added.)

- When Ray left Canada and went to Birmingham, at Raul's direction, he rented a room from a Mr. Cherpes, who told Huie, "You couldn't imagine a nicer guy to have around—quiet, neat, paid his bill promptly every week, talked mostly about the weather . . . I thought he was just a good fellow temporarily out of work."[620] That Huie had the decency to report these rebuttals of the official false profile is commendable and shows that he apparently had a slight streak of honesty about him (probably because he expected that they would buy a copy of his book since their names would be in it); yet to forgive him for continuing down his chosen path of brazen dishonesty more than offsets whatever value that sliver of candor might have had.

- When he returned to Canada after the assassination, his first landlady in Toronto, Mrs. Szpakowski, described Ray as the ideal roomer:

"He was quiet, kept to himself, made no unusual demands. He paid his rent in advance and on time." Even after seeing Ray's photo in the newspaper on April 19 when he had finally been identified, she passed it off as an error. As the first author of a published book on the subject, Clay Blair Jr., noted in 1969, she decided that "he was such a gentleman, he couldn't be a killer."[621]

Yet, despite these witnesses' testimony, Huie seemed to register surprise each time he heard the same story from so many people who had gotten to know him, all claiming that Ray was a genuinely nice guy. In these cases, Huie instinctively knew that he could not report otherwise due to the risk of being called out by the people he had interviewed. But he knew that the unnamed Canadian lady would never do that, since she would only embarrass herself in doing so; likewise, the Mexican prostitute, whom he undoubtedly presumed would never read his articles anyway, would never contradict anything he might write about her experience with Ray. For those reasons, he decided to exploit those opportunities to twist and reshape innocuous testimony into evidence of extreme racism and vicious criminal behavior, unaware of course that the HSCA would eventually expose them, well after the damage was done.

While Huie quickly dispatched the more positive statements by witnesses regarding Ray's persona, he abruptly segued to the negatively reframed statements.. Yet Huie—and the subsequent authors determined to sustain his lies—took the questionable statements of a few fellow prisoners who had known him and were willing to tell Huie what he wanted to hear. Ignoring their lack of credibility and conflicted motives—they had simply hoped to cash in on their own notoriety with the famed checkbook journalist—Huie used the words of the most incredible, obviously dishonest people to override the veritable accounts of credible people. As he repeatedly demonstrated throughout his book, he proceeded to write an account intentionally biased against Ray, who was supposed to be his primary client.

The fact that all of these early fiction writers had clearly acted against Ray's interests from the start—intentionally going out of their way to do so—is conclusive proof that they were all involved in a continuing blatant conflict of interest. The Haneses were undoubtedly the least culpable in that, and had attempted to balance their actions between Ray's and Huie's interests, but they still failed Ray by putting Huie in the middle of the massive conflict of interest.

Despite hearing all of these personal accounts—from people who interacted with James Earl Ray, who had gotten to know him well, even intimately—it still had apparently not occurred to Huie that James Earl Ray was anything but a deranged violent racist and vicious killer. The fact that

Huie created this paradox is bewildering, given that he had assured Ray early on that he would be true to Ray's story, and even help him to repair his very damaged reputation. The worst thing about this paradox is that it has apparently gone unnoticed, not only by most readers of his book, but especially the critics of the official story, whose failures to aggressively pursue this enigma have contributed to its perpetuation.

The real reason for the contradictions was that Huie's first priority was to follow the FBI's script, which profiled a loathsome, violent man, despite what he was being told about Ray's opposite behavior and his rather withdrawn, introverted, distinctly unaggressive personality. That unavoidable inconsistency—combined with Ray's lack of a record of physical violence toward others—must be considered as unassailable proof of the deliberate amalgamation of lies designed to replace the truth about the actual essence of the man whom the FBI had labeled "extremely dangerous." James's brother Jerry stated, in explaining James's lack of a violent temperament, that he had never been violent in his life:[622]

> Never. He never had. He never had—the most violent thing he ever did was rob a store, you know, the Kroger store. That's the most violent ever, but there never was no [*sic*] violence used in that, you know. And in fact, before that he was always, you know, like a burglar. You know, like breaking in and stealing money, but then when he got with that—I mentioned his name before—Owens. Owens did robbery, see, so then he went in on the robbery.

The general public would never learn about the persona of the real Ray and how he was so unlike the fictional, fearsome, aggressively threatening, mythological Ray. After recounting those vignettes of real people coming to like the real Ray, the novelist Huie, referring to Ray as a "crafty criminal," stated that Ray decided to kill Dr. King so that he could "make the Top Ten" [FBI's most wanted list], deliberately leaving evidence at the scene to identify himself as the killer, the only way to attain that distinction. Moreover, he declared that Ray intended to escape to Portuguese West Africa, from where he could not be extradited.[623] By the time he wrote that passage just halfway through his book, he continued to refer to Ray as the presumed killer, as he was ordered to do by his anonymous handlers, certainly not by any insights he had gained as to the real persona of his subject.

By the time he was three-quarters of the way through the book, Huie added more prose to what he had written earlier when he opined on Ray's motive for murdering Dr. King: "*His motivation was his yearning to wear boots too big for him.*" (Emphasis added.) Huie then reiterated his most damaging descriptions of his ex-client, saying that he was a "dull criminal, ashamed of himself," but somehow, despite his backward demeanor, a man who felt that he ought to be on the FBI's Ten Most Wanted list, who deserved to be considered one of the more interesting criminals of all time, whom others would enjoy reading about.[624] Huie's narrative at this point has become a series of unconnected non sequiturs, the gravity lost completely in such pithy sentences as: "But with the passage of time truth becomes more and more difficult to recall and to enunciate. Many men outside prison prefer fantasies to truth."[625] Here Huie almost seems to be repeating a mantra that he had memorized (perhaps while visiting FBI HQ).

Huie stated that in coming up with his conclusion that James Ray sought "recognition," he interviewed the head of the International Society of Hypnosis, Reverend Xavier von Koss, in the South Bay area of Los Angeles, whom Ray had sought out in January 1968. Reverend von Koss stated that he had attempted to hypnotize Ray (who had introduced himself as Eric Galt) but that he "quickly encountered very strong subconscious resistance. He could not cooperate. This, of course, is always the case when a person fears that under hypnosis he may reveal something he wishes to conceal."[626]

While Ray resisted subconsciously being hypnotized, he had stated that he wanted to use hypnosis to solve problems, mentioning that those that might take thirty minutes at the conscious level could be reduced to thirty seconds. Reverend von Goss explained that "Galt" seemed interested in general self-improvement and deduced therefore that he belonged to the "recognition" type, that he valued recognition more than anything else, including sex, money, or self-preservation. That he could come up with that description for a man who—through the use of numerous aliases and getting plastic surgery to change his facial features, even avoiding registering to vote, for fear of being discovered—as an escaped fugitive actually sought anonymity is startling.

Huie took that to the next level when he deduced that Ray's way of getting recognized was to aim for getting the first position of the FBI's Ten Most Wanted list.[627] Huie (who never met or even talked over the telephone with Ray) ventured an array of intimate details of how Ray thought, and on that subject he asserted that Ray thought that criminals in the FBI's Ten Most Wanted list was comparable to actors winning an Academy Award, or models aspiring to be in a fashion magazine's Ten Best-Dressed Women's list. In the same way, Huie imagined, criminals would compete with their peers to attain the exalted and rarefied status and recognition of being made the number-one criminal of the FBI's top-ten listing.[628] By his own words,

Huie portrayed himself as either remarkably prescient about the aspirations of the most hardened criminals, especially about a man he had never met (in stark contrast to what he had been told by credible, real people who did know him), or, conversely, exceptionally obtuse and hallucinatory about a man whom he was out to destroy.

Huie's fictionally based book became the foundation upon which not only other later authors, but even the government itself, based its "factual references." In a clear-cut example, the Department of Justice relied on Huie's book for much of the background and movements—including Huie's prevarications of Ray's "stalking" of King, and the unsubstantiated charges of racism—of James Earl Ray in its original report. As noted by Mark Lane:

> In just the opening pages of Section IIC, it cited that book more than twenty times as the source of information about Ray. The report relied upon Huie's description of Ray's relationship with a Canadian woman who Ray considered asking for assistance in securing a passport [but changed his mind when he found out about her being a government worker]. Huie had written that Ray told the woman that people who "know niggers hate them."[629]

Ray had vigorously denied ever making such a statement and the unidentified woman confirmed that, meaning that Huie could only have made it up out of whole cloth. To do that required the most egregious cunning and guile. Yet that lie was used as the cornerstone of the government's argument for the original portrayal of Ray being a racist stalker and the HSCA's equivocation on the racism charge ten years later, though not the stalker part, which should have also been rejected. The irony of that depiction—coming as it did from the FBI's blatant instructions to Huie in the first place—meant that the racist canard had started in the same downtown Washington building, the Department of Justice, as where it eventually returned. It was only determined later, by the 1976–78 HSCA hearings on Capitol Hill, that indeed it was a lie perpetrated by Huie, but of course it was delivered with deliberate understatement. Though the lie was finally rescinded—the official government position amended, and the government technically acknowledged that James Earl Ray was not the racist he was purported to have been —most of the public have still not received that message.

A profound irony was thus created. The elaborate lie originally created by Hoover and high-level FBI officials, published by an ethically challenged writer of fiction but accepted by the public hungry for a satisfactory explanation—one that stood unchallenged for a decade—had become so widely accepted that its whispered retraction in 1979 failed to correct the record, and thus still stands today in the minds of most people. Worse than that, the double irony was that the lie was originated by the real racists then running the FBI. The triple irony was that they were the real perpetrators of the murder of Martin Luther King Jr., not the man they had set up to take the fall.

The greatest of the paradoxical ironies is that the HSCA's jettison of Ray's "racist mentality" as the underlying motive in 1978 was finally replaced with the only other one that has since surfaced, as noted above by Huie: *"That he yearned to wear boots too big for him."* This is simply another way of saying that Ray's primary motive was his desire to achieve great notoriety, to be elevated to the top position on the FBI's Ten Most Wanted list so that he would be recognized as the most famous criminal in America, a profile that is completely incongruous with his quiet and introverted persona. If nothing else, for Huie to have singlehandedly propagated such an enormous deception—since repeated by numerous other fiction writers—was his own greatest achievement.

Another Mysterious Character, or "Raul" Stand-in? Jules Ricco Kimble (a.k.a. "Rolland" or "Rollie")

Dr. Philip H. Melanson, through a Canadian journalist named Andy Salwyn, the Montreal bureau chief for the *Toronto Star* in 1967–68, identified another man who had frequented the same Montreal neighborhood where James Earl Ray had briefly lived during the summer of 1967: a mysterious American from Louisiana named Jules Ricco Kimble. The HSCA also investigated this man, who was not cooperative with the investigators—as someone of his background might be expected to be—because he was a convicted murderer who had acknowledged that he knew Ray. But instead of piquing their interest, according to Melanson, their inquiry was nonetheless "both perfunctory and misleading." Kimble had even admitted (albeit vaguely) that he had participated in the King assassination, and that both he and Ray had been summoned by the CIA to come to Montreal in 1967, apparently so they could reevaluate them for possible assignments. He must have been a little too hot to handle for the HSCA investigators, given how he disappeared afterward.[630]

The HSCA was seemingly content to avoid pursuing this witness and did their utmost to avoid a number of potential leads enumerated by the authors cited below in their extensive research of this man. The committee ultimately came to the curious conclusion that despite a number of confluences in their travels and actions, there was "no evidence to support a Ray-Kimble connection or to indicate that Kimble was involved in any plot to kill Dr. King."[631]

Kimble was scrutinized more fully by authors John Larry Ray and Lyndon Barsten in their 2008 book *Truth at Last*. It was they who raised perplexing questions about why James would have driven his old Plymouth all the way from St. Louis to Montreal (1,200 miles) when another large Canadian city, Toronto, was less than 800 miles away, if all he wanted to achieve was to be in a large city in Canada, out of US law enforcement's direct reach.[632] Choosing to put himself in the same neighborhood as another man, George "Benny" Edmondson, who had also recently escaped from the same Missouri prison from which James had escaped, suggests that both of them were directed there by persons unknown. In Benny's case, he was recaptured on June 29, 1967, and returned to Jeff City Prison—but, amazingly, was almost immediately released on bond and then allowed to return to Montreal, live under an alias of "Alex Bormann," and marry a woman he had met as a fugitive a few weeks before that. Then, in still another twist, Benny felt comfortable enough to complain to the FBI when Huie's book was published because he had revealed his new alias.[633] A cynic might think that it seemed as if he were doing a favor for the FBI by doing a dry run for Ray's handlers to use as a template for his own escape.

James Earl Ray's brother, John Larry Ray, believed that during James's previous military service in Germany, he had been unwittingly subjected to secret intelligence experiments related to the CIA's MKULTRA program and that as part of that conditioning, he was made to understand that severe retributions would be exacted if he were to ever talk about them. As noted previously, while in Germany, his military records indicated that he had been given spinal taps, portrayed along with other miscellaneous medical ailments (such as gonorrhea, headaches, tonsillitis, boils, sore throat, etc.) as though such procedures were routine. If true, that would explain a lot about his reticence to fully reveal his reasons for settling in the Montreal neighborhood that he chose. It was near McGill University, where in 1959, according to CIA documents obtained by researcher Lyndon Barsten, the CIA had established a program called Subproject 68, run by Dr. Ewen Cameron at the Allen Memorial Institute.[634]

Lyndon Barsten interviewed Jules Kimble, who told him in a recorded telephone conversation that he and James were both ordered to go to McGill's Allen Memorial Institute by the CIA in 1967 to undergo hypnosis. The Royal Canadian Mounted Police verified Kimble's statement through their own investigation.[635] Kimble also stated to Barsten that he and James Earl Ray were subjected to "narco-hypnosis" treatments by an employee of Allen Memorial Institute as part of Subproject 68 of the CIA's mind-control program MKULTRA. Barsten noted that since this was a top-secret project in 1968, it implicitly meant that Kimble must have had first-hand knowledge of what was going on there at the time.[636]

Ray had gone there previously, in 1959, to hide out; and now, in the summer of 1967, shortly after he broke out of prison, he made his way back to that same neighborhood. The Montreal journalist whom Melanson interviewed, Andy Salwyn, was "adamant" that Kimble and Ray were together in Montreal in July 1967. He produced a witness (identified by Melanson using a pseudonym to protect her privacy), a nurse who had briefly dated Kimble and knew him only as "Rollie." She told Salwyn that he had a police-band radio in his car, that he carried guns in the trunk of the car, and that he made a number of phone calls from her apartment. In fact, she produced a phone bill that contained the numbers he had called, which she gave to the RCMP, unfortunately not first making a copy of them since they would turn up missing from the RCMP files. Salwyn obtained the numbers and had his colleague Earl McRae call each one. They turned out to be five bars in Texas and New Orleans (where Ray claimed to have met "Raoul" in a bar in December 1967).

When Melanson tried to exact more information from the RCMP, he was met with stiff resistance by officials. But he was told by the chief information officer of the RCMP that he "was the only individual, Canadian or American, who had ever requested data on the King case."[637] Evidently, this either meant that even the HSCA had not expressed interest or that their investigators did not meet the qualification he stated, as "individuals." Andy Salwyn went to Washington to testify to the HSCA, but he met with similar intransigence when the committee staff "questioned him in closed session for less than ten minutes" while they "grilled him sharply about his own data, almost as if he were a hostile witness." He stated that it was apparent to him that the committee had the RCMP's investigative file, which Dr. Melanson verified, because he showed that the HSCA's Final Report contained citations to that file.

The HSCA report, however, was dismissive of everything Salwyn had presented, orally or within his written files, which they erroneously referenced as an "article" in the *Toronto Star*; this was despite the fact that the story was killed before ever being published due to the mysterious disappearance of Salwyn's source material in the offices of one of the *Star*'s lawyers when a legal secretary misplaced them.[638] Their confusion on that aspect was reflective of a more general state of bewilderment about—or disinterest in pursuing—this entire disturbing lead, possibly because of efforts by the CIA to close that gate.

When Melanson called HSCA Chief Counsel G. Robert Blakey—who had by then returned to Notre Dame as a professor—to discuss it, he too dismissed Salwyn's testimony as "bullshit," and then he opined, "I'm as sure Ray killed Martin Luther King as I am of my birthday."[639] In their efforts to ignore this story, the HSCA stated that Kimble had been arrested in New Orleans on July 26, 1967 (omitting the fact that he posted a $500 bond and was immediately released). Moreover, although they did acknowledge the evidence that Kimble had been in Montreal in September 1967, they presumed—with no evidence to support or refute it—that he must have just arrived there, as though he couldn't have been there in August, when they knew Ray was there. They also ignored the documented fact that Kimble had also been back in New Orleans in December 1967, when Ray was known to have been there.[640]

The Kimble story is but one of many that had gotten too close to possibly becoming exculpatory evidence in the official frame-up that had begun immediately after King's assassination, run by people skilled in maneuvering the hapless victim. From all outward appearances, it seems the intent was to ensure that due process was systematically denied, rather than ever having been the goal for James Earl Ray. There must have been a lot of pressure put on the HSCA to drop this line of inquiry, because it was clear to all members and their staff of attorneys and investigators—and certainly to Chairman Stokes—that it could only, inextricably, lead to a case of high-government-sponsored conspiracy, and that was a result that could not stand. The very idea of that dark and foreboding rabbit hole would have been declared off limits by the powerful forces that had been behind the very plot that they were supposedly investigating. It should have never been a surprise to anyone that Kimble was declared out of bounds and quickly dismissed from the committee's agenda.

The Mysterious Randy Rosen (Randolph Erwin Rosenson): Another Raul Assistant?

In November 1967, James Earl Ray, before leaving Mexico to return to California, while cleaning his car to ensure the border guards would find nothing incriminating, had found a business card tucked under the cellophane of an open cigarette pack stuck between the front passenger seat and the center console of the Mustang. The printed names and address on the front side of the card had been scribbled over, but he noted that the letters "L.E.A.A." were still visible.* On the other side of the card, someone had written "Randy Rosen, 1180 Northwest River Drive, Miami, Florida."[641] Although James said that he had no recollection of ever meeting anyone by that name, his brothers Jerry[642] and John[643] believe he had met Rosen (Rosenson) in New Orleans on his trip there with Charlie Stein in December 1967. In fact, John stated that James met him, along with Raul, in the Playboy Club (Le Bunny Lounge) on Canal Street[644] and later met high-level associates of Carlos Marcello at his main headquarters in the Town and Country Motel.[645]

John Larry Ray also stated that James had some involvement with another infamous character there named Edward Grady Partin, a union official who had been "turned" into a witness against Jimmy Hoffa (whose lawyer, Z. T. Osborn, would be "suicided" right after agreeing to represent James). Ed Partin—whose rap sheet included charges ranging from armed robbery to kidnapping and rape—had also previously corrupted a deputy sheriff from Baton Rouge named Herman Thompson, an association that would be documented in a federal lawsuit.[646] As James determined on his own—and would unsuccessfully plead with his attorneys to investigate—the Baton Rouge telephone number he had been given as a backup to Raul's New Orleans number was the listing for "Herman A. Thompson." (James had picked up a talent for checking telephone numbers against the phone book by reading them backward, using the last two digits and, when finding a match, checking the rest of the number.)[647]

James Earl Ray had been circumspect about admitting anything related to his gangland contacts, beginning in Chicago, but in Montreal and New Orleans, as well. As noted elsewhere, it had to do with warnings he had received, even as far back as the 1940s, after his army service, never to divulge any of his covert associations for fear of severe, possibly fatal, reprisal. That admonishment would have prevailed with Rosenson, Kimble, and everyone else he had been in contact with in New Orleans. That obviously hindered his own credibility and undermined his defense, but seeing what happened to his new lawyer Osborn, he was reminded of the severe consequences that would be inevitable if he did go over that line. For those reasons, he maintained

---

* The Law Enforcement Assistance Administration (LEAA) was created in 1968 as a provision of the Omnibus Crime Control and Safe Streets Act, replacing an earlier similar program to provide federal funds in the form of block grants and discretionary funds to states for disbursement to local areas for crime-fighting purposes. One such initiative was reported to be for supporting specific local programs as "testing innovative strategies to resolve continuing problems" as a means to reduce crime. At the street level, this program was known for being a method to fund informers, for example.

that he never met Rosen and submitted statements indicating that the card must have been left there by Raul the last time they rode together in the car. In 1974, his brother Jerry determined, through one of the attorneys he had worked with, that the full name of that person was Randolph Erwin Rosenson, who had been convicted of narcotics charges and had been suspected of smuggling drugs from Mexico.

Ray had dutifully reported this to the FBI in 1968, before finding out that Rosen was actually Rosenson, and again to the HSCA in 1977, then divulging both names. He continued to deny to his attorneys and investigators—yet admit to his brothers—that he had ever met this man and claimed that the card and cigarette pack had been inadvertently left in the car by Raul, therefore that Rosen/Rosenson was one of Raul's associates. James felt that it was not important to admit he had met him but that this was yet another potential lead that would prove "Raoul's" existence if it had been vigorously pursued. But the HSCA staff, in its efforts to avoid going in that direction—still denying the existence of Raul—only attempted to find a direct connection between Ray and Rosenson, even discovering that they were in Los Angeles and Birmingham at the same times in 1967, and again in Birmingham in 1968 when Ray purchased the rifle(s) as guided by Raul.[648]

It did not take the HSCA investigators long to find Rosenson. Inexplicably, they decided to put him up in a Knoxville, Tennessee, hotel near the Brushy Mountain Prison where Ray was serving time, for an extended period, from May through July 1977. The hotel was owned by a friend of Governor Blanton, chosen for what was apparently another instance of political payback for which Governor Blanton had become infamous—in this case, apparently, a favor being repaid by someone on the committee. Rosenson's importance as a witness was reflected in the fact that the HSCA staff interviewed him six times. He also appeared before the full committee in executive session (the records, including audiotapes, of which have still not been made public).[649]

A few months later, by September 1977, Rosenson had disappeared completely (a rumor at the time was that he had been put into the Department of Justice's Federal Witness Protection Program).[650] Rosenson's disappearance at that propitious time suggests that someone decided it was the only way possible to permanently cut this lead, and that should be considered a marker for how critically important it had to be, to justify such an extraordinary action. Rosenson's disappearance came concurrently with another possibly related event: Ray's wife Anna—whom he had married in prison with King's friend Reverend James Lawson officiating—received an anonymous telephone call informing her that she and Ray needed to drop the Rosenson matter, and the search for audiotapes of his HSCA interview, if she wanted to remain "healthy." Those tapes are among the committee's classified documents that were hidden from the public for a period of fifty years, which means they will not be accessible until the year 2029.[651]

The HSCA only released heavily redacted files for certain documents regarding the Rosenson enigma, but some of the finer points were revealed in records that did become public. One was the HSCA's determination that Rosenson "traveled in many of the same New Orleans circles as Ray's associate Charles Stein . . . both of them were known to the New Orleans Police Department for similar criminal conduct, [and they] also had mutual acquaintances, frequented the same bars, and had retained the same lawyer"—who, it should be noted, was yet another top-tier New Orleans criminal lawyer, G. Wray Gill. And Gill even brought in another famed attorney named Camille F. Gravel; the mere fact that these men were able to retain lawyers of that caliber raises even more suspicions.[652]

In one of the "Murkin" case files (the FBI's code name, "MURder of KINg") obtained by Harold Weisberg, it was noted that Charles Stein had at one point indicated that he had actually met Raul in New Orleans on the December 1967 trip he made with Ray; however, he subsequently backpedaled on that claim, possibly because of someone's reminding him not to go there.[653] In an article published by the *New York Times* on April 26, 1968, Charles Stein was quoted as having said that the real purpose of that trip was for Ray to "talk business with 'a man with an Italian name.'" Stein also stated that "Galt had told him the man's name, but I don't remember right now what it was."[654] (Though Stein referred to an Italian name, it is reasonable to infer that he meant a Latin name, which would include Spanish or Portuguese names as well as possibly others. Raul Coelho, as referenced elsewhere, was an immigrant from Portugal.)

A portion of the Murkin File obtained by Weisberg stated:

> There was also a more recent episode in the saga of the traveling carnival man [Rosenson], one never mentioned by HSCA. It was Ray who indicated in a letter to the author that Rosenson "was in the Andrew Johnson Hotel in Knoxville when I escaped [from Brushy Mountain Prison in Petros, thirty-five miles outside of Knoxville] in June 1977." This was confirmed by Stan DeLozier, a reporter for the *Knoxville News-Sentinel* who had done a story on Rosenson in 1978 when he was being questioned by HSCA. DeLozier managed to dig up information which HSCA either did not have or chose not to reveal.

He interviewed Rosenson's Knoxville lawyer, Gene A. "Chip" Stanley, Jr. Stanley confirmed that Rosenson had been convicted in New Orleans of drug offenses and customs violations.[655]

The fact that Rosenson had been convicted of dealing in drugs and smuggling intersects with what Ray had consistently claimed about "Raoul." It was the very point that had attached Ray to Raul all along and was the basis for Ray's consistent claim that Raul had financed his travels for nearly a year, starting with jobs moving contraband across the Canadian border, then the Mexican border. From that, the nature of the smuggling was being moved up a notch, to gun smuggling, and it was on that hook that Raul had promised Ray a bigger paycheck of $12,000 and a passport to allow him passage out of the country. The information the HSCA did compile and present for public inspection left strong suggestions that Rosenson, being from New Orleans, was Raul's close associate there. Further, it might account for the person who had handled many of Ray's telephone calls in Raul's absence; it also suggested that he had apparently traveled in the background, with or without Raul, to places where Ray was staying, monitoring him throughout his travels.

The HSCA tempered their findings, though—instead of "drug offenses and customs violations," it became merely unspecified "criminal conduct" in New Orleans in Rosenson's criminal record to intentionally obfuscate the relationship he apparently shared with Raul. It was the linkage to Raul that the investigators were obviously hiding; Ray had never claimed to have ever met Rosenson personally. Considering the significant investment made by the HSCA in the Rosenson matter—three months in the Knoxville hotel, six interviews plus another in executive session, the apparent induction of him into the US Federal Witness Protection Program—and the fact that the biggest secrets were either partially or wholly redacted only causes this lead to take on much more prominence than it otherwise might have. The similarities with the also-aborted Kimble investigation combine to make both of these ignored leads highly suspect, suggesting that the linkages were among the strongest exculpatory evidence in Ray's favor, thus too dangerous for the committee to pursue.

Regardless of the intensive examination done in the Kimble / Rosenson / Raul / Stein / Ray nexus, and the need to keep much of it secret for fifty years, the final word on this subject by the HSCA was succinctly stated: "The committee concluded that Rosenson was not involved with Ray in a conspiracy to assassinate Dr. King" [and in so doing, they implicitly dropped even the possibility of Raul's existence from further consideration].[656]

Preparing the Public Persona of James Earl Ray

A vigorous propaganda campaign was conducted immediately after the arrest of James Earl Ray, during the last half of 1968 and into 1969. It was a concerted effort by President Johnson—axiomatically, it could have only existed through his creation and sustenance, whether directly ordered or by his acquiescence to the FBI's initiative—to instill a sense of finality in the public mind that the killer of Martin Luther King Jr. had been identified and justice would prevail. A large part of that message was devoted to convincing the public that there were no accomplices, that there was no high-level, organized collusion with other parties (the only exception was that advanced by William Bradford Huie, and subsequently by his fictional descendants, who charged that anonymous and amorphous racists might have offered a cash reward), and certainly no governmental resources involved in King's murder.

One example of this appeared when a major story titled "Ray Alone Still Talks of a Plot" was published in the *Washington Post* on Sunday, March 16, 1969, in the immediate aftermath of the minitrial and in the midst of the vigorous public outcry that resulted from what was generally perceived by many as a great injustice, due to pervasive suspicions that others were involved in Dr. King's murder.[657] The front page of the National News section, G-1, was dedicated to this story, with a large photo of the "confessed murderer" emblazoned in the middle. The lead paragraphs stated:

> The only person directly tied to the investigation of the James Earl Ray case—who still insists there was a conspiracy to kill the Rev. Dr. Martin Luther King Jr.—is James Earl Ray himself.
>
> And Ray—convicted thief, forger, prison escapee, user of countless aliases and possessor of an elaborate psychiatric record—has what may charitably be called a credibility problem.

In a later paragraph, the article names William Bradford Huie as the ultimate authority—"the most knowledgeable person about the details of the alleged plot"—and the fact that he could not name one conspirator (despite the fact that Ray had repeatedly begged Huie to track down "Raoul" and had given him the necessary leads to do so).

Yet the article then erroneously stated that "He has never specified names, places or dates of any known consequence . . . A full trial of the case, contrary to what some critics feel, would not have revealed much more than what prosecutors presented at the guilty plea hearing." That statement is contradicted by what James wrote in his own book, that he had repeatedly given (or tried to in Foreman's case) all of those details, complete with telephone numbers he still remembered. Given the beyond merely incompetent, purposefully conflicted lawyering that Ray had had, it should be clear to all by now that this wasn't just some benign and misinformed effort by a newspaper editor to provide incisive analysis of the major story of the week. It was clearly designed to instill another layer of mythology within the public mind about how James Earl Ray was not worth further discussion, that he had had his day in court and that justice had been served.

Part IV

The Trials and Retrials (1969–1999)

Chapter 10

CRIMINAL TRIAL ABORTED

> Dick Cavett: *"A lot of people in the legal profession were astounded at how you got [James Earl Ray] to change the plea [from "not guilty" to "guilty"]."*
> Percy Foreman: *"I didn't get him to change the plea. [Laughing] I simply told him that I thought he would be executed if he didn't."*
> —*The Dick Cavett Show*, August 9, 1969

The Manipulation of the Patsy, Continued

The worst, most cunning, and successful manipulations of James Earl Ray came after the murder of Dr. King and were the result of a part of the plot that was supposed to have never been needed. If Ray had minded his handler Raul, he would not have left the crime scene fifteen minutes early to get his spare tire fixed and his gas tank refilled. That act saved his life but also made it necessary for some high-powered lawyering to ensure he would spend the rest of his life in prison.

The story begins with the enigmatic way he was immediately hooked up with his first attorney, former FBI agent and CIA operative Arthur Hanes, who brought him documents to sign that had already been prepared by the checkbook journalist, William Bradford Huie. Looking at these events in retrospect, they were occurring so rapidly that they had all the appearances of having been in the works for a considerable period of time; that they were possibly being set up in the weeks between the assassination and the arrest of Ray in London.

There was, figuratively, a full-court press deployed by Tennessee and federal officials—and by extension, through the FBI's pressure on UK officials—to ensure that James Earl Ray would either be executed for his alleged crime or that he would spend the rest of his natural life in prison. The latter course was finally selected because it offered the potential of avoiding a trial entirely, prompted by the possibility that Ray might be found not guilty by a jury due to the lack of physical evidence or credible witnesses to testify that he was the shooter.

Among the first indications of the frailty of the legal case against Ray was that while still incarcerated in London, he was not permitted to consult with his chosen attorney, Arthur Hanes Sr., before the extradition hearing on July 2, 1968, despite the fact that Mr. Hanes had gone to London within ten days of his arrest for that very purpose. All of the evidence presented against him was in affidavit form and therefore not subject to cross-examination. The only witness from the United States was Mr. Arthur Bonebrake, an FBI special agent, who was not there to ensure that Ray's legal interests were being protected.

Ray might have avoided extradition altogether if he had been given sound legal advice, regardless of the charges and publicity, since the extant treaty between the US and the UK, dating from 1931, prohibited extradition for cases involving political crimes. Furthermore, just as in JFK's murder—where the use of the term "conspiracy" allowed President Johnson and FBI Director Hoover to have the FBI take jurisdiction away from local law enforcement agencies, and where the initial charging document was based upon that same term despite being dropped immediately afterwards—the sole basis for Ray's extradition from England was that he was allegedly acting as part of a conspiracy to murder Dr. King. That premise was dropped as soon as Ray was returned and put into the Shelby County jail, putting the legality of the extradition itself into question.[658] Moreover, Ramsey Clark, the attorney general, refused to permit Ray's lawyer, Mr. Hanes, to accompany Ray on the flight from London to Memphis, nor was Hanes present when Ray arrived in Memphis. All of these legal lapses were directed by the highest federal officials, indubitably from the man to whom Attorney General Ramsey Clark reported: Lyndon B. Johnson, the president of the United States.

When Ray arrived back at the Shelby County jail, he was taken to a specially prepared cell, in which he was confined for over eight months as he awaited his day in court. It was a standard-sized cell, six by eight feet, with a bed in one corner and a toilet and sink in the opposite corner, located within a block of six cells. Ray described it as an environment "straight out of a police state handbook."[659] It was freshly painted to cover the walls and every window, which were fitted with steel plates to keep out any natural light. The lighting was provided by bright floodlights that burned twenty-four hours a day, causing him to lose all track of day or night. Two visible CCTV cameras monitored his movements in the cell and the surrounding cellblock, and live feeds were sent to two televisions within the cell block to allow guards to constantly surveil Ray's every move within the cell, even when he was on the toilet and in the shower stalls in an adjoining area.[660]

Two guards, a city policeman, and a county deputy sheriff were also on constant duty to ensure that he wouldn't attempt an escape. There was also a visible microphone aimed at his cell that the sheriff said was always turned off when his attorney met with him, although Ray did not believe that. Ray later testified that not only had the guards overheard his conversations with his attorneys, but that his lawyer Percy Foreman spoke very loudly during their conversations, as if to make sure his comments were recorded. But there was little need for that since, according to one of Ray's metaphors, the microphones were so sensitive that the guards "could hear a roach walk across the floor."[661]

After a couple of months of this treatment, Ray began to suffer insomnia, restlessness, fatigue, and nosebleeds due to the absence of fresh air and sunlight, so finally Hanes wrote to the judge, calling the conditions "cruel and unusual punishment." The prosecutor told the court that all of it was necessary, and that according to the closed-circuit television feeds, the prisoner was getting eight and a half hours of sleep per night. As Ray observed, that finding was based upon the presumption that a person lying on his back motionless, trying to sleep, was actually asleep. Judge Battle found on November 22 that this treatment was "reasonable," but he did allow that if the bright lights were an irritant, Ray could have a mask to wear to cover his eyes.[662] Specifically, Judge Battle wrote in his decree that:

> [A] great percentage of the security complained of is for the benefit of the defendant to protect him, as well as preserve him, for attendance at his trial; that the measures taken for security and protection of the defendant are reasonable;
>
> The Court fails to find any evidence that anything is being done to the defendant that tends to upset his nervous system or his appetite or his ability to sleep;
>
> The Court further finds from the proof that the guards remove themselves some twenty-four to twenty-seven feet from the place where defendant and his counsel confer and they also turn off the microphone when Mr. Hanes enters the cell block; and the Court takes judicial knowledge that the defendant and his counsel can confer under such conditions without being overheard.[663]

In the unoccupied cell across the guard's walkway from Ray's own cell, a strange contraption was installed that looked to him like an old X-ray machine.

It spooked him such that he would "sometimes make deliberately misleading statements to Hanes about the King case for the benefit of any eavesdroppers who might be connected to the machine. While speaking untruths, I wrote down the correct information on paper for Hanes to read."[664]

During this period, Ray had begun having doubts about Hanes's dedication to his job of representing Huie's interests rather than putting his own first. It began with the book contracts that Hanes had negotiated with Huie. They allowed Hanes to provide Huie with whatever information Ray had shared with him, and if he failed to do that, it would nullify the contract. Ray had never been comfortable with that, but since he did not expect Huie's articles to be published before the trial, he had never made an issue of it.

Days before the criminal trial was set to begin, the first of Huie's articles appeared in the November 12, 1968, edition of *Look* magazine, giving his portrayal of the crime and the "innocent until proven guilty" suspect to a nationwide audience hungry for the slightest morsels of insider information about what was expected to be the murderer of a national martyr. Ray became angry with Hanes when he realized that Huie had proceeded to publish details that revealed too much of the defense. Also, the prosecution's original list of sixty-seven witnesses suddenly ballooned to 377 as a result of that article. Ray felt that it looked foolish that his attorney had given away too many strategic details before his trial and that this would result in giving the prosecutors key information to use against him, and the opportunity to manipulate witnesses, providing them with a map to win a guilty verdict.[665]

Ray Switches Attorneys, Opts for "Texas Tiger," Friend of LBJ and Attorney General Ramsey Clark

Ray also fought with Hanes about whether he would be allowed to testify, which Ray felt was essential to getting his story across, especially about having been manipulated by "Raoul." Hanes disagreed, but for reasons that Ray didn't know about at the time: it was Huie, behind the scenes, who had insisted that Ray not be allowed to testify, because he did not want Ray's story to become public during the trial, as it might impede sales of the magazine articles and book that he planned to write. To head off that possibility, Huie asked Ray's brother Jerry to come to Huie's home in Hartselle, Alabama, where he offered to give him, and James, $12,000 to keep James from testifying. Jerry then went to Memphis to convey the offer to James, who not only rejected it outright, but decided then and there to fire Hanes, just a few days before the trial was to have started.[666]

The question then became, who should they select to replace him? Almost simultaneously, the day before the trial was to have started, Houston attorney Percy Eugene Foreman showed up unannounced at the Shelby County jail, and, like Huie and Hanes, to Ray, "he seemed to be motivated mainly by money." Among Foreman's many deceptions, the one most crucial was how he had framed his entrée as James Earl Ray's new attorney: in the same edition of *Look* magazine (April 15, 1969) as Huie's third, and last, article, "Why James Earl Ray Murdered Dr. King," Foreman wrote his own article, which wrongly asserted that ". . . the brothers of James Earl Ray sought me out and handed me a letter from him, beseeching me to represent him."[667]

The Rays all deny that any of them went to Foreman. James stated that "Foreman showed up at the Shelby County Jail the day before the trial was to begin. He wasn't listed in the jail record as representing me. I never requested to see him. Yet the sheriff promptly ushered him into my presence."[668] Further, Ray stated that the unusual circumstances of Foreman's debut performance should have forewarned him about his true purposes, which Ray explained as the courts ". . . knew him to be a man willing to make a deal."[669]

Foreman's *Look* article also laid out his premise from the start: that his client was guilty, beyond any doubt, and that his sole objective was ". . . not to spring him, but to try to save his life. I then, over several weeks, spent 40 hours in conversation with him, endeavoring to bring him to believe that I knew more about the law than he did, after which I saved his life in the only way I thought it could be saved. I consider that no mean achievement." That ridiculous premise was undermined by the fact that the state of Tennessee, at that point, had not executed anyone for a decade, as an ongoing debate on the merits of capital punishment had still not been resolved when Ray's case was being "adjudicated" (if that term could even be stretched enough to apply to it). According to Wikipedia, "Between 1960 and 2000, the death penalty however was not applied in this state—the death penalty was reinstated there in 1975, but executions only resumed in 2000."[670]

According to his own book, Ray said that Jerry told him that he had seen Foreman on a TV talk show and that he "looked to me like he knew his business."[671] Foreman asked them to not call him "Mr. Foreman," but the "Texas Tiger."

Foreman told Ray that Huie and Hanes were personal friends who were out to exploit Ray and said, with feigned indignanty, that "if you stick with them you'll be barbecued." Then he intimated that hiring him, Foreman, would ensure that Ray would have a chance to testify and promised that there would be no literary contracts entered into until after the trial, adding that he could finance the defense fee of $150,000 that would be arranged after the trial with book authors. Foreman sold him on the deal by explaining that he had tried a thousand murder cases and only a few had been lost, with only one defendant ever executed; Ray's case, he said, "was the easiest he'd ever seen."[672]

On November 11, 1968, Ray went to court, with both attorneys present, before Judge Preston Battle. The judge agreed to the change but then warned Ray that he wouldn't permit further changes in counsel.[673] At that point, Huie's first article in *Look* magazine had already appeared in newsstands, a few days before the edition date of November 12, 1968. As noted above, while it still purported to support Ray's own story, it had already been set to undermine it, especially in how he was already being portrayed as a "southern racist."

When he finally moved to Memphis for the trial, Foreman chose the luxurious Peabody Hotel for his residence, famed for the Peabody Duck March twice a day, where a line of five ducks—one drake and four hens—march through the hotel lobby on their way to the fountain where, for nearly ninety years, they go to spend the day splashing in the pool until they return to their residence on the roof at 5 p.m. It is undoubtedly one of the finest, most elegant hotels in the South, and it probably made Foreman very conscious of the need to finance his months-long stay there.

A few weeks later, Foreman met with the Haneses and obtained the entire file on Ray, consisting of thousands of pages of documents, photographs, transcripts of interviews, and trial briefs. According to Ray, he spent about ten minutes rifling through the file before going out to dinner with the Haneses. Arthur Hanes Jr. said, "He wasn't interested in the case. He wanted to drink some Scotch, eat some dinner and talk about his famous cases. He also told us about how he made speeches all over the country." Ray said that Foreman never discussed the case with him, and that he had also told him that he never asked for a client's statement until he had investigated the state's case.[674] He pointedly never asked Ray if he had murdered Dr. King, indicating that he was never really interested enough in the answer to that basic issue.

After that, Ray heard very little from Foreman for nearly six weeks, then finally, on December 18, to his surprise, deputies appeared at his cell to escort him to Judge Battle's courtroom, where he heard Foreman requesting that the state help pay for his defense, that there were no funds available to cover his investigation and no prospect of obtaining funds through future publishing contracts; all of it was in direct contradiction to what he had stated to Ray when they originally met. Ray found out later that this was not the first discussion that Foreman had with the judge about the case and that all of it had been preengineered by Foreman as a way to get the public defender insinuated into the case, relieving Foreman of having to do all the grunt work involved in preparing a murder defense for trial. When the judge agreed to appoint a public defender to assist the formidable Foreman, according to Ray's account, "Lo and behold—public defender Hugh W. Stanton Sr. just happened to be sitting at the front of the courtroom."[675]

According to Huie's own account, he first met with Foreman on November 27, 1968, to discuss the transfer of the literary contract with Hanes to Foreman. Instead of the previous split, giving Ray a percentage cut, his new proposal was for Huie to retain 40 percent of the proceeds and Foreman to take the remaining 60 percent. Ten weeks later, on February 3, 1969, the contracts were signed, just as Foreman set it up.[676] Excluding Ray from any interest in the contract also meant that he would not even be aware of its existence.

At the next hearing a month after the first one, in late January 1969, the "Texas Tiger" Foreman called in sick, leaving only Stanton Sr. and his son Junior there to represent Ray. It probably had something to do with how he was still working on the new literary contracts, which had still not been finalized. Judge Battle, not pleased with this turn of events, declared that, if Foreman's illness should continue, Stanton Sr. would have full authority, as cocounsel, to conduct all future responsibilities of the lead counsel, with or without the presence of Foreman.[677] This was only two months into his representation of Ray; Percy Foreman's deceits were just beginning to show through his polished veneer. He didn't see Ray for a week after that, for reasons unknown, but when he did, he seemed to have overcome his illness, even looking "chipper" to Ray.

The purpose of his visit, however, was another surprise for Ray, since it was about how he had finagled the publishing contracts with Huie away from Hanes to transfer the monetary rights to himself, contrary to everything that he had promised Ray from the beginning. At their first meeting, before he talked Ray into changing lawyers, he had derided the Haneses for having signed those contracts with Huie and had even promised Judge Battle, in court, that he would not sign any such contracts. Yet later, Ray found out that at exactly the same time that he was making those promises back in November, he had already told Huie that he would do so.[678]

During that visit, Foreman presented a $5,000 check from Huie made payable to Ray and himself, which, he said, was needed to hire still another lawyer, John Jay Hooker Sr., a prominent Nashville attorney and major figure in the Tennessee Democratic party, whose son happened to be a friend of

Robert Kennedy. Ray later found out that he had obtained a second check in the same amount, on which Foreman forged Ray's signature.

A few weeks later, in February, Foreman got Ray to sign yet another contract authorizing all funds accruing from all publishing contracts to be paid directly to Foreman under the pretext of being only for the purpose of redirecting any revenue away from Hanes to himself; its real effect was to enable Foreman to enter into new contracts that would similarly undermine Ray's interests. By this point, after seven months of debilitating confinement in his brightly lit jail cell, Ray's resistance was flagging, and so he signed the contract.

His brother Jerry Ray, in his 1999 testimony at the King family's civil trial against Loyd Jowers, explained James's dilemma with his lawyers this way:

> Because he couldn't give these lawyers like Haynes—every time you give him some information, a phone number or something, he'd give it to Huie. And he said "how can I get a trial when they know everything I'm going to testify to." And so when he got rid of Arthur Haynes [*sic*—Hanes], then he got Percy Foreman, and Percy Foreman came in and said this is going to be the easiest case I ever had in my life. There's no evidence at all against him, and he did that up until about a month before the guilty plea. Then he started crying saying they're going to execute him, they're going to do this, do [that]. And so James asked him to resign from the case because he was determined to go to trial anyway, and Foreman wouldn't resign. And Judge Battle said if he fired Foreman, he had to go to trial with a public defender.[679]

Then Foreman—obviously by now obsessed with Ray's becoming his personal cash cow, milking it for all it was worth—went to Judge Battle, behind Ray's back, and asked the court to allow him to have a *Life* magazine photographer take pictures of Ray behind bars, and also get the court's blessing to have Huie interview Ray in jail. The judge denied both requests, to Ray's relief, but by this point, his opinion about Foreman's techniques had gone full circle and he had already begun to distrust him. He knew he was now stuck with him because of Judge Battle's earlier warning, when Ray had fired Hanes, that there would be no more attorney changes after that.

Ray would find out, many years later, that during this same period, Foreman had persuaded Huie that there had been no conspiracy, there was never any handler named Raul, that James Earl Ray was the only killer of Martin Luther King Jr., and that Huie should therefore change the narrative and the title of his book to reflect that, which probably didn't require much convincing anyway.[680] (That was Ray's impression, anyway, but it probably didn't require a lot of convincing, since Huie had already secretly begun to take that position, even before writing his first *Look* article.) It was then that the title, *They Slew the Dreamer*, was changed: "*They*" was dropped, replaced by "*He*." Along with that cover change, on the inside of the book, all suggestions that there might have been a conspiracy were summarily diminished or dropped, replaced by the dual themes of "southern racist hoping to collect a reward," and/or "vicious stalker who had suddenly grown a strong need for recognition."

Ray had started his acts of slipping little fibs into his story line back when the Haneses were his lawyers, knowing that anything he told them would end up in Huie's articles and book, so he led them off course with, usually, inconsequential untruths. The first was when he misled Huie about his prison break, telling him he had gone "over the wall" when he had really escaped in a very large breadbox from the prison bakery, in order to keep that fact, and the names of his accomplices, out of the story for their protection. Then he began going further astray with his natural streak of sarcasm, when asked to describe his movements on April 4, 1968, the day King was shot. He wrote, as a joke, that he had been sitting in the Mustang outside of Jim's Grill when the shot happened, and then "Raoul" came running out of the building wearing a white sheet, dropped the bundle with the rifle, and jumped into the car. Ray's dry wit got him into trouble like this on more than this occasion.[681]

Then he found out that Foreman didn't use that statement at all, but handed it over to still another author wanting to write a book about it, Gerold Frank, who was also an FBI-friendly journalist who could be counted on to support the official line, as drafted by the highest echelon of that organization. Frank dutifully included this point in his book, along with Ray's other statements incriminating himself through the purchases of all the items in the bundle dumped in the doorway alcove in front of Canipe's store.[682] It was stories like these that came back to bite Ray, by rendering everything else he ever said about Raul suspect to those same authors, all of whom would have been told by the plotter/handlers that Raul did not exist and not to indicate otherwise.

How the "Texas Tiger" Fooled His Own Client to Plead Guilty

On February 13, Foreman presented Ray with yet another contract to sign, claiming it was simply evidence that he had advised Ray to let him negotiate a guilty plea on his behalf, so that Foreman could use it to get a delay in the trial as a waiver of his habeas corpus right to a reasonably fast trial. Ray made it clear that in signing it, he would never actually plead guilty. But at the subsequent hearing, it was revealed that Foreman had signed a secret contract with Huie and his publisher to the effect that "Ray is expected to plead guilty on or about March 10, 1969, to the charge of murdering Dr. Martin Luther King" and that Foreman was to be paid $1,000 for writing a post-plea article for inclusion with Huie's last *Look* magazine article scheduled for April.

It was then that Foreman began pressing Ray to plead guilty as the only means to avoid being found guilty at a jury trial and sentenced to death. He told him that the court clerk was planning to rig the jury, by selecting only blacks known to be very angry and bent on revenge, and/or business people who only wanted their jury service to be over as soon as possible so they could get back to minding their businesses. Ray was not persuaded by these arguments and told him that blacks were more interested in getting to the truth than convicting him simply because he had been accused of the crime. To Foreman's point that the prosecution witness Charles Quitman Stephens was to be a star witness—testifying that he saw Ray immediately after the shot as he ran out of the bathroom—Ray replied that everyone knew he had been too drunk to see, or remember what he allegedly saw, to be believable.[683]

After Ray threatened to fire him and act as his own counsel, Foreman reminded him of Judge Battle's earlier statement about not allowing him to change attorneys again, and also raising the specter of his brother and father being arrested—as having aided James in his plot—as well as reminding him that he would not present an aggressive defense of Ray in a courtroom if that was what he wanted to do.

Against this extreme pressure, Ray tried one more gambit to avoid pleading guilty by suggesting that Foreman contract with Huie to pay him $150,000, of which he would give his brother Jerry $500, funds that James would then use to retain another lawyer to take the case to trial. Foreman refused, saying that he was already entitled to all proceeds of all publishing contracts, but he put forth a counteroffer: if Ray pled guilty, he would take a $165,000 fee from Huie and his publishers and Ray and Jerry would get $500 with which to find another lawyer to appeal the agreement.[684]

Judge Preston W. Battle had discussions with Percy Foreman throughout this period, starting in December 1968 and into January and February 1969. Despite admitting that there were many unanswered questions concerning the murder of Dr. King, and even acknowledging that he could have refused to accept the plea bargain agreement, Judge Battle raised many unresolved issues himself—after the fact—yet went ahead with it anyway: "It was entirely in my power to do so. But my conscience told me that it better served the ends of justice to accept the agreement. Had there been a trial, there could always have been the possibility, in such an emotionally charged case, of a hung jury. Or, though it may appear far-fetched now, he could have been acquitted by a jury."[685]

The pressure that Foreman had begun to put on Ray to plead guilty by seeking the delayed trial, coming after four months of his taking the case, was done for his own purposes, giving himself more time to manipulate Ray into a standoff and eventually completely waiving his right to a trial. Early researcher Harold Weisberg—in the first edition of his book, in 1970—described Foreman's extensive, well-executed manipulations in a profoundly incisive analysis that will elude anyone reading only the books written by famed novelists:

> It was carefully arranged and staged, the arranging taking some doing. When it could not be pulled off by the date set for trial, March 3, Foreman asked for and got a further extension, until April 7, on the grounds that he had not been able to study the case completely and prepare a defense. This, it will soon be apparent, was tantamount to fraud. That was not the reason he required and was given the extension. I repeat—*I emphasize*—there is no available reason to believe Foreman intended to take this case to open trial, none that he made any preparation to, none that he even really tried to analyze and assess the evidence available to him. In his own way, without so intending, he has come close to confirming this . . .
>
> His intent could not have been what he said it was, to serve the ends of justice. He frustrated justice.
>
> What he contrived, a very daring and almost impossible thing, did not require him to prepare the case, to do any work. If he could not pull it off, he need only have gone back into court and told the judge he could not proceed, that he and his client could not agree on tactics and strategy. Hanes had already laid the foundation for this. Ray's legal history would have tended to confirm it. At worst, there would have been a further delay. This would not have hurt Ray. It might have served his purpose, if Hanes's opinion, that he wanted delays, is correct.[686]

All during this period, Ray tried valiantly to get Foreman to aggressively pursue a strong defense. He gave him every piece of information that might assist in such an investigation, including names, dates, and telephone numbers—including the telephone number of Raul in New Orleans that Ray had used to call him while he was in Mexico, and a Baton Rouge number listed under the name Herman A. Thompson. Hadn't he looked into these? Foreman responded that if any phone numbers were to be used as evidence, he would obtain them from his friend, Meyer Lansky, the mobster who had everyone's number.[687] The fact that Foreman had another friend, Lyndon B. Johnson, who was also very accomplished in this same kind of meticulous manipulation—perhaps even assisting him as he was known to have done with a number of others involved in the same case, as detailed elsewhere—would have been discreetly managed as personal matters not materially pertinent.

Some of the techniques that Johnson had used during his lifetime of public manipulation were being played out in the background, giving credence to his anonymous involvement, not only of the measures Foreman used against Ray, but even in the placement of Foreman onto the scene at that precipitous point on the timeline. All of it replicated how Johnson had previously forced his partner in crime, Billie Sol Estes, to accept Johnson's personal attorney and with the same kind of tactics to accept a guilty verdict and prison time to ensure his credibility would be forever destroyed. For example, instead of ever acting aggressively on Ray's behalf to prepare for a strong defense, Foreman repeatedly applied pressure on him to knuckle under, to plead guilty and accept a ninety-nine-year sentence in order to avoid the death sentence. Even pleading guilty under the alternate option of a life sentence was never pursued, since it would have carried with it the chance of an early parole, but of course none of that was ever presented to Ray.

Still another tactical similarity was how Foreman constantly increased the pressure on Ray: that was done as Johnson had repeatedly practiced, through leaking (actually planting) canards to the press, such as suggestions of an imminent plea bargain, that something was in the works to increase the perception of momentum, creating a constant flurry of breaking activity with a refrain of extreme urgency. Foreman, just as LBJ had similarly done throughout his career, had begun using wire service contacts (UPI and AP) and a reporter for the *Huntsville* (Alabama) *Times*, with the understanding that he—attorney Percy Foreman—would never be named, but the story would always be attributed to "a source close to the case."[688] It was as if his old Texas friend were somewhere in the background, pushing him to use every device he had up his own long sleeves to ensure their stooge would never again see the light of day.

Foreman had even gone to St. Louis to attempt to get Ray's family to back his effort to get Ray to plead guilty. Even when they all refused to do that, he still claimed that they had agreed to do so when he next visited Ray in jail. In the meantime, Foreman had tried multiple tricks to get Ray to plead guilty, telling him that if he did, the agreement would be quickly overturned by a higher court, but he would be left with the promise of not being given a death sentence; however, if he didn't, his brothers John or Jerry might even be brought into it, as a "conspiracy of brothers" (which eventually was attempted), or even that his seventy-seven-year-old father could be rejailed. Finally, Foreman told him that, if he really insisted on testifying at a trial, he wouldn't attempt to put on a strong defense.[689]

For weeks on end following his new lawyer's appointment, Ray endured suffering through his solitary and inhumane confinement—totaling eight months, which he had come to realize would not end until he gave up and capitulated to his demands—while Foreman continued these tactics, constantly pressuring Ray to agree to the guilty plea. He told him that going to a jury trial would inevitably produce a guilty verdict of first degree murder that would guarantee him the death penalty. This was despite the fact that Tennessee was one of many states teetering on the edge of doing away with capital murder, and that it had been many years since any prisoner had been executed.

In late February, feeling ground down by the constant monitoring and the lack of sleep, sunshine, or fresh air—all exacerbated by the constant glare of the floodlights, and understanding the futility of his situation with an attorney he couldn't replace—Ray reluctantly accepted Foreman's promises that a guilty plea would quickly be overturned. Worn down by the inhumane treatment he was being given during his months-long prison confinement, Ray finally acceded to the constant pressure to accept a plea bargain for a ninety-nine-year prison sentence to avoid the alternative that Foreman had also promised if he didn't: a death sentence. Ray had resisted the risky promise for months but finally capitulated as a result of the extreme pressure and torture.

On March 8, 1969, the *Washington Post* reported in an article headlined "Ray Hearing Set; Guilty Plea Hinted" that "Ray will plead guilty in exchange for a 99-year sentence instead of a possible death penalty. Asked about this, Ray's lawyer, Percy Foreman of Houston, Tex., replied, 'It's none of your business.'" The article also noted Judge Battle's orders against "pre-trial publicity" and cited another article in *The Huntsville Times* that stated that "a source close to the case [obviously Foreman himself] said the guilty plea would be 'the only way Ray can escape the death sentence.'"[690] That unnamed source explained further that a jury would be empaneled and each juror would be asked if he or she could abide by the court's recommendations, implicitly meaning only those who would cooperate in this sham would be selected for the jury. Further, the source said, the court "would then accept a plea of guilty and recommend the sentence of 99 years . . . the jury would [then] be allowed to leave the courtroom to confirm the sentence." [691] Under that preset scenario, the result would be guaranteed in advance, and the procedures outlined by Ray's own counsel—absolute assurance of prison for the rest of his client's life, with no risk of him ever having a fair trial—would ensure that the real plotters would never be caught and that the patsy would rot in jail until the day he died.

Once he signed the paper saying Foreman had advised him to plead guilty, a constant stream of stipulations (called "stips") were given to Ray to sign, fifty-five in all, essentially ratifying the state's case in complete detail. Every time he objected to a stip, he marked it in pencil, then he had to initial each page to indicate he agreed with all of them other than the ones checked, and Foreman would take them back to the prosecutors for revision to conform to Ray's objections. After several days of this, the stips were reduced to a few, which Judge Battle would read and resolve at the hearing. When Ray later sued Foreman for ineffective counsel, he discovered that Foreman had erased many of the penciled check marks where Ray had objected. [692] Gerold Frank, unsurprisingly, included the details about those fifty-five stips in his book, naturally writing nothing about Ray's objections to them. [693]

On March 10, 1969, the hearing was conducted as laid out in advance, except that the script was not followed precisely by the accused, which we will examine next. Despite the contorted immediate outcome, the longer-term effects on the judicial process helped ensure that future investigators would discover the discrepancies and find evidence of high-level government misconduct. In a stunning development, Dr. King's own family and closest advisers saw it immediately, as evidenced by an article the next day in the *Washington Post*, headlined "Mrs. King Urges Conspiracy Probe." Within the article, Coretta Scott King called for "all concerned people" to press on, and "continue until all who are responsible for this crime have been apprehended." Further, Reverend James Orange of the SCLC was convinced that Ray was merely a patsy, saying that "I think they should set that man free." [694] For a brief period, that sentiment was ubiquitous within the African American community, as noted on March 12, 1969, in the *Daily World*: "The Murder Cover-up Outrages Nation," which asserted that there had been a large-scale conspiracy, and that the legal proceedings in Memphis "were an attempt to cover up other participants in the conspiracy." Quoting William L. Patterson, former chairman of the Civil Rights Congress, the article continued, "[the] unseemly haste with which James Earl Ray . . . was convicted is in itself almost irrefutable evidence of the conspiratorial character of a monstrous crime . . . there exists on a national scale a conspiracy to behead leadership of militant, black-led organizations fighting to secure the enforcement of the constitutional rights and human dignity of black Americans."[695]

The Denial of Ray's Appeal:
How the Tennessee Judicial System Was Rigged

The injustice done to James Earl Ray before his appeal was only half the story of his mistreatment, which went beyond the merely expeditious and perfunctory manner that was apparent to those giving it the most cursory review. As explained by John Avery Emison, there was a significant legal anomaly that any competent attorney interested in defending his client would have aggressively exploited to turn the stream of legal roadblocks around and finally obtain what Ray had always been denied: a fair trial. It involved a discrepancy between the transcripts and the voice recordings of the hearing and an effort that had been made by someone to patch over the transcript with verbiage that did not exist on the tape recordings.[696] This inconsistency involved Ray's response to the following question asked him by the judge:

> **The Court:** "Has any pressure of any kind by anyone in any way been used on you to get you to plead guilty?"
> **J.E.R.:** "Now, what did you say?"
> (Some years later, an enhanced audio analysis was conducted on the only remaining tape recording, which was unclear because Ray was not near the microphone. Experts concluded that his statement was either "I don't know what to say" or "I don't know what to think." The court reporter at the time, Charles E. Koster, was standing closer to Ray and also had a clearer recording, but it was no longer available for inspection.)[697]

Ray had been coached to respond to that question with a simple "No." After he went off script with an equivocal nonanswer, Judge Battle continued on, evidently not paying too much attention to the defendant's answers, as he persisted in asking the other questions in the script that both of them were following; the court reporter originally recorded it correctly, with the response noted above. However, at some later point, Ray's response was changed by someone, to state: *"No. No one, in any way."* (Emphasis added.)

Fortunately, the original response had been recorded in the very first book on the case, a little-known 1969 book titled *The Strange Case of James Earl Ray: The Man Who Murdered Martin Luther King,* by Clay Blaire Jr.[698] It was also corroborated in another book in 1971, titled *A Search for Justice,* by John Seigenthaler.[699] The alternate, secretly revised transcript that ensured the defendant would never get a new trial first appeared about ten weeks after the aborted trial, on May 26, 1969, and was repeatedly used in subsequent hearings involving both state and federal appeals courts and the Tennessee Supreme Court for many more years before the cunning maneuver by someone within the Tennessee judicial system was discovered. Indeed, the judge in one of those hearings, L. Clure Morton, on a filing of a writ of habeas corpus, cited those specific (revised) words—never spoken by James Earl Ray—as proof that Ray had "entered a voluntary, knowing and intelligent plea of guilty," apparently not realizing that he had based his decision on a brazenly fabricated statement that should have—on its own—justified giving Ray a new trial.

Harold Weisberg—in 1970, even before the fudged transcript had been discovered—explained the perfunctory nature of the hearing: "*At no point did he admit the killing. At no point was he ever asked!*" Weisberg also stated that the prosecutor, Phil Canale, even admitted that there was no proof of a conspiracy, despite the fact that Ray's own lawyer, Percy Foreman, had done that; according to Weisberg, Foreman "uttered no single word on behalf of his client." Moreover, he stated that Foreman's defense was "one of the most unusual 'defenses' and jury-examinations in legal history," and that "It was not the *prosecution* who sought to guarantee Ray's lifetime incarceration but his *defender*, the man who was 'sure' the judge 'would excuse' any juror unwilling to pledge, *in advance of presentation or consideration of any evidence whatsoever*, first, to find the accused guilty and, next, to agree to a life-plus sentence."[700] (Emphasis in original.)

The five witnesses called were only asked questions that proved, indeed, that Dr. King had been murdered and that there was reason to believe that Ray, or property belonging to him, had been around the scene of the crime. But no witness placed him there at that point in time, much less stated that he saw Ray commit the murder. Yet despite the virtually complete lack of proof of Ray's guilt, the assistant prosecutor gratuitously asked FBI agent Robert G. Jensen, "Did the investigation made by the FBI culminate in the arrest of James Earl Ray?" which allowed Jensen to respond with "Yes sir, it did." Weisberg wryly observed that the word "culminate" allowed anyone to venture that all sorts of "nothingness" might have "culminated" in Ray's arrest, even though the FBI placed him in Mexico when he was actually in Canada, and in Portugal when he was in England, also accusing him of robbing banks when he was hundreds or thousands of miles away from them; he finally summed up the so-called trial of James Earl Ray thusly:

> We know what Ramsey Clark, J. Edgar Hoover and the FBI, the rest of the federal government [implicitly including LBJ, the man to whom they both reported] and the Memphis authorities got out of it. They got a corrupt decision that seemed to buttress them. The official record is made to seem to support them. The crime is "solved." What they did not get is the support and approval of the broad mass of the people. Only a few of those calling themselves liberals and intellectuals and those either without interest or unable to evaluate the obvious really support public authority in this case.[701]

Thus, the evidence presented now includes the essential proof that the doctored document was only one item of many that were deliberately fabricated for the purpose of framing James Earl Ray: taken together, the sum total of physical evidence and credible witness testimony reveals a widely dispersed edict from someone at the pinnacle of a powerful, unified aegis, thus revealing the scope of an historical, epochal, albeit ugly, truth.

The enormous combined and coordinated efforts of the federal, state, county, and city officials guiding the effort—and the various geographic districts of the state and federal judiciaries—were focused as only a powerfully coordinated resolve could accomplish. The objective was to ensure that James Earl Ray would be denied any chance, even the outward appearance, of getting a routine criminal trial (never mind a truly fair one).

At this juncture, we pause to note how the books by the fiction writers barely even mentioned anything about this critical issue. Consider how much space the bestselling book by Hampton Sides allocated to Ray's "trial": *One sentence*, which skipped over all the messy details and simply stated that Ray "pleaded guilty" and "received a ninety-nine-year sentence."[702] So much for traipsing through the weeds of what really happened—it might interfere with the syrupy telling of great myths.

The Dead-End Appeals by James Earl Ray for a New Trial

In the immediate aftermath—only three days later—of the original "trial" so cunningly orchestrated by the "Texas Tiger" Percy Foreman, James Earl Ray wrote to Judge Battle repudiating the hearing and requesting a new and proper trial. At this point, Ray had no attorney representing him. as he had summarily fired Foreman after his "day in court." Battle did not respond to the letter before leaving for a Florida vacation. When he returned on March 31, 1969, he found a second letter from Ray, dated March 26, in which he asked Battle to consider it a formal application "for a reversal of the 99-year sentence." He also asked the judge to appoint an attorney, or a public defender, to assist Ray in future pleadings, explaining to Battle that "I understand on one avenue of appeal, I have only 30 days in which to file." [703]

Battle then showed the letter to the Assistant Attorney General James Beasley, who had presented the case against Ray, informing him also that three lawyers—J. B. Stoner, Richard J. Ryan, and Robert H. Hill Jr.—had all expressed an interest in representing Ray. The propriety of the judge involving the prosecutor to assist in determining who should represent Ray as his defense attorney in future proceedings was at least questionable, arguably even outrageously unethical. According to Ray's later attorney Mark Lane, "[t]he legal canons of ethics proscribe such conduct. Battle could not ethically call upon the prosecutor to play a role in the determination of counsel for Ray. Beasley should not have responded." [704]

When Beasley attempted to call Judge Battle, he couldn't get through, so he visited Battle's chambers and found the judge dead, his head on his desk, on top of the last letter from James Earl Ray. The timing of Battle's death could not have been more curious, and suspicious. He had begun second-guessing his own handling of the trial, and if his superiors in the state judicial system—up to and including Governor Ellington—had any doubts about his intentions to possibly capitulate and grant Ray a new trial and a new lawyer to pursue getting a free and fair trial, they would not have been pleased. In fact, given the stakes involved, that would have probably been at least a career-ending decision, had he lived to make it, and given the desperation and fury of some of the men involved in getting the case put on ice at that point, it might possibly have even been a life-ending one if any of the anxious men at the top determined that there was no other option.

John Emison first raised the "ugly question that cannot be avoided" regarding Judge Battle's mysterious death, noting that six years after the fact, it was revealed in hearings of the Congressional Church Committee that the CIA had developed a "heart attack gun" in the early 1960s. When someone there decided that a key person might need to have an early death, that gun could deliver a tiny frozen needle, only a quarter inch long and with the diameter of a human hair. Upon entering the body it would thaw and deliver a toxin that induced a heart attack but then became undetectable at autopsy. In 1969 it was still unknown outside of the Agency. [705]

Just before he died, Judge Battle had a visit from one of the three attorneys asking to represent Ray. Richard J. Ryan, who had asked the judge to set a date for a hearing on Ray's request and had taken the liberty of filing a formal application for a new trial on Ray's behalf, explained why, with the judge's death, there should have been no question that a new trial was in order:

> We had thirty days to get [the application for a new trial] in and we filed it in a timely fashion. The law of Tennessee is really clear on this question. *If a judge should die or go insane after an application for a new trial is filed and before he rules upon it the application is automatically granted.* There has never been an exception in Tennessee since that statute was adopted by the legislature.[706] (Emphasis added by author.)

In the meantime, Judge Arthur Faquin Jr. was appointed to be Battle's successor. This was evidently a politically driven maneuver to forestall any consideration whatsoever of the pending application. As attorney Ryan explained, Faquin's response to the request was perfunctory, passive, and knee-jerk; no explanation was offered for why the statutory rule was not enforced:

> He just said at the hearing held at the end of May 1969 that Ray had pleaded guilty voluntarily and that was it. The laws of Tennessee just did not apply anymore. The reason is that there was a conspiracy to kill Dr. King, probably the FBI or CIA were in on it and they did not want this case being re-opened.[707]

Attorney Richard Ryan's candor—especially in describing the FBI and CIA conspiracy—is a stunning turn of events and must have electrified the entire Tennessee judiciary at the time. Ray's new attorneys, Ryan, Hill, and Stoner, then appealed the denial to the Tennessee Court of Criminal Appeals in Jackson, Tennessee, presided by the newly appointed (by Governor Ellington) appellant justice William H. Williams, who had previously been the Shelby County criminal court judge. Williams sided with the lower court without explanation, except to state that the petition was "not well taken" and "is hereby denied."[708]

After that perfunctory ruling, Ray's new lawyers took the appeal to the Tennessee Supreme Court, which was then composed of four justices (three of whom had been appointed by Governor Ellington). In an unusual move, probably to remove the decision from the normal course of handling through the state judicial system—and perhaps at the insistence of the powerful men who had managed this case from its inception—Governor Buford Ellington (known to be a fowl-, rabbit-, and duck-hunting crony of Lyndon Johnson) appointed a fifth "special justice" to rule on the appeal, a man who—based upon the hunting metaphors that appeared in his ruling—might have also been in the Johnson-Ellington hunting party.

Judge Erby L. Jenkins was brought in on a temporary basis, for the specific purpose of writing the court's unanimous opinion to deny Ray a fair trial again. Judge Jenkins must have had a reputation for being a great and crafty wordsmith who could write a magnificent denial that would never be forgotten by either Ray or any of his lawyers. Examples of his talent for sweeping rhetoric based upon faulty logic, erroneous stipulations, and an inaccurate presumption of the competence, veracity, and effectiveness of Ray's counsel, the "Texas Tiger"—ergo, the question of whether due process had prevailed—follow:

> The defendant upon the advice of his well-qualified and nationally known counsel pleaded guilty to murder in the first degree, the offense with which he was charged, a cold-blooded murder without an explained motive.
>
> Consequently, his right to appeal was waived, because it is well settled in Tennessee that when a defendant pleads guilty and fully understands what he is doing, as we believe this defendant did, there can be no legal ground to justify the granting of a new trial. Otherwise the doors of our state prisons would remain ever ajar to those who are incarcerated therein on a plea of guilty, and who becoming dissatisfied, seek relief on motions for new trial. The dockets of our courts would become congested with such procedure, and these cases would never be closed. There must be a conclusion to litigation sometime, even in a criminal case, in spite of the liberal interpretations of the law by some of our courts. To allow such procedure would be permitting those defendants to toy with the courts.
>
> The defendant, in his motion for a new trial, if considered in its most favorable light could be construed as such, alleges that he was misled into entering a guilty plea, and in his petition for certiorari he alleged that he did not knowingly and voluntarily waive his right to appeal. The substance of the above allegations is that the defendant was deprived of his constitutional right

(Sixth Amendment) to have the assistance of counsel. However, there is not one fact in petitioner's brief to support the above allegations.

[...]

In the trial court the petitioner was represented by competent counsel. He entered a plea of guilty on the advice of his counsel, and there is no doubt that his counsel explained to him that the penalty for murder in the first degree in Tennessee carried the death penalty, and that such plea was made with an eager ear, a willing mind and a willing heart.

The defendant, after due and thoughtful consideration and after being properly advised, entered a plea of guilty to murder in the first degree, and then took the known offered sentence of ninety-nine years, rather than taking the calculated risk of receiving a more severe penalty at the hands of a jury. He now seeks to back out of this trade with the State and asks for a new trial. There is nothing from which it can be inferred that the defendant was misled, or that his guilty plea was made involuntarily without knowing the consequences thereof, thus the defendant is precluded from any appellate relief.

[...]

In Tennessee, a reasonable person does not shoot and kill an unarmed, unsuspecting and innocent victim without just punishment and retribution under our law. The defendant, by his own voluntary and uncoerced action received such, or what he thought was then just punishment, and will now not be heard to complain.

This well planned and well executed killing would indicate the defendant to be of at least or over-average intelligence, and certainly of such intelligence as to understand what he was doing when he went to the "bargaining table," to decide his fate—whether to plead as he did or take his chances at the hands of a jury. He made the bargain. There is no claim that the State or the court below coerced or influenced him in any manner to make this decision. It was his and his alone, with the aid of the advice of his chosen private counsel. Whether or not they made a mistake in judgment is not for us to say.

In Tennessee, as in all other liberty loving civilized countries, ambush killers are not looked upon with much favor, to say the least. In a country where you do not shoot a sitting duck or a fowl unless in flight; where a rabbit or other game of the field is allowed its chance to run; and where one does not shoot down his fellowman unless that man has committed an overt act that would justify the defendant in so doing, jurors are inclined to deal harshly with such defendants. The defendant and his attorney, with his years of experience, knew this, and in the light of this knowledge of human nature to react violently against those who have committed unprovoked violence, they made the decision to plead guilty and such plea, in the opinion of the court, should stand.

The next question for consideration is whether the proceedings, at the time the defendant entered his guilty plea, were such a "farce" or "sham" that it can be said that the defendant was denied due process. The concept of due process of law as contained in the Fourteenth Amendment is concerned solely with whether or not the State played any part in the wrong done the accused [citation omitted].

[. . .]

The Court finds that the defendant willingly, knowingly and intelligently and with the advice of counsel entered a plea of guilty to murder in the first degree by lying in wait, and this Court cannot sit idly by while deepening disorder, disrespect for constitutional authority and mounting violence and murder stalk the land and let waiting justice sleep.

Therefore, the petition for certiorari is denied.[709]

Despite all the histrionic rhetoric about how the defendant had such great lawyering—"well qualified and nationally known counsel"—the due process of law and the concerns about how "mounting violence and murder stalk the land" and the injected irony about letting "waiting justice sleep," this decision ignored the conditions Ray was subjected to for eight months in jail, with no natural light, no fresh air, no privacy for basic human hygienic or toiletry functions; it made a mockery of how Ray had supposedly not been coerced by the state to make the decisions he did. To state that "There is no claim that the State or the court below coerced or influenced him in any manner to make this decision" ignores the fact that his earliest lawyers had indeed made attempts with the lower courts to remove those conditions, which were repeatedly rejected with essentially the same kind of banal language employed by Justice Jenkins.

The fact that the trial court's transcript had been intentionally revised, and Ray's own attorney had been inserted into that position through high-level political manipulation to ensure that the courts would deny him a fair trial in the first place—and that he would never get one, assuring that he would spend the rest of his life in prison—renders this decree among the worst, most contemptible examples of judicial malpractice in US history. (See Appendix B: James Earl Ray Appeal. Note that among the many bases listed for the appeal was someone's intentional revision of the court transcript—at page 17—to hide the evidence of how Ray had attempted to insert his objection to the judge's question as noted above. This single issue should have been sufficient to force a retrial.) These maneuverings have all the signs of being directed from above by some very powerful persons, or person, who must have exercised great power indeed to be able to control not only the law enforcement, but the judicial systems as well, of every level of government: federal, state, county, and city.

The worst part of this decision by the Tennessee Supreme Court was that it was made during a tumultuous time of confusion and growing public knowledge of the political wrangling behind the closely guarded negotiations between the prosecution and defense; the outing of Percy Foreman as a swindler who was not interested in defending his client; the involvement of US Attorney General Ramsey Clark (whose strings were being pulled by President Johnson) and Tennessee Governor Buford Ellington, with King's widow, Coretta, caught in the middle.[710]

Proof of Foreman's double-cross on his client came only a few months later, when he virtually admitted—as noted in the epigraph of this chapter, on the Dick Cavett television show—that he had indeed coerced Ray into taking the guilty plea in the *Look* magazine article of April 1969. The "Texas Tiger" sold Ray under the pretext that it was his only way to avoid the electric chair, while falsely promising that the sentence would be quickly modified to allow him an early release, despite the fact that it was an admission of his guilt; it was also done after Ray had been subjected to eight months of torture designed for the very purpose of destroying his will to fight on and robbing his mind of the last threads of rationality.

Foreman even reiterated in the *Look* article that had Ray not taken the guilty plea, it would have been his "duty" to take the stand against his own client, in violation of the sacred attorney-client relationship, and testify against Ray. Despite all of that, the august "Special Justice" Erby L. Jenkins would declare that "There is no claim that the State or the court below coerced" James Earl Ray into making the decision to plead guilty." The federally sponsored—and state-sanctioned—cruelly inhumane treatment given to James Earl Ray was nearly unmatched by any other case in American history, with the notable exceptions of Sirhan B. Sirhan and Lee Harvey Oswald. All three of these cases were comparable to what one might expect to find in German history, circa 1936–1945, or in the Stalinist era of the Soviet Union.

The Final Appeal by James Earl Ray

The legal wrangling continued throughout the next two decades as futility remained a constant impediment to any attempt by his attorneys for delayed justice. The objective of their efforts would eventually move from the criminal courts to the civil courts and from justice for James Earl Ray to the more esoteric framework of nominal awards for his memory and vindication for the King family's enormous loss and a measure of solace for the rest of the country. But for the equitable requital of the injury to the American culture, it was a Pyrrhic victory, the only consolation being that the real legacy of Dr. King was sustained through it all and finally recognized with a national holiday dedicated to his memory, an ironic memorial from the next generation of officialdom, as partial and implicit recognition of the failures of their own predecessors.

Dr. William Pepper, in a final move to extract some modicum of justice for James Earl Ray, petitioned the Tennessee Court of Appeals to give him a new trial in 1994. His petition was referred to Judge Joe Brown. Four years later, after Brown had spoken out about his concerns over the inconsistencies in the ballistics evidence, which indicated to him that the Remington 30.06 rifle that Ray had purchased in Birmingham could not have been the murder weapon, the state judiciary officials took him off the case. The African American Brown was an avid hunter and firearms expert who subsequently starred in a reality television show, *Judge Joe Brown,* which ran for fifteen years. The judicial officials who took him off the case must have known that he would not play along with the official thirty-year-old myth that had become sanctified as the official verdict of Ray's guilt despite his never having been given a fair trial. Judge Brown appeared in a number of videos now available on YouTube, including one in which he stated that the "Remington 760 GameMaster they have in the Civil Rights Museum was not the murder weapon; it's not even close."[711] It could not be more clear that the mission of the original plotters was still alive in 1998 and is undoubtedly just as true today: the evidence is clear, as even more truths are revealed year by year that have gradually exposed the fundamental lies. The original myth still endures.

Researcher Dick Russell thoroughly investigated the removal of Judge Brown (which the mainstream media ignored) and reported his findings in *High Times* in 1999 ("A King-Sized Conspiracy: The Judge Investigating The 30-Year-Old Assassination of Martin Luther King Turned Up So Much Evidence of Government Complicity and Cover-Up That He's Been Yanked Off the Case. And You Won't Hear About That in Any Other Publication in America").[712] Russell's article is based upon a series of quotations from Judge Joe Brown:

> As [Judge Joe] Brown puts it, "What you've got in terms of the physical evidence relative to ballistics is frightening. First, it's not the right type of rifle. It's never been sighted in. It's the wrong kind of scope." And furthermore, "With a 30.06, it makes a particularly difficult shot firing at a downward trajectory in that circumstance."
>
> Above all, according to Brown, "Metallurgical analysis excludes the bullet taken from the body of Dr. King from coming from the cartridge case they say was fired in that rifle. That bullet was originally sent to the FBI [lab] intact. What came back was fragments —but there was a piece of the intact bullet. In the last four years that photograph, which was marked into evidence, is missing. A number of items were removed from this case. There was one incident where [Brown's own] court had to send one of its bailiffs to physically stop an individual from removing the bullet fragments from the courthouse."
>
> [. . .]
>
> "You want to say." remarks Judge Brown, "that a three-time loser, an escaped convict with no obvious financial resources and no technical knowledge, is going to not only miraculously learn how to become a good marksman? This one individual is able to acquire the resources to get identities of deceased individuals, come up with very good forgeries for passports and fake identification. and somehow acquire funds for a very expensive itinerary and travel schedule? Then he gets himself caught because he goes through Heathrow Airport, but does not know whether he is a citizen, an alien or has Commonwealth status? Now, be real! You have to be the worst culpable moron to go for that story. An analysis suggests that what you've got in this case was a stooge whose task was to throw everybody off the trail."

[...]
The Court of Criminal Appeals that ousted Brown included, the judge says, "former prosecutors involved in the James Earl Ray case, who had sat on or were sitting on that bench." They accused Brown of being too involved in personally grilling witnesses, though the Tennessee rules of evidence explicitly allow that.

Mr. Russell's article finishes with these words quoted from Judge Joe Brown:

> "The federal government ought to do an investigation. It's obvious, from looking at everything in the existing case file, this matter is not resolved. The reason we must go forward . . . is for the children. Generation X is coming of age, and there's going to be leadership which will come out of this generation and the one behind it. They will do things to offend the power structure, just like we did in the '60s . . . . To protect this new generation from this type of response by the system, we must do something profound so that somebody is brought to justice as a deterrent.
>
> "A demand needs to be made as to why this farce has been perpetrated among the people," Brown goes on, "I'm probably going to catch all kinds of hell for these remarks, but I really don't care that much about being a judge, if I've got to sit there and keep my mouth shut when I see this kind of injustice. They can take this job and shove it!"

The delay in getting the justice that Judge Brown referenced—to the children of Generation X—was instead kept in the same polluted can, one that has since been kicked down the road to the Millennial generation. It should be evident to all that the American culture was coarsened and debased by the officials involved in the miscarriage of justice in this case and the other treasons carried out fifty years ago, and—if Shakespeare's axiom, that eventually "the truth will out," has the least validity—it is time now for that to materialize.

Dick Russell's account of the official deceit and deception used by Tennessee authorities, to keep a respected judge from an honest inquiry into the murder of Dr. King—thirty years after the fact—and the fact that they went to great lengths to keep the American people uninformed of their insidious manipulations should be all the evidence needed to impel a congressional investigation of the crime, even now, half a century later.

Chapter 11

HSCA CONGRESSIONAL INVESTIGATION

"Robert Blakey was a purported expert on organized crime who had taught at both Notre Dame and Cornell law schools. As my investigation proceeded during these early days, I reviewed a copy of a most unusual affidavit executed by Blakey on February 4, 1976 [shortly before being appointed as senior counsel to the HSCA]: Blakey, as an expert witness, contended that Moe Dalitz had no connection with organized crime."
—Dr. William F. Pepper *(The Plot to Kill King,* p. 35)

OFFICIAL CONCLUSION of HSCA REPORT
Report of the Select Committee on Assassinations of the US House of Representatives:
The Committee Believes, on the Basis of the Circumstantial Evidence Available to it, that there is a Likelihood that James Earl Ray Assassinated Dr. Martin Luther King, JR., as a Result of a Conspiracy.

The Sordid History of the House Select Committee on Assassinations (HSCA)

That Robert Blakey would execute such an affidavit was disconcerting to Dr. Pepper, but it was not the only basis for his concerns, as we will now further explore. That it was done just months before his appointment as the senior counsel to the HSCA—put in charge of guiding its investigation—in the face of Moe Dalitz's nationwide reputation as one of the Mafia's major kingpins sets the stage for everything else presented here about how the HSCA was managed.

Even after the deaths of J. Edgar Hoover, Clyde Tolson, and Lyndon Johnson, the forces that had been assembled to execute the assassination, then the cover-up, were still at work a decade later, continuing the cover-up to ensure that the case remained buried forever.

In 1976, eight years after Dr. King's murder, as public pressure mounted in reaction to the debacles of the 1960s—the three major assassinations, the recognition of the disastrousness of the Vietnam War (the false-flag attack on the USS *Liberty* was still a state secret), followed in short order by the Watergate scandals that took down a president whose crimes paled in comparison to those of his predecessor—the House Select Committee on Assassinations (HSCA) was created to investigate the JFK and MLK assassinations. At that point, apparently, the consensus was that the RFK assassination did not merit their attention because the alleged "lone-nut" killer had been caught red-handed. (It all seemed so simple then, when people still generally accepted government pronouncements without question.)

Much of that public pressure emanated from the 1975 House "Church Committee," formally called the Select Committee to Study Governmental Operations with Respect to Intelligence Activities. The abuses of power under the administration of Lyndon B. Johnson by the FBI and CIA during the previous decade had finally become sufficiently exposed, specifically the harassment of Martin Luther King Jr. and a number of others similarly treated, which became the catalyst for the creation of the HSCA. The Church Committee had already revealed the major abuses—Dr. King's harassment under the FBI's COINTELPRO program; the CIA's extended version of that unconstitutional affront to American citizens MHCHAOS, the murderous raid on Black Panther Fred Hampton's apartment, the CIA's Operation Mockingbird, the CIA's plots against Fidel Castro, and their systematic withholding of incriminating documents on JFK's assassination to the Warren Commission.[713]

Congressman Thomas N. Downing (D-VA) had spearheaded the legislation that created the HSCA and became its original chairman but initially intended to investigate only JFK's assassination. To gain support from black representatives, it was extended at Mark Lane's urging to include Dr. King's assassination. That the bill was initiated by Representative Downing was a surprise for most of his House colleagues, because he usually did not take leadership positions on controversial matters or even most routine legislation, and he was nearing retirement.[714] But he was uncharacteristically troubled with deep doubts about the innocence of his government in the series of assassinations, and sufficiently concerned about the need to investigate them further, that he became a major sponsor of the HSCA bill. In fact, before he retired, he appointed a tenacious chief counsel, Richard A. Sprague, to head the inquiry, who had quickly assembled a staff of researchers, investigators, and lawyers by the end of 1976.

The political infighting that started the process—with a number of congressmen whose biggest clients were the CIA and the FBI—successfully defanged those who were the most active and aggressive members and staff who were actually serious about the mission. Even after its passage, a number of congressmen remained strongly opposed to any such investigation and did everything they could to undermine it, including a few who smeared Sprague with hypocritical innuendo. One of them, Robert E. Bauman (R-MD), piled on in this effort to sabotage the work of the committee, which he stated was "perhaps the worst example of Congressional inquiry run amok," and claimed that Sprague had a "checkered past."[715] Three years later, in the middle of his own reelection campaign, Bauman had to resign his seat after being arrested for soliciting sex from a sixteen-year-old boy in a rare and highly public case of karma involving his own deserved political suicide.

In the middle of this hullabaloo, and before the investigation began, the Memphis mayor—evidently warned that revisionist measures were suddenly needed—ordered that all the files of the MPD's domestic intelligence division be destroyed. Those files contained much of the still-secret details related to the conduct of the police and fire department's handling of the protection and/or surveillance of Dr. King, such as why black officers were pulled off their assignments. On September 10, 1976, 180 boxes of those files were burned.[716] Three reporters and their publishers, all compromised by their "mouthpiece links" to the FBI and CIA—George Lardner, Jr. of the *Washington Post*, Jermiah O'Leary of the *Washington Star*, and David B. Burnham of the *New York Times*—joined in a campaign to discredit Sprague and undermine the fledgling committee. Burnham, for example, dug deep into the Philadelphia newspaper archives and reported anew stories from ten to fifteen years earlier that alleged, for example, that Sprague had mishandled a homicide case many years previously involving the son of a friend.[717]

A longtime friend and crony of Lyndon Johnson (who had died four years earlier), Congressman Henry Gonzalez (D-TX), having no interest in aggressively pursuing reinvestigations, replaced Downing as chairman of the HSCA and immediately attempted to fire Sprague as chief counsel, calling him "an unconscionable scoundrel." The real reason for his removal, according to what Sprague told HSCA researcher Gaeton Fonzi, was because of his intent to rigorously investigate the details of the CIA operations related to the assassinations, including getting access to all of its employees and all pertinent records from that period of time. The highest-level CIA officials balked at that but eventually offered to provide him information if he signed a secrecy agreement. Sprague refused, saying, "How can I possible sign [a secrecy] agreement with an agency I'm supposed to be investigating?"[718]

Two subcommittees were created: one on the assassination of President John F. Kennedy, with Richardson Preyer of North Carolina as its chairman, and another on the assassination of Martin Luther King, with Walter E. Fauntroy as its chairman. The staff was divided into two task forces designated to assist each of the subcommittees.

Walter Fauntroy, in his testimony at the 1999 civil trial *King v. Jowers*, explained how the HSCA was damaged from the start because of these strategic disagreements between members and journalists who were being used by the CIA and FBI to help protect their interests. He explained that a six-month delay in getting started was due to a disagreement between the chairman of the full committee, Mr. Gonzales, and the chief counsel, Richard Sprague. He confirmed that it centered around Sprague's intent to seek access to all government records, not only from the FBI, but the records of the CIA and military intelligence as well, which caused much controversy among some members of the committee whose allegiance to those entities seemed to be higher than that to the mission of the committee. The delays throughout 1977 ultimately caused the committee's failure to complete its work and forced it to close down prematurely, by the end of the 95th Congress (1977–79). By this time, it was clear that there would be no support for a continuance in the 96th Congress.[719]

Gonzales ultimately resigned from his position and Sprague was fired. Before he resigned, Gonzalez appointed someone more to his liking to become the new chairman, Louis Stokes of Ohio. Sprague met with Stokes on March 29 and subsequently agreed to resign. He was replaced by G. Robert Blakey, and the HSCA immediately changed course in its capitulation to the CIA's insistence on defining what information would be revealed to the committee.

Unfortunately, and partly because the loss of at least six months on the timeline, a compromise was reached that resulted in the suspension of an aggressive investigative process of the assassinations under Sprague, to be replaced by a more evaluative process under Robert Blakey. The already-compromised process was stunted from the start, and neither of the so-called "investigations" was successfully resolved, in Representative Fauntroy's opinion: "We admittedly concluded our investigation without having thoroughly investigated all of the evidence that was apparent."[720]

The Investigation's First Rule of Order: "No Conspiracy Angles"

Unfortunately, some lessons are learned too late. Mr. Blakey's realization of how his committee had been hijacked by the very forces behind the treasons they were attempting to investigate was among them. The ponderously lengthy evaluative role undertaken by the committee merely reinforced with verbiage what had already been decided years before, by the same forces. Faced with the choice of bucking the system to find essential truths or standing down and reinforcing myths, the committee capitulated to the easier, more sanguine, and comforting avenue, not the hard-questioning, confrontational attitude of the previous chief counsel, Mr. Sprague.

By 1967, the men in charge of the highest levels of government had dealt with a constant barrage of criticisms of the Warren Report on the assassination of President Kennedy and had grown so tired of the very word "conspiracy" that attempts were made to denigrate anyone who even used it. The CIA, reacting to efforts by New Orleans District Attorney Jim Garrison to conduct an honest and thorough investigation of the JFK assassination, introduced a new and dismissive term that was intended to ridicule anyone having the temerity to even question their mythologies: conspiracy theorists.

That term was created in a memorandum written not only to their own employees, but also for their many stringers in the journalism and publication worlds, who were paid to replicate whatever message the powers that be wanted to be written. Specifically, the memorandum coined the terms "conspiracy theories" and "conspiracy theorists" and included recommendations for discrediting and ridiculing such theories (see Appendix D).

After six months of internal squabbling over which direction to proceed, leaving only eighteen months to complete their work, the committee effectively gave up any semblance of an actual investigation before their work was started. It was never verbalized or committed to paper, but the understanding from the start was that any hint of looking for a conspiracy could not stand.[721]

Altogether, the committee brushed aside over twenty-four individuals and organizations that were stipulated as possible "conspiracy" candidates or witnesses who had come forward in their attempts to call out leads they had become involved with. The highly credible John McFerren, previously noted, was one such witness, and two others, tagged as "criminal candidates"—Randy Rosenson and Jules Ricco Kimble—were also included in that listing. All of them were summarily dismissed in one fashion or the other, invariably because the committee chairman could not overcome his conviction that only James Earl Ray could have possibly been the demented lone assassin.

However, another witness they did interview in executive session—James Cooper Green, mentioned in Chapter 8—was not only omitted from the list, his testimony is nowhere to be found in the HSCA report or any of its hearing records. In fact, it was withheld completely, and those documents are still not scheduled for release until 2029, along with all the remaining classified documents.[722] That would have been true for JFK documents as well, were it not for the 1992 JFK Act, passed on the heels of Oliver Stone's 1991 movie *JFK*, which caused the schedule to be moved forward to October 2017, twenty-five years after the law was signed. (As 2017 drew to a close, the CIA continued to obfuscate and delay a full release, evidently many of those records still holding many "National Security" secrets despite the official conclusion that the killing of the president over fifty-four years ago was done entirely by a lone gunman with no significant contacts to any other government entity.)

The reason behind the Jim Green documents being classified might be explained by an article written by C. D. Stelzer on May 9, 2001, in a magazine called the *Riverfront Times* titled "Maybe in Memphis," which detailed Green's background, split between small-time crime and later law enforcement. Having been subpoenaed to appear before the congressional committee, Green said Paul (a.k.a. Ray's handler "Raul"), another FBI agent, and former assistant director Cartha DeLoach paid a visit to him in his hotel room, for the purpose of preparing him for what he should and should not say at the closed session ("executive session") hearing the next day. Green stated that he was warned to limit his testimony to "his knowledge of a St. Louis-based conspiracy."[723] Clearly, DeLoach and Paul were there to ensure that nothing would be said to point to "Raul" (i.e., "Paul").

But Green worried that limiting his testimony—as DeLoach and Paul/Raul had instructed him—and thereby not telling the whole truth would put himself at risk of perjury. When he began testifying, as he was revealing names and events, Paul and DeLoach entered the hearing room, obviously to intimidate him. Chairman Stokes began haranguing him as well, then asked him why he had to refer to notes, further angering Green. He stated that he told them, "I was laying on top of this building and I saw James [Earl Ray] walking and that he was not in the area when the shots [*sic*] were fired." When Stokes accused him of not being truthful, Green said he replied, "Look, I don't even have to be here!" got up, and left the room.[724] The joint appearance of DeLoach and Raul at that hearing should have set off dozens of red flags and front-page news headlines (in a fair and perfect world, where real news preempted "fake news" stories).

The HSCA's Elaborate Effort to Dismiss Ray's Claims: There Shall Be No "Raul"

As should by now be apparent, throughout this narrative and as demonstrated within this chapter regarding the HSCA's final conclusions, the FBI's preestablished plan even before the assassination was to subvert any suggestion of a wide-ranging conspiracy. Allowing any leads in that direction could potentially—perhaps inevitably—lead directly back to themselves. The proof of this lies in the fact that every one of the many leads to Ray's handler, Raul, would be stopped as soon as it appeared. Most of them were directly related to the fact that Ray had become dependent on Raul for his financial wherewithal; the most compelling evidence for how the HSCA purposefully avoided that lead was how it indefatigably attempted to associate him—and his entire family—with a series of bank robberies that he, and they, had nothing to do with.

The only attempt by the HSCA to explain where all the cash was coming from to finance Ray's extensive travels and purchases of a one-year-old Mustang, a new gun, cameras, binoculars, and assorted other expenses was to assert his involvement in the bank robbery in Alton, Illinois. Had they bothered to ask the local police there, they would have found that none of the Rays had been considered as possible suspects in that robbery. The day after this assertion was made in the committee hearings, by Representative Floyd J. Fithian (D-IN)—suggesting that Ray and his brother Jerry had pulled off the robbery—Jerry went to the bank with a television reporter in tow to meet with bank and police officials to deny the accusation. Police department spokesman Lieutenant Walter Conrad stated that neither James nor Jerry was ever a suspect.[725]

Given that the committee hadn't done so, Dr. Pepper also personally called the bank president and local sheriff, both of whom stated that James had nothing to do with it, nor was he ever a suspect.[726] Furthermore, Dr. Pepper found out from them that they knew who the real culprits were but lacked enough evidence to convict them. The worst part of it was that both of them stated that they had never even been contacted about Ray's possible involvement in that robbery: not by the FBI, not by the *New York Times* or the *Washington Post*, and not even by the HSCA investigators. After a decade of using this canard, when Dr. Pepper tried to inform the HSCA of his critically important findings, they ignored him, too.

With that, the committee simply revised its accusations, replacing Jerry's name with brother John, and then began an effort to tie him into a whole series of other unsolved bank robberies—committed *after* King's murder, completely unrelated to the crime being investigated—in their efforts to incriminate James vicariously, now through John. Before it was over, the committee produced huge blow-up maps of the city of Alton and the surrounding area, plotting different homes once inhabited by the Ray family, as if such stupendous exhibits themselves might prove his and/or his brothers', uncle's, or grandfather's guilt for every bank robbery ever committed in the area. It soon became clear that the committee, led by its chairman, Louis Stokes, had actually become obsessed with proving their contention that James had robbed that bank regardless of the lack of such evidence and the insistence of the local police that he was not a suspect.[727]

Not only did the Final Report of the HSCA obsessively insist that the Ray family had to be the primary suspects in that robbery, as well as the several others they felt he, or they, might have committed, they purposefully *ignored* the fact that over a hundred police or FBI documents were actually placed into evidence that identified fifteen *other* names of *actual* suspects, to wit: Ralph Robert Page, Charles William "Chuck" Baze, Gary Dale Vandergriff, Robert W. Vandergriff, Joe Mack Sparrowk, Vincent Myron Ruyle, Harold Richard Covington, Louis Eugene Carter, Clinton Allen Bramlet, Jerald Swetland, John Kenneth McClintock, Robert L. Stanton, Jackie Lee Crider, Willie Lee, and Edward Richard Cesarz. Additionally, numerous others were also named as persons of interest (none having the surname "Ray" or otherwise having any connections to the family) or suspects for one or more of the other *later* robberies.[728] Why the committee even allowed all of these documents to be put into evidence—essentially helping to disprove their own unsupported and ridiculous theories—can only be attributed to the guiding principle they worked under, similar to other official cover-up operations such as the Warren Commission's. Bury the readers in officious-looking paperwork: it will help make the investigation look "thorough."

In its zeal to create the notion of a "Ray family conspiracy"—as a replacement of the "Raul" explanation for the basis of James's financial wherewithal, involving James, Jerry, John, and even their sister, Carol Pepper—the FBI (and a decade later, the HSCA) used a variety of bogus pieces of "evidence." Much of it apparently came from the original myths fed by the FBI's senior officials to the fiction writers Huie, Frank, and McMillan, as it then appeared in their books, which was then regurgitated and portrayed as "evidence" by the FBI originally and the HSCA a decade later in their tenacious effort to aggressively avoid investigating Raul.

There was a measured degree of acknowledgment in the HSCA's appendices to its Final Report of the FBI's previous incompetence and criminal actions, as shown in the excerpt below. But it is all in the context of the FBI not having sufficiently, vigorously pursued its investigation in a legally correct manner to show the Ray family's alleged criminal acts, thereby rendering the HSCA's task so much more difficult, which became their excuse for their own inability to make their case. That was clearly the purpose behind the following snippets, which were taken directly from the HSCA's files as referenced in the citation below, augmented only by the author's attempt to clarify, as noted by the use of secondary brackets [ ]:

> "[C]andor requires the comment that the evidence indicates that the performance of the FBI, as well as the Justice Department, was flawed, not in pursuit of the fugitive but in the search for others who may have been involved in the assassination. For example, there is reason to question the adequacy of the FBI's response to substantial evidence of contacts between Ray and his brothers, Jerry and John, at various times between his escape from prison and the assassination. That evidence includes such items as:
>
> (1) Statements of several witnesses [*coming from fellow prisoners or disreputable ex-cons, as noted elsewhere*] pointing to meetings between Ray and a brother;
>
> (2) denials by Jerry and John of pre-assassination contact with James that are in conflict with information established independently [*see above, and Weisberg's response, below*];
>
> (3) Missouri State Penitentiary records indicating John visited James the day before he escaped [*another lie created by the FBI, see Weisberg's response, below*];
>
> (4) information that Jerry, on two occasions, admitted knowledge of a conspiracy in the assassination [*information furnished by McMillan and denied by Jerry*]; and
>
> (5) Ray's statement to a salesman in a gun store, just 6 days before the assassination, that he wished to exchange the rifle on advice from his brother [*actually, Ray said his "brother-in-law" and it was in relation to his excuse that "the deer in Wisconsin are bigger," which was caused by Ray's not being able to provide a better excuse for returning the original rifle, as he was told to do by "Raoul"*].
>
> "Coupled with these indications of a possible family based association that pointed toward a criminal relationship were the indications that the mysterious Raoul might actually have been one or both of the brothers. Even so, the FBI never made a

concerted effort to check out the possibility of a Ray family conspiracy in the assassination. Instead, it treated the brothers and other relatives almost solely as information sources as to James' whereabouts.

"In fact, the Bureau became so preoccupied with the fugitive search that on May 13 Mr. Hoover recommended—with the concurrence of Mr. DeLoach, Mr. [Assistant Director Alex] Rosen, and Mr. Tolson—the placing of electronic surveillance devices in the homes of John Ray, Carol Pepper—a sister—and John's place of business—the Grapevine Tavern in St. Louis.

"This clearly illegal action was never endorsed by the Department of Justice but the request itself is disturbing enough. Not only does it show a lack of concern for the constitutional rights of the relative[s], it establishes the Bureau's lack of interest in a possible conspiracy involving the brothers. Had the taps picked up evidence of such a conspiracy, the illegality of the surveillance would almost surely have tainted the evidence in any subsequent conspiracy trial. Internal FBI memoranda, moreover, indicate that Mr. Hoover and his assistants were well aware of the problem but made the request in any event. While the FBI was proposing unlawful electronic surveillance, it apparently failed to take advantage of a legal way to accomplish the same objective. There is nothing in the FBI files to indicate consideration was given to title III of Public Law 90–351. Signed on June 19, 1968, it empowered the Department of Justice to conduct court-ordered electronic surveillance in the investigation of a variety of crimes, including murder.

"The committee has uncovered two incidents in which the constitutional rights of Ray himself were also apparently a matter of little concern to the FBI:

"The first occurred while Ray was [a]waiting trial in Shelby County, Tenn. On September 30, 1968, Judge W. Preston Battle issued an order emphasizing Ray's written communications with his attorney at the time, Arthur Hanes, Sr., were privileged. Battle directed that they could be monitored only for the purpose of detecting attempts to break prison security but not in order to learn their full content. Nevertheless, during the month of October at least three Ray-to-Hanes letters were intercepted, photocopied, passed along to the FBI's Memphis field office and subsequently transmitted to FBI headquarters in Washington.

"The second occurred shortly after Ray pled guilty in March 1969. Ray was interviewed by the agents-in-charge of the Memphis field office for the purpose of obtaining information on an assassination conspiracy. Ray was not accompanied by an attorney nor was he informed of his Miranda rights — that is, his right to have an attorney, paid or appointed, present; his right to terminate the interview at will; his right to remain silent; and the fact that the Government could use his statements against him. Of course, the use of Ray's self-incriminatory statements in a later conspiracy prosecution would have depended on the ability of the Government to survive a motion to suppress them. So not only were Ray's rights disregarded but the FBI again was risking destruction of valuable evidence in a conspiracy case if one was ever to be made." [729]

There is only one explanation for why the HSCA persisted in its use of this stale, tattered, bald-faced lie, even to the extent of putting forth these statements of FBI incompetence and illegalities, as a sorry excuse for its unsuccessful prosecution of the Ray family's "criminality." It was nothing more or less than an indirect admission of its own incompetence, thus the need for putting it into the permanent public record and thereby becoming an official excuse for the still-unsolved crime. It can only mean that the committee found no other possible rationale for the source of Ray's financial wherewithal, given their absolute refusal to pursue Ray's consistent plea for them to check out "Raoul."

Caught without a reasonable explanation for Ray's otherwise inexplicably ample funds, sufficient to live for a full year driving around three countries—acquiring, in cash, a nearly new Mustang—and living it up like a redneck playboy, they desperately clung to that bank robbery. Evidently, they were pledged to support the theory originally created by an acclaimed novelist at the behest of the FBI. Nothing could stand in the way of "proving" that originally tainted false narrative, not even the truth as presented by the local officials who had intensively investigated the robbery. [730]

Therefore, for posterity, the committee concluded in its Final Report, despite what the Alton police had repeatedly tried to explain to them, that Ray had indeed financed his travels and purchases from this robbery, one for which he had never been convicted, much less charged, tried, or even implicated. [731] That conclusion—including the extended implicit presumption that his brother (though which one remains unclear) was also guilty, not only in the bank robbery, but that he had also been the mysterious "Raoul"—ultimately became the enduring, preposterous official government position, which remains intact today.

Moreover, this absurd result seemed to satisfy the mainstream media's need for a quiet closure, which also allowed them to ignore all subsequent developments over the past four decades. Coincidentally, it was an early example of a covert mission established by government fiat: one designed to permanently replace the classical "integrity of journalism" standard once taught in bygone times at universities, generally among the first precepts taught in Journalism 101. Reporting unvarnished truths is no longer as important as shaping public opinion; political correctness became the accepted norm in the mid-1960s, during the administration of Lyndon B. Johnson, beginning with the creation of a euphemism especially for his lies: "credibility gap." About the same time, lapdogs replaced watchdogs and fealty to governmental dictates became paramount to the anachronistic concept of a vigilant press that once understood the reason for its constitutional role as the Fourth Estate.

The HSCA's Accomplishments, Writ Small: Harold Weisberg's Conclusions and Summary

The best summary of the Martin Luther King Jr. "reinvestigation" portion of the HSCA proceedings can be found in the final sixty pages of Volume VIII of its Final Report. Some of the points made below reference the previous section regarding the bank-robbery explanation and add further clarity to the conclusions presented above. They were written into this public record by one of the most prolific researchers of the time, Harold Weisberg, and excerpts of his incisive analysis are presented below:[732]

- "The committee pursued a series of mutually exclusionary conjectures about the King assassination. All are from FBI files, [and] all were proven false by prior FBI investigation . . ." [p. 607]
- [Among the many fabricated stories proffered by different writers and accepted as fact] "one was manufactured by Raymond Curtis [a fellow prisoner of James Ray's]. Curtis is a virtual hero in the 'biography' of James Earl Ray by George McMillan . . . Curtis began with an effort to defraud *Ebony* magazine based on a false story of a 'contract' offer to kill King. *The FBI's records characterize Curtis as a pathological liar.* [Emphasis added.] This did not deter the committee's giving credence to the McMillan/

Curtis theory, which became the committee's official conjecture, the basis of its Ray investigation." [p. 608]

- "No public records of the committee disclose any investigation of the King assassination. Like the FBI before it, the committee conducted a Ray investigation instead." [p. 608]
- [In the Justice Department's Office of Professional Responsibility's zeal to appear thorough], "it just had to have some criticism of the FBI's performance. That one attributed the alleged 'contract' or 'bounty' to an unidentified businessmen's group. The 'group' was not identified because it did not exist . . . In fact, once Dr. King was killed the jails of the country were rife with these and similar fakes, made up by the Curtises for money and by others in hope of special treatment, like a reduction in sentence." [p. 609]
- "As the committee worked its way through the thicket of baseless, fabricated stories proven false by the FBI investigation, it used these known falsehoods for self-promotion and headlines . . . In the end the committee fixed up and diligently leaked 'plots' which refute each other . . . also straight from FBI files which also reflect its impossibility, is that James Earl Ray's brothers, John and Jerry, combined in bank robberies to finance James Earl Ray." [p. 609]
- "The allegation of a Ray family conspiracy in the King assassination provides the committee with . . . the appearance of something to show for its work . . . [and] require[s] *a beginning that is not fact and what did not exist, Ray family closeness if not intimacy.* [Emphasis added.] Confronted with the total absence of any evidence that John and James Earl Ray were ever close, the committee merely pretended they were, wanting to believe it. In fact, they never were. In their adulthood they almost never saw each other. This is disclosed by the committee's own evidence. One example is Exhibit MLK F-634, a Missouri penitentiary prisoner visitor card in the name of John Ray. The committee represented that this card shows by his signature that John Ray visited James Earl Ray on April 22, 1967, the day before the escape. In fact, there is not a single signature after any of the nine visits recorded. There is no contradiction to the Ray family testimony, that Jerry Ray did not have a visitor's card and that he and others as well as John used the card obtained by John Ray. So far from close to James Earl Ray was John that he did not even obtain permission to visit James at the Missouri penitentiary until James had been there for several years." [pp. 611–612]

- "In the absence of any evidence at all, the committee 'narrated' Jerry Ray as the 'Raoul' James Earl says was his criminal associate and financier, with the alternative that 'Raoul' was a 'composite' of John and Jerry. The allegedly wealthy co-conspirator and fellow bank robber Jerry Ray drove only a variety of troublesome secondhand cars from the time of James Earl's 1967 prison escape . . . . There is nothing in Jerry Ray's life or style of life indicative of his ever having had any of the alleged bank-robbery money. The committee has made no effort to show that he did. It merely assumed and alleged this, in contradiction to what it also withholds, the results of the FBI's investigation." [pp. 612–613]

- "While the committee's number of robberies attributed to [the Ray family's three brothers: James, and / or John and Jerry] varies, the committee finally fixed upon five. *Of these five, four were long after James was captured, long after he entered a guilty plea, and can have no relevance to the crime or any legislative purpose other than prejudicing.* [Emphasis added.] The only one of these robberies that was not long after the guilty plea is that of the Bank of Alton, Illinois. All that connects the Ray brothers to this is the committee's longing and need. After the committee publicized this conjecture, Jerry Ray surrendered himself and asked to be tried. He was told he was not and never had been a suspect." [p. 614]

- "Before the committee fixed upon this 'conspiracy theory,' the FBI, during its 1968 investigation, leaked the identical conjecture in its effort to appear to account for James Earl Ray's financing other than he had, by his being financed by those with whom he had a criminal association." [p. 614]

- "Based upon this ['evidence'] the committee had John jailed and demanded that his parole be canceled. Based on this it also accused him of perjury for denying he had robbed four banks long *after* James was convicted for the King assassination ('After' is emphasized [in the original document] because the committee's legislative authority is limited to the actual assassination. It does not include an investigation of bank robberies)." [pp. 615–616]

- "The committee's 'modus operandi' [meaning the commonalities of all the bank robberies, as Weisberg put it] is unique only when banks are robbed with toothpicks or feathers. The committee's exhibits include nothing more unique than that weapons were used, masks and hats were worn, and that none of the banks in question was robbed by a single man. There is no other uniqueness in what is hyped into an allegedly distinctive 'modus operandi' and 'conclusive' proof of John Ray's alleged guilt." [p. 624]

- "From the committee's own charts, Exhibits MLK F-648 through 652, the robbers of these banks did not even use the same weapons in the robberies. The allegedly 'solid evidence' is contradictory on this and on other essential details. Although the committee took executive session testimony from alleged co-conspirators, no transcripts of their testimony are included in the narration text and exhibits released to the press . . . No less surprising, given the nature, thrust and significance the committee gives its conjectures about John Ray's alleged share in $114,880 of bank robberies, the committee withheld from the press its Exhibit F-86a-g, 'John Ray Bank Statements' . . . " [p. 625]
- [In one of the FBI's original, and later the HSCA's, most egregious actions]: "In the course of trying to frame John Ray on the Ladonia robbery, the perjury [committed by Clarence Haynes, one of the actual, convicted bank robbers] helped put the innocent Ernest Turley away for eight years. This ruined Turley's life and that of his entire family in tragic ways. In executive session John Ray testified to Haynes' perjury and to the frame-up . . . The committee wanted to use Haynes against John and exploited the opportunities provided by keeping John's testimony secret. The committee leaked an angled account of the Turley framing, wrote a compassionate letter to the governor and told the St. Louis *Post-Dispatch* how its good heart and investigative diligence would lead to the exoneration of the innocent Turley. This became page-one news in the St. Louis *Post-Dispatch*."[pp. 625–626]
- "By keeping knowledge of Haynes's perjury from its public record, the committee could and did pretend he was a dependable witness who gave what Mr. Blakey described as 'conclusive' proof. The committee did know Haynes was a perjurer, had framed an innocent man, did withhold all of this at its December 1 hearing and did regard Haynes as a credible witness against John. The real credit is due John Ray. His testimony to Haynes's perjury is over several pages ending on page 51 of the suppressed transcript. In seeking to make some use of this testimony, the committee merely omitted the uncongenial pages from those it used on December 1 and withheld from its press kit. By this means, the committee also suppressed John's testimony to the means by which the FBI suborned Haynes perjury." [The committee also suppressed the

release of Haynes's testimony, thereby hiding his lies that were used against both Turley and John Ray. Pp. 626–627]

- [To further illustrate how the committee "framed" John Ray, Weisberg quoted the actual perpetrator of the robberies, who denied that he had been involved in any of them, and then summarized the charade as follows]: "In order to protect its fragile concoction of perjuries and fabrications procured in an effort to make it appear that the committee's conspiracy theorizing had some basis, the committee first held all its hearings in total secrecy and then shouted down John's counsel each time he sought to inform the committee of its error." [p. 635]

- "The committee actually took the position that any effort to correct its error is contemptuous and that it has a license to err because the role of counsel is restricted to the committee's concept of a witness's Constitutional rights. In essence, the committee's position is that when an innocent man is being framed by a Congressional committee, the man's counsel has no right to object—because no Constitutional right is abridged by a committee frame-up . . . It severely limited if it did not entirely preclude the possibility of correcting factual error. The committee's report was already drafted based on preconceptions. The John Ray hearing could not have any significant influence. It was intended as a rubber stamp . . . Faced with the need to come up with something else and certain that the Rays were without means or influence, the committee fixed upon its 'conspiracy theory' of a Ray family conspiracy . . . the committee held its hearings entirely in secret. Secrecy prevents general knowledge of the fact that the committee never really investigated the crime or the performance of the executive agencies involved in the official investigation. Secrecy also hides the fact that there was no Ray family conspiracy in the King assassination." [pp. 636–637]

- "Having taken as its own the FBI's fugitive investigation and assumed that the FBI's assumed killer is the actual killer, the committee can hardly criticize the FBI for not solving the killing. The committee has reduced itself to complaining that the FBI did not validate the unfounded conjectures the committee wants to be believed so that the committee will not stand naked, exposed as having wasted its funding and not met its mandate after unprecedented support by the Congress, even those in the Congress who had deep doubts about the committee and its proposals." [p. 637] "In turn, this meant harsh treatment by the committee to stifle John Ray and his counsel. Despite the committee's shouting down, overt threats, gavel banging and baseless personal insults, the committee was unable to prevent some exposure of itself. It was proven to have misrepresented what it presented as evidence and it misquoted its own records in further misrepresentation as part of its effort to breathe the semblance of life into its Pinocchio before the press and on coast-to-coast broadcast. In this effort the chairman's behavior was such that he was forced to surrender the chairmanship." [p. 637]

- "While pretending it wanted only truth, the committee actually banned truth and fact by insisting that only its questions and predetermined answers to them were relevant. When it could not completely stifle Ray's counsel by threat and gavel, it merely alleged that correction could be made in the five minutes it allotted at the end. As this memorandum reflects, five hours would not provide an adequate time for correction of the false record manufactured by the committee." [p. 637–638]

- "This censoring was of the public record. Those of means could buy a transcript. It was broadcast in full from coast-to-coast and tape-recorded. Yet the committee withheld the full transcript from Ray and his counsel to make correction of it difficult if not impossible for what remained of the committee's life and for the brief interval before the report would be issued. This served to prevent the destruction of the committee's baseless prefabricated case, the kind of case once believed limited to the Gestapos and KBBs of the world." [p. 638]

- "A more meager accomplishment for a Congressional investigation is impossible to imagine . . . The committee's secret awareness of its nakedness, or its singular lack of any real accomplishment, is what drives it to have some slight claim to *anything* of its own. [Emphasis in original.] Thus its persecution of the resourceless and powerless rightwinger, John Ray. His only real crime is being the vulnerable brother of the accused assassin—with whom he was never close and with whom neither the FBI nor the committee proved he had any contact of any kind for the year prior to the assassination of Dr. King." [p. 655]

Harold Weisberg also noted a number of highly irrational precepts the committee posited by drawing the conclusions they did. For example, after allegedly robbing the Alton bank with one of his brothers, the next day Ray supposedly took his share of the loot (totaling $27,250, his share at most being $13,625) and bought a $200, six-year-old clunker and thus began his whirlwind tour of Canada, before returning to the US within a few months and giving the car to Jerry, who junked it. Only then did he proceed to Birmingham to buy a nearly new $2,000 Mustang to resume his five-month tour of the North American continent before suddenly deciding to stalk Dr. King in preparation for murdering him by loading his brand-new rifle with one single bullet, a gun he had purportedly only fired a few times using a telescopic sight that had never been properly adjusted.[733]

Also noted by Weisberg was how Chief Counsel Blakey, seemingly acting as judge, jury, and sheriff of Kansas City, wrote to the Parole Commission there about how they needed to revoke Jerry Ray's parole—based upon his and the committee's presumptuous conclusions of Jerry's purported guilt—having offered no evidence whatsoever of his involvement in the four bank robberies for which they had "convicted" him. The parole board not only immediately revoked his parole based upon this completely baseless letter, they even placed him in solitary confinement for three months before finally paroling him again a few months later. As Jerry waited for the parole to become effective, he had to reside in a halfway house, vulnerable to further pressure from the committee to keep his mouth shut.[734]

This Kafkaesque moment, as the chief counsel demanded that the brother of the accused commit perjury by confessing to robberies Jerry had nothing to do with, was something that even the novelists couldn't have made up. The statement Jerry was asked to sign included not only those four robberies, but an acknowledgement that he had also committed five more than that, plus a statement that "it is believed" that John was also involved in the Alton bank robbery, which they had "determined" James had committed. That was the only one of the eleven total bank robberies that—had it been true that he had done it—would have been at all germane to the case that Blakey's committee was supposedly investigating. All of this harassment of John and Jerry Ray was the result of Blakey's revenge against them caused by their refusal to confess to the four bank robberies that the committee conjectured one or the other of them pulled.

But, beyond the Keystone Cops analogy that one's mind conjures at this point, the reason the committee had for attempting to make the case in the first place was their single-minded determination to "prove" that the Alton bank robbery was the source of James's funds for his free-spending almost year's vacation of freedom and travels: from Chicago to Toronto and Montreal, Canada; back into the deep south, Birmingham, Alabama; from there to Texas, Mexico City, Acapulco, Puerto Vallarta, Los Angeles, New Orleans (and return to LA, back again to NOLA), and then on to Birmingham and Atlanta, return to Birmingham, and finally to Memphis. Even after the murder of King, he would return back to Atlanta, then travel to Toronto again, and on to London, Lisbon, Portugal, and back to London, where he was finally arrested. That all of these travels—his purchases of the Mustang, expensive cameras, and related equipment; the rifle(s); suits and other clothes; plastic surgery on his nose; dance, locksmithing, and bartending lessons; and everything else—were all purchased with funds he mysteriously acquired. As the committee struggled to come up with a compatible explanation, it became painfully obvious that it was all simply unbelievable: thus the elaborate lengths by an august congressional committee to explain it with unsupportable deceits while carefully ignoring all clues leading back to "Raoul," because he had been declared out of bounds.

The entire ludicrous story was necessary because they could not countenance what James Earl Ray plaintively, patiently, repeatedly, and consistently stated: that all those funds came from "Raoul," who they obviously knew would lead them to places they did not want to go.

An Example of HSCA's Skulduggery—Two Birds, One Stone: Their Attempt to Dismiss the FBI's Blackmail of King and the Existence of "Raoul"

In Chapter 7, we noted how the FBI-induced violence caused Dr. King to cancel the sanitation worker march and—responding to the FBI's planted news leak about how he had stayed at the Holiday Inn Rivermont—caused him to change to the Lorraine Motel the following week. The HSCA responded to that point with the following treatise:

> "If its purpose was to cause Dr. King to take a room at the Lorraine, its intent remained sinister, no matter what the reasons were for the choice of lodgings. On the other hand, if the purpose was to embarrass Dr. King, it was simply one of many COINTELPRO initiatives that had no connection with the assassination.
>
> "An examination of Ray's conduct in Memphis led the committee to conclude that the latter is the more credible alternative. Dr. King returned to Memphis and checked into the Lorraine on the morning of April 3, 1968. Ray arrived in Memphis on the evening of April 3. Yet Ray chose to stay at the New Rebel Motel and did not check into the roominghouse at

422 ½ South Main Street until the afternoon of April 4. To assume the FBI's purpose on March 29 was to set Dr. King up for assassination at the Lorraine is to assume that the Bureau had control over Ray's movements. Ray's presence at the New Rebel on April 3 was evidence that it did not have such control. The committee concluded, therefore, that the drafters of the March 29 memorandum did not intend to set Dr. King up for assassination at the Lorraine." [735]

The circular logic demonstrated within this statement, that Ray's choice of motel the evening before the murder showed that "the FBI did not control his movement," is a classic non sequitur: he was only a few miles away, it not being necessary for him to be any closer at that point (or any other point, since he was completely oblivious to King's whereabouts), and he was brought there by the FBI's man Raul, on his—and their—schedule. If Ray had gone to the Lorraine or to Bessie's rooming house the first night, they would have used that as more "evidence" of him "stalking" Dr. King. That flawed logic, once rejected, sends one back to their first alternative: a sinister intent, by the HSCA's own countercircular logic.

The HSCA "Investigation": An Anatomy of a Kangaroo Court Proceeding

As most people would expect, the imprimatur automatically conferred on an investigation commissioned by congressional decree should produce a final reckoning guaranteed to resolve all remaining questions related to the subjects of the inquiry. But that was not the case in 1979, when the HSCAs (JFK and MLK) finally delivered its report of its two-year investigation.

Despite the aura of official sanctimoniousness in the summary Final Report as it pertained to the Martin Luther King Jr. investigation, one need only review a few of the underlying documents—Volumes VII and VIII in particular—for a fuller assessment of the inner workings that produced that result. [736] In the latter volume, there were 672 pages in the referenced document. The first 600 consist almost entirely of speculative, wishful, but unsubstantiated charges of a "possibility" that James Earl Ray had collaborated with his two brothers in not only his escape from prison, but in conducting a series of bank robberies throughout central Illinois and Missouri starting before—but mostly even well *after*—Ray began his lengthy travels around the United States, Canada, and Mexico as the means for his financial resources to fund those travels.

Much of this committee dialogue, and the resulting minutes and reports, was centered not on James Earl Ray's attitudes toward blacks *before* Dr. King's murder, but on those of his brothers, even *after* the assassination. But the cited incidents began thirty years *before* the hearing—and *twenty* years before the assassination—as when committee counsel, Mark Speiser, asked John Ray about his attitudes expressed in a letter he had written to George McMillan about how black soldiers who had married white girls in Germany were allowed to ride in the first-class part of the ship coming home back after the war, while white soldiers who did the fighting but who had not married were consigned to the second-class section of the ship.[737] According to John Ray, it wasn't just him or James who objected, it was practically the whole ship. Apparently their view, in a nonracial context, was simply that the honors were being conferred on men handling logistical or clerical tasks while the heroes of the war were shunted aside, into the lower bowels of the ship.

As previously noted, the HSCA finally—ten years after the theme had originally been set by the novelist William Bradford Huie—recanted the earlier finding of the FBI in 1968, and the original Justice Department's task force, that the murder of Martin Luther King Jr. was the result of James Earl Ray's racism. The irony of that finding, originally put forth by the primary planner and instigator—who *was* a genuine racist, as detailed in the first chapters of this book—could not be more surreal.

Even Hampton Sides noted the irony, albeit unwittingly, when he wrote that Hoover had told Attorney General Ramsey Clark in a meeting on June 20, 1968, that "We are dealing with a man who is not an ordinary criminal, but a man capable of doing any kind of sly act . . . Ray is not a fanatic [like] Sirhan Sirhan. But he is a racist and detests Negroes, and Martin Luther King . . . I think he acted entirely alone, but we are not closing our minds that others might be associated with him. We have to run down every lead."[738] After stating that, Hoover proceeded to do exactly what he stated they could not do, "closing our minds that others might be" involved, while discarding everything that did not conform to the preestablished paradigm.

In a memorandum summarizing his conversation with Ramsey Clark, J. Edgar Hoover stated with aplomb, and considerable helpings of duplicitousness, cynicism, and irony mixed in:

> I said I think Ray is a racist and detested Negroes and Martin Luther King and there is indication that prior to the Memphis situation, he had information about King speaking in other towns and then picked out Memphis.[739]

By projecting his own racial attitudes and animus toward Dr. King onto the patsy, Hoover could be assured that the real motive would accurately be stated as the proximate cause behind the murder, because he would have uniquely understood it. The only difference was the identity of the real perpetrator.

Despite the intrinsic lies about Ray's faux "legend"—which we have conclusively demonstrated to have been baseless—that comment from Hoover himself actually validates the main thesis of this book. Because it shows that at this early date (just days after Ray was arrested in London), and before either Hanes or Huie had been put into their respective positions as the attorney and author representing Ray, and before any other substantive story about him had been written by anyone else—ergo, before anyone had even evaluated Ray's persona in depth—J. Edgar Hoover had already framed him according to the theme that would be repeated again and again by the chosen authors of books and newspaper and magazine articles. It proves that the die had already been cast, and from then on, James Earl Ray was officially christened as a racist hater of "Negroes" and a stalker of Martin Luther King, both false legends that would endure for half a century. Perhaps for eternity, if the fifty-year-old house of cards does not finally collapse, and soon.

Cartha DeLoach Fumbles Through His Testimony

The obsequious Cartha DeLoach, certainly aware of the massive obfuscation efforts to frame Ray for the murder, would later gloat: "From the time we found that photograph at the bartender's school, his fate was sealed . . . [Ray] was a loner, an egotist, a bigot, a man who in prison had said he was going to kill Dr. King, a man who wanted to be known, a man who *stalked* Dr. King: The evidence was overwhelming."[740]

Not content to leave it at that, DeLoach claimed that Hoover's own feelings about King—which belied the fact that he was (to borrow a phrase from Hoover's quote about Ray) "a racist and detested Negroes and Martin Luther King"—actually *intensified* the manhunt. DeLoach wrote: "Truth be told, the old feud did have an impact—it drove us to prove, at every moment, that we were doing all we humanly could do to catch King's killer . . . The FBI had never pursued a fugitive with greater patience and imagination."[741]

At the HSCA hearings in 1978, this exchange with staff counsel, Mr. Peter Beeson, occurred, as to where DeLoach was in the FBI's pecking order:

> **Mr. Beeson:** "So in 1968 at the time of Dr. King's
> assassination you were No. 3 man in the Bureau underneath

> Mr. Tolson and Mr. Hoover and had direct supervisory responsibility for the activities in both the Domestic Intelligence Division and the General Investigative Division, as well as other divisions, correct?"
>
> **Mr. DeLoach:** "The facts aren't exactly correct, Mr. Beeson. We didn't play the numbers game. There was no No. 3 or no No. 4 man. There were two Assistants to the Director. I was assistant to the Director in charge of Investigative Activities and Crime Records, which included public relations; and Mr. John P. Mohr was an Assistant to the Director in charge of General Administrative Matters. In fact, your chart is incorrect; it puts me on a parallel with Mr. Tolson. I reported to Mr. Tolson."
>
> **Mr. Beeson:** "All right. Well, we certainly would like to clarify it for the record."

Yet despite denying that anyone at the FBI ever played "the numbers game," when DeLoach wrote his memoirs, the very first paragraph of the first chapter claimed otherwise:

> Shortly after the death of President John Kennedy, I became the official FBI liaison to President Lyndon Johnson. *I was given this assignment because of my position as third in command in the FBI, second only to Hoover's old friend, Clyde Tolson.* Within a few months I began to realize how far LBJ was willing to go to use the FBI for his own political purposes.[742] (Emphasis added.)

These first interactions with the committee set the pattern for DeLoach's later responses to various members and were testament to the fact that his prevarications and circumlocutions were just getting started. Throughout his testimony, he attempted to diminish his own role and his knowledge or influence in anything unrelated to his administrative duties as he pretended to be the lord of the filing cabinets and the clerks who maintained them.

In the questioning by Representative Fauntroy, reference was made to a memorandum from William Sullivan to Alan Belmont summarizing the initial December 23, 1963, "major planning conference," previously noted. The memo, dated the next day (December 24, 1963), described the results of that meeting, and it would have been considered a milestone kind of meeting that probably everyone working there would have indelibly remembered, but not Mr. DeLoach:

Mr. Fauntroy asked Cartha DeLoach: "Were you aware of a conference which was called, in a memo dated Christmas Eve in 1963, a conference held in the Atlanta office [*sic*: to be clear, the conference, with personnel from the FBI field office in Atlanta, among other field offices, was held the previous day at FBI headquarters in Washington][743] with the seat of government personnel which had as its purpose how best to carry out an investigation to produce results without embarrassing the administration, the Bureau, and how to come up with a complete analysis of the avenues and approaches to neutralize King as an effective Negro leader, and concerning some development of his continued dependence upon the Communists? Were you aware of that?"

Mr. DeLoach [probably breathing a sigh of relief that Fauntroy misstated the location of that meeting, allowing him to evade the question, rather than correcting him, replied]: "No, sir, Mr. Fauntroy, I was not. As you could observe from the memorandum, this was not sent through me for consideration or approval and was only sent to my office later on, for review or just simply for information, after Mr. Hoover had already approved it, or after the action had taken place."

Having claimed to have no knowledge of this "Atlanta" meeting, DeLoach continued answering in the negative to a series of follow-up questions, effectively denying that he ever had any inkling of this major campaign within the FBI to neutralize Dr. King—despite the obvious fact that, as the FBI's "personal liaison to the president," he would have clearly been squarely in the middle of that effort.

Fauntroy's line of questioning included a reference to the related FBI objective of intervening to force the appointment of a successor to King once he was effectively removed from his position. Through another series of gaffes in getting their evidence properly labeled and supplied to the witness, it became apparent that the thrust of this question was thereby lost, and therefore never even properly asked, thus it was never answered by the witness:

Mr. DeLoach: "Which exhibit is that, Mr. Fauntroy?"
Mr. Fauntroy: "That is actually exhibit F-437B—I'm sorry— which you do not have and which I will not trouble you with."
Mr. DeLoach: "All right."

Mr. Fauntroy: "But you don't recall Mr. Sullivan ever having expressed that view, or Mr. Hoover?"

Mr. DeLoach: "No, sir."

Mr. Fauntroy: "Do you recall 438D?"

Mr. DeLoach: "'D' as in David, Mr. Fauntroy[?]"

Mr. Fauntroy: "'D' as in David, which references . . . "

Mr. DeLoach: "I don't see that, sir."

Mr. Fauntroy: "Sorry. We do not have 438D; and I won't trouble you with that, save to reference a memo of January 8, 1964, which began, 'It is your responsibility as Assistant Director in charge of and having the DID to report to you, *a reference to the importance of developing a new leader once you had discredited Dr. King*'—not you, but the FBI—according to the memo. [Emphasis added.]

"It might be important if you have 438D, to provide it to the witness, because here in Mr. Hoover's writing he indicates that he is glad to see that Mr. Sullivan has finally seen the light, though it is dismally delayed, that he struggled for months to convince him that the Communists had very definite influence over Dr. King.

"I would like to move now, Mr. [. . .]"

Mr. DeLoach: "Mr. Fauntroy, before you move on, this memo apparently was not sent to me, and I was not a party to it."

Mr. Fauntroy: "So you were not aware of it?"

Mr. DeLoach: "No, sir; it was sent back to my office, for information apparently after Mr. Hoover had ordered the action to be taken."

Mr. Fauntroy: "But now you are aware, at least from the record, that a campaign was under way at that time?"

Mr. DeLoach: "From what you told me, yes."[744]

Mr. DeLoach undoubtedly breathed more than one sigh of relief at the bungled questioning, giving him wide berth to evade responsive answers to unasked questions, because despite his denial, he knew all about that point, as we observed in Chapter 3. Even before Sullivan made a recommendation to Hoover—that if they succeeded in removing Dr. King from his position, they should to be ready to submit the name of Dr. Samuel R. Pierce Jr. to the NAACP as his replacement—he had already reviewed that with DeLoach and Tolson, and both of them had approved it.[745] Chairman Louis Stokes would call that idea—to not only remove "a leader for a whole race of people, destroying that man," but then also attempt to choose his replacement— "pure, unadulterated arrogance."[746]

Yet, when DeLoach was finally caught in this lie during his testimony, he managed to evade it, thanks to the bungled questioning and the fumbled preparations for confronting him on it. In fact, DeLoach was the architect of that particular skullduggery, as proven by the correspondence referenced in earlier chapters. "Deke" DeLoach was always one of the slickest of the sychophants serving Hoover and Johnson, and his skills in that area obviously brought him the deference the committee members showed to him throughout this unproductive session, including that of the chairman, who was outraged by the FBI's attempt to manage Dr. King's replacement but nonetheless accepted DeLoach's denial of knowledge. Deke technically won this confrontation through his ability to prevaricate, his ersatz bearing, and silver tongue, yet that performance was one of his lesser deceits.

How the HSCA's Failures Revitalized the Original Deceits and Myths of King's Murder

The HSCA's primary achievement—nearly the *only* one—in its "investigation" was in finally correcting the keystone point of the record, in removing the racism motive as the alleged killer's primary reason for killing King. That point was examined in previous chapters, where we showed that the HSCA investigators reinterviewed several witnesses whose actual testimonies to the HSCA were at variance with what they had purportedly told the early authors of books written (by Huie, Frank, and McMillan) in 1968 through 1976, which had been mislabeled as nonfiction rather than the much more proper genre in which they should have been sold, novels, based upon enough partial fact to make them believable to a credulous public anxious to understand still another lone-nut assassination.

As unbelievable as it sounds, despite the fact that the HSCA investigators categorically demolished the "Ray as southern violent racist" canard, a number of later authors, including Gerald Posner and Hampton Sides, ignored that point and continued the same meme in their increasingly novelistic works of fiction over the last twenty-five years. Not only did Hampton Sides continue the previous deceits—adding even more, as noted throughout this narrative—he did it with such aplomb in *Hellhound on His Trail* that reviews such as the following ensured heightened marketing success:

> "Sides' book, meticulously researched, reads like nothing so much as a novel, and no wonder," wrote Steve Yarbrough, *The Oregonian*'s reviewer . . . "I have rarely read a better work of narrative nonfiction. Even those of us who witnessed the civil

rights movement and were fortunate enough to hear Martin Luther King Jr. speak, as I did, have likely forgotten much about this time period, which Sides' fine book brings brilliantly back to life. Following King's murder, many American cities exploded as the anger and rage of a denied minority reached critical mass."[747]

In archetypical irony, Sides himself wrote a column on April 3, 2011, in the *Washington Post* titled "Remembering Martin Luther King as a man, not a saint," about the need for writers to avoid hyperbole in his remembrance:

> Today, King is enshrined in the pantheon of our greatest heroes—an icon, a saint, untouchable . . . We have no use for Hallmark heroes — airbrushed, Photoshopped, simon-pure. We need to see King in all his pathos, imperfection and messy ambiguity. In the end, that's the only way we can relate to his struggles or appreciate his greatness.[748]

Yet his own unconstrained hyperbole has set the historical record in the pantheon Sides described. Clearly, his brand of the hybrid book genre—a recipe of a few time-worn partial "facts," blended with copious portions of fustian hyperbole—has established the generally accepted mythological historical record which 90 percent of the population accept as the ultimate truth.

The story Sides presented in his book perpetuated the myth previously rejected by the HSCA's Final Report, because books like his ignored the only true accomplishment of that unfortunate expenditure of public resources. Readers of Sides's book would never know that the official government report rejected the meme of Ray's racism four decades ago because that point got trampled under the stampede of the public's preference for history presented as novelettes.

The many factually based books—written by such authors as Weisberg, Lane, Melanson, Emison, and Pepper—were insufficient to correct the record left by Huie, Frank, McMillan, and later by Posner, Sides, and others. The latter of these works exploited the fact that the HSCA's findings were effectively hidden by the dearth of publicity by mass media. The inevitable result was the same hyperbole presented within Sides's book, which he himself then lamented in his referenced article.

But that should have been expected when, despite having knocked down the foundation of Ray's guilt by rejecting the racism motive, the

HSCA then failed to replace it with anything that would support the rest of the faux theory of Ray's guilt. Moreover, in failing to present a more complete deconstruction of all the myths built around that failed premise—and continuing to pursue alternatives to the provenance of Ray's financial wherewithal to the extent of becoming an irrationally malicious obsession to prove it had to be the conjured bank robberies—the committee's original purpose was lost long before its anticlimactic conclusions were ever written.

It is much easier for writers of fiction to bend the facts and write books that read like a novel if they do not need to present scrupulously cited points within thickets of elucidative detail. The original FBI plotters and their successors understood that, and their selection of writers to tell the official story that they wanted told was based upon that foundation. Besides, they *wanted* the facts to be bent—even filtered, modified, and hidden—free of any hint of embarrassing dirty details. It was critical to the cover-up mission that the official story be written by acclaimed, well-known novelists who would be schooled in the well-established quasi-factual details and themes that were to be presented. If they had to cite a few nonexistent people and events that never occurred—or ignore real ones—so be it.

The Different Ways Ray's Trip to New Orleans Was Presented

The HSCA should at least be commended—by ignoring the mishmash presented by the first three fiction writers about how Ray wound up in Selma—for establishing that, as he had promised in New Orleans, "Raoul" sent Ray a letter sometime in late February telling him he was to drive east, join him in New Orleans, and continue on to Atlanta. Ray called New Orleans shortly thereafter and received more complete information about the trip:

> [Ray's statement to the HSCA]: "I know there was mention of me to go to New Orleans to make contact there . . . I have some recollection of a little more detail in the phone call than I usually got, but I don't know other than going to New Orleans, I don't know if there was any mention of possibly going somewhere else or not. There was mention of Atlanta but I don't know when that was first raised. I don't know if it was Los Angeles or where. I know it was raised in Birmingham . . ."[749]
>
> [Additional excerpts from the HSCA report cited in the previous endnote continue in the following indented paragraphs]:

"Ray states *that he was unaware of Dr. King's presence in Los Angeles* just before Ray left to meet Raoul. (Emphasis added.)

[. . .]

"Ray was a full day late getting to New Orleans but until he arrived in town he says he made no effort to contact Raoul and tell him he was behind schedule. (HSCA 4) Upon arrival he called the contact number and was told that Raoul had gone on to Birmingham and would meet him there at the Starlight Lounge the next day.

[. . .]

"After dropping off Martin's packages somewhere on the edge of New Orleans, he left town and spent the night in a motel somewhere between New Orleans and Biloxi, Miss.

[. . .]

"The next morning he was back on the road headed for Birmingham, but somehow he got lost and wound up spending the night in Selma, Ala. Ray strongly denies the charge that he was in Selma because Dr. King was in the area; he says that he accidentally got off the main highway onto a smaller road to Montgomery, and that he spent the night in Selma simply because that happened to be where he was when it got dark."

Probably the best single example of creative wordsmanship was how Huie, then Frank, McMillan, Posner, and Sides, attempted to portray Ray's trip from Los Angeles to Selma, as though Selma were supposedly a primary destination. Huie simply alluded to the stop in Selma as something Ray decided to do after reaching New Orleans, and allegedly reading in a newspaper that Dr. King would be in that area, which was a baseless charge; Frank simply wrote, without explanation, that Ray went to New Orleans, then to Selma, and incorrectly stated that King had planned to be in Selma on March 22 [*sic*] but went to Camden instead [*sic*],[750] overlooking the historical fact that he had never done either of those stops.

Then McMillan repeated not only Huie's lie about Ray's reading a nonexistent article in a New Orleans newspaper, but Frank's lies about King supposedly being scheduled to be in Selma [*sic*], and actually appearing in Camden [*sic*], as though he had no time to recheck King's actual itinerary in the seven years he took to write his book.[751] Posner then retold the lies about New Orleans newspapers that supposedly reported Dr. King's purported plan to be in Selma on March 22 (despite his well-known plan to be in Memphis on that very day, until being snowed out) and then wrote a lengthy footnote about how impossible it would have been for Ray to have become lost on his journey to Birmingham. Posner stated that it would not be easy to get lost on such a trip since there is a straight route (i.e., I-59) between the two, but he failed to notice the evidence presented and accepted by the HSCA that Ray did not take that route; instead, he went east toward Biloxi, before turning north, out of New Orleans.[752] He merely provided more proof of how easy it is to write a fictional account of real events by citing facts sparingly and ignoring actual evidence to make arguments seem more convincing than what actual evidence demonstrates.

By the time Hampton Sides wrote his fiction, the trip was transformed completely, now making Ray's stay in New Orleans (his actual destination) as an inadvertent rest stop, yet another marker for his stalking premise. As Sides portrayed it, he followed *"a southerly route across the prickly deserts of the Southwest,"* stopping *"for one night in New Orleans."*[753] (Emphasis added.) Here he is treating the New Orleans stop as having been a random point along his journey, a handy spot for a bit of rest before heading on to Selma, his supposedly true destination. While this little twist does not sound like much of a deceit, it is a major one in his revisionist context, considering that New Orleans was really very much out of the way—arguably at least 100 miles south of any direct route, 200 miles total—for what was purported to be a trip from Los Angeles to Selma. Thus, the story was remade to be the opposite of the truth.

Raul's original instruction was for Ray to go to New Orleans to meet him; when Ray got there, he called Raul's telephone number and was told that Raul had changed plans; now they were to meet in Birmingham on March 23. It was actually Selma that then became an inadvertent rest stop. This was merely an attempt to resurrect Huie's original account, created as only someone gifted in creative writing techniques could reframe the entire trip around the false assertion that Ray stayed overnight in Selma for the purpose of his hoping to stalk King there.

The summary presented in the HSCA's Final Report reads as though it were copied, nearly verbatim, from Huie's fabricated account. Clearly, the primary methodology of the HSCA "investigation" was to simply follow the original fiction as written by authors Huie, Frank, and McMillan during the previous decade.

How the HSCA Regurgitated the FBI-Inspired Fiction

The HSCA's rejection of Ray having a racist motive required a little back-filling in order to support his only other possible rationales. That was done by replacing racism with the possibility that Ray might have been involved with other shadowy figures who could have promised him other rewards for taking the extraordinarily violent action—especially for someone who had never done anything like it in his life—of shooting King using a high-powered rifle with a misaligned scope (one that was, incidentally, never shown to have been the murder weapon, and indeed it has been proven that it could not have been). Instead of racism, it was conjured, Ray might have been intrigued by having his name in a lot of newspapers, thus making it into the FBI's Ten Most Wanted list (though he had carefully chosen a number of aliases to avoid that very thing) and being given a large reward for his efforts (though nothing like that ever occurred either, other than book contracts that would be used against himself to pay for his deceitful lawyers).

Despite its finding of a possible conspiracy, the HSCA went out of its way to hedge its conclusions, seemingly trying to appease all viewpoints, a common approach of consensus by committee: reaching conclusions designed to be all things to all people to avoid displeasing any of its members. It stated, in well-parsed, ultimately meaningless prose:

> The committee recognized that despite the results of earlier investigations, a respectable body of public opinion supported the theory that the King assassination was the product of a conspiracy. In addition, the committee was faced with a variety of well-publicized conspiracy allegations, most based on speculation and not grounded on fact, and many of them inconsistent with one another.[754]

Ignoring the fact that the original official story itself was also based upon unfounded speculation, the HSCA proceeded to use the fictional accounts as the guide by which it conducted the "investigation." The report also referenced a 1977 Justice Department Task Force conclusion that "proposed varying interpretations of Ray's ultimate motivation; it, too, agreed that he acted alone in the assassination." A referenced footnote stated: "The task force report, while noting in Ray 'a strong racist attitude toward Blacks,' concluded that his motive was a combination of 'apparent hatred for the civil rights movement; his possible yearning for recognition, and a desire for a potential quick profit.'"[755] It must have been very hard for the employees of the Justice Department to jettison the near decade-long narrative and see through the fog that had been left in the wake of so many acclaimed books that seemed to have made sense to them.

Driven as it was to re-prove James Earl Ray's guilt rather than to actually reinvestigate the case with open minds and a desire to find out the truth—by throwing out the tainted evidence in favor of fleshing out real facts from more credible witnesses—the committee decided to craft language to advance a persuasive rationale as a way to justify their intransigence:

> [I]f it was established that Ray were driven by a psychological need for recognition in the criminal community, his involvement in a notorious crime such as the assassination, without the help or urging of others, would likewise be understandable. Nevertheless, to the extent that a theory tied to Ray's racism or some other motive did not provide a satisfactory rationale, other explanations had to be sought. And with each additional explanation, its consistency with a lone assassin theory had to be tested anew.
>
> In its examination of the question of motive, the committee was aware that its ability ultimately to resolve this issue was necessarily limited. Ray consistently denied his involvement in Dr. King's murder. The committee, therefore, did not have access to the most probative evidence—Ray's own explanation for his conduct. In the absence of a confession, the committee was forced to rely on the testimony of others and on an analysis of Ray's conduct. This evidence was valuable, but it was unsatisfactory for the purpose of understanding the complexities of Ray's psyche, which might lead to firm conclusions on the issue of motive.[756]

There was a reason, of course, for why the committee "did not have access to the most probative evidence—Ray's own explanation for his conduct." It might have been because they chose instead to read the books of fiction, instead of actually listening to what Ray had attempted to explain. That they even noted his plaintive plea, in the process of summarily dismissing it, was as much as one might expect: "Ray consistently denied his involvement in Dr. King's murder" suggested that even the possibility was so ridiculous that it didn't merit any elucidation, much less a cursory rebuttal. That was made more emphatic when it was then stated, "[i]n the absence of a confession, the committee was forced to rely on the testimony of others," which of course gave them the justification for having to turn to the likes of the fiction authors Huie, Frank, and McMillan, the self-proclaimed "experts."

The crux of the HSCA's case came down to this statement in their MLK Report, Volume IV, p. 5.:

> The examination of Mr. Ray by the committee was based on the evidence from which *it might be inferred* that Ray, in fact, first, stalked Dr. King; participated in the assassination itself; was not in the gas station as he said at the time of the assassination; and the suggestion that the mysterious individual named Raoul, who, according to Ray, masterminded the assassination plot, probably did not exist.[757] (Emphasis added.)

James Earl Ray as the "Stalker"

The committee attempted to show that Ray started stalking Dr. King beginning in Los Angeles the week of March 16—at a point when both Dr. King and Ray were, coincidentally, in that city—despite the fact that Ray left Los Angeles on the 17th, the day following King's arrival. In the process, the committee made a series of factual errors, as noted below.

Just before he left Los Angeles, Ray had completed a change-of-address form at a Los Angeles post office to catch any mail (with his alias name "Eric Galt") that might be on its way there and have it forwarded to General Delivery in Atlanta, where Raul had told him they would next be residing after their planned New Orleans meeting. The HSCA report noted that Ray had claimed he didn't even know that Atlanta was King's home and that it was where the SCLC headquarters was located. It then stated that "Mr. Ray was somewhat taken aback" when Chairman Louis Stokes produced a change-of-address card submitted by Ray on the 18th, [*sic*] under the Galt alias, then erroneously stated that the "announcement [of King's scheduled departure on the 18th] appeared in the written press on the 17th," the same date that the postal form was dated and the day Ray actually left Los Angeles. Yet the announcement of King's planned departure was not reported until the following day, March 18, and indeed Stokes had quoted from an article in the *Los Angeles Herald-Examiner* that had appeared on that day.[758] The committee staffers had prepared a huge blow-up copy of the postal form, but *without the date*. Mark Lane later got a copy of the original form, which clearly showed that it was indeed dated March 17, not 18 as Stokes had implied. Their report began with how they decided early on to embrace the Ray legend as originally created by Huie:

> The committee considered allegations that Ray stalked Dr. King for a period of time preceding the assassination, and it

> developed evidence indicating a high probability that Ray did, in fact, pursue Dr. King from Los Angeles to Atlanta and ultimately to the Lorraine Motel in Memphis. In all likelihood, the stalking began about March 17, 1968, the day that Ray left Los Angeles and drove eastward.[759]

The disconnect buried within that sentence is that (in this instance) the committee acknowledges that Ray left Los Angeles the day after King arrived there, and the day before King left, without having made any attempt to even see Dr. King, much less begin stalking him. That should have undermined the stalking premise once and for all, since Ray did not attend any of King's speeches there. The entire argument was based upon Ray's purported stalking that began in Los Angeles, yet they admit he left without having made any effort to do *any stalking* there. The HSCA's artfully worded report states that Dr. King "was in Los Angeles the week of March 16, 1968." That part was true; he had actually arrived there on that specific date.[760]

But if Ray had really wanted to stalk Dr. King as early as his stay in Los Angeles—as the HSCA and authors like Huie, McMillan, Frank, Posner, Sides, Hancock and Wexler, McMichael, et al. would have us believe—does it not follow that he would have begun to actually do that in Los Angeles? He was only a few miles away from him on the 16th and 17th, yet he was packing up on the 16th and leaving for New Orleans on the 17th, just as Dr. King was delivering a speech in Anaheim on the 16th,[761] and another at Second Baptist Church in Los Angeles on the 17th, before flying off to Memphis on the 18th.[762] Why wouldn't such a devious stalker have begun his stalking then, when King was only a few miles away, rather than allegedly rushing (as all of these authors have claimed) out of town, setting off on a grueling 2,200-mile drive—alone—to Selma to begin stalking King? As noted by Dr. Pepper, the stalking theory put forth by so many authors (as well as Chairman Stokes of the HSCA) suffers a problem in this juxtaposition with Ray's actual actions in leaving town just as Dr. King arrived and made himself available for anyone already there who might be interested in actually engaging in stalking activities.[763]

In Chapter 7 we scrutinized the centerpiece argument of the alleged stalking when Huie put Dr. King in Selma, on Ray's way to Birmingham, and found it to be a fabrication of Huie's vivid imagination, which was built on multiple instances of deception and outright lies. Chief among them was his statement that Ray had gone to Selma because he allegedly somehow knew King would be there on March 22, 1968, the very date that Dr. King was scheduled to be in Memphis for a march supporting the sanitation workers, which he missed because of the freak snowstorm in Memphis that closed the airport there.

Huie simply invented the fiction that King was to be in Selma on the 22nd, and that it had been reported in a New Orleans newspaper the day before, when Huie knew Ray had been in New Orleans. The alleged article, on page 58 of the newspaper presented in Chapter 7, mentioned *nothing* about his being in or near Selma at any time. Huie's lies built a platform that the seven authors noted above and many others would repeat in similarly distorted fashion in book reviews, news articles, movies, and videos, and none of them contained an ounce of truth. James Earl Ray was never conscious of Dr. King's whereabouts, much less ever intending to do him harm.

The HSCA's Adoption of Huie's Lies: The "Stalking King in Selma" Lie, Part A (The *New Orleans Times-Picayune* Nonstory)

As a brief recap of that elaborate lie that is somehow still alive, the HSCA report stated:

> During the Witness [*sic*] journey from Los Angeles to Atlanta, Georgia, the only published report that the Witness could have learned of Dr. King's itinerary in order to have learned *then proceeded in the direction of Dr. King's location* was published in the *New Orleans Times-Picayune* on March 21, 1968. The published article stated Dr. King was then in the State of Mississippi attending a rally at Jackson State College. EXHIBIT, FOUR. (Emphasis added.)

That part was true, but the implication was left that it somehow revealed his plan to go to Selma, which cannot be inferred from that article, since it said nothing about King going to Alabama:

> As committee Documents reveal, *the Witness on departing New Orleans on March 22 traveled through the State of Alabama, not Mississippi.* (Emphasis added.)

That statement was written in such a way as to suggest that the route chosen was a much more sinister choice than any alternative route. Evidently, whoever wrote that sentence had never looked at a map of that area, since it is impossible for anyone driving from Louisiana to Alabama to do so without first traversing Mississippi, and in order to go to Birmingham, of course, one must drive into the state of Alabama. But starting out to that destination from New Orleans requires one to drive in a northeasterly direction; therefore, the first decision one must make is whether to proceed by going north or east, then transition to the other direction later by following the available roads. That simple choice is not in any way enigmatic, it is merely essential. The report continued:

> As the committee's Documents [*sic*] further reveal, through the State's [*sic*] stipulations to the Witness guilty pleas & other evidence, the Witness [*sic*] spent the day of March 21, 1968 in New Orleans, Louisiana. [This is a rather rare example of at least one true and factual statement in these proceedings.]

The HSCA—clearly taking Huie's fictional account as their agenda—adopted the theme of Ray's alleged stalking obsession, while permanently entering the Huie lie into the Congressional Record that "Dr. King was in Selma" when he had not even been in the state of Alabama when Ray entered it.[764] The report continues:

> Since Atlanta was the national headquarters of the SCLC, as well as Dr. King's home, the committee found Ray's anticipated travel to that city as the first significant indication of his interest in tracking the activities of Dr. King.
> Ray's probable stalking of Dr. King continued with his trip to Selma, Ala., following his departure from Los Angeles. Dr. King was in the Selma area on March 21 [*sic*]. Ray admitted being in Selma on March 22 (a motel registration card for his Galt alias confirms his stay there), but his explanation for being there was not convincing. He claimed that while driving from New Orleans to Birmingham, allegedly to meet Raoul, he got lost and had to spend the night in Selma. The committee noted, however, that in 1968 there were two direct routes from New Orleans to Birmingham, and that Selma was on neither of them. It was situated in between the two routes, about 45 miles out of the way. The committee further determined that it would have been difficult for Ray to have become lost between New Orleans and Birmingham.

For the congressional committee to question whether someone might make a wrong turn or not, and to assert that it would have been difficult to believe that anyone might ever become lost on a four-hundred-mile journey over several different highways on a very stormy day from one city to another, requires considerable hubris; to infer from that an evil intent requires the same, on the part of the person who posited the premise.

As for the difference in mileage (HSCA staffers said forty-five miles, Hampton Sides said sixty), anyone with a computer today can obtain information from readily available computerized maps, choosing several routes available in 1968, and *leaving New Orleans going east initially* indicates that the alternate distances from New Orleans to Birmingham for three different routes range from 380 miles to 410 miles, a disparity of only thirty miles. A possible route that Ray might have taken, which would go through downtown Selma, was approximately 387 miles.[765] Ray had testified to the committee that after delivering the packages for Ms. Martin's daughter and calling his contact number for Raul, he was told by the intermediary to go on to Birmingham the next day; he then went to a motel "on the edge of New Orleans" that was on the highway to Biloxi, Mississippi:

> The next morning, he was back on the road for Birmingham, but somehow he got lost and would end up spending the night in Selma, Ala. Ray strongly denies the charge that he was in Selma because Dr. King was in the area; [*sic*] he says that he accidentally got off the main highway onto a smaller road to Montgomery, and that he spent the night in Selma simply because that happened to be where he was when it got dark.[766]
>
> [Asked if Dr. King was in Selma when you were there, Ray answered]: I have no idea. *William Bradford Huie says he was in that area*, but I don't have any independent knowledge of that. (Emphasis added.)

The key to the complete falseness of Huie's assertions of Ray's stalking King—repeated by numerous authors and even the HSCA's investment of untold hours of inquiry and how they perpetuated the myth—lies in James Earl Ray's final comment above: he had never showed any signs whatsoever of being interested in Dr. King's whereabouts. Huie had simply invented that story because it fit nicely in his frame-up story of Ray being a cunning stalker and wannabe famous murderer of an icon.

The "Stalking King in Selma" Lie, Part B
(The *Selma Times-Journal* Nonstory)

The fact that the article never mentioned anything about King being in Selma was because he had *never planned to be in Selma on that day*. It was always a lie that Huie created. The entire story was fiction, yet after he fabricated it using sleight of hand magician's tricks, numerous other authors repeated it, even the HSCA investigators ten years later. And the committee chairman, Louis Stokes, also bought it hook, line, and sinker. The HSCA report officially sanctioned the lie when it stated:

> CHAIRMAN LOUIS STOKES, next picked up the Witness [*sic*] alleged stalking of Dr. King by pointing out that the Witness was in Selma, Alabama, registered in the Flamingo Motel on March 22, 1968. Then offering as proof the Witness was following Dr. King in the form of an article from the *Selma Times-Journal* dated March 21, 1968. The article stated that Dr. King would be in the Linden-Camden, Alabama, area on March 21, 1968.[767]

Even if there were such an article and this were a true account (which is not a given in light of Huie's other prevarications and the unavailability of an archived record of that article), the article in this locally circulated newspaper would have been in the previous day's edition, on March 21, printed while Ray was still in New Orleans.

When Ray arrived in Selma the following evening, even if he did come across a day-old newspaper and noticed the article, it proves nothing. At that point, Ray was already there—not because the article had induced him to be, but because of his wrong turn—and besides, Dr. King had already left Alabama, having only stayed overnight once, two evenings before that, in the northeast-central area of the state—in Bessemer outside Birmingham (roughly 100 miles away). Dr. King boarded a flight back to his home in Atlanta the morning of Thursday, March 21, to prepare for the next day's planned trip to Memphis. *More than a day later*, James Earl Ray would drive into the southwestern end of the state, as he made his way toward Birmingham. Not only was Ray unaware of Dr. King's whereabouts, the evidence shows that he couldn't have cared less about where King was, except in Huie's deluded mind.

Why Would Ray Return to Atlanta?
Raul Told Him to Proceed to Memphis

Also, as noted previously, after Ray had traveled from Los Angeles to New Orleans, then Birmingham, he proceeded to Atlanta with Raul, arriving there March 24. He stayed there while Raul made a quick trip to Miami before they joined up again to return to Birmingham on March 29–30, where he purchased the rifle(s). Less than a week before Martin Luther King Jr. was shot in Memphis, Ray was in Birmingham, Alabama, at Aeromarine Supply Company, following Raul's instruction to purchase a rifle with a telescopic sight as a model for him to offer to convey to the alleged paymaster for the "gun-smuggling operation." At Raul's insistence, he then returned it the next day for a more powerful one, before he had even taken a practice shot with the first one. This was the only time Ray had reverted to using an alias of a non-Canadian since he began using the Galt name. These transactions were completed using a new assumed name, Harvey Lowmeyer, phonetically similar to the name of his brother Jerry's fellow prisoner in Illinois, Harvey Edward Lohmeyer, who stated that he had never known James Earl Ray. Ray admitted never having met Lohmeyer personally but stated that he knew about him through his brother and that the name had just stuck in his head.[768]

The HSCA tried to discredit this statement, on the basis that he hadn't been in Quincy, Illinois, in nine months, as though he could not possibly have simply remembered a name for that long. But their real purpose was to posit that brother Jerry was actually the "real" Raul:

> Ray's use of the Harvey Lowmeyer alias also corroborated the possible involvement of a brother in the rifle purchase. Ray told the committee he got the name from a friend or criminal associate in Quincy, Ill. Ray's last known visit to Quincy, however, had been in June and July of 1967, 9 months earlier. Further, the actual Harvey Lohmeyer told the committee in an interview that while he knew John Ray and Jerry Ray from a period of overlapping prison terms at Menard State Penitentiary in Chester, Ill., in the late 1950's, he did not know James Earl Ray. The committee, therefore, believed it more likely that James got the idea for this alias from either John or Jerry Ray. In the absence of any evidence that James stockpiled aliases, Ray's use of "Harvey Lowmeyer" for the rifle purchase suggested contact with one or both brothers at that time.[769]

To strengthen their argument that his brother Jerry was the real Raul, they brought in the "Texas Tiger," Ray's ex-lawyer Percy Foreman, who gave them the needed testimony:

> I cross-examined James Earl Ray for hours and the only name that he ever mentioned other than his own at any phase or time of his preparation for the killing . . . Dr. Martin Luther King . . . the only person's name that he ever mentioned to me was his brother, Jerry.
>
> Jerry was with him when he bought the rifle in Birmingham, the one he did not use because it was a low caliber. He took it back and traded it for a more powerful one that would be more likely to kill an individual. The smaller caliber was more suited for killing small animals. And Jerry was not with him, according to Ray's statement, when he bought the gun that killed Dr. Martin Luther King; but he was with him the day before at the same place where he bought another rifle for that purpose.[770]

According to James, he absolutely did inform him of "Raoul" numerous times and even provided him his telephone contact numbers as a way of tracking him down. Foreman is simply reverting to his customary duplicity in making this outrageously false testimony. The fact that Percy Foreman was considered to be more credible than James Earl Ray is, at best, a lamentable notion in this context. That Foreman's deception and sworn lies, given all of his proven deceits in hijacking Ray's "trial"—which he successfully quashed as he railroaded him into a ninety-nine-year sentence—was simply another in a long series intended to place the blame on an unwitting patsy. For five decades it has succeeded, proving that the elaborate cover-up remains in place and probably will continue to do so, until a president with enough power, conscience, compassion, and determination decides to right this wrong.

When James Earl Ray left Birmingham on March 30 (with no need to return to Atlanta, despite the HSCA's insistence), Raul having instructed him to do so, he made his way north and west to Memphis in a leisurely drive with stops along the way in motels in Decatur, Alabama (March 30), Florence, Alabama (March 31), Corinth, Mississippi (April 1), the Desota Motel in Southhaven, Mississippi (April 2), and finally the Rebel Motel outside of Memphis on April 3. But the HSCA, in its zeal to prove that Ray had been shadowing Dr. King—as "proven" by the novelist Huie—chose to believe that he had not set out on his journey to Memphis, but had returned to Atlanta again, for inexplicable (real) reasons. The only (transparently false) reason for this was to suggest he did it for the purpose of stalking Dr. King, but that fails because King was in Washington on March 31. He would not return to Atlanta until April 1—when Huie, the FBI, and then the HSCA all attempted to assert that Ray then left Atlanta again. That was because the news of King's return to Memphis had been publicly announced—therefore it was previously only known to "insiders" and FBI "informers"—thus, the "official" narrative required it.

The Atlanta story was simply another fabrication by Huie, who used it as another "proof" for his spurious argument that Ray had been stalking Dr. King. In Huie's efforts to create a stalking theme, he wrote that Ray had driven 150 miles east from Birmingham to Atlanta on March 31, but the next day—hearing of King's plans to go to Memphis—then reversed course and drove back to Alabama, this time 280 miles to a motel near Florence, Alabama. Ray vehemently denied this, but the FBI—and ten years later, the HSCA, as well—accepted Huie's version, clearly for the same reason that he had originally conceived it.

To prove this, the HSCA investigators produced a receipt from Piedmont Laundry dated April 1 (a Monday), the only evidence offered that he went back there to "stalk and attempt to kill King" with his new gun that he had still not even test-fired. He had dropped laundry off there, but he did that on March 29,[771] a Friday, before he left for Birmingham. It was an inconvenient fact that the records of Ray buying the gun in Birmingham on the 29th and then returning to the same store the next day for an exchange presented a problem for the FBI—thus their need to explain this. The anomaly of Ray's apparent absence from Atlanta before Dr. King had announced his plan to return to Memphis was thus avoided.

The most likely explanation, given the multiple instances of fabricated evidence, was that it had been purposefully modified by someone to support a trail for Ray that would conform to that of a venal stalker of Dr. King. That would conform to the many other instances recounted within these pages—false testimony based upon the lies of fiction writers, or ex-fellow prisoners wishing to cash in on Ray's infamy—that had been created to support that theme, since there was nothing genuine in his past to prove it. As demonstrated numerous times, evidence was destroyed or manufactured many times—and witnesses suborned—to fit the official version of the story, and to conform to the false story line originally laid out by the novelist William Bradford Huie.

In a letter to Harold Weisberg, James Earl Ray objected strongly to this canard, writing the following note, in which the first sentence was written in the lawyerly context of a third person:

> The fact is that the defendant left no laundry at the above mentioned cleaners on April 1, nor was he even in Atlanta, Georgia on that date, rather in Alabama . . . . I mention this one incident because all those associated with the prosecution has [*sic*] for some reason zealously insisted that I admitted to being in Atlanta until April 1, rather than the correct date of March 28, 1968 [having left there on March 29].
>
> [Note by Weisberg]: Since Dr. King didn't decide "publicly" to return to Memphis until April 1, 1968, and the defendant [Ray] was asked to go to Memphis March 30, it might indicate that close associates or, more probable, the professional buggers who were tapping his phone were the only ones aware he would return to Memphis period. Possibly that is one of the purposes of the adversary trial system, to resolve questions such as the aforementioned.[772]

This is a very interesting and important statement, and it is evidence of a significant insight of Ray's: that the reason someone went to the trouble of attempting to show that Ray went back to Atlanta after buying the gun in Birmingham was that the public would not yet be aware of King's plan to go to Memphis, and that he could know that only because his handlers knew that by then. They had to eliminate that possibility from the record, therefore they could not let him begin his journey to Memphis until after April 1.

In his 1972 book, Gerold Frank added even more confusion to the mix when he stated that Ray had gone back to Birmingham even earlier, on March 27 (two days before Ray said he went there with Raul) going to two other gun stores and being described by a clerk named Clyde Manasco as being "in his early thirties, with dark hair, something of a receding forehead, and a sharp nose."[773] All of Frank's descriptions simply muddied the waters even more with a series of inexplicable contradictions, starting with that description of Ray's nose: evidently, the plastic surgery had not been as effective as Ray had thought. But according to this account, in yet another confusing statement never mentioned again, Manasco even recognized him from being there previously, then added still another contradiction when he proceeded to describe Ray as having good familiarity with high-powered rifles (a direct contradiction to the Aeromarine salesman's claim that he had no knowledge of rifles):

> His particular interest appeared to be the speed and trajectory of bullets. Manasco's employer, Quentin Davis, had tried to answer some of his questions, too—what rifle would give the flattest and longest trajectory? How far would a bullet drop at one hundred yards? At two hundred yards? What rifle would he recommend for accuracy? [774]

Frank added still another "fact" undiscovered by anyone else—like the one above, apparently not considered credible enough by the HSCA to have even explored—of his appearance in yet another gun store in Bessemer, Alabama, on March 29. This incident compounded the confusion by repeating the same general description (describing him as "about thirty or so," which in both cases was ten years less than his real age of forty in 1968) and similar questions that paradoxically reflected a good working knowledge of rifles in general and particularly the specifications of different models of expensive rifles.

Frank then completely contradicted his own descriptions of Ray when he quoted a man who he described as an observant customer who had briefly engaged Ray in a conversation: *"That guy obviously doesn't know a damn thing about guns. He's got no business buying a rifle."* [775] (Emphasis in original.)

This was exactly what Don Wood, the son of the store's owner, testified to a decade later at the HSCA, and, according to researcher Lyndon Barsten, the only person the Woods had ever met who had less knowledge about rifles than Ray was the HSCA investigator who visited them to ask about Ray's own knowledge; [776] Wood's testimony directly undermined the premise of James Earl Ray being an expert sharpshooter, yet, in still another major contradiction, the FBI and prosecutors had always tried to portray Ray as exactly that to support the premise of him being King's killer. Among the numerous other errors in Frank's book was the reference to the first rifle that Ray bought being a "Remington .243," when in fact it was a .243 caliber Winchester, as affirmed by the HSCA [777] and all of the other, more consistently accurate books noted previously. The only reality proven by Frank's book was that it contains more sloppy errors and fabricated untruths than even Huie's original fiction.

Had Ray actually returned to Atlanta after buying the second rifle, it should have been expected that he would have returned to the room that he had previously rented there, which he had already rented for the following week, before he left on March 29. There was no indication, nor did the committee attempt to show, nor did the proprietor, James Garner, admit that; he did state that he and a maid had gone into the apartment to change the linens on April 1, finding that it was not occupied. Garner did find the note that Ray had left on the 29th, which stated that he would return later to pick up his personal effects, including a television set.[778] Had Ray returned there, surely Garner would have run into him then, and there would have been no need for the note he testified finding then.

According to Ray, when he originally rented the room, Garner had to move Ray to another unit the next day, having found that the room he gave him the previous night had already been rented.[779] Ray also said that the only time Garner had seen Raul (since Raul left the next day for Miami and didn't return until they left for Birmingham on March 29) was when they checked in, but Garner didn't remember him because he was intoxicated that evening. Garner gave the HSCA investigators a statement "in which he says he 'recalls seeing Mr. Ray but no one answering the description of Raoul.'"[780] Another possible explanation for his nonrecollection of Raul might be "what was the description of Raoul that was given to Garner" (i.e., the question of its accuracy, given that neither the FBI then, nor the HSCA investigators ten years later, were actually interested in finding Raul). There are other possible explanations about how the question was posed to him that might also have something to do with Garner's failure to remember Raul, including the intimidation tactics that were used by investigators of all of the 1960s assassinations to steer interviewees in directions other than toward the unambiguous truth.

The HSCA similarly manipulated its findings regarding Ray's rental of the room in Memphis. Its "final report" erroneously stated that Ray had rejected the first room offering, Room 8, located toward the front of the building because "it offered neither privacy nor the possibility of a view of the Lorraine Motel located to the rear of the building."[781] Instead, the report stated that Ray told Mrs. Brewer that he wanted only a sleeping room and she escorted him to Room 5-B, in the other wing of the buildings toward the rear, but found no evidence that he examined the view from the window. In the following paragraph, the HSCA returned to the stalking meme, noting, "Ray's monitoring of Dr. King was also indicated by his purchase of a pair of binoculars after renting the room. Ray admitted purchasing binoculars on the afternoon of April 4, 1968,"[782] Ray's explanation, that he had been instructed by Raul to purchase the binolulars, was ignored; then, as if to dig into that point to give it more emphasis, he stated that his "admission was corroborated by a sales receipt from the York Arms Co., 163 South Main Street, Memphis, dated April 4, 1968 . . ."[783]

Now doubling down, as if this were the Rosetta Stone that would seal the verdict against him, the report stated that all of it was further corroborated by the statement of the sales clerk, Ray's fingerprint found on the binoculars, and that it was all part of the bundle of evidence found outside Canipe's.

Finally, the HSCA "validated" the error-filled books about the view of Dr. King's balcony when it stated:[784]

1. [Oblivious to the visual obstruction of how the side window actually faced the adjacent building, requiring one to lean out the bedroom's window], the report stated that the binoculars "would have enabled Ray to keep a close watch on movement at the Lorraine Motel from the rear of the roominghouse."

2. [Ignoring the fact that a tree branch directly in back of the rooming house's bathroom window and the brush growing between it and the Lorraine had been cut down the following morning], the report stated: "Ray could have observed the Lorraine either from room 5-B, by leaning slightly [*sic*] out of the window, or from the bathroom at the end of the hall."

3. [Despite not finding Ray's fingerprints anywhere in Room 5-B or the bathroom of the rooming house],[785] the report noted that "a dresser had been pushed from in front of the window and that a chair had been moved up to the window, indicating that Ray had, in fact, used the window for surveillance of the Lorraine."

4. [The disproven stalking theory was strengthened] by stating: "Thus, there is compelling circumstantial evidence that from March 17, 1968, Ray tracked Dr. King's movements from Los Angeles eastward, and then followed him to Selma, Ala., Atlanta, Ga., and ultimately Memphis, Tenn., where he rented a room from which he could observe Dr. King and purchased a pair of binoculars to assist him in his observations."

5. Finally, the report used all of these inaccuracies to state: "The committee concluded that these were activities performed by Ray in preparation for assassinating Dr. King."

All of it, as demonstrated previously, was the product of Huie's hubris.

Just as every other investigative agency and judicial authority had done in the decade following the King assassination, so did the HSCA when it adopted the five erroneous conclusions above, all of which we either have debunked or will debunk in this book.

Huie Returns—An Extended Mission to Prove Ray's Guilt

Nine years after Ray had fired him, just prior to the HSCA hearings in 1977, William Bradford Huie contacted Ray's attorney Jack Kershaw with a new proposition: in exchange for Ray admitting his "involvement" in King's murder, Huie would pay him an unspecified amount of money. Attorney Kershaw told the committee that he had attended a meeting in the offices of "a Nashville publishing company" with Huie and "other persons" whom he did not recognize but said that "two of them appeared to be government types." The original offer was for $50,000, but by the time it was proffered to Ray's brother Jerry at a later date, the same offer had been increased, as noted below.[786] That would indicate a major effort was being made—apparently to aid the HSCA in obtaining a seal of finality—to incentivize Ray to accept a deal that would guarantee a closed case. In the absence of external stimuli, what would have motivated Huie—well after his "work" was finished—to "re-prove" Ray's guilt?

As a result of Kershaw's report of Huie's offer to Ray, Ray had his brother Jerry call Huie to ask for more specifics, while taping the conversation. Huie's proposal was conditional on Ray confessing to the murder of Dr. King, telling him now that Huie would pay him $220,000 plus promise his efforts to have the (then-) Tennessee governor Ray Blanton issue him a pardon to free him from prison. Huie said, "I know how to sell him on doing that. He's got problems."[787] It would later be revealed that Governor Blanton was found guilty of multiple crimes, including conspiracy and extortion, for such actions as selling pardons for convicted criminals and dispensing state-controlled liquor licenses for political favors and cash. He would also be infamously included in a published list of the "Ten Most Corrupt Politicians in U.S. History."[788]

At the 1999 civil trial *King v. Jowers*, Jerry Ray testified about the offer Huie made, practically begging him with visions of freedom for both of them and a promise that they could, figuratively, go anywhere in the world and live out their lives in halcyon bliss on a big bucolic ranch that they could call their own:

A. [Huie] made an offer, and we got it on tape. He made an offer that we taped for $220,000 if I get him in to see James.

Q. Well, he wasn't paying $220,000 for a visit.

A. No, no.

Q. What was the offer?

A. $220,000 if he would tell him about killing King and he had to give him, you know, a story about that he killed King and that—he said that's the only way a book will sell if you write a book that he killed King.

Q. What would James do with $220,000 if he was in prison?

A. Well, he said that—he explained that—he started off with that Blanton was the governor, and he said we get James out through Blanton and you and James both can live good in another country.

Q. So he was going to arrange a pardon?

A. Yes, through Governor Ray Blanton.

Q. Did you record that telephone conversation?

A. Yeah, it was all taped. Me and Mark Lane taped it.

Q. And was there a transcription of that recording?

A. Yes.

Q. Let me show you this transcription. (Document passed to witness.)

Q. Would you tell the Court and the jury what is the heading of that transcription, the date, time and place?

A. It's October 29, 1977, a.m.—9:45 a.m. Jerry William—Jerry Ray or William Ray, Bradford Huie, Oak Ridge, Tennessee, rural Scottish Inn.

Q. Would you just look through that transcription and see if you recognize it as the transcription that was made of the tape recording of that conversation?

A. Yeah, that's it.

MR. PEPPER: Plaintiffs move the transcription into evidence. (Whereupon, the above-mentioned document was marked as Exhibit 20.)

Q. (BY MR. PEPPER) What happened to the tape of that conversation?

A. Mark Lane made the tape and he turned the copy over to the House Assassination Committee that was investigating the King assassination [and that] of Kennedy at the [same] time, and he kept the other one.

> **Q.** So the House Select Committee on Assassinations had a copy of that tape recording?*
> **A.** Yes, had a copy of it.
> **Q.** That same committee decided that there was no Raul?
> **A.** Yeah.[789]

To evaluate the larger context of this offer, one must consider why Huie would offer that much money (stated above in 1977 dollars, the equivalent of over $900,000 in 2018).[790] Even if his planned book had sold in record numbers, it would represent an enormous investment that entailed an extremely problematic, incalculably high, and ambiguous risk. At that point, ten years after the fact, he had already written one book that was *not* the bestseller he had expected, because after Ray's guilty plea, the story quickly became old news, overtaken by the massive number of new articles. If anything, there would be even less public interest in whatever else Ray might have said about his guilt, so why would Huie have still conceivably expected that he could make that deal work? Perhaps the funding came not from the checkbook journalist who was good at recruiting vulnerable people, but certain governmental entities that would have needed to achieve a final closure that only such a public confession could possibly bring.

At one point in the FBI's investigation of Governor Blanton, they decided to push the envelope, testing how far Blanton might go in his hunger for more pay-for-play shenanigans. According to blogger Dirk Langeveld, on his Downfall Dictionary website, the attempt failed, but not without a counteroffer being made:

> Undercover agents, testing how far the administration would go, met with a [Blanton] bodyguard and asked how much it would take to secure the release of James Earl Ray, who had murdered [*sic*] civil rights icon Martin Luther King, Jr. The bodyguard responded that Ray was too high-profile a prisoner for clemency, but it was possible that he could be allowed to escape for the right price.[791]

Coincidentally, Ray did escape, in June 1977, from Brushy Mountain Tennessee State Prison shortly after that incident, but Blanton evidently did

---

* Mark Lane made a copy of the transcript of that recording and sent it to the HSCA, but it was evidently insufficient to prompt anyone to question the ongoing covert double-dealing to railroad Ray.

not facilitate it, since he actually forced the FBI—which was then actively investigating Blanton—to withdraw their SWAT team, variously reported as thirty to fifty men sent (uninvited) to capture or, more likely, kill Ray. The prisoner-turned-journalist J. J. Maloney, from the *Kansas City Star*, described the escape in a series of articles in which he expressed his own astonishment that such a large contingent of federal agents were sent to recapture four or five escapees from a state prison. Moreover, he made the point that they were assembled so quickly, it appeared that they had advance notice. Maloney—a former fellow inmate of Ray's—was convinced that the SWAT team was sent there to "shoot to kill." [792] The FBI's alarm was apparently related to their fear that Ray's possible revised testimony—either to the fledgling HSCA inquiry, or related to this escape and any legal proceedings it might lead to—might result in his getting renewed public attention for the fact that he had never gotten a fair trial for King's murder, because it was a certainty that given the opportunity, he would again recant his coerced 1969 testimony.

The absurdity of such a deal—getting Ray to finally confess to a murder for which he had always denied his involvement, in exchange for which Huie would pledge his help in using that confession to obtain his freedom—is more than a little bizarre. This travesty was occurring simultaneously with the HSCA investigators intentionally overlooking the incriminating behavior of still others who were supposed to be trying to determine the actual truth of MLK's murder. That paradox included Ray's first two attorneys and officials of the city of Memphis, Shelby County, the state of Tennessee, and US federal authorities. It is ultimately more proof that so many people, and agencies, were involved in counteractive operations that could only be due to orders from their superiors, based upon their own objectives for intentionally misdirected "justice." Governor Blanton was merely one example of an ethically challenged politician; he was unique among them for the fact that he got caught. [793]

HSCA Investigators Cannot Accept Ray's Story: His Attempt to Get Spare Tire Fixed Won't Compute

When James Earl Ray suddenly remembered, as he sat in the Mustang outside of Jim's Grill about 5:45 p.m. on April 4, that he needed to have his spare tire fixed, he took an action that undoubtedly, and serendipitously, saved his life. He drove off just minutes before he would have otherwise undoubtedly been shot while making his "getaway." Yet that same action ultimately landed him in prison for the rest of his life amid an incredibly tangled legal morass; furthermore, the multiple paradoxes indirectly help to prove his innocence while exposing traces of the enormous conspiracy put into place by very powerful politicians, all of whom were much luckier than Governor Ray Blanton.

The HSCA chose to disbelieve Ray's story about deciding to get his flat tire fixed approximately fifteen minutes before Dr. King was shot. They clearly recognized that to believe it would have undermined the official story of his being a lone southern racist filled with hate for King and destroyed the case against his being the assassin. They rightly feared that doing so would open a can of worms that could not possibly be resolved within their eighteen-month mandate.

The fact that the FBI's files containing the statements signed by the two witnesses as referenced in Chapter 8—Ray Hendrix and William (Bill) Reed—were missing made it impossible to validate Ray's story at the time. When Ray made his statement, there was no other available evidence to support it, which made it easy for the HSCA to ignore his story. Thanks to it being misfiled (intentionally or not; more likely, purposefully hidden), there was nothing else that vindicated him and his association with Raul. Once that opportunity had passed, it was too late to ever bring it back.

But there was much more to this story, and a closer examination of it produces arguably the best single example of how the HSCA used age-old sorcerer's trickery, smoke and mirrors, or what logicians call selective preference to con its audience (the entire American population) into looking the other way. The result was a successful effort to discredit Ray's key piece of exculpatory evidence. Below we will dissect their methodology in pathological detail in order to explain it coherently:

- James Earl Ray decided, on the spur of the moment, to leave the vicinity of the Lorraine Motel in his Mustang to go to two service stations in his attempt to get his flat tire fixed and the gas tank refilled. The first of these was a Texaco station at the corner of 2nd Street and Linden Avenue in Memphis, four blocks north and one block east of the Lorraine Motel, owned by Lance McFall and his son Phillip McFall. But he did not get out of the car; rather, he simply drove into the service station lot and asked the attendant if he could get his tire fixed and was told no, not right away, because they were too busy at that time, so he drove off, going to another station. He had not even thought of reporting that first stop to the committee, since it seemed inconsequential to him.[794]
- Yet the committee summoned the McFalls so they could publicly deny ever serving Ray that evening. Ten years afterward, it is

reasonable to presume their memory of the innocuous nonevent described by Ray was hazy at best—especially if they had not personally been involved in the five- to ten-second exchange Ray had with "an attendant"—and therefore they could not possibly be positive about what had happened that evening.

- The reason the committee had become interested in this non-story in the first place was due to the appearance of a con man named Coy Dean Cowden, who was a friend of the prominent black Memphis congressman Harold Ford (D-TN), a member of the committee. Cowden was a chronic alcoholic who frequently checked himself in to the Memphis Veterans Hospital to dry out. Their procedure was to temporarily put such patients into the psychiatric ward, and while there, Cowden became friends with one Renfro Hays, a private investigator who had worked on Ray's case when he had been represented by Arthur Hanes Sr. Together, the two of them decided to play a hoax that they figured would lead to making both of them a lot of money. Hays told Cowden about how Ray had claimed that he had visited a gas station in the area, so they decided that Cowden would claim that he had seen him at McFalls' station at the time, which would make his testimony valuable to sell to the highest bidder.[795]

- Renfro Hays and Coy Dean Cowden then found a buyer, the *National Enquirer,* which ran a story about the purported incident in its edition of October 11, 1977.[796]

- Cowden repeated the story to Mark Lane, who recorded it and played the recording to Ray while he was in prison at Brushy Mountain. Ray explained to Lane that he had not gotten out of the car and walked around, as reported by Cowden in his fictional account.[797]

- Cowden was then asked to explain himself to the HSCA, where he choked and decided to come clean and admit it was a hoax. The committee seemed to love hearing that story—how they could turn it around, to use it against Ray for not having reported his first stop at the McFalls' service station—as they needed somehow to kill Ray's main alibi as quickly as possible.[798]

- Despite Cowden's admissions, which should have negated only his lies, Ray's testimony then became easy to dismiss. Thus, the committee deemed all of it a hoax, dismissing Ray's testimony with it, since the witness statements (Hendrix and Reed) that the

FBI had suppressed, which would have verified all of it, were then unknown to Ray's attorneys.

- Unfortunately for the sake of genuine justice, the committee did not mention Cowden's record of being a regular patient at the VA psychiatric ward and his problems with alcohol, nor the fact that they had to sequester him in advance to ensure that he would be sober for the hearings and his television appearances (including CBS's *Face the Nation*, where he shared the stage with HSCA Chairman Stokes and panel member L. Richardson Preyer, to strengthen his credibility, which should have been nonexistent) as he boasted about having conned Mark Lane into believing his story.[799]

- An article in the August 19, 1978, edition of the Memphis *Commercial Appeal* also ran the story, blending fallacies and facts when it reported that "Ray had said" he was at McFall's station (which he hadn't, as explained above, and below again: it was only the first of two service stations he briefly visited and did not think it was consequential), and therefore the newspaper article deduced that he had lied "to mask his guilt, which can only mean that the state has been right all along."[800]

- Despite the fact that Ray had never mentioned anything about going to the McFalls' station in his testimony to the HSCA, or anyone else, the hoax that was invented by the drunken Cowden and the psychotic Hays was then used by the committee against Ray to "prove" that he had not gone to that service station to get his flat fixed. This despite the fact that he had only stopped there briefly, then left immediately to go to another station, and had never claimed otherwise, which allowed the McFalls' testimony to take on a significance that was never there, except for the fake witnesses and thus the committee's purposeful deceit. The damage done to Ray's already-shattered credibility by this outrageous hoax—and the resulting maelstrom of misinformation—was incalculable, and remains so.

None of the then-famed investigative journalists (Woodward or Bernstein, Jack Anderson, or anyone else having comparable credentials) came forward to point out the leaps of logic, the suppression of evidence, the many indications of the questionable credibility of several witnesses who were being held up as paragons of virtue: in addition to Cowden and Hays, there was the drunken Charlie Stephens, whose more truthful wife had been locked away in a mental hospital against her will and despite her actual intact sanity.

The Redoubtable Chief Inspector Eist, Ex-Scotland Yard, Testifies

Another witness, a former chief inspector from London named Alexander Eist, was, according to researcher Harold Weisberg, brought to the committee's attention through the FBI's collaboration with Scotland Yard. But the committee—having already been apprised of Eist's damaged reputation in England, due to being charged with corruption and forced to retire two years earlier—had withheld his name as a witness until the last minute as a surprise for Ray's attorney, Mark Lane.[801] When Representative Samuel Devine (R-OH), on August 18, 1978, began reading Eist's deposition, which had been taken by committee staff on August 4 in London, Lane quickly left the committee room and called an attorney in London to inquire about his credibility. Lane was told that Eist was "corrupt, and 'a disgrace to the England police force' and had been forced off the job for unlawful conduct."[802] Eist had claimed in his testimony that while Ray was in his custody—though not actually asserting that he had murdered Dr. King—he did make certain admissions to him, including that he had panicked as he left the scene in Memphis and threw the rifle down when he saw policemen nearby, and that he "just hated black people. In fact, he said he was trying to go to Africa to try to shoot some more."[803]

A flurry of news stories about Eist's testimony appeared in papers across the nation in the next few days, including the *Dallas Morning News* and the *San Francisco Chronicle* on August 19. Two days after the incident, on Sunday, August 20, an article by one of the primary mouthpieces of the FBI and CIA, Jeremiah O'Leary, titled "British Policeman, Upset by Attacks, Sticks to Story on Ray," appeared in the *Washington Star*.[804] Despite a very brief acknowledgement that Eist's record with Scotland Yard was blemished by the 1976 charges of conspiracy to commit corruption, the article was written in a way that put much greater emphasis on his lengthy service and the awards he had accumulated during the twenty-eight years he was employed there, as though his earlier problems were just a hiccup and his integrity had never been in doubt.

Many articles—instead of explaining that Eist's superiors felt his actions were reprehensible enough to justify very strong corrective action (i.e., termination of his employment), and believing that they had sufficient evidence against him to prove corruption—phrased the outcome as "he had been found innocent," a kinder, gentler way to say that the judge, upon evaluating the case against him, determined that the evidence presented was simply insufficient to lock him away for a very long term. On the same day as O'Leary's article, another story, "British Ex-Detective Defends Testimony for King Hearing" by Raymond Snoddy, appeared in the *Washington Post*, which confirmed that charges were indeed filed against Eist, despite the fact that the judge ultimately decided there was insufficient proof to convict him. But a few more details emerged in the *Post* article, which stated that "[Mark] Lane said he had been told that Eist 'had been placed on trial for taking bribes and for involvement in jewel robberies and that in court he fabricated testimony.'" [805] It is entirely possible that just as Ray's innocence remained unproven for the rest of his life, the opposite might have occurred in the case of certain witnesses against him, whose guilt could not be proved for technical reasons and that allowed them to remain free through sheer luck of the draw.

Harold Weisberg, in a state of high agitation the day following Eist's testimony by deposition, wrote a memo to FBI HQ/FOIA staff person Quin Shea—dated August 19, 1978—stating, in part:

> I know of no case in which any withheld name was not public knowledge prior to the FBI's withholding and no case in which the affidavits provided even claimed that the withheld names were not public knowledge and in the sense in which they were withheld.
>
> Yesterday's bizarre spectacle before and by the House assassins [*sic*] underscores the harm that results from unjustified, unnecessary and misrepresented withholdings falsely and baselessly attributed to a need to prevent the disruption of relations with foreign police.
>
> Yesterday's is also the fourth case I recall of bad material being provided to the House assassins [*sic*] by the FBI in what has become a clear disinformation operation in which FOIA is misused to preclude truthful and factual information from being available to offset the disinformation.
>
> On the face of the story by Alexander Anthony Eist, retired Scotland Yard Inspector, aired on coast-to-coast TV and to the nation by other press means without the most rudimentary checking—merely on the FBI's referral—*is inherently without credibility and to a subject expert is blatantly false . . . It has to have known the Eist stuff is total fabrication as it relates to anything other than his police employment. In plain English I allege a Cointelpro operation against the knowledge people can have via the committee and that any resulting reduction in the committee's credibility serves FBI interests.* [Emphasis added.] In

this I am ascribing motive to the foreign-police withholdings
. . . The fact of these cooperative arrangements is well know
[*sic*] . . . What Eist says he passed on has not been provided.
It may be in London Legat files if not hidden also somewhere
in FBIHQ. There is more like this and I intend to include all
of it.[806]

The point Weisberg seems to be making in this memorandum is that the
FBI, in proffering testimony from the "foreign police," was knowingly going
outside US jurisdiction for the purpose of suborning perjury from a willing
source who would otherwise be subject to severe penalty for lying under
oath, and that these cooperative arrangements were well known to exist.
These astonishing charges by Weisberg have apparently never seen the light
of day since he wrote that memo—years after his own book was published—
which was then buried deeply within the files of the National Archives, where
precious few previous authors have evidently ventured.

The most troubling part of Weisberg's assertions is what he did not
say. If Hoover, Tolson, and DeLoach went to all the trouble they apparently
did to get Eist's perjurious testimony into the record, does it not follow
that the assertions he made were part of the fabrication? For example: "Ray
just hated black people. In fact, he said he was trying to go to Africa to
try to shoot some more." Given that even the HSCA gave up on proving
that Ray was a racist—based upon testimony of many highly credible people
who emphatically denied that, from his Canadian girlfriend Claire Keating
to Dexter King—it may be reasonably concluded that Ray would never
have made such a scurrilous comment. Ergo, where could it possibly have
come from? Who fed that to Eist in the first place? Whether or not it was
Hoover himself or one of his minions who did that—knowing Hoover would
approve—is a moot point. It could only have come from the one with the
power to have directed that operation.

But despite the blemishes on Eist's record and the clearly duplicitous
maneuvering by the FBI—thankfully caught and recorded by the indefatigable
Weisberg—certain committee members still believed his testimony and
pressured the committee to bring him to Washington to redeem himself.
After having originally tried and failed to keep his blemishes secret—thanks
wholly to Mark Lane's inspired telephone call and good luck in reaching his
London attorney friend at that moment—the committee now agreed to pay
for his plane tickets, hotel, and all travel expenses to come to Washington.
Three months later, on November 9, 1978, Eist testified before the committee
in a bizarre appearance where he was treated to softball questioning by the

committee as they obsequiously asked him about his lengthy service and the various awards honoring him, led by staff counsel Alan Hausman (this interview was partially recorded on short video clips available at the WPA Film Library website). But there were no questions about the basis for the charges filed against him, and nothing about the specific circumstances of how he really left his employment at Scotland Yard—only the passive acceptance of his claim to have experienced thyroid problems.[807]

Eist proceeded to perjure himself about such spurious charges as Ray supposedly admitting that he hated blacks, Ray's purportedly being worried about a conspiracy charge, how Ray allegedly expected to become a national hero, and how Ray had not shown any remorse for King's murder—about which any innocent man should not be expected to have. Having gone out of their way to patch over their original gaffe, now the HSCA staff paid him to put the same truculent testimony into the record, twice, but even more important, going out of their way to keep Ray's plaintive rebuttal out, a clear violation of his constitutional rights.[808] The committee decided that Ray would not be allowed to respond to any of these charges—officially condoning the railroading of him by denying him the opportunity to respond to his accuser and rebut the scurrilous charges, despite the highly incriminating damage done to him.[809] This story was reported in the *Knoxville News-Sentinel* on November 10, 1978.

As part of his circumlocution, Eist made statements to the effect that Ray's purported offensive comments were always made only in his presence, when no other guards were around, which had to be on those occasions when the other guard was on personal breaks, given that there were always two guards on duty during the period of Ray's custody by Scotland Yard. That such procedures were the routine was confirmed by other guards, which makes Eist's testimony even more suspect: it meant that Ray would only utter those words to him, and no one else; ergo, he would always wait for the other guard to leave so he could make the ugliest remarks that anyone had ever heard from him, as though he saved them just for Eist. One such guard, Christopher Baxter, stated under oath that:

> *My recollection is that RAY made no such direct admissions in my presence.* Detective Chief Superintendent CARTER has put certain matters to me which apparently have been suggested as comments made by RAY to Sergeant EIST at some stage whilst EIST was keeping surveillance upon RAY whilst RAY was in custody in London. Having heard details of those alleged comments by RAY to EIST, *I have no recollection whatsoever to any*

of these matters being mentioned by RAY to EIST in my presence at any time.[810] (Emphasis added.)

The overly zealous members of the HSCA—obviously looking for any possible ways they could claim to have investigated the murder of King—affirmed that James Earl Ray was the guilty assassin, having found in Eist, Cowden and Hays, Charlie Stephens, and all the other incredible "witnesses" the perfect tools, and fools, by which they could jettison his inconvenient alibi once and for all.

Despite his damaged credibility, Eist was referenced in a number of the later books—by authors Gerald Posner, Hampton Sides, Stuart Wexler, and Larry Hancock, and most recently by Pate McMichael—without any comment whatsoever regarding the blemishes on his record nor the devious plotting by FBI officials to go outside the province of US legal jurisdiction to procure his perjured testimony. Neither did they point out the worst of it, that Ray was never allowed to formally respond in front of the committee to the charges posited in person by Eist against him, all of which Ray, plaintively and futilely, denied had ever occurred. Only his lawyers and prison guards would ever hear his rebuttal.

Within this single vignette, added to the rest of the runaway train called the HSCA, the invisible hands of the highest-level plotters named in this book, even long after their deaths, are clear, dark, and visible; it was a scene that might have been described by John Milton in his most eloquent lines from *Paradise Lost*, drawing a picture of the most extreme kind of evil: "As one great Furnace flam'd, yet from those flames, No light, but rather darkness visible."

The Mysterious "Raul": Real or Imagined?

The HSCA—like the Memphis Police Department, the FBI, and the first Justice Department Task Force before it—summarily disregarded Ray's insistent plea that someone investigate the person named Raul, whom he had identified as his handler. Had an intensive search for this person actually been undertaken back in 1968, or even a decade later, Raul would have undoubtedly been found, just as he was four decades afterward when Dr. William F. Pepper found him. Upon locating him in Yonkers, New York, Pepper began photographic surveillance of him; Pepper's apartment was burglarized shortly thereafter, and those photos were the only things stolen. Pepper's witness, Glenda Grabow, with confirmation of her testimony by her husband, Roy, identified the man from his original Immigration

Naturalization Service photograph, as did James Earl Ray himself.[811] But the FBI would have never betrayed its own undercover man, so rather than doing anything to trace Raul, they did everything to protect him from being implicated while steadfastly denying that he ever existed.

By treating Raul as a fictional character from the start, they were able to make the statement ten years later that because of Ray's intransigence, they "did not have access to the most probative evidence." The real reason they had evaded this possibility was that had any of the investigators identified Raul, and charged and tried him, it would have meant the following:

- They could not have left unsettled such mysteries as why Ray—after finally reaching Montreal in July 1967, three months after his prison escape, from where he had planned to go to Europe and Africa to find a country without reciprocal extradition laws with the US—would then suddenly decide to return to the US after all. When he arrived in Canada, he had vowed to himself that he would never return, to avoid the risk of being returned to prison for the rest of his life. Ray would have needed big incentives to return to the US under any circumstances. Had the HSCA pursued the leads previously noted and found the solid evidence Ray repeatedly offered to track him down and thereby verified Raul's existence, they might have understood why Ray changed his mind.

 All Ray had to do in exchange for Raul's offer to become his benefactor was to ask no questions, meet when and where Raul specified, and do the petty crimes that he would be assigned. Ray wrote to Harold Weisberg:

 > Well, I didn't know what to do. If I took Raoul's proposition, I had to go back to the States and risk the Missouri Pen again. I didn't want to do that. I had sworn I'd never go back. But I was running out of capital again, and I didn't want to risk another hold-up in Canada. I couldn't get on a ship. I couldn't get I.D. So I told Raoul okay I'd meet him in Windsor. But I didn't know then whether I'd meet him or not. The woman in Ottawa seemed to like me. She was my last chance. I hadn't had time to talk to her in Montreal about the passport. So now I was going to Ottawa and tell her something about myself, and if she'd help me get the passport, I wasn't going to meet Raoul.

- They would leave another mystery unresolved, undoubtedly because doing so would lead into dangerously revealing significant additional information that was inconsistent with the desired results: about how Ray had ordered a new suit at a tailor's shop in Montreal on July 21, 1967, but before it was made—and before Ray left Canada for Birmingham a month later—the tailor was given instructions to forward it to 2608 S. Highland Street in Birmingham, the exact address where Ray would rent a room in a rooming house in late August from a man named Peter Cherpes.[812] How would Ray know about that address before he had even arrived in Birmingham to rent the room? Had Raul already arranged for Ray's accommodations there?

- They would accept incoherent scenarios without question, including the fact that McMillan tried to show, with nothing to support the assertion, that "Raoul" was a name made up by Ray, which McMillan decided was merely an "alter-ego" for Ray—ironically, a Hispanic name that he would have likely never heard of back in his time spent around Alton, Illinois, and Hannibal, Missouri.[813]

McMillan proceeded to treat James's return to the United States as though it were nothing extraordinary, despite the fact that doing so put him at much greater risk of getting caught and returned to prison. It was an incredible act for him to return under the circumstances. But McMillan, in ignoring the disconnect, as did the HSCA two years later, thus avoided having to explain why Ray—safely residing in Montreal and having begun a good relationship with a "beautiful" woman (according to Huie) who cared for him—would suddenly decide to chuck his new carefree life and put himself at great risk by returning to the United States.

McMillan had lied about many of the stories he made up about James Earl Ray, saying that he had gotten them from Jerry Ray, such as "The whole thing about Raoul and running drugs from Canada was bullshit."[814] Jerry vehemently denied ever saying this, but it was just one of many things McMillan claimed Jerry had told him, undoubtedly declaring his own credibility greater than that of the ex-con Jerry.

- How they avoided even trying to explain why, after Ray had given Hanes, Huie, and Foreman (and later the HSCA investigators) Raul's New Orleans telephone number, none of them ever pursued it as a positive lead.[815]

After firing Hanes and Huie, Ray then tried to give Percy Foreman the New Orleans and Baton Rouge contact numbers.

Foreman turned him down, telling him that if he needed any telephone numbers, he would get them from his mobster friend, Meyer Lansky.[816] None of them wanted anything to do with checking those numbers, and they didn't even attempt to explain it because they knew they couldn't under their "no Raul" premise.

- They could not so glibly leave unexplained why, of all places in America, Ray would choose the heart of Dixie—Birmingham, Alabama—to return to, at least temporarily (Raul had asked him to go to Mobile, but Ray chose the larger nearby city because he felt he could more easily remain anonymous there).[817] He was never a southerner in any sense; it was only because he had grown up along the Mississippi River, in central-northern Illinois, that he was even attached to anything with a southern name. Perhaps his handler, Raul, was told to get him back to that city as a means to strengthen his credibility as a southern racist?

  McMillan had thought about that one and came up with a logical reason for his having selected Birmingham. His answer was consistent with the series of lies he posited about Ray's purported racism and being a fan of George Wallace: McMillan stated that Ray would have believed that, after the dust settled, Wallace would certainly pardon him eventually.[818]

  That led into another chance for McMillan to expound on how "Jimmy was getting caught up in the Wallace campaign," again according to a fabricated conversation with Jerry Ray, when no other evidence of that was in existence. Putting things into Jerry Ray's mouth became McMillan's favorite technique, and it was repeated extensively by subsequent authors as well as the HSCA investigators, who extended it to Ray's other brother, John Larry ("Jack") Ray.

- The two trips that James made from Los Angeles to New Orleans seemed to have put some of the fiction writers into a quandary. By ignoring Ray's statements that he was responding to Raul's requests, they needed to come up with some other reason for those trips. George McMillan offered up the notion that he was "hauling drugs from New Orleans to Los Angeles, and that he made several trips," not just the one in December 1967 and the second on March 17, 1968 (although that one had no return trip to LA).

  That must have gotten McMillan a bonus, since Ray was in Los Angeles for four months; it might come in as a handy device to explain some other things. But then he discarded that and stated that a better reason could be politics. Here McMillan offered even more reason to believe that Ray was a deeply committed George Wallace enthusiast, an idea that James scoffed at, given that he was a fugitive on the run, afraid of being caught and unable to even use a legitimate name. McMillan then posited what should be an absurdly ridiculous suggestion: that Ray agreed to go on a 4,000-mile round-trip journey to New Orleans if Marie Martin and her cousin Charlie Stein agreed to sign the Wallace petition. Stein—who had been described as a "hippie"—supposedly went along with this and signed the petition and supposedly said, "I figured Ray was getting paid for votes."

But McMillan set forth still another preposterous possibility: "an emotionally persuasive one . . . that he made it simply for the reason Rita [*sic*—another sloppy error from his book—he meant Marie] had asked him to make it, for the children, to unite them with their mother."[819] One can only sigh at the extended explanation of how Ray had allegedly fantasized back in Jeff City of wanting to run an orphanage, about doing something for "the children" that he had dreamed of for years. After repeatedly arguing that Ray was a vicious, irredeemable racist and violent sociopathic killer, now he states that Ray really had a soft spot for the innocent little children who needed a few breaks in life. McMillan probably got another bonus (from taxpayer funds) for his creativity in coming up with this explanation for why Ray twice drove the 2,000 miles to New Orleans—plus a return trip the first time—simply because there was no "Raul" allowed in the book deal he was working on.

- They would not have to explain the curious matter of why James Earl Ray went back to the Aeromarine Sporting Goods store the day after buying one rifle and returned it for a larger bore, using the excuse that he had bought it for his brother-in-law's use in deer hunting. When the salesman pointed out that the first rifle would be adequate for that task, Ray's response was that the rifle was needed because it was to be used for Wisconsin deer, which were so much larger than Alabama deer, therefore they required a more powerful rifle.

As noted elsewhere, the salesman stated that Ray's knowledge of firearms (at least rifles) was practically nonexistent, so the question about the first gun's adequacy becomes even more curious. The real reason for the exchange—why Raul insisted on it—was undoubtedly to ensure that the salesman would indelibly remember his customer, "Harvey Lowmeyer," when the FBI came calling in a week or so to inquire about him.

- They would not have had to invent wild alternate theories to explain where James had gotten the funds to do all the traveling he did, across Canadian and Mexican borders, into such places as Montreal, Quebec, and Ottawa; then to Birmingham, New Orleans, Mexico City, Acapulco, Puerto Vallarta, Los Angeles, returns to New Orleans and Birmingham, then his first trip to Atlanta and finally Memphis, where he stayed in hotels for weeks at a time. And about the fact that he bought a one-year-old Mustang for $2,000 cash; that he paid his rent on time for apartments or rooms in all of those cities, and more in between them; that he bought a precision rifle, a good quality camera with projector, and other assorted items, all for cash.

- They couldn't have then quite so easily denied that Ray had left the area around the Lorraine Motel at least fifteen minutes before the shooting. Due to the FBI's hiding exculpatory evidence of the witnesses—Ray Hendrix and William (Bill) Reed—who gave statements confirming that they saw James's car leave the area exactly when he said he did, they had no evidence before them to prove that he had not left; ergo, as they erroneously concluded, he did not. This fact *alone* should now be considered *prima facie* evidence of the FBI's complicity, not only in the cover-up, but even significant credible circumstantial evidence of their own role in the conspiracy to murder King, as well.

- The HSCA not only ignored this series of actual leads, but then created oxymoronic alternatives to replace them. The committee actually convinced itself of the fiction that Ray, aided and abetted by one of his brothers (though it was unclear which one), had robbed an Alton, Illinois, bank—against all the evidence and statements by the police there that they were *never* suspects—yet the HSCA staffers had gone to great lengths to reinforce that story. All of this proved that the real intent of the committee was to paper the files sufficiently to help strengthen the case against James Earl Ray so they could put it back to bed.

- Above all else, by denying the existence of Raul, it left Ray as being the only suspect, another lone-nut canard that must have seemed like a successful paradigm to the plotters, given its previous success in the "Big Event" in Dallas (and soon to be repeated in Los Angeles).

- Finally, through their conclusion that Ray was the "sole assassin," by rejecting any hint of a conspiracy out of hand, everything else related to the FBI's previous efforts to neutralize King would be kept out of the news: the illegal surveillance of Dr. King, through repeated acts of breaking and entering his offices, residences, and hotels all over the country; the harassment campaigns, including haranguing and taunting him and his family; and Hoover's other well-known efforts to destroy him completely in the eyes of his supporters—even pushing him to commit suicide—along with all their other previous illegal and despicable methods used against him.

Excerpts from the HSCA Testimony of Frank C. Holloman

Despite the feckless attempt of the congressional hearings to resolve the continuing deficiencies of both the JFK and MLK assassinations, there were some revealing moments in their interviews with Memphis Police and Fire Department Commissioner Frank C. Holloman. It appears that the early works of some of the first researchers had left their mark in Mr. Holloman's conscience, yet although his aplomb before the committee was tested, it was never completely breached.

A decade after the King assassination, on November 10, 1978, Commissioner Holloman appeared before the HSCA to defend himself from "the malicious and viciously slanderous portrayal of me through a despicable character in Abbie Mann's television film 'King' and in the grossly libelous treatment of me in Mark Lane's book, all based on an unproven and ludicrous theory and unfounded allegation." Holloman gave his testimony to congressmen who attempted to break through his detached bearing by asserting their incredulity at his allowing the security detail assigned to Dr. King to be withdrawn, even as the most of the surveillance detail continued.[820]

- [Congressman Fauntroy from the District of Columbia made a number of statements that led to a question:] Mr. Holloman, you are well aware of the allegations of conspiracy that have been woven around your presence in Memphis, based and attributing sinister motives to a number of actions which were or were not taken, and you are aware that one of our responsibilities is to assess the validity of those sinister allegations. What has remained unresolved for me is the many things of which you have testified you were not aware. You said, for example, that while you were aware of security being assigned to Dr. King, as the chief executive officer you were not aware of that security being dropped at 5 p.m. on April 3. You have testified that you were not aware of any specific threats on the life of Martin Luther King, Jr. with respect to his return to Memphis, and that your reason for approving the security was that you were concerned about the previous appearance of Dr. King in Memphis around which violence erupted. Is that true; at least in those two instances you were not aware of withdrawal of security, you were not aware of specific threats on the life of Dr. King?

- Holloman: If I did not so testify, I should have testified or I will testify that what you have said is my recollection . . . But as to a fact, I cannot say that I was not advised. I said my recollection is that I was not advised of that situation.[821]

- Fauntroy: You have also testified that you cannot recall who communicated to you a threat on the life of Detective Redditt. Your recollection is that it was a Secret Service officer, and while you do not remember the specific reference to the Mississippi Freedom Democratic Party allegation, that you have the feeling that there were two allegations or two threats on Redditt. Is that your testimony?

- Holloman: Yes, sir, that is my recollection, and that was my testimony of my recollection.

- Fauntroy: And you really are not aware even though you know that your presence and the allegation around your presence has been the subject of public concern for several years.

- Holloman: Yes, I am very well aware of that.

- Fauntroy: But you can't remember under any circumstances who communicated to you or whether or not in fact there were two threats communicated to you.

- Holloman: If I could recall that, then that would resolve in my mind, and I wish I could resolve it in my recollection.

- Fauntroy: You further testified that you were not aware of the COINTEL program during the period that you were responsible as the chief executive officer in Memphis . . . [And] you had no knowledge whatever of any activities on the part of the FBI as communicated through memos or otherwise to FBI agents relating to civil rights leaders?

- Holloman: Not that I can recall, sir.
- Fauntroy: Were you aware of undercover agents of the Memphis PD working with the Invaders, among the Invaders?
  - Holloman: Yes, sir.
- Fauntroy: Were you aware that such undercover personnel were on the scene at the Lorraine?
  - Holloman: Yes, sir.
- Fauntroy: And finally, you are aware, as other members have indicated . . . of how troubling it is to us as we evaluate this allegation of conspiracy that no all-points bulletin [APD] was issued, and your testimony is that you were unaware of whether or not such a bulletin had been issued?
  - Holloman: My recollection was that there was not such an APB issued at the time.
- Fauntroy: And your recollection is that it never occurred to you to do that?
  - Holloman: That is my recollection that it did not occur to me at that time to do it, myself. I was depending upon the commanding officer of the police department to do what was necessary under the circumstances.

[. . .]

- [Congressman Stewart B. McKinney from Connecticut stated his concerns about the fact that] [A] great many people have written that there was either a conspiracy or complicity on the part of the Memphis Police Department and the FBI in the assassination of Martin Luther King . . . You sat with J. Edgar Hoover, and I understand from your testimony that you interpreted his jottings on memorandum [*sic*] and so on to make sure they were carried out; is that correct? [822]
  - Holloman: Yes, sir.
- [Congressman McKinney continued:] I have had the experience on this committee of reading many of Mr. Hoover's jottings, and his jottings for not even making a telephone call were northern Siberia [i.e., cryptic, but often voluminous—ed.]. Yet here you had a police department that totally failed to function when a national leader was killed. You stayed on until November of 1970, and nobody was demoted, fired, removed or anything else. Why?
  - Holloman: As I have already testified, I cannot explain that, sir. I would say that it was a dereliction on my part that I didn't . . . Mark Lane has made the allegation or made the

original allegation that the conspiracy evolved itself around the fact that I removed Detective Redditt from the security detail . . . he had nothing whatsoever to do with security.

- [Congressman McKinney responded:] I worked very hard this morning eliciting from Detective Redditt that he was never really on a security detail except when he resumed [duty] he was on at the airport, that he was in fact a Black officer hired essentially to report, to the police department the activities of those surrounding Martin Luther King, those of the [SCLC] and those surrounding the sanitation strike . . .

To clarify this point, Redditt was always on surveillance duty, not protective duty, to Dr. King or his associates. Nonetheless, what is suspicious about his abrupt removal, and that of the two black firemen (Norvell E. Wallace and Floyd E. Newsom) who were reassigned to other stations for seemingly spurious reasons,[823] was that their removal appeared to be for the purpose of eliminating all black fire and policemen from the area before the assassination took place.

Newsom was convinced that he and Wallace were "detailed" out to other stations to remove them from the scene that day. He stated that in his normal duty station he was one of five men assigned to a company that required five men to operate the equipment, and his absence rendered that equipment inoperable. He said his transfer to a four-man pumper company at Fire Station No. 31 made him the fifth man on that detail, resulting in it being overstaffed. Wallace made a similar statement regarding the fact that the pump truck he had been reassigned to at Fire Station No. 33 was already adequately staffed. It was well known within the MFD that both men actively supported the sanitations workers strike and had attended the rallies.[824]

These inexplicable personnel duty changes had the appearance, therefore, that all three of them were removed from Fire Station No. 2 the day of the assassination to avoid having them in positions that might have led to their spontaneous reactions to rush to King's aid or defense. That was especially true in Newsom's case, as he personally decided to attend King's rally the night before at the Mason Temple where King made his last speech.[825]

- [Holloman finished his testimony with this comment (excerpted from a lengthier statement):] The erroneous inference has been left that I was an active participant in the conspiracy to murder Dr. King. I had not a scintilla or iota of a desire or motive to see any harm come to Dr. King and I categorically deny any implications in his death either directly or indirectly. One of the greatest disappointments in my life has been that Dr. King was assassinated in Memphis. My actions before and after this death give unequivocal evidence of that statement. In addition, no reasonable and prudent person could possibly believe any director of fire and police would want such an assassination to occur in his city knowing full well the riotous conditions which would follow immediately.

[. . .]

There apparently has been a persistent effort to prove a theory or allegation that the FBI engaged in a conspiracy to assassinate Dr. King and that I, because of my past association with the FBI, was a party to that conspiracy. It is unbelievable to me that the FBI would even entertain such an idea. It is ludicrous and preposterous that I would be a party to such a thing either directly or indirectly. And now lately, as reported in the news media, the ridiculous charge has been made that former and off-duty FBI agents assassinated Dr. Martin Luther King. Anyone, for whatever evil or ulterior purposes, can dream up preposterous theories and charges. Proving those theories or charges with truth and facts is another matter and has not been accomplished.

I have been deeply disturbed that in view of my public service and reputation in the community, I have been viciously and deliberately maligned and slandered—apparently without recourse.[826]

It would seem that in the fullest context of the revelations we have summarized here, Frank C. Holloman's pitiful plea of his own innocence rings hollow. His strong reaction contained no remorse about what he had to know was going on during the period during which he served Hoover as his right-hand man, "interpreting his jottings"—and undoubtedly helping to facilitate some of those very same criminal acts that were required to complete the chief's instructions in the process. His denials, or inability to remember certain details—particularly the removal of the black police officers and firemen—suggest it was either an unusually defensive act (indicative of guilt) or that he really couldn't remember key actions or decisions only he could have executed (denoting incompetence). Especially troubling were his many memory lapses about his basic responsibility to ensure Dr. King's protection was never compromised throughout his stay. Despite being so well prepared to defend himself, his answers in the rest of his lengthy testimony often ended with "no recollection," even occasionally conceding his own dereliction of duty.

Short of repeating the entire transcript of his testimony—which can be easily obtained from the websites referenced in the endnotes—it is sufficient to say that given his many years of serving at the right hand of J. Edgar Hoover, and having the responsibility of interpreting Hoover's cryptic notes (and ensuring that his instructions were fulfilled) on every piece of correspondence he reviewed, Frank Holloman's role for eight years at FBI HQ was as Hoover's chief facilitator. His denials worked only because the worst of Hoover's crimes had still not become known; only the more blatant technical misuses of power had been revealed by 1978. Clearly, he would have had multiple direct connections to the "SOG" when he worked directly for Hoover, and the linkages would have remained after he moved to Memphis. It follows that the most odious of his orders would have been communicated through the secret channels, never committed to paper, either in person or via secured telephone, ensuring that all parties would be assured of complete discretion. It should be implicitly understood that Holloman's long service as Hoover's right-hand man, and his subsequent position in complete control of the Memphis police and fire departments, was not happenstance. He was working for Hoover during 1956 and 1957, when Hoover's "Prayer List" was taken by Clyde Tolson to Memphis and given to Russell Adkins as an FYI note of future plans to be developed.

Most people hearing or reading Holloman's testimony in 1978 would have probably agreed with his sentiments, because most people at that time would not have yet become aware of the brazenly criminal actions committed by the highest-level officials of the FBI throughout the forty-eight-year Hoover regime, a period that had lasted until Hoover died in 1973. The real persona of J. Edgar Hoover and his minions did not begin surfacing until many years later, led by early researchers including Harold Weisberg and Mark Lane, then after another decade, through books by William C. Sullivan and David J. Garrow in 1981, which revealed some of the tiniest slivers of Hoover's darker side. Not until the books by Curt Gentry in 1991 and Anthony Summers in 1993, and others since, would the real persona of Hoover become more widely known.

An Early Author's Capitulation to "The Powers That Be"

Unfortunately, David J. Garrow's partial revelations of Hoover's malfeasance and assorted criminal acts abruptly stopped with King's assassination. He did not address the closing episode of King's life; there is little reflection evident as to the forces that came to bear on King's murder in Memphis within Garrow's book, despite the intensive examination of them up until that point. There were no references to James Earl Ray, Eric Galt, or any of Ray's other aliases within his 1981 book, yet Garrow portrayed himself as the expert in later interviews on the subject. In not connecting anything he had examined up to 1968 with what happened next, he created a major disconnect. It was as if all of the lawlessness of the premier law enforcement agency in the United States stopped early in 1968. But it didn't; it was just getting up to speed and would continue for many more years. This point was referenced in Chapter 3, where we cited the revelations made by whistleblower Frederick Whitehurst, as noted in the 2004 book *The FBI & American Democracy: A Brief Criminal History* by Athan Theoharis. Some indications of its continued existence still leak out on occasion.

Garrow acknowledged that Johnson was behind Hoover's continuing smear efforts because he had exploited the perquisite of receiving fresh files—the recordings and transcripts thereof—directly from Cartha DeLoach, who routinely delivered them personally to the White House.[827] Garrow also noted Reverend Abernathy's lament that the SCLC did not hold Johnson responsible for Hoover's activities because they had considered Johnson a friend. He wrote that Abernathy and his associates were unaware of the fact that the Bureau's conduct was actively backed by the president himself.[828]

Unfortunately for him, however, Garrow's place in history will forever carry an asterisk because of how he criticized the King family for its "ignorance" in not accepting the official government story. Despite everything else he had discovered—even "how hostile the Johnson White House was toward King," and LBJ's fear that King might run for the presidency, either in 1968 or some future election[829]—it was still insufficient to cause him to recognize the intensity of Johnson's and Hoover's obsession to neutralize Dr. King. That apparently led him to minimize the possibility that either of them had anything to do with murdering King; evidently, he gave them both the benefit of the doubt and presumed that—despite the very facts of their combined vitriol, some of which he had personally chronicled—they would accomplish King's destruction through more conventional extralegal methods, like simply besmirching his reputation.

Garrow's naïveté was possibly due to how he had evidently fallen for the lies placed in the early books by authors Huie, Frank, and McMillan, never admitting his own ignorance about Ray. In a taped segment on MSNBC's *Time and Again*, broadcast on April 3, 1997, he asserted, "I think it's very sad that the King family and the King children are so uninformed of the history that they could be open to believing that Mr. Ray was not involved in Dr. King's assassination. Mr. Ray was someone of long-standing racist, segregationist affiliations, and as the House Assassinations Committee very correctly concluded nineteen years ago, Mr. Ray was probably the trigger-man for a wider segregationist conspiracy to kill Dr. King." [830] These multiple errors belie an uncritical, gullible mindset ill-befitting a scholar who had previously demonstrated an evaluative ability that seems to have since disappeared.

Even more lamentable than that is Mr. Garrow's willingness—despite everything he had reported about the FBI's many illegal and unconstitutional efforts to destroy Dr. King—to not accept the facts presented in the many books written by honest and truth-seeking researchers. His conclusions demonstrate his complete unawareness of the numerous anomalies present in the "Ray did it as a lone nut" canard. Like many others beguiled by the authors of the FBI's fictions (which were part and parcel of the brazen attacks on Dr. King that he himself chronicled), his own ill-informed statements suggest that he based his opinions upon the easy-to-read, quasi-fictional books.

Dexter King's response to Garrow's comments began: "The fact of the matter is, I guess I'm really not surprised, because Mr. Garrow, for whatever reason, is doing his job, and frankly he is an agent for those forces of suppression, who do not want this truth to come forward . . . I think what is really appalling here is that Mr. Garrow has built a platform on exploiting my father's legacy; if it were not for my family, Mr. Garrow would not have gained access to my father's papers and many other things that have given him a platform to speak out . . . I met Mr. Ray, he is not a segregationist, I've met segregationists, this man was not born in the South as the media portrayed at the time, the fact of the matter is he was born in Illinois, I met his family, they are not people who strike me as racists; the fact of the matter is that this man was set up, and we need to deal with this so that we can move on. The American public deserves the right to know, and certainly the family of the victim deserves the right to know what happened to their loved one. We need to stop living in denial in this country and once and for all face this injustice." [831]

It wasn't until the early 1990s that a greater part of Hoover's demented reign started to be revealed, when several books were published that took it to another level, including those by Anthony Summers, Curt Gentry, Mark North, and Athan Theoharis. Later in that decade, the first of William F. Pepper's books brought more information to the fore, causing most people who were paying attention to come to the realization that the men running the FBI during the entire period were all contaminated by Hoover's and

Tolson's chronic criminality. Their unscrupulous disregard of the very laws they were responsible for enforcing can no longer be denied, though many people still prefer to let sleeping dogs lie.

The HSCA's Intrinsically Compromised Mission

A hint of how the highest leadership of the 1968 Justice Department—the then-attorney general of the United States, Ramsey Clark—failed due to his compromised position (that of working under Lyndon Johnson while trying to supervise J. Edgar Hoover) was revealed in his response to a question posed to him by an HSCA member regarding how Ray obtained his finances. This short excerpt of a lengthy answer illustrates the larger context through the circumlocutions of his answer.

> Representative Fithian: An awful lot of people have a great deal of difficulty accepting the fact that a fugitive from Missouri State Penitentiary could finance himself and do all these things, and go to several continents, and get passports and operate as long as he did, including the assassination of Dr. King, without some kind of assistance from somewhere.
>
> Now, just as a general proposition, and then more specifically, if you were directing an investigation of this nature, what kinds of steps would you have personally directed be taken with regard to assessing the conspiracy angle; and second, then, do you believe that those steps or alternative steps that could be looked upon now as thorough were actually undertaken by the FBI.
>
> Mr. Clark: I can't tell you whether they did all—your investigation makes you privy to far more information I think on that subject than I have.
>
> Your question, what would I have done to investigate conspiracy, is really very difficult. Naturally I feel modestly—I think I was a splendid Attorney General. But I can't tell you that I have had vast experience in criminal investigation. I haven't. I have had probably more than most who served as Attorney General, but I would have to begin as pretty much a beginner.[832]

Clark had experienced other regrettable public statements, as when he immediately declared there was no conspiracy involved, even before the investigation was barely underway, not to mention the trial that never was.

Worse yet, as researcher Harold Weisberg noted, "Clark is the great liberal who proclaimed publicly there was no conspiracy to assassinate King while simultaneously charging in an indictment that Ray was part of a conspiracy. He thus contrived the federal jurisdiction without which this enormous, historic debasement of the law and justice would have been impossible." [833]

In his conflicted actions, AG Clark was undoubtedly speaking directly on behalf of President Johnson to effectively ensure that any jury that might ever be assembled would already be disposed to pronounce the accused guilty, while simultaneously ensuring that the case would be "investigated" by an FBI fully under Johnson's and Hoover's control. Furthermore, under the watchful eye of his friend Governor Ellington, the case would be handed back for prosecution to the Tennessee judicial system. It was a repeat of the way the FBI took over the Oswald case, a state crime in 1963, completely out of the FBI's jurisdiction, except for the fact that it was also initially declared a Communist conspiracy, even though that was simultaneously being vociferously denied. This was yet another pattern that would be repeated again, just two months later, with Robert Kennedy's assassination.[834]

The HSCA: Mission Unaccomplished

During its over two-year existence, the HSCA had a staff of lawyers and the subpoena powers to get to the bottom of both John F. Kennedy's and Martin Luther King Jr.'s assassinations, but they failed to even get near solving either one. The only thing they managed to do in the first case was to find a smidgen of the available evidence that proved a conspiracy had existed: an audiotape that indicated more than three shots were fired during the attack on JFK. In the case of Dr. King's murder, despite their feckless efforts to find anything more substantive, they merely decided that James Earl Ray was indeed the guilty assassin. Their findings, examined below, seemed to have been designed to ignore the numerous signs pointing to Ray's involvement being only of an unwitting nature, as a pawn set up through an extensive plan engineered by the CIA and FBI, with assistance of military intelligence units.

Given the sacrosanct levels of high-level government officialdom being implicated in the crime, their unsuccessful search for the truth of both of these treasons should come as no surprise. It was remarkably like the Warren Commission twelve years before, the same trick used and perfected by ancient sorcerers, magicians, and gypsies, through metaphorical shell games, to further stretch a veil of elaborate deceits embroidered and gilded over officially sanctioned murderous treasons.

The most likely candidate for the original person who picked James Earl Ray to be the patsy was James Jesus Angleton, who was the head of the counterintelligence division of the CIA and had overseen the agency's experiments with mind-control operations, and those run in parallel by the army, as noted in Chapter 4. In addition to researcher Lyndon Barsten, whose pioneering work on this point has been referenced throughout this narrative, authors John Avery Emison[835] and Philip H. Melanson[836] have also suggested variations of that possibility. Once selected by Angleton and his CIA operatives, Ray would become a puppet, unknowingly managed by men at the highest levels of the FBI and military intelligence.

This kind of disciplined, well-coordinated interagency planning and execution could only have been deployed through an even higher-level authority: thus, axiomatically, the only person who could have realistically been the source of such an order was the then-president of the United States, Lyndon B. Johnson.

Senior Counsel Blakey's Lamentable Experiences

John Simkin, the creator of a leading British research center, Spartacus Educational Forum, summarized the turnaround experienced by Professor Blakey in the decades since the HSCA completed its work:

> Blakey was shocked in 2003 when declassified CIA documents revealed the full identity of the retired agent who had acted as the committee's liaison to the agency, George Joannides, who had also overseen a group of anti-Castro Cuban exiles in Dallas [Directorio Revolucionario Estudiantil, or DRE] in the months before the assassination, when Lee Harvey Oswald was in contact with them.
>
> Blakey was furious when he discovered this information. He issued a statement where he said: "I am no longer confident that the Central Intelligence Agency co-operated with the committee . . . . I was not told of Joannides' background with the DRE, a focal point of the investigation. Had I known who he was, he would have been a witness who would have been interrogated under oath by the staff or by the committee. He would never have been acceptable as a point of contact with us to retrieve documents. In fact, I have now learned, as I note above, that Joannides was the point of contact between the Agency and DRE during the period Oswald was in contact with DRE.

That the Agency would put a 'material witness' in as a 'filter' between the committee and its quests for documents was a flat-out breach of the understanding the committee had with the Agency that it would co-operate with the investigation."

In August 2013, Blakey told the Las Vegas Sun: "They (the CIA) held stuff back from the Warren Commission, they held stuff back from us, they held stuff back from the ARRB. That's three agencies that they were supposed to be fully candid with. And now they're taking the position that some of these documents can't be released even today. Why are they continuing to fight tooth and nail to avoid doing something they'd promised to do?"[837]

Despite his protestations of being shocked to find out how he had been manipulated into his position and then how the CIA "held stuff back from us," we still have the unresolved and inexplicable quandary noted on the first page of this chapter, including the epigraph there: How is it that a person who is held out to be an expert on organized crime would even verbalize—much less put into an affidavit—his belief that Moe Dalitz had no connection with organized crime? Indeed, how could someone put into the position Blakey was, as senior counsel, not have been aware of the lengthy CIA background of the liaison they had assigned to the HSCA, George Joannides?

And why would the HSCA's senior counsel be either the instigator or irresponsibly unaware of the clandestine assignments given to the previous FBI informer and HSCA undercover agent Oliver Patterson, as described by Dr. Pepper in his book *The Plot to Kill King*? According to Pepper, the HSCA staff—under either the implicit or explicit authority of Blakey—assigned Patterson the task of befriending Ray's brother Jerry in order to spy on him by going through his personal effects, reading anything he might write or correspondence he might receive, and obtaining such things as his hair samples. Furthermore, Patterson was told to give an interview to the *New York Times* reporter Anthony J. Marro on August 7, 1978, and "to accuse Mark Lane of being gay, state that Lane had told him [Patterson] that he knew there was no person named Raul, and further allege that his [Patterson's] own undercover work had confirmed James Earl Ray's guilt." Caught by the fact that a friend of Patterson's, Susan Wadsworth, discovered the plot and informed Lane about it, who then confronted Patterson about it, he agreed to cooperate with Lane; when Marro arrived at a St. Louis hotel for the interview, he found himself in a room filled with reporters and photographers and ran away, with Lane in pursuit asking him if he wanted the truth. Lane, Wadsworth, and Patterson then held a news conference to expose all the details of this journalistic travesty.[838] The shameful conduct perpetrated against Mark Lane, as documented in affidavits signed by Susan Wadsworth and Tina Denaro and the sworn statements of Patterson himself, should have put the parties involved in personal legal jeopardy. But though Blakey issued a pro forma denial of the allegations and promised to conduct a complete investigation of the incident, nothing further was ever produced. Patterson's allegations—in the absence of such "complete investigation"— stand as the last word on the matter.

Finally, it was reported by James Earl Ray himself that Blakey's own alleged conflicts of interest enabled him to personally profit from his experience on the committee, even while precluding all other staff members from that opportunity by requiring them to sign agreements to not publish any information obtained while working for the HSCA. Two examples were cited: (1) A $10,000 payment as a "consulting fee" for helping Bantam Books publish *The Final Assassinations Report* in 1979; and (2) Blakey's own book, *The Plot to Kill the President*, published in 1980. By eliminating any competition, Blakey had assured a greater market share for himself in advance of signing his own contract.[839]

Beyond these instances of generally aberrant and conflicted behavior on the part of the senior HSCA staff and officials are the specific, inexplicable actions taken to ignore specific leads and suborn perjury of witnesses. The most egregious examples of the HSCA's mishandling of witnesses—e.g., Andy Salwyn, Harry Avery, and John McFerren—or protecting potential participants—e.g., Randolph Rosenson (a.k.a. Randy Rosen), Raul Coelho, Jules Ricco Kimble, and Frank Holloman—are clear evidence that the original intent of the committee had been hijacked by powerful politicians who had no interest in finding the truth of Dr. King's murder.

That is the most compelling proof that the real genesis of the plot resided at the very highest level of power in existence in 1968: within the Oval Office of the White House. It was because the plot against Martin Luther King Jr. originated at the pinnacle of power that, even fifty years on, it remains unsolved.

Chapter 12

CIVIL TRIALS: FOUR MORE DECADES OF DELAYED AND DENIED JUSTICE

"Dexter Scott King, one of Dr. King's sons, said he had come to accept Mr. Pepper's theory that the assassination was carried out through a vast conspiracy involving agents of the Mafia and the Federal Government, with the knowledge of President Lyndon B. Johnson."
—Kevin Sack, *The New York Times*, March 25, 1998[840]

In the absence of a free, fair, and open trial where the accused is accorded certain fundamental constitutional rights—all of which were waived in the case of James Earl Ray—and the numerous failed attempts made by or on behalf of Mr. Ray to rectify his status, he was given three substitute proceedings: a stacked-deck "minihearing" at which the ordinary rules of law were officially suspended, a mock trial where they were partially restored but only for dramatic effect, while he was still alive, and a simulacrum civil trial after his death in 1998, as a sort of postmortem vindication.

In 1992, Dr. William F. Pepper contracted with Thames Television in London for the production of an unscripted television trial that was conducted according to Tennessee law and criminal procedure. It included twelve jurors and two alternates from a pool of US citizens and included the cumulative findings known at that time, including such key points as the fact that the prosecution's star witness, Charles Q. Stephens, was incoherent and falling-down drunk at the time of the shot and that Dr. King's room at the Lorraine had been switched from the original secluded room to the one on the balcony.[841]

In April 1993, HBO broadcast that mock trial, which found that James Earl Ray did not murder Martin Luther King Jr. That television show, though ignored by virtually the entire mass media, was the subject of a newspaper article by Carl Rowan, a syndicated black journalist and television pundit, which appeared in a number of newspapers, including the *Baltimore Sun* on April 7, 1993, titled "After 25 Years, Truth Begins to Emerge." Now, after twenty-five more years—fifty years since the murder of Dr. King—Rowan's article has proven to be eerily prescient, coming to the same conclusions that we are reaching now (the only difference is that specific names have been added to his assertions). Mr. Rowan wrote:

> This absorbing HBO "trial" is a great public service, because it makes available to ordinary Americans facts, evidence, testimony that make it clear that while Ray is a scoundrel, he is also the pawn, the fall guy, in a murder perpetrated by powerful law-enforcement figures who could manipulate the courts, lawyers and politicians.[842]

Rowan then proceeded to outline all of the reasons why James Earl Ray could not possibly have been the sole murderer of King. One of his major points was how Memphis police turned over a whole bullet to the FBI for analysis and it came back mangled, cut into three pieces, rendering it impossible to ever match bullets from Ray's rifle. The homicide detective, Thomas H. Smith, who led the MPD investigation testified that he had gone to the morgue, put his hand on the back of Dr. King under his lower left shoulder blade, and felt an object, "it felt just like a bullet to me, the lead jacket of a bullet." When asked whether it was in one piece he replied, "Yes, sir, it was still round [in one piece]."[843]

Furthermore, Rowan pointed out that Ray:

- could not have made the changes in King's plans to stay at the Lorraine;
- could not have had all black policemen and firemen reassigned so they would not witness the murder;
- could not have ordered the electronic spying on King;
- could not have ordered the cutting of bushes the next day to demolish the crime scene; and
- could not have suppressed the evidence that the gunman had shot from where those bushes were the previous day, rather than the fabrication that it was done from the rooming-house bathroom.

Carl Rowan, twenty-five years ago, effectively demolished the official story in this single column, which was so shunned by the rest of the mainstream media of the day that what should have been a major blockbuster story was consigned to the back pages of a few newspapers and one broadcast program. As previously noted, the December 16, 1993, ABC news program *Prime-Time Live* with anchorman Sam Donaldson included an interview with Loyd

Jowers in which he revealed his long-held secret of having been involved in a conspiracy to murder King, which set up James Earl Ray to take the fall. The results of these productions evolved into Pepper's first book, *Orders to Kill*, in 1995.

The preparations for the eventual civil trial in 1999 began several years before; James Earl Ray was deposed in March 1995 and would die in 1998, before the trial commenced. The King family's understanding of the real story of Dr. King's murder also grew during this period, which led to their efforts to increase the public's awareness of their findings. On June 20, 1997, in a *New York Times* article headlined "Son of Dr. King Asserts L.B.J. Role in Plot," by Kevin Sack, the King family admitted that they now suspected that President Lyndon Baines Johnson and J. Edgar Hoover were behind the murder of Dr. Martin Luther King. This was the first time that Johnson's name was publicly connected to the murder of Dr. King by a prominent member of the King family:

> Three months ago, Dexter Scott King declared that he and his family believed that James Earl Ray was not guilty of the murder of his father, the Rev. Dr. Martin Luther King Jr. Tonight, in a televised interview, Mr. King asserted that President Lyndon B. Johnson must have been part of a military and governmental conspiracy to kill Dr. King.
>
> "Based on the evidence that I've been shown, I would think that it would be very difficult for something of that magnitude to occur on his watch and he not be privy to it," Mr. King said on the ABC News program "Turning Point."
>
> Mr. King, who heads the Martin Luther King Jr. Center for Nonviolent Social Change in Atlanta, suggested that the Army and Federal intelligence agencies were involved in his father's assassination, in Memphis on April 4, 1968. "I am told that it was part and parcel Army intelligence, C.I.A., F.B.I.," he said in the interview. "I think we knew it all along."

Dr. William Pepper represented the King family in the 1999 trial, *King Family vs. Loyd Jowers*, in which Jowers was being sued for the wrongful death of Dr. King. Pepper produced over seventy witnesses during the trial, which lasted four weeks. Jowers, too ill to attend, testified by deposition that James Earl Ray was a scapegoat and was not wittingly involved in the assassination. Jowers also testified that Memphis police officer Earl Clark had fired the fatal shots (although since then, it has been established that Clark's role was only to take the rifle from the actual shooter and dispose of it). On December 8, 1999, the Memphis jury found Jowers's testimony believable, taking less than an hour to find in favor of the King family for the requested sum of $100.

That Tennessee civil court jury determined that the supposedly confessed assassin, James Earl Ray, could not have acted alone in the murder of Dr. Martin Luther King Jr, and the jury was convinced that Ray had not willingly acted at all. Ray had died the year before, having spent over thirty years in jail waiting for an actual trial, having been denied his constitutional right to one after finally giving in to his attorney's insistence for a guilty plea in exchange for an empty promise that the plea would be quickly overturned and Ray would wind up with a guarantee that he would never face the death penalty (Ray's eight months of inhumane torture had a lot to do with how Percy Foreman was able to pull off that swindle).

The fact that the trial took place more than three decades after the event, despite the momentous and profound verdict, explains why it was virtually ignored by the mainstream media. A book and PDF document available on the Internet, *The 13th Juror—The Official Transcript of the Martin Luther King Assassination Conspiracy Trial*, provides the complete details as a virtual transcript of that trial. Within it, an explanation is given of why the jury essentially found James Earl Ray innocent of the murder, just as the King family had long suspected was the case.[844] It is the only one of the three major assassinations ever successfully adjudicated in a courtroom setting, and the results of that trial prove the truths revealed within this book, which include many more facts, and compelling additional testimonies, than were then available.

Among the many momentous statements of highly credible people who voluntarily came forth to seek a modicum of long-delayed justice, we will present a small portion. Readers who want to pursue more are urged to either acquire the book referenced above, *The 13th Juror,* or refer to the King Center website (www.thekingcenter.org) for access to the complete transcript.

Consider the testimony of just two of the over seventy such witnesses who testified:

- Witness **Nathan Whitlock**, a Memphis taxi driver and professional musician who has performed throughout North America, a man who had received a number of commendations and awards from two Tennessee governors, Senators Al Gore and Jim Sasser, Mayor Willie Herenton, and a number of others in recognition of his achievements, including having saved a man's life. Whitlock swore under oath that he was told in 1979 personally by Frank Liberto that Liberto had been involved in Martin Luther King's assassination. His testimony stated:

> He told me, he said, "I didn't kill the nigger, but I had it done." I said, what about that other son-of-a-bitch [Ray] up there taking credit for it? He says, "ahh, he wasn't nothing but a troublemaker from Missouri, he was a front man." I didn't know what that meant. Because "front man" to me means something different than what he was thinking about. I said, a what? He said, "a setup man." [845]

- Witness **John McFerren**, the country store owner described in Chapter 8, came forward to testify at the civil trial and provide lengthy background description of his many years on the front lines of the civil rights fight, and how being placed on the embargo list by the Ku Klux Klan had forced him to purchase groceries for his store from the likes of Frank Liberto, acknowledged to be part of the underworld. McFerren described the incredible methods he had to create in order to buy things like bread and lettuce for his country store, including how he had to modify his car into a hot rod in order to outrun the KKK, which was trying to starve him and his customers:

> During that time, I made friends with the underworld. What I mean by the underworld, they [the KKK] run me out of every wholesale house in Memphis but Malone & Hyde. The bread companies wouldn't sell nothing to me. There was a young bread man who said, tell you what you do, you meet me out there on Summer Avenue and I'll sell you the bread off the truck.
>
> I would come to Memphis and meet him on Summer Avenue in Memphis [in 1960–62] in a 1955 Ford car. That's what I had. I would come to Memphis and meet him on Summer Avenue and get bread. The Klan would get after me every night or two . . . I'm a top mechanic myself on the old models. To make a car run fast and turn curves faster, if you noticed, a 1955 Ford has got a solid frame in the front. We took the torch and cut two inches out of the frame in the front. That brought the front wheels in and let the back wheels be wider, and . . . when it would go around a sharp curve, it would slide around. At that time . . . I could drive just like I was standing still, and when they'd get after me, I'd cut over in them back roads, and them new cars couldn't turn good like me. [846]

McFerren further explained how he similarly bought meats and produce for his store:[847]

Q. Where have you always bought your merchandise?

A. Well, I bought all over Memphis. I'd buy from Frank Liberto's Produce, I'd buy from the meat houses, Morrell Meat Company, Fineberg Meat Company. I know everyone in Memphis.

Q. How many years had you been buying produce from Mr. Liberto?

A. Since 1906 [*sic*—transcription error, should be 1960] or 1961.

Q. Since 1960 or 1961 he ran that warehouse?

A. He was there then, but I didn't know his name. When I first started going there, I didn't know his name like I did later.

Q. What day of the week—do you recall what day of the week did you go to pick up your produce in the year 1968?

A. It was on a Thursday, around five-fifteen.

[. . .]

Q. So Liberto's warehouse was your last pickup?

A. Was the last pickup.

Q. You would get there around five-fifteen?

A. I got there that day at five-fifteen exactly.

Q. We're coming to that day. April 4 was a Thursday, the day Martin Luther King was assassinated was a Thursday.

A. That's correct.

[The discussion continued, until McFerren described hearing Frank Liberto take a telephone call.][848]

Q. Five twenty-five to five-thirty you heard him talking on the telephone?

Q. He received a phone call. What did you hear him say once again?

A. Shoot the son-of-a-bitch on the balcony.

Q. Shoot the son-of-a-bitch on the balcony. Then what happened after that?

A. [. . .] Mr. Liberto told him to go to his brother in New Orleans and get his $5,000.

McFerren then told how he didn't initially think too much of it until he heard how Dr. King was murdered, on a balcony. By the following Sunday, he decided to tell his story to Reverend Baxton Bryant, a white Nashville minister. At his urging, McFerren agreed to tell his story to the FBI and later met with two agents, who questioned him for "two or three hours" over his story. Then the next day, a Monday, two other "little young FBI" agents came to his store and questioned McFerren "half a day," followed by a mob-connected store owner from New Orleans named Robert Powers (in his testimony at the 1999 trial, McFerren misstated his name as "Powell"), who had called him and asked how to get to his house "through the back roads." Shortly after that, a milk truck "ran my mama down, caught her on the road, run over the truck," and two other goons beat McFerren up.

In 1977, an investigator for the HSCA, Gene Johnson, came to his house to interview him; when he later returned with documents for him to sign, McFerren said that "he had gotten a little hostile towards me," which led him to conclude that someone had gotten to Johnson and changed his attitude. McFerren had been scheduled to testify to the committee, but a few days before he was supposed to go to Washington, Johnson called him to say they had changed their minds, his testimony was not needed.[849] The reason for that change of attitude will be examined shortly.

Over seventy other credible witnesses testified to various points of contention, including Mrs. Coretta Scott King (Dr. King's widow), Dexter Scott King (Dr. King's son), Yolanda King (Dr. King's daughter), Andrew Young (Dr. King's senior associate, later mayor of Atlanta and UN ambassador), and many others, all having impeccable credentials and reputations.

At a 1999 press conference, Coretta Scott King issued the following statement after the trial:

> There is abundant evidence of a major high level conspiracy in the assassination of my husband, Martin Luther King, Jr. . . . the conspiracy of the Mafia, local, state and federal government agencies, were deeply involved in the assassination of my husband. The jury also affirmed overwhelming evidence that identified someone else, not James Earl Ray, as the shooter, and that Mr. Ray was set up to take the blame.

Dr. King's son, Dexter King, was subsequently interviewed by a reporter who stated, "There are many people out there who feel that as long as these conspirators remain nameless and faceless there is no true closure, and no justice." Dexter King replied, "No, he [Loyd Jowers] named the shooter. The shooter was the Memphis Police Department Officer, Lt. Earl Clark, who he named as the killer. Once again, beyond that you had credible witnesses that named members of a Special Forces team who didn't have to act because the contract killer succeeded, with plausible denial, a Mafia contracted killer."

Though the result of this civil trial—James Earl Ray being posthumously declared innocent—brought a bit more finality to the family of Dr. King, it was an event that was virtually ignored by the mainstream media, thus leaving James Earl Ray with the legend, in the public consciousness at least, of being just another lone assassin. This is one pattern that is like the sore thumb, a common denominator of all the 1960s assassinations, so much so that it alone should be considered as what the plotters considered their "signature."

Representative Walter Fauntroy's Testimony at the Civil Trial

In Chapter 11, we noted Walter Fauntroy's testimony in the civil trial about the reasons for the HSCA's failure to achieve substantive results in getting to the bottom of the assassinations of President Kennedy and Martin Luther King Jr. Much of it was due to the controversies related to the CIA's and FBI's undermining of the committee through the use of journalists whose professional integrity had been subverted through Operation Mockingbird, redirected to protecting governmental secrets and covert operations, as well as House colleagues who were similarly compromised by the same methods. The committee was lucky enough to even survive that onslaught, but their effectiveness was irreparably damaged when the original senior counsel and staff director, Richard Sprague, was fired and replaced by Robert Blakey. Instead of an aggressive investigation, the committee assumed a position similar to that of the Warren Commission, one which merely "evaluated" the reports of the FBI and their own circumscribed investigators.[850]

Fauntroy also stated that among the leads not explored or questions never resolved were:[851]

- No credible witnesses placed James Earl Ray at the scene.
- The origin of the shot—allegedly the window of the rooming house, never proven, or from the bushes below, as stated by three credible witnesses—was never established.
- The bullet allegedly fired was never traced to the gun that had Ray's fingerprints on it.
- The competence of Ray being able to have pulled off the jailbreak, then travel all over the country, acquiring three passports all by himself without help, and acquiring at least $10,000 to sustain himself, never made sense to him.

- The fact that it was established (from Ray's army records) that he couldn't hit a target a hundred feet away with an M-1 rifle, but had become an expert to hit a deadly shot from two hundred feet away at Dr. King, "disturbed" Mr. Fauntroy.
- The testimony of John Paul Speaker [*sic*: "Spica"] had never been investigated, regarding the supposed $50,000 offer of a "bounty" for the murder of King; all of it had been turned over to the FBI and Justice Department for follow-up, but never concluded, which left "many of us with reservations about closing the investigation."
- Finally, Mr. Fauntroy stated that "I was never satisfied with the conclusion on whether there was a Raul or not a Raul" (it was always a given that there was no Raul, according to official government dogma).

During the period Fauntroy referenced (1976–79), the worst of the FBI abuses had not yet been revealed. At the time of this testimony (1999), he noted the books by David Garrow and Curt Gentry, which "greatly upset" him because the latter described the connections among Hoover, Carlos Marcello, Texas oilmen "Clint Merchaser" [*sic*: Murchison], and "E. L. Hunt" [*sic*: H. L. Hunt], which prompted him to recall the expunged testimony of John McFerren. "I was really upset about that during the investigation and had been assured that really it was just Mr. Laberto's [*sic*: Liberto's] word against Mr. McFarran's [*sic*: McFerren's] word." [852]

That testimony goes directly to the underhanded way that the committee staff "disinvited" John McFerren to testify to the committee. He had been assured by staffer Gene Johnson on his first visit that he would be called on to testify, but by the time Johnson returned to McFerren's store to get sign-offs on his statements, he had had a "change of attitude," which revealed the inner struggle of the committee. They knew that McFerren would be seen by the committee as a highly credible witness and they obviously feared his testimony so much that they invented this excuse, knowing that in putting him on the stand against Liberto, there was no doubt about which witness the committee would believe. Yet, due to McFerren's statements that he thought he had seen James Earl Ray as an employee of Liberto's (based upon a sketch of the "suspect" that bore a resemblance to Ray), he was portrayed in the final HSCA assessment as having "questionable credibility" and his testimony was summarily dismissed:

> "On the basis of witness [Liberto's, naturally] denials, lack of corroborating evidence and McFerren's questionable credibility,

the committee concluded that his allegation was without foundation and that there was no connection between his story and the assassination of Dr. King." [853]

This suggests—*proves* is not an overstatement—that someone on the HSCA staff (or Chairman Stokes himself?) was put there to avoid this kind of dilemma. Fauntroy was a very credible and honest man and would have never condoned this kind of subterfuge—it is apparent in his words that he did not understand the underlying reasons why McFerren was cut from the witness list, because that explanation would have never worked with him.

Mr. Fauntroy also admitted feeling that "we were dealing with very sophisticated forces" during this time, and later, learning the extent of the FBI surveillance practices, he decided to look into the possibility that his own home and offices in his church had been bugged. Sure enough, he found that a maid at his church, apparently masquerading as a church member, had given him a television set for his church office in the early 1960s, and it had "stayed in my office throughout the sixties, even while I was in Congress." When he had his office checked for bugs, he stated that they "found a bug on [the television] that enabled persons to drive around the block of the church and pick up anything that was going on in the church . . . it sort of signaled me what we joked about a lot in the sixties, namely that, you know, Uncle Bubba is listening—I mean J. Edgar Hoover is listening. So that was amusing, and I learned also that there was a bug in my phone at home that wore out [after] about three years. A fellow told me it [takes] about 500 hours, and I do recall that every time the phone would get a little funny, I would call and the same fella would show up to repair it so those kinds of laughable things were sort of in my mind." [854]

What Walter Fauntroy Told James Douglass After the Trial

James Douglass got to know Congressman Walter Fauntroy—one of the more honest and serious pursuers of truth on the committee. He wrote about Fauntroy's experiences during his two-decade-long service, including the two years when he chaired the subcommittee formed to reinvestigate the assassination of Martin Luther King Jr.

Fauntroy claimed that it became apparent that he and the committee were all being surveilled throughout that period by "very sophisticated forces," with "electronic bugs on his phones and TV set." He also stated that the original lead investigator for the HSCA, Richard Sprague—who was committed to mounting an aggressive investigation, including a review of all

FBI, CIA, and military intelligence records—was forced to resign. He was then replaced by the mild-mannered professor G. Robert Blakey, who decided to pursue a more evaluative methodology, rather than an investigative type. A portion of Mr. Douglass's interview with Fauntroy follows:

> When I interviewed Fauntroy in a van on his way back to the Memphis Airport [after the civil trial of *King v. Jowers*], I asked about the implications of his statements in an April 4, 1997 *Atlanta Constitution* article. The article said Fauntroy now believed "Ray did not fire the shot that killed King and was part of a larger conspiracy that possibly involved federal law enforcement agencies," and added: "Fauntroy said he kept silent about his suspicions because of fear for himself and his family."
>
> Fauntroy told me that when he left Congress in 1991 he had the opportunity to read through his files on the King assassination, including raw materials that he'd never seen before. Among them was information from J. Edgar Hoover's logs. *There he learned that in the three weeks before King's murder the FBI chief held a series of meetings with "persons involved with the CIA and military intelligence in the Phoenix operation in Southeast Asia." Why? Fauntroy also discovered there had been Green Berets and military intelligence agents in Memphis when King was killed. "What were they doing there?" he asked.*[855] (Emphasis added.)

With those words, Mr. Fauntroy undoubtedly referenced the testimony of another one of the witnesses called by Dr. Pepper at the civil trial, Mr. Douglas Valentine, the author of *The Phoenix Program*, which he summed up as follows: "The Phoenix Program was created by the CIA in Vietnam in 1967 as part of a recognition that the war could not be won militarily and that a second other war had to be waged against what was called the Vietcong infrastructure which was a jargon for the shadow government of the Vietcong."[856] A few excerpted sentences from that seminal book will explain it further:

> Central to Phoenix is the fact that it targeted civilians, not soldiers . . . Under Phoenix . . . due process was totally nonexistent. South Vietnamese civilians whose names appeared on blacklists could be kidnapped, tortured, detained for two years without trial, or even murdered, simply on the word of an anonymous informer.[857]

In his testimony at the *King v. Jowers* trial, Mr. Valentine stated that many of the military intelligence officers and enlisted men assigned to the Phoenix Program in Vietnam, upon returning to the United States, were assigned to various surveillance and other operations in the civil rights movement.[858] Moreover, he stated that some of them surveilled such notable antiwar protesters as Abbie Hoffman and Jerry Rubin; others were employed as agent provocateurs, to incite riots, which allowed the police to arrest those who were provoked to take criminal actions. One of those individuals revealed that credible rumors had circulated within the 111th Military Intelligence Group that some of its members were in Memphis surveilling Dr. King on April 4, 1968, and took photographs of the assassination. Valentine also stated that he had not previously known about the 902nd MIG[859] but learned about it in 1996, after interviewing a man named Phillip Manual, who in 1975 was a Senate investigator. Although Mr. Manual would not discuss his past, nor anything about the 902nd MIG, Valentine did learn that he had been in Memphis on the day of the assassination and had conveyed the information about an alleged threat to the life of Detective Redditt to MPD Lieutenant Eli Arkin, who subsequently relieved Redditt from his post surveilling Dr. King.[860]

Carthel Weeden—the fire department captain in charge of Fire Station No. 2—finally testified about assisting two men with army credentials but wearing civilian clothes who went to the roof of the fire station the morning of April 4. They surveilled the area and took photographs of everyone coming and going into buildings in that area. However, according to his informers, Dr. Pepper stated that the actual assassin was caught in the act of shooting, but the photographs were never published[861] (which possibly means they may still be safely filed away for future archeologists trying to make sense of twentieth-century America to discover). One of those team members told Dr. Pepper that it was not James Earl Ray who was in that photograph.[862]

Fauntroy also spoke about the time in June 1977 that Ray escaped from the Brushy Mountain State Penitentiary in Eastern Tennessee. He had heard that the FBI—uninvited by the state—sent a SWAT team there (of allegedly thirty men), ostensibly to help catch the escapee, but actually for the purpose of shooting him, to prevent him ever talking again. This was at the point where the HSCA was finally getting organized and preparing to take Ray's testimony. Fauntroy spoke to Chairman Stokes about this and he alerted Governor Blanton to the danger, which resulted in the SWAT team being removed from the scene.[863]

Concurrently with the HSCA's attempts to tepidly "reinvestigate" the King assassination with limited resources and a constricted timetable,

President Jimmy Carter had appointed Andrew Young to be the US ambassador to the United Nations, and Brady Tyson was appointed to be an aide to Young. In June 1978, through his work at the U.N., Tyson had become a friend of Daniel Ellsberg, famous for having leaked the Pentagon Papers—the secrets of how and why the Vietnam War had come about—and through their discussions it became apparent that Tyson and Young had also discovered some truths about "who, what, why, and how" had been behind the assassination of Martin Luther King Jr. Eventually, Ellsberg documented the results of his conversations with Tyson in an affidavit, stating:

> I asked Tyson whether he thought there had been a conspiracy and who he thought might have done it. He said very flatly to me, "We know there was a conspiracy and we know who did it . . . It was a group of off-duty and retired FBI officers working under the personal direction of J. Edgar Hoover." He said further that this was a group working secretly and known to almost no one else in the FBI.[864]

Upon further questioning by Ellsberg, Tyson told him, "That has turned up in Walter Fauntroy's (HSCA) investigation and he's told us." Tyson also told Ellsberg that when Fauntroy originally pressed Carl Albert, the Speaker of the House (and longtime Lyndon Johnson crony, wise to his methods) to be assigned not only to the HSCA, but to appoint him to head the MLK investigation, Albert told him, "Walter, you don't want that job." When Fauntroy replied that yes, he did want it, Albert whispered his own response: "Walter, they will kill you . . . the FBI."[865]

The morning after Ellsberg gave his affidavit, Dr. Pepper left a copy with former Attorney General Ramsey Clark, who discussed it with Tyson, whose response was to deny the specifics of the allegations. Immediately thereafter, led by Fauntroy, Andy Young, Brady Tyson, and another aide, Stoney Cooks, began backpedaling on the information in the Ellsberg affidavit—all of them denying any knowledge of FBI involvement in the assassination. Eventually, with everyone apparently now in denial because of a lack of solid evidence, it became a pet theory advanced by Brady Tyson. Toward the end of the HSCA's existence, in November 1978, all four of them testified before the HSCA, categorically denying any actual proof of the FBI's involvement. It appeared that they had all spoken too openly about what they had been discussing behind the scenes and did not expect that it would become exposed to the public.[866]

It would not be unreasonable to speculate that the involvement of so many high-level officials, and former officials, forced everyone involved to "close ranks" to effectively "let the sleeping dog lie," lest the culmination of the HSCA's work lead directly to a constitutional crisis that might threaten the continued existence of the country.

Representative Fauntroy later planned to write a book about his experiences on the HSCA and the subsequent developments, but as soon as that became known, he was quickly put on notice by the Justice Department that it wasn't such a good idea. It was a subtle and indirect warning, brought about by a notice that he was being investigated for financial misdeeds. According to him, his attorney could not understand why the DOJ would make such a fuss about a technicality involving one misdated check. Fauntroy's interpretation: "Look, we'll get you on something if you continue this way . . . I just thought: I'll tell them I won't go and finish the book, because it's surely not worth it." [867]

1990s Developments: An Ex-FBI Agent, Donald G. Wilson, Steps Forward Thirty Years Later, Offers More Proof of Raul's Existence

Similar to Ray's finding a card in his Mustang with Randy Rosen's name and address in November 1967, a few months later, in April 1968, a young FBI agent found multiple papers with still other leads in Ray's Mustang. Thirty years later, in 1998, ex-FBI agent Donald G. Wilson contacted Dr. William F. Pepper and the King family to inform them of this evidence and would later write a book, *Evidence Withheld*, describing the incident in detail. Wilson had personally been on the FBI detail dispatched to the apartment complex to recover the Mustang left by James Earl Ray on April 11, 1968—six days after Ray had abandoned the vehicle. Wilson stated that even before they were sent to the apartment complex to check on the car, he and his partner had spotted a person, one day after the assassination, who matched the description of the suspect. They radioed the field office for permission to apprehend the person, but it was refused without explanation.

Donald Wilson claimed that he was among the first agents on the scene and conducted the earliest search of the abandoned car, even before it was taken to the Atlanta FBI's garage, where it would be examined more intensely. Wilson said that as he opened the passenger-side door, a small white envelope fell from underneath a door panel in Ray's car, but he never turned it over to the FBI and did not disclose its contents until he revealed them to Dr. Pepper and the King family twenty-nine years later, in 1997.

Within the envelope was a page torn from a 1963 Dallas telephone book. The telephone numbers on the page included the listing for H. L. Hunt and other members of the Hunt family. In handwriting on the page margins, another telephone number was written, along with the name "Raul" and the letter "J" as well as the number of Jack Ruby's club. A second piece of paper included several names and sums of money related to each name, as though it were some kind of payoff list, with Raul's name and date for payment to be made. A third piece of paper contained the telephone number for the Atlanta FBI. Combined, the papers represented a possible sketch of persons in the Atlanta FBI office and key people in Dallas who were connected to the JFK assassination.

Wilson claimed that he didn't immediately tell his superiors about what he found because he didn't want them to know that he had tampered with the crime scene, and later, it was because Ray had already confessed. He also stated that he knew instinctively that if he had turned in the evidence he found, it would quickly disappear and perhaps never be recoverable. After having decided to keep it secure, he was also cognizant of the fact—as Jim Marrs's book *Crossfire* attested, among numerous others—that there was a long list of convenient deaths of other witnesses who had come forward in the JFK assassination, and he didn't want to join that list as it pertained to the King assassination. After Wilson finally did come forward, the response of the Department of Justice (a misnomer in many cases) and the FBI was "immediate and vitriolic," and within twenty-four hours, press releases were leaked to the effect that *"We never even heard of an FBI agent named Donald Wilson."*[868] (Emphasis in original.)

Coming out of retirement to assist in the verbal assault on Mr. Wilson was none other than the long-retired FBI Assistant Director Cartha "Deke" DeLoach, whom many people within the FBI, according to an article by Rowland Evans and Robert Novak, considered "to be guilty of 'right-wing bias and blatant opportunism.'"[869] Others boiled it down to a single adjective: *unctuous.*

Attorney General Janet Reno Orders "Reinvestigation" of MLK Assassination

The last in the series of government "investigations"—in a grand finale of officious slap-downs, the Justice Department Task Force in 2000—was an elaborately conducted, clearly preestablished denial of everything brought out in the 1999 Memphis civil trial of *King v. Jowers* plus the evidence brought forth by former FBI agent Donald G. Wilson. Originally prompted by the March 1998 disclosures by Wilson, US Attorney General Janet Reno ordered a new investigation of the merits of this newly found evidence on August 26, 1998.

Subsequently, the verdict of the 1999 civil trial that exonerated James Earl Ray was added to the DOJ reinvestigation. On June 9, 2000, the DOJ released a 150-page report that summarily rejected the findings of that jury—mostly by attacking the credibility of witnesses giving testimony and the evidence that supported them—while also dismissing the evidence brought forward by Donald Wilson.[870] The following excerpts from the DOJ report summarize the position of the government regarding Donald Wilson:

> During our meeting, Wilson refused to provide the original documents he said he took from Ray's car. Rather, he gave us two original documents the following day, only after he learned that a search warrant for them was about to be executed. One document was a torn page from a 1963 Dallas, Texas telephone directory that refers to figures associated with the assassination of President Kennedy, along with the name "Raul." The other was a piece of paper with handwritten figures and words, including the name "Raul."
>
> We considered a variety of factors in assessing the credibility of Wilson's claim and the authenticity of these documents. First, we evaluated whether Wilson's statements about the documents to the King family, Dr. Pepper, the District Attorney, the media, and our investigation have been consistent. We also analyzed whether independent evidence exists to support the accuracy of Wilson's claims. In that regard, we reviewed original law enforcement records and attempted to interview all law enforcement and civilian witnesses who were present at the scene when Ray's car was discovered or who had information about the Mustang. We also assessed the overall plausibility of Wilson's claims, including whether it was likely that a law enforcement officer would steal and then hide potential evidence regarding Dr. King's assassination for 30 years and, when finally disclosing it, continue to conceal the existence of a potentially crucial piece of evidence.
>
> We further analyzed the two original documents obtained from Wilson. In an attempt to resolve the central issues related to the authenticity of the papers—whether they came from Ray's Mustang in 1968 and who authored them—we had the United States Secret Service (USSS) laboratory scientifically analyze the documents and the handwritten notations on them.

Further, we considered James Earl Ray's failure to recall the documents and the likelihood that he would have possessed a torn page from a 1963 Dallas telephone directory with notations that suggest a connection between the assassinations of Dr. King and President Kennedy.

B. The Origin of The Allegations

1. April 1968: The Discovery of Ray's Mustang

On April 11, 1968, residents of a public housing project alerted the Atlanta Police Department to an abandoned, white Ford Mustang in the project's parking lot. Two police detectives responded and found the Mustang locked. They unlocked the driver-side door with a coat hanger to obtain the vehicle's identification number. A records search revealed the car was registered to Eric Galt, an alias used by James Earl Ray. The FBI was notified and arrived on the scene approximately two hours after the Atlanta police detectives. Federal agents arranged for the Mustang to be towed to a government garage where it was searched and processed for evidence.

On April 11, 1968, Donald Wilson was a new FBI agent assigned to the Atlanta field office. Records reflect that he had been an agent for less than a year and on that date was assigned, along with three other agents, to search for Western Union money orders relevant to the murder of Dr. King. According to Wilson, he joined the FBI in part because of his concern with the racism he observed while attending college and law school in the South during the 1960s. He believed the FBI would provide him an opportunity to protect civil rights. Shortly after becoming an agent, however, Wilson became disillusioned, concluding that the FBI had racist policies and little regard for individual liberties.

Wilson nonetheless had a successful career with the FBI for ten years, receiving several promotions and awards. He abruptly resigned in 1977, on the same day he gave written notice. Notes from an exit interview reflect that Wilson stated that he left "because of personal values and career objectives" and refused to "elaborate further."

The Justice Department report also acknowledged that the apartment searches they conducted were illegal black bag jobs and therefore kept the identities of the two senior agents who conducted them secret, evidently excusing the behavior because they were just following orders—illegal orders that had issued from none other than J. Edgar Hoover himself. The report indicated that "Both agents who participated in the search unequivocally told our investigation team that Wilson had no part in the 'black bag' job and one specifically recalls delivering the fruits of the search to the FBI field office himself. Since each has admitted participation in an unauthorized activity, neither has a motive to deny Wilson's involvement. Nor would it have been unusual for Wilson to have learned of the activity from office gossip afterwards." [871]

The context of their use of that word "unauthorized" should be clear. It was another deception, a completely opposite mischaracterization of a word, which allowed the point to be swept aside in order to advance an even larger deceit. A better word would have been "unconstitutional," but more important, to say that "neither has a motive to deny Wilson's involvement" is ridiculous: *both* of them would have had such a motive, given that their actions were illegal. Wilson's response to those assertions reads, in part:

> I was indeed instructed to assist in this search which included, in addition to me, FBI special agents John Reynolds and Donald Burgess. Burgess and Reynolds tried to dress as "hippies" as Ray's room was located in an area which at that time was populated by "hippies" of the 1960s. They still looked out of place given their age at the time and their appearance gave great amusement to many of the Atlanta agents upon seeing their "hippie disguise." The plan called for Reynolds and Burgess to conduct the illegal entry and collect items they deemed relevant.
>
> When finished, Burgess was to go to a nearby public phone booth under the pretext of making a call and leave the materials in a bag. My role was to go to the phone booth which I had under surveillance, retrieve the evidence and then proceed back to the FBI office and hand deliver the items to the Agent in Charge, Frank Hitt. I did so and also at that time was introduced to Assistant FBI Director Mr. William Sullivan who was on the scene to personally supervise the King investigation. Prior to carrying out this assignment I asked agent Burgess, that since we had no search warrant, could we later find ourselves confronted with a legal problem. He responded by telling me, *"Hey kid, we are the FBI . . . we do whatever the hell we want."*
>
> After this investigation was completed I specifically asked agent Burgess if I should dictate a FD 302 [a report describing

investigative results] as to my retrieving the evidence and hand carrying it back to the Atlanta office. He replied, *"Since you are to be transferred soon to your second office, don't bother as it will be an inconvenience as you might have to return to testify ... don't worry about it kid, I'll take care of it."* I also discussed the preparation of FD 302's regarding my presence at Capital Homes as well as my role in the burglary of Ray's room with Assistant Agent in Charge Jack Keith [who advised him] *"Hey kid, it's not necessary, don't worry about it."*[872] (Italics in original.)

Despite this, and regardless of the fact that Wilson had intimate knowledge of the crime scene, even naming the names that the DOJ refrained from giving, and had physical evidence to support his claim, Wilson was senselessly attacked by peers and faceless minions of the Clinton administration. The administration's faux civil rights division turned a blind eye to this witness's honest attempt to furnish evidence that could be—and should have been—used to resolve a case that had already been mishandled for over thirty years.

The Reno Justice Department—undoubtedly with the imprimatur of President Clinton and Vice President Al Gore Jr.—in its examination of a trial that many close observers hailed as the most intensive adjudication of evidence and witnesses ever conducted of Dr. King's assassination, summarily dismissed the many substantive leads presented by Ray's attorneys in the case, all accumulated over three decades of privately conducted investigations. It was as if an "all hands on deck" order were given at the highest possible level for every agency and employee in the government to close ranks and use whatever methods it took to close the case with finality. The closing was formalized by the Justice Department's June 2000 report, presenting with finality all the obligatory denials resulting from governmental agencies caught red-handed in treasons committed by their leadership.

In the civil trial *King v. Jowers,* over seventy witnesses—most of them having impeccable credentials and expertise compared with most of the original government witnesses—came forward to try to expose the truth. All were essentially refuted by the Clinton/Reno "investigation" as being unreliable and noncredible. Two of those witnesses were Nathan Whitlock and John McFerren, both of whom were exemplars of honorable men with unblemished reputations, but whose testimonies, as summarized above, were maligned and denigrated by the Reno-appointed task force.

The following paragraph is representative of the dozens of pages produced by the DOJ in 2000, in a style repeated throughout. It consisted of a series of half-truths, non sequiturs, circumlocutions, abstractions, fallacious reasoning, denials of objective facts presented by DOJ bureaucrats as being subjective, therefore debatable, and nonsubstantive opinions. The complete obtuse report is available at the DOJ website for those wishing to experience an incomparable example of banal bureaucratese:

> Nonetheless, we examined the trial evidence relating to these far-ranging conspiracy claims. We found that it was both con-tradictory and based on uncorroborated secondhand and third-hand hearsay accounts. Nor did we find any credible, concrete facts to substantiate any of the conspiracy allegations. Because there was no reliable evidence presented at trial relating to a conspiracy to assassinate Dr. King involving either Jowers, the government, African American ministers, or anyone else, and because we know of no information to support such allegations, we find no justification for further investigation.[873]

To say that "there was no reliable evidence presented at trial" must have been a surprise for the jurors, since the 1999 jury felt otherwise. While the original conspiracy allegations investigated by the HSCA were in some cases specious on their face (e.g., in one case, asserting that Reverend Ralph Abernathy was behind one such conspiracy), in others presented by such witnesses as McFerren and Whitlock, they had been perfunctorily explored and summarily dismissed by the HSCA twenty years earlier.[874] For example, the rationale for why the DOJ in 2000 would not take seriously the documents that Donald Wilson had come forward with over thirty years after he found them under the upholstery of Ray's abandoned Mustang; their report included this curious statement:

> Further, we considered *James Earl Ray's failure* to recall the documents and the likelihood that he would have possessed a torn page from a 1963 Dallas telephone directory with nota-tions that suggest a connection between the assassinations of Dr. King and President Kennedy. (Emphasis added.)

In contradiction of everything presented to them, the DOJ again blamed the victim for not remembering this evidence, even though it was never claimed that it had been left there by Ray, or that he ever had any knowledge of it, or even any reason to expect it to have been there. The materials found by Wilson were clearly left there—not by Ray, but by Raul, as a passenger in Ray's car on one of their several trips together, apparently left there inadvertently by Raul, under the upholstery or behind a door panel, and simply never discovered by Ray. The brilliant attorneys and investigators at the Department of Justice had evidently decided that through his negligence in not properly cleaning his car and finding this material, Ray's guilt was proven once again, and the new evidence was thus summarily discarded and deemed inconsequential.

As detailed previously, regarding the incident where Ray *did* find a card—apparently also left by Raul—having the name and address of "Randy Rosen" (Randolph E. Rosenson) under the front passenger seat in 1967, even in the opposite context, the HSCA had found a way to similarly dismiss it as being of no value to them (although not before interviewing Rosenson secretly in a Knoxville hotel, after which he mysteriously disappeared). The differences in their treatment of Rosenson and Wilson regarding similarly found evidence from the Mustang were more than offset by the similarities in how the substantive evidence presented in both cases was first ridiculed and then dispatched without follow-up.

According to Weisberg, he was told by Arthur Hanes that the FBI found, in the trunk of the Mustang, "a man's clothing, much too small for Ray. It would fit a man who weighs 125 pounds." Weisberg then noted that that was consistent with the size of the man whom Grace Stephens described as fleeing the rooming house; it is also consistent with the descriptions of Raul by the witnesses noted by Dr. Pepper. Raul had also left the Mustang's ashtray full of cigarette butts, none of which were ever examined for fingerprints, probably because all the investigators knew that Ray was a nonsmoker.[875] The ashtray enigma—as obvious a contradiction as possible—was consistently ignored by all so-called investigators because it never led in the right direction for them and they were apparently afraid of where it might lead.

Another point—originally made in 1969 by Clay Blair Jr., the author of the first credible book on Ray—that was never pursued by any law enforcement agency was that someone who claimed to be Eric S. Galt telephoned the Alabama Highway Patrol's license division on February 28, 1968, to ask that a duplicate license be sent to the address of his rented room in Birmingham. Ray was still in Los Angeles on that date, yet, according to Peter Cherpes, the manager of the rooming house, an unknown person retrieved the envelope containing that duplicate on March 2 or 3 and paid the twenty-five-cent fee to the license division on March 6. This incident pointed clearly to an accomplice of Ray's who had specific knowledge of Ray's alias, his Birmingham address, and the fact that he had obtained that license.[876]

But the DOJ could never acknowledge any of these pieces of evidence, because it would be incongruent with their mission and a concession that there was a "Raoul" after all, which had always been off-limits. Their many claims that Ray had never produced any evidence of Raul's existence was also belied by the fact that he had offered, through his lawyers, the telephone number contacts that he had for Raul. That they ignored all of this, and the many fingerprints that were left "unidentified" in other locations, and now the documents brought forth by Wilson—of "credible, concrete facts to substantiate any of the conspiracy allegations"—which they continued to deny, is the best documentation of how they had circumscribed their own "investigation."

Clearly, the same cover-up continues even now, given that the original fifty-year-old fictional mythology still prevails. Together, that adds up to sixty years of official deceit. The perpetuation of the myth into the twenty-first century appears to have been directly guided by successor-clones of the original FBI plotters, given that—as repeatedly annotated within this narrative—their renditions are obviously based upon the same discredited fictions originally created by the earlier authors. Regardless of the source of their motivation, and whether they were being led or were merely following their own misguided pecuniary interests, Posner, Waldron, Sides, and the other lesser-knowns would take up the task and add startlingly brazen additional bits of disinformation to keep the myth alive.

US Department of Justice Denies All Leads: Shades of 1984's Ministry of Truth?

The Department of Justice wrote a lengthy report filled with disinformation, obfuscation, and perfunctory dismissals of exculpatory evidence of Ray's innocence in its attempt to discredit Donald Wilson and deny the validation of the evidence. Formally titled "UNITED STATES DEPARTMENT OF JUSTICE INVESTIGATION OF RECENT ALLEGATIONS REGARDING THE ASSASSINATION OF DR. MARTIN LUTHER KING, JR.," it grouped Wilson's evidence with all other testimony and evidence presented at the 1999 civil trial *King v. Jowers* and collectively rejected all of it.

It also contained many references to Ray's allegedly inconsistent testimony, without citations of where the alleged statements were made. One example was that "descriptions of Raoul are completely inconsistent. During his lifetime, Ray gave as many as six conflicting descriptions."[877] Given that those discrepancies would have been planted by Huie in his zeal to portray Ray as the stalker/killer, that should have been enough to throw them out, but assuming there was any truth to the assertion, the confusion would undoubtedly have been related to the inhumane treatment Ray was given as a prisoner for the eight months prior to his "trial." During the entire period of his incarceration, nearly three decades of often abusive treatment, it is unlikely that anyone would have been completely consistent about such a subjective question (i.e., without benefit of photos or identification documents, it would be difficult for anyone to remember precisely another person's height, weight, hair or eye color, facial features, etc., having seen them on relatively few occasions under different circumstances, some of which were subject to change over a ten-month period). But discrediting someone on that basis was certainly easy.[878]

Yet the DOJ report stated that the photograph was not a correct representation of Raul: "The contrast in Raul's picture is so pronounced that the facial features are indistinct, large areas are entirely washed out, and all details are obscured. Thus, the representation of Raul appears more like a block print than a photograph and stands out markedly from the others. The representation of Raul lacks sufficient clarity to reflect accurately his actual appearance. In fact, the representation is so poor that it bears no resemblance to the original photograph and, most probably, does not approximate his appearance when it was taken."[879] Given their own acknowledgement of the numerous deficiencies in the photograph, their criticisms of Ray's inconsistencies in his descriptions of him, without benefit of any photograph, are incomprehensible.

Next, the DOJ report portrayed the "New York Raul" as someone who could not speak English when he immigrated to the United States in 1961 and slowly learned to speak it for over a decade, not getting English lessons until 1975. Yet both Ray and witness Glenda Grabow stated that he spoke English well throughout the 1960s period. In fact, Ms. Grabow testified that she wrote out a transcript of a conversation that she had with him on April 20, 1995, where he greeted her, after not having spoken to her in three decades, with the name that he had uniquely called her, "Olinda," when they knew each other in Dallas over thirty years earlier.[880] That was sufficient to prove that Raul acknowledged his identity to her. Many others also confirmed that the photo matched the Raul whom James had previously identified, including Glenda's husband and brother, both of whom also knew him from 1962–63, and also the owner of Jim's Bar, Loyd Jowers—who had seen him in the grill, with Raul, on April 4, 1968—and Sid Carthew, the UK merchant seaman who had met both James and Raul at the Neptune Bar in Montreal. Even Raul's own daughter inadvertently confirmed the same thing when, after looking at the photo of Raul, stated, "anyone could get that picture of my father."[881]

Part V

The Case Unravels, Slowly (1999–2018)

Chapter 13

HIDDEN LIES EMERGE, LBJ'S CRIMES CONVERGE

"On March 31 [1968], in an act that I long regarded as unrelated to the events of this story, Lyndon Johnson announced before a nationwide radio and television audience that he wouldn't seek reelection. Fifteen days earlier Robert Kennedy had announced his intention to challenge Johnson for the presidency." [882]

—Dr. William F. Pepper, Esq.

More Revelations of Lyndon Johnson's Connections from Washington to Dallas, Houston, New Orleans, and Memphis: Jack Valenti and Jack Ruby—Partners in Porn?

In earlier chapters, we noted Lyndon Johnson's documented close connections to an assortment of men and women who were involved in key positions of the widely based plot to kill Dr. King. Chief among them of course was his longtime friendship with his neighbor J. Edgar Hoover, the most obvious of these key figures, who had been obsessed for at least a decade with "neutralizing" Martin Luther King Jr. Hoover, of course, had his own line of acolytes ready, willing, and able to do their part in planning, executing, and/or covering up the assassination: Tolson, DeLoach, Sullivan, Papich, Holloman, and all the men and women attached to them, down to the local FBI agents in Atlanta, Memphis, and other cities around the country.

James Angleton at the CIA took a similar lead within that organization when Richard Ober was put in charge of Operation CHAOS in 1967 to accomplish similar—even far more intrusive and expansive—spying operations on American citizens. All of the hullabaloo over Johnson's edict to stop illegal wiretaps and electronic bugging by the FBI in 1966 was proven to be a ruse, because within a few months, he simply transferred much of it upriver to Langley. Also previously noted was how the head of army military intelligence, William Yarborough, at about the same time, brought his own sleuths into the fold, all under the coordinated efforts of the FBI as the lead federal agency in advancing the plot. The fact that the FBI had led "Operation Memphis" from the beginning—from the original meeting conducted at FBI headquarters on December 23, 1963, only one month after JFK's assassination—put it in control of the entire plot, indubitably with the blessing of the newly installed president.

At the state and local level, another very close longtime Johnson associate, Tennessee governor Buford Ellington, was crucial in corralling select state officials in both judicial and law enforcement circles—all politically propelled into their respective areas of responsibility, anxious to accommodate their superiors—in discreetly setting the stages as needed. Hudley Crockett, the governor's press secretary, marveled at how close Ellington was to Johnson, including the fact that he had an open invitation to stay at the White House whenever he went to Washington, and how they often talked about events and politics on the telephone and hunted birds together in Texas.[883]

Ellington's power over the state judiciary through his appointments to judgeships at the district, appeals, and state supreme courts was critical to the plan to deny James Earl Ray any chance of a fair trial. This power is an undeniable fact, proven beyond a shadow of a doubt by how Ray spent the last thirty years his life in prison cells, having been denied his constitutional rights to prove his innocence before a fair judge and an impartial jury through a competent, honest, diligent, and uncompromised attorney.

But Johnson's reach went well beyond the established political, judicial, and law enforcement hierarchies. It was even more entrenched in the underworld's hierarchy of power. He had his own long-standing connections to gangsters even before becoming the majority leader of the Senate, but after that he kept himself at least one step removed from the dirty work by delegating much of that to the Senate Secretary Robert G. "Bobby" Baker. According to Peter Dale Scott, "While working for Johnson, Baker became the epitome of Washington wheeler-dealer sleaze. Repeatedly, he fronted for [among others] syndicate gamblers Cliff Jones and Ed Levinson in investments that earned super profits for himself and another military-industrial lobbyist, his friend Fred Black Jr. In exchange, he intervened to help Jones and Levinson obtain casino contracts with the Intercontinental international hotel system (before Castro, when Jones and Levinson, both associates of Meyer Lansky, had the casino in the Havana Hilton)."[884]

The next level in the "triangle of influence" led by Johnson, vicariously through Baker, included Clint Murchison, James Hoffa, Carlos Marcello, the Mafia godfather of New Orleans, and Johnson's longtime lobbyist friend Irving Davidson,[885] "a dapper Washington public relations man who did business with government officials in Israel and Latin America."[886] But that was only one of multiple direct ties Johnson had to Marcello, whose territory included Louisiana, Mississippi, Alabama, Arkansas, Tennessee, Oklahoma, and Texas. Another was directly through Jack Halfen of Houston, Johnson's original Texas connection to the Mafia, who began funneling campaign funds to Johnson in the 1940s. When Halfen was imprisoned for income tax fraud in 1954, he told US Marshal J. Neal Matthews that the mob had already given LBJ $500,000 in cash and campaign contributions just in the first five years of Johnson's career in the Senate.[887] Halfen had run a gambling syndicate in Houston and had conducted payoffs to the mob of $100,000 per week before his conviction. The finances flowing from illegal slot machine profits and bookies using the Marcello racing wire services throughout Texas were a major part of the foundation of Johnson's rise to the top of the political empire.[888]

Many other tentacles of these groups can be traced to other mobsters, including Sam Giancana (the Chicago syndicate), Santos Trafficante (Florida), Meyer Lansky, and Johnny Rosselli (Las Vegas and Los Angeles), who were among the few top crime figures never wiretapped or bugged by the FBI even as Robert Kennedy's Justice Department aggressively pursued mob figures throughout the rest of the United States.[889] The FBI's reticence had less to do with insufficient cause than it did with the mob's coercive power over the vulnerable director of the FBI, J. Edgar Hoover.

At the center of the Louisiana/Texas portion of the gossamer web of underground connections were some of the wealthiest of the oil billionaires, such as Clint Murchison, Sid Richardson, and H. L. Hunt, all of whom were connected at the highest levels directly back to Johnson and Hoover. Dallas Mafia boss Joseph Civello had paid off many policemen there and had long associations with Dallas County Sheriff Bill Decker and Jack Halfen.[890] Dallas restaurateur Joe Campisi eventually replaced Joseph Civello as the Mafia leader of Dallas; both Campisi and Civello were deputies of Carlos Marcello and were the heads of Dallas's Mafia family. As noted by John H. Davis, this was "a reality that J. Edgar Hoover tried to keep from the attention of the Warren Commission and which the commission itself suppressed by not mentioning it in its report or published exhibits."[891]

Farther down this Texas section of the web, working under the mafiosi chiefs noted above, were a number of men working the seamier sectors of the mob's underbelly. They were men who could be counted on for steady revenue streams and "special jobs"—for which one of them, Jack Ruby, would become infamous when the plan to kill the patsy on the scene went awry and Lee Harvey Oswald managed to escape from his post at the Texas School Book Depository. Ruby was called upon to fix that problem as only he could do because of his close ties with many of the police and the top officials of the department; he was also the proprietor of popular strip clubs, one of which was the Carousel, on Commerce Street in downtown Dallas, conveniently located across the street from the Adolphus Hotel.

Another of the local lieutenants was Jack Valenti, who had cofounded an advertising company in Houston and had ties to a mob-connected oil executive before moving to Washington to work as a top aide to the newly sworn-in President Johnson on November 22, 1963. According to an FBI investigation conducted shortly after Johnson's highest-level aide, Walter Jenkins, was arrested for sexual perversion charges, the accusation was telephoned in to the FBI from someone who accused Valenti of the same conduct. The FBI's file was replete with references to Valenti's ties to mafiosi from Houston and Las Vegas and indicated that both his father and father-in-law had their own long histories of run-ins, even both having been sent to prison for frauds dating back to 1937. A February 2009 Internet news article noted some of Valenti's own mob connections:

> [A] document in Valenti's file refers to this [unnamed] individual as a "top hoodlum and leading gambling figure of the Houston area," and says he had been "a friend of long standing" with Valenti. A document dated Dec. 20, 1963, states that the "top hoodlum" conducted "a lucrative bookmaking operation" and was "employed by [name redacted], who has also been investigated under the Anti-Racketeering Program. [Name redacted] is an extremely wealthy individual who heads [redacted] in Houston, which is a private oil producing company." [892]

A second article on this subject appeared in the *Washington Post* ten days later, adding further details on Valenti's storied past. This article stated that one of Valenti's Houston friends was a "top hoodlum and prominent gambler" and that FBI agents had evidence that this mobster underwrote the cost of Valenti's wedding and honeymoon at the Tropicana Hotel-Casino in Las Vegas. The article also noted a call from an unnamed individual who suggested the FBI investigate Valenti as a "sex pervert" based upon the fact that he was known to have swum nude in the White House pool with other males.[893] It is not clear whether the file also noted that this was done with the president's blessing and encouragement, and that he had done the same thing on numerous occasions, practically demanding that his guests partake in the fun, allegedly as a test of their manhood. According to an FBI memo dated Nov. 12, 1964, the FBI's investigation turned up evidence that Valenti had a reputation as a homosexual and that he had had an affair with a photographer for "a number of years." A week later, Hoover reported those findings to the president, and subsequently Johnson told DeLoach that Valenti was "all right." After further panicked calls between Johnson and DeLoach, it was decided to leave the matter with Valenti alone, but by then Johnson had received a request from Bill Moyers to have the FBI investigate two other administration employees who, according to Moyers's memo, were "suspected as having homosexual tendencies."

Other rumors (not published in these articles, possibly because they were too hot to handle) persisted about an alleged partnership between Carlos Marcello, Jack Valenti, and Jack Ruby in another lucrative sideline that they had purportedly developed, this one involving the production of pornographic films, but their specialty in this line was said to be well beyond the "Debbie Does Dallas" variety. The allegations—never proved in a court setting, possibly because of their ties to powerful politicians—involved underage girls.

Coincidentally, one of the girls allegedly involved in this purported enterprise was the same Glenda Grabow who positively identified Raul, whom she knew by his nickname, "Dago," in Houston, Texas, during 1962–63. She would later identify him by his full name, Raul Coelho. In 1962, she was fourteen years old. She met him at a service station on the corner of East Haven and College Boulevard as she walked back and forth to school. At that point, she said, he was about thirty years old, stood about five feet nine inches, and weighed about 155–160 pounds, having dark brown hair with a reddish tint. Glenda married a young man named Roy at age fifteen, and together they became friends with two other young men, one called Armando and another named Felix Torrino. Armando was "Dago's" cousin and both of them had immigrated to the United States in the early 1960s from Portugal.[894]

Raul had spent much time at the Alabama Theater, where he had become involved in the production of "Lolita" pornography films. He had been seen there with Carlos Marcello, as well as Jack Ruby and Jack Valenti. That enterprise was evidently set up by Marcello and run by Valenti and Ruby.[895] In a telephone call Ms. Grabow made to Raul (whom she had tracked down in Yonkers, New York) on April 20, 1995, she immediately knew she had found the right "Raul" when he called her "Olinda," the same name he had uniquely called her over thirty years previously. In their six-minute conversation (documented by her telephone bill, which Pepper included as Appendix E in his 2016 book), she even alluded to Valenti when she asked him, "Have you heard from Jack V—lately?"[896]

In an angry meltdown by Raul in the early 1970s, Ms. Grabow witnessed him react to a photo of Martin Luther King Jr. by shouting, "I killed that black son of a bitch once, and it looks like I'll have to do it again." Even more astounding was the fact that in the late 1970s Ms. Grabow had also gotten to know the Houston attorney Percy Foreman, who a decade earlier had inserted himself—just as James Earl Ray fired his first lawyer, Arthur Hanes—into the position of Ray's lead attorney. Foreman had developed his reputation as one of the nation's foremost mobster-lawyers by then.[897] He confided to Grabow that he had also personally known Raul "for some time" and that he had always known that Ray had been "set up" for Dr. King's murder but he had been selected as a "sacrifice" for the sake of American citizens. Foreman had taken a liking to Ms. Grabow, but she maintained her distance. Finally, he told her and her husband that if they did not leave Houston, "they would be dead within a year." They did leave, but shortly after that, as she was driving on an expressway, one of her wheels—of which it was determined that every lug nut had been loosened—fell off and she narrowly escaped being run over by a semitruck pulling a long trailer.[898]

In his otherwise stultifying book *Killing the Dream*, Gerald Posner—as part of his attempt to continue strengthening the long-discredited myths and to discredit Dr. Pepper's truthful revelations—took up Ms. Grabow's story. His first shot was particularly inane, about how he doubted that her use of Raul's nickname "Dago" meant that she had never known his real name, as if that was pertinent to whether her story was true or not.[899] But then he proceeded to reveal many other points he had taken from viewing a two-hour video of an interview with Ms. Grabow by a previous investigator for Dr. Pepper, Jack Saltman, which had included his naming Jack Valenti as being directly involved in the production of filmed child pornography (a point that Pepper had not made).

Furthermore, Posner stated that the video revealed many other facets of the Houston underworld of the early 1960s, including the assertion that Raul had routinely met with Jack Valenti, Jack Ruby, and Carlos Marcello and that Ruby had "molested her once in a car." From the statements made in Posner's book, it can be inferred that a number of underaged girls had been photographed nude, and that Valenti was working on the film production side of this Mafia sideline business while Ruby was working on the magazine side. Posner even quoted Raul: "He said he wanted to make a million dollars with Jack Valenti."[900]

Incredibly, Posner had opened up this arena, presenting to a much wider audience the possibility of a direct, solid connection between LBJ's special assistant Jack Valenti and Jack Ruby—the murderer of Lee Harvey Oswald— and Carlos Marcello, the Mafia don of New Orleans. Those ties implicitly connected the JFK assassination and the MLK Jr. assassination five years later, something that had never been done with substantive evidence before, yet it was done by the major denier of *both* of them. Dr. Pepper indicated[901] that he considered doing the same but decided against it because they were both overly complex enough; fortuitously, Posner stumbled into the middle of it and unwittingly made the point for posterity.

Posner's strongest refutation of all of this was that it was impossible because the real Raul could not have done all of this traveling because he was working in his car factory job at the times he was supposedly seen in Texas.[902] Short of a lengthy discourse about CIA methods for setting up these kinds of operations, suffice to say that Dr. Pepper has presented compelling evidence that this "Raul" was indeed the same man whom Ray and several other persons positively identified and affirmed as being a photographic match, strengthened by Grabow's statements regarding their 1995 telephone conversation. Furthermore, to the question of his factory worker duties, it perhaps never occurred to Posner that those records might have been fudged; they would have probably been among the least difficult records ever modified in the history of covert operations. For Posner to leave that as his last word is particularly unconvincing.

Yet he still ignores the far more curious point raised by Pepper: why would the US government—as Pepper proved they had done—provide extended protective services to a "retired automobile plant worker," to personally visit him and his family multiple times in their home, giving them legal advice and counseling them on how to respond to inquiries, while monitoring their telephones on their behalf?[903]

Posner also stated that "It was impossible for Grabow to have seen Valenti in Houston during *most of the time* she claimed, since he was living and working in Washington, DC, in a high-profile job in the Johnson administration." (Italics added.) What he failed to note was that Valenti did not go to Washington until he flew there with the Johnson party on November 22, 1963. That left the entirety of 1962 and previous years and the first eleven months of 1963. Moreover, he could have continued running that side operation remotely, even after that. It was during this 1961–63 period of time that Ms. Grabow was still under age; the fact that they continued their relationship for over a decade later is not germane to that point. Valenti was obviously not the chief cameraman, or the technician processing the film, or supervising the shipping department; there was no reason he had to be part of the production crew, as his role was apparently that of a part-time manager, and evidently a part-owner of the enterprise under the wing of mafioso-capo Carlos Marcello.

It was a rather banal effort on Posner's part, as he attempted to deny the plausibility of such sordid connections while simultaneously revealing even more of the dirty details of this piece of the Marcello-Ruby-Valenti-Foreman-Johnson-Raul-Ray associations. This despite providing significant evidence to support—and failing to produce substantive evidence to rebut—Pepper's case.

But there was one other curious assertion by Posner (assuming he actually did converse with Valenti about the matter—unlike others with whom he claimed to have talked, but which they denied). According to Posner, when he presented this material to Jack Valenti, he was "flabbergasted to hear about the accusations" and denied all of it. "It's just pure fantasy, completely and utterly false. It's either malicious or the product of someone who is disturbed."[904] Of course he denied it: who in their right mind would concede something like this just because some erstwhile author wanted to get his response?

Regarding Valenti's point about the involvement of someone "disturbed": while there is no proof of it for obvious reasons, one possible candidate for that "disturbed" description—the person who might have been the most likely culprit for the entire operation, not just this dirty little slice of it—might have been the president himself. That Lyndon Johnson liked this particular kind of entertainment was well known, and reports have become available that suggest that he might have had a special way of viewing this kind of shameless child pornography. It would have been while sailing down the Potomac, alone on the presidential yacht *Sequoia*, just him and the crew who operated the boat, even though it would have only been the crew that might have enjoyed the nighttime aquatic sightseeing.

Just such a secretive account of Johnson's multiple instances of this kind of "entertainment" was reported in an article by Patrick Gavin, in a November 2010 post on *Politico*: "Lyndon Johnson would put a film projector on this table and come up here and watch certain risqué movies . . . reportedly in a robe and in his underwear so he was relaxed and alone, and they would sail to Mount Vernon." A video of the present owner of the *Sequoia* giving a minitour of the boat and making this same point is available, at the time of this writing, on YouTube.[905] Johnson's secretiveness about it (how the article noted that he watched it alone, not with a few friends) might be explained if the film involved very young girls—i.e., child porn—as the Marcello-Valenti-Ruby productions were stated to be.

Traces of Official Government Malfeasance: The Existential Patterns from Then and There to Here and Now

Long before Martin Luther King's assassination, the plotting to conduct the murder and cover-up began. One of the early tasks on that timeline was anchored to the creation of the faux legend of James Earl Ray, as the purported "stalker" of Dr. King.

But as we have seen, the stalker-legend of James Earl Ray fails on a number of points, starting with the reality we have exposed in the previous chapters, that there was never a factual basis for the assertion:

- Ray was never a violent southern racist. That was a lie which was fabricated out of whole cloth by a series of fiction writers—he was neither southern nor racist nor violent, as attested to by numerous early researchers including Harold Weisberg, Mark Lane, Dr. William Pepper, and the family of Dr. King including his son Dexter King, Reverend Lawson, and others.
- Ray was never a demented stalker. This was an elaborately spun deceit invented originally by William Bradford Huie and repeated by a half-dozen other later fiction authors, each adding more lies to the original set created by Huie, as we have demonstrated in earlier chapters.
- Ray had never indicated a hatred of Martin Luther King: another lie also promulgated by the early fiction writers.
- Ray had never expressed an interest in the hobby of shooting rifles, especially of ever making any efforts whatsoever to become a skilled sharpshooter. Indeed, as the salesman who sold the GameMaster to Ray on March 30 (less than a week before the murder in Memphis) told HSCA investigators, Ray didn't really know anything about firearms, "I mean nothing."
- The entire Ray legend is based on the premise that this man— with no rifleman skills—took a new rifle with its misaligned scope, loaded it with only one bullet, and then fired it from an awkwardly difficult position at the end of a bathtub sideways out the window and hit Dr. King: All of it is absurdly implausible, if not impossible.
- Finally, the keystone to the cover-up has also been revealed: all evidence of the existence of Ray's handler, Raul, was either summarily dismissed or aggressively ignored, and/or evidence was fabricated and introduced to replace Ray's own assertions.

Specifically, regarding the keystone issue of the provenance of these deceits, we have exposed the following cracks in a figurative wall designed by high-level FBI officials and constructed by the three earliest fiction writers and adopted in large part by the HSCA investigation. The biggest illustration of how the diabolical story line was created through the deceits planted by the FBI's handpicked fiction writer, William Bradford Huie, was the fact that all subsequent investigations of the crime were largely based upon his articles and book, as proven by the numerous references to his "findings" throughout all of it, including the HSCA report, which accepted as fact that Ray's "stalking" of King began in Los Angeles on March 16. As we have demonstrated, Ray left town the next day and was never in the same city as King again until the day of King's assassination, and even then he was oblivious to King's presence there.

- The tendentiously directed authors, and the FBI and HSCA investigators, went to incredible lengths to ignore the mayor and police officials and the bank president of the Alton, Illinois, bank, who repeatedly explained that neither James, Jerry, nor John Ray had anything to do with the robbery of that bank.
- It was the arrogance of the FBI and HSCA investigators—with their federal credentials—that led them to decide that they could summarily dismiss these yokels and ignore the realities, to continue the pursuit of a dead end while rejecting Ray's claims. They had no other basis to explain the source for James's extensive travels and purchases and they were desperate. It is arguably the most obvious crack in the stone wall upon which they built their case.
- True investigators would have made a more aggressive attempt to track the leads left by Raul, to determine his identity and pursue him vigorously. They could have started by tracking the telephone numbers furnished by Ray[906] to at least verify—or reject, if they were proven to be fictitious—his identity, the locations of his other telephone callers and/or recipients, and related information pertaining to those findings. Yet they did not do this, as proven by the complete lack of any evidence to the contrary.
- Another related enigma—specific failures to pursue potential leads that might have traced back to Raul—was the numerous unidentified fingerprints that could not be matched to Ray or other known persons. That was the case with various documents and letters, the items found in the green bundle dropped in front of Canipe's store, the Mustang, and the furnishings, door handles, and door and window frames within the five main rooming houses or apartment locations where Ray had stayed. For a single example, the day after the assassination, several more prints were lifted in room 5-B and the bathroom of Bessie Brewer's

rooming house, including two from the dresser. Only one of the dresser prints matched a Memphis police officer, and the other one was never identified. The failure to try to resolve this—and the numerous other similar unidentified prints—would tend to corroborate Ray's story, by virtue of the fact that they could not absolutely rule out Raul's presence, despite having come to that very conclusion.[907]

- The investigators could have tracked down more people who had interactions with both Ray and Raul: the owners, bar managers, and customers at the various establishments where the two had allegedly met, starting with the Neptune Bar in Montreal and various others in Birmingham, New Orleans, and Atlanta. That might have led them to some of the witnesses eventually identified by Dr. William Pepper, including Glenda Grabow and Sid Carthew. There is no indication in the available documents that this was ever attempted.[908]
- Failing that, at least in later years—i.e., after Don Wilson came onto the scene—instead of summarily dismissing his evidence in their zeal to maintain the long-discredited official story, they might have consulted with Pepper, who actually managed to track down Raul, practically singlehandedly, though many years after the fact and having to act without subpoena or arresting powers.[909]

Unfortunately, none of the investigators—neither the original FBI nor the subsequent DOJ task force in 1976–77, the HSCA personnel in 1977–78, nor the Justice Department investigators again in 1999–2000—were ever interested in finding Raul, for reasons outlined in the previous chapters. The wall built by the early authors—like figurative masons placing mortared bricks, setting each of them to secure a strong and solid wall meant to endure for decades, even centuries—was doomed to fail from the start. It was because the stonewall they built—and added to at each of these points, with vivid imagery, eloquent phrases, but hollow words—was weakened by a foundation of lies and deceits. It was figuratively a wall built on quicksand and has long since become fractured and cracked, and is now a crumbling pile of debris, yet still maintained by government decree.

The Stonewall of Myth Crumbles: A Pathological Report

Within these pages, we have attempted to complete the stonewall's deconstruction, allowing people interested in finding the truth to conduct a pathological examination of its remains. Now, as we put all of it under a microscope, one fact becomes immediately obvious: a concerted effort was made to portray James Earl Ray as an expert sharpshooter and diabolical, cunning stalker by those writing the script, even going to great lengths to create new or rewrite old documents and fabricate imaginary dots to connect to their tale, dots that had never been there to being with.

Multiple writers were drafted and assigned to make the case stick, put there by the FBI immediately afterward: Huie, Frank, and McMillan were all clearly assigned to that task from the start, as demonstrated by their own memoranda, guided by DeLoach, Belmont, and Sullivan. An examination of the background of each of these writers—especially the first of them, Huie—will help set the context for these assertions:

- In 1950, William Bradford Huie had become the chief editor of the formerly great literary magazine *American Mercury,* founded by H. L. Mencken. In its golden age, it published essays by such writers as Clarence Darrow, W. E. B. DuBois, William Faulkner, F. Scott Fitzgerald, Langston Hughes, Sinclair Lewis, Eugene O'Neill, Carl Sandburg, and William Saroyan.[910]
- Huie managed to turn the publication from an iconic literary jewel to a FBI/CIA rag.[911] During Huie's time there, the magazine went into a sharp decline, undoubtedly a result at least partly caused by his choice of writers, one of whom was J. Edgar Hoover (though he was known to assign such tasks to a ghostwriter from his "SOG" staff).
- By 1955, Huie was forced out of his position and the magazine was driven further into the ground, subsequently becoming a chronicle of racism and anti-Semitism before finally being buried for good. He would write two novels, *The Revolt of Mamie Stover* and *The Americanization of Emily* in the 1950s, both about how certain people had profited from the war. Both would later be made into movies.
- Huie's 1955–56 stories of the Emmett Till murder came along just in time for him to restart a career based on his creative writing skills and "checkbook journalism" methods, previously described by other authors as "appalling" and even acknowledged by Huie as having been "distasteful."
- According to Lyndon Barsten, Huie and Hoover had known each other since the 1930s, well before they began collaborating on the *American Mercury* articles in the early 1950s.[912] Regardless of

precisely how and when their association began, there is abundant evidence that it existed a decade or two before 1968. Hoover was very much aware of Huie's reputation as a checkbook journalist and took care to write negative comments about that on FBI files, even entire memoranda to various others on his staff, to get the official take on file, if for any reason their relationship might come to light in future years.

- Huie's close associations with his friends at the highest levels of the FBI were strengthened during this period as he wrote other magazine articles and books requiring information from FBI files. His long-term relationships led to Huie's selection by Hoover and Tolson to be the first of the major authors to set the parameters for the faux portrayal of James Earl Ray as a vicious southern racist and stalker of Dr. King.

- Huie's lengthy associations with both the FBI and the CIA left little doubt where, when, and why the source of his initiative to destroy James Earl Ray had originated. It is the absence of any plausible and realistic self-interest in doing what he did that is the biggest proof of the origin of his goal, clearly revealed by the result. It is the fact of his aggressive pursuit of his own "client" with clearly fabricated evidence designed to mislead an entire population—contrary to what should have been his natural interest, one of supporting Ray's story as he had promised to do—that becomes the most compelling proof of his framing of Ray for King's murder.

- The beleaguered Ray would gladly walk into this trap, with the promise of a famed attorney to be paid, in exchange for his life story, which, he erroneously presumed, would only be written after the attorney had secured his freedom.

- The reason Ray finally sacked his first attorney and attempted to end Huie's access to information about the defense case was that he realized, too late, that Hanes was feeding Huie privileged information and both of them were passing it on to the FBI. But that wasn't the worst of it, as Huie himself revealed publicly in his November 1968 *Look* magazine articles, which were written months before Ray's sabotaged "trial." They were clearly written to prejudice readers—ergo, the jury—against his client, ensuring a guilty verdict, presuming that he had ever gotten to trial.

- Eight years after the fact, in 1976, Huie proved again that he was still acting on behalf of handlers when he came forward with offers to Jerry Ray that he would pay him and James $220,000 if only they would agree to a clear confession of his guilt in the murder, by writing an article, with Huie, titled "Why and How I Killed Dr. King." Clearly, someone was desperate that the case be closed forever, and a fee like that was dangled to them for that purpose.[913] Curiously, this effort came just before the HSCA investigation commenced, and so it was the most likely catalyst.

The second author selected by the FBI, Gerold Frank, was also specifically selected for that role. In the prologue of this book, a memorandum was referenced, from Cartha DeLoach to Clyde Tolson on March 11, 1969—two days after Ray's fake "trial"—recommending that the Bureau "choose a friendly, capable author" to write a "carefully written 'factual' book" in order to ensure the "true history" of the case, evidently to repeat and strengthen what Huie had already begun in 1968. In an addendum the following day, DeLoach specifically recommended Gerold Frank, who had recently written *The Boston Strangler* and had asked for the "Bureau's cooperation in the preparation of the book on a number of occasions." It was the truth-seeking author Dr. Philip H. Melanson who was the earliest to prove that the FBI was instrumental in arranging for the succession of servile scribes assigned the task of writing the official history of King's assassination according to the themes it stipulated.[914]

Before the third FBI-approved author, George McMillan, even started writing his 1976 book, he told Jeremiah O'Leary (one of the Bureau's highest-level mouthpieces) of the *Washington Star*, back in 1969, that his book would merely focus on James Earl Ray's life story, as though his role in the MLK assassination had been proven beyond a shadow of a doubt, and the official story was the final word and needed no further investigation; his task was to support the narrative through piling on about Ray's allegedly loathsome family history.[915] Moreover, in the same year, McMillan even told the *New York Times* that "I have always believed James Earl Ray did it alone. And I have never investigated any aspects of a conspiracy, which has left me free to work on his biography."[916]

By making the presumption of Ray's guilt from the start, McMillan accepted without question the government's case and proceeded to examine Ray's psyche, going to great lengths—despite having no credentials to do so—to psychoanalyze his subject without ever having talked to him. He did this through some conversations with Ray's brother Jerry, although many of his statements that purportedly came from Jerry were vehemently denied by him.[917] Jerry's explanation for agreeing to talk to McMillan was that he knew that George was a big spender with a large expense account. In order to keep the money flowing, Jerry played him by feeding him disinformation but never said anything that would have incriminated James.[918] As noted elsewhere, McMillan had his own extensive connections to the CIA, as did his wife Priscilla, who had even greater connections and whom he credited within the book, saying it could not have been done without her assistance.[919]

We may logically extend that premise one additional step and further presume that the mission of all of the authors named above who contributed to the creation or sustenance of that mythical legend was to effectively replace truthful facts with whole lies and half-truths. It can therefore be reasonably concluded that they—and the later authors who carried the same baton— were following instructions from someone in a position to do so, given that there is nothing to suggest that any of them had some other axe to grind against Ray. Not only is it logically traceable to the FBI (and its partners, the CIA and the 902nd MIG), it would be illogical to attempt to suggest such a motive within any other entity or person. As demonstrated elsewhere, the FBI had been writing the entire script behind the scenes throughout the lead-up—beginning in 1957, to the execution in 1968, and then the cover-up as well—ergo, the result was inevitable.

The evidence presented shows that the preassassination conspiracy had gone on for ten years, although only in an conceptual, embryotic stage for the first half of that period.. It also proves that the postassassination cover-up was clearly still in place ten years after the fact, during the HSCA proceeding, and again in the DOJ report of 2000; it clearly continues today by virtue of the still-standing previously documented shams and the directed official indifference to ever getting to the truth. The cover-ups by elaborate and officious documents were created through use of the same techniques as previously done by the original fiction writers: selective preference, omission of exculpatory evidence, ignoring credible witnesses, and creation of unsubstantiated alternate theorems (all misdirected theories, of course), all of which have been thoroughly proven in this book.

Lyndon Johnson's "Worst Nightmare"

From the moment he became president on November 22, 1963, on the tarmac at Love Field in Dallas, Lyndon Johnson lived in fear of the possibility that either Robert or Edward Kennedy might ever become president. This point was made by William Sullivan, who served as an assistant FBI director for a decade, 1961–1971, in his memoirs. Johnson felt particularly threatened by Bobby and was so afraid of the possibility of a groundswell of support for RFK's nomination as vice president at the 1964 Democratic Convention in Atlantic City that he went to lengthy manipulative efforts to prevent any chance of that.[920]

Johnson made sure that Bobby's appearance there would be the last day of the convention, well after the selection of the vice presidential nominee. He also arranged for a special surveillance team of FBI agents headed by DeLoach to accompany him there, to be on call to assist Johnson in whatever way he asked, and to spy on any delegate who was not on the "All the Way with LBJ" bandwagon. The FBI infiltrated the convention with agents posing as news reporters and with the cooperation of the management of NBC News; Assistant Director DeLoach reported, "Our agents were furnished press credentials."[921] This was among the many misuses of FBI, Secret Service, CIA, military, and other government personnel routinely exploited by Johnson for his personal accommodation. Such misuses were simply accepted and not even reported to anyone, and even if they were, they were whispered, such that they were likewise never mentioned in the press.

By the end of 1967, Lyndon Johnson's presidency—emanating from his cabinet members and department heads—had become as dysfunctional as the president himself, struggling to maintain a semblance of purpose. As many of the holdovers from JFK's administration had already done, some of Johnson's own aides had left, including his topmost assistant, Bill Moyers. The latest, highest-profile cabinet official, Secretary of Defense Robert McNamara, had either been fired or voluntarily resigned (no one, including him, seemed to know which). But in McNamara's case at least, it was undoubtedly a mutually agreed-upon decision, both he and Johnson seemingly disgusted with the other, as evidenced by McNamara's eventual attempt to blame the whole sorry mess of Vietnam on what he called the "Fog of War," which caused him and the president to make so many bad decisions. Bad decisions and vague excuses for all of them seemed to become the repeated meme.

Much of the disillusionment was due to the growing public anger over the lives of so many young men lost in an unnecessary, unwinnable, completely futile war in Vietnam that had nothing whatsoever to do with national security. It was merely one cause of Johnson's growing credibility gap, which was the only thing in ascendancy at that point. In February, a new play called *MacBird!* opened in New York City that compared the president to the murderous Shakespearean character Macbeth; by the middle of March 1968, his national approval rating had sunk to 36 percent and support for his handling of Vietnam sank to 26 percent. That is roughly the percentage of people who would support anything a president might do, for people who still valued the banal show of patriotism in the face of the dirtiest of deeds being committed. In a closed-door meeting of Senate Democrats, Missouri Senator Stuart Symington laid it on the line when he said: "Lyndon Johnson could not be elected dogcatcher."[922]

In September 1967, *Newsweek* magazine (which had until then been among Johnson's strongest supporters) reported that "He is the first President in U.S. history to be beset simultaneously with a major war abroad and a major rebellion at home—neither of them going well or holding forth any promise of the kind of sudden and dramatic improvement that alone could reverse the rising tide of anger, frustration and bitterness that is cresting around the White House. He is also a President whose own personality has become an issue in itself—an issue, indeed, that seems increasingly to be producing almost as much criticism and contention as the war in Vietnam and the tumult in the ghettos."[923]

Some of Johnson's staff had reported that he had begun to talk about dropping out of the 1968 election, including his top aide Marvin Watson (who had filled the vacant Moyers position), who said LBJ had privately told him that in January 1968. It was at this point that the Vietcong initiated the Tet Offensive, a surprise attack launched simultaneously throughout South Vietnam, setting off bombs and attacking even the "invulnerable" American embassy in Saigon. It was a huge operation that shook even the most strident supporters in the US, who finally came to realize that the president had led them down the primrose path. Finally, the majority of Americans began to understand President Johnson had brazenly lied to them about the light at the end of the tunnel and the enemy body counts.

That was also the impetus for Robert Kennedy to reevaluate his position against running for president that year. On March 12, Minnesota Senator Eugene McCarthy won 40 percent of the votes in the New Hampshire primary, nearly beating the incumbent president. Two weeks after RFK announced his candidacy for the presidency, President Johnson announced his departure from the reelection campaign. Johnson made his stunning announcement on March 31, 1968, after mouthing a series of sentences that were organized into mind-numbing paragraphs with a few bulleted lists randomly included. His speechwriters must have found it frustrating to create speeches having any trace of soaring rhetoric that were consonant with his drawling Texas dialect, absent the usual corny colloquialisms he preferred. His talk went on for over 4,000 words before he finally came to the best twenty-one-word sentence he had ever uttered:

"Accordingly, I shall not seek, and I will not accept, the nomination of my party for another term as your President."

Parties immediately broke out all over the nation, especially in bars in college towns and cities across the country. There has arguably never been such a spontaneous, decentralized, and widespread celebration, before or since. People of all political stripes, young and old, were literally dancing in the streets, according to the president himself.

Nexus: The 1968 Springtime Assassinations

Like most people who were startled by Johnson's unexpected announcement, as noted in this chapter's epigraph, to Dr. Pepper it was something he had "long regarded as unrelated to the events of this story." His clear implication may be interpreted to mean that it is no longer his current attitude. And that suggests he believes that there is a connection between Johnson's action on March 31 to the assassination of Dr. King four days later, and of Robert Kennedy two months after that. If so, he is not alone in that point of view.

For a man so obsessed with winning his first term in the Oval Office to then sacrifice his presidential powers without a fight meant that he had undergone a powerful transformation. That he voluntarily gave up the office for which he had lusted over his entire lifetime could only mean that he had to surrender it in order to accomplish even greater objectives. His primary concern at that point would have undoubtedly been to ensure that his tenure as president would be enshrined forever in a legacy befitting one of the "greatest presidents of all time." Only a position in the same tier as George Washington, Abraham Lincoln, and Franklin D. Roosevelt in the pantheon of US presidents would be adequate for him, at least in his own mind.

But to accomplish that, he would have to ensure that no one then alive and in a powerful position to succeed him—anyone who might wish to destroy the myth of his "greatness"—would ever be allowed to follow him into the White House. Robert F. Kennedy and Martin Luther King Jr. were the men he feared the most, because he knew that they knew the truth about those myths.

When he made his announcement, he must have feared defeat two days later in the next primary election, April 2 in Wisconsin. The nightly news shows had reported that the entire state had been covered by the energized band of "McCarthy kids," and the entire country eagerly awaited the results of that contest. Robert Kennedy's groundswell of support was already beginning to displace McCarthy's lead there, and he was expected to quickly become the leading candidate in the remaining contests and probably head into the summer convention as the foregone winner. This eventuality was precisely what Lyndon Johnson had long dreaded: "[T]he thing I feared from the first day of my Presidency was actually coming true, Robert Kennedy had openly announced his intention to reclaim the throne in the memory of his brother. And the American people, swayed by the magic of the name, were dancing in the streets."[924]

RFK's Assassination and the Mysterious Delay in the FBI's Long-Awaited Announcement of the Capture of James Earl Ray

After the disastrous Tet Offensive in February 1968, Americans began losing whatever confidence they still had in President Johnson's performance overall (about 35 percent), and specifically regarding his Vietnam War policies (now about 23 percent). Six months before the convention, many antiwar activists had become involved in the nascent campaigns of war opponents Senator Eugene McCarthy (D-MN) and Senator Robert Kennedy (D-NY), and extensive planning had already begun for protest demonstrations in Chicago. More than 100 antiwar groups planned to attend, led by the Youth International Party (known as the YIPPIES), which had a goal of bringing 100,000 young people to Chicago for the occasion. They applied for a permit, but the city, as dictated by its dictator mayor, Richard J. Daley, rejected it. But that didn't stop them from coming.

By the following month, Johnson had come to the realization that he had lost virtually all the political capital he had begun his presidency with and must have also known that he risked losing the backing of his own party, never mind the entire country, in the November election. Both of those prospects were unthinkable to him, especially the notion of losing it to Robert Kennedy. In addition to the politico talk of a Benjamin Spock/Martin Luther King presidential ticket from the year before, now there were even rumors and rumblings—should RFK win the nomination—of a combined ticket of Robert F. Kennedy and Martin Luther King; while that might have been unlikely in 1968, the prospect of either of them ever becoming president would have sent chills up LBJ's back as the worst possible scenario that could ever occur. It would have certainly meant the destruction of his own future and that of the legacy he had planned for so long.

Four days after Johnson's announcement, Martin Luther King Jr. was murdered in Memphis. Two months after that, not coincidentally, the man Johnson had most feared might become president—Robert F. Kennedy—was also assassinated. Shortly after midnight on June 5, 1968, just after he celebrated winning the California primary, he was shot in Los Angeles. He did not die immediately—he held onto his life by a very small thread all that day and into the next until he finally died.

All across the nation on June 5, most people of goodwill grieved and prayed for him to survive. But all day long as RFK lay in the hospital, President Johnson fretted, not about whether he would live, but when he would die. The *New York Times* would later report that "Johnson repeatedly phoned the Secret Service to ask if Kennedy had died. He paced the floor for hours, phone in hand, muttering: 'I've got to know. Is he dead? Is he dead yet?'"[925] Joseph Califano wrote in his memoirs that Johnson himself made several calls to the Secret Service to ask them to check on whether Bobby was dead yet and asked Califano to call Larry Levinson, another aide, to do the same.[926] Califano was even more candid with Robert Caro, who substantively added to that colloquy by stating that Califano and Levinson, following the president's orders, repeatedly made such calls, prompting Levinson to ask, in exasperation, "Joe, is this something that he's wishing to have happen? Why is he asking it that way?"[927] This is another of many examples of how people who worked closely with Johnson were very imperceptive about some of the president's most odious character traits, at least until they were exposed to lengthy, pounding repetitions of such behaviors.

The recorded official history of the capture of James Earl Ray is that he was arrested just moments before Robert Kennedy's funeral mass, on June 8, 1968. At least two books have claimed otherwise, one by a former FBI official whose reputation for honesty is not beyond reproach. William C. Sullivan's 1979 memoir (published two years after his own suspicious death—being shot by a hunter who had purportedly mistaken him for a deer) stated: "Ray was in custody in London for two days before Hoover released the story to the press. He waited until the day of Bobby Kennedy's funeral to break the news so that the FBI could steal the headline from Kennedy one last time."[928] Curt Gentry's biography of J. Edgar Hoover indicated that "DeLoach had told one of the Bureau's favored journalists about the arrest the evening before."[929] According to a 395-page FBI file on the King assassination that was mysteriously included in the tranche of JFK assassination files released on October 26, 2017, Ray was arrested on June 8 at 11:15 a.m. in London (6:15 a.m. in New York).[930] The official records, however, appear to have been "fudged" if one accepts what James Earl Ray wrote in an affidavit just before the hearing with Judge Battle, that he was arrested on June 6 and held "incommunicado" for four days.*

---

* James Earl Ray's Affidavit, 26 March 1969:"On or about the 6th day of June 1968 I was arrested at the Heathrow airport, London England, Subsequently I was charged with homicide in the United States and ordered held for immigration hearing. After being held incommunicado for approximately 4 days I was taken before an English magistrate and ordered held for an extradition hearing.... After I was returned to Memphis Tenn and confined in the Shelby County Jail, I was denied access to legal counsel, or sleep, until I submitted to palm prints."

It was after Robert Kennedy's body had lain in state on June 7 and 8 in St. Patrick's Cathedral in New York City that the news broke, just as the coffin was being carried down the steps of the Cathedral. Suddenly, an FBI agent broke through the line of honorary pallbearers just behind the coffin and took the arm of the attorney general, Ramsey Clark, telling him that Deke DeLoach needed to talk to him: "It's urgent that you call him immediately!"[931] Clark left the funeral and called DeLoach, who told him that James Earl Ray had been arrested in London. Furthermore, he stated that Scotland Yard had refused to delay the announcement for the funeral service. The announcement on radio and television immediately redirected the country's attention away from Robert Kennedy's assassination (including all of the still-developing cover-up story related to Sirhan, adding more confusion to that case) and back toward the hot news flash coming from England that the other patsy had finally been caught.

Ramsey Clark apparently found out for himself that there was a discrepancy in the timing of the news stories shortly afterward, because he decided that the story he had gotten from DeLoach was a lie. Clark was correct about the "discrepancy" though he did not understand it, and neither did anyone else until—after the first edition of this book was published—I discovered the affidavit of James Earl Ray described in the above footnote. Sullivan was correct about the arrest coming two days earlier than reported, but he blamed it on Hoover "so that the FBI could steal the headline from Kennedy one last time." I believe that it was Johnson's idea, because he famously liked to set up such charades, and the purpose was to take the public's attention away from Robert Kennedy's funeral just as his body was removed from the church. Clark was furious at the way DeLoach had set him up, obviously unaware that "Deke" was merely acting as the messenger from the President, famously skilled in the art of deception.[932] After that incident, Clark refused to ever use DeLoach again in the remaining six months of his term.[933] That incident, and Ramsey Clark's fury, might have led to a comment that Johnson made to writer Leo Janos, which reflected Johnson's disappointment with Clark's failure to become a team player: "Disgust tinged Johnson's voice as the conversation came to an end. 'I thought I had appointed Tom Clark's son—I was wrong.'"[934]

A friend of RFK's, Paul Schrade, who was with Kennedy when he was shot—and was himself shot by Sirhan B. Sirhan—never believed that Kennedy was shot by the accused assassin. Schrade believes that Sirhan was set up in a very sophisticated conspiracy to eliminate Robert Kennedy. On the occasion of a February 2016 parole hearing for Sirhan, Schrade stated that "a second unidentified shooter killed Kennedy."[935] This revealing article stated:

The AP noted that "Schrade's voice cracked with emotion during an hour of testimony on his efforts to untangle mysteries about the events of June 5, 1968." The 91-year-old Schrade, a Kennedy family friend, was working as the labor chairman of the senator's presidential campaign in 1968. He was walking behind Kennedy when the Democratic candidate was shot four times. In part because Kennedy was struck from behind, Schrade has long advanced the argument that Sirhan fired shots that night — but not the ones that killed Kennedy. The fatal bullets, Schrade argued, were fired from a different shooter's gun.

After the Assassinations, Johnson Attempts to Restart His Campaign

In yet another startling development, according to LBJ biographer Robert Dallek, shortly after the assassinations of Martin Luther King Jr. and Robert F. Kennedy, Lyndon Johnson acted to put himself back into the race. Soon after RFK's assassination on June 5, at a time when Nixon was leading Humphrey in the polls, Johnson began putting feelers out about the possibility that he could reenter the race, not as a last-minute campaign, but to make it known that he would certainly accept being "drafted" during the convention, as a sort of "knight on a white horse" candidate, purporting to be the only one who could recapture the White House. That led several top aides within his administration, and various party leaders, to state that if his latest "peace efforts" showed promise quickly enough, he might have a chance to save the presidency for the Democrats after all. Dallek wrote that weeks before the 1968 Democratic National Convention was scheduled to begin, "Humphrey wanted to give a speech in which he put some daylight between himself and Johnson on Vietnam. He hoped to convince 'the large number of antiwar voters that he would somehow be more ready to compromise on Vietnam than the President.'" [936] But when Humphrey let Johnson preview the speech, Johnson was angered because he felt Humphrey had betrayed him by casting doubt on the wisdom of Johnson's venture in the first place.

Then Johnson met on July 26 with the presumptive Republican nominee, Richard Nixon, who urged Johnson not to give in to pressure from Humphrey to soften his Vietnam positions; in return, he would not publicly criticize Johnson's policies. Clark Clifford summed up Nixon's response as giving "us his support in return for inflexibility in our negotiating position, and thereby freeze poor Hubert out in the cold. Humphrey wants to change the policy, but the President won't let him say so." [937]

It was at this point, around the end of July and the early weeks of August 1968, that Johnson had come close to a decision to throw his big Stetson back into the ring, giving serious thought to actually attending the Democratic National Convention the end of the month. He planned to arrive there as a surprise guest, to the acclamation of the excited and ecstatically happy delegates, thankful to him for his personal sacrifices all for the sake of continued service to his country. He thought it would become a triumphant moment in his personal and presidential history. It was then that he put a number of aides and speech writers to work planning the "Draft Johnson" movement, similar to how he had meticulously planned many other "surprise" events over the course of his career.

Next, Johnson sent his high-level aides Harry McPherson and Larry Levinson to Hollywood to begin working on a film glorifying his life and extensive achievements, all of which led up to the magnificent program he had brought to the country, called the "Great Society." By maximizing the good things and playing them up for all they were worth while minimizing the fact that many of them were already being defunded in order to reallocate scarce funds to his war, Johnson felt that the country would finally come to its senses and better appreciate the value of having such a great and magnanimous president as he had been for yet another four years. He discussed all of this with Chicago's mayor, Richard Daley, who proclaimed his excitement: "That's what I'm for," Daley said. "I'm for a draft, and I'll start it if there is any chance he will do it." [938]

Johnson's longtime aides John Connally and Warren "Woodie" Woodward affirmed that "[Johnson] very much hoped he would be drafted by the convention," and, moreover, he even sent his de facto chief of staff at that time, Marvin Watson, to Chicago "to assess the possibility of that convention drafting LBJ . . . I want to get it on the record," Connally said, "that even though there had been a withdrawal, Marvin Watson was up there for the specific purpose of talking to delegates at Mr. Johnson's (direction)." [939] John Connally also stated that "I personally was asked to go to meet with the governors of the southern delegations, with Buford Ellington, Farris Bryant, and that group, to see if they would support President Johnson in a draft movement in 1968 . . . I believed it strongly enough that I went before all those southern governors and asked them if they would support Johnson in a draft, and they said, 'No way.'" [940]

The continuing evening news stories, meanwhile, suggested that the thousands of young people headed to Chicago would create violent clashes between themselves and the police, with the delegates caught in the middle. For that reason, there had been considerable pressure among many party leaders to have the convention be moved to Miami, the site where the Republican National Convention was scheduled to meet in early August, three weeks before the Democratic convention's schedule. That proposal had even been supported by Humphrey, but Chicago Mayor Richard J. Daley was adamantly opposed to it and promised that peace would be maintained. Moreover, he also promised that if it were moved, he would withhold support for the party's candidate, presumed to be Hubert Humphrey, the then-vice president. President Johnson, a good friend of and in mind-sync with Mayor Daley, was also against moving it and was rumored to have said, "Miami is not an American city."[941]

Johnson not only caused the convention to remain in Chicago despite the high risk perceived by practically everyone else, but he began—just as he had done four years earlier for the Atlantic City convention, and many other projects he deemed so critically important, like the Dallas motorcade in November 1963—micromanaging all arrangements, down to the requirement that Humphrey's son-in-law had to personally appear each morning in line for tickets to get into the convention center, for all members of the family. Johnson also rejected every one of Humphrey's recommendations for the entire program—the scheduling issues, the speakers, the content of the all-important platform— even for the lower-level officers to be appointed to manage the entire affair.[942] Afterward, he denied having taken over the entire operation, which only affirmed to many people—those not previously convinced—the entire premise of the "credibility gap" term that had been created by journalists to describe the intrinsic worthlessness of his words.[943]

Of course, history did not quite take that course, and instead of a triumphal presidential draft movement, the 1968 Democratic Convention is remembered, hands down, as the worst of all time. On August 28, over 10,000 student protesters gathered in Chicago's Grant Park. One man lowered the city-owned American flag, which caused several policemen to confront the man and, in the melee that followed, begin to beat him. The demonstrators reacted to that by throwing rocks and other objects at the police and hurling words and threats, as well. The scenes of police attacking the protesters with tear gas and mace, and the protesters yelling chants and throwing rocks, were all captured on live television and broadcast throughout the country. These scenes outside the convention center were intermixed with the news broadcasts showing the nominating speech for Senator George McGovern, which was being given by Connecticut senator Abraham Ribicoff.

Ribicoff made reference to the violence outside when he said that with "McGovern as president of the United States, we won't have Gestapo tactics in the streets," as was then being witnessed by people across the country on live television. Then the cameras showed Mayor Daley shouting at Senator Ribicoff and the senator screaming back to the mayor, "How hard is it to accept the truth?" Those images inflicted sustained damage to not only the city of Chicago because of the police behavior that was unleashed by Daley, but even more so to the Democratic Party, for decades afterward, arguably due entirely to the intransigence of President Johnson in not agreeing to move the convention to a less confrontational venue.

What was Really Behind Lyndon Johnson's Actions: Protection of His Legacy?

The question of what caused Lyndon Johnson to decide not to run for reelection—just four days before Martin Luther King Jr. was murdered, and two months before Robert F. Kennedy was assassinated—then almost immediately deciding to reverse his decision, is perplexing yet possibly quite explainable. The nub of the matter—LBJ's actions beginning March 31, 1968, and ending five months later on August 28, 1968—comes down to what changed during that period. The only substantive matters were related to those assassinations and the series of primary elections that had just begun, with his poor performance in the first primaries and signs of trouble brewing in the ones remaining. By the end of June, the primary season was over, his two most feared political enemies were dead, and in early July he had begun planning the resumption of his political career, only three months after having declared to the nation that he was unequivocally ending it.

What could possibly explain these seemingly unconnected, inexplicable events, all of which occurred in the months leading up to the 1968 Democratic National Convention, one of the most tumultuous and violent periods of American history? Was it mere coincidence, the result of a serendipitous changing of the president's enigmatic mind? Or was it the product of a deeper, hidden strategy, a plan that had been worked out well in advance as an attempt to accomplish higher-priority goals while removing the president from having to participate in the time-consuming primary elections that would surely take a toll on him personally? In the end, he would be able to then make a triumphant return just in the nick of time, which would ensure greater popularity, and would be ready to mount a strong campaign in the general election, one that would pit him against a man whose position on Vietnam would be no different than his own.

One of the most insightful and prolific bloggers of our age, David Martin, writing as "DC Dave" at his website of that name, offered the following explanation in an article titled "Did Lyndon Step Down So Bobby Could Be Killed?":

> But how would it have looked, no matter how hard the government and the press sold the notion that it was just the work of another lone, crazed gunman, for another Johnson rival for power to be removed by assassination? It might have been out of the question at the time for anyone to state publicly any suspicions about LBJ's guilt in the JFK murder, the reality was that it was in the back of almost everyone's mind. This latest outrage would have surely brought it to the front. Whether it was Johnson's decision or he was made an offer that he could not refuse by his handlers, he had to disavow any further interest in retention of power so that the serious threat that RFK represented could be removed. Put bluntly, for the November 22, 1963, coup to stick, keeping Bobby out—permanently—trumped keeping Lyndon in for another four years.[944]

As it happens, there were some people in the RFK camp who could already see which way the wind was blowing. The following quote is from *Sons and Brothers: The Life and Times of Jack and Bobby Kennedy* by Richard D. Mahoney:

> . . . some around Bobby began to talk openly about the inevitable. French novelist Romain Gary, then living in Los Angeles, told Pierre Salinger, "Your candidate is going to get killed." When Jimmy Breslin asked several reporters around a table whether they thought Bobby had the stuff to go all the way, John J. Lindsay replied, "Yes, of course, he has the stuff to go all the way, but he's not going to go all the way. The reason is that somebody is going to shoot him. I know it and you know it, just as sure as we're sitting here. He's out there waiting for him."

The only thing wrong with Lindsay's prediction, as it turned out, was that it was not a "he" but a "they," the official story notwithstanding.

In a pure, fair, and perfect world—where contrived myths could never be sustained, where they were always immediately discovered and replaced with truths, a world in which powerful logic, fairness, and sound reasoning would always automatically prevail—DC Dave's explanation would be axiomatic. Of course, in that world, such atrocities would never occur in the first place, but we digress.

At the Pinnacle of the Pyramid: Puppeteers Create Posterity

We have outlined how William Bradford Huie's mission was originally designed by the highest-level officials of the FBI, and how a number of subsequent authors have repeated the same themes, decade by decade, ever since. The original meme was clearly created for the very purpose of setting the stage for those future authors of books supporting the official myth. They could only have gotten their marching orders from other, even more powerful forces who undoubtedly signed off on Huie's selection as the first author; those powers, obviously, were higher in the hierarchy than the assistant directors of the FBI who carried them out. The orders could have only emanated from the head of the FBI, J. Edgar Hoover, and only with either the acquiescence or the active instigation of his longtime friend, neighbor, and cohort, President Lyndon B. Johnson.

The essential truths revealed throughout this book can be summarized thusly:

- We showed how the collaboration between President Lyndon B. Johnson and his decades-long friend and neighbor J. Edgar Hoover worked to achieve their mutual objectives—the series of three major assassinations of their sworn enemies—and began well before Johnson ascended to the presidency in 1963. It undoubtedly began as early as 1960, when Johnson enlisted Hoover's help in forcing John F. Kennedy to accept him as his vice presidential nominee, even after he had decided to put Senator Stuart Symington into that position.
- We noted how the plot to kill Dr. King was begun, exactly one month after the first objective was completed: JFK's assassination. Hoover called together some of the highest-ranking FBI officials, including several from the Atlanta, Birmingham, and Memphis field offices, on December 23, 1963, to discuss the various measures to be taken to neutralize Dr. Martin Luther King Jr. At that point the ultimately fatal measure was also initiated—though not openly discussed there—as proven by what happened next: reservations for first-class cabins on the SS *United States* were obviously secured

at about that point for a cruise that would begin only five months later. Clyde Tolson and Russell Adkins set off in May 1964 for a four-month ocean cruise to begin hammering out the most critical points of the agenda required for a plot to assassinate Dr. King.

- We explained how the much-vaunted collaboration of Johnson and King was actually a very temporary marriage of convenience to accomplish their only mutual goal that happened to coincide during 1964–65. As soon as Johnson decided to make Vietnam his last stand, that association was over. His comment about the "G—D— N—r Preacher" marked the complete destruction of that partnership. Hoover's own infamous comment, that King was "the most notorious liar in America," was uttered about the same time.

- We exposed how the direct connection between J. Edgar Hoover and William Bradford Huie, from at least the early 1950s—probably even well before that, according to one source—was established. Based upon their long-term symbiotic relationship, it can be reasonably inferred that getting Huie on board with the plan to frame James Earl Ray was not only begun before Dr. King's assassination, but that it was undoubtedly a major point of the original action plan developed by Tolson and Adkins on their 1964 ocean voyage. Aware of Huie's checkered reputation, Hoover went out of his way to write negative comments and memoranda into the FBI's files for the record.

- We also detailed how the later additions of at least two more fiction writers—Gerold Frank and George McMillan—followed: all were recruited to write their FBI-dictated accounts for the purpose of solidifying and expanding on Huie's original frame-up of Ray, with the knowledge that their fame would guarantee a wide audience, while the real story told by earnest researchers would never be taken by major publishers—warned away by the CIA's "Mockingbird"-inspired conspiracy-debunking (see Appendix D) program—ensuring their fable would win in the end. In Huie's case, with the release of three *Look* cover stories, starting even before Ray's phony trial, his conviction—in the public's mind, thus the jury's—would be assured before the legal process had even begun.

- We reviewed how the many other personal connections were used—which allowed orders to be conveyed without written records—to ensure the plot's success: beginning with Johnson and Hoover at the top, and from there to Tennessee governor Ellington; Hoover's companion and associate director Tolson to Russell Adkins, Frank Holloman, and Mayor Loeb, who were all keys to the creation of an invisible web that interconnected the politicians, the Tennessee justice system, and law enforcement apparatus; all the way down to the Missouri prison warden who was bribed, and the prisoner who enticed Ray to escape. That invisible network was extended further, through Johnson's linear connections to Yarborough at the Pentagon, thus the MIGs noted within, and to the CIA's Helms and Angleton, and thus vicariously to Angleton's RCMP counterpart, Leslie "Jim" Bennett.

- We disclosed how Johnson's 1967 creation of the CIA's Operation CHAOS, with its secret spying on approximately 7,500–10,000 American civilians, was facilitated by the purported "national security" crisis that was used for the ultimate justification: Dr. King being portrayed to all of these warrior/officials as a Communist dupe who was a danger to the continuation of the republic. Ultimately the plot was sold, to anyone who might have had misgivings, on the basis of it being the ultimate patriotic act they could perform for their beloved country.
- We examined the extreme lengths taken first by the FBI and then the HSCA investigators to ignore every single lead which they were presented that led back to the man named "Raoul." This despite Ray's consistent claim that "Raoul" existed, never wavering from his statements that he had been guided and financed by him. We saw how they were both connected—Ray and Raoul—to secret units of military intelligence and the CIA (in Ray's case, back to his army service in Germany), even the RCMP in Montreal, and in Raoul's case, directly to the FBI.
- Finally, we put the enduring cover-up under the microscope. We saw how the original initiative—well after the deaths of the original plotters, Johnson and Hoover—to establish the HSCA was subverted from the start. Moreover, how that could only have been done by the highest officials at Langley, and how they assured that congressional leadership—Henry Gonzales, a longtime Johnson crony, among others—would emasculate anyone who might get out of line. Thus, Gonzales himself finally resigned in order to ensure that Richard Sprague would be fired. The six-month leadership battle initiated at Langley ultimately

doomed the original mission—to aggressively reinvestigate both JFK's and MLK's assassinations—and reduced it to just more "re-evaluations" of the previous tainted whitewashes left by the FBI. The cover-up was extended and strengthened as recently as 2014, when the brick structure that once housed Bessie's roominghouse was completely gutted and rebuilt, raising the floor level by at least one foot, and moving the bathtub away from the wall by at least 10–12 inches, evidently to better present the scene as the perfect sniper's lair.

Ultimately, the multimillion-dollar product of the HSCA exercise was just a very lengthy essay filled with half-truths, whole lies, non sequiturs, abstractions, and circumlocutions put together by talented wordsmiths into manuscript form as designed by the professorial Robert Blakey. As William Shakespeare might have said about its actual value, "Much ado about nothing."

The cunningly created scenario designed by Hoover and Tolson, polished up and finished by Huie, had never even occurred to James Earl Ray until he heard the news on his car radio as he drove out of Memphis. As he listened to the radio, hearing news broadcasts about the alleged killer being a white man about his age and matching his description—a fugitive from justice, just like him—driving a white Mustang just like his, it hit him like a lightning bolt: he knew that he had been *had* by his handler "Raoul." He could not have imagined the level of enmity, contempt, and wrath he had created in the minds of his handlers and highest-level plotters when he left the crime scene fifteen minutes before the crime was committed; he was supposed to have been killed on the spot as he sat in the Mustang waiting for Raul, and now they would have to track him down and expend an enormous amount of time, energy, money, and political muscle to ensure that he was found, jailed, and given a perfunctory hearing sans civil rights that would ensure he would spend the rest of his life in prison. Having to invoke "Plan B" because of Ray's lack of discipline must have been very upsetting to a lot of people, some of the highest level officials in Washington, and now they had to react spontaneously to come up with a recovery strategy (which undoubtedly explains why there were so many inexplicable fumbles and delays in the FBI's response to the wayward patsy's actions).

But Ray was still not conscious of the fact that it had been a very elaborate, carefully planned scheme, involving many people, having its primary origins in Washington, DC. Even after three decades of imprisonment, when he eventually died, the notion that he had been the victim of an elaborate charade designed by the nation's top law enforcement agency had probably never occurred to him. He might have correctly concluded, from the inhumane nature of his imprisonment, that those conditions could have only been directed by the highest-level politicians of the state of Tennessee, the county of Shelby, and the city of Memphis. He certainly knew from the moment of his incarceration that he had become the designated patsy in one of the most outrageous of the 1960s assassinations, which may have given him a hint of the plot's origins.

Another of Johnson's sycophants, his attorney general, Ramsey Clark,[945] had a vocal malfunction in 1968 when he declared there was no conspiracy involved, even before the "investigation" was complete, not to mention the "trial." That pronouncement was at odds with the legal precepts used to extradite Ray from the United Kingdom, which was predicated on the basis of a conspiracy as a means to avoid any reference to what might be considered a political crime, a fact that would clearly impede an expedited legal process. Of course, Clark was speaking on behalf of President Johnson in pronouncing the accused guilty, and for that he has earned much sympathy.

Connecting Dots: A Summary from Dallas to Memphis

The efforts of LBJ's defenders, then as now, have served to hide Johnson's deceit and nefarious maneuvers, thus his most secret and criminal actions throughout his presidency. The time has come for those crimes and treasons to be brought out of the closets in which they have been hidden for five decades and exposed to the light of truth. The nation has been seriously harmed, and the public's right to know has been denied, for far too long. The public's trust in the federal government is at an all-time low as a direct result of the compounded hidden lies and buried crimes. The LBJ legend can no longer stand the truth test, and it is therefore imperative that it must be corrected, the sooner the better.

On the basis of everything else presented, it should now be clear that the entire plot to kill Dr. King was conceived and dictated by the FBI's two highest officials, J. Edgar Hoover and Clyde Tolson, in accordance with a plot approved by Lyndon B. Johnson, president of the United States. The details were most likely laid out into a playbook by the FBI's assistant directors, William Sullivan and Cartha DeLoach, under the guidance of Tolson, the chief operating officer directly liaised with Angleton at the CIA and Yarborough at the Pentagon. Only under these authorities could such a plan—involving the military assets being used, the intelligence apparatus being controlled by the CIA, and the law-enforcement arm (Hoover's FBI) under which the plot was managed—have possibly been executed.

The numerous connections to high-level FBI personnel—who would have routinely delegated certain aspects of their work to subordinates, perhaps not as well trusted by the higher-ups—might explain a number of mysterious deaths during the period of the HSCA's deliberations (1977–78). Gary Revel, an investigator who worked on the HSCA investigations during this period, wrote the following summary of this aspect of the extended cover-up during this period on his website:

> William Sullivan's goal was to testify before the public HSCA hearings and lay his cards on the table, so to speak. He was going to give the committee and the American people the truth about J. Edgar Hoover's hatred of Martin Luther King Jr. as well as his hatred for President John Kennedy and Presidential Candidate Robert Kennedy. Sullivan's knowledge of how the FBI worked with the CIA, when it came to J. Edgar Hoover's plans to neutralize the human rights activities of African-American leaders and their supporters, was unique. This knowledge and the evidence he was prepared to present would have given the HSCA the direction it needed to truly uncover and prosecute the perpetrators of the JFK and MLK assassinations. It is no wonder that those who had the most to lose if the truth came out were not unhappy to hear of his "accidental murder." The official record says that Robert Daniels mistook William Sullivan for a deer while deer hunting and shot and killed him before Bill could make his revelations public.[946]

Moreover, in an email to me dated March 29, 2017, Mr. Revel stated:

> I am still trying to unravel the bizarre happenings of that year. My brother, and my cousin's husband, Ivan Riley, as well as William Sullivan and 5 other FBI or former FBI officials who could have been valuable to my investigation, died mysteriously or were simply killed during 1977. Sullivan and the other 5 were scheduled to testify before the committee. Donald Kaylor was a fingerprint expert who had worked on the JFK assassination evidence. Alan Belmont and Louis Nichols were both special assistants to J. Edgar Hoover. JFK assassination document examiner and expert James Cadigan was another. J. M. English, an expert on the

rifle that supposedly killed President John F. Kennedy and head of the FBI Forensic Sciences Laboratory was also terminated. Those who travel to a place beyond reason and continue to try to defend the official stories of lone assassins despite contradictory evidence produced from thorough investigations simply haven't gotten it yet. When there are so many coincidences any reasonable person will just know that something is amiss. The "Lone Gunman Theory" is just that, a theory. Neither James Earl Ray nor Lee Harvey Oswald were ever tried and convicted for the assassinations and, in the case of Robert F. Kennedy's assassination, Sirhan Sirhan was clearly railroaded with a "Kangaroo Court" and with the deck stacked against him.

Earlier, we noted the presence of a number of famed criminal attorneys, all connected directly to the mafioso godfather Carlos Marcello and Lyndon Johnson. Among them were Percy Foreman of Houston and G. Wray Gill and Camille Gravel, both New Orleans attorneys representing men who had fallen under suspicion for their connections to the frame-up of Ray but who were both mysteriously excused by the HSCA. Gill in particular had figured in the pre- and post-JFK assassination events and had employed Lee Harvey Oswald's CIA handler David Ferrie to investigate the methods used by Robert Kennedy in his attempts to deport Marcello, both legally and in his previous extralegal actions of simply capturing him and having him flown to Guatemala. Within two months, Ferrie flew down to Guatemala to smuggle Marcello back to New Orleans.

We described Marcello's reputed business dealings with Johnson's aide Jack Valenti, in collaboration with Jack Ruby, the well-known accused assassin of Oswald. Also noted was the serendipitous appearance of Percy Foreman at the Shelby County jail, even before James Earl Ray had fired his first attorney, Arthur Hanes. Left unexplained, yet not inexplicable, was how Foreman was able to finagle an uninvited and highly irregular visit with Ray, timed exactly to the point at which Ray had just decided to fire Hanes. Perhaps that was the product of one piece of covert intelligence yielded by the microphones placed in Ray's jail cell—planted there as only someone wielding a lot of political power in Tennessee could have possibly arranged. It was these ties, through Johnson's friends Percy Foreman and Governor Buford Ellington, that provide the insights into how the overall network functioned. At its center, the Louisiana/Texas nexus of the gossamer web of underground connections created, managed, and facilitated events before and after Dr. King's assassination.

It should also be clear by now that all three of the major political assassinations of the 1960s were perpetrated by essentially the same men, using related resources, comparable methods of operation, and analogous motives. And they were all executed with the active provocations of the two men at the very head of the hierarchy, Lyndon B. Johnson and J. Edgar Hoover. Only the combined power wielded by them could have reasonably equipped—with the eager assistance of intelligence officials from the military, the CIA, and key members of the Dixie Mafia—the facilitators and street-level operatives with the kinds of resources, and spheres of influence in the local communities involved (Dallas, Memphis and Los Angeles), to have succeeded in accomplishing their multiple missions. The most powerful man in America circa 1963–1968 was Lyndon B. Johnson. That it was he who instigated all of these major treasons should by now be indisputable.

More Traces of the Continuing Cover-Up

Beginning in 2012, a $27.5 million, two-year renovation of the Lorraine Motel—and the rooming-house across Mulberry Street from which William Bradford Huie and several other servile authors claimed the fatal shot had been fired—was conducted. The buildings now comprise the National Civil Rights Museum, and the renovations were done mostly to enhance the visitor's learning experience, although ulterior goals were also achieved, as we will see. During the renovation, the interior (including floors and wood joists) of the buildings that once housed Bessie Brewer's rooming-house was completely gutted and rebuilt with steel framework and solid concrete floors. Only the room 5-B and the bathroom were recreated, almost as they were originally built; all other boarding rooms were eliminated to create open spaces for the exhibits.

It is a stunning revelation to observe that, when the second floor was rebuilt, it was obviously raised from the level it had been, by at least a foot, and the bathtub was moved away from the East-facing wall (with the small window) by approximately ten to twelve inches. The only conceivable purpose in making those changes was to create a scene that is much more conducive to a shooter being able to comfortably fire an accurate shot from that location. It stands in stark contrast to what we referenced in Chapter 8, where Harold Weisberg's description was cited, of how "impossible" an accurate shot would have been to be fired from there. The renovations have removed those impediments, and the rearrangement, incorrectly, now portrays it to be a perfect sniper's lair, with plenty of room for a man to position himself between the bathtub and window and have the windowsill at a perfect height to fire a rifle from

1968

2017

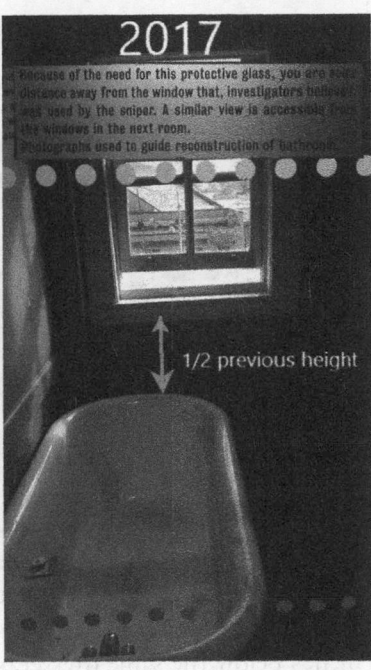

Because of the need for this protective glass, you are some distance away from the window that, investigators believe, was used by the sniper. A similar view is accessible from the windows in the next room.

Photographs used to guide reconstruction of bathroom.

1/2 previous height

The top of the bathtub in 1968 was nearly two feet below the windowsill; now it is approximately one foot below the window. The bathtub—originally flush to the wall below the window—was moved approximately 10–12 inches away from the wall.

that position. In order to make those "improvements" to the "crime scene," subtle physical changes, shown clearly in the photographs to follow, had to be made in the interior, which reveal traces of the continued cover-up. Yet, despite all the revisionism, no one actually fired a shot from there, least of all James Earl Ray, as explained elsewhere by eyewitnesses—all of whom placed the shooter in the brushy area behind the rooming house—people who had been carefully avoided by police and FBI investigators.

Since the entire second floor had been replaced but the outer brick walls had not, the windows remained exactly where they were originally, and that gave away the fact that the new floor was approximately one foot, or more, higher in elevation than it had been originally. The fact that there was no other apparent need for this change—together with the related fact that the bathtub was also moved away from the wall in the process—can only mean that this was a key part, and the ultimate purpose, of the design.

The top of the doorway to the left was about a foot below the top of the adjacent window in 1968. Now it is roughly even with the top of the window. The large wall section above the fireplace mantle and fascia in 1968

Room 5-B of the Rooming House (Before / After Renovations)

has nearly disappeared after the renovations because the fireplace, mantle, and fascia had to be rebuilt on a higher plane, yet adjacent to the windows, which remained in their original position. The bottom of the window was roughly even with the top of the dresser in 1968; today, it is approximately twelve inches below the same dresser, sitting higher than previously.

All of this indisputably revealing evidence proves that the reconstruction was done with the same cunning and guile as the original crime and cover-up were carried out and was actually the latest extension of that effort. For those who believe that the crimes of fifty years ago were committed by rogue agents untethered to official governmental sanctions, this stunning evidence stands as ultimate proof that the crimes of "then and there" are inextricably connected to the same governmental conduct here and now. Of course, it should be acknowledged that the people who made those decisions decades later had nothing to do with Dr. King's murder; the catalyst of their motivation—as Lyndon B. Johnson had always known it would become—was simply to protect the legacies, thus the legitimacy, of government institutions and its historical leadership. His own would thus be ensured, as well.

As noted previously, this phenomenon has been repeated time and again, as new evidence or witnesses appear, or events occur; the fact the reactions produce the same results is proof enough of the existence of a sub-rosa network within the "Deep State" assigned to keep state secrets secret. The cost of moving that floor a foot higher and relocating the bathtub was undoubtedly one of its most minor expenditures.

EPILOGUE

"The arc of the moral universe is long, but it bends toward justice."
"Truth crushed to earth will rise again."
—*Martin Luther King Jr.*

Dr. King's quotes, like the eventual rendering of William Shakespeare's prophecy in *The Merchant of Venice,* that eventually the truth will out, may be of comfort in the long run. But the counterpoint to that, as John Maynard Keynes reminded us, is that "in the long run we will all be dead."

Like the assassinations of John and Robert Kennedy, the conspiracy to kill Dr. Martin Luther King Jr. involved elements within the federal government as well as within the contemporaneous criminal underworld. Beginning in 1965, King's speeches against the Vietnam War had become increasingly forceful, and by late 1966 and into 1967, he was calling the US government "the greatest purveyor of violence in the world." [947] That kind of rhetoric, during that era, was viewed as increasingly radical by the broadcast media and considered as tantamount to near treason in the minds of many people who felt that the government could do no wrong. To them, Dr. King's use of that kind of language was unforgiveable, no matter how much the charge has since become accepted—and in retrospect even understated, considering the still-hidden government deceits underpinning the war's rationalizations.

By the spring of 1968, the revolutionary atmosphere had been stoked by three summers of race riots and nearly continuous antiwar protests. The fears and anger that swirled throughout the country—fueled by the provocative statements of the highest-level Washington officials, the very ones who considered themselves to be the "true patriots"—led to the most explosive and tumultuous political environment of modern US history. Many government officials and a few sycophants in military leadership, anxious to prove their fealty, agreed with their superiors that Dr. King's charisma and grassroots power could potentially lead to a national revolt that might even threaten the continuance of the government itself.

William Bradford Huie's original fictional story—clearly commissioned and directed by high officials of the FBI—became accepted by a public hungry for another overly simplistic answer to a senseless tragedy. In time,

Huie's tale became a legend that was repeated and expanded, over and over again, by many other authors, each adding more fictional figments from their own repertoire. The original myths were strengthened with every positive book review and newspaper article and subsequent books by other similarly guided authors. Eventually, they collectively blended together in a generally accepted popular narrative with a life of its own. The lies and deceits at its foundation—long buried by the myths—gradually replaced practically the entire truth of actual events and have now become what is known as "official history." Unfortunately for future generations, the lessons lost will inevitably haunt the American culture for many more lifetimes.

The Trade-Offs between Discretion and Brutal Honesty

James Douglass, writing in *Probe* magazine in 2000, lamented the fact that thirty-two years (now fifty) after Martin Luther King Jr. was assassinated by a conspiracy conducted by agencies of his own government, the case remained unresolved due to a continuing cover-up by officials of that government. Not only was that fact proven to be true then, it still remains true now, nearly five decades after Dr. King's assassination and two decades after Douglass's lament.

The essence of Mr. Douglass's poignant essay is included here (with emphasis added on key points, for purposes that will become apparent):

> *[A] court extended the circle of responsibility for the assassination beyond the late scapegoat James Earl Ray to the United States government.*
>
> What I experienced in that courtroom ranged from inspiration at the courage of the Kings, their lawyer-investigator William F. Pepper, and the witnesses, to amazement at the *government's carefully interwoven plot to kill Dr. King. The seriousness with which U.S. intelligence agencies planned the murder* of Martin Luther King Jr. speaks eloquently of the threat Kingian nonviolence represented to the powers that be in the spring of 1968.
>
> Perhaps the lesson of the King assassination is that our government understands the power of nonviolence better than we do, or better than we want to. In the spring of 1968, when Martin King was marching (and Robert Kennedy was campaigning), King was determined that massive, nonviolent civil disobedience would end the domination of democracy by

> corporate and military power. *The powers that be took Martin Luther King seriously.* They dealt with him in Memphis.[948] (Emphasis added throughout.)

With those words, Mr. Douglass illustrates why he is widely considered to be one of the most thoughtful and articulate authors in the truth finder field today. However—and not to minimize his very important works— unfortunately Mr. Douglass omitted closing that circle of responsibility, which, as he implicitly noted in the first paragraph, had only been extended by the court to include unnamed officials. He stopped short of naming the names of the actual people who constituted *"the powers that be"* in charge of the *"US intelligence agencies"* and all the other involved *"agencies of government,"* just as he also refrained from doing that in his magisterial and (otherwise) incisive 2008 opus titled *JFK and the Unspeakable: Why He Died and Why It Matters.* For understanding the deep and expansive context behind the 1960s assassinations, his work is indispensable and of unquestioned value.

And such subtle grace and presumed innocence is expected of a journalist, or a jurist, and it is the proper standard for treating a live person accused of a crime, pending a specific finding by a jury. But since most of the people who have been implicated in these deeds are now dead and no longer within reach of earthly justice—having escaped it in their time as mortals—we are long past the point where such exigencies of due process, or the niceties of polite manners and graciousness, are still pertinent.

This kind of tepid discretion only further slows the already lengthy process of rendering historic truths, especially when the evidence—already stale and fragmented as a result of the enormous cover-ups put into place by the diabolically powerful culprits—finally dribbles out piecemeal over many years. Given that traditional court remedies are no longer possible, the excessive caution not only hinders achieving real justice, it impedes the ability of the general public to learn enough to avoid repeating the deadliest mistakes of the past.

The 1960s madness will never be reconciled by books that stop short of naming the men who choreographed the worst crimes of that era. The many books that direct us to the doorstep of only one of the agencies used to facilitate these crimes (the one in Langley, Virginia), despite the fact that it was only one of several, will never produce that result.

For half a century, the slaying of Dr. King remained a misunderstood enigma, successfully chalked up as just another meaningless lone-nut 1960s assassination. But over time, the story became understood by most cognitively aware people to be just another myth that the public accepted in lieu of what was presumed to be a much more disturbing, but hidden, reality. The myth of Ray as the "lone nut, hateful racist and stalker" was indeed a well-orchestrated lie that replaced what would—and should—have been the shattering, epochal event that many people at the time privately suspected it was.

Looking back on the story that never was—the innocence of James Earl Ray—it finally becomes clear. He was merely another patsy, just like Lee Harvey Oswald and Sirhan B. Sirhan. All were men framed by the most shrewd, cunning, devious plotters within the federal bureaucracy in Washington, men who would dare to impute their own motives (purportedly racist in Ray's case, rabidly anti-Communist in Oswald's, and schizoid/anti-Semitic—against RFK's allegedly too pro-Israel views—in Sirhan's). The reality was that all three of them were simply unsuspecting but malleable, vulnerable men who had been exposed to the earlier mind-control experiments secretly conducted on unwitting soldiers, prisoners, mental patients, and ordinary men and women by the CIA's diabolical "Black Sorcerer," Sidney Gottlieb. In Ray's case, he was particularly vulnerable, throughout his one year of "freedom" after his prison break, as a fugitive on the run.

It was triply ironic that all of these "lone-nut" false portrayals—a hateful racist, a fervent anti-Communist, and a loathsome, demented anti-Semite—were primary character traits of one of the main plotters himself: the FBI director, J. Edgar Hoover. At least the first two characteristics were shared by his patron, President Lyndon Baines Johnson.

Thanks in large part to the countless hours and the meticulous, indefatigable work of the many earlier researchers and authors cited throughout this book, we now know that James Earl Ray took the fall for a very sophisticated murder plot, of which he was completely unaware until after it was executed. We also know now that—in every so-called investigation by federal, state, and local law enforcement agencies—there was an explainable reason for why no real attempt was ever made to even acknowledge Ray's repeated pleas to find the man named "Raoul," who had guided him for nearly twenty thousand miles around the North American continent. There were many missed opportunities to follow that lead, even by the simplest measures, such as tracing the telephone numbers that Ray provided to his attorneys. The only serious work, of sorts, was the felonious attempt by the FBI—and later, to an even greater and more outrageous level, the absurdly counterproductive attempt by the HSCA—to deviously pin the Alton, Illinois, bank robbery on James, followed by a whole string of later bank heists allegedly done by his brothers—all equally baseless—to try to prove that "Raoul" was really a composite of his brothers Jerry and John.

Furthermore, we know that in addition to the participation of the Dixie Mafia in the plot, there were two sniper teams associated with the 902nd and the 111th MIGs; there were also numerous signs of the CIA's involvement, and the fact that the FBI was the guiding force throughout virtually all facets of the murder and subsequent cover-up. We know that all of it stemmed from a long-planned, highly coordinated, well-executed plot that brought all of these elements together under the auspices of well-placed politicians and employees of the federal, state, and local governments. We even know the names of the men, from the top of the hierarchy through the middle levels and down to the local, street-level operatives—most of whom have been named in the previous chapters—responsible for the murder of Dr. King.

The only thing we don't know is how much longer this shamefully despicable lie—putting the blame on an innocent, vulnerable man who was set up months, even years, in advance—can remain in the nation's most secret closets. But it should now be understandable to all that the longer the nation's foundation continues to rest upon fabricated myths, built on top of fractured and crumbling truths—compounded with a patchwork of new, ever-greater lies to extend the original cover-up—the weaker and more vulnerable it will become.

APPENDIX A

Motives of Critics of Dr. Pepper

Pondering the Motives of Critics Who Attack Dr. William F. Pepper: The Best Original Researcher of MLK's Murder

Unfortunately, there are organizations whose specialty seems to be directed at screening new books as part of their stealthy mission, which many have come to believe might be their primary *raison d'être*: that of "keeping state secrets secret." To accomplish this, while portraying themselves as "truth seekers," they are known to somewhat arbitrarily dismiss certain sources that go too far into areas that they prefer to keep out-of-bounds. The organization "Kennedys and King," (previously known as CTKA—paradoxically named "Citizens for Truth in the Kennedy Assassination") is one such entity. While there are a number of contributors to it whose works do not cross those circumscribed territories—because the subject matter conveniently does not—many others are apparently assigned the role of keeping researchers/authors on a very narrow path, as though there were invisible boundaries that cannot be breached.* As with all myths, it is necessary to include enough truth to make them believable to a large audience, and that did not go unnoticed by the mythmakers who created this organization, or other similar entities.

Such was the case with Dr. Pepper's works, in a review written by Martin Hay dated August 1, 2016, shortly after Pepper's latest book, *The Plot to Kill King*, was published. In his opening commentary, Hay wrote:

> Over the years, this reviewer has adopted something of an agnostic position when it comes to areas of Pepper's work. Whilst there is undoubtedly great value in what he has uncovered and accomplished, it nonetheless remains true that there a number of legitimate reasons for doubting important elements of Pepper's research.

---

* Refer to the website below for my essay "A Response to the CTKA review of *LBJ: The Mastermind of the JFK Assassination*" by Joseph Green for a detailed account of one such review, which I have charitably called an unsupported "hatchet-job." (www.lbjmastermind.com — Tab: Response to the Trolls)

On that weak platform, the "reviewer" set forth to disparage many of the people who had come forward with pertinent information, and some of the collateral witnesses or suspects whom Dr. Pepper interviewed as a result of the his arduous, decades-long investigation. In doing so, it seemed as if the memory lapses of decades-long events, and the relatively inconsequential character flaws in a number of them, completely disqualified them from being considered at all believable in the considered opinion of this reader of books and self-styled critic.

Clearly, though this review was written in such a way as to give Dr. Pepper some general recognition for his long-term commitment to solving King's murder, the reviewer apparently decided that Pepper was getting too dangerously close to an unstated but apparent long-standing objective of his sponsors: exposing partial truths while keeping to its real agenda of protecting the nation's highest state secrets, one of which is the criminality of the 36th President. In this specific instance, the reviewer's obvious objective was to invalidate the case Dr. Pepper had made against a number of key figures whom he—through witness Ron Adkins—had implicated as having been involved in the murder of Dr. King: such luminaries as Rev. Samuel "Billy" Kyles, Rev. Jesse Jackson, Memphis Mayor Henry Loeb, Memphis Police and Fire Department Chief Frank Holloman, FBI Director J. Edgar Hoover, FBI Associate Director Clyde Tolson, and a number of others who worked either for one of them or were associated with the Dixie Mafia. And, by direct extension, President Lyndon B. Johnson.

The sworn depositions of witness Ronnie Lee Adkins, a.k.a. Ron Tyler, run over 111 pages in the book, consisting almost entirely of (reduced) deposition pages, four to each book page, for a total of nearly 400 pages. In other words, Dr. Pepper went to an incredible amount of time, expense, and patience to carefully extract information from this man, and others— and document it for all time, and present it to a public hungry for the very rare truths and hard-to-find facts amongst the jetsam found in many of the best-selling but fictional books written about this case—because Pepper had considered him, and them, as reasonably credible witnesses wanting to provide truthful testimony. Since the Adkins' deposition was taken over forty years after the event (it is dated December 10, 2009), some basic errors and inconsistencies should be expected.

But the reviewer evidently had a much higher standard than that, as demonstrated by his declaration that *"calling Adkins' story hard to believe would be a vast understatement. In fact it is, in this reviewer's opinion, so utterly lacking in credibility that it hardly seems worth wasting time on a detailed deconstruction . . . Accepting this man's word without verification is, as far as this reviewer is concerned, completely unthinkable."* (Emphasis supplied).

As for what possible motives Mr. Adkins might have had for going to all the trouble of sitting through the hours of intensive, memory-searching interviews, followed by even more intense, on the record, very detailed testimony under oath—at the risk of perjury or contempt charges—in the depositions, we have nothing other than this rather haughty pronouncement. That such an assertion could be made, devoid of any specific reasoning whatsoever about any possible motive Adkins might have had for willingly undergoing what can only be concluded was an extraordinary act of masochism, should be enough to abrogate the charge and validate Adkins's testimony.

Let's examine specific examples of the deceptive methodologies used in the delusive "review," among an assortment that the reviewer referenced, some of which have already been addressed within the narrative of this book:

- The first relates to his assertion that because Adkins had stated that Jesse Jackson was responsible for ensuring that the Lorraine Motel would change Dr. King's room to the one having a balcony, when the manager had claimed that he had received a telephone call from someone at the Atlanta SCLC to make that change, this "error" should discredit Adkins's testimony. Consider, just for a moment, the possibility that both could be true, that Jackson had been instructed to make certain, in person, that this long-distance telephonic instruction would actually be carried out, given that the caller was (apparently, assuming the call really was made from Atlanta) too far away to do that. Had the reviewer given it a few seconds to sink in, he might have realized that its critical importance to the objective might require on-site "back-up" assurance: the term used by the spooks is called "planned redundancy," and it is a key element of covert operations that helps to assure that all elements of a carefully crafted plan are executed in accordance with that plan. Qualified reviewers of books about such operations should implicitly understand that elementary concept and would have not used it to make a fallacious point.
- Another example relates to the incident that became the catalyst for ensuring Dr. King's appearance in Memphis: that he would come to Memphis to lend his support for the sanitation workers. Two of them, Echol Cole and Robert Walker, were crushed to

death when the compactor mechanism of the trash truck was (according to the official city report) "accidentally" triggered. The fact that city rules forbade black employees to seek shelter from rain anywhere but in the back of their compressor trucks, and the meager financial settlement offered their families after the incident, ultimately led to Dr. King's decision to return to the city to lead a protest march. According to Dr. Pepper's witness, Ron Adkins, that incident was no "accident": it was purposefully done as part of the larger plan to assure King's return to Memphis for that very purpose. Other than citing the "official findings" (which, like so much of this case, is rightfully suspect—to the point of arguably a lie that should be reinterpreted as the opposite of what it asserts), there is no evidence presented to doubt the veracity of Adkins's sworn testimony based upon his "insider knowledge." It isn't a stretch—given all the other component parts of a very elaborate, detailed plan—to believe that the plotters would come up with a subplot such as this, to ensure that King would respond to a request to appear in Memphis to play homage to these men, killed in a tragic accident caused in part by dangerous working conditions. And it needn't have to be conditioned to a particular day, merely one "on the next rainy day." To deny the possibility of that, again based on the same arbitrary dismissal of all of Adkins's testimony, with the flippant statement: "But in Ronnie's world, this was no accident, 'Somebody pulled the hammer, pulled the lever on the truck and mashed them up in there'" is merely another instance of "selective preference."

• In another passage, the reviewer makes a number of misstatements and factual errors when he asserts: "In Adkins' narrative there is no mention of or accounting for Raul and he names some extremely unlikely individuals as part of the plot. He even has MPD officer Tommy Smith . . . *waiting in his car on Main Street and then dropping the bundle of evidence in the doorway of Canipe's.*" (Emphasis added.)

First, regarding Adkins's not "accounting for Raul," the question must be asked: "Why would he?" As another elementary point about people involved in covert operations, they are all compartmentalized, to assure that anyone without a "need to know" is purposefully kept from knowledge of all aspects of the operation, and there are multiple reasons for that which most minimally informed people already know. There was no reason that Adkins would have had any reason to know about Raul, or even Ray, for that matter; his knowledge was confined to the events he witnessed as a teenager over approximately two years at his father's side. That should be self-evident to anyone who gives it a moment's thought, so we will leave it at that and save the reader from a lengthy discourse about that point.

Second, his statement that Tommy Smith was the one who dropped the "bundle of evidence in the doorway of Cannipe's" is, simply, *incorrect.* In his deposition (part 2), at page 163 (book page 643), the actual statement reads as follows: "*The guy that was with* Tommy Smith when I saw Tommy at the red light is the one I was told put the gun there." The reviewer actually cited page 256, the narrative supplied by Dr. Pepper, in explaining the witness' testimony, however even that clearly states, "He [Adkins] was told that *the officer who sat with* Lieutenant Tommy Smith was the man who dropped the bundle in front [of] Canipe's." (Emphasis added in both of the above sentences.) *Nowhere* does the witness, Adkins, say anything about it being Tommy Smith who deposited the bundle of evidence. In evaluating this rather glaring error, one must ask themselves whether it was simply an oversight—merely a reading slippage whereby the five key words were somehow skipped—or, lacking sufficient concrete reasons to discredit the witness, the exercise of a license to misinterpret certain statements, being extended by the organization that assigned the reviewer this project, was just another trashing tool? There can only be two possible explanations for this kind of factual misrepresentation; not being able to prove it one way or the other, we'll leave it at that and let the reader decide which seems more appropriate.

- One of the reviewer's statements dismissing Dr. Pepper's witness was this: "*There are also logical problems aplenty with Adkins' story. Like why on Earth would Hoover have had the names [sic: initials] JFK, RFK and MLK put on a [prayer] list and handed to Russell Adkins Sr. in 1956? Was anyone even referring to them by their initials back then?*"

  That "prayer list" he referenced (as we described in Chapter 5) was conveyed to Russell Adkins by none other than Hoover's and Adkin's mutual friend, Senator Joe McCarthy, at Clyde Tolson's request, as a little "head's up" alert about possible future "targets" that would eventually follow; since McCarthy died in 1957, it is presumed to have been sent in 1956 at the latest. As most minimally informed people know, the practice of politicians using their initials as a short-cut ID started with FDR (first elected in 1932), so we turned for guidance on this practice to a book by William Safire titled *Safire's Political Dictionary:**

Ted Sorensen wrote: "JFK—as he persuaded the headline writers to call him, not to imitate FDR but to avoid the youthful 'Jack.'"

(The following statement followed in Safire's statement, so we include it here): *Even before his association with FDR*, LBJ was preoccupied with initials: Lady Bird Johnson, Lynda Bird and Luci Baines all carried the same initials, as did his ranch and his dog Little Beagle Johnson. (Emphasis added.) Also, on another page of this book, p. 467, he stated that Johnson was also called "Big Daddy," which was undoubtedly an endearing term that he himself had also started, for prurient reasons that we have previously noted.

So, to answer the reviewer's question: "Yes," at least in the case of JFK, whose appearance in the headlines began at least in the early 1950s, it can safely be intuited that the use of his initials had begun well before 1956, and his brother Robert, being as close to "Jack" as he always was, had probably been coincidentally influenced to do the same. As for MLK, who knows? Perhaps Mr. Hoover just wanted to use the same script style to make matters easy for others to understand, knowing that they would figure it out in due course; indeed, it may have simply been Hoover's choice as a cryptic device that would not be sufficient to prove his criminal intent, or merely one of his many other inexplicable fetishes. Not to be pedantic about it, but, one might raise the question, "How does this question even merit such a diversion?" Answer: It's called "piling on" and serves the purpose of throwing in everything, including a metaphoric "kitchen sink," to try to destroy the credibility of Dr. Pepper and his masterful book.

- Then there was this hodge-podge of assorted questions:
  - *Once Dr. King's assassination was decided, why did it take four years for so many presumably intelligent people to formulate a plan?*

---

* Safire, p. 343

This is probably one of the easiest questions to answer, except that a thorough explanation must necessarily be lengthy. The—much too obvious—answer to this question is probably because it was a rather sophisticated plan, involving a lot of complicated subplans, thus, planning meetings (called "prayer meetings," probably because they had long been on J. Edgar Hoover's "prayer list" as well as the fact that many took place in a church).

As every project manager knows (but evidently not all book reviewers), they would first have to lay out a macroplan and, as consensus agreements were made, then add detailed subparts: identification of the tasks (and consequent risk evaluations), time lines, and specifications for potential assignments, then the nomination of carefully chosen "recruits," followed by the required approvals, to get to a microlevel detailed subplan for each of them. They were undoubtedly not working with standard business planning devices such as PERT Charts to conduct this work, but they still had to go to great lengths to make their plans, some requiring great lead times, such as carefully selecting, then setting up, a patsy. In this case, high-level sleuths were clearly involved to first produce a list of several potential candidates, then select the one most suitable for such a sacrifice. These were men (most likely James J. Angleton chief among them, as explained elsewhere) who were knowledgeable about each candidate's past, and his present whereabouts, who selected James Earl Ray.* The plan required the assistance of the prison warden to set up a carefully controlled escape, and this would require its own time line. A "handler" and other facilitators were also needed for this purpose, and they would need to be given specialized training for that purpose; then additional plans would be needed to make subsequent contact with the "patsy" in carefully preplanned—but seemingly

---

* In Chapter 6, we examined evidence that James Earl Ray's military career included time spent in an organization formed in 1947, largely out of the old OSS (Office of Strategic Services), which then became the CIA, and a short-lived unit called the 7892nd Infantry, which has been identified as having experimented with various mind-control and "reprograming" operations, an outgrowth of the CIA's MKULTRA program headed by Sidney Gottlieb, at the direction of Director Allen Dulles.

serendipitous—meetings . . . in this case, the first was at the Neptune bar in Montreal in July, 1967.

This part of that plan would be the lengthiest "task"— the key "critical path" upon which everything else depended. From there, the handler would make the patsy dependent upon him for financial backing from then on through the period leading up to the scheduled killing of MLK. These meetings were explained at length in Adkins's deposition, for example in pp. 25-50 (book pages 608-615). The general instruction from Clyde Tolson himself was "Make it happen in Memphis . . . so we can control it" (i.e., by the local officials named elsewhere and various members of the Dixie Mafia, the FBI, CIA, and military intelligence). The 3½-month ocean cruise in the summer of 1964, where the plan was carefully pieced together by Tolson and Russell Adkins Sr., was the first major task. Tolson also placed an early order for "five or six" rifles and had them shipped from Oregon to Memphis, and this was all done in 1964, probably to ensure that there would be no record of them, or if there was, that they would have sufficient time to have it erased, or if necessary to get replacement rifles acquired elsewhere. And then there was the matter of recruiting "FBI informants" who would cooperate for their own self-serving reasons (mostly monetary and career-building), as well: Jesse Jackson and Billy Kyles being two of them, according to this witness, which the reviewer finds so incredible.

Another one of the "action items" that might have had a long lead time would have been related to the money Hoover collected and then gave to Clyde Tolson for necessary expenses, such as the bribe of $25,000 to the warden at the prison where James Earl Ray was incarcerated. That occurred in November, 1966, so that one single component was done almost eighteen months before the killing date. Another eighteen months before that would likely be required, in simply getting the plan underway; the patsies screened and winnowed down to one; the key highest level team players identified and agreed to; getting the money set up, the financiers and highest-level Washington plotters behind it satisfied that the mission was being handled tightly; the required street-level men selected, all from diverse backgrounds and positions—all of whom had to "pass muster" and be implicitly trusted to keep their lips sealed—accounts for three of the four years that have been questioned. Getting Hoover's retired lieutenant Frank Holloman appointed as police and fire commissioner, in time to control that end of the operation, would have also been a key item on the "To Do" list. We could extend this elementary exercise further into the weeds, but this should be sufficient to make the point: it was a very sophisticated plan, created and managed by men having decades of experience in the skullduggery required for successful political assassinations. So the short answer to Mr. Hays's simplistic question is "Yes, four years seems about right."

- *How did they come to decide that "pissing off" the sanitation workers was the best way of getting Dr. King into Memphis?*
Who knows? But there had to be a pretext, something that would "piss off" some group of people enough to practically demand an appearance by Dr. King. The long-term animus toward this group by Memphis Mayor Henry Loeb probably had something to do with the choice.

- *Why was it necessary for 16-year-old Ronnie to carry the rifle to the scene on the back of his motorbike? Who thought that was a good idea? What if he had been stopped by police officers not in on the plot? Why did Junior not just take the rifle with him in the first place?*
Again, the answer to this question will never be known for certain, but if the police were to find a rifle on a 16-year-old, it might have raised fewer questions than if it were found in the trunk of a car of a middle-aged man whom they might have liked to frame for something, or possibly was already the subject of a "Wanted" poster.

- *And what exactly was Earl Clark doing in the bushes if he wasn't the shooter? Would it have been so difficult for Junior to have handed the rifle to Jowers himself? It should be noted that there is no support anywhere in the record for the notion that there were three people hiding in the shrubbery.*
Earl Clark was there as a "spotter" assisting the shooter and to take the rifle immediately after the shot, allowing the shooter to escape the scene. Jowers waited at the back door of the restaurant for the rifle to be brought to him by Earl

Clark.* Clark received the gun from the shooter, in a similar fashion as what is known to have happened in Dallas, after the shooter on the grassy knoll quickly handed his gun to an accomplice to dispose of, knowing that the shooter (in both cases) would be preoccupied with his own immediate escape, whereas the "helper" could deal with the weapon a bit more dispassionately. As to the question of "the record," there was a lot more information than that, which was also either never recorded or subsequently deleted.

In his final assessment, Hay stated: "Yet none of these arguments preclude the possibility that Jowers' confession was invented as part of a money-making scheme that backfired." Rather than accepting just a scintilla or two of Jowers's testimony, given the raw fact of his actual presence at the scene throughout the murder, and Dr. Pepper's more seasoned and intelligent judgment of Jowers's credibility—based on intensive interactions with him over a long period of time—this review simply throws it all out, "the baby with the bathwater." Then, despite lauding Pepper's success at advancing the case in the civil trial of *King v. Jowers*, and bringing out facts and witnesses that should have been done in 1969, the reviewer returned to disputing the credibility of many other witnesses, going through a litany of reasons why one should not believe any of them. In each case, the reviewer's specious reasoning, flawed critiques, and use of "selected preference" biases—as demonstrated here merely for one such witness—could easily be used to rebut all of the others, but in the interest of brevity, we will resist that temptation.

Finally, Mr. Hay concludes his treatise with what seems to be a startling, and stunning, embracement of the work of the famed prevaricator-plagiarist Gerald Posner,† when he offers the following as another exhibit in his defamation of Dr. Pepper's latest and most complete book: "Gerald Posner [has] delighted in quoting Pepper's former investigator Ken Herman as stating

---

* See pp. 664-665 of the King Family Trial Transcript (available at the King Center website: http://www.thekingcenter.org/sites/default/files/KING%20FAMILY%20TRIAL%20TRAN-SCRIPT.pdf).

"LOYD JOWERS: Yes, I met him—yes, I was at the back door.
"ANDREW YOUNG: Out of the storeroom?
"LOYD JOWERS: Yeah.
"ANDREW YOUNG: And he came up from the woods back there or bushes?
"LOYD JOWERS: From the bushes.
"ANDREW YOUNG: And he handed you the rifle?"

† As noted in Prologue. Also see: http://www.miaminewtimes.com/news/posner-plagiarizes-again-6367387

that 'Pepper is the most gullible person I have ever met in my life.'" Given Dr. Pepper's enormous accomplishments, his long history of the pursuit of truth and justice in the face of unrelenting resistance, and his prestigious general legacy, there is another way to interpret that comment, which is not very complimentary about Mr. Herman's own gullibility and hubris.

Posner's *Killing the Dream* book, as was also true in his previous *Case Closed* tome, is rife with half-truths, whole-cloth lies, and made-up "testimony," as previously documented at the very website where Mr. Hay has posted this document; it is therefore curious that he would offer as "evidence" of Pepper's "gullibility" anything that Posner wrote and expect readers to believe its veracity. But Hay's attitudes about Pepper seem, alas, to have been shaped more by Gerald Posner than anyone else, which is a troubling indicator of the degree to which he has gone to smear Pepper's latest and greatest book. As anyone—being well informed of the overall details of the MLK murder case, and then viewing this unfortunate sideshow—who looks at this vignette will soon realize, it is not Dr. William F. Pepper, Esq., who is the "gullible" one at this table, as Mr. Hay could understand by simply looking into a mirror.

There were other instances of long and rambling discourses—seemingly pointless statements, non sequiturs, leaps of logic, gaps of reasoning, and illogical conclusions—but rather than going through all of the machinations used to discredit important new evidence that Dr. Pepper has painstakingly presented (to borrow the reviewer's own phrase above) *hardly seems worth wasting time on a detailed deconstruction.* To suggest that his pronouncement that critical witnesses—whom Dr. Pepper personally vetted through lengthy hours of intense interviews and the time, expense, and trouble involved in taking sworn depositions, upon which their credibility was firmly established—should be rejected because the reviewer felt that he gave erroneous statements is a bit conceited: indeed, as noted above, in multiple instances, it was the reviewer himself who unnecessarily created his own confusion.

The enormous work and tenacious efforts of Dr. William F. Pepper, in his stellar record of accomplishments for over four decades, should not be minimized or devalued by shoddy, ill-informed "book reviews" having a preordained mission. It is easy to declare oneself the "decider" of what research is acceptable, or not, and what books and authors are to be believed, or not, as has long been the stated "purpose" of the ironically named organization that published this drivel. But it is the unfortunate result of the checkered history of their reviews that causes many in the "research community" to believe that their true purpose is to channel newer readers in certain directions that do not necessarily go where actual "truths" might be found. Like shepherds leading their flocks to well-controlled pastures, the administrators of that organization thus ensure that the "sheeple" grazing in their domain are led into well-marked "safe corners," thus ensuring that the most-prized secrets of the estate are safely withheld.

The people who finance and run the noted websites have succeeded in their efforts to dissuade many people from reading important works, not only Dr. Pepper's, but many others that point directly back to the very cabal that was responsible for the 1960s treasons. Their high-handed, brutal but perfunctory, error-filled "book reviews"—as exemplified above—suggest that they are not motivated by passion for exposing truths, so much as perpetuating myths and plumbing for payoffs. It raises questions about whether their existence has been derived from financial subsidies provided by officials who represent the successors of that selfsame cabal. If so, their real mission is revealed by the product they have created: are they the embodiment and an extension of the same "invisible government" that they purportedly decry?

APPENDIX B

James Earl Ray's 1968 Appeal

IN THE CRIMINAL COURT OF SHELBY COUNTY, TENNESSEE

```
...........................
                                :
JAMES EARL RAY,                 :
      Petitioner                :
                                :
                                :
    VS                          :
                                :
                                :          No. H.C. 661
STATE OF TENNESSEE              :
      and                       :
                                :
LEWIS TOLLETT, WARDEN           :
State Penitentiary at           :
Petros, Tennessee,              :
                                :
      Defendants                :
                                :
...........................
```

AMENDED PETITION FOR POST CONVICTION RELIEF

Comes now your petitioner, JAMES EARL RAY, by and
through his attorneys, J. B. STONER, RICHARD J. RYAN, and
BERNARD FENSTERWALD, JR., and respectfully shows to the Court
that he is being illegally and wrongfully restrained of his
liberty by the Warden of the Penitentiary of the State of Tennessee, located near Petros, Tennessee, in Morgan County.

Petitioner asks that this AMENDED PETITION be substitu-
ted for and should replace one filed on April 13, 1970.

Petitioner states that his names is JAMES EARL RAY; that
his present address is the Brushy Mountain Prison at Petros, Ten-

nessee; that he is under confinement being sentenced on the charge of murder under Criminal Court Docket No. 16645 of Shelby County, Tennessee; that the sentence was pronounced by the late Honorable Preston Battle on March 10, 1969, in Division III of the Criminal Court of Shelby County, Tennessee; that the sentence was for a term of ninety-nine (99) years; that he is confined to the Brushy Mountain Penitentiary at Petros, Tennessee, in the custody of Warden Lewis Tollett who is presently charged with the custody of petitioner; that said custody began on or about March 25, 1970; that prior to that date your petitioner was confined in the State Penitentiary in Nashville, Tennessee, in the custody of William S. Neil, Warden.

Petitioner would show that he heretofore filed a Motion for a New Trial; that prior to the hearing the presiding Judge, the Honorable Preston Battle died; that an Amended Motion was filed suggesting the death of the trial Judge; the State of Tennessee filed a Motion to Strike and it was granted by the succeeding Judge, the Honorable Arthur Faquin, said judgment being appealed to the Court of Criminal Appeals and the Supreme Court of the State of Tennessee which was subsequently affirmed and the Petition to Rehear denied.

Your petitioner was represented by the following attorneys at the various stages of his case: in the extradition proceeding in London, England, by Messrs. Michael Eugene (Solicitor) and Roger Frisby (Barrister), while in incarceration from July to November, 1968, by Messrs. Arthur Hanes, Jr., and Arthur Hanes, Sr., of Birmingham, Alabama, from November 12, 1968 through March 10, 1969, by Mr. Percy Foreman of Houston, Texas, assisted by court-appointed Public Defender of Memphis and his staff; on appeal in 1969 by Messrs. J.B. Stoner of Savannah, Georgia, Richard J. Ryan of Memphis, and Robert Hill of Chattanooga; currently by petitioner is represented by Messrs. Stoner, Ryan, and Bernard Fensterwald, Jr., of Washington, D. C.

Your petitioner charges that his rights of "due process" guaranteed him by both the State and Federal Constitution have been grossly violated.

He avers that his rights to counsel guaranteed him by the State and Federal Constitution at all stages of the criminal proceedings against him have been grossly violated.

He also avers that he has not been accorded the "equal protection" guaranteed him by the Fourteenth Amendment to the United States Constitution.

As a result of these violations, petitioner avers that his plea of guilty was involuntary, and offers the following facts and supporting evidence in support thereof:

I. DUE PROCESS DENIED IN PROCEEDING WHEREBY PETITIONER WAS EXTRADITED TO MEMPHIS.

a. Petitioner was not permitted to consult Arthur Hanes, Sr., counsel of his choice, before the extradition hearing in the Bow Street Magistrate's Court, London, on June 28, despite the fact that Mr. Hanes had gone to London for that very purpose.

b. While incarcerated in London, petitioner was denied the right to communicate orally or in writing with persons who might assist him. For example, he was denied the right to communicate with Mr. Heath, Leader of the Opposition in Parliament.

Page 3

c. Virtually all of the evidence presented in England against petitioner was in affidavit form and hence, not subject to cross-examination. Only one witness from the United States was offered and cross-examined; he was Mr. Arthur Bonebrake, an FBI Special Agent, who testified at greatest length on civil rights matters in the United States, though he repeatedly admitted that he was incompetent to give expert testimony with respect to such matters. [See Exhibit A for Mr. Bonebrake's testimony.]

d. If petitioner had had competent counsel in England, he could not have been extradited for the murder of Dr. King, even if he had perpetrated the crime, because under the Anglo-American extradition treaty of 1931 and the applicable doctrines of international law, extradition is not granted in cases of political crimes.

e. Mr. Ramsey Clark, Attorney General of the United States, refused to permit the petitioner's lawyer, Mr. Hanes, to accompany him on the flight from London to Memphis; therefore, Mr. Hanes was absent and unavailable when petitioner arrived in Memphis. This decision on the part of the U.S. Attorney General was arbitrary and capricious, and it resulted in a denial of due process to petitioner at the hands of U.S. authorities even before petitioner arrived in the United States.

II. DUE PROCESS - TRIAL BY PRESS

a. Petitioner would like to remind the Court that this was a case that attracted international attention due to the prominence of the person murdered, and that the Trial Judge deemed it necessary to take unusual and rigorous steps in an effort to

Page 4

prevent either the State or this petitioner from being prejudiced by the welter of lurid publicity which attended this case.

b. In order to keep him from being totally indigent and to finance at least a part of the cost of his defense, petitioner made certain agreements between himself, his attorneys, and Mr. William Bradford Huie, whereby he would assist Mr. Huie in the preparation of certain magazine articles, books, etc., re the charges against petitioner. [See Exhibits B through F, attached hereto.]

c. Despite a promise to petitioner that he would not publish anything prior to trial, and despite an order by the Trial Judge that no such pre-trial publication be made, William Bradford Huie did publish two long articles in Look Magazine prior to the original trial date of November 12, 1968.

d. Huie not only broke his pledge to petitioner, he also misquoted and distorted what was told him by petitioner. For example, petitioner told Huie that his principal prior to the date of Dr. King's killing had "dark, red hair;" in Huie's articles, the principal was a "blonde."

e. The substance of Huie's pre-trial articles in Look Magazine [Appendixes G and H] was widely distributed, directly and indirectly. As Huie then stated that Dr. King's murder resulted from a wide conspiracy, the article had the effect of warning potential witnesses that there were powerful conspirators free to wreak vengeance if they said anything.

f. Huie's pre-trial publicity, and the indirect publicity deriving from it, would have made it difficult for an unbiased jury to be picked for petitioner's trial.

g. For these reasons, the Trial Judge charged Huie with contempt of court; unfortunately, the Trial Judge postponed action on the charge, and he died before Huie could be tried by him on this charge.

III. DUE PROCESS - EXCULPATORY INFORMATION WITHHELD FROM PETITIONER

a. Petitioner avers that much exculpatory information was withheld from the petitioner. A few of the more crucial items are:

1. the plain fact that no identifiable bullet was removed from Dr. King's body;

2. that Dr. King suffered a second and more damaging wound than the one to the jaw, proving that the missile was frangible or fragmentable; and

3. that, immediately after the crime, the State's chief eye witness, Charles Quitman Stevens could not and would not identify petitioner as the killer.

b. Much of the exculpatory material was contained in 200-odd pages of affidavits and other documents presented to the Bow Street Magistrate's Court in connection with the extradition proceeding. These documents were returned to the United States custody at the completion of the extradition proceeding; they have been sequestered and made unavailable to Ray's lawyers and to Ray himself, although urgent and repeated requests for them have been made to both the British and U.S. Governments. [See Exhibits I and J].

c. During preparation for trial, petitioner filed a motion for the State to produce ballistic and weapons tests and reports thereof. By order dated September 9, 1968, the Trial Judge denied the motion, thus wrongfully depriving petitioner of information vital to his defense. [See Exhibits K and L for said Motion and Order.]

IV. DUE PROCESS - UNAVAILABILITY OF WITNESSES

a. The State provided the petitioner with a list of 360 "potential witnesses" in various States of the Union and in a number of foreign countries. Although the State made the statement that it actually intended to use only "80 or 90" of these "potential witnesses," it would not give the list of 80 or 90 to petitioner, nor, despite numerous requests, would the Trial Judge order it to do so. Further, Trial Judge refused to permit petitioner's attorneys to take depositions from any witnesses, here or abroad. This combination of factors amounts to a denial of petitioner's right to due process, both under the Constitution of Tennessee and under Articles V and XIV of the U.S. Constitution.

b. Petitioner believes that at least one crucial witness, Mrs. Grace Stevens, was wrongfully incarcerated in the (Tennessee) Western State Mental Hospital solely because she might have testified favorably to petitioner.

Page 7

V. UNREASONABLE SEARCH AND SEIZURE

Petitioner has reason to believe that an illegal search and seizure was made by the FBI of his rented premises at 107 14th st., N.E., Atlanta, Georgia, and that the fruits of this search and seizure were introduced in evidence at his trial on March 10, 1969. [For a discussion of this matter before Trial Judge on February 7, 1969, see Exhibit M, pp. 16-19 of the transcript for that date.]

VI. RIGHT TO COUNSEL

Under both Tennessee and Federal law, right to counsel means effective right to counsel. Petitioner avers that his effective right to counsel was negated in the following specific ways:

a. During his incarceration in Memphis, he was physically prevented from having private conversations with his attorneys. Not only were there guards present at all times, but also his quarters (where lawyer-client conversations were permitted) were permanently and admittedly "bugged;" it was said that the microphones were cut off during such conversations, but there was no way for either petitioner or his lawyers to verify this. Further, all written communications, even between lawyer and client, was subject to censorship. A motion to grant private communication was made by petitioner [Exhibit O] but denied by the Trial Judge [Exhibit P].

b. A series of conflicts of interests prevented a series of competent attorneys from providing effective counsel to petitioner.

Page 8

Petitioner first chose Arthur Hanes, Sr., of Birmingham, Alabama, as his counsel-of-choice. At their very first meeting, Hanes required petitioner to sign two documents: 1) a general power of attorney; 2) a fee contract whereby Hanes would get 40% of all future proceeds to be derived from the sale of petitioner's story in the form of magazines, books, movies, etc. [See Appendix   ]. Lawyer Hanes knew that his 40% might come to a tidy sum, as he had already contracted with Author William Bradford Huie for the magazine and book rights before he departed for London for his meeting with petitioner.

Upon petitioner's return to the United States, Lawyer Hanes presented petitioner with a new-contract, whereby a new carving up of petitioner took place:

Huie	40%
Hanes	30%
Ray	30%

but, as Hanes got 40% of Ray's 30%, it came out:

Huie	40%
Hanes	42%
Ray	18%

To finance the deal, Look Magazine advanced Huie $30,000; Huie paid the $30,000 to petitioner, who, in turn, signed it all over to Hanes as his legal fee.

This contract forced petitioner to provide Huie with what was against petitioner's interest, i.e., falsehoods, as he dared not tell the whole truth if he wished to live.

From Huie's standpoint ---- and also from Hanes' standpoint in large measure ---- there could be no real income if

Page 9

all of petitioner's story were told in open court where it became
part of public domain. Specifically to Huie, it meant that he had
to get part of petitioner's story in print before any trial, hence,
he risked contempt of court to publish two articles in Look ----
all to petitioner's detriment. Petitioner is informed, and therefore alleges, that the author Huie made the statement that your
petitioner "must not take the witness stand in his expected trial,
because if he did take the witness stand, then he (Huie) would
have no book."

      To Hanes, it meant basically the same thing, i.e.,
although he could try the case on a not-guilty plea, he could not
permit petitioner to take the stand and tell his whole story from
the witness stand. Thus, Hanes was protecting his own mercenary
interests and those of Huie, rather than protecting the life and
liberty of petitioner.

      As November 12th and the opening of the trial neared,
petitioner and Hanes were unable to agree as to petitioner's
taking the stand. At this point, Attorney Percy Foreman entered
the case, but improperly. Although he knew that petitioner still
retained Arthur Hanes, Foreman was persuaded by petitioner's
brother, Jerry Ray, to visit Memphis and petitioner without informing Hanes or receiving any request, either orally or in writing,
from petitioner. In fact, Jerry Ray had written petitioner in
England as to the acceptability of Foreman as counsel, and he had
received an emphatic "no," because petitioner knew Foreman to be
very friendly with U.S. Attorney General Ramsey Clark and his
father, retired Justice Tom Clark.

Page 10

However, in Memphis on November 10, 1968, Foreman persuaded petitioner to discharge Hanes and retain him as counsel. Foreman said that he could break the Huie-Hanes contract; whereupon, petitioner agreed orally with Foreman at their first meeting on November 10th, that a fee of $150,000 should be paid out of future "earnings" for Foreman's legal assistance through the trial and on appeal, all the way to the U.S. Supreme Court if necessary However, Foreman then turned around and renegotiated the Hanes-Huie arrangement, inserting himself for both Hanes and petitioner thus, he had a 60% interest and Huie had a 40% interest in petitioner's "earnings" from books, magazines, etc. In short, Foreman rapidly assumed the same conflict of interest that had immobilized Hanes as an effective advocate, with one exception: he was greedier than Hanes, taking petitioner's 18% for himself.

Petitioner alleges that in the establishment of conflict of interest between petitioner and Hanes and Foreman, as evidenced by Exhibits B through F, that the said prior attorneys actually represented Huie and their own financial interests and not his, your petitioner's.

Petitioner further avers that these attorneys entered into contracts with Huie who was desirous of obtaining the exclusive rights to the facts of the petitioner's version of the case, and this could not be accomplished if there was an open trial of the case, as the facts of such a public trial would thereby become public knowledge. Petitioner avers that Attorney Foreman conceived the diabolical idea that if he could induce petitioner to plead guilty, these ends could be thus achieved.

Petitioner charges that attorneys Hanes and Foreman had a responsibility over and above that to their client. As agents

Page 11

of the court, they had an obligation to see that justice was done.
They should have refrained from making sharp financial transactions
and then fitting their court performance to their financial interests. They ignored their responsibilities to their client and
their profession.

Petitioner's failure to have _effective_ and _honest_ counsel
is in reality a greater disservice to him than having incompetent
counsel and is a gross denial of his rights under Article I, Section 9, of the Constitution of the State of Tennessee and the 6th
and 14th Amendments to the Constitution of the United States of
America. This failure to have effective representation made petitioner's plea of guilty, a farce, a sham, and a mockery of justice.

4. As difficult as it may be to believe, the Public
Defender and his office aided the prosecution more than the petitioner.

On December 18, 1968, the Trial Judge appointed the
Public Defender, Mr. High Stanton, Sr., to assist Foreman in preparing his defense of petitioner, who had been adjudged indigent.
At their very first meeting on December 18th, Stanton suggested
to Foreman that they should attempt to work out a guilty plea.

Petitioner avers that the Trial Judge appointed the
Public Defender to assist in his, petitioner's, preparation of
his defense, not to persuade his counsel-of-choice to enter a
plea of guilty.

Page 12

VII. THE DEAL

After Stanton's conference with Foreman on December 18th, he went to work to see what kind of a deal he could work out with the other interested parties for a plea of guilty and a "reduced" sentence.

On December 26th, Stanton phoned Foreman that the best he can do was a sentence of 99 years. When this word was passed to petitioner, he vehemently rejected the deal.

During January and February, 1969, Foreman visited petitioner often. His theme was always the same: accept the deal or go to the electric chair. Eventually, petitioner was persuaded and signed a letter authorizing Foreman to make a deal. On February 21st, Foreman took the formal plea of guilty to District Attorney Canale. On February 28th, Asst. District Attorney Beasley gave Foreman the stipulations which must accompany the plea. On or about February 28th, Foreman returned with petitioner's approval of the stipulations. In early March, District Attorney Canale consulted the U.S. Department of Justice which gave its approval to the deal. Next the District Attorney consulted Mrs. King and the Reverend Abernathy who did not "approve" the "deal" but said that they did not object to petitioner's not going to the electric chair, as they disapproved of capital punishment in general. Mrs. King and the Reverend Abernathy have both consistently expressed the view that they believe that the Reverend King was murdered as the result of a conspiracy.

Finally, Messrs. Foreman and Canale took the deal to the Trial Judge who gave his approval, but only because the deal provided 99 years imprisonment rather than a life sentence. Ironi-

Page 13

cally, after sentence had been pronounced, Judge Battle proclaimed to the court that it had been a good deal. After all, according to him, it avoided the possibility of acquittal or a hung jury, and, after all, no one has been put to death in Tennessee in over a decade.

VIII. PETITIONER ACCEPTED DEAL UNDER DURESS AND BRIBERY

a. Petitioner charges that his attorney, Percy Foreman, instituted a course of action toward him designed to pressure petitioner into pleading guilty. Your petitioner avers that his attorney's action was not taken for the welfare of petitioner but was done by his said attorney so that he could collect large sums of money from the writer or writers with whom he had contracted.

b. Although petitioner was very loathe to plead guilty to a crime which he did not commit, he was equally loathe to disregard the consistent and persistent advice of his chosen and experienced counsel. Personalities and differences in age and education - petitioner only finished eighth grade - certainly took its toll in the process of persuasion and acceptance.

c. Petitioner avers that attorney Foreman pressured him toward a plea of guilty all during the months of January and February, finally warning him without equivocation that 'the only way to save his life was for him to plead guilty.'

d. Having changed lawyers once, and having been warned by the Trial Judge that he would not be permitted to do so again except under the most exceptional circumstances, and fearful of ignoring the advice of his chosen counsel and the Public Defender, petitioner finally gave in and consented under extreme duress to a plea of guilty.

e. Petitioner avers that Attorney Foreman told him that chances of conviction were "100%" and chances of the electric chair were "99%."

f. Later, on a national TV program (Dick Cavett, August 9, 1969), Attorney Foreman bragged of his handling of the guilty plea:

> Cavett: ...... a lot of people in the legal profession were astounded at how you got him to change the plea.
>
> Foreman: I didn't get him to change the plea. I simply told him that I thought he would be executed if he didn't. [Laughter.]

g. What Attorney Foreman did not tell the TV audience was that, when the agreement for the guilty plea became unhinged on March 9th, the day before the trial, that he seasoned his duress with a touch of bribery to get petitioner "back in line." Specifically, petitioner desired to change his mind and return to his original plea of "not guilty." When Attorney Foreman heard of this, he rushed to the jail and spent 2-1/2 hours with petitioner, arguing with him to stick with the "guilty plea."

Furthermore, Attorney Foreman said (and confirmed in writing) that if petitioner persisted in his demand for a "not guilty" plea and a trial that he (Foreman) would insist on execution of his contractual rights to all of petitioner's future earnings from literary, movie, etc. rights; Foreman estimated these to be approximately one half million dollars; Foreman had some basis for this estimate as he thought he had worked out movie

Page 15

rights alone with producer Carlo Ponti for $175,000, plus 13% of
proceeds. Attorney Foreman informed petitioner, however, that if
he stuck with the guilty plea "and no embarrassing circumstances
take place in the courtroom, I am willing to assign to any bank,
trust company or individual selected by you all my receipts under
the above assignment in excess of $165,000.00". It has never been
explained as to whom the circumstances were not to be "embarrassing." Foreman? Canale? The United States? [See Exhibits Q and
R for two letters of March 9, 1969, from Percy Foreman to petitioner.] Thus, bribery was added to duress.

IX. CRUEL AND UNUSUAL PUNISHMENT

Petitioner avers that he was subjected to cruel and
unusual punishment in violation of the Constitutions of Tennessee
and the United States, and that this punishment contributed
directly to his plea of guilty to a crime which he did not commit.
Specifically, petitioner avers that:

a. He was kept in solitary confinement in Memphis for
nine months.

b. He was cut off from all fresh air and daylight
during this long period of time.

c. He was under constant surveillance, 60 minutes of
every hour, 24 hours of every day during that period. The surveillance consisted of bright lights, guards within eye and ear
shot, closed circuit TV and concealed microphones at all times.

d. Despite protests, he was subjected almost constantly
to radio and TV noises from the guards' radio and TV sets.

Page 16

e. As a result of this cruel and unusual punishment, he could not get proper rest. He became extremely nervous and suffered from chronic headaches and nosebleeds.

f. The Trial Judge denied a motion by petitioner to correct or ameliorate certain of these conditions.

g. Because of his distress and nervousness, he became incapable of making rational and intelligent decisions with respect to his defense. He became wholly dependent on Attorneys Foreman and Stanton and their judgement. Eventually, his resistance was worn down and he was induced to bow to their insistence on a plea of guilty.

XI. DID PETITIONER IN FACT AGREE IN COURT THAT HE WAS VOLUNTARILY PLEADING GUILTY?

At the hearing on March 10, 1969, Judge Battle posed this question to petitioner:

"Has any pressure of any kind by anyone in any way been used on you to get you to plead guilty?"

According to the transcript prepared by the Clerk of Court, petitioner replied:

"No, no one, in any way." [Exhibit Q.]

However, in the only published version of the court proceeding [See Exhibit R, *The Strange Case of James Earl Ray*, by Clay Blair, Bantam Press, 1969, at p. 210, the exact same question is answered:

"Now, what did you say?"

and the judge, without repeating the question, went on to the
next question.

Yet, on this crucial question of duress, still another
"official" version of the transcript, that of Miss Marty Otwell,
Court Reporter, Memphis, completely omits both the question and
answer. [See Exhibit S]. Miss Otwell had been approved by
Judge Battle as official court reporter for petitioner.

Petitioner avers that he recalls that the question was
asked, but that, because of its importance, he wanted to be sure
that he understood it exactly. To the best of his memory, the
question was not repeated, and he was given no further opportunity
to answer it.

Petitioner further avers that the record on this point,
at best, is very unclear, and that, as set out above at some
length, continuous and heavy pressure was brought to bear by his
counsel. The pressure had been particularly heavy on the previous
day, March 9, and it had been supplemented with bribery.

XII. FRAUD ON THE COURT

Petitioner avers that the Court as well as he has been
defrauded by the actions of counsel in this case, and cites the
following specific examples:

a. Despite a prohibition against pre-trial publicity,
Look Magazine published highly prejudicial articles by author

Page 18

Wm. Bradford Huie, who had received his information from Attorney
Arthus Hanes.

b. On November 12, 1968, when Judge Battle enrolled
Percy Foreman to practice before the court as petitioner's counsel,
Foreman made no mention of fee. However, when he reported to the
court on December 18, 1968, as to progress in his investigation
of the case, he made these statements:

"I intend to stay in this case as long as your Honor
will permit me so to do and without compensation. If compensation should become available, it will do so without
my committing any of what I consider a lawyer's responsibility or a client's rights." [Transcript, p.3]

"... and I will keep this court advised if any
contracts of any kind are signed or agreed upon."
[Transcript, p. 6]

"If I were willing to sell this man's life for some
royalties on a picture and on a book, magazine articles,
it would be logical for money but I don't practice law
for money now. There was a time when I did." [Transcript,
p. 23].

Again, on February 7, 1969, he told the court:

"... because I want it said at the conclusion of
this trial that I did not receive anything for my
part of this case...." [Transcript, p. 21]

As Exhibits B-F indicate, from the very beginning
Foreman had every intention of extracting as much money as possible out of the case. Petitioner avers that at their very first
meeting, Foreman demanded and he verbally agreed to $150,000 if
that much could be realised from the sale of literary rights.
In time, this sum was increased considerably and, at one point,
Foreman had a written contract for all of petitioner's and Hanes'
percentage of the future rights.

Page 19

Petitioner further avers that he knows of no evidence to indicate that these mercenary agreements, so full of conflict of interest, were ever revealed to the court as promised.

    c. Attorney Foreman's Motion for Enrollment, granted on November 12, 1968, contained this promise:

> "That he will, if admitted, secure the services of a lawyer licensed by the State of Tennessee to associate with him in the defense of said cases."

Yet, petitioner avers, that no such lawyer was ever engaged. The first mention that petitioner heard of a Tennessee lawyer in private practice was on or about March 1st when Foreman said that he wanted Attorney John J. Hooker, Sr., of Nashville, associated with the plea of guilty. Under the circumstances, petitioner declined the services of the eminent lawyer, as he needed no further assistance in pleading guilty.

    d. Attorney Foreman stalled the court for months with the argument that he personally needed to interview all 360 of the State's prospective witnesses. Petitioner believes it to be a fact that Foreman personally interviewed less than 10% of these witnesses (if, indeed, that many) and that the extensions of time were sought solely to pressure him into a plea of guilty.

    e. Later, on the Dick Cavett show of August 8, 1969, Attorney Foreman discussed petitioner's case and made at least two statements which petitioner urges are further frauds on the court of which Foreman is an officer:

    1. He outlined certain serious crimes which he alleges petitioner perpetrated; if petitioner had perpetrated such crimes he could be prosecuted and might

be convicted; and public disclosure of such alleged crimes is a gross breach of a lawyer's responsibility toward a client. Foreman's statement as to petitioner was as follows:

"Well, he [petitioner] ran three packets of narcotics from Windsor down to Detroit. He ran one tire full of jewelry from Laredo, Texas, into Mexico.

2. Attorney Foreman also made this statement on the same show:

"Well, there are few people in my 42 years and not one has committed a murder that ever committed his second one. Of course, there are paid killers, but they are an asset to society usually by the type of people they kill, at least most of them. [Laughter].

Such is the lawyer who persuaded petitioner to plead guilty.

XIII. PUBLIC INTEREST

No two cases are exactly alike and petitioner believes that his case is somewhat exceptional from the viewpoint of public interest.

The public is grossly dissatisfied with the proceeding in Memphis whereby petitioner plead guilty. They do not believe that he killed Dr. King, certainly not by himself. If there was a conspiracy, they wish to know the identity of the conspirators, and why they have not been tried and convicted.

Page 21

Under our American system of law, all suspects are to
be tried in court by an adversary proceeding. Here, due to the
duplicity of petitioner's attorneys, petitioner was tried, not in
court, but in the press in advance of a trial date. There was no
adversary proceeding, only a stipulation of the record.

Petitioner avers further that he has never had a trial
and has never been accorded his day in court. By way of being more
explicit, petitioner would show to the court that he was induced
to plead guilty when, in fact, he was and is not guilty of the
crime of murder.

XIV. **TRIAL JUDGE INTENDED TO HEAR MOTION FOR
NEW TRIAL AT TIME OF HIS DEATH**

Petitioner avers that Judge Battle intended to hold a
hearing on petitioner's Motion for a New Trial at the time of his
death. In fact, he had on his desk two letters from petitioner
which he considered the equivalent of such a Motion. He had
promised petitioner's new counsel, Mr. Richard Ryan of Memphis,
on that very day that he would arrange for Mr. Ryan to visit
petitioner in jail and work out details of the Motion before the
thirty-day time limit ran. Unfortunately, Judge Battle dropped
dead before he could complete these arrangements on that day.

Your petitioner avers that another Judge, the Hon.
Arthur Faquin, serving in place of Judge Battle, ruled that since
he had pleaded guilty, there could be no motion for a new trial
heard, and refused to set aside the judgment. Yet, in a reply
brief of May 13, 1969, District Attorney Canale admitted that
Judge Battle, had he lived, could have given petitioner relief

Page 22

on a Motion to Withdraw his plea of guilty if the proper and required grounds were present." Also, by an order dated March 13,
1969, Judge Battle ordered all evidence retained by the State,
obviously anticipating further legal moves in the case.

The case was carried to the highest appellate courts of
this State and finally the Supreme Court of Tennessee affirmed the
Judgment of the Criminal Court of Shelby County. This was done
despite the statutes of Tennessee which require a new trial where
the presiding Judge has died before passing on such motions. The
prior decisions of the Supreme Court of Tennessee had held this to
be a wholesome law since the judge who heard the case was the only
Judge who could properly and legally authenticate the record in the
case for review by the Supreme Court.

XV. DELAY

Your petitioner further charges that this matter was
brought to the attention of the Judge who originally presided in
this case, and before the death of Judge Battle, and to the attention of the successor Judge and the District Attorney General,
within a short time thereafter; the matters contained in this com-
plaint were brought to the attention of the Court and the prosecution promptly, so that delay could not have been petitioner's
motive, nor could the passage of such a short period of time have
impaired the chances of the prosecution in presenting whatever case
they have or may have not had. Petitioner hereby makes his
affidavit a part of this petition and is filing the same with
this petition.

He would show to the court that the State's case has not been
prejudiced, and that he has obtained no unfair advantages by
reason of his plea of guilty.

Page 23

XVI. RELIEF

Petitioner avers that he only pleaded guilty because of the above-stated reasons and not because he was in fact guilty.

PREMISES CONSIDERED, PETITIONER PRAYS:

1. That he be allowed to file this petition;

2. That the Writ of Habeas Corpus issue requiring the warden, Lewis Tollett, to have the person of the petitioner before this Court at such time and place as this Court may require and order, so that the legality of his restraint may be inquired into;

3. He prays that he be allowed to withdraw his plea of guilty and that the judgment upon which he is being restrained, be set aside and for nothing held and that he be granted a trial on his plea of not guilty;

4. That the Public Defender be ordered to make all files on this case available to present counsel for petitioner;

5. That an evidentiary hearing be granted under Section 40-3809 of Tennessee Statutes;

6. That for such evidentiary hearing, a Court Reporter be appointed under Section 40-3801 of the Tennessee Statutes;

7. He prays for such other, further and general relief as the equities and justice of the case may demand.

JAMES EARL RAY
(Petitioner)

J. B. STONER
(Attorney for Petitioner)

R. J. RYAN
(Attorney for Petitioner)

B. FENSTERWALD, JR.
(Attorney for Petitioner)

Page 25

[Exhibit I]

BOW STREET MAGISTRATES COURT

Bow Street,

London, W.C.2.

1st May 1969

Dear Sir,

I am directed by the Chief Magistrate to reply to your letter of the 23rd April concerning the proceedings at this Court against James Earl Ray.

There is not available any complete transcript of the proceedings and the arguments at the time of Ray's appearance. Certain oral evidence was given including the making of a statement by Ray, but all copies of that were sent to the Secretary of State at the Home Office in London for transmission to the State Department at Washington, together with the papers which had been sent to this Court from Washington. As far as I know the Home Office has not retained copies of those papers.

It is possible that you might be able to obtain some assistance from the solicitors in London who acted on behalf of James Earl Ray. Their name is Michael Dresden & Co., 32 Tavistock Street, London, W.C.2.

Yours faithfully,

Chief Clerk

RECEIVED

AS OF

MAY -5 1969

BY ROBERT W. HILL, JR.

Robert W. Hill, Jr.,
418 Pioneer Building,
Chattanooga, Tennessee 37402.

[Exhibit J]

DEPARTMENT OF STATE

Washington, D.C. 20520

December 10, 1969

Mr. James E. Ray, 65477
Station-A-West
MSB H-3
Nashville, Tennessee

Dear Mr. Ray:

I regret the delay in a further response to your letter of August 14, 1969.

The Department has recently received the transcript of the extradition proceedings, and a copy will be sent to you shortly along with the request for inspection and copy of record, a copy of which is enclosed for your information.

With respect to affidavits submitted by the United States Government to the Bow Street Court in support of the extradition request, the court has returned those documents to the United States. The Deputy Attorney General has advised the Department of State that these documents are considered part of investigative files of the Department of Justice and are exempt from disclosure under subsection (e)(7) of section 552 of Title 5 of the United States Code. Accordingly, those affidavits have been returned to the custody of the originating agency. Any further inquiries, therefore, should be addressed to the Department of Justice.

Sincerely yours,

J. Edward Lyerly
Deputy Legal Adviser

Enclosure

APPENDIX C

Senator Robert Byrd's Speech, March 29, 1968

MEMPHIS RIOTS AND THE COMING MARCH ON WASHINGTON

Mr. President, we have been hearing for months now that Dr. Martin Luther King, Jr. has been planning a march on Washington and a "civil disobedience campaign" in the Nation's Capital in April.

Yesterday, Mr. President, the Nation was given a preview of what may be in store for this city by the outrageous and despicable riot that Martin Luther King helped to bring about in Memphis, Tenn.

If this self-seeking rabble-rouser is allowed to go through with his plans here, Washington may well be treated to the same kind of violence, destruction, looting and bloodshed.

In Memphis, people were injured, stores were looted, property was destroyed, terror reigned in the streets, people were beaten by hoodlums, at least one Negro youth is known to have been killed, and massive rioting erupted during a march which was led by this man. It was a shameful and totally uncalled-for outburst of lawlessness, undoubtedly encouraged to some considerable degree, at least, by his words and actions, and his presence. There is no reason for us to believe that the same destructive rioting and violence cannot, or that it will not, happen here if King attempts his so-called poor people's march, for what he plans in Washington appears to be something on a far greater scale than what he had indicated he planned to do in Memphis.

When the predictable rioting erupted in Tennessee, Martin Luther King fled the scene. He took to his heels and disappeared, leaving it to others to cope with the destructive forces he had helped to unleash.

He was due in Washington today, to conduct discussions in furtherance of the demonstration planned for this city. However, as a result of the tragic happening of yesterday, he canceled the conferences in Washington for today. Nonetheless, I do not believe that the implications of the ugly events of yesterday will be lost on local residents—despite the widespread sanction and support that has been offered to King by churches, the YMCA, and many other organizations in the Nation's Capital. I hope that well-meaning Negro leaders and individuals in the Negro community here will now take a new look at this man who gets other people into trouble and then takes off like a scared rabbit. If anybody is to be hurt or killed in the disorder which follows in the wake of his highly publicized marches and demonstrations, he apparently is going to be sure that it will be someone other than Martin Luther King.

Mr. President, what occurred yesterday in Memphis was totally uncalled for—just as Martin Luther King's proposed march on Washington is totally uncalled for and totally unnecessary. He himself has been publicly quoted as saying that he thinks nothing constructive, so far as congressional action is concerned, can come out of his campaign here. Yet he says he is coming anyway. Why? To bring about another riot?

Mr. President, the main difference that I see now between what Martin Luther King plans here and what happened in Memphis yesterday is that the Memphis riot he precipitated might best be described as a hit-and-run riot, in view of his flight, while he has promised that his demonstration in the Federal City may last all summer.

Ostensibly, Martin Luther King went to Memphis to do the same sort of thing he has promised to do here—to "help poor people." He has billed his Washington march as a "poor people's crusade." In Memphis he went to lead striking garbage workers in a march to "help" them, but today, in the aftermath of Thursday's stupid and tragic occurrence, the Negroes he purportedly wanted to help are far worse off than they would have been in he had never gone there, for many are in jail and many are injured—and most certainly race relations have been dealt a severe setback across the Nation, as they have been in Memphis.

Is Washington now to be subjected to the same destruction and bloodshed?

Martin Luther King had no business in Memphis, he should never have gone there for the purposed of leading the protest march—just as he never should come here for the purpose of conducting a poor people's demonstration. There can be no doubt that he must be held directly responsible for much of what took place in Tennessee, and he will have to bear the onus for whatever takes place in Washington if he carries through on his threatened demonstration here.

King, himself, has talked of a crisis-packed situation in connection with his projected Washington demonstration and the erection of his proposed "shantytown," wherever it is to be located, whether among the Tidal Basin's cherry trees, on the Mall, in the District of Columbia Stadium, or elsewhere.

This man, who suffers from the delusion that only his eyes have the divine insight to detect what is wrong in our country, claims he wants to dramatize the plight of the poor. He has declared:

> Bitter experience has shown that our Government does not act
> until it is confronted directly and militantly.

With this as his deceitful theme, King intends to demand greater and more unrealistic governmental subsidies in a year when the Federal Government is already spending over $25 billion annually to help the poor.

His plan for creating a crisis-packed situation, which he so often foments, is to bring 100 initial demonstrators to the Nation's Capital on April 22 to pressure Congress and Federal executives for more adequate health care and education, increases in jobs and incomes, and numerous other actions. Larger masses of people will begin moving in on April 26, according to a news story written by Willard Clopton, which was published in the *Washington Post* of March 28, 1968.

Never before in history has an administration, a Congress, or a Nation's citizenry as a whole devoted as much effort and action toward alleviating the problems of poverty and discrimination. Yet, in the midst of this, the pious Dr. King ominously declares:

> We have a national emergency. The prospects of cities aflame
> is very real indeed, but I would also remind America of the
> continuing violence perpetrated daily by racism in our society.

If King goes through with his plans now, he will indeed crate a crisis-packed situation in Washington, just as his presence created an explosive situation in Memphis.

There are very real dangers, Mr. President—as yesterday's rioting clearly showed—in the sort of irresponsible actions King indulged in in Memphis, and in what he is planning here. The warning signals should be raised, if, indeed, they have not already been. There are dangers from the leader himself, as he so thoroughly demonstrated by not being able to keep down violence in Memphis despite his vaunted policy of nonviolence. And there is certainly danger in the type of gathering he envisions here.

Mr. President, I call attention to one paragraph in an article written again by Willard Clopton, entitled "Riot Spurs Review of March Here," which was published in the *Washington Post* this morning. The paragraph reads as follows:

> One of the Campaign's organizers said of the Memphis erup-
> tion, "It looks like we were 'had' by the extremists . . . We
> weren't prepared." He indicated that the SCLC's usual precau-

tions against violence such as the posting of numerous marshals and monitors, were overlooked yesterday.

King intends to create a black hole of despair with people packed together with pigs and chickens in a "shanty town" lacking sanitation. Surely he must know that to change hearts it is not necessary to turn stomachs. It can be assumed that, however, if yesterday's flight by King from the disorder he had helped to generate was any indication of what he might do here, the "Messiah" himself will not share the squalor he plans and that instead he will be conducting a lay-in at a posh Washington hotel to dramatize some imaginary discrimination there.

In his typical fashion, King intends to build a powder keg village and then plead that no one play with matches nearby lest destruction occur. He lays down the fuses around such a situation, however, with his semantic storehouse of volatile phrases such as "bloodless war," "direct action program," "crisis-packed situation," "dramatic confrontation," "attention-getting activities," "pressure," and "civil disobedience."

King's semantic gyrations have not fooled the American public, because violence has followed him like his shadow. Just as Shakespeare's Iago goaded Othello, the Moor, into committing outrage, King, the ever-correct phrasemaker, manages with saccharin words to produce sanguinary results.

He preaches nonviolence as a characteristic of disobedience. But the new civil disobedience is "civil disturbance." Riots, bombing, and violent protest typify the civil disobedience of today.

The marches in Milwaukee and Chicago last year were chaotic, and the Memphis march Thursday was disastrous. King has called for nonviolence here, but there are people allied with the poor people's campaign who call for the overthrow of the American Government by violence. Martin Luther King may have been a powerful man in the civil rights movement up to now, but it seems almost impossible to expect that he can control such large groups of militant activists as those he expects to join him in the demonstration here. Or, Mr. President, does he really expect to control them?

Both Stokely Carmichael and H. Rap Brown, if he can get out of jail, have agreed to march with Dr. King on the latter's terms—nonviolence—but how can we, or King, be sure of this? How can we be sure that another Memphis will not erupt? How can we be sure that King's lieutenants will not again have to say, "It looks like we were 'had' by the extremists. We were not prepared."

It is a well-known fact that riots begin when there is some uniting spark to excite a mob. All it would take in a situation like a Washington camp-in would be for some incident to turn the modern Coxey's Army King in raising into an angry, and ugly mob.

If Dr. King's plans to obstruct passage into the departments of the Government and buildings on Capitol Hill are carried out, it is certain that these actions will be met with a counterforce. There would be violence, and there is a great possibility that someone could be injured or killed.

Washington citizens and businessmen are concerned about their city. They do not want Washington to be torn apart by riots or discord.

Washington businessmen have been meeting with District officials and among themselves to draw up plans for the possible coming of the campaign. Hotel Association President Hudson Moses was quoted in the Washington Post on March 1 on what the city might lose as a result of the demonstration. He said:

> Several of our members told me they have had group cancellations specifically because of the march. . . . It will cost this city millions of dollars in indirect loss of business and taxes.

Martin Luther King's main target, in Washington, Mr. President, is the Congress, because it has not passed all of the broad legislation that he seeks.

From the beginning, this Washington march and demonstration—if it really seeks the goals that King claims for it—has been poorly conceived and poorly planned. It must be obvious to anyone that people who have to be recruited and trained will not be coming to Washington of their own volition. This will be no spontaneous demonstration, Mr. President, no grassroots movement. This task force he wants to bring here, by King's own admission, must be recruited and "trained."

Some of the recruits, it is said, will come from cities that went up in flames last summer. One can only assume that they will be riot-hardened veterans. One can properly ask, I think: What sort of "training" are they now being given?

Why, Mr. President, do citizens, if their cause and their grievances are just, have to be trained? It seems to me that there is something very sinister here. I am aware, as I have indicated before in these remarks, that Dr. King has said that his tactics will be nonviolent. But when he sets the stage for violence, how long can his "trained" army and the malcontents, disrupters, militants, and hoodlums already here be expected to remain nonviolent in Washington's long, hot summer?

Mr. President, they may have learned their lessons well from King, who once said:

> I do feel that there are two types of laws. One is a just law and one is an unjust law. I think we all have moral obligations to disobey unjust laws. I think that the distinction here is that when one breaks a law that conscience tells him is unjust, he must do it openly, he must do it cheerfully, he must do it lovingly, he must do it civilly, not uncivilly, and he must do it with a willingness to accept the penalty.

King lovingly breaks the law like a boa constrictor. He crushes the very life from it. His willingness to accept the penalty, which is supposed to set him apart from the common lawbreaker, can be judged by his irritation at a court decision which upheld a 5-day jail sentence for King recently. Faced with the prospect of accepting the penalty, King intoned that the decision would "encourage riots and violence in the sense that it all but said that Negroes cannot redress their grievances through peaceful means without facing the kind of decision that we face." Analyze this comment, if you will. Although King states the court decision did not declare that Negroes could not redress their grievances, he seems to say just the opposite and warns that the dire consequences are riots and violence. The English language is like putty in King's hands, but his incantations are loaded with hidden land mines.

Apparently, the hoodlums in Memphis yesterday followed King's advice to break laws with which they did not agree. This has been a cardinal principle of his philosophy—a philosophy that leads naturally to the escalation of nonviolence into civil disobedience—which is only a euphemism for lawbreaking and criminality and which escalates next into civil unrest, civil disorder, and insurrection.

Mr. President, I have previously urged, in discussing this matter with the Justice Department, that the Federal Government seek a court order to enjoin Martin Luther King and his pulpitless parsons from carrying out their planned poor people's campaign in the Nation's Capital. In the light of yesterday's bloody chapter of violence which erupted with the visit of Martin Luther King to Memphis, I again urge that the Federal Government take steps to prevent King from carrying out his planned harassment of Washington, D.C. An ounce of prevention is worth a pound of cure. It is time for our Federal Government—which in recent years has shown itself to be virtually spineless when it comes to standing up against the lawbreakers, the hoodlums, and the Marxist demonstrators—at least to let the Nation know, in no uncertain terms, that it will not allow this Nobel Peace Prize winner to create another Memphis in the city which serves as the seat of the Government of the United States.

Law-abiding citizens, both Negro and white, in Washington and elsewhere, deserve no less from a government, the first duty of which is to preserve law and order.

APPENDIX D

CIA Document 1035–960
Concerning Criticism of the Warren Report

CIA Document #1035–960
RE: Concerning Criticism of the Warren Report

1. Our Concern. From the day of President Kennedy›s assassination on, there has been speculation about the responsibility for his murder. Although this was stemmed for a time by the Warren Commission report, (which appeared at the end of September 1964), various writers have now had time to scan the Commission›s published report and documents for new pretexts for questioning, and there has been a new wave of books and articles criticizing the Commission›s findings. In most cases the critics have speculated as to the existence of some kind of conspiracy, and often they have implied that the Commission itself was involved. Presumably as a result of the increasing challenge to the Warren Commission›s report, a public opinion poll recently indicated that 46% of the American public did not think that Oswald acted alone, while more than half of those polled thought that the Commission had left some questions unresolved. Doubtless polls abroad would show similar, or possibly more adverse results.

2. This trend of opinion is a matter of concern to the U.S. government, including our organization. The members of the Warren Commission were naturally chosen for their integrity, experience and prominence. They represented both major parties, and they and their staff were deliberately drawn from all sections of the country. Just because of the standing of the Commissioners, efforts to impugn their rectitude and wisdom tend to cast doubt on the whole leadership of American society. Moreover, there seems to be an increasing tendency to hint that President Johnson himself, as the one person who might be said to have benefited, was in some way responsible for the assassination.

Innuendo of such seriousness affects not only the individual concerned, but also the whole reputation of the American government. Our organization itself is directly involved: among other facts, we contributed information to the investigation. Conspiracy theories have frequently thrown suspicion on our organization, for example by falsely alleging that Lee Harvey Oswald worked for us. The aim of this dispatch is to provide material countering and discrediting the claims of the conspiracy theorists, so as to inhibit the circulation of such claims in other countries. Background information is supplied in a classified section and in a number of unclassified attachments.

3. Action. We do not recommend that discussion of the assassination question be initiated where it is not already taking place. Where discussion is active [business] addresses are requested:

a. To discuss the publicity problem with [?] and friendly elite contacts (especially politicians and editors), pointing out that the Warren Commission made as thorough an investigation as humanly possible, that the charges of the critics are without serious foundation, and that further speculative discussion only plays into the hands of the opposition. Point out also that parts of the conspiracy talk appear to be deliberately generated by Communist propagandists. Urge them to use their influence to discourage unfounded and irresponsible speculation.

b. To employ propaganda assets to [negate] and refute the attacks of the critics. Book reviews and feature articles are particularly appropriate for this purpose. The unclassified attachments to this guidance should provide useful background material for passing to assets. Our ploy should point out, as applicable, that the critics are (I) wedded to theories adopted before the evidence was in, (I) politically interested, (III) financially interested, (IV) hasty and inaccurate in their research, or (V) infatuated with their own theories. In the course of discussions of the whole phenomenon of criticism, a useful strategy may be to single out Epstein's theory for attack, using the attached Fletcher [?] article and Spectator piece for background. (Although Mark Lane's book is much less convincing that Epstein's and comes off badly where confronted by knowledgeable critics, it is also much more difficult to answer as a whole, as one becomes lost in a morass of unrelated details.)

4. In private to media discussions not directed at any particular writer, or in attacking publications which may be yet forthcoming, the following arguments should be useful:

a. No significant new evidence has emerged which the Commission did not consider. The assassination is sometimes compared (e.g., by Joachim Joesten and Bertrand Russell) with the Dreyfus case; however, unlike that case, the attack on the Warren Commission have produced no new evidence, no new culprits have been convincingly identified, and there is no agreement among the critics. (A better parallel, though an imperfect one, might be with the Reichstag fire of 1933, which some competent historians (Fritz Tobias, AJ.P. Taylor, D.C. Watt) now believe was set by Vander Lubbe on his own initiative, without acting for either Nazis or Communists; the Nazis tried to pin the blame on the Communists, but the latter have been more successful in convincing the world that the Nazis were to blame.)

b. Critics usually overvalue particular items and ignore others. They tend to place more emphasis on the recollections of individual witnesses (which are less reliable and more divergent--and hence offer more hand-holds for criticism) and less on ballistics, autopsy, and photographic evidence. A close examination of the Commission's records will usually show that the conflicting eyewitness accounts are quoted out of context, or were discarded by the Commission for good and sufficient reason.

c. Conspiracy on the large scale often suggested would be impossible to conceal in the United States, esp. since informants could expect to receive large royalties, etc. Note that Robert Kennedy, Attorney General at the time and John F. Kennedy's brother, would be the last man to overlook or conceal any conspiracy. And as one reviewer pointed out, Congressman Gerald R. Ford would hardly have held his tongue for the sake of the Democratic administration, and Senator Russell would have had every political interest in exposing any misdeeds on the part of Chief Justice Warren. A conspirator moreover would hardly choose a location for a shooting where so much depended on conditions beyond his control: the route, the speed of the cars, the moving target, the risk that the assassin would be discovered. A group of wealthy conspirators could have arranged much more secure conditions.

d. Critics have often been enticed by a form of intellectual pride: they light on some theory and fall in love with it; they also scoff at the Commission because it did not always answer every question with a flat decision one way or the other. Actually, the make-up of the Commission and its staff was an excellent safeguard against over-commitment to any one theory, or against the illicit transformation of probabilities into certainties.

e. Oswald would not have been any sensible person's choice for a co-conspirator. He was a "loner," mixed up, of questionable reliability and an unknown quantity to any professional intelligence service.

f. As to charges that the Commission's report was a rush job, it emerged three months after the deadline originally set. But to the degree that the Commission tried to speed up its reporting, this was largely due to the pressure of irresponsible speculation already appearing, in some cases coming from the same critics who, refusing to admit their errors, are now putting out new criticisms.

g. Such vague accusations as that "more than ten people have died mysteriously" can always be explained in some natural way e.g.: the individuals concerned have for the most part died of natural causes; the Commission staff questioned 418 witnesses (the FBI interviewed far more people, conduction 25,000 interviews and re interviews), and in such a large group, a certain number of deaths are to be expected. (When Penn Jones, one of the originators of the "ten mysterious deaths" line, appeared on television, it emerged that two of the deaths on his list were from heart attacks, one from cancer, one was from a head-on collision on a bridge, and one occurred when a driver drifted into a bridge abutment.)

5. Where possible, counter speculation by encouraging reference to the Commission's Report itself. Open-minded foreign readers should still be impressed by the care, thoroughness, objectivity and speed with which the Commission worked. Reviewers of other books might be encouraged to add to their account the idea that, checking back with the report itself, they found it far superior to the work of its critics.

BIBLIOGRAPHY

Periodicals

Bernstein, Adam, "H. Weisberg, 88, Critic of JFK Report," the *Washington Post*, February 25, 2002

Chevigny, Paul G.. "Politics and Law in the Control of Local Surveillance," *Cornell Law Review* V. 70, April 1984

Cornwell, Rupert, "Obituary: Sidney Gottlieb." *Independent*, Culture Section. March 15, 1999. http://www.independent.co.uk/arts-entertainment/obituary-sidney-gottlieb-1080920.html

Dallas Morning News (AP), "Ray admitted murder, ex-inspector says," August 19, 1978

Douglass, Jim, "The Martin Luther King Conspiracy Exposed in Memphis," *Probe Magazine*, Spring 2000. https://ratical.org/ratville/JFK/Unspeakable /MLKconExp.html

Farney, Dennis, "What makes Jackson run?" *Des Moines Register*, January 6, 1984. https://www.newspapers.com/image/130828889/

Goodman, George, "Dr. King, One Year After 'He Lives, Man!'" *Look* magazine, April 15, 1969, pp. 28–31

Hattem, Julian, "Top Dem: Don't name new FBI HQ after J. Edgar Hoover," *The Hill.com*, April 20, 2016. http://thehill.com/policy/national-security/277057-top-dem-dont-name-new-fbi-hq-after-j-edgar-hoover

Holley, Peter, "Sirhan Sirhan Denied Parole Despite a Kennedy Confidant's Call for the Assassin's Release," the *Washington Post*, February 11, 2015

Huie, William Bradford, "The Story of James Earl Ray and the Conspiracy to Kill Martin Luther King" (Parts I and II), *Look* magazine, November 12–26, 1968

Huie, William Bradford, with Percy Foreman and Arthur J. Hanes, "Why James Earl Ray Murdered Dr. King," *Look* magazine April 15, 1969, pp. 102–104; 106; 109-110; 112.

Janos, Leo, "The Last Days of the President: LBJ in Retirement," *The Atlantic*, July 1973. http://www.theatlantic.com/magazine/archive/1973/07/the-last-days-of-the-president/376281/

Jilani, Zaid, "What the 'Santa Clausification' of Martin Luther King Jr. Leaves Out," *The Intercept*, January 16, 2017

Knoxville News-Sentinel UPI, "House Probers Do Not Plan to Recall Ray, Chairman Says," November 10, 1978

Langeveld, Dirk, "Leonard Ray Blanton: Pardons for a Price," *The Downfall Dictionary*, February 7, 2009. http://downfalldictionary.blogspot.com/2009/02/leonard-ray-blanton-pardons-for-price.html

Leuchtenburg, William E., "A Visit With LBJ: An hour and a half of growing astonishment in the presence of the President of the United States, as recorded by a witness who now publishes a record of it for the first time," *American Heritage* magazine, May–June 1990, pp. 47–64.

Los Angeles Times, "Dr. King Urges US to Admit Vietnam War is 'Mistake,'" March 18, 1968

Meroney, John, "What Really Happened Between J. Edgar Hoover and MLK Jr.," *The Atlantic*, November 11, 2011

Meyers, Jim, "FBI Probed Hollywood's Jack Valenti for Mob Ties," *Newsmax.com*, February 9, 2009. http://www.newsmax.com/InsideCover/fbi-valenti-probe/2009/02/09/id/328179/

Mitchell, Jerry, "Could Lies about Emmett Till Lead to Prosecution?" Jackson (MS) *Clarion-Ledger*, Feb. 6, 2017

Mitchell, Jerry, "Some Fingerprints Still Untested in MLK Killing," Jackson (MS) *Clarion-Ledger*, April 4, 2013

O'Leary, Jeremiah, "British Policeman, Upset by Attacks, Sticks to Story on Ray," *The Washington Star*, August 20, 1978

Oregonian, The, "The Best Books of 2010," December 25, 2010

Oshinsky, David M.,"Fear and Loathing in the White House" *New York Times*, October 26, 1997

Pear, Robert, "President Reagan Pardons 2 Ex-FBI Officials in 1970's Break-Ins," *New York Times*, April 16, 1981. http://www.nytimes.com/1981/04/16/us/president-reagan-pardons-2-ex-fbi-officials-in-1970-s-break-ins.html

Pearce, John, "Negroes Plan Capital March: Army of Poor Will Move in April," New Orleans *Times-Picayune* (AP), Section 2, p. 29 (p. 58 on digital copy). http://phw02.newsbank.com/cache/arhb/fullsize/pl_011062016_0952_56749_118.pdf

Perrusquia, Marc, "Six:01," Memphis *Commercial Appeal*, April 2013 http://archive.commercialappeal.com/news/investigations/martin-luther-king-jr-the-last-32-hours-328547301.html

Phillips, Kristine, "In the latest JFK files the FBI's ugly analysis on Martin Luther King Jr. filled with falsehoods," the *Washington Post*, November 4, 2017 https://www.washingtonpost.com/news/retropolis/wp/2017/11/04/in-the-latest-jfk-files-the-fbis-ugly-analysis-on-martin-luther-king-jr-filled-with-falsehoods/?tid=pm_pop&utm_term=.49ad807437d1

Real Clear Politics, "Ten Most Corrupt Politicians in U.S. History," May 22, 2012

Rowan, Carl, "After 25 Years, Truth Begins to Emerge," the *Baltimore Sun*, April 7, 1993. http://articles.baltimoresun.com/1993-04-07/news /1993097035_1_james-earl-ray-hbo-real-trial

Russell, Dick, "A King-sized Conspiracy," *High Times*, 1999

Sack, Kevin, "Hidden Evidence Claimed in King Slaying," the *New York Times*, March 25, 1998

Sack, Kevin, "Son of Dr. King Asserts LBJ Role in Plot," the *New York Times*, June 20, 1997

San Francisco Chronicle, "Ex-Cop Says Ray Boasted He Shot King," August 19, 1978

Shannan, Pat, "Former CIA Participant Says He Was Part of It, Raul Identified as FBI Agent," *Media By-Pass: The Uncensored National News*, Vol. 9 No. 5 May 2001, p. 32

Sides, Hampton, "Remembering Martin Luther King as a Man, Not as a Saint," the *Washington Post*, April 1, 2011

Snoddy, Raymond, "British Ex-Detective Defends Testimony for King Hearing," the *Washington Post*, August 20, 1978. https://www.washington-post.com/archive/politics/1978/08/20/british-ex-detective-defends-testimony-for-king-hearing/f31ac029-cb10-4290-953a-c8754d6ab9a3/

Stelzer, C.D., "Maybe in Memphis," *RFT Riverfront Times*, May 9, 2001. http://www.riverfronttimes.com/stlouis/maybe-in-memphis/Content? oid=2471896

Stephens, Joe, "Valenti's Sexuality Was Topic For FBI," the *Washington Post*, February 19, 2009. http://www.washingtonpost.com/wp-dyn/content /article/2009/02/18/AR2009021803819.html

Time magazine, "The King Assassination Revisited," and ""I'm Gonna Kill That Nigger King," January 26, 1976, pp. 16–18; 23.

Tompkins, Steve, "Army feared King, Secretly Watched Him," Memphis *Commercial Appeal*, March 21, 1993. http://jfk.hood.edu/Collection/ Weisberg%20Subject%20Index%20Files/A%20Disk/Army%20Intelligence/Item%2012.pdf https://ratical.org/ratville/JFK/ArmyFearedKing.html#s8

Books

Barnes, Ben, with Lisa Dickey. *Barn Burning Barn Building*. Albany, Texas: Bright Sky Press, 2006

Blair, Clay Jr. *The Strange Case of James Earl Ray: The Man Who Murdered Martin Luther King*, New York, NY: Bantam Books, 1969

Branch, Taylor. *At Canaan's Edge: America in the King Years 1965–68*. New York: Simon & Schuster, 2006

Califano, Jr., Joseph A. *The Triumph & Tragedy of Lyndon Johnson*. New York: Simon & Schuster, 1991.

Caro, Robert A. *The Years of Lyndon Johnson—The Path to Power*. New York: Alfred A. Knopf, 1982.

Caro, Robert A. *The Years of Lyndon Johnson—Means of Ascent*. New York: Alfred A. Knopf, 1990.

Caro, Robert A. *The Years of Lyndon Johnson—The Master of the Senate*. New York: Alfred A. Knopf, 2002.

Caro, Robert A. *The Years of Lyndon Johnson—The Passage of Power*. New York: Alfred A. Knopf, 2012.

Cohen, Michael A. *American Maelstrom: The 1968 Election and the Politics of Division*. New York: Oxford University Press, 2016

Dallek, Robert. *Flawed Giant: Lyndon Johnson and His Times, 1961–1973*. New York: Oxford University Press, 1998

Davis, Deborah. *Katherine the Great*. New York: Harcourt, Brace and Jovanovich, Inc., 1979

Davis, John H. *Mafia Kingfish: Carlos Marcello and the Assassination of John F. Kennedy*. New York: McGraw Hill, 1989.

DeLoach, Cartha. *Hoover's FBI: The Inside Story by Hoover's Trusted Lieutenant*. Washington, DC: Regnery, 1997

Demaris, Ovid. *The Director: An Oral Biography of J. Edgar Hoover*. New York: Harper's Magazine Press, 1975.

Emison, John Avery. *The Martin Luther King Congressional Cover-Up: The Railroading of James Earl Ray*. Gretna, LA: Pelican Publishing Company, Inc., 2014

Frank, Gerold. *An American Death; The True Story of the Assassination of Dr. Martin Luther King, Jr. and the Greatest Manhunt of our Time*. New York: Hamish Hamilton, 1972

Garrow, David J. *The FBI and Martin Luther King, Jr*. New York: W.W. Norton & Co., 1981

Gentry, Curt, *J. Edgar Hoover: The Man and the Secrets*. New York: W.W. Norton, 1991

Goodwin, Richard N. *Remembering America*. Boston: Little, Brown and Company, 1988

Halberstam, David. *The Best and the Brightest*. New York: Random House, 1972

Halberstam, David. *The Fifties*. New York: Villard Books, 1993

Haley, James Evetts. *A Texan Looks at Lyndon: A Study in Illegitimate Power.* Canyon, TX: Palo Duro Press, 1964.

Hancock, Larry and Stuart Wexler. *The Awful Grace of God.* Berkeley, CA: Counterpoint, 2012

Hersh, Burton. *Bobby and J. Edgar: The Historic Face-Off Between the Kennedys and J. Edgar Hoover that Transformed America.* New York: Basic Books, 2008

Huie, William Bradford. *He Slew the Dreamer—My Search, with James Earl Ray, for the Truth About the Murder of Martin Luther King.* New York: Delacorte Press. 1968, 1969, 1970

Kearns Goodwin, Doris. *Lyndon Johnson and the American Dream.* New York: Harper & Row, 1976

Kessler, Ronald. *Inside the White House.* New York: Pocket Books, 1995

Lane, Mark, and Dick Gregory. *Murder in Memphis: The FBI and the Assassination of Martin Luther King.* Charlottesville, VA: The Lane Group, 2015

Lasky, Victor. *It Didn't Start with Watergate.* New York: The Dial Press, 1977

Livingstone, Harrison Edward. *Killing the Truth: Deceit and Deception in the JFK Case.* New York: Carroll & Graf Publishers, 1993

Mahoney, Richard D. *Sons & Brothers: The Days of Jack and Bobby Kennedy.* New York: Arcade Publishing Co., 1999.

Maxwell, William J. *F.B. Eyes: How J. Edgar Hoover's Ghostreaders Framed African-American Literature.* Princeton, NJ: Princeton University Press, 2015

McGhee, Millie. *Secrets Uncovered: J. Edgar Hoover, Passing for White?* Riverside, CA: Inland Empire Services, 2000

McGhee, Millie. *What's Done in The Dark.* Auburn, NY: Allen Morris Publishing: 2005

McKnight, Gerald D. *Breach of Trust: How the Warren Commission Failed the Nation and Why.* Lawrence, KS: University Press of Kansas, 2005.

McKnight, Gerald D. *The Last Crusade: Martin Luther King, Jr., the FBI, and the Poor People's Campaign.* Boulder, CO: Westview Press, 1998

McMichael, Pate. *Klandestine: How a Klan Lawyer and a Checkbook Journalist Helped James Earl Ray Cover Up His Crime.* Chicago: Chicago Review Press, Inc., 2015

McMillan, George. *The Making of an Assassin: The Life of James Earl Ray.* Boston: Little, Brown and Company, 1976

Melanson, Philip H. *The Martin Luther King Assassination: New Revelations on the Conspiracy and Cover-Up, 1968–1991.* New York: Shapolsky Publishers, Inc. 1991

MLK The Truth LLC. *The 13th Juror: The Official Transcript of the Martin Luther King Assassination Conspiracy Trial.* Seattle, WA: Amazon Digital Services, 2009

North, Mark. *Act of Treason: The Role of J. Edgar Hoover in the Assassination of President Kennedy.* New York: Carroll & Graf Publishers, Inc., 1991

Pepper, William F. *The Plot to Kill King: The Truth Behind the Assassination of Martin Luther King, Jr.* New York: Skyhorse Publishing, 2016

Posner, Gerald. *Killing the Dream: James Earl Ray and the Assassination of Martin Luther King Jr.* New York: Random House, 1998

Ray, James Earl. *Who Killed Martin Luther King? The True Story by the Alleged Assassin.* Washington, DC: National Press Books, 1992

Ray, Jerry and Tamara Carter. *A Memoir of Injustice.* Walterville, OR: Trine Day LLC, 2011

Ray, John Larry and Lyndon Barsten. *Truth At Last: The Untold Story Behind James Earl Ray and the Assassination of Martin Luther King Jr.* Guilford, CT: Lyons Press, 2008

Reynolds, Barbara A. *Jesse Jackson: The Man, the Movement, the Myth.* Chicago: Nelson-Hall, Inc. Publishers, 1975

Safer, Morley. *Morley Safer, Flashbacks: On Returning to Vietnam.* New York: Random House, 1990

Safire, William. *Safire's Political Dictionary.* New York: Oxford University Press, 2008

Scheim, David E. *Contract on America: The Mafia Murder of President John F. Kennedy.* New York: Zebra Books/Kensington Publishing Corp., 1989

Schlesinger Jr., Arthur M. *Robert Kennedy and His Times.* New York: Ballantine Books, 1978

Scott, Peter Dale. *Deep Politics and the Death of JFK.* Berkeley: University of California Press, 1996

Seigenthaler, John, and James D. Squires, Jack Hemphill, and Frank Ritter. *A Search for Justice.* Nashville, TN: Aurora, 1971

Sherrill, Robert. *The Accidental President.* New York: Pyramid Publication, Inc., 1968

Shesol, Jeff. *Mutual Contempt: Lyndon Johnson, Robert Kennedy and the Feud That Defined a Decade.* New York: W. W. Norton & Co., 1997

Sides, Hampton. *Hellhound on His Trail: The Stalking of Martin Luther King Jr. and the International Hunt for His Assassin.* New York: Doubleday, 2010

Sullivan, William C., with Bill Brown. *The Bureau: My Thirty Years in Hoover's FBI.* New York: W. W. Norton & Co., 1979

Summers, Anthony. *Official and Confidential: The Secret Life of J. Edgar Hoover.* New York: G. P. Putnam's Sons, 1993

Swearingen, M. Wesley. *To Kill a President.* Self-published, 2008

Theoharis, Athan. *From the Secret Files of J. Edgar Hoover.* Chicago: Ivan Dee, 1991

Theoharis, Athan. *The FBI & American Democracy: A Brief Criminal History.* Lawrence, KS: University Press of Kansas, 2004

Thomas, Evan. *The Man to See.* New York: Simon & Schuster, 1991

Timmerman, Kenneth R. *Shakedown: Exposing the Real Jesse Jackson.* Washington, DC: Regnery Publishing Co., 2002

Turner, William W. *Hoover's FBI.* New York: Dell, 1971

Turner, William W. *Rearview Mirror.* Granite Bay, CA: Penmarin Books, 2001

Valentine, Douglas. *The Phoenix Program.* New York: William Morrow & Co., 1990

Weiner, Tim. *Enemies: A History of the FBI.* New York: Random House, 2012

Weisberg, Harold. *Frame-Up: The Assassination of Martin Luther King.* New York: Skyhorse Publishing, (1970) 2013

Wilson, Donald G. *Evidence Withheld.* Parker, CO: Outskirts Press, 2013

Library and Internet Sites

Civil Rights Digital Library: http://crdl.usg.edu/collections/holloman/ See also https://books.google.com/books?id=8h406aDUeL4C&pg=PA161&lpg=PA161&dq=memphis+TN:++frank+c.+holloman

CNN.com. Brief History Of Chicago's 1968 Democratic Convention: http://www.cnn.com/ALLPOLITICS/1996/conventions/chicago/facts/chicago68/index.shtml

Democracy Now! "EXCLUSIVE . . . Jennifer Dohrn: I Was The Target Of Illegal FBI Break-Ins Ordered by Mark Felt aka 'Deep Throat,'" June 2, 2005. http://www.democracynow.org/2005/6/2/exclusive_jennifer_dohrn_i_was_the

Department of Justice (DOJ): https://www.justice.gov

Encylopedia.com: Riots, Urban, of 1967: http://www.encyclopedia.com/history/dictionaries-thesauruses-pictures-and-press-releases/riots-urban-1967

Famous Trials Website—The Emmett Till Murder Trial—1955: http://famous-trials.com/emmetttill/1759-chronology

Gary Revel website: http://garyrevel.com/News/mystery_helicopter.html

Hood College—Weisberg Collection (Murkin Conspiracy File): http://jfk.hood.edu/

King Center: King family trial transcript. See: http://www.thekingcenter.org/sites/default/files/KING%20FAMILY%20TRIAL%20TRANSCRIPT.pdf

LBJ Library Oral History Interviews:
Hubert H. Humphrey: http://www.lbjlibrary.net/collections/oral-histories/humphrey-h.-hubert.html
Nicholas D. Katzenbach: http://www.lbjlibrary.net/collections/oral-histories/katzenbach-deb.-nichola.html

Martin, David, DCDave.com, "Did Lyndon Step Down So Bobby Could Be Killed?" September 23, 2014: http://www.dcdave.com/article5/140923.htm

Mary Ferrell Organization (References to HSCA hearings, report volumes, and Final Report: https://www.maryferrell.org

National Archives: Findings on MLK Assassination (References to HSCA Hearings, Report Volumes and Final Report): https://www.archives.gov/research/jfk/select-committee-report/part-2a.html)
For MLK Records released October 26, 2017: https://www.archives.gov/files/research/jfk/releases/docid-32397527.pdf
For the FBI report: "Martin Luther King, A Current Analysis (3/12/1968)": https://www.archives.gov/files/research/jfk/releases/104-10125-10133.pdf

Orange County Register: http://www.ocregister.com

Spartacus Educational
http://spartacus-educational.com/JFKdavidsonI.htm
http://spartacus-educational.com/JFKblakey.htm
http://spartacus-educational.com/JFKassassinationsC.htm
http://spartacus-educational.com/JFKdowningT.htmTennessee Encyclopedia of History and Culture John and Viola McFerren: http://tennessee-encyclopedia.net/entry.php?rec=864

Wikipedia: *The American Mercury,* William Ayers, Cartha DeLoach, Frank Holloman, Iago, Henry Loeb, Operation CHAOS, President John F. Kennedy Assassination Records Collection Act of 1992, Louella Parsons, Clyde Tolson

William H. Williams Collection of Criminal Court Papers 1968–1992, Collection #5689, Southern Historical Collection, The Wilson Library, University of North Carolina at Chapel Hill: http://finding-aids.lib.unc.edu/05689/

WPA Film Library: https://www.wpafilmlibrary.com/videos/168341

YouTube videos:

"Conspiracy 5/11—Who Killed Martin Luther King Jr." https://www. youtube.com/watch?v=hmoPSUTazvQ

"Jessie Jackson Killed Martin Luther King Jr." https://www.youtube.com/watch?v=teEplUjU0Bw

"Judge Joe: James Earl Ray Didn't Assassinate Martin Luther King Jr." https://www.youtube.com/watch?v=HcJ_szc3TEA

"LBJ Watched 'Risque' Films" https://www.youtube.com/watch?feature=player_embedded &v=mCt9Zh7mDzg

"Martin Luther King's son Dexter meets James Earl Ray, Patsy-Assassin of his father" https://www.youtube.com/watch?v=rDVMu7nGVuU

"What's Done in the Dark - A Millie L McGhee Story" https://www.youtube.com/watch?v=hACX6T2aPFY, or https://www. youtube.com/watch?v=rDVMu7nGVuU

Zerohedge.com: http://www.zerohedge.com/news/2015-02-23/1967-he- cia-created-phrase-conspiracy-theorists-and-ways-attack-anyone-who- challenge

AFTERWORD

DID FAMED ATTORNEY / LBJ FRIEND PERCY FOREMAN BLACKMAIL JIMMY CARTER USING HIS SECRETS FROM RAILROADING RAY?

After the original edition of this book was published, the author began taking a closer look at the clearly unethical and illegal methods used by Percy Foreman during his purported "defense" of James Earl Ray. Though that edition included numerous instances of Foreman's clearly incompetent and/or antagonistic attitude regarding James Earl Ray and his family, the level of Foreman's sordid corruption was understated in that volume. That point is redressed here by a brief but intense look at other accounts of Percy Foreman's lengthy record using illegal methods to "win" cases at any cost. In James Earl Ray's case, he would reverse that methodology, betraying Ray, thus ensuring that he would rot in prison.

It would take nearly another decade, but eventually Percy Foreman practically acknowledged his own nefarious, highly illegal actions when he used his knowledge of the secrets of Martin Luther King's assassination – and the official cover-up – to present his "Get out of Jail" card, apparently directly to Jimmy Carter, the newly-elected president of the United States.

The "Official" Legend of Percy Foreman

At the top of the pyramid of the most famed Texas criminal lawyers stands the "legendary" Percy Foreman, who compiled a spectacular record of acquittals in seemingly unwinnable cases. Supporting that legend is the 1969 Foreman biography by Michael Dorman, King of the Courtroom: Percy Foreman for the Defense.

Even at the publication date of that book, nearly twenty years before Foreman's death when he was still actively involved in legal work, the author stated that his subject had represented "more accused killers than any man in history—upwards of 1,000." Yet, of that number, only fifty-five had gone to prison for their deeds and only one had been executed. According to author Dorman, the credo fastidiously followed by Foreman was:[949]

> [A defense attorney] should never allow the defendant to be tried. Try someone else—the husband, the lover, the police or, if the case has social implications, society generally. But never the defendant.

To illustrate Foreman's technique, in one of his most famous cases, in 1966 he defended a lady named Candy Mossler and her young paramour Melvin Powers – who was also her nephew – for the murder of Candy's multimillionaire husband, Jacques Mossler. Percy began that trial by stating to the jury that, "If each one of the 39 knife wounds had been inflicted by a different person, there still would be three times that number of people left with real or imaginary justification to want the death of Jacques Mossler." He then noted some of Mossler's alleged character traits that might have given unnamed other persons reason to want him dead: "Mossler was a ruthless businessman, a sexual deviate and a Jekyll and Hyde," without producing one scrap of evidence to support any of those accusations.[950] By painting the victim as a closeted homosexual, Foreman declared it was inevitable that his poor wife was forced to seek male companionship elsewhere. And that created, in the minds of the jurors, a strawman suspect—an unidentified homosexual lover apparently jilted by Jacques—who had supposedly become so upset that he furiously stabbed Mossler thirty-nine times.

Further distancing his clients from the aura of guilt, he managed to convince the jury that, if anything, the elderly dead man had certainly deserved to die. Falsely portraying Jacques as an irredeemable bully who, among other things, used to snap a bullwhip at his young wife's feet to make her dance—it was merely a story that apparently originated as a hallucination within Foreman's mind.

But he wanted to make that bold point stick, and endure for the entire trial, so he acquired a number of bullwhips, and arranged them on the defense table in front of the jury. Throughout the trial, they remained displayed in front of the jurors as reminders of the allegedly vicious husband. Foreman often picked them up as he went to great lengths to refresh the point during the course of the trial, coiling and uncoiling them individually, then shuffling through them as visual reminders of the original point, occasionally snapping one of them against the table to add emphasis to an important assertion. By the time the judge gave the jury their instructions, all twelve of the jurors had become convinced that Jacques, who had previously succumbed to the lovely young lady, had supposedly morphed into a wretched, homosexual philanderer with no redeemable character traits. Thus, the poor young wife and her proxy-lover—though acknowledging her incestual relationship with her even younger nephew, while pointing out they were not on trial for that—were the real victims of the tragic event. Against a massive amount of evidence of their guilt, Foreman's tactics prevailed when the jury found both Candy and Mel were not guilty of the murder of Jacques.[951]

A Fellow Texas Attorney's Scathing Rebuttal of Foreman's Conflicted "Legacy"

Contradicting Percy's purported legend—as written in the biography referenced above, of a scrupulously dedicated and "honorable" lawyer—was another Texas attorney, who had also attained stature near the top of that "famed Texas lawyers" pyramid. David Berg documented how Percy Foreman was a duplicitous and consummate liar. In his 2013 memoir *Run, Brother, Run,* Berg wrote that Foreman used a standard two-pronged approach in many cases, the first of which matched what author Dorman referenced, above. Berg's description of Foreman's second prong, however, crossed over all ethical boundaries:

> In case character assassination alone might fail, he reached into his stable of "reserve witnesses," as he called them: former clients and others who repaid his favors by swearing to have been with his defendant at the time of the crime. It wasn't just opposing prosecutors who knew that Foreman operated this way: his colleagues and even attentive laymen understood that *he would do anything, no matter how dishonest, to win a trial.* (Italics added by author).[952]

His use of the higher-risk "second step" option was reserved for cases in which the standard "try someone else" maneuver became impossible. But Percy did pull it out of his quiver in another infamous case, when he defended the hitman Charles Harrelson (father of famed actor Woody Harrelson) in a murder trial that took place immediately after destroying James Earl Ray's chance of getting a fair trial in 1969.[953]

Charles Harrelson's Business Card[954]

Among Harrelson's numerous murders was the contract murder of Alan Berg, the brother of David Berg, whose book referenced above was primarily about that case. In that courtroom, just when things were looking very tenuous for Foreman and his murderous client, new witnesses were introduced to present "evidence" of Harrelson's innocence. The three "witnesses" included Charles' father and two neighbors, all of whom might have been models for rednecks in the 1972 movie *Deliverance*. Together, they averred that Charles Harrelson was one hundred miles away, in Trinity, Texas at the very time the murder occurred. They could make such an assertion because the notary public (a.k.a. "justice of the peace") J. V. Price had noted the time on the "bill of sale" which he notarized, a very unusual practice. He also wrote it out in pencil, a practice generally used to obfuscate the authenticity of a document since "… it couldn't be dated by any scientific testing."[955] Through what was clearly the use of the most brazen deceits—the fabrication of the bogus bill of sale and the accompanying subornation of perjury by three witnesses, as well as the use of his standard tactic, blaming the murder on the victim himself—Percy Foreman had sprung the murderous Harrelson when the jury came back with the verdict of "not guilty."[956]

In yet another one of Harrelson's murder trials—for killing Sam Degelia, whose business partner needed him dead so he could collect his life insurance proceeds—Foreman again resorted to suborning perjury by coaching a woman in his debt to falsely testify that she had been with Harrelson in another town, far from the crime scene at the time of the murder. That caused the jury to become deadlocked, forcing the judge to declare it a mistrial. But when the new trial was held, the Texas Rangers—outraged by the brazen lies created by Foreman and his fake witness to free the murderer Harrelson—assembled evidence proving that the witness had lied about her whereabouts, and sent a Ranger to sit in the gallery prepared to arrest her if she dared show up again to repeat her lies. She chose to prolong her vacation in Aruba until after that trial. Despite Percy Foreman's best effort to set this serial killer free, Harrelson was finally found guilty of the murder and sentenced to fifteen years in prison.[957]

These were merely a sampling of Percy Foreman's lengthy, scurrilous record of using unethical and criminal tactics to "win" at all costs. In the interest of brevity, many other, equally appalling instances have been omitted.

Percy Foreman's Lifetime of Deceit—And How He Managed to Avoid His Own Prison Term

Foreman's choice of the clientele to whom he offered his services throughout his career, and the fraudulent methods he often used in doing that, brought with it a high risk of exposure and the potential of a consequent end to that career. In one extraordinary 1970s instance, Percy Foreman became involved as a central player in a case of massive fraud involving a number of other famed Texas lawyers, millionaires, and security specialists. One of the reasons it was "extraordinary" was about how it received a flourish of media coverage on the front end, but that soon became dampened, and by time it was adjudicated it had practically become a secret.

The following excerpts, from an article titled "H.L. Hunt's Long Goodbye" in the March 1975 edition of *Texas Monthly*, explain the basics and how it all started with a traffic stop:[958]

- The intrigue surfaced routinely enough four years ago [1971], when a suburban Dallas policeman stopped Jon Joseph Kelly for running a stop sign. Kelly, a twenty-five-year-old Houston man, identified himself as a private detective. The patrolman noticed a tape recorder in Kelly's back seat. "When I asked him if he was working on a divorce case," the policeman later recalled, "he stepped on the gas and took off. If he hadn't panicked, I wouldn't have hauled him in and none of this would have come out."
- The FBI discovered that Kelly and a sidekick, Patrick McCann, had placed wiretaps in the homes of four Hunt Oil executives, among them Paul Rothermel, H. L. Hunt's chief security man.

Rothermel, a former FBI man and an attorney, claimed that in 1969 he had persuaded Hunt to change his will to the greater benefit of the second Mrs. Hunt and her children. Since then, odd things had been happening; and Rothermel believed that the older Hunt sons were behind it. Kelly and McCann, however, remained mute—until they got three years in prison. Then they fingered two of the older Hunt sons, Nelson Bunker and W. Herbert Hunt, as the plotters and paymasters.

- Nelson and Herbert were indicted on wiretapping charges, but only after a curiously long-time lag. They have since admitted that they ordered "legal investigations" of Rothermel and the other executives, but not wiretaps. They contend their motive was not to spy on their father's will-making, but to trace millions of dollars which were allegedly siphoned off into dummy companies. They backed up their charges with a suit against Rothermel and two other company officials. Since then Kelly has sued Nelson and W. Herbert Hunt, complaining they ruined his reputation and career.

The original charging document stated that in mid-December 1971, Foreman had entered into a contract with the plaintiff, Jon Joseph Kelly, but, unbeknownst to Kelly, it was launched to enable Foreman to conduct a fraud against him. The gist of the lawsuit, asserting that Foreman was at the very center of a conspiracy, stated that he "surreptitiously conspired in Houston, Texas to disregard his ethical and lawful duty to the Plaintiff and to the Court and to sell his allegiance for cash dollars to be paid in a clandestine manner" and is further described in this excerpt of the charging document:[959]

The defendants conspired together and concocted a scheme to cover up certain criminal activities of NELSON BUNKER HUNT and W. HERBERT HUNT by paying PERCY FOREMAN vast sums of money [$100,000 total paid in early 1972], to betray Jon Joseph Kelly, a client he was then representing, and by guile, treachery, artifice and deceit, as well as intimidation and threat of force, to thereby dupe, use and frighten the Plaintiff and prevent hm from giving testimony regarding the criminal activities of NELSON BUNKER HUNT and W. HERBERT HUNT. It was agreed by the conspirators that they would pay FOREMAN who would then pretend to defend the Plaintiff, when in truth and in fact, and unbeknownst to Plaintiff, FOREMAN was really working exclusively for the conspirators and against the best interests of the Plaintiff . . .

The lawsuit asked for actual, exemplary and punitive damages "in the sum of at least ONE HUNDRED MILLION AND NO/100 ($100,000,000.00) DOLLARS."

Foreman was cast in that document as the central key conspirator . . . representing the other defendants, who, ". . . by word and deed [did] deter Plaintiff by misrepresentation, threats of physical harm, threats of economic ruin, intimidation of will, and other furtive methods from becoming a witness in or attending in a Court of the United States or testifying to a matter pending therein freely, fully and truthfully."

From Civil Suit to Criminal Indictment

That civil lawsuit, filed in 1972, led to a criminal indictment by a federal grand jury in July, 1975, naming the aforementioned Jon Joseph Kelly as a victim and the following persons were charged with multiple counts of obstruction of justice: Ralph Shank (a Dallas attorney), Charles Tessmer (a Dallas attorney), B. H. Timmins, Jr. (a Dallas attorney), Edward J. Hudson, (a Houston millionaire), Percy Foreman (a Houston attorney), Nelson Bunker Hunt and W. Herbert Hunt, (sons of the late H.L. Hunt, all millionaires of Dallas, Texas).[960]

In an article published in the *New York Times* July 22, 1975, more insights are revealed; the description included in this excerpt further explains the background of the criminal charges:

> The indictments handed up today allege that the Hunts promised Mr. Kelly, Mr. McCann and Mr. Everett amounts ranging from $800 to $1,250 per month while in prison if they did not testify before a grand jury concerning the Hunts involvement in the wiretapping case.[961]

Percy Foreman's Case is Given a Change of Venue

One year later, in July 1976, a motion to separate Percy Foreman from the original case and change the venue for his case from the Northern District of Texas to the Southern District (Houston) was granted by Halbert O. Woodward, the District Judge of the Northern District. The following restriction—rather odd, considering the public interest in such a development—was added, to ensure that this maneuver would be kept out of the public purview:[962]

> "This document contains neither recommendations nor conclusions of the FBI. It is the property of the FBI and is loaned to your agency; *it and its contents are not to be distributed outside your agency.*" (Emphasis added.)

The fact that only Percy Foreman's case was cut and moved from Dallas to Houston, when other defendants, also from Houston, were not, suggests that there were other reasons behind the move, a point that will be revisited below.

Percy Foreman Receives His "Get Out of Jail" Card

Led by the legal and PR team of the Hunt brothers, mounting political pressure was brought to bear in Washington to keep their names out of the press, and of course that meant they would also need to go to extraordinary lengths to avoid a trial. Although a search of various newspaper archives yields no significant articles, it has been independently reported that, just before the trial for the six other defendants was scheduled to begin, Senator James O. Eastland (D-MS) had been employed to quietly negotiate settlements with the Justice Department, allowing the defendants to plead no contest to a lesser charge and pay a nominal fine.

Less than a year later, on June 6, 1977, the same federal judge as before, Halbert O. Woodward, referencing an order from the US Attorney General (Griffin Bell, appointed by Jimmy Carter), *dismissed without explanation the indictment against Percy Foreman*:[963]

The fact that Percy Foreman had gotten off "scot-free" compromised the prosecution's ability to mount a strong case for the other defendants, ensuring that all of it would be handled without the normal level of media attention that might be expected to a case that had originally burst upon the scene with headlines in the national press, as previously noted.

Both Cases Mysteriously Disappear

Federal criminal cases generally wind their way to a specific outcome: a trial or a pre-trial settlement. The unusual intervention of the highest level of the Executive Department, only five months into the Carter administration, to

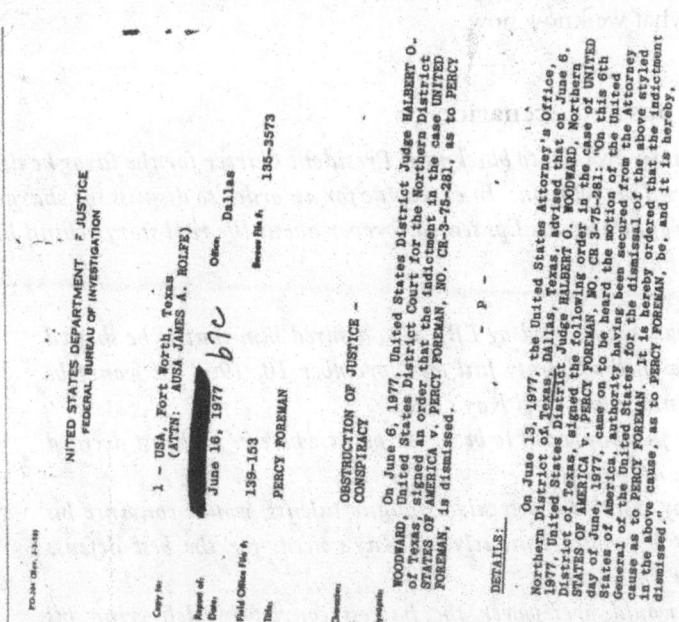

The memoranda—had they not been suppressed—that might have rocked the nation's constitutional foundation and exposed the real story of Martin Luther King's murder.

dismiss the single-most key conspirator who designed the cover-up, without a whimper from either side, must be considered most unusual.

It is reasonable to conclude that only the most powerful authority in Washington in 1977, the President himself, could have intervened to throw the case against Percy Foreman out. The fact that it came directly from his Attorney General Griffin Bell, nearly secretly—without even a hint of explanation of its rationale—means, axiomatically, that it had to have Carter's backing, either explicitly or at the very least with his acquiescence.

All of which evokes the image of "the 800-pound elephant in the room" and raises the rhetorical question of: *"What was the rationale?"*

The only realistic answer to that question is that it was something so potentially catastrophic to the continuance of the government—another of the "constitutional crises" that had been so common during LBJ's presidency—that there was no other option. If the president had publicly admitted the reason, could the country survive, with much of the population—especially blacks, still recovering from Martin Luther King's murder and the then-new revelations about the FBI's harassment of King amid new suspicions of Hoover's involvement in his murder—already primed for revolt? There is one reasonable explanation that is not only plausible, but maybe the only one possible, given what we know now.

Consider this possible scenario:

That Percy Foreman decided to blackmail President Carter for the favor he did for his friend President Johnson: In exchange for an order to dismiss the charges against him he would keep his lips sealed forever about the real story behind his defense of James Earl Ray:

- *how he had been called by LBJ, who assured him that if he showed up at the Shelby County Jail on November 10, 1968, he would be ushered into James Earl Ray's cell;*
- *that Ray just happened to be at the point where he had just decided to change attorneys;*
- *that Percy, using his best silver-tongue talents, would convince his prey that he would uniquely fill Ray's needs for the best defense lawyer in the country;*
- *that he would over-power the hapless convict by delivering his customary sales job ("I've defended over 1,000 murderers and only 1 got the electric chair.")*

- *And that, of course his service to his country would earn him his usual princely fees.*

This construct would also explain the reason for the first step taken by Judge Woodward a year earlier—to separate Foreman from the rest of the defendants—was so that he could be given "special" treatment without involving the others.

And, indubitably not verbalized at that point, but the brilliant lawyer had probably already figured out on his own, that there was also a tacit, nearly automatic advantage to him, in case he ever needed it: A permanent "Get out of jail" card that he could use whenever he wished. All he needed to do was ask—whomever was the president at the time.

ENDNOTES

1. McKnight, *The Last Crusade*, pp. 7–8.
2. Branch, p. 758.
3. Ibid., p. 14.
4. Ibid., p. 305.
5. Branch, p. 309.
6. Caro, *The Path,* p. xix.
7. Caro, *Master of the Senate*, p. 156.
8. Branch, p. 33.
9. Branch, pp. 33–34; Caro, *The Passage of Power,* pp. 560–567.
10. Shesol, pp. 11–12.
11. Kessler, *Inside the White House*, p. 33.
12. Kearns Goodwin, p. 148.
13. Davis, Deborah, p. 146.
14. See (among other sites) http://www.zerohedge.com/news/2015-02-23/1967
    -he-cia-created-phrase-conspiracy-theorists-and-ways-attack-anyone-who-
    challenge.
15. See JFK: Researching the Researchers (https://jfkresearch.me/).
16. Livingstone, pp. 386–396.
17. Pepper, pp. 29–30; Ray, James Earl, pp. 160; 243–247; 250.
18. In Huie's case, because his ethical challenges related to his reputation as a
    "checkbook journalist" were widely known, the FBI's files did not reflect
    their association with him. In fact, their memos and notations indicated
    that Hoover and his underlings were very cognizant of his reputation and
    apprehensive about revealing any suggestion that they had assisted him in
    any way. Yet the fact of his immediate involvement with Hanes as soon
    as Ray was arrested, and the way he clearly went out of his way to create
    for Ray a "stalking legend," inherently meant that his mission was pre-
    established; otherwise, there would have been no reason for him to have
    set out from the start to do what he ultimately did: dismiss the notion of
    Raul's involvement while going well beyond a factual basis—while creating
    a whole series of brazen lies—to support his case, framing James Earl Ray
    as the lone assassin.
19. Halberstam, *The Fifties,* p. 441. Also see Famous Trials website for the
    Emmett Till Murder Trial—1955: http://famous-trials.com/emmetttill/1759
    -chronology.

20. *Jet* magazine, October 6, 1955 pp. 8–10: http://jetcityorange.com/emmett-till/index4.html.
21. Op. cit. (Halberstam), p. 435.
22. See http://www.clarionledger.com/story/news/local/journeytojustice/2017/02/06/could-lies-about-emmett-till-be-prosecuted/97557668/.
23. Lane, p. 282.
24. McMillan, p. 226.
25. Ibid.
26. Emison, p. 103.
27. McMillan, p. 176.
28. Ibid.
29. Ray, Jerry, and T. Carter, pp. 46–47.
30. Pepper, p. 35.
31. See http://www.miaminewtimes.com/news/posner-plagiarizes-again-6367387.
32. Ibid.
33. Sides, p. xiv.
34. Ibid.
35. See https://www.archives.gov/files/research/jfk/releases/docid-32397527.pdf, p. 307 (Ref. *Life* magazine, May 3, 1968).
36. Theoharis, *From the Secret Files,* p. 1.
37. Ibid., p. 2.
38. Ibid., p. 2–11.
39. North, p. 21.
40. Turner, *Hoover's FBI,* pp. 251, 253.
41. Sullivan, pp. 80–81.
42. North, pp. 21–22 (Ref. to Fred J. Cook, *The FBI Nobody Knows.* NY: Macmillan Co. 1964, pp. 4–5; William C. Sullivan and Bill Brown, *The Bureau: My Thirty Years in Hoover's FBI.* NY: W. W. Norton, 1979, p. 184; Welch, Neil J. and David W. Marston, *Inside Hoover's FBI.* Garden City, NY: Doubleday & Co., 1984, p. 43).
43. Summers, pp. 433–434.
44. Ibid., p. 434.
45. Ibid., pp. 12, 254–258; 434.
46. Gentry, p. 217 (f/n).
47. Gentry, pp. 217–218.
48. Ibid.
49. Summers, p. 77.
50. Gentry, p. 189.
51. Op. cit. (Summers). Also see Wikipedia entry for Clyde Tolson.
52. Gentry, p. 190.
53. Halberstam, *The Fifties,* p. 336.

54. Gentry, p. 218. There are a number of YouTube videos that provide additional background insights into the social life of Hoover and Tolson, including one that references the New Year's Eve party (1936) they attended at the Waldorf-Astoria Hotel as guests of Walter Winchell, later going to the Cotton Club in Harlem. A number of witnesses at the time describe incidents in New York, New Orleans, and Las Vegas, where Hoover and Tolson's relationship was described, including alleged photographs held by the Meyer Lansky and others that showed them together in a "compromising position." See, for example, "Racist Homosexual J. Edgar Hoover #1": https://www.youtube.com/watch?v=FbSuabv0yY8.

55. Ibid.

56. Sullivan, p. 94.

57. Op. cit. (Also see Wikipedia entry for Walter Winchell.)

58. Halberstam, *The Fifties*, p. 336.

59. Sullivan, pp. 124–125.

60. Halberstam, *The Fifties*, p. 337; Gentry, pp. 217–218, 658–659; Summers, p. 79; Demaris, p. 21.

61. North, pp. 23–24 (Ref. Schott, *No Left Turns*, New York: Praeger Publishers, 1975, p. 162; Rutledge, Leigh W., *The Gay Book of Lists*. Boston: Alyson Publications, 1987 pp. 48–49; Dennis Altman, *The Homosexualization of America*. Boston: Beacon Press, 1982, p. 130; Vern L. Bullough, *Homosexuality: A History*. New York: Garland STPM Press, 1979, p. 179).

62. North, pp. 21–22.

63. Shannan, Pat. "Former CIA Participant Says He Was Part of It, Raoul Identified as FBI Agent." *Media By-Pass: The Uncensored National News*, Vol. 9 No. 5 May, 2001, p. 37.

64. Sullivan, pp. 61–64.

65. Ibid.

66. Sides, p. 375.

67. Weisberg, pp. 249–251.

68. Sullivan, pp. 145–146.

69. Summers, pp. 350–351.

70. Ibid.

71. See: *What's Done in the Dark* A Millie L McGhee Story (see https://www.youtube.com/watch?v=hACX6T2aPFY, orhttps://www.youtube.com/watch?v=rDVMu7nGVuU).

72. Swearingen, p. 254.

73. See http://members.tripod.com/~american_almanac/hoover.htm#1.

74. Maxwell, p. 40.

75. Op. cit.

76. Summers, p. 23.

77. Ibid.

78. Weiner, p. 199.

79. Ibid., p. 200.
80. Ibid.
81. Gentry, p. 441.
82. Ibid.
83. Gentry, pp. 580–581.
84. Ibid.
85. Ibid.
86. Demaris, p. 79.
87. Leuchtenburg, William E. "A Visit With LBJ," *American Heritage* magazine, May/June, 1990, p. 56.
88. Ibid. p. 62.
89. Halberstam, *The Best and* . . . p. 446.
90. Caro, *Master of the Senate,* p. 229; Gentry, p. 217.
91. See http://spartacus-educational.com/JFKdavidsonI.htm.
92. See Wikipedia: Louella Parsons.
93. Haley, p. 234.
94. North, p. 248 (Ref. Rowe, *Bobby Baker Story*, pp. 45, 72).
95. Caro, *The Path* . . . p. 295.
96. Ibid., pp. 3–5; 11–12; 16; 21; 95; 348;484.
97. Ibid., p. 298.
98. Demaris, pp. 76–77.
99. Weiner, p. 198.
100. Ibid., p. 199.
101. Ibid.
102. Gentry, p. 406.
103. Ibid., p. 500.
104. Ibid., p. 505.
105. Swearingen, p. 11; Turner, *Rearview* . . . p. 43–44.
106. Gentry, p. 501.
107. Meroney, John, "What Really Happened Between J. Edgar Hoover and MLK Jr.," *The Atlantic,* November 11, 2011.
108. Scott, pp. 230–232 (Ref. Baker, Bobby, *Wheeling and Dealing,* 80).
109. Lasky, *It Didn't Start* . . . , pp. 135–137.
110. Hersh, Burton, *Bobby and J. Edgar* . . . , pp. 206–209.
111. Mahoney, p. 278 (citing Guthman and Shulman, p. 130).
112. Summers, *Official and Confidential*, pp. 312–313).
113. Op. cit. (Mahoney).
114. Theoharis, p. 99.
115. Gentry, pp. 567–569.
116. Ibid.
117. Ibid., p. 570.
118. Barnes, p. 108.
119. Ibid.

120. Meroney, "What Really Happened Between J. Edgar Hoover and MLK Jr.," *The Atlantic,* November 11, 2011.

121. Weisberg, *Frame Up* . . . p. 237.

122. Demaris, p. 198.

123. Ibid., p. 199.

124. Garrow, pp. 165.

125. Ibid.

126. Turner, *Rearview Mirror* . . . p. 46.

127. Op. cit. (Garrow).

128. Sherrill, p. 42.

129. Lasky, Victor, *It Didn't Start* . . . pp. 196–198.

130. Ibid.

131. Safer, p. 96 (Iago is one of the major characters in Shakespeare's play Othello and was "one of Shakespeare's most sinister villains, often considered such because of the unique trust that Othello places in him, which he betrays while maintaining his reputation of honesty and dedication." —Wikipedia).

132. Weisberg, *Frame Up,* pp. 242–243.

133. Branch, pp. 368; 420–421; 563–564.

134. Turner, *Rearview Mirror* . . . p. 48.

135. Garrow, p. 168.

136. Branch, pp. 400–403.

137. Sullivan was an alumnus of American University, and though many considered him to be the most qualified successor to Hoover, for many years he had swallowed his scruples in serving his megalomaniac boss, apparently in furtherance of his own career. Gradually, he began to distance himself from Hoover—generally because he felt Hoover's rabid anticommunism policies impeded more important work on extremist organizations (both left and right ends of the political spectrum) and organized crime threats to the country—and thus fell into disfavor with Hoover and the other sycophants who served him. According to his *New York Times* obituary (11/10/77), Sullivan was "the only liberal Democrat ever to break into the top ranks of the bureau." When he testified to the Senate Intelligence Committee in 1975, he stated, in reference to Hoover's illegal COINTELPRO activities, "Never once did I hear anybody, including myself, raise the question, 'Is this course of action which we have agreed upon lawful, is it legal, is it ethical or moral?'" Two years later, during the period in which numerous witnesses to the House Select Committee on Assassinations were murdered, Sullivan himself apparently became one such target (out of six officials in the FBI alone), when he was mysteriously shot to death as he went for a morning walk. As noted by investigative reporter Robert Novak in his 2007 memoir, *Prince of Darkness*: "On November 9, 1977, days before he was to testify to the House Select Committee on Assassinations, twenty minutes before sunrise, sixty-five-year-old William C. Sullivan was walking through the

woods near his retirement home in Sugar Hill, New Hampshire, on the
way to meet hunting companions. Another hunter, Robert Daniels, Jr., a
twenty-two-year-old son of a state policeman, using a telescopic sight on
a .30 caliber rifle, said he mistook Sullivan for a deer, shot him in the neck,
and killed him instantly." Novak wrote of his own doubts about that story:
"Sullivan came to our house in the Maryland suburbs in June 1972 for
lunch and a long conversation about my plans for a biography of Hoover (a
project I abandoned as just too ambitious an undertaking). Before he left,
Bill told me someday I probably would read about his death in some kind
of accident, but not to believe it. It would be murder."

138. Op. cit.(Branch), p. 565.
139. Ibid.
140. Ibid.
141. Ibid.
142. Ibid., pp. 566–567.
143. Theoharis, pp. 132; 153–154.
144. Branch, p. 564.
145. Transcript, Nicholas D. Katzenbach Oral History Interview I, 11/12/68,
by Paige E. Mulhollan, Internet Copy, LBJ Library. See http://www
.lbjlib.utexas.edu/johnson/archives.hom/oralhistory.hom/katzenbach
/katzenbl.pdf.
146. Op. cit. (Branch).
147. Ibid.
148. Ibid., pp. 172–173.
149. Ibid., pp. 173–174.
150. Ibid., p. 175.
151. Ibid.
152. Ibid.
153. Ibid.
154. Ibid., pp. 175–176.
155. Ibid.
156. Sullivan, p. 131.
157. Branch, p. 180.
158. Ibid., p. 216.
159. Ibid., p. 218.
160. Ibid., p. 219.
161. Ibid., p. 220.
162. Ibid., p. 354.
163. Weisberg, *Frame Up* . . . p. 43.
164. Branch, p. 419.
165. Ibid., pp. 419–420.
166. Ibid., p. 420.
167. Garrow, p. 169.

168. Ibid.
169. McKnight, *The Last Crusade* . . . pp. 7–8.
170. Ibid., p. 8.
171. Branch, p. 305.
172. Caro, *The Master of the Senate,* p. 711.
173. Ibid., pp. 712–713.
174. Ibid., p. 719.
175. Garrow, pp. 125–126. This letter can also be seen at the website Letters of Note: http://www.lettersofnote.com/2012/01/king-like-all-frauds-your-end-is.html.
176. Sullivan, p. 142.
177. See Kristine Phillips, the *Washington Post,* November 4, 2017:. https://www.washingtonpost.com/news/retropolis/wp/2017/11/04/in-the-latest-jfk-files-the-fbis-ugly-analysis-on-martin-luther-king-jr-filled-with-falsehoods/?tid=pm_pop&utm_term=.49ad807437d1.
178. National Archives website: https://www.archives.gov/files/research/jfk/releases/104-10125-10133.pdf.
179. Op. cit. (Sullivan), p. 144.
180. Ibid.
181. Theoharis, *From the Secret Files* . . . p. 109.
182. Ibid., p. 9.
183. Ibid.
184. Turner, *Rearview Mirror* . . . p. 51.
185. Ibid., pp. 51–52.
186. http://www.publiceye.org/liberty/felt.html.
187. Ibid.
188. Swearingen, fourth page of Introduction; Theoharis, *The FBI and American Democracy,* p.156.
189. http://www.nytimes.com/1981/04/16/us/president-reagan-pardons-2-ex-fbi-officials-in-1970-s-break-ins.html.
190. Wikipedia.com (William Ayers). (Ref: Jeremy Varon, *Bringing the War Home: the Weather Underground, the Red Army Faction and Revolutionary Violence in the Sixties and Seventies,* Berkeley: University of California Press, 2004, p. 297).
191. *Democracy Now!* "EXCLUSIVE . . . Jennifer Dohrn: I Was The Target Of Illegal FBI Break-Ins Ordered by Mark Felt aka 'Deep Throat,'" June 2, 2005: http://www.democracynow.org/2005/6/2/exclusive_jennifer_dohrn_i_was_the.
192. See http://thehill.com/policy/national-security/277057-top-dem-dont-name-new-fbi-hq-after-j-edgar-hoover and http://abcnews.go.com/US/hoover-battle-18b-fbi-headquarters/story?id=39640360.
193. Branch, pp. 260–261.
194. Ibid., p. 287.

195. Ibid.

196. Ibid., pp. 324–326.

197. Ibid., p. 326.

198. Ibid., pp. 324–329.

199. Halberstam, *The Fifties,* p. 407.

200. Janos, Leo. "The Last Days of the President: LBJ in Retirement," *The Atlantic,* July 1973.

201. Ibid.

202. Goodman, George, "Dr. King, One Year After 'He Lives, Man!'" *Look,* April 15, 1969, p. 29.

203. King, Jr., Martin Luther. "Beyond Vietnam" (Speech at Riverside Church, New York City, April 4, 1967).

204. Ibid.

205. "A Tragedy," the *Washington Post,* April 6, 1967.

206. Op. cit.

207. See History.com: "Thousands protest the war in Vietnam—Oct 21, 1967": http://www.history.com/this-day-in-history/thousands-protest-the-war-in-vietnam.

208. Pepper, p. 8.

209. Ibid., p. xii.

210. Garrow, p. 182.

211. Ibid., p. 207.

212. Gentry, p. 567.

213. Garrow, pp. 102–103.

214. Pepper, Appendix K (p. 679).

215. Ibid., p. 274.

216. Ibid., pp. 240, 274.

217. Emison, p. 185.

218. Ibid.

219. Ibid.

220. Transcript, Hubert H. Humphrey Oral History Interview I, 8/18/71, by Joe B. Frantz, Internet Copy, LBJ Library.

221. Halberstam, *The Best . . .* p. 446.

222. Op. cit. (Emison).

223. Ibid., pp. 186–187.

224. Ibid., p. 187.

225. Ibid. (Ref. Lyndon B. Johnson Library, Recordings and Transcripts of Conversations and Meetings, Tap WH6503.03, March 8, 1965, 8:10 a.m.).

226. Ibid., p. 188.

227. McKnight, p. 47.

228. Society of Former Special Agents of the FBI. See:https://books.google.com/books?id=8h406aDUeL4C&pg=PA161&lpg=PA161&dq=memphis+TN:++frank+c.+holloman.

229. Op. cit.
230. See Wikipedia, "Henry Loeb" and Frank, pp. 12–13.
231. Pepper, p. 622 (Appendix I: Deposition of Ron Tyler Adkins, p. 80).
232. Ibid., p. 566 (Appendix I: Deposition of Ron Tyler Adkins, pp. 78–79).
233. Ibid., pp. 556–557 (Appendix I: Deposition of Ron Tyler Adkins, pp. 39–42).
234. Ibid., pp. 557–558 (Appendix I: pp. 44–46).
235. Ibid., pp. 558–562 (Appendix I: pp. 48–65).
236. Ibid., p. 564 (Appendix I: pp. 70–72).
237. Ibid., p. 619 (Appendix I: pp. 68).
238. Ibid., p. 620 (Appendix I: p. 71).
239. McKnight, p. 46.
240. Ibid. (Citation states "Police intelligence units like the DIU have historically been referred to as 'red squads.'" See Paul G. Chevigny, "Politics and Law in the Control of Local Surveillance," Cornell Law Review 70 [April 1984], p. 736.)
241. Op. cit., Pepper, pp. 564–565 (Appendix I: pp. 73–75).
242. Lane and Gregory, p. 108.
243. Ibid.
244. Ibid., pp. 296–303 (Appendix Two: Speech of Senator Robert C. Byrd).
245. Pepper, pp. 564–565 (Appendix I, pp. 73–75), 644 (Appendix p. 169).
246. Ibid., p. 644.
247. Lane, pp. 108–109.
248. Pepper, pp. 565–566 (Appendix I: pp. 77–78).
249. Ibid, p. 565 (Appendix I: p. 74).
250. Ibid, p. 611 (Appendix I: pp. 36–37).
251. Emison, pp. 188–197.
252. Ibid.
253. Ibid.
254. Ibid., p. 197.
255. Ibid., p. 199.
256. Ibid., pp. 98, 262.
257. Ibid.
258. Garrow. p. 157.
259. Ibid. pp. 151–155.
260. Branch, p. 97.
261. Garrow, p. 158.
262. Ibid.
263. Ibid.
264. Ibid., pp. 159–160.
265. Pepper, pp. x, 245, 276,284.
266. Ibid., p. 245.
267. Ibid., pp. 242–243.
268. Ibid., pp. 245, 564–585, 608–657.

269. Ibid., p. 246, 605–622.

270. Ibid., p. 578 (pp. 126–127 of deposition).

271. Ibid., p. 41; 240–241.

272. Ray, John and Lyndon Barsten, p. 73.

273. Op. cit., (Pepper), pp. 248–249.

274. Ibid., pp. 324–325.

275. Emison, pp. 95–96.

276. Ibid., p. 99.

277. Wikipedia: Operation Chaos (Ref: Athan Theoharis, Richard H. [2006]. *The Central Intelligence Agency: Security Under Scrutiny*. Greenwood Publishing Group. pp. 49, 175, 195, 203, 322). See: https://en.wikipedia.org/wiki/Operation_CHAOS.

278. Op. cit. (Emison, p. 99).

279. Ibid. pp. 97–98.

280. Caro, *The Path* . . . pp. 183–8, 200, 235, 262, 280.

281. Op. cit. (Emison pp. 97–98).

282. Ibid.

283. Encylopedia.com: Riots, Urban, of 1967. http://www.encyclopedia.com/history/dictionaries-thesauruses-pictures-and-press-releases/riots-urban-1967.

284. Pepper, p. 326.

285. Tompkins, Steve, "Army feared King, secretly watched him," Memphis *Commercial Appeal,* March 21, 1993. See:http://jfk.hood.edu/Collection/Weisberg%20Subject%20Index%20Files/A%20Disk/Army%20Intelligence/Item%2012.pdforhttps://ratical.org/ratville/JFK/ArmyFeared King.html#s8.

286. Emison, p. 120.

287. Ibid., p. 121.

288. Jilani, Zaid, "What the 'Santa Clausification' of Martin Luther King Jr. Leaves Out," *The Intercept,* January 16, 2017: https://theintercept.com/2017/01/16/what-the-santa-clausification-of-martin-luther-king-jr-leaves-out/.

289. Op. cit. (Tompkins).

290. See, for example, Richard Goodwin, *Remembering America*, pp. 402–403, where Goodwin states, in first person narrative: "I was sitting in Bill Moyers's office, awaiting his arrival for a conference to discuss the next year's budget, when Bill walked in, his face pale, visibly shaken. 'I just came from a conversation with the president. He told me he was going to fire everybody that didn't agree with him, that Hubert (Humphrey) could not be trusted and we weren't to tell him anything; then he began to explain that the communist way of thinking had infected everyone around him, that his enemies were deceiving the people and, if they succeeded, there was no way he could stop World War Three.'" Numerous other references

to similar statements can be found in other pages of the entire Chapters 21 and 22, a total of thirty-five pages, as well as the works of other authors who observed Johnson first-hand, including Arthur Schlesinger Jr.'s works.

291. Pepper, pp. 323–324.
292. Ibid., pp. 134–135.
293. Ibid.
294. Pepper, in Appendix A, p. 317.
295. Op. cit. (Tompkins).
296. Op. cit. (Pepper), p. 123.
297. Ibid., pp. 124–125.
298. Op. cit. (Tompkins).
299. Ibid.
300. Ibid.
301. Pepper, pp. 123–135.
302. Op. cit. (Tompkins).
303. Emison, p. 99.
304. Op. cit. (Wikipedia: Operation CHAOS).
305. Op. cit. (Emison, p. 99).
306. Ray, John Larry, and Lyndon Barsten, p. 17.
307. Ray, James Earl, p. 23.
308. Ray, John Larry, and Lyndon Barsten, p. 19.
309. Ibid.
310. Ibid., pp. 19–20.
311. McMillan, p. 110.
312. Op. cit. (Ray and Barsten), pp. 19–20.
313. Ibid., p. 24.
314. According to the first sentence of his obituary in the UK's *Independent* newspaper, "Sidney Gottlieb was living vindication for conspiracy theorists that there is nothing, however evil, pointless or even lunatic, that unaccountable intelligence agencies will not get up to in the pursuit of their secret wars." http://www.independent.co.uk/arts-entertainment/obituary-sidney-gottlieb-1080920.html.
315. Op. cit. (Ray and Barsten), pp. 24–25.
316. Ibid., p. 27.
317. Ray, John Larry, and Lyndon Barsten, pp. 83, 79.
318. Ray, James Earl, pp. 30–32; Pepper, p. 39.
319. Frank, p. 183; McMillan, p. 143; Posner, p. 112; Sides, p. 342.
320. Ray, James Earl, p. 30–32; Ray and Barsten, p. 41 (see also Pepper, p. 39).
321. Ray and Barsten, p. 41.
322. King Assassination Documents—FBI Central Headquarters File, Section 49: http://www.maryferrell.org/showDoc.html?docId=99621&search=walter_rife#relPageId=105&tab=page, p. 98.
323. Ray and Barsten, p. 42.

324. Ibid.
325. Op. cit. (Frank, p. 183; Posner, p. 111; Sides, pp. 342–343).
326. Sides, p. 343.
327. Ray, James Earl, pp. 39–53.
328. Ray and Barsten, p. 63.
329. Pepper, pp. 40–41.
330. Op. cit. (Ray), pp. 45–50.
331. HSCA MLK Report, Volume VIII, p. 62.
332. Ray, James Earl, pp. 58–59.
333. Weisberg, p. 197.
334. Ibid.
335. McMillan, p. 173.
336. Ibid., Weisberg, pp. 334–335.
337. Gentry, p. 567.
338. Op. cit. (Ref. Church Hearings, Vol. 6, p. 50).
339. Weisberg, p. 46.
340. Weisberg, p. xii.
341. Lane, p. xxvi; John Larry Ray and Lyndon Barsten, p. 125,.
342. Op. cit. (Weisberg), p. 46.
343. Ibid. pp. 42–43.
344. Lane, p. 159.
345. Op. cit. (Weisberg).
346. Ibid., p. 44.
347. Ibid.
348. The incongruity of that release was not explained; however, it might have related to the fact that files from both of these events became intertwined during the 1976–79 period of the HSCA investigations of both assassinations. https://www.archives.gov/files/research/jfk/releases/docid -32397527.pdf.
349. Ibid., p. 278.
350. Ibid., pp. 151–170.
351. Ray, James Earl, p. 108.
352. Ibid., p. 107.
353. Halberstam, *The Fifties,* p. 434.
354. Op. cit. (from archives.gov/files/research/jfk/releases), p. 179.
355. Ibid. p. 180 (the *Washington Post,* "Ray Interviewer Cited for Contempt," February 2, 1969, p. A-3).
356. Weisberg, p. 318.
357. Ray, John Larry, and Lyndon Barsten, pp. 19–25.
358. Frank, p. 38.
359. McMillan, p. 172.
360. Ibid.
361. Ibid., p. 150.

362. Op. cit. (Ray, John Larry, and Lyndon Barsten, p. 64).
363. McMillan, pp. 185–186.
364. HSCA MLK Report, Volume IV, pp. 154–157; 193–195.
365. Ray, Jerry, and Tamara Carter, pp. 44–47.
366. Lane, p. 248.
367. Emison, p. 29.
368. Op. cit., p. 249.
369. Emison, p. 78.
370. McMillan, pp. 206–207.
371. Ray, James Earl, p. 169.
372. Op. cit. Ray, Jerry, and Tamara Carter, pp. 44–48.
373. Lane, p. 251.
374. Ray, Jerry, and Tamara Carter, pp. 16–17.
375. National Archives, *Findings on Martin Luther King Jr. Assassination*: https://www.archives.gov/research/jfk/select-committee-report/part-2b .html).
376. Emison, pp. 76–77 (Cit. HSCA, *MLK Hearings*, vol. VIII, p. 245.
377. Ibid.
378. Emison, p. 77.
379. Ray, James Earl, pp. 17–18.
380. See, for example, *Murder in Memphis*, by Mark Lane and Dick Gregory, p. 224.
381. Sides, p. 374. (It should be acknowledged that Sides did mention the name "Raoul," on pages 390–391 in the 397-page narrative, but only for the purpose of stating that this was either an alias for his brother Jerry or simply a figment of Ray's imagination to dismiss it, apparently to avoid the implications of it being real, therefore ignoring it in order not to complicate the book with too many potential distractions to put his readers' entertainment at risk.)
382. Ibid., pp. 374–375.
383. McMillan, pp. 11–12.
384. Ibid., p. 12.
385. Ray, John Larry, and Lyndon Barsten, p. 83.
386. Melanson, pp. 6–7.
387. Ibid., pp. 7–8.
388. Ibid., pp. 8–9. Also see Brasscheck TV, "The Assassination of Martin Luther King": http://www.brasschecktv.com/videos/assassination-studies-1/the -assassination-of-martin-luther-king.html.
389. Pepper, p. 296.
390. Op. cit., p. 34 (Ref. HSCA Vol. 9, p. 421).
391. Ibid., p. 27.
392. Ibid., pp. 35–37.
393. Weisberg, p. 198.

394. Huie, pp. 94–95.

395. Ibid., pp. 83–84.

396. Huie, p. 75.

397. Ray, James Earl, pp. 80–81.

398. Ibid., p. 82.

399. Huie, p. 80.

400. Ibid.

401. Ibid., p. 81.

402. Ibid.

403. Op. cit. (Ray, Barsten), p. 85.

404. Huie, p. 100.

405. Ibid.

406. Ibid.

407. Huie, William Bradford, "The Story of James Earl Ray and the Conspiracy to Kill Martin Luther King," *Look* magazine, November 12, 1968. (See Weisberg, pp. 54–55 regarding Neptune Bar meetings.)

408. Emison, p. 132.

409. Huie, William Bradford, "The Story of James Earl Ray and the Conspiracy to Kill Martin Luther King," *Look* magazine, November 26, 1968.

410. Huie, William Bradford, "The Story of James Earl Ray and the Conspiracy to Kill Martin Luther King," *Look* magazine, April 15, 1969 (p. 106).

411. Huie, pp. 100–105.

412. Branch, p. 722.

413. Ibid.

414. Huie, p. 104.

415. Weisberg, pp. 60; 189.

416. Pepper, p. 31.

417. Pearce, John, "Negroes Plan Capital March: Army of Poor Will Move in April," *The New Orleans Times-Picayune,* (AP) Section 2, page 29 (p. 58 on digital copy) http://phw02.newsbank.com/cache/arhb/fullsize /pl_011062016_0952_56749_118.pdf.

418. Branch, p. 719.

419. Branch, p. 722.

420. Ibid.

421. Branch, p. 722; McKnight, p. 52; Garrow, p. 191; Wilson, p. 159.

422. Sides, p. 96.

423. Ibid., p. 97.

424. Ibid., pp. 97–98.

425. McMichael, p. 159.

426. Branch, pp. 722–727.

427. Huie, p. 118.

428. Branch, pp. 730–731.

429. Lane and Gregory, p. 98. (Also Pepper, p. 623 - Appendix I, p. 85.)

430. Branch, p. 733.
431. http://garyrevel.com/News/mystery_helicopter.html.
432. Op. cit.
433. Ibid., p. 734.
434. HSCA MLK Report, Volume VI, pp. 380–400 (Stegall's name appears at p. 394): https://www.maryferrell.org/showDoc.html?docId=95658&search=stegall#relPageId=403&tab=page.
435. Op. cit., pp. 736–737.
436. Perrusquia, Marc. "Six:01," Memphis *Commercial Appeal*. April 2013 (Story section).
437. Frank, pp. 30–31.
438. Branch, p. 760.
439. Lane and Gregory, p. 99.
440. Pepper, p. 34.
441. Ibid., pp. 132–133.
442. Lane and Gregory, p. 100.
443. Reynolds, p. 142.
444. The King Center, King Family Trial Transcript.pdf (Position 127 on Transcript): http://www.thekingcenter.org/sites/default/files/KING%20FAMILY%20TRIAL%20TRANSCRIPT.pdf.
445. Pepper, pp. 240–241.
446. Emison, p. 126.
447. Op. cit. (Pepper), pp. 240–241.
448. Ray, James Earl, p. 92.
449. Ibid.
450. HSCA MLK Report, Volume VIII, p. 656.
451. For one example, he had only used the alias "John Willard" once, to register at Bessie Brewer's rooming house. Another example was that Ray made up another alias, "Doug Collins," which he was known to have only used once, to join the Rabbit's Foot Key Club in Los Angeles. See HSCA MLK Report, Volume IV, p. 145: https://www.maryferrell.org/showDoc.html?docId=95656&relPageId=149&search=wallace.
452. Op. cit. (HSCA MLK Report, Volume VIII), p. 658.
453. Ibid., pp. 656–659.
454. Ray, John Larry, and Lyndon Barsten, p. 108.
455. Huie, William Bradford, "The Story of James Earl Ray and the Conspiracy to Kill Martin Luther King," *Look* magazine, April 15, 1969 (p. 106).
456. Ibid.
457. HSCA MLK Report, Volume II, p. 34.
458. Weisberg, p. 151.
459. Pepper, pp. 84, 171, 297. (Also naming the Admiral Benbow Hotel and the Holiday Inn midtown as other favorites.) Weisberg, p. 178, 282 (Weisberg pointedly noted, "Huie could not have fabricated more skillful deception

and, simultaneously, more seriously damaged his own case . . . . In short, Huie here argues against himself. He really says Ray had to be the creature of a conspiracy.")

460. Ibid., p. 279; 297.

461. Huie, pp. 116–117.

462. Posner, p. 324.

463. Ibid.

464. Lane, Gregory, p. 105.

465. Ibid.

466. Ibid., p. 106.

467. Pepper, pp. 247–249.

468. Ibid.

469. Emison, pp. 113–115.

470. Pepper, pp. 126–127.

471. Ibid., p. 125.

472. Ibid., p. 128.

473. Ibid., pp. 128–129.

474. Ray, James Earl. p. 93.

475. Ibid., pp. 93–94.

476. Shannan, pp. 35–36. (For MPD officer Strausser's role as the assassin, See Pepper, pp. 224-237)

477. Op. cit. (Ray).

478. Huie, pp. 116–117.

479. HSCA MLK Report, Volume IV pp. 196–197.

480. Weisberg, p. 150.

481. Frank, p. 324.

482. Huie. p. 169.

483. Sides, p. 147.

484. Weisberg, pp. 166–167.

485. Ibid.

486. Emison, p. 53.

487. Sides, p. 164.

488. Weisberg, p. 168.

489. Huie, p. 171.

490. Emison, p. 73.

491. Ibid.

492. Posner, p. 324.

493. Sides, p. 144. Interestingly, Sides also referenced the same edition of that paper on pp. 202–203 without mentioning anything about the phantom photograph.

494. Frank, p. 44. Out of twenty-nine photographs that Frank did include in the photo section of his book, his caption / comment accompanying picture #5 also incorrectly stated that the six men were entering Room 306. A

thirtieth photo was listed in the "Photo Credits" page, acknowledging Jim Sherin, but that photo was not included anywhere within the book. But when the same photo (#5, of the men entering a room on the balcony) was printed in the Marc Perrusquia article referenced elsewhere, the photo was correctly identified as being the room next door to 306, belonging to Reverend and Mrs. Cotton: Room 307.

495. Weisberg, pp. 170–175.
496. Frank, p. 38.
497. Op. cit. (Weisberg).
498. Sides, p. 150.
499. Op. cit. (Pepper, 178); Emison, p. 45, 237.
500. Perrusquia, Marc. "Six:01" Memphis *Commercial Appeal*. April, 2013 (Story section).
501. Ibid. (Timeline section).
502. An example of the latter can be found in Donald G. Wilson's book, *Evidence Withheld*, where on page 4 he writes, "On Tuesday, April 2, King, Abernathy and Bernard Lee traveled to Memphis." The fact is, they traveled to Memphis on Wednesday, April 3. Unfortunately, he evidently relied too heavily on the error-filled Posner book (p. 16) for this information.
503. Op. cit. (Sides).
504. Ibid. pp. 160, 164.
505. Pepper, p. 175. (This fact was affirmed by witness Charles Hurley in sworn testimony, as noted by Dr. Pepper.)
506. Ibid., p. 256.
507. Ibid., pp. 175–295.
508. Frank, p. 63.
509. Weisberg, p. 154.
510. Huie, pp. 171–172.
511. Weisberg, pp. 154–155.
512. Op. cit. (from archives.gov/files/research/jfk/releases), p. 267.
513. Ibid.
514. Weisberg, pp. 155–156, 294, 338; Lane & Gregory, pp. 168–170; Ray and Barsten, pp. 74–75.
515. Pepper, pp. 293, 297–298.
516. The King Center: King Family Trial Transcript.pdf (Position 244–246 on Transcript): http://www.thekingcenter.org/sites/default/files/KING%20 FAMILY%20TRIAL%20TRANSCRIPT.pdf.
517. Frank, pp. 100–101.
518. Pepper, p. 246.
519. Ibid., pp. 246–247.
520. Op. cit. (King Family Trial Transcript): Position 1656–1657 on Transcript.
521. Ibid. (Positions 1658–1660 on Transcript).
522. Pepper, p. 178.

523. Ibid., pp. 149–155.
524. Ray, James Earl, pp. 94–96.
525. Pepper, pp. 175, 184, 270.
526. The King Center: King Family Trial Transcript.pdf (pp. 408–418; 1067–1070): http://www.thekingcenter.org/sites/default/files/KING%20FAMILY%20TRIAL%20TRANSCRIPT.pdf).
527. Ibid.
528. Tennessee Encyclopedia of History and Culture—John and Viola McFerren: http://tennesseeencyclopedia.net/entry.php?rec=864.
529. Ibid.
530. Pepper, pp. 82–84, 168–169, 289, 303–304.
531. Ibid.
532. Ibid., pp. 167–170.
533. Pepper, pp. 261–262.
534. Pepper, p. 698 (Ref. Shelby depo. p. 46, line 18–19).
535. Ibid., p. 700 (Ref. Shelby depo, p 53 [lines 23–24] and 54 [lines 1–10]).
536. Ibid. (Shelby depo, p. 53 [lines 9–13]).
537. Ibid., p. 266.
538. Ibid., p. 262.
539. Gentry, p. 606 (Ref. HSCA MLK Assassination Reports, Vol. VI, p. 107).
540. HSCA MLK Report, Volume VI, pp. 108–109.
541. Ibid., p. 112.
542. Ibid., p. 116.
543. Ibid., p. 118.
544. Ibid., pp. 119–120.
545. Ibid., pp. 120–121.
546. DeLoach, p. 35.
547. "JESSIE JACKSON KILLED MARTIN LUTHER KING JR": https://www.youtube.com/watch?v=teEplUjU0Bw.
548. Pepper, p. 625.
549. Op. cit., "Jesse Jackson . . ." (13:30–16:55 min.).
550. Ibid. (13:55–14:03 min.; 24:25–25:00).
551. Ibid. (25:30 - 26:10).
552. Ibid. (30:00–30:40).
553. Ibid. (25:00–25:30).
554. Ibid. (30:30:30:41).
555. Ibid. (32:15–32:30).
556. Ibid. (35:00–35:45).
557. Ibid.
558. Ibid. (21:00–21:45).
559. Ibid. (12:00–12:28; 14:03–14:15).
560. Ibid. (15:50–16:10).
561. Ibid. (16:10 - 16:35). Also see Thomas, Evan, *The Man to See*, p. 464.

562. Timmerman, pp. 90–91.

563. Op. cit., "Jesse Jackson . . ." (17:00–17:14 min); Thomas, Evan, The Man to See, p. 464 [extended additional portion of quote supplied from book].

564. Op. cit., "Jesse Jackson . . ." (17:30–17:44 min).

565. Thomas, p. 465.

566. It is interesting that the HSCA (in Volume IV of the MLK Report, pp. 196–197) stated that "it has been charged that Dr. King was purposefully placed in room 306, the only room to which a marksman in the roominghouse [*sic*] bathroom would have had an unobstructed view. A white man disguised as a Black man and posing as an official of SCLC is alleged to have requested that Dr. King be assigned to 306." In a different context, of course, that statement might have been essentially correct.

567. Pepper, p. 192.

568. Reynolds, p. 82.

569. Ibid., p. 83.

570. Farney, Dennis, "What makes Jackson run?" *Des Moines Register,* January 6, 1984: https://www.newspapers.com/image/130828889/.

571. Ibid.

572. Ibid.

573. Op. cit. (Reynolds), p. 83.

574. Ibid.

575. Ibid.

576. Ibid.

577. Lane and Gregory, p. 284 (Ref. *New York Post*, February 19, 1977).

578. Ibid.

579. See: "Conspiracy 5/11 - Who Killed Martin Luther King Jr." (@ 1:35–1:40): https://www.youtube.com/watch?v=hmoPSUTazvQ or "Martin Luther King's son Dexter meets James Earl Ray, Patsy-Assassin of his father": https://www.youtube.com/watch?v=rDVMu7nGVuU.

580. Ibid. (@2:08–2:14).

581. http://spartacus-educational.com/JFKblakey.htm.

582. Mitchell, Jerry, "Some Fingerprints Still Untested in MLK Killing," Jackson (MS) *Clarion-Ledger,* April 4, 2013.

583. Goodman, George, "Dr. King, One Year After 'He Lives, Man!'" *Look,* April 15, 1969, p. 31.

584. Ray, James Earl, p. 97.

585. National Archives, "Findings on MLK Assassination": https://www.archives.gov/research/jfk/select-committee-report/part-2c.html.

586. Op. cit. (Ray), pp. 90, 97.

587. HSCA MLK Report, Volume III; Section: X - Atlanta I. See: https://www.maryferrell.org/showDoc.html?docId=95655#relPageId=218&tab=page.

588. Huie (op. cit.), *Look* magazine, April 15, 1969 (pp. 106–109).

589. Pepper, p. 68; The King Center: King Family Trial Transcript.pdf (Position 437 on Transcript).

590. Ibid. (Position 549–552 on Transcript); Pepper, pp. 256, 300.

591. Pepper, pp. 68–69.

592. Op. cit. (King Center Transcript).

593. Ray, James Earl. pp. 101–102.

594. Ibid., pp. 104–105.

595. Ibid., pp. 105–106.

596. Ibid.

597. HSCA Report on Martin Luther King Jr. Assassination, p. 334: https://www.maryferrell.org/showDoc.html?docId=99886&search=Huie_and+Hanes+a+long+time+before+James+Earl+Ray#relPageId=158&tab=page.

598. FBI AIRTEL Memorandum dated 9/2/1968 from SAC-Birmingham to Director, FBI (Op. Cit., https://www.maryferrell.org. Pages 158–159 of 223 pages).

599. Ibid.

600. Huie, p. 41.

601. Ray, James Earl, pp. 117, 126.

602. Ibid., p. 65.

603. Emison, p. 81.

604. Ibid. (Ref. HSCA MLK Hearings, vol. IV, p. 117).

605. Ibid., pp. 81–82.

606. Huie, p. 45.

607. Op. cit., HSCA Report, pp. 328–330 (See: http://www.archives.gov/research/jfk/select-committee-report/part-2b.html).

608. Ibid.

609. Emison, p. 101.

610. Huie, pp. 41, 44.

611. Ibid., p. 44.

612. Ibid., pp. 42–43.

613. Ibid., p. 22. (Also see *Look* magazine, November 12, 1968, p. 100.)

614. *Look* magazine, November 12, 1968, p. 100.

615. Huie, pp. 23–24.

616. Ibid.

617. See Huie's first magazine article: "The Story of James Earl Ray and the Plot to Assassinate Martin Luther King," *Look* magazine, November 12, 1968, p. 100.

618. Huie, pp. 26–27.

619. Ibid. (Also see *Look* magazine, November 12, 1968, p. 100.)

620. Ibid., p. 57.

621. Blair, p. 189.

622. The King Family Trial Transcript (Op. cit., Position 1252 on Transcript).

623. Op. cit. (Huie), p. 100.
624. Ibid., p. 145.
625. Ibid., p. 205.
626. Ibid., pp. 91–93.
627. Ibid., p. 100.
628. Ibid., p. 89.
629. Lane and Gregory, p. 281.
630. Melanson, pp. 177–182.
631. Ibid., pp. 46–47.
632. Ray and Barsten, p. 47.
633. Ibid., p. 63.
634. Ibid.
635. Ibid., p. 48.
636. Ibid., p. 85 and fourth photo page after p. 148.
637. Op. Cit. (Melanson), p. 45.
638. Ibid., p. 46.
639. Ibid.
640. Ibid., pp. 47–49.
641. Ray, James Earl, pp. 79, 237–242.
642. Ray, Jerry, and T. Carter, p. 96.
643. Ray, John, and Lyndon Barsten, p. 95.
644. Ibid.
645. Ibid., p. 102.
646. Ibid., p. 96 (Amant v. Thompson, 390 U.S. 727 [1968], argued before the Louisiana Supreme Court on April 4, 1968, the same day that MLK was assassinated.)
647. Ray, James Earl, pp. 72–73.
648. Op. cit. (HSCA Findings on MLK Assassination, p. 393).
649. See: Murkin Conspiracy File, Weisberg Collection, Hood College, p. 4 of 21 http://jfk.hood.edu/Collection/Weisberg%20Subject%20Index%20Files /O%20Disk/Otmoor%20Productions%20BBC/Item%2010.pdf.
650. Ray, James Earl, p. 238–240.
651. Ibid.
652. Ibid., pp. 240–242.
653. Op. cit. (Murkin Conspiracy File, Weisberg Collection).
654. Op. cit. (from archives.gov/files/research/jfk/releases), pp. 309–310 (Ref. *The New York Times*, "Galt Trip From Coast to New Orleans Recalled by Companion," April 26, 1968).
655. Ibid.
656. Op. cit. (HSCA Findings on MLK Assassination, p. 393).
657. Op. cit. (from archives.gov/files/research/jfk/releases), p. 215 (Ref. *The Washington Post*,"Ray Alone Still Talks of a Plot," March 16, 1969, p. G-1).
658. Ray, James Earl p. 271.

659. Ibid., p. 115–116.
660. Ibid.
661. Lane and Gregory, p. 189.
662. Op. cit. (Ray, James E.), p. 116.
663. Order on Motion to Remove Microphones, T.V. and Lights filed November 22, 1968, Appendix J, Folder No. 7, in the William H. Williams Collection of Criminal Court Papers #5689, Southern Historical Collection, The Wilson Library, University of North Carolina at Chapel Hill.
664. Op. cit. (Ray, James E.).
665. Ibid., p. 117.
666. Ibid., pp. 117–118.
667. Foreman, Percy, "Against Conspiracy," *Look* magazine, April 15, 1969, p. 112.
668. Op. cit. (Ray, James E.), p. 118.
669. Ibid.
670. https://en.wikipedia.org/wiki/Capital_punishment_in_Tennessee.
671. Ibid., p. 118.
672. Ibid., p. 119.
673. Ibid., p. 119.
674. Ibid., pp. 120–121.
675. Ibid., p. 121.
676. Huie, pp. 191–193.
677. Op. cit. (Ray, James E.), p. 122.
678. Ibid., p. 123.
679. The King Family Trial Transcript (Op. cit., Position 1258 on Transcript).
680. Op. cit. (Ray, James E.), p. 124.
681. Ibid., p. 126.
682. Frank, p. 241.
683. Op. cit. (Ray, James E.), pp. 127–128.
684. Ibid., Ray, p. 133.
685. Ibid., pp. 90–91. (Also see: http://jfk.hood.edu/Collection/Weisberg%20 Subject%20Index%20Files/R%20Disk/Ray%20James%20Earl%20 Tennessee/Item%2003.pdf.)
686. Weisberg, *Frame-Up,* pp. 73–74.
687. Ray, James Earl, pp. 128–131.
688. Op. cit., Weisberg, p. 74. (Weisberg included, within a footnote, the following profound insight: "The leak is another exact parallel to the mishandling of the Presidential assassination investigation, where everything of any consequence was carefully leaked in advance to a compliant press that, in accepting the information, was itself corrupted . . . The vaunted and vain J. Edgar Hoover, the greatest investigator of them all, could not find a single culprit. To see the one most guilty, he need only have opened his eyes when he shaved.")
689. Op. cit., Ray, p. 131.

690. See https://www.archives.gov/files/research/jfk/releases/docid-32397527 .pdf, p. 181 (Ref. "Ray Hearing Set; Guilty Plea Hinted," *Washington Post*, March 8, 1969, p. A-1).

691. Ibid.

692. Op. cit., Ray, pp. 131–132.

693. Frank, pp. 428–432.

694. Op. cit. (archives document ref. Ray Hearing/*Washington Post* article), p. 182.

695. Ibid.

696. Emison, pp. 165–184.

697. Ibid., pp. 181–182.

698. Blair, Clay Jr., pp. 209–244.

699. Seigenthaler, John, and James D. Squires, Jack Hemphill, and Frank Ritter. *A Search for Justice*. Nashville, TN: Aurora, 1971, pp. 183–187.

700. Weisberg, pp 103–104.

701. Weisberg, pp. 103–104; 128; 383.

702. Sides, p. 390.

703. Lane, p. 253.

704. Ibid.

705. Emison, p. 207 (Ref. "Intelligence: Of Dart Guns and Poisons," *Time*, September 29, 1975).

706. Lane., p. 254.

707. Ibid.

708. Judge Williams's Response to Motion for Appeal, Folder No. 8, in the William H. Williams Collection of Criminal Court Papers #5689, Southern Historical Collection, The Wilson Library, University of North Carolina at Chapel Hill.

709. Ibid. (See Memorandum Denying Petition for Certiorari, Re; James Earl Ray, 1970.)

710. Emison, p. 209 (Ref. Associated Press news story as printed in the *High Point Enterprise* [North Carolina], March 15, 1969).

711. You Tube: "Judge Joe: James Earl Ray Didn't Assassinate Martin Luther King Jr.,". https://www.youtube.com/watch?v=HcJ_szc3TEA.

712. Russell, Dick. "A King-sized Conspiracy," *High Times*, 1999, pp 48, 50, 70. (See: http://www.dickrussell.org/articles/king.htm.)

713. See Spartacus Educational HSCA: http://spartacus-educational.com /JFKassassinationsC.htm.

714. Lane, p. 260.

715. Ibid., p. 267; See also Spartacus Educational—Thomas Downing: http:// spartacus-educational.com/JFKdowningT.htm.

716. Lane, pp. 265–266.

717. Ibid.

718. Op. cit. (Spartacus Educational HSCA).

719. Op. cit. (The King Center: King Family Trial Transcript.pdf (Position 1354 on Transcript)).

720. Ibid.

721. Pepper, pp. 34–35, 61–62, 80–82.

722. Shannan, p. 35.

723. Stelzer, "Maybe in Memphis".

724. Ibid.

725. Ray, James Earl, p. 193.

726. Pepper, p. 198.

727. Ibid., pp. 216–221.

728. HSCA MLK Report, Volume VIII, pp 74–170. See https://www.maryferrell.org/showDoc.html?docId=95660&search=covington#relPageId=76&tab=page.

729. HSCA MLK Assassination Hearings Vol. VII, pp. 9–18. See https://archive.org/stream/HSCAMLKReport/HSCA%20MLK%20Report,%20Volume%207_djvu.txt.

730. Pepper, p. 288.

731. Ibid.

732. Op. cit. (HSCA MLK Report, Volume VIII. pp. 607–668).

733. Ibid., p. 614.

734. Ibid., p. 617.

735. HSCA Final Report: D. NO FEDERAL, STATE OR LOCAL GOVERNMENT AGENCY WAS INVOLVED. IN THE ASSASSINATION OF DR. KING, pp. 410–411 (https://www.history-matters.com/archive/jfk/hsca/report/pdf/HSCA_Report_2D_Agency.pdf).

736. See Mary Ferrell Foundation, HSCA MLK Report, Volume VIII: http://www.maryferrell.org/showDoc.html?docId=95660&search=walter_rife#relPageId=1&tab=page.

737. Ibid., pp. 40–41.

738. Sides, p. 375.

739. HSCA Final Report, p. 326. See http://www.archives.gov/research/jfk/select-committee-report/part-2b.html#fbi.

740. HSCA MLK Assassination Hearings Vol. VII, p. 39.

741. DeLoach, pp. 256–258.

742. Ibid., p. 3.

743. Ibid.; Garrow, p. 102.

744. HSCA Report on the Martin Luther King Jr. Assassination, Vol. VII (p. 57). See https://archive.org/stream/HSCAMLKReport/HSCA%20MLK%20Report,%20Volume%207_djvu.txt.

745. Gentry, p. 568.

746. Ibid. (Second footnote).

747. See "The Best Books of 2010", *The Oregonian,* December 25, 2010: http://www.oregonlive.com/books/index.ssf/2010/12/best_books_of_2010.html.

748. Sides, Hampton. "Remembering Martin Luther King as a Man, Not as a Saint," the *Washington Post,* April 1, 2011: https://www.washingtonpost.com/opinions/remembering-martin-luther-king-as-a-man-not-a-saint/2011/04/01/AFvQjTXC_story.html.

749. HSCA MLK Report, Volume III, Section: IX - The Drive East, p. 207. See https://www.maryferrell.org/showDoc.html?docId=95655#relPageId=211&tab=page.

750. Frank, p. 310.

751. McMillan, p. 289.

752. Posner, pp. 219–220.

753. Sides, pp. 95–96.

754. Op. cit. (HSCA Final Report).

755. Ibid.

756. Ibid., p. 327.

757. HSCA MLK Report, Volume IV, p. 5. See https://www.maryferrell.org/showDoc.html?docId=95656&search=hearings_vol+IV#relPageId=9&tab=page.

758. Ibid. Also see Ray, James Earl, p. 190.

759. HSCA Final Assassinations Report, p. 296. See https://www.history-matters.com/archive/jfk/hsca/report/html/HSCA_Report_0163b.htm.

760. Pepper, p. 295.

761. See Orange County Register: http://www.ocregister.com/articles/-294602--.html.

762. His speech there included the following, according to Wikipedia: "March 17, 1968: Martin Luther King, Jr., spoke at Second Baptist two weeks before he was assassinated. Delivering the sermon at the Sunday worship service, Dr. King spoke against the Vietnam War, declaring that the United States was involved in a 'senseless, reckless, immoral and unwinnable war.'[*] He noted that John F. Kennedy had been courageous in admitting he made a mistake after the Bay of Pigs fiasco, and continued, 'It is time for somebody in Washington to say we made a mistake in Vietnam.'[*] Dr. King also said that white racism was 'still a glaring reality in our country,' and charged that the U.S. Congress, dominated by the rural South, 'stands as a stubborn force in the way of social progress.'"[See https://en.wikipedia.org/wiki/Second_Baptist_Church_(Los_Angeles)] *(Citation: "DR. KING URGES U.S. TO ADMIT VIETNAM WAR IS 'MISTAKE,'" *Los Angeles Times,* March 18, 1968).

763. Op. cit., Pepper.

764. HSCA Final Report, p. 297. See http://www.maryferrell.org/showDoc.html?docId=800&search=garner#relPageId=327&tab=page.

765. Beginning where he had stayed in a motel in the outskirts of New Orleans "on the highway to Biloxi" according to Ray, across Mississippi and into Alabama on I-10 (which opened in 1965, according to the website www. aaroad.com/guide, citing "61 Miles of Interstate Will Open During 1965," *Times Daily* (Florence, AL), May 11, 1965) to Alabama Highway 41 North, then to Highway 22 North into Selma. From there, continuing on Highway 22 North to Highway 25 North and then Highway 31 North.

766. HSCA MLK Report, Volume III, Section: IX - The Drive East, p. 209.

767. HSCA MLK Report, Volume III, pp. 568–569.

768. Ray, James Earl, p. 91.

769. Op. cit. (National Archives, *Findings on Martin Luther King Jr. Assassination*, p. 356).

770. Ibid.

771. Ray, James Earl, p. 191.

772. Weisberg, p. 517.

773. Frank, p. 34.

774. Ibid.

775. Ibid. p. 36.

776. Ray and Barsten, p. 73.

777. Op. cit., Frank, pp. 36–37; National Archives, *Findings on MLK*, p. 355.

778. Op. cit., Ray, p. 191.

779. Ibid., p. 90.

780. HSCA MLK Report, Volume IV, p. 6.

781. HSCA Final Assassination Report, p. 299: https://www.history-matters .com/archive/jfk/hsca/report/html/HSCA_Report_0165a.htm).

782. Ibid.

783. Ibid.

784. Ibid.

785. Weisberg, pp. 208–209.

786. Pepper, pp. 184–185.

787. Op. cit. (Ray, James Earl), pp. 201–202.

788. "Ten Most Corrupt Politicians in U.S. History," Real Clear Politics, May 22, 2012. An excerpt from that article reads: "Blanton's most serious acts of corruption occurred just shortly before his term was to expire as pardons were delivered for 24 convicted murderers and 28 prisoners of other crimes in what many believed were performed in exchange for money. To stop Blanton's pardon spree, the Lieutenant Governor and State House Speaker claimed the state constitution was unspecific as to when a newly elected Governor must be sworn in. As a result, [New Governor Lamar] Alexander was sworn in three days before his scheduled inauguration to get Blanton out before he could pardon anyone else."

789. Op. cit., The King Center: King Family Trial Transcript.pdf (Position 1266 on Transcript).

790. See http://www.saving.org/inflation/inflation.php?amount=1&year=1977 ($1.00 worth $4.06 in 2016).

791. Langeveld, Dirk, "Leonard Ray Blanton: pardons for a price," *The Downfall Dictionary*, February 7, 2009: http://downfalldictionary.blogspot.com/2009/02/leonard-ray-blanton-pardons-for-price.html.

792. Op. cit. (Ray, James Earl), p. 173.

793. Ibid., pp. 201–202.

794. Ibid., p.195.

795. Ibid., pp. 194–195.

796. Ibid., pp. 202–203.

797. Ibid., p. 194.

798. Ibid.

799. Ibid., p. 203.

800. Ibid.

801. Ibid., pp. 192–193.

802. *Dallas Morning News*, "Ray admitted murder, ex-inspector says," August 19, 1978.

803. Ibid.

804. See https://ia800402.us.archive.org/0/items/nsia-EistAlexanderAnthonyScotlandYardInspector/nsia-EistAlexanderAnthonyScotlandYardInspector/Eist%20Alexander%20A%2028.pdf.

805. Snoddy, Raymond, "British Ex-Detective Defends Testimony for King Hearing," the *Washington Post*, August 20, 1978.

806. National Archives Website: https://archive.org/details/nsia-EistAlexanderAnthonyScotlandYardInspector Item A-24) https://ia600402.us.archive.org/0/items/nsia-EistAlexanderAnthonyScotlandYardInspector/nsia-EistAlexanderAnthonyScotlandYardInspector/Eist%20Alexander%20A%2024.pdf.

807. WPA Film Library website: https://www.wpafilmlibrary.com/videos/168341.

808. *Knoxville News-Sentinel* 11-10-78 "House Probers Do Not Plan to Recall Ray".

809. Op. cit. (Ray, James Earl), pp. 222–224.

810. See Statement of Witness Christopher Baxter dated December 13, 1978: https://archive.org/stream/nsia-EistAlexanderAnthonyScotlandYardInspector/nsia-EistAlexanderAnthonyScotlandYardInspector/Eist%20Alexander%20A%2044#page/n0/mode/2up.

811. Pepper, p. 199.

812. Weisberg, p. 55, 57, 180, 339.

813. McMillan, p. 246.

814. Ibid., p. 257.

815. Op. cit.(Weisberg).

816. Ray, James Earl, p. 128.

817. Ibid., p. 65.

818. McMillan p. 259.

819. Ibid., p. 280.

820. HSCA MLK Report, Vol. IV, pp. 325 +. See https://www.maryferrell.org /showDoc.html?docId=95656&search=hearings_vol+IV# relPageId=333&tab=page.

821. Ibid., p. 327.

822. Ibid., p. 329.

823. Lane, pp. 278–279 (name misspelled as "Newsum"); See King Family Trial Transcript (Op. cit.), pp. 302–303.

824. Ibid., pp. 125, 278.

825. Ibid.

826. HSCA MLK Report, Vol. IV, pp. 327–335.

827. Garrow, p. 168.

828. Ibid., p. 169.

829. Ibid., p. 207.

830. See YouTube video "Martin Luther King's son Dexter meets James Earl Ray, Patsy-Assassin of his father," @ 5:25: https://www.youtube.com/ watch?v=-wHQZ1zyVxY.

831. Ibid., @ 5:50–9.00 on timeline.

832. See "Full text of HSCA Report on Martin Luther King Jr. Assassination," pp. 153–155:.https://archive.org/stream/HSCAMLKReport/HSCA%20 MLK%20Report,%20Volume%207_djvu.txt.

833. Weisberg, p. 411.

834. The same thing occurred with Robert Kennedy's assassination, when the "investigation" was handled yet again with FBI and CIA oversight, through a specially installed "team" called the "SUS" (Special Unit Senator) that included CIA operatives handling all of it. See Turner, William W. and Jonn G. Christian. *The Assassination of Robert F. Kennedy: A Searching Look at the Conspiracy and Cover-Up 1968–1978.* New York: Random House. 1978. Republished in 2006 by Carroll & Graf, with a substantially revised and updated Introduction; O'Sullivan, Shane. *Who Killed Bobby?* New York/London: Union Square Press (Sterling Publishing Co.), 2008.

835. Emison, pp. 24, 95, 98–100.

836. Melanson, p. 37.

837. See Spartacus Educational G. Robert Blakey: http://spartacus-educational .com/JFKblakey.htm.

838. Pepper, pp. 35–37.

839. Ray, James Earl, p. 204.

840. Sack, Kevin, "Hidden Evidence Claimed in King Slaying," the *New York Times*, March 25, 1998, para. 9.

841. Pepper, pp. 83–84.

842. Rowan, Carl, "After 25 Years, Truth Begins to Emerge." the *Baltimore Sun*, April 7, 1993. See http://articles.baltimoresun.com/1993-04-07/news/1993097035_1_james-earl-ray-hbo-real-trial.

843. See The King Center: King Family Trial Transcript.pdf (Position 247 on Transcript): http://www.thekingcenter.org/sites/default/files/KING%20FAMILY%20TRIAL%20TRANSCRIPT.pdf.

844. Ibid. (Position 55 on Transcript).

845. Ibid. (Position 224 on Transcript).

846. Ibid. (Position 184–185 on Transcript).

847. Ibid. (Position 190–191 on Transcript).

848. Ibid. (Position 196 on Transcript).

849. Ibid. (Position 200–204 on Transcript).

850. Op. cit., The King Center: King Family Trial Transcript.pdf (Position 1354 on Transcript).

851. Ibid. (Positions 1355–1361 on Transcript).

852. Ibid. (Positions 1363 on Transcript).

853. See HSCA Findings on MLK Assassination, p. 387. https://www.archives.gov/research/jfk/select-committee-report/part-2c.html#rosenson).

854. Ibid. (Positions 1366 on Transcript).

855. Op. cit. (Douglass, Jim, "The Martin Luther King Conspiracy Exposed in Memphis").

856. Op. cit., The King Center: King Family Trial Transcript.pdf (Position 1323 on Transcript).

857. Valentine, p. 13.

858. Op. cit., The King Center: King Family Trial Transcript.pdf (Position 1324 on Transcript).

859. According to Wikipedia, "The 902d Military Intelligence Group is a United States Army group commanded by a colonel, under the command of the United States Army Intelligence and Security Command, and with an operational focus on counterintelligence. The unit is headquartered at Fort Meade, Maryland. The 902d Military Intelligence Group .

860. Op. cit. (Position 1325–1332 on Transcript).

861. Pepper, p. 180.

862. Ibid., p. 281.

863. Op. cit., The King Center: King Family Trial Transcript.pdf (Position 1383 on Transcript).

864. Pepper, pp. 61–62.

865. Ibid.

866. Ibid., pp. 68–70.

867. Op. cit. (Douglass, Jim, "The Martin Luther King Conspiracy Exposed in Memphis").

868. Wilson, p. 108.

869. See: https://ipfs.io/ipfs/QmXoypizjW3WknFiJnKLwHCnL72vedxjQkD DPlmXWo6uco/wiki/Cartha_DeLoach.html.

870. Department of Justice (DOJ): https://www.justice.gov/crt/united-states-department-justice-investigation-recent-allegations-regarding-assassination-dr#over.

871. Op. Cit., DOJ Report Section D.6. p. 39, para. 2. Also see Wilson, p. 92 and https://www.justice.gov/crt/v-wilsons-allegations.

872. Ibid.

873. Department of Justice (DOJ): https://www.justice.gov/crt/list-attachments-0#toc.

874. National Archives "Findings on MLK Assassination": https://www.archives.gov/research/jfk/select-committee-report/part-2c.html#rosenson.

875. Weisberg, pp. 338–339, 432–433, 453.

876. Blair, p. 136.

877. See Department of Justice (DOJ) VI. RAOUL AND HIS ALLEGED PARTICIPATION IN THE ASSASSINATION: https://www.justice.gov/crt/vi-raoul-and-his-alleged-participation-assassination, Section E.1.

878. Ibid., Section C.3.a. In Ray's book (p. 63) he stated that Raoul had "slightly wavy dark red hair that might have been the result of a dye job." Also see Appendix B, James Earl Ray's 1968 Appeal, Sect. II-d. referencing Ray's assertion that he told Huie that Raul's hair was red but Huie changed that to blonde, purposefully creating the inconsistency later cited by the HSCA for which they had to blame Ray since they would not accept the fact of Raul's existence.

879. Ibid.

880. Pepper, p. 200.

881. Ibid., p. 204.

882. Pepper, p. 8.

883. Emison, p. 185.

884. Scott, p. 218 (Ref. Reid and Demaris, *The Green Felt Jungle*, pp. 217–220).

885. Op. cit. (Scott), p. 219.

886. Ibid. (ref. Moldea, Dan E., *The Hoffa Wars*, New York: Paddington Press, 1978).

887. Mahoney, p. 383; Scheim, p. 247.

888. Davis, p. 518.

889. Scott, p. 144.

890. Scott, pp. 128, 161.

891. Davis, John H., p. 403.

892. Meyers, Jim, "FBI Probed Hollywood's Jack Valenti for Mob Ties," *Newsmax.com*, February 9, 2009.

893. Stephens, Joe, "Valenti's Sexuality Was Topic For FBI," the *Washington Post*, February 19, 2009.

894. Pepper, pp. 117–119.
895. Pepper, pp. 114–119, 199–200.
896. Ibid., p. 378.
897. Ibid., p. 117.
898. Ibid., pp. 116–117.
899. Posner, p. 303.
900. Ibid., p. 304.
901. Pepper, p. 203.
902. Op. cit.
903. Pepper, pp. 202–204, 304–305.
904. Op. cit., p. 305.
905. See YouTube, "LBJ Watched 'Risque' Films":. https://www.youtube
.com/watch?feature=player_embedded&v=mCt9Zh7mDzg.
906. Ray, James Earl, pp. 128, 198.
907. Emison, pp. 57–58.
908. Pepper, pp. 115–120; 204.
909. Pepper, pp. 198–202.
910. See Wikipedia: *The American Mercury*.
911. Ibid.
912. Ray and Barsten, p. 134.
913. Pepper, pp. 74, 185.
914. Melanson, p. 184–185.
915. Emison, p. 104.
916. Ray, James Earl, p. 166.
917. Ray, Jerry, and Carter, T., pp. 44–47; Pepper, p. 294.
918. Pepper, pp. 294–295.
919. McMillan, p. 309.
920. Sullivan, pp. 58–59; Dallek, pp. 162–165.
921. Summers, *Official and Confidential*, pp. 344–345.
922. Cohen, p. 109.
923. *Newsweek*, September 4, 1967.
924. Kearns Goodwin, p. 343.
925. Oshinsky, David M., "Fear and Loathing in the White House" the *New York Times*, Oct. 26, 1997.
926. Califano, pp. 299–300.
927. Caro, *The Passage* . . . , p. 587.
928. Sullivan, p. 146.
929. Gentry, pp. 606–607.
930. See https://www.archives.gov/files/research/jfk/releases/docid-32397527.pdf, p. 105.
931. Gentry, p. 607.
932. William H. Williams Collection of Criminal Court Papers, #5689, Southern Historical Collection, Box #4 (The Wilson Library, University

of North Carolina–Chapel Hill) (For access via internet to summary document see: https://finding-aids.lib.unc.edu/05689/ "Folder 4")).

933. Ibid.

934. Janos, Op. cit. The context might have related in part to Clark's 1968 review of the Warren Report, in which Clark couldn't find "anything new" to tie the assassination to Fidel Castro, since there wasn't any such linkage to find. Yet President Johnson would have naturally expected him to find something (real or otherwise) nonetheless.

935. See Peter Holley, "Sirhan Sirhan denied parole despite a Kennedy confidant's call for the assassin's release," the *Washington Post*, February 11, 2015: https://www.washingtonpost.com/news/post-nation/wp/2016/02/10/this-kennedy-confidant-has-spent-decades-calling-for-the-release-of-rfks-killer/?postshare=9771455345625972&tid=ss_fb.

936. Dallek, *Flawed Giant* . . . p. 571.

937. Ibid.

938. Ibid.

939. Ibid., p. 572.

940. Ibid.

941. See http://www.cnn.com/ALLPOLITICS/1996/conventions/chicago/facts/chicago68/index.shtml.

942. Op. cit., Dallek, p. 574.

943. Ibid.

944. See Martin, David, DCDave.com, "Did Lyndon Step Down So Bobby Could Be Killed?" September 23, 2014: http://www.dcdave.com/article5/140923.htm.

945. It is more than a little ironic that Ramsey Clark gave this dust-jacket blurb to Dr. William Pepper for his latest book: "No one has done more than Dr. William F. Pepper to keep alive the quest for truth concerning the violent death of Martin Luther King." Though it is certainly true, the irony of Clark being the attorney general during that sordid episode, and reporting to Johnson, while Hoover reported to him, theoretically put him into the unique position to have possibly solved this mystery nearly five decades ago. He must have felt a little hamstrung in that position.

946. http://garyrevel.com/.

947. Martin Luther King Jr., April 4, 1967. See http://kingencyclopedia.stanford.edu/encyclopedia/documentsentry/doc_beyond_vietnam/.

948. Op. cit. (Douglass, Jim, "The Martin Luther King Conspiracy Exposed in Memphis").

949. Dorman, Michael, *King of the Courtroom: Percy Foreman for the Defense,* New York: Delacorte Press, 1969, pp. xi-xii

950. Ibid., p. 173.

951. Ibid., pp. 173-175; 207–208; (also see: https://www.nickdavies.net/1988/09/05/death-of-a-legal-legend/).

952. Ibid. pp. 150–151.

953. Berg, David, *Run, Brother, Run,* New York: Scribner, 2013, p. 217

954. Ibid., p. 216.

955. Ibid. p. 189.

956. Ibid. pp. 157–195.

957. Ibid., pp. 202–203.

958. See "H. L. Hunt's Long Goodbye" *Texas Monthly,* March, 1975: https://www.texasmonthly.com/articles/h-l-hunts-long-goodbye/.

959. See: Harold Weisberg collection – Hood College Library, Frederick Md: Percy Foreman folio, Item #11.

960. http://jfk.hood.edu/Collection/Weisberg%20Subject%20Index%20Files/F%20Disk/Foreman%20Percy/Item%2011.pdf.

961. Ibid. (Item #10).

962. *The New York Times* July 22, 1975 titled "2 Hunts Indicted with 5 in Dallas" p.21.

963. Op. Cit. (Item #10).

964. Ibid. (Item #25).

INDEX